Lecture Notes in Computer Science 1239
Edited by G. Goos, J. Hartmanis and J. van Leeuwen

Springer
Berlin
Heidelberg
New York
Barcelona
Budapest
Hong Kong
London
Milan
Paris
Santa Clara
Singapore
Tokyo

David Sehr Utpal Banerjee David Gelernter
Alex Nicolau David Padua (Eds.)

Languages and Compilers for Parallel Computing

9th International Workshop, LCPC'96
San Jose, California, USA, August 8-10, 1996
Proceedings

Springer

Volume Editors

David Sehr
Utpal Banerjee
Intel Corporation, 2200 Mission College Boulevard, RN6-18
Santa Clara, CA 95052, USA
E-mail:(dsehr/banerjee)@gomez.sc.intel.com

David Gelernter
Yale University, Department of Computer Science
51 Prospect Street, New Haven, CT 06520, USA
E-mail: gelernter@cs.yale.edu

Alex Nicolau
University of California, Department of Information and Computer Science
Irvine, CA 92717, USA
E-mail: nicolau@ics.uci.edu

David Padua
University of Illinois, Department of Computer Science
1308 West Main Street, Urbana, IL 61801, USA
E-mail: padua@cs.uiuc.edu

Cataloging-in-Publication data applied for

Die Deutsche Bibliothek - CIP-Einheitsaufnahme

Languages and compilers for parallel computing : 9th international workshop ; proceedings / LCPC '96, San Jose, California, USA, August 8 - 10, 1996. David Sehr ... (ed.). - Berlin ; Heidelberg ; New York ; Barcelona ; Budapest ; Hong Kong ; London ; Milan ; Paris ; Tokyo : Springer, 1997
(Lecture notes in computer science ; Vol. 1239)
ISBN 3-540-63091-0

CR Subject Classification (1991): D.1.3, D.3.1, D.3.4, F.1.2, B.2.1

ISSN 0302-9743
ISBN 3-540-63091-0 Springer-Verlag Berlin Heidelberg New York

Typesetting: Camera-ready by author
SPIN 10548814 06/3142 – 5 4 3 2 1 0 Printed on acid-free paper

Foreword

My association with the Workshop on Languages and Compilers for Parallel Computing began in 1988, when the first one was hosted by Cornell University. That year the number of attendees was small enough to accomodate in a conference room, and the list read like a "who's who" of high-performance computing. We heard excellent presentations on a variety of topics, and the discussion was extremely lively. As a graduate student presenting his first paper, let alone a paper about Prolog, I was more than a little intimidated to address that group. But despite a few tough questions, I survived mostly intact and gained an insight into just how valuable interchanging ideas with such people can be. This workshop, because it brings together people from across the range of parallel computing, serves the purpose of generating new ideas and thoroughly reviewing existing ones. This workshop has traditionally drawn the best machine architecture, systems software, and algorithms people in the field to accomplish those tasks.

Moreover, having twice presented my work on Prolog, this workshop has always held a special place for me by its presentations tackling high performance computing through "non-traditional" approaches. In the past, papers have been presented running the gamut of non-imperative languages, including functional, logic, and constraint languages. Program transformation systems, visual programming aids, and other tools to aid parallel program development have also found a home in the workshop.

Of course the primary focus remains high-performance scientific and engineering computing, so Fortran retains a place of honor in the workshop. Because of this, many great papers on dependence analysis, loop transformations, instruction scheduling, and the like have been presented. As the technology for parallelizing Fortran has become more mature, though, the workshop has made room for explicit parallelism and data distribution directives, as well as venturing into C and more recently C++. In the current volume we find several papers addressing C and C++, and one even addressing extensions to those languages.

This year the ninth workshop was held from August 8 to August 10, 1996 at the Red Lion Hotel in San Jose, California. The attendance this year was approximately 100 people, representing fifteen U.S. states and ten other countries. Although the workshop has grown well beyond the size to fit in a conference room, it continues to have a single track and a relatively leisurely schedule. A very successful addition this year was the poster session, which afforded considerable interaction for poster session authors. The sponsor this year was my employer, Intel Corporation.

No effort such as this comes to fruition without the efforts of many. I would first like to thank the members of the committee, Utpal Banerjee, David Gelernter, Alex Nicolau, and David Padua, for having given me the chance to host the workshop and work with them. I would also like to thank the referees, especially those who gave reviews with very short notice. It is through the efforts of such conscientious reviewers that we are able to keep the workshop going. A very special mention goes to the two people who worked most closely with me on site arrangements, Karen Kmetz and Diane Proudfoot; they gave extremely gracious and helpful responses to even my most ridiculous requests. Also deserving many thanks are my colleagues Knud Kirkegaard and Peter Jensen, who helped with a variety of tasks. Dr. Robert Colwell, recently appointed an Intel Fellow, more than earned my thanks by consenting to give his terrific keynote speech. A last note of thanks goes to my superiors at Intel for allowing me the time to work on this task, and to Intel for sponsoring the event.

March 1997

David Sehr

Program Chair

List of Referees

Tarek Abdelrahman
Tito Autrey
Eduard Ayguadé
Milind Bhandarka
Dong-Yuan Chen
William Chen
Fabien Coelho
Béatrice Creusillet
Luiz De Rose
Rudi Eigenmann
Milind Girkar
John Grout
Junjie Frank Gu
Attila Gursoy
Mohammad Haghighat
Jay Hoeflinger
François Irigoin
Roy Ju
Knud Kirkegaard
Venkata Krishnan
Robert Kuhn
Jaejin Lee
Yong-Fong Lee
Calvin Lin
Bret Andrew Marsolf
Samuel Midkiff
Jose Moreira
Trung Nguyen
David Padua
Yunheung Paek
Vishesh Parikh
Paul Petersen
Bill Pottenger
Lawrence Rauschwerger
Martin Rinard
Hideki Saito
Dale Schouten
David Sehr
Ajay Sethi
Xiaowei Shen
Nicholas Stavrakos
Ernesto Su
Pedro Trancoso
Jenn-Yuan Tsai
Peng Tu
Pen-Chung Yew

Table of Contents

Automatic Data Distribution and Locality Enhancement

Program Analysis

Compiler Algorithms for Fine-Grain Parallelism

Instruction Scheduling and Register Allocation

Parallelizing Compilers

Communication Optimization

Compiling HPF

New Languages and New Compiler Techniques

Run Time Control of Parallelism

Poster Session Papers

Cross-Loop Reuse Analysis and Its Application to Cache Optimizations

Keith Cooper, Ken Kennedy, and Nathaniel McIntosh *

Department of Computer Science
Rice University
Houston, Texas USA

Abstract. In this paper we describe the design of a data-flow framework for detecting *cross-loop reuse*. Cross-loop reuse takes place when a set of data items or cache lines is accessed in a given loop nest and then accessed again within some subsequent portion of the program, usually another outer loop nest. In contrast to *intra-loop* reuse, which occurs during the execution of a single loop nest, cross-loop reuse is hard to analyze using traditional dependence-based techniques. The framework we have constructed is based on a combination of array section analysis (to capture array access patterns at a high level) and data-flow analysis (to deal with intra-procedural control flow). The framework is designed to account for cache size when gathering reuse information, and when used in an interprocedural setting, the framework also provides a mechanism for summarizing the effects of procedure calls.

Cross-loop reuse information can be used to drive a number of transformations that enhance locality and improve cache utilization, including loop fusion and loop reversal. Although these transformations are not new, their impact on cache behavior has not always been possible to predict, making them difficult to apply. As part of this paper we report the results of a comprehensive experimental study in which we apply our techniques to a set of ten programs from the SPEC95 floating point benchmark suite. We were able to obtain modest performance gains overall for several of the programs, based mostly on improvements in cache utilization.

1 Introduction

One of the major trends in computer architecture over the last decade has been the widening gap between processor speed and memory latency. Main memory latencies for modern-day workstations are approaching 100 cycles and beyond, compared with the 1-5 cycle latencies of a decade ago. This huge speed difference has had a number of consequences in the world of computer architecture, chiefly that system designers have had to rely increasingly on cache memories as a means to avoid latency and increase overall memory bandwidth. This is particularly true for shared-memory multiprocessors, since transfers between a processor and

* This work was supported in part by ARPA (Army Contract DABT63-95-C-0115).

memory must pass through additional levels of interconnection, resulting in even longer latencies.

Compiler researchers have also been attacking this problem; they have developed a number of optimizations that seek to enhance cache utilization, including loop interchange, loop tiling, and unroll-and-jam [8, 20] [2]. For most of these techniques, the compiler first analyzes a loop nest to find out what sort of reuse it contains, and then applies transformations to expose or improve the reuse in some way. Accurate information on loop-level reuse is a critical component for these methods; if the compiler can't detect the reuse, then there is no way for it to determine how or when to apply transformations.

Loop-level reuse analysis is most often based on *dependence analysis* [4, 21]. Dependence analysis can provide very detailed information about the memory access patterns within a loop, but applying it to larger regions within a procedure is difficult, especially if the region in question contains control flow or procedure calls. As a result, dependence analysis is not well suited to detecting cross-loop reuse.

Transformations also exist that exploit cross-loop reuse, primarily loop fusion and loop reversal [21]. Because of the shortcomings of existing reuse analysis methods, however, there has been no effective way until now to detect situations where these transformations can be profitably applied.

In this paper we describe a compiler framework for detecting useful cross-loop reuse. Rather than operating on the granularity of individual statements or array references, as is the case with dependence analysis, our framework uses array section analysis to reason about reuse in terms of entire regions within an array. The information derived from array section analysis is then used as input to a data-flow solver, which deals with intra-procedural control flow.

An outline of the remainder of this paper is as follows. In Section 2 we describe the details of our framework. In Section 3 we outline how the information provided by the framework can be applied, and in Section 4 we describe the results of some preliminary experiments using our framework. In Section 5 we discuss related work, and finally in Section 6 we offer our conclusions on this work.

2 Analysis framework

We now describe the details of our analysis. In Section 2.1 we outline some of the key design goals for the problem we are solving, and discuss how we accomplish these goals. In Section 2.2 we discuss array section analysis, an important component of our framework. Section 2.3 introduces the control flow representation used by our data-flow solver. In Section 2.4 we describe the domain over which our data-flow solver operates (i.e. the sets propagated during the analysis). Sections 2.5, 2.6 and 2.7 describe the actual data-flow equations used, along with

[2] Much of this work has been geared towards optimizing scientific programs, since these programs often make relatively poor use of cache memories, and since they are amenable to compile-time methods such as dependence analysis.

their inputs and the details of the solver. In Section 2.8 we discuss incorporation of cache size constraints. In Section 2.9 we briefly cover the algorithmic complexity of some of the operations performed in the framework. Finally, in Section 2.10 we describe how this framework can be used in an interprocedural setting.

2.1 Important design considerations

At a high level, the goal of our framework is to determine, given a point X within the program being analyzed, the set of array regions accessed on all paths that reach X; in many respects, this problem is similar to the well-known compiler optimization problem of "available expressions". We attack this problem, not surprisingly, with data flow analysis.

We do not use a traditional data-flow solver, however, since our problem is unusual in some important respects. First, the problem requires that we explicitly take into account the loop structure of the program, as opposed to treating all control flow in an identical fashion. This is due to the fact that a given subscripted reference may access a different region in an array depending on how much of the surrounding loop context is taken into account (see section 2.2).

A second aspect of the problem that complicates the analysis is that we want to take into account the size of the cache. The tools we have developed for this sub-task are difficult to combine with traditional flow analysis techniques. The solver we use allows us to develop a framework for detecting reuse without considering cache size constraints, and then factor in the cache size if necessary (see section 2.8).

2.2 Array sections

Array section analysis is a technique for summarizing the region(s) within an array that are accessed during some portion of the program [2, 5, 7, 15]. These summary representations provide a compact way of capturing the array access patterns, making them attractive for applications in which large portions of the program need to be considered. Our particular implementation represents array accesses using *Data Access Descriptors* [3], or "DAD"s.

The region within an array accessed by a given subscripted reference depends on the context that surrounds the reference. For example, consider the reference `a(i,j)` in Figure 1. If we consider this array reference in isolation, then it can be thought of as accessing the single element at `a(i,j)`. If we take the `do i` loop into account, then the reference can be thought of as accessing the vector `a(1:n,j)`, and so on.

We use the term *array section at level M* to refer to the region within an array that is accessed at a given loop level. More formally, given a subscripted reference nested within N loops, the array section at level M for the reference is the region accessed within the array when A) the loop induction variable(s) at levels M-1 and below are viewed as invariants, and B) the induction variables at levels M and above are allowed to vary.

2.3 Control flow representation

Rather than using a standard control flow graph (CFG), this framework uses an *interval-flow graph*, developed by Reinhard von Hanxleden and Ken Kennedy [14]. This allows us to take the loop structure of the program into account explicitly. The interval-flow graph (IFG) can be constructed by starting with a normal CFG and then partitioning the nodes and edges in the graph into categories based on Tarjan interval analysis [18] [3].

A Tarjan interval $T(h)$ is a set of CFG nodes that corresponds to a loop within the program, where h is a unique header node (with $h \notin T(h)$). Intuitively, $T(h)$ together with h form a strongly connected region within the CFG. When $x \in T(h)$, we say that $\text{HEADER}(x) = h$.

Each interval-flow graph $G = (N, E)$ has a unique root node, ROOT, that can be viewed as the header node for the interval corresponding to the entire procedure. We define $\text{LEVEL}(n)$ as the loop nesting level of node n, counting from the outside in, where $\text{LEVEL}(\text{ROOT})$ is defined as 0. For a given interval $T(n)$, we define $\text{CHILDREN}(n)$ as the set of nodes $\{ p \in T(n) : \text{LEVEL}(p) = \text{LEVEL}(n)+1 \}$, that is, the nodes in the interval headed by n that are immediate descendants of n. Figure 1 shows an example program fragment along with its interval-flow graph.

Each edge $(x \rightarrow y)$ in the IFG is placed into one of the following categories:

ENTRY: iff $y \in T(x)$; this corresponds to an edge from an interval header x to a node within the interval.

CYCLE: iff $x \in T(y)$; this corresponds to an edge from within an interval back to the header of that interval.

JUMP: iff $\exists h : x \in T(h),\ y \notin \{ T(h) \cup h \}$; this corresponds to a jump out of a loop (i.e. an edge from a node in one interval to a node outside the interval that is not the header node).

FLOW: iff $\forall h : x \in T(h) \iff y \in T(h)$; this corresponds to an intra-interval edge (i.e. an edge that is none of the above).

To refer to the predecessors and successors of a given node, we use the following terminology:

$\text{PREDS}(n)$: The set of nodes $\{ x : \exists e \in E,\ e = (x, n) \}$

$\text{SUCCS}(n)$: The set of nodes $\{ x : \exists e \in E,\ e = (n, x) \}$

The $\text{PREDS}(n)$ and $\text{SUCCS}(n)$ notation may be further qualified by adding a superscript containing the desired edge type. For example, $\text{PREDS}^F(n)$ is the set of nodes that are at the source of a FLOW edge whose sink is n.

[3] The interval-flow graph is not be confused with interval-based data-flow analysis. With the interval-flow graph, there is no notion of collapsing intervals in the CFG into single nodes, as in interval-based data-flow analysis.

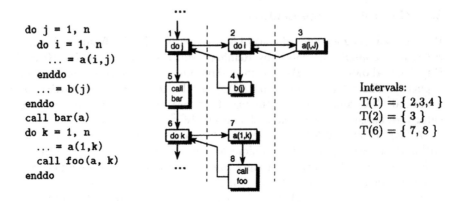

```
do j = 1, n
  do i = 1, n
    ... = a(i,j)
  enddo
  ... = b(j)
enddo
call bar(a)
do k = 1, n
  ... = a(1,k)
  call foo(a, k)
enddo
```

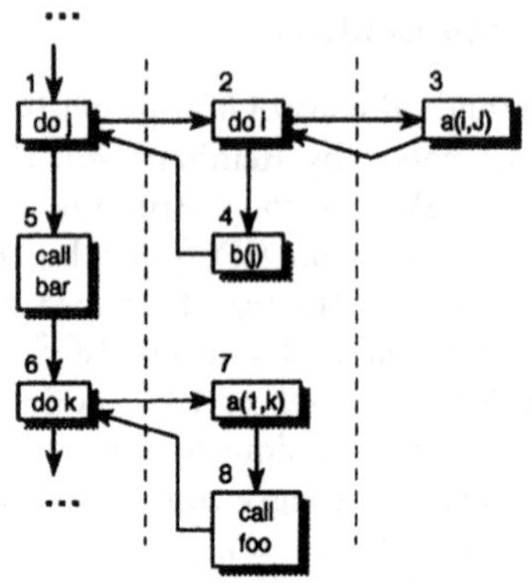

Intervals:
T(1) = { 2,3,4 }
T(2) = { 3 }
T(6) = { 7, 8 }

Fig. 1. Example sub-program with interval-flow graph

After construction of the IFG, the graph is post-processed to insure that each interval has at most one CYCLE edge, i.e. for each non-empty interval $T(h)$ there exists a unique $n \in T(h)$ such that $(n, h) \in E$. This sometimes requires the insertion of *synthetic* nodes and edges; see [13] for details.

In addition, we define two types of partial orderings on N, as follows:

FORWARD/BACKWARD: Given a FLOW/JUMP edge (m, n), a FORWARD order visits m before n, whereas a BACKWARD order visits m after n.

UPWARD/DOWNWARD: Given $m, n \in N$ such that $m \in T(n)$, an UPWARD order visits m before n, whereas a DOWNWARD order visits n before m.

These two orderings are orthogonal and may be combined (for example, a FORWARD and DOWNWARD order).

2.4 Data-flow universe

The universe for this data-flow problem consists of sets of array section descriptors, where each descriptor is composed of the name of the array in question and a symbolic representation of the region accessed within the array. We call these sets *reuse summary sets*. An example of a reuse summary set might be

$$\{\ a(1:10),\ a(75:n),\ b(1:n)\ \}$$

As can be seen from the set above, a reuse summary set may contain more than one region within a given array. The interpretation of the set depends on the context; it may represent a set of array sections available on entry to a given block, generated within a given loop, etc.

2.5 Initial information

For each basic block n that contains one or more array references, we compute the set $GEN_{INIT}(n)$. This reuse summary set contains an array section for each array reference within the block. The sections initially assigned to $GEN_{INIT}(n)$ are computed with respect to the innermost loop level. During the analysis, when the section is propagated up out of an enclosing loop, the region of the section is reconstructed to take the loop in question into account.

During the computation of the initial set for a block, we attempt to coalesce sections that are adjacent or identical. For example, we might try to collapse the set { `a(i,j), a(i+1,j)` } into { `a(i:i+1,j)` }. This coalescing is only performed when it will result in no loss of precision, however.

$$GEN_{IN}(n) = \bigwedge_{p \in PRED^F(n)} \{\ GEN_{OUT}(p)\ \} \tag{1}$$

$$GEN_{LOC}(n) = \begin{cases} GEN_{OUT}(\text{LASTCHILD}(n)) & \text{if } n \text{ is an interval header} \\ GEN_{INIT}(n) & \text{otherwise} \end{cases} \tag{2}$$

$$GEN_{OUT}(n) = GEN_{IN}(n) \vee GEN_{LOC}(n) \tag{3}$$

$$REACH_{IN}(n) = \begin{cases} REACH_{IN}(\text{HEADER}(n)) & \text{if PREDS}^{B}(n) \neq \emptyset \\ \bigwedge_{p \in PRED^F(n)} \{\ REACH_{OUT}(p)\ \} & \text{otherwise} \end{cases} \tag{4}$$

$$REACH_{OUT}(n) = REACH_{IN}(n) \vee GEN_{LOC}(n) \tag{5}$$

Fig. 2. Reuse equations

2.6 Reuse equations

Our goal for the flow analysis is to compute the set $REACH_{IN}(n)$ for all of the nodes in the IFG. The set $REACH_{IN}(n)$ corresponds informally to the set of array sections that reach node n on all paths from ROOT to n. We compute $REACH_{IN}$ using the equations in Figure 2; evaluation of the equations is controlled by the algorithm in Figure 3. All sets are initially empty (with the exception of GEN_{INIT}).

Intuitively, $GEN_{IN}(n)$ corresponds to the set of sections accessed by the nodes prior to n within the interval that contains n. $GEN_{LOC}(n)$ corresponds to the set of sections accessed within n (if n is not a loop header) or the sections accessed within the interval headed by n (if n is a loop header). $GEN_{OUT}(n)$ combines GEN_{IN} and GEN_{LOC} to form the set of sections that flow out of

n (taking into account only the nodes in the interval containing n). The GEN values are computed starting with innermost loops and working outwards.

$REACH_{IN}(n)$ corresponds to the set of sections reaching n from within n's interval and (possibly) from some previous loop outside n's interval. $REACH_{OUT}(n)$ is the set of sections flowing out of n, where the sections may be generated locally or they may reach n from some previous loop somewhere in the program.

---

procedure *ComputeReuse*

inputs: interval-flow graph $G = (N, E)$
$GEN_{INIT}(n)$ for all $n \in N$
outputs: $REACH_{IN}(n)$ and $REACH_{OUT}(n)$ for all $n \in N$

begin
  forall $n \in N$ in UPWARD and FORWARD order:
    compute equations 1, 2, and 3
  forall $n \in N$ in DOWNWARD and FORWARD order:
    compute equations 4 and 5
end

Fig. 3. Procedure for computing reuse equations

2.7 $\bigvee$ and $\bigwedge$ operators

In the equations above, the $\vee$ and $\wedge$ operators play an important role. The $\wedge$ operator is used to merge together sets of sections at join points, and the $\vee$ operator is used to merge together local information with incoming information (i.e. models the effects of passing through a block).

The left hand side of Figure 4 illustrates a situation where the $\wedge$ operator would be applied. In this case, the analysis needs to merge together the sections reaching the node X from its two predecessors M and N, taking into account the fact that the particular path to X is unknown.

The right hand side of Figure 4 shows a situation where the $\vee$ operator is needed. The sections flowing out of X need to be combined with the sections locally generated at Y, but in this case we know that flow of control *must* reach Y if it reaches X.

2.8 Incorporating cache constraints

If the goal is to predict reuse without regard to cache size or other resource constraints, then we can implement the $\vee$ operator as set union and the $\wedge$ operator as set intersection. The resulting information, however, does not give any hint as to distance between successive uses of array data (only that some set of array locations are reused). In many situations we would like to know whether

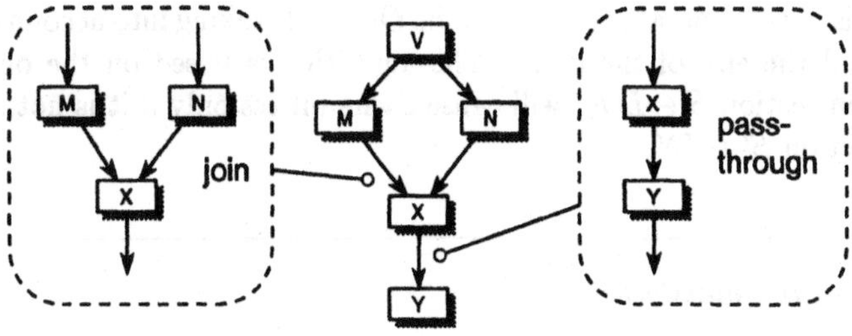

Fig. 4. Control flow

the distance between the successive uses is small enough that the reused items will be found in cache, for some fixed cache size. This section describes how we modify our framework to take cache size and organization into account.

Array section age: First, we introduce the concept of the "age" of an array section with respect to a particular point in the program. We define the age of a given section as the number of cache misses that have taken place since the first element of the section was brought into the cache.

During the analysis, we associate age values with each of the sections in a reuse summary set. When an array section is first added to a reuse summary set (corresponding to the point where it is first brought into the cache) we assign it an initial age value based on its volume. As the section is propagated to other points in the program, other accesses will start to displace the section from the cache; when this happens, the age of the section is incremented. Eventually the age of the section reaches a cutoff, at which point we consider the section "dead" (i.e. totally displaced from the cache), and it is eliminated from its reuse summary set.

In order for this scheme to work, we need to have a mechanism for determining the number of cache lines accessed by an array reference within a loop; this is in fact a research problem all by itself [10]. Our approach is to estimate the volume of the DAD for the reference, using a simple technique similar to the RefCost algorithm developed by Carr, McKinley, and Tseng [8].

Cache organization: Our framework is not equipped to predict cache conflicts due to limited associativity; we instead conservatively assume that cache conflicts will reduce the amount of reuse that takes place by a fixed factor. We currently estimate the "effective" size of the cache (used in the analysis) by multiplying the actual cache size by $1 - \frac{1}{2S}$, where S is the set associativity of the cache.

$\vee$ operator for finite caches: For the finite cache case, we use a more sophisticated $\vee$ operator that models the cache effects when execution passes through a given node (shown in Figure 5). Given the set of sections flowing into block N (IN) and the set of sections accessed locally within N and N's descendants

(*LOC*), this new ∨ operator computes the *OUT* set, taking into account the level of reuse and the size of the cache. The algorithm is based on the observation that a given section $S \in LOC$ will cause cache misses only if it is not contained in some section $S' \in IN$.

```
procedure FiniteCache-∨

inputs:    IN (incoming reuse summary set)
           LOC (reuse summary set for locally accessed data)
outputs:   OUT (outgoing reuse summary set)

begin
   volume ← 0
   R ← ∅
   forall x ∈ LOC:
      if ∃ y ∈ IN such that x is contained in y then
         R ← R ∪ { y }
      else
         volume ← volume + (cache line volume of x)
      endif
   endfor
   OUT ← LOC ∪ (IN - R)
   forall x ∈ OUT:
      increment age value of x by volume
      remove x from OUT if age exceeds cache size cutoff
   endfor
end
```

Fig. 5. ∨ for finite cache case

∧ operator for finite caches: We also modify the ∧ operator when estimating reuse for a finite cache. Set intersection is still the basis for the operator, but the age values of the sections must be adjusted as well. In particular, when the reuse summary sets for two incoming paths are merged together by the ∧ operator, we may encounter an array section that appears in both sets, but has a different age value in each one. In this case, the ∧ operator chooses the larger of the two ages for the section in question when forming the result.

For example, consider the graph fragment in Figure 4. Suppose that we are applying the ∧ operator to the sections reaching block X from its predecessors M and N, and suppose that blocks V, M, and X contain array accesses (each to a different array), and that N contains no accesses. When we apply the ∧ operator, both input sets will contain the section from V (we assume here that the number of accesses in M is relatively small), however the age of the sections from V that arrive at X along the edge $M \rightarrow X$ will be larger than the age of the corresponding sections flowing through the edge $N \rightarrow X$ (due to the additional data brought into the cache in M). The $\wedge$ operator selects the larger age, in order to be conservative.

2.9 Complexity

Generating the GEN_{INIT} set for each block requires that we build a DAD for each array reference in the procedure. This process requires $O(D^2 * N)$ time per reference, where D is the number of dimensions of the array and N is the nesting depth of the reference. Each DAD takes $O(D^2)$ space, and most operations involving DADs (union, intersection, containment, comparison) take $O(D^2)$ time.

The flow analysis framework itself considers each node and edge in the IFG exactly twice. The $\wedge$ and $\vee$ operators for the unlimited-cache case are linear in the number of sections in the sets being operated on, but for the finite-cache case, $\vee$ takes $O(N^2)$ time in the worst case (where N is the number of sections in each set), since since each section in the set may have to be compared with every other section.

In practice, we have found that the time required by the framework is comparable to the time that it takes to perform dependence analysis for the procedure.

2.10 Interprocedural analysis

Array section analysis was originally conceived of as a means of summarizing the effects of procedure calls within loops; as a result, it is relatively straightforward to extend our framework to work in an interprocedural setting.

When invoked in the context of whole-program analysis, we use the following strategy. We analyze procedures starting with the leaves in the call graph and working up to the root, visiting a procedure only after all of the procedures it calls have been visited. When a procedure call is encountered within the IFG of the subroutine being analyzed, we take the previously computed $REACH_{OUT}$ set for the callee and use it as the GEN_{LOC} set for call (applying array reshapes if necessary, and translating the summary into the name space of the caller by substituting actuals for formals, etc).

Summarizing call sites in this fashion is generally feasible only if the framework is being run with cache size constraints taken into account (without the size constraints, the reuse summary sets grow very large in the upper regions of the call graph).

Currently we are restricted to propagating information upwards in the call graph; we do not, for example, take advantage of context within calling routines to reason about reuse within a callee. Our analysis does not currently handle programs whose call graphs contain cycles.

3 Applications of cross-loop reuse information

This section describes some of the ways in which cross-loop reuse information can be used by a compiler. It should be noted that exploiting cross-loop reuse information tends to be more difficult than exploiting loop-level reuse information; the larger the region over which the reuse is taking place, the more more obstacles that must be overcome if restructuring is to be applied.

3.1 Locality-enhancing loop transformations

Cross-loop reuse can be used to predict the profitability of locality-enhancing transformations involving pairs of adjacent loop nests. These transformations include (but are not limited to) loop fusion and loop reversal.

Loop fusion: Loop fusion is the dual of loop distribution; it combines two adjacent loops with identical headers into a single loop. Loop fusion has the potential to convert cross-loop reuse into loop-level reuse, which can greatly enhance cache utilization.

Our framework can supply enough information to cheaply predict the profitability of loop fusion. The compiler can examine the $REACH_{IN}$ set for a given loop nest to see what sections reach the loop. If the intersection of the $REACH_{IN}$ set with the GEN_{LOC} set of the loop is sufficiently large and the sections in the $REACH_{IN}$ set originate from the immediately preceding loop nest, then loop fusion will be profitable (the degree of profitability will be dependent on the volume of the intersection).[4] Once it is established that the transformation is profitable, then the compiler can apply the more costly dependence-based techniques to determine whether fusion is safe [21].

Loop reversal: A weaker but slightly more widely applicable technique is loop reversal. This optimization can provide benefits only in proportion to the size of the cache, thus it works best for very large (presumably secondary or tertiary) caches. Consider two consecutive outer loops that both access a single large vector (i.e. larger than will fit in the cache). Even though the vector is reused, there is no cache reuse, since when the second loop begins execution, the first elements of the vector have long since been flushed from cache. However if we reverse the second loop, then the last elements of the vector from the previous loop are likely to still be in cache. This optimization relies on the *traversal order* component of the DAD representation, which captures the direction and stride of the access in each array dimension (see [3] for the details). One advantage of loop reversal is that the loops to be optimized do not have to be directly adjacent (there may be intervening code, provided that it does not destroy the reuse between the loops).

3.2 Transformation selection

Even if the compiler can cheaply predict when a transformation is going to be profitable, there still remains the problem of deciding the sequence of transformations to apply within a procedure. A given loop nest may be optimized in

[4] This requires that we tag each section with the ID of the loop in which it originated.

several different ways (fused with its predecessor or with its successor, for example). Selecting the optimal set of transformations is a very difficult problem; optimizing temporal locality using loop fusion alone is NP-hard [16]. As a result, the compiler must resort to heuristics to choose the set of transformations to apply.

4 Experimental results

In this section, we report the results from an experimental study, in which we apply our techniques to ten programs from the SPEC95 floating point benchmark suite [19]. Our experimental infrastructure consists of a Fortran transformation engine, including the cross-loop reuse analysis framework, and an execution-driven simulator for gathering instruction counts and cache statistics.

4.1 Compiler

The phases in our compiler are shown in Figure 6. The compiler operates in a source-to-source fashion, reading and writing Fortran code. All of the analysis and transformation steps shown are performed automatically.

Phase	Remarks
1. Front end processing	read and typecheck Fortran source build AST (abstract syntax tree)
2. Local analysis	build IFG for each procedure compute GEN_{INIT} for all $n \in$ IFG
3. Cross-loop analysis	run cross-loop framework for each function
4. Transformations	apply loop reversal and loop fusion based on cross-loop reuse info
5. Output	generate transformed Fortran source

Fig. 6. Compilation stages

Our transformation selection procedure is as follows. For each loop nest N, we create a hash table (the "reuse score table") whose entries are tuples of the form $\langle L, R\rangle$, where L is a loop ID number and R is an estimate of the number of cache lines reused from loop L. We generate the reuse score table for a loop N while computing the value of equation 3 in Figure 2; when a section $x \in GEN_{IN}(N)$ intersects with a section $y \in GEN_{LOC}(N)$, we compute the volume of the intersection of x and y, determine the loop L' in which x originated, and update the L' entry in N's table. We calculate the total score for a loop by summing the values of all of the entries in its reuse score table.

We then use a greedy algorithm to select the loops to optimize; we first consider the loop nest with the highest reuse score value, optimize it if possible, then consider the loop with the next highest score, and so on. We first apply loop fusion, then loop reversal. In order to concentrate our results primarily on cache effects, we limited loop fusion to the outermost loop in each pair of adjacent loop nests.

4.2 Simulator

Our cache simulator is based on the SPARC Performance Analysis Toolkit; it is layered on top of the tool **shade** [9]. **Shade** provides an extensible mechanism for writing execution-driven simulators; it operates by interpreting a SPARC executable and passing a trace of the instructions to a user-written trace analyzer. In our case, the trace analyzer counts instructions and simulates a particular cache configuration.

After the source-to-source transformer is run, the target programs are instrumented with calls to runtime routines to tag outer loop nests and to demarcate the regions of the program's address space containing array data. The instrumented programs are then compiled using the Sun **f77** Fortran compiler (version SC4.0 18/Oct/95).

The simulator deals with *data* cache behavior only; it does not simulate an instruction cache. Simulated cache characteristics were as follows. We used a 64Kbyte, 4-way set-associative L1 cache with a line size of 32 bytes, and a 1024Kbyte L2 cache, also 4-way set-associative with a line size of 32 bytes. An LRU replacement policy was used within each cache set. Both caches are write-back, with an allocate-on-write-miss policy.

Program	Functions	Lines	Data (KB)	Runtime (secs)
applu	16	1869	32,309	25
apsi	96	4576	9,381	61
fpppp	38	2408	454	6
hydro2d	42	1597	8,630	182
mgrid	14	448	7,464	192
su2cor	36	1700	23,806	551
swim	6	254	14,392	15
tomcatv	1	119	14,407	181
turb3d	23	1294	25,360	337
wave5	104	7036	41,403	65

Fig. 7. Program characteristics

4.3 Benchmark programs

Figure 7 gives some of the summary characteristics of the programs we used for our experiments. "Functions" is the number of procedures in the program; "Lines" is the number of non-comment source lines. "Data" is the total size of all the arrays used by the program, in kilobytes. "Runtime" shows the approximate wall clock running time on an unloaded SPARCStation 10 with 256 megabytes of memory. The "training" input files were used for these runs, in order to yield more reasonable simulation times [19].

Program	Instructions	L1 hits	L1 misses	L2 hits	L2 misses	P-cycles
applu	329,240	66,962	5,962	4,731	1,231	487,340
apsi	2,333,872	362,521	5,427	5,413	4	2,388,462
fpppp	240,043	23,771	38	36	2	240,583
hydro2d	5,543,080	1,186,888	218,461	16,091	202,371	23,917,370
mgrid	12,566,952	3,445,822	119,285	102,698	16,587	15,086,762
su2cor	23,341,356	6,425,969	1,215,323	1,024,815	190,508	50,735,226
swim	481,252	119,409	8,784	21	8,763	1,270,132
tomcatv	6,398,033	1,647,655	172,041	26,139	145,901	19,790,523
turb3d	14,453,171	2,568,151	84,751	34,275	50,475	19,338,681
wave5	2,700,459	564,179	38,124	30,988	7,106	3,650,179

Fig. 8. Simulation data for original programs [thousands]

4.4 Results

Figure 8 gives the raw instruction counts and cache metrics for the original untransformed programs. All numbers are in thousands. The "Instructions" column contains the total dynamic instruction count for the program. The L1 and L2 cache metrics are for accesses to array data only (i.e. they exclude accesses to scalars, compiler-generated spill code, etc). The "P-cycles" term in the final column is an approximation of the overall execution time of the program; it combines the total instruction count with the projected stalls due to cache misses. It is computed as follows:

$$\text{P-Cycles} = \text{IC} + (M_1 * P_1) + (M_2 * P_2)$$

where "IC" is the total instruction count, M_k is the total number of misses at level k, and P_k is the additional miss penalty at level k. For the purposes of our study, we assume a level 1 miss penalty of 10 cycles, and an additional level 2 miss penalty of 80 cycles (a miss to main memory takes a total of 90 cycles, in other words).

Figures 9, 10, and 11 show the results for the transformed programs using purely static reuse analysis. Figure 9 gives a summary of the specific transformations applied to each of the programs. The numbers show for "candidates" indicate the total number of loops in the program that were determined to be legal candidates for fusion or for reversal. Figure 10 shows the raw data for the transformed programs (again, all numbers are in thousands). Figure 9 compares the transformed programs to the original programs in each category, showing

		fusion		reversal	
Program	loops	fused	candidates	reversed	candidates
applu	168	2	4	20	111
apsi	298	1	2	5	150
fpppp	39	0	0	0	6
hydro2d	163	3	14	5	136
mgrid	57	0	1	7	36
su2cor	118	0	0	3	47
swim	24	0	4	0	22
tomcatv	16	0	2	0	8
turb3d	64	0	0	0	33
wave5	377	14	27	27	212

Fig. 9. Transformation summary

Program	Instructions	L1 hits	L1 misses	L2 hits	L2 misses	P-cycles
applu	330,029	67,138	5,814	4,582	1,232	486,729
apsi	2,333,872	360,505	5,411	5,399	4	2,388,302
fpppp	240,042	23,518	39	37	2	240,592
hydro2d	5,542,709	1,197,341	218,262	18,518	199,744	23,704,849
mgrid	12,561,752	3,448,549	116,891	100,306	16,577	15,056,822
su2cor	23,341,354	6,423,729	1,217,500	1,027,017	190,482	50,754,914
swim	481,490	119,409	8,784	21	8,763	1,270,370
tomcatv	6,397,215	1,647,651	172,044	26,143	145,901	19,789,735
turb3d	14,668,168	2,555,806	95,870	45,379	50,490	19,666,068
wave5	2,686,798	559,578	38,891	31,779	7,081	3,642,188

Fig. 10. Simulation data for transformed programs [thousands]

Program	Instructions	L1 hits	L1 misses	L2 hits	L2 misses	P-cycles
applu	0.23	0.26	-2.48	-3.14	0.08	-0.12
apsi	0	-0.55	-0.29	-0.25	0	0
fpppp	0	-1.06	2.63	2.77	0	0
hydro2d	0	0.88	-0.09	15.08	-1.29	-0.88
mgrid	-0.04	0.07	-2.00	-2.32	-0.06	-0.19
su2cor	0	-0.03	0.17	0.21	-0.01	0.03
swim	0.04	0	0	0	0	0.01
tomcatv	-0.01	0	0	0.01	0	0
turb3d	1.48	-0.48	13.11	32.39	0.02	1.69
wave5	-0.50	-0.81	2.01	2.55	-0.35	-0.21

Fig. 11. Percent change between original and transformed

percent change; as can be easily seen, there is very little overall change in program performance.

After a closer inspection of the results, we found that the framework appeared to be missing a number of important transformation opportunities, due primarily to situations loop bound values could not be determined at compile time (forcing the compiler to conservatively assume no reuse). To explore this hypothesis, we ran a new set of experiments in which the compiler incorporated profiling data into the analysis framework.

Profiling data was gathered by running each program on the given input file and gathering the minimum, maximum, and average value for the loop bounds, loop step, and overall trip count. For loops whose bounds were constant at run-time, the compiler substituted in the bounds from the profiling data when computing the GEN_{LOC} set for the loop in question. It should be emphasized that profiling data was only used in the portions of the analysis that determine profitability of transformations, not the safety of the transformations.

Figures 12, 13, and 14 show the results with the profiling information. By using profiling data, the compiler was able to compute more accurate estimates of the number of cache lines accessed in each loop nest, and was able to detect reuse in situations where previously it had to conservatively assume no overlaps. The number of loops fused went up from 20 to 24, and the number of reversed loops went up from 67 to 84. The results in Figure 14 indicate that two programs, `tomcatv` and `hydro2d`, showed improvements in performance as a result of the transformations. In both cases, the speedup is due to improved cache behavior; both programs show significant reductions in both L1 and L2 misses overall.

5 Related work

A number of researchers have developed compiler techniques useful for improving cache behavior [1, 6, 8, 17, 20]. Almost all of these techniques apply to individual loop nests, however, and are not designed to detect or exploit cross-loop reuse. Two exceptions are *loop fusion* and *affinity regions*.

Kennedy and McKinley have proposed using loop fusion to improve locality and cache behavior [16]. In a subsequent study, McKinley, Tseng, and Carr included loop fusion in their repertoire of transformations for an experimental study on compiler cache optimizations [8]. This study used dependence analysis to test for the profitability of loop fusion; loop reversal was not used as a locality-enhancing transformation.

Affinity regions are a mechanism that allows a compiler or user to give locality-improving hints to the loop scheduler for a parallel program running on a shared-memory multiprocessor. By placing a set of consecutive parallel loops within an affinity region, the user or compiler is informing the loop scheduler that cross-loop reuse exists and that it should try to assign iterations to processors in such a way that the reuse is preserved. Compile-time identification of affinity regions was proposed by Appelbe et al [1].

		fusion		reversal	
Program	loops	fused	candidates	reversed	candidates
applu	168	2	4	20	111
apsi	298	1	2	5	150
fpppp	39	0	0	0	6
hydro2d	163	5	14	20	136
mgrid	57	0	1	7	36
su2cor	118	0	0	5	47
swim	24	1	4	1	22
tomcatv	16	1	2	0	8
turb3d	64	0	0	0	33
wave5	377	14	27	26	212

Fig. 12. Transformation summary (with profile)

Program	Instructions	L1 hits	L1 misses	L2 hits	L2 misses	P-cycles
applu	329,562	67,122	5,813	4,584	1,229	486,012
apsi	2,333,873	362,635	5,289	5,277	4	2,387,083
fpppp	241,000	23,518	39	37	2	241,550
hydro2d	5,581,854	1,195,747	209,575	30,474	179,101	22,005,684
mgrid	12,561,753	3,446,434	118,673	102,110	16,563	15,073,523
su2cor	23,342,471	6,423,530	1,217,698	1,027,185	190,514	50,760,571
swim	480,793	119,411	8,783	29	8,754	1,268,943
tomcatv	6,396,957	1,663,997	155,700	23,096	132,603	18,562,197
turb3d	14,453,171	2,567,901	84,701	34,225	50,476	19,338,261
wave5	2,705,524	559,560	38,909	31,797	7,081	3,661,094

Fig. 13. Simulation data for transformed programs, with profile [thousands]

Program	Instructions	L1 hits	L1 misses	L2 hits	L2 misses	P-cycles
applu	0.09	0.23	-2.49	-3.10	-0.16	-0.27
apsi	0	0.03	-2.54	-2.51	0	-0.05
fpppp	0.39	-1.06	2.63	2.77	0	0.40
hydro2d	0.69	0.74	-4.06	89.38	-11.49	-7.99
mgrid	-0.04	0.01	-0.51	-0.57	-0.14	-0.08
su2cor	0	-0.03	0.19	0.23	0	0.04
swim	-0.09	0	-0.01	38.09	-0.10	-0.09
tomcatv	-0.01	0.99	-9.49	-11.64	-9.11	-6.20
turb3d	0	0	-0.05	-0.14	0	0
wave5	0.18	-0.81	2.05	2.61	-0.35	0.29

Fig. 14. Percent change between original and transformed (with profile)

Our data-flow framework resembles that of Gross and Steenkiste [11]. However their framework is geared towards finding parallelism as opposed to detecting useful reuse for cache optimizations. Our techniques are also similar to those developed by Gupta, Schonberg, and Srinivasan for optimizing communication placement for programs running on distributed-memory multiprocessors [12].

6 Conclusions

In this paper we have presented a framework for predicting cross-loop reuse. The framework combines two existing tools: array section analysis and data-flow analysis. By using array sections, we can exploit the characteristics of the program's array access patterns without resorting to potentially costly procedure-wide dependence analysis. By using data-flow analysis, we can gracefully handle intra-procedural control flow. Our framework also provides a mechanism for taking into account a fixed cache size when predicting reuse, should this be required.

This work opens up the possibility of systematically applying cross-loop transformations to improve cache utilization, since it provides a means of cheaply predicting the profitability of loop fusion and particularly loop reversal.

Our experimental results suggest that for programs that exhibit cross-loop reuse, our analysis framework is able to detect this reuse at apply cross-loop transformations to exploit it. For programs running on uniprocessors, our results translate into modest improvements in overall execution time; we would expect to see more significant gains for shared-memory multiprocessors, where small increases in second-level cache utilization can sometimes result in significant performance improvements.

7 Acknowledgements

The authors would like to thank Kathryn McKinley, Jerry Roth, Taylor Simpson, and Phil Schielke for their comments on earlier drafts of this paper.

References

1. B. Appelbe and B. Lakshmanan. Program transformations for locality using affinity regions. In *Proceedings of the Sixth Workshop on Languages and Compilers for Parallel Computing*, Portland, OR, August 1993.
2. V. Balasundaram. *Interactive Parallelization of Numerical Scientific Programs.* PhD thesis, Dept. of Computer Science, Rice University, May 1989.
3. V. Balasundaram. A mechanism for keeping useful internal information in parallel programming tools: The data access descriptor. *Journal of Parallel and Distributed Computing*, 9(2):154–170, June 1990.
4. U. Banerjee. *Dependence Analysis for Supercomputing.* Kluwer Academic Publishers, Boston, MA, 1988.
5. M. Burke and R. Cytron. Interprocedural dependence analysis and parallelization. In *Proceedings of the SIGPLAN '86 Symposium on Compiler Construction*, Palo Alto, CA, June 1986.

6. D. Callahan, S. Carr, and K. Kennedy. Improving register allocation for subscripted variables. In *Proceedings of the SIGPLAN '90 Conference on Programming Language Design and Implementation*, White Plains, NY, June 1990.
7. D. Callahan, J. Cocke, and K. Kennedy. Analysis of interprocedural side effects in a parallel programming environment. *Journal of Parallel and Distributed Computing*, 5(5):517–550, October 1988.
8. S. Carr, K. S. McKinley, and C.-W. Tseng. Compiler optimizations for improving data locality. In *Proceedings of the Sixth International Conference on Architectural Support for Programming Languages and Operating Systems (ASPLOS-VI)*, San Jose, CA, October 1994.
9. R. Cmelik and D. Keppel. Shade: A fast instruction-set simulator for execution profiling. Technical Report SMLI 93-12; UWCSE 93-06-06, Sun Microsystems Laboratories, Inc. and University of Washington, 1993.
10. J. Ferrante, V. Sarkar, and W. Thrash. On estimating and enhancing cache effectiveness. In U. Banerjee, D. Gelernter, A. Nicolau, and D. Padua, editors, *Languages and Compilers for Parallel Computing, Fourth International Workshop*, Santa Clara, CA, August 1991. Springer-Verlag.
11. T. Gross and P. Steenkiste. Structured dataflow analysis for arrays and its use in an optimizing compiler. *Software—Practice and Experience*, 20(2):133–155, February 1990.
12. M. Gupta, E. Schonberg, and H. Srinivasan. A unified data-flow framework for optimizing communication. In *Proceedings of the Seventh Workshop on Languages and Compilers for Parallel Computing*, Ithaca, NY, August 1994.
13. R. v. Hanxleden. *Compiler Support for Machine-Independent Parallelization of Irregular Problems*. PhD thesis, Dept. of Computer Science, Rice University, December 1994.
14. R. v. Hanxleden and K. Kennedy. Give-N-Take — A balanced code placement framework. In *Proceedings of the SIGPLAN '94 Conference on Programming Language Design and Implementation*, Orlando, FL, June 1994.
15. P. Havlak and K. Kennedy. An implementation of interprocedural bounded regular section analysis. *IEEE Transactions on Parallel and Distributed Systems*, 2(3):350–360, July 1991.
16. K. Kennedy and K. S. McKinley. Maximizing loop parallelism and improving data locality via loop fusion and distribution. In *Proceedings of the Sixth Workshop on Languages and Compilers for Parallel Computing*, Portland, OR, August 1993.
17. W. Li and K. Pingali. Access normalization: Loop restructuring for NUMA compilers. In *Proceedings of the Fifth International Conference on Architectural Support for Programming Languages and Operating Systems (ASPLOS-V)*, Boston, MA, October 1992.
18. R. E. Tarjan. Testing flow graph reducibility. *Journal of Computer and System Sciences*, 9:355–365, 1974.
19. J. Uniejewski. SPEC Benchmark Suite: Designed for today's advanced systems. SPEC Newsletter Volume 1, Issue 1, SPEC, Fall 1989.
20. M. E. Wolf and M. Lam. A data locality optimizing algorithm. In *Proceedings of the SIGPLAN '91 Conference on Programming Language Design and Implementation*, Toronto, Canada, June 1991.
21. M. J. Wolfe. *Optimizing Supercompilers for Supercomputers*. The MIT Press, Cambridge, MA, 1989.

Locality Analysis for Distributed Shared-Memory Multiprocessors

Vivek Sarkar* Guang R. Gao ** Shaohua Han ***

Abstract. This paper studies the locality analysis problem for shared-memory multiprocessors, a class of parallel machines that has experienced steady and rapid growth in the past few years. The focus of this work is on estimation of the memory performance of a loop nest for a given set of computation and data distributions. We assume a distributed shared-memory multiprocessor model. We discuss how to estimate the total number of cache misses (compulsory misses, conflict misses, capacity misses), and also the fractions of these cache misses that result in local vs. remote memory accesses. The goal of our work is to use this performance estimation to guide automatic and semi-automatic selection of data distributions and loop transformations in programs written for future shared-memory multiprocessors. This paper also includes simulation results as validation of our analysis method.

1 Introduction

Shared-memory multiprocessors represent a class of parallel machines that has experienced steady and rapid growth in the past few years. An important advantage of shared memory architectures is ease of programming. Under a shared memory model, programmers can access the entire memory via a global shared address space, avoiding the need for specifying explicit data movement through message passing, which can be tedious and error-prone. Caching is a critical mechanism for boosting the performance of shared memory processors. Since all inter-processor communication is indirect (implicit) through memory loads and stores, it is very important to reduce the frequency of cache misses into non-local (remote) processor memories.

This paper studies the locality analysis problem for shared-memory multiprocessors. Our interest is in estimating the memory performance of a loop nest for a given set of computation and data mappings. The computation and data

* Laboratory for Computer Science, Massachusetts Institute of Technology, Cambridge, MA 02139. Email: vivek@lcs.mit.edu.

** Dept. of Electrical Engineering, University of Delaware, Newark 19711. Email: ggao@eecis.udel.edu.

*** School of Computer Science, McGill University, Montreal, Canada H3A 2A7. Email: shaohua@cs.mcgill.ca.

mappings may be derived automatically by a compiler with (or without) guidance from user annotations and directives [2, 3, 15]. We assume a distributed shared memory model with caching.

The program model considered in this work is a perfect loop nest, where array references contain affine subscript expressions. Given a computation mapping and a data mapping for a loop nest, we are interested in estimating the total number of cache misses (compulsory, capacity, and conflict) that will be incurred, and in estimating how many of them will result in non-local memory accesses (remote cache misses).

The major results of this paper are twofold:

- We extend the method of estimating uniprocessor cache misses in [8] to estimate the number of non-local (remote) misses for different cache organizations (e.g. fully associative, direct-mapped and set-associative) under our program and machine models (Section 4 and 5). Our estimation methods are simple and efficient. Simulation results are presented to validate these methods.
- In addition, we present some new results on exact solutions of number of cache misses under certain conditions. In particular, we present exact solutions for some restricted cases of an array dimension subscript expression[4] involving three index variables. Furthermore, in cases where an array dimension only involves two or fewer index variables — a frequent case in real programs — we provide an alternative proof based on the concept of reuse vectors and reuse spaces for the exact solution presented in [8].

The rest of the paper is organized as follows. Section 2 describes the machine model and program model assumed in our work. Section 3 states the locality analysis problem that is addressed by this paper. Section 4 summarizes our solution for estimating total, local, and remote compulsory misses assuming a unit line size, an unbounded cache, and at most one reference per array variable. Section 5 extends the results from section 4 to the case of misses in a direct-mapped cache. Section 6 identifies cases in which our estimates are provably exact. Section 7 presents simulation results for an example loop nest to validate our method and to demonstrate how these estimation techniques can be used to select data distribution and computation mapping. Section 8 discuss how the techniques presented in sections 4 and 5 can be extended to the cases of non-unit cache line size, multiple references per variable, and set-associative caches. Section 9 summarizes related work, and section 10 contains our conclusions.

2 Machine Model and Program Model

2.1 Machine Model

Our target machine model is based on a distributed non-uniform shared-memory multiprocessor architecture (NUMA) as shown in Figure 1. This model supports

[4] We assume that partial or full linearization is performed before locality analysis to eliminate coupling among multiple dimensions in an array reference.

a global shared address space. As shown in the figure, we assume that each processor has a local memory that forms a part of the shared memory of the whole machine. A program can issue a load or store operation to directly access any data in the entire machine although the memory is physically distributed across the processors.

Each processor may have a hierarchy of caches which can hold both local and remote data. In this discussion, as shown in the figure, we assume that there are two levels of caches for each processor. We assume that cache coherence is maintained automatically by the hardware and/or the operating system. In this paper, we focus on counting misses in the second-level (L2) cache since it is the level that typically interfaces with local and remote memories. Without loss of generality, the term "cache" with be used in this paper to mean a second-level cache. However, our analysis method is equally applicable to a single-level cache or alternative memory hierarchy organizations.

A cache miss to local memory (called a *local miss*) costs less than a cache miss to remote memory (called a *remote miss*). It is important to consider this distinction in a locality cost model for a NUMA machine. Let N be the number of processors. Throughout our discussion, we assume that the cache geometry is specified by: L = number of array elements per line (block), S = number of sets, and k = degree of associativity

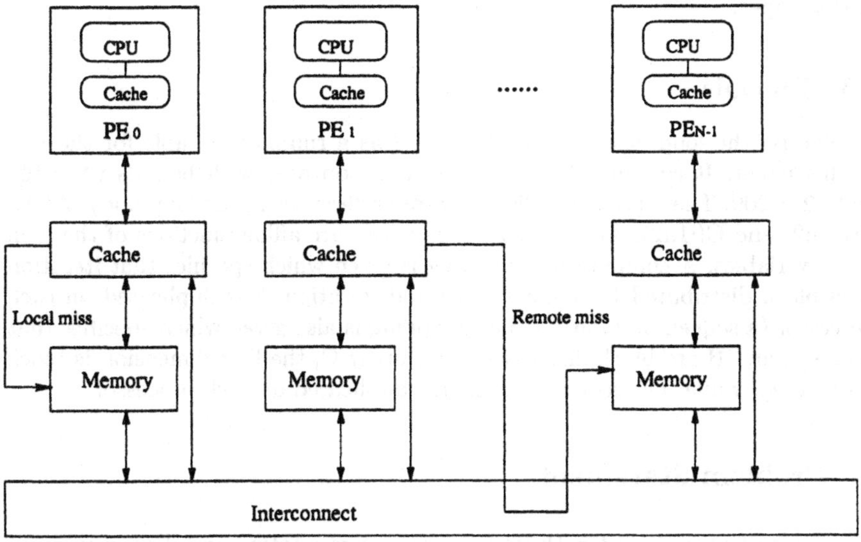

Fig. 1. Multiprocessor Model

2.2 Program Model

For the program model, our focus in this paper is on locality analysis of array references in a single perfect loop nest. Our analysis is applicable to array references with affine subscript expressions. In this paper, we assume that all loop bounds expressions are invariant (rectangular), though the extension to trapezoidal loop bounds is straightforward using techniques such as those presented in [6].

We assume that a computation mapping $\mathcal{C}$ is given (either by a compiler or a user) which specifies partitioning of iterations onto processors, and a data mapping $\mathcal{D}$ is given which specifies partitioning of array elements onto processor local memories. Both $\mathcal{C}$ and $\mathcal{D}$ have the form $(d_1, \ldots, d_m)$, where m is the number of iteration/array dimensions, and each d_j is one of BLOCK, CYCLIC, CYCLIC(n), or $*$. Similar formulations of these mappings have been used elsewhere [11, 3, 7]. In this paper, we assume that the mapping of global data addresses to local memories stays fixed during program execution.

In the rest of our discussion, we assume that a loop is sequential if its computation mapping is $*$ and is parallel (i.e. a doall loop) otherwise. This does not mean that our locality analysis is restricted to doall loops as the only form of parallelism. However, when a loop containing loop-carried dependence is executed on a parallel machine, it becomes necessary to introduce synchronization among iterations. The amount of extra cache traffic generated at a synchronization point depends on the underlying memory consistency model and cache consistency protocol. A detailed discussion of these issues is beyond the scope of this paper.

2.3 Example

We use the loop nest shown in Figure 2 as a running example for the rest of this paper. It contains a two-dimensional loop nest with bounds n1 = 100 and n2 = 200. There are three distinct array references in the loop body: A(i1), B(i1+i2) and C(i1,i2). All subscript expressions are affine functions of the loop index variables. A computation mapping is given which specifies that iteration $i1$ is block distributed (a parallel loop) and iteration $i2$ is duplicated on each processor (a sequential loop). A data mapping is also given which specifies that arrays A and B are block distributed. For array C, the first dimension is block distributed, while the second dimension is duplicated on each processor.

3 Problem Statement

Given a perfect loop nest with its associated computation and data mappings, and a parallel machine model, our goal is to estimate:

1. Number of *total cache misses* incurred, $M(i)$, for each processor i (includes compulsory misses, capacity misses, collision misses, and false-sharing misses)

```
parameter(n1=100,n2=200)

! Data mapping
real*8 A(n1), B(n1+n2), C(n1,n2)
distribute A(block), B(block), C(block,*)

! Computation mapping
distribute i1(block), i2(*)

! Loop nest
  do i1 = 1, n1    ! parallel loop
    do i2 = 1, n2 ! sequential loop
      A(i1) = A(i1) + B(i1+i2) + C(i1,i2)
    end do
  end do
```

Fig. 2. Sample loop nest

2. Number of *local cache misses*, $LM(i)$ (cache misses in processor i's local memory)
3. Number of *remote cache misses*, $RM(i) = M(i) - LM(i)$ (cache misses into remote memories)

This estimation can be used to guide automatic or semi-automatic selection of data and computation mappings for parallel programs that execute on NUMA machines.

4 Single Reference Per Variable, Unit Line Size, Unbounded Cache

In this section, we address the problem of locality analysis for the case of single reference per array variable, assuming that the cache is large enough so that no capacity or collision misses occur and only compulsory misses need to be considered. We also assume that the cache line size is one word, so that there will be no false sharing misses. Although this is a restricted case, it serves as a basis to develop our solution methodology for the more complex cases considered later in the paper.

4.1 Estimating Number of Total Misses

The total number of misses per processor is estimated as follows for a single array variable X:

1. Identify $I_C(i)$, the *local iteration space* for processor i from the *computation mapping*, C .

2. For each array variable, X, estimate the number of distinct accesses (DA) for X's array reference in the local iteration space, $I_C(i)$, which equals the number of total (compulsory) misses incurred by processor i for accesses to X.
   We can use the heuristic bound method from [8] for this estimation, or the exact methods for special cases discussed later in section 6.

The sum over all variables X of the number of misses estimated in step 2 is reported as the total number of misses (we know that there can be no cache line overlap across distinct variables because the cache line is assumed to be one word). Note that the number of total misses will depend on the computation mapping (due to $I_C(i)$), but not on the data mapping, since no distinction is made between local vs. remote misses when counting total misses.

To illustrate our method, consider the loop nest in Figure 2. For step 1, we identify the local iteration space for processor i from the computation mapping to obtain $I_C(i)$ as follows:

```
! Local iteration space for processor i (assuming P=4):
  do 10 i1 = i*100/4 + 1, (i+1)*100/4
    do 10 i2 = 1, 200
10    A(i1) = A(i1) + B(i1+i2) + C(i1,i2)
```

In this example, the iterations of the outer loop i1 are evenly distributed across all four processors, i.e. processor 1 is assigned iterations 1 to 25, processor 2 is assigned iterations 26 to 50, and so on.

For step 2, consider reference $B(i1 + i2)$ to array B. It is clear that this reference exhibits temporal locality e.g. B(1+2) and B(2+1) access the same array element. We estimate the total number of misses due to B(i1+i2) as the number of distinct accesses to B, DA_B by using the method from [8] as follows (f^{lo} and f^{hi} are the low and high bounds of the expression i1+i2 in the local iteration space):

$$\begin{aligned} f^{lo} &= (25i + 1) + 1 \\ f^{hi} &= (25(i + 1) + 1) + 200 \\ DA_B &= (25(i + 1) + 200) - (25i + 1 + 1) + 1 = 224 \end{aligned}$$

The array references $A(i1)$ and $C(i1, i2)$ are simple and it is easy to use the same technique to obtain the estimates, $DA_A = 25$ and $DA_C = 5000$. So, the number of total cache misses for processor i is estimated as $M = DA_A + DA_B + DA_C = 25 + 224 + 5,000 = 5,249$, which is exact.

In this example, DA_A, DA_B, DA_C are independent of processor i, but this need not be true in general. The cost function for number of misses may take different values on different processors. Also, the cost formulae we derived can be extended to contain symbolic expressions as needed e.g. when the number of iterations is unknown.

4.2 Estimating Number of Local Misses

The number of *local* misses (c.f. section 3) for a processor is the number of its cache misses incurred on data located in the processor's local memory. Recall that the estimated number of *remote misses* can simply be obtained from the estimated number of total misses and estimated number of local misses as $RM(i) = M(i) - LM(i)$. Given both the computation and data mappings, the number of local misses for a single variable (with a single reference) can be estimated by performing the following steps:

1. Identify $I_c(i)$, the *local iteration space* for processor i from *computation mapping, C*, as before.
2. Identify lower bounds and upper bounds f^{lo} and f^{hi} for each dimension of the array reference from $I_c(i)$.
3. Identify lower bounds and upper bounds d^{lo} and d^{hi} for each dimension of *local subarray* for processor i from *data mapping, D*.
4. Estimate the number of distinct accesses in the local array region consisting of the intersection of lower and upper bounds from step 2 and 3.
   We can use the heuristic bound method from [8] outlined in section 4.1 to do the counting, or the exact methods for special cases discussed later in section 6.

Let us use the example in Figure 2 to illustrate the steps outlined above. We will estimate the number of local misses on processor 0 for array B. Note that array B has 300 elements, and is block distributed among the four processors.

For step 1, the local iteration space for processor 0, $I_C(0)$ is defined by the following linear inequalities:

$$1 \leq i1 \leq 25$$
$$1 \leq i2 \leq 200$$

For step 2, the lower and upper bounds of accesses to array B in $I_C(0)$ is given by

$$2 \leq i1 + i2 \leq 225$$

For step 3, the local subarray of B on processor 0 is $B(1:75)$.

In step 4, the intersection of bounds from step 2 and step 3 yields the range, 2...75. We then estimate the distinct number of accesses for B in this subarray, $DA = 75 - 2 + 1 = 74$, as the number of local misses to array B from processor 0. For processors 1, 2, 3, the number of local misses is 75, rather than 74. Hence the number of remote misses is 150 for processor 0 and 149 for processors 1, 2, 3.

5 Single Reference Per Variable, Unit Line Size, Direct-mapped Cache

In the previous section, we developed cost functions to estimate the number of local and remote *compulsory* misses for a single array reference. Counting compulsory misses can be viewed as counting misses for an idealized cache of unbounded size in which no capacity or collision misses occur. When we deal with real caches with finite capacity and a limited degree of set-associativity, it is not sufficient to estimate the number of compulsory misses; we also need to estimate the number of local and remote *capacity* and *collision* misses [12].

In section 5.1, we address the problem of counting capacity misses by estimating the number of total misses for a fully associative cache with S lines. In section 5.2, we estimate the number of total misses for direct-mapped cache with S sets/lines of unit size. In section 5.3, we develop cost functions to estimate the number of local (and hence, remote) misses for a direct-mapped cache.

5.1 Capacity Misses

As a prelude to analyzing the case of a direct-mapped cache with S sets/lines of unit size (discussed in Section 5.2), we first consider the case of a fully associative cache with S lines of unit size. A fully associative cache is a set-associative cache with only a single set. In this case, all memory accesses "collide" on the single set representing the fully associative cache. The limited capacity of S lines can cause additional misses to occur, compared to the compulsory misses analyzed in Section 4. This special case of collision misses is also referred to as *capacity* misses.

We present a heuristic method to estimate the capacity misses. The basic idea is to first determine how many loop iterations will fill the whole cache — which we will call the "locality group" below — and estimate the number of misses within a locality group. Since we know the total number of iterations in the entire loop nest, we can find how many "locality group instances" it can be divided into. Then, if we conservatively ignore the reuse among distinct locality group instances, the total number of misses can be easily estimated.

We start by formalizing the notion of the *locality group* of a loop nest. The locality group is the largest innermost subspace of the iteration space that is guaranteed to incur no capacity or collision misses if it starts execution with a clean (empty) cache. The locality group can be specified by two parameters, (m, B), as follows:

1. $m \geq 0$, the number of innermost loops in the locality group.
   m can be determined by using the techniques outlined in Section 4 to estimate the number of distinct lines accessed by progressively larger subspaces of the iteration space (innermost loop, inner two loops, and so on) till we reach a case where no loops remain or one iteration of the m + 1st loop overflows cache.

2. $B \geq 1$, the largest number of iterations (block size) of the outermost loop in the locality group such that no capacity or collision misses occur.
   Note that B may, in general, only be a fraction of the total number of iterations in the outermost loop of the locality group. In other words, only the first $m-1$ inner loops in the group span their complete iteration ranges without incurring capacity or collision misses. For a given m, B can be estimated by solving a simple linear equation obtained by setting the estimated number of distinct lines to the number of lines available in cache, and applying the floor ($\lfloor\ \rfloor$) function to convert the interpolated B value to an integer value.

Thus, the locality group consists of the m innermost loops, with B iterations of the outermost loop in the locality group and complete iterations of all other loops in the locality group. B is properly defined only when $m \geq 1$. $m = 0$ indicates that a single iteration of the loop nest overflows the cache. The locality group can also be viewed as an innermost "tile" of the iteration space such that no capacity or collision misses occur within the tile. In fact, if the tiling transformation is performed on the loop nest prior to locality analysis, we would expect the locality group to be identical to a single tile from the tiling transformation.

Consider the example from Figure 2 for $S = 1024$. In this case, we can determine easily that the locality group consists of both loops (therefore $m = 2$) using the procedure outlined above for step 1. For the outermost loop, we have $B = 4$. We can obtain this value of B by setting up the following linear equation for b based on the total number of distinct accesses M(b) :

$$M(b) = DA_A(b) + DA_B(b) + DA_C(b) = (b) + (199 + b) + (200b) = 1024$$

which simplifies to $202b + 199 = 1024$, thus yielding the solution, $b = 825/202 = 4.08$. Therefore, we set $B = \lfloor b \rfloor = 4$. The validity of our computation can be easily confirmed since 5 iterations of the outermost i1 loop overflows a fully associative cache with 1024 lines.

Given the locality group, we develop the following approximate procedure to estimate the total number of capacity misses by ignoring any reuse that occurs across locality group instances. We first estimate the total number of cache misses (compulsory misses) incurred within the locality group, then divide the estimate by the number of iterations in the locality group, and finally multiply by the total number of iterations in the loop nest so as to get a pro-rated estimate for the entire local iteration space. The pro-rated estimate is conservative because it ignores possible reuse among different instances of the locality group.

Continuing with our example from Figure 2, the number of cache misses within the locality group is $M = DA_A + DA_B + DA_C = 4 + 203 + 800 = 1007$. Since the locality group has $4 \times 200 = 800$ iterations, this amounts to an average of $1007/800 = 1.26$ misses/iteration. For the entire local iteration space, this estimation results in $1.26 \times 5,000 \simeq 6,294$ cache misses.

5.2 Collision Misses

We now tackle the harder problem of locality analysis for a direct-mapped cache with S sets/lines of unit size. Intuitively, a direct-mapped cache is at the opposite end of the spectrum from a fully-associative cache because it effectively divides the memory space into cyclic "regions" such that an entire region is directly mapped to a single cache line. For example, locations $a, a+S, a+2S, \ldots$ all map to the same cache line. In other words, if a particular array reference pattern maps to only one or a few such "regions" in memory, then the available cache size is effectively reduced. Our approach is to first estimate the cache utilization efficiency, η, for a particular array reference, and then use it to estimate the *effective* cache size, ECS.

To start with, consider a simple array reference with a single stride T as follows:

```
      DO 10 i = . . .
10       A(T*i + c) = . . .
```

We are interested in estimating
$\eta(T)$ = cache utilization efficiency of stride T
= fraction of sets accessed over a large no. of iterations

For example, consider the array reference, A(2i). It is obvious that the array reference will only utilize at most every alternate line in the cache. Therefore, the "effective" cache size usable by A(2i) is only 50 percent of the total cache size, i.e. $\eta = 1/2$.

For the case of a direct-mapped cache with S sets/lines of unit size, we have proved that

$$\eta(T) = \frac{1}{gcd(T,S)}$$

It is well known that a stride value that is a power of two leads to poor efficiency. In that case, $gcd(T,S) = min(T,S)$ (since S is also usually a power of two), thus making $\eta(T)$ small.

The basic idea in our method is to use the cache utilization efficiency to estimate the effective shrinking of a direct-mapped cache with S lines to an "equivalent" fully associative cache with $S' \leq S$ lines. Recall that the solution for a fully associative cache is based on the notion of locality groups. With cache utilization efficiency known, we can find the *effective* locality group accordingly, and thus estimate the number of collision misses.

Our overall approach to estimating locality cost for a direct-mapped cache with S sets/lines of unit size is as follows:

1. For each index variable i of the m innermost loops, examine each array reference that contains i, and estimate $\eta(T)$ for the stride T of i in that array reference.
   The value of m used in this step comes from the locality group (m, B) obtained for a fully associative cache with S lines.

2. For each array variable, choose the minimum among the estimated $\eta(T)$ values from step 1 as the cache utilization efficiency for the variable.
3. Set effective cache size $S' = \lfloor \eta_{avg/min} S \rfloor$, where $\eta_{avg/min}$ is the average value taken over all array variables of the minimal cache utilization efficiency obtained in step 2.
4. Identify the effective locality group (m', B') assuming a fully associative cache with S' lines of unit size, and report the estimated number of capacity misses for (m', B') as the predicted number of misses for a direct-mapped cache with S lines/sets of unit size.

In the above steps, the minimum $\eta(T)$ value is used for each array variable, so that the estimation is conservative. $\eta_{avg/min}$ is estimated as the average of the min values based on the assumption that cache usage is divided equally among all the array variables. If needed, the average can be refined to a weighted mean by considering a non-uniform partitioning of the cache for different array variables.

Continuing with our example from Figure 2. For step 1, note that index variable $i1$ has efficiency $\eta = 1$ for all array references. Index variable $i2$ has efficiency $\eta = 1$ for array B, but efficiency $\eta = 1/gcd(100, 1024) = 0.25$ for array C (assuming that the array is stored in a column-major layout as in Fortran). In step 2, we choose $\eta = 1$ for array A and B, and $\eta = 0.25$ for array C. In step 3, we estimate $\eta_{avg/min} = (1 + 1 + 0.25)/3 = 0.75$ and $S' = \lfloor 0.75 \times 1024 \rfloor = 768$. Finally, in step 4, we use $S' = 768$ to obtain an effective locality group with $m' = 2$ and $B' = 2$. The number of cache misses for the effective locality group is $M = 202 \times 2 + 199 = 603$. Since the effective locality group has $2 \times 200 = 400$ iterations, this amounts to an average of $603/400 = 1.51$ misses/iteration. For the entire local iteration space, this estimation results in $1.51 \times 5,000 \simeq 7,538$ cache misses.

Program transformations such as array dimension padding [4] and array copying [14] can be used to improve the cache utilization efficiency. In this paper, our focus is on analysis of locality costs. The analysis can be applied before and/or after such locality-improving program transformations.

5.3 Estimating Number of Local Misses for a Direct-Mapped Cache

The number of *local* misses can be estimated by performing the steps listed earlier in section 4.2, but substituting the effective locality group (as defined in section 5.2) in place of the local iteration space. The steps to be performed are as follows:

1. Identify $I_c(i)$, the *local iteration space* for processor i from *computation mapping*, C, as before
2. Identify $I_g(i)$, the iteration space for the *effective locality group* (m', B') for $I_c(i)$, using the techniques outlined in section 5.2.
3. Identify lower bounds and upper bounds f^{lo} and f^{hi} for each dimension of the array reference from $I_g(i)$
4. Identify lower bounds and upper bounds d^{lo} and d^{hi} for each dimension of the *local subarray* for processor i from *data mapping*, D

5. Estimate the number of distinct accesses in the local array region consisting of the intersection of lower and upper bounds from step 3 and 4, i.e., the number of local misses in the effective locality group.
6. Use the number of local misses in the effective locality group to obtain a pro-rated estimate of local misses for the entire local iteration space.

We illustrate this approach by using the same example that was used in section 4.2, namely that of estimating the number of local misses on processor 0 for array B. From section 5.2, we know that the effective locality group is (m',B') = (2,2), and so $I_g(0)$ is defined as follows:

```
! Effective locality group for processor 0:
  do 10 i1 = 1, 2
    do 10 i2 = 1, 200
10    A(i1) = A(i1) + B(i1+i2) + C(i1,i2)
```

In step 3 above, we identify the lower and upper bounds for array B from $I_g(i)$ as $B(2:202)$. As in section 4.2, the intersection of bounds in step 5, yields the subarray $B(2\ldots75)$. Therefore, the number of local misses to array B in the effective locality group is 74. For the entire local iteration space in step 6, the total number of local misses to array B is estimated as $74 \times 25/2 = 925$ cache misses.

6 Exact Methods for Estimating Number of Total Compulsory Misses

In this section, we focus on exact methods for estimating the total number of compulsory misses. The estimation techniques used in prior sections were based on upper bounds presented in [8]. [8] also contained a closed-form exact formula for a single array reference in a two-dimensional loop nest. In section 6.1, we study the case of three-dimensional loop nest, and state conditions under which the bounds introduced from [8] are provably exact. In section 6.2, we introduce the concepts of reuse vectors and reuse spaces, and demonstrate how to use these concepts to prove the correctness of the exact formula for two variables. An interesting possibility for future work is to use these concepts to obtain more precise or exact estimates for more general cases of three or more variables.

6.1 Using the Heuristic Bound as an Exact Count

Under certain conditions, the heuristic bounds for DA described in section 4.1 become tight – they give the exact number of distinct accesses. In this section, we discuss these conditions and state some results.

Theorem 1. *Consider a subscript expression $f = ai + bj + ck$ in one dimension of array A in a perfect nest of three loops $1 \le i \le n_i$, $1 \le j \le n_j$, $1 \le k \le n_k$, such that*

1. $0 < a \leq b \leq c$,
2. $gcd(a, b, c) = 1$.

If $a = 1$, and $n_i \geq max(b, c)$ then the bounds from [8] are exact.

Proof. (Sketch) Note that $f^{lo} = 1 + b + c$, and $f^{hi} = n_i + bn_j + cn_k$ when $a = 1$. We will prove that each number in $f^{lo} \ldots f^{hi}$ belongs to the range of f. Consider what happens when index k is incremented by 1, and the value of f increases from $1 + b + c$ to $1 + b + 2c$. Since $a = 1$ and $c < n_i$, each number in this interval (of length $\leq c$) will be covered when index i steps through $1 \ldots n_i$. A similar argument can be used for the successive increments of j and k.

Theorem 2. *Consider subscript expression $f = ai + bj + ck$ as in Theorem 1. If $g = gcd(a, b, c) > 1$, and one of $(a/g, b/g, c/g)$ equals 1, then the bounds from [8] are exact.*

Proof. (Sketch) Let $f' = a'i + b'j + c'k$, such that $(a', b', c') = (a/g, b/g, c/g)$, and $f = gf'$. There is a one-one correspondence between values in the range of f and values in the range of f' Therefore, f and f' have the same number of distinct accesses. Since f' satisfies the conditions for Theorem 1, the proof of this theorem follows from Theorem 1.

Theorems 1 and 2 assume that coefficients a, b, c are all positive. The theorems can easily be extended to negative coefficients. Details have been omitted for the sake of brevity.

6.2 Exact Solution for Two Loops Using Reuse Space and Reuse Vectors

Consider a single one-dimensional array reference embedded in two perfectly nested loops as follows:

```
 do 10 i1 =  . . .
   do 10 i2 = . . .
            . . .
10        ... A[f(i1, i2)] ...
```

We examine the array reference $A(f(\mathbf{i}))$ where f is a function of the subscript index vector $\mathbf{i}$. Note that iterations $\mathbf{i} \prec \mathbf{i}'$ reuse an array reference if and only if $\mathbf{i}$ and $\mathbf{i}'$ map to the same array location i.e. $f(\mathbf{i}) = f(\mathbf{i}')$ We define RV, the set of reuse vectors, to be the set of $(\mathbf{i}' - \mathbf{i})$ vectors such that iteration $\mathbf{i}'$ will reuse the same array element accessed by iteration $\mathbf{i}'$, where $\mathbf{i} \prec \mathbf{i}'$. That is:

$$RV = \{\mathbf{i}' - \mathbf{i} \mid \mathbf{i}, \mathbf{i}' \in I \text{ and } \mathbf{i} \prec \mathbf{i}' \text{ and } f(\mathbf{i}) = f(\mathbf{i}')\}$$

In other word, $\mathbf{r} \in RV$ means that iteration $\mathbf{i} + \mathbf{r}$ must access the same array location as iteration $\mathbf{i}$. We also make the following observation:

$$\mathbf{r_1}, \mathbf{r_2} \in RV \Rightarrow \mathbf{r_1} + \mathbf{r_2} \in RV$$

We also define the reuse space, RS, to be the set of iterations which reuse a previously accessed array location

$$RS = \{\mathbf{i}+\mathbf{r} \mid \mathbf{i} \in I, \mathbf{r} \in RV\} \cap I$$

where I is the iteration space. Alternatively, $RS = I - \cup_{\mathbf{r} \in RV}(I+\mathbf{r})$. We can observe that $I - RS$ = set of distinct accesses. This implies that RV can be used to obtain more precise estimate of DA.

We have determined the existence of a unique minimal reuse vector, RV_{min}, for the case of two loops. Assume that the subscript expression is:

$$f = a_1 i_1 + a_2 i_2, 1 \le i_1 \le B_1, 1 \le i_2 \le B_2 \tag{1}$$

where i_1 and i_2 are two index variables. Without loss of generality, we assume both a_1 and a_2 are positive. A closed-form solution for RV_{min} is obtained as follows (see [10] for details):

$$RV_{min} = (a_1/gcd(a_1, a_2), -a_2/gcd(a_1, a_2)). \tag{2}$$

The above expression for RV_{min} can be used to show that

$$|RS| = (B_1 - a_2/gcd(a_1, a_2))(B_2 - a_1/gcd(a_1, a_2)). \tag{3}$$

We can make use of the reuse space, RS, to estimate the number of *total* compulsory misses for our idealized cache. Note that the set of iterations that exhibit reuse is simply RS, and the number of hits, is the size of this set, $|RS|$. Therefore, the number of misses is simply $|I| - |RS|$, where $|I|$ is the total number of iterations for the loop set.

Let us examine our example. We will estimate the number of local misses on processor 0 for array B. The computation mapping identifies the local iteration space for processor 0 as

```
    do 10 i1 = 1, 25
      do 10 i2 = 1, 200
10      ... = ... + B(i1+i2) + ...
```

The reuse space space for local iterations is as follows:

$$RV_{min} = \{(1, -1)\}$$
$$RS = \{2 \dots 25\} \times \{1 \dots 199\}$$

The size of reuse space $|RS|$ = 24x199 = 4776. Therefore, the number of misses is simply $|I| - |RS|$, where $|I|$ = 25x200 = 5000. So, the total number of misses equals to 5000-4776 = 224, which is exact as we had seen earlier.

7 Verification and Simulation

In the previous sections, we proposed a series of simple methods to estimate local and total cache misses in a loop nest for a given data/computation mapping. In this section, we will demonstrate how these methods can be applied to guide selection of data and computation mapping.

Supposing we have a loop nest and a group of candidates of data/computation mappings on a NUMA-like machine. We estimate local and total cache misses first for each candidate. Given these estimated results, we should pick the candidate data and computation mapping which yields the best data locality. Consider the following loop nest which has the same data reference pattern as the previous example but has no loop-carried dependence:

```
parameter(n1=100,n2=200)
real*8 A(n1), B(n1+n2), C(n1,n2)
do i1 = 1, n1
  do i2 = 1, n2
    C(i1,i2) = A(i1) + B(i1+i2)
  end do
end do
```

Assume that we have four processors and that arrays A and B are BLOCK distributed. We consider two possible cases for array C — (BLOCK, *) or (*, BLOCK). Thus, the two possible data mappings on processor 0 are:

- *D1:* A(1..25), B(1..75), C(1..25, 1..200)
- *D2:* A(1..25), B(1..75), C(1..100, 1:50)

For computation mappings, we consider two cases — *i*1 loop parallel or *i*2 loop parallel. The *i*2 loop parallel case also includes a loop interchange to move the parallel loop outwards. Thus, the two possible computation mappings on processor 0 are:

- *C1:* i1(BLOCK), i2(*)

```
do i1 = 1, 25          ! parallel loop
  do i2 = 1, 200       ! sequential loop
    C(i1,i2) = A(i1) + B(i1+i2)
  end do
end do
```

- *C2:* i1(*), i2(BLOCK)

```
do i2 = 1, 50          ! parallel loop
  do i1 = 1, 100       ! sequential loop
    C(i1,i2) = A(i1) + B(i1+i2)
  end do
```

We now examine four possible candidates of data/computation mappings : C1-D1, C1-D2, C2-D1, and C2-D2. Assuming unit cache line size, we then estimate both local and total cache misses for each candidate using the cache models examined in section 4 and section 5. The results are presented in the following three tables, where *EstLocal*, *EstRem* and *EstTotal* represent estimated local, remote and total cache misses, *SimLocal*, *SimRem* and *SimTotal* represent simulated local, remote and total cache misses, and *Err* represents relative error between *EstTotal* and *SimTotal*. The simulation results were obtained using the Powersim [16] tool, with an extension to cause the entire cache to be flushed after each locality group instance.

Table 1: Fully Associative Cache With Unbounded Lines

Mapping	EstLocal	EstRem	EstTotal	SimLocal	SimRem	SimTotal	Err
C1-D1	5099	150	5249	5099	150	5249	0.0%
C2-D1	1349	3900	5249	1349	3900	5249	0.0%
C1-D2	1349	3900	5249	1349	3900	5249	0.0%
C2-D2	5099	150	5249	5099	150	5249	0.0%

Prioritized ordering of mapping choices is (best to worst):

- Estimated — C2-D2 and C1-D1, C2-D1 and C1-D2
- Simulated — same as Estimated

Table 2: Fully Associative Cache With 1024 8-Byte Lines

Mapping	LocalGroup	EstLocal	EstRem	EstTotal	SimLocal	SimRem	SimTotal	Err
C1-D1	(2, 4)	5488	806	6294	5465	978	6443	2.3%
C2-D1	(2, 8)	1869	4425	6294	1781	4662	6443	2.3%
C1-D2	(2, 4)	1738	4556	6294	1715	4728	6443	2.3%
C2-D2	(2, 8)	5619	675	6294	5531	912	6443	2.3%

Prioritized ordering of mapping choices is (best to worst):

- Estimated — C2-D2, C1-D1, C2-D1, C1-D2
- Simulated — same as Estimated

Table 3: Direct-mapped Cache With 1024 8-Byte Lines

Mapping	LocalGroup	EstLocal	EstRem	EstTotal	SimLocal	SimRem	SimTotal	Err
C1-D1	(2, 2)	5950	1588	7538	5981	2094	8075	6.7%
C2-D1	(2, 5)	2240	4800	7040	2094	5927	8021	12.2%
C1-D2	(2, 2)	2200	5338	7538	2128	5947	8075	6.7%
C2-D2	(2, 5)	5990	1050	7040	6086	1935	8021	12.2%

Prioritized ordering of mapping choices is (best to worst):

- Estimated — C2-D2, C1-D1, C2-D1, C1-D2
- Simulated — same as Estimated

By examining the above tables, we make the following observations:

- For the case of unbounded cache capacity, the estimated results are identical to the simulated results. Thus the heuristic bounds of compulsory misses are exact for this example.
- For the other two cases of limited cache capacity, the relative error between *EstTotal* and *SimTotal* for this example is 2.3% for a fully-associative cache and within 12.2% for a direct-mapped cache. Thus our estimates are quite accurate. While our estimates will always be conservative for an integral number of locality group instances, they can be lower than the simulated values when the iteration space does not contain an integral number of locality group instances, as in this example.
- For all three cases, the prioritized ordering dictated by estimates is identical to the prioritized ordering obtained from the simulation results. This is our primary objective in locality analysis. The cost estimates point to C2-D2 as the combination with the fewest number of remote and total misses. This selection is borne out by the simulation results in which C2-D2 is indeed seen to be the combination with the lowest memory cost. This validates the use of our locality analysis technique in guiding the selection of computation and data mappings.

8 Extensions

The method proposed in the paper can be extended to deal with more realistic cache models and program models, such as caches with non-unit line sizes (with the possibility of false-sharing), loops with multiple references to the same array variable, and general set-associative cache organizations. We summarize these extensions below.

8.1 Non-unit Line Size

Let us look at cache organizations with non-unit line size. With a cache line size $L > 1$, a single cache miss fetches L contiguous words. Subsequent accesses to other words in the same cache line results in spatial locality. One complication for non-unit line sizes in a multiprocessor context is the effect of *false sharing.* Below, we discuss locality analysis for two cases: read-only variables and read-write variables.

Estimating Number of Misses for Read-only Variables False sharing is not an issue for read-only variables since multiple processors can cache their own copies of the shared cache line. Therefore, we can simply extend the solutions for estimating the number of distinct accesses (DA) to the number of distinct lines (DL) based on the solution outlined in [8].

In section 5.2, we outlined a method to estimate $\eta(T)$ for a direct-mapped cache with S lines/sets. It needs to be extended for the $L > 1$ case as discussed in [8]. More precise estimates of $\eta(T)$ are possible when cache block alignment offset, number of loop iterations, and degree of cache associativity are also taken into account.

Estimating Number of Misses for Read/Write Variables (False Sharing) We make a conservative estimate of false sharing overhead. We estimate the number of *misses* for a falsely-shared line (a line that may be written concurrently by multiple processors) to equal the number of *accesses* to that line. This represents the worst case scenario in which a falsely shared cache line is invalidated after each access. For a single array reference, false sharing can only occur at the boundaries between two processors' iteration sets. From the computation and data decomposition we can identify the falsely shared lines for a given cache organization. After completing the estimation outlined in section 5, we add in false sharing misses for boundary lines.

8.2 Multiple References per Array Variable

We now consider the case when the loop body contains multiple references to the same array variable. Consider the following example and its local iteration space for processor i

```
   do 10 i1 = i*100/4 + 1, (i+1)*100/4
10   A(i1) = A(i1) + A(i1-1) + A(i1+1)
```

The three references to array A, $A(i1-1)$, $A(i1)$ and $A(i1+1)$, are said to be ***uniformly generated*** [9]. It is easy to see that the overwhelming majority of the three references overlap with each other. A simple extension to the previous solutions is to perform locality analysis for a single reference in a uniformly generated set, and assume that the other references need not be counted separately because of the large overlap. In the above example, we may just perform locality analysis on $A(i1)$ and then ignore array references $A(i1-1)$ and $A(i1+1)$.

For multiple uniformly-generated sets, we can combine the solutions from the above methods by taking one representative reference from each uniformly generated set, and using the technique illustrated in this subsection to combine their effects. In practice, this is a good trade-off between precision and compile-time cost.

Extending the above formulae bounding the number of distinct accesses (DA) to the number of distinct lines (DL), is trickier than for a single reference because two access functions may yield elements that fall in the same cache line, even if the functions have no elements in common. We refer the readers to [8] for a brief discussion on how to do the estimation in this case.

8.3 Set-associative Caches

We considered locality analysis for a fully associative cache in section 5.1 and for a direct-mapped cache in section 5.2. A set-associative cache is a hybrid of these two cases. Consider a k-way set associative cache with S sets. We can apply similar ideas in section 5.2 to this case.

The steps outlined in section 5.2 are modified as follows. In steps 1 and 2, $\eta_{avg/min}$ is estimated just as for a direct-mapped cache with S lines. This estimation is safe since the cache has S k-way sets. However in step 3, the effective cache size is now computed as $S' = k\lfloor \eta_{avg/min} S \rfloor$ since we compute the locality group as for we have a fully-associative cache of $k \times S$ lines. Step 4 remains the same.

9 Related Work

Due to space limitations, this section only contains a brief discussion of previous work that is most relevant to this paper. Most of the references cited below perform locality analysis in the context of uniprocessor execution, and do not deal with identifying local vs. remote misses.

Ferrante, Sarkar and Thrash [8] provide simple closed-form formulae that bound the number of distinct accesses (DA) and distinct lines (DL) for a single array reference in a given sequential loop nest. They show how to extend these bounds for multiple references to the same array variable. They also provide an exact closed-form solution for computing DA for a single array reference contained in two loops. These bounds provide an estimate of the number of cache misses incurred by a given loop nest. They also showed how to analyze set conflicts in the case of direct mapped and set associative caches with non-unit line sizes.

Wolf and Lam [18] propose an algorithm that improves the locality of a loop nest by transforming the code via interchange, reversal, skewing and tiling based on a mathematical formulation of reuse and locality, and a loop transformation theory that unifies the various transforms as unimodular transformations. Their goal is to find the best combination of loop interchange, skewing, reversal and tiling that maximizes the data locality within loop nests, subject to the constraints of direction and distance vectors. Unlike our approach of locality analysis by estimating a count of the number of cache misses, they measure the locality of a transformed code by intersecting the reuse vector space with the localized vector space.

In [5], Bailey presents a thorough analysis of the behavior of a direct-mapped cache with strided data access, and gives a formula for estimating cache efficiency. Using cache efficiency, the compiler can detect unfavorable strides and automatically adjust array dimensions through padding techniques. However, this work does not address the overall problem of locality analysis (estimating the number of misses) for array references in a loop nest.

Bacon et al [4] focus on techniques for improving uniprocessor data locality by restructuring data declarations, as opposed to restructuring the computation without changing the data layout. They provide a padding algorithm for selecting appropriate padding amounts, which takes into account various cache and translation lookaside buffer effects collectively within a single framework.

Jeremiassen and Eggers [13] develop compiler algorithms that analyze parallel programs and restructure their shared data to reduce the number of false sharing misses. The algorithms analyze per-process shared data accesses, pinpoint the data structures that are susceptible to false sharing and choose an appropriate transformation to reduce it. The transformations either group data that is accessed by the same processor or separate individual data items that are shared. Restructuring can reduce false sharing, but it may also have a negative impact on spatial locality. Thus it is hard to estimate how much pay-off restructuring can get.

Agarwal, Krantz and Nararajan [1] present a theoretical framework for automatically partitioning parallel loops to minimize cache coherency traffic on shared-memory multiprocessors. They derive an optimal hyperparallelpiped tiling of iteration space for minimal communication for loops with general affine index expressions in multiprocessors with caches. The tiling specifies both the shape and size of iteration space tiles. Their solution addresses a limited problem statement – that of partitioning a loop nest with perfect load balance. They restrict their analysis to the case of a unit line size and do not take cache size considerations into account.

Verghese et al [17] study the performance improvements provided by OS supported dynamic page migration replication on CC-NUMA (cache-coherent non-uniform memory access) machine. The operating system can improve data locality by migrating and replicating pages. Page migration is used to keep data local to the process when it is moved, and page replication is required where data is heavily-read-shared between many processors. To support page migration and replication, cache-miss information has to be sampled and collected at a fixed rate, that involves both time and space overhead. Page migration and replication also cause kernel overhead and space overhead.

10 Conclusions

In this paper, we presented techniques for estimating the locality cost (number of misses) on a NUMA-style distributed-shared-memory multiprocessor for a loop nest with given computation and data mappings. These techniques build on past work on locality analysis for uniprocessor execution. A prototype implementation of many of these analysis techniques has been completed at IBM, and the compile-time cost of this analysis has been found to be very small. We believe that these techniques will be very useful in guiding automatic and semi-automatic selection of computation and data mappings on current and future NUMA-style distributed-shared-memory multiprocessors. Our future work plans include studying ways of relaxing the assumption of no reuse across multiple instances of a locality group for more precise locality analysis.

References

1. Anant Agarwal, David Krantz, and Venkat Natarajan. Automatic Partitioning of Parallel Loops and Data Arrays for Distributed Shared Memory Multiprocessors. *International Conference on Parallel Computing*, 1993.
2. S. Amarasinghe and M. Lam. Generating efficient communication for distributed memory machines. In *Proceedings of ACM SIGPLAN'93 Conference on Programming Language Design and Implementation*, June 1993.

3. J. M. Anderson and M. S. Lam. Global optimizations for parallelism and locality on scalable parallel machines. *ACM SIGPLAN '93 Conference on Programming Language Design and Implementation*, pages 112–125, June 1993. Albuquerque, NM.
4. David F. Bacon, Jyh-Herng Chow, Dz ching R. Ju, K. Muthukumar, and Vivek Sarkar. A Compiler Framework for Restructuring Data Declarations to Enhance Cache and TLB Effectiveness. *CASCON '94 conference*, November 1994.
5. David H. Bailey. Unfavorable Strides in Cache Memory Systems. *Scientific Programming*, 4:53–58, 1995. RNR Technical Report RNR-92-015, NASA Ames Research Center.
6. Utpal Banerjee. *Dependence Analysis for Supercomputing.* Kluwer Academic Publishers, Norwell, Massachusetts, 1988.
7. R. Berrendorf, M. Gerndt, and M. Mairandres. Programming Shared Virtual Memory on the Intel Paragon Supercomputer . *Proceedings of Fifth Workshop on Compilers for Parallel Computers*, 1995. Internal Report KFA-ZAM-IB-9509, Research Centre Juelich, Germany (also http://www.kfa-juelich.de/zam/ZAMPeople/gerndt.html).
8. Jeanne Ferrante, Vivek Sarkar, and Wendy Thrash. On Estimating and Enhancing Cache Effectiveness. *Lecture Notes in Computer Science*, (589):328–343, 1991. Proceedings of the Fourth International Workshop on Languages and Compilers for Parallel Computing, Santa Clara, California, USA, August 1991.
9. D. Gannon, , W. Jalby, and K. Gallivan. Strategies for cache and local memory management by global program transformation. *Journal of Parallel and Distributed Computing*, 5:587–616, 1988.
10. Shaohua Han. Cache Misses Prediction for Array References in Loop Nest. Technical report, School of Computer Science, McGill University, 1996. Master's thesis in progress.
11. High Performance Fortran Forum. *High Performance Fortran. Language Specification – Version 0.4*, December 1992.
12. M. D. Hill. *Aspects of Cache Memories and Instruction Buffer Performance.* PhD thesis, Univ. of California at Berkeley, November 1987. Tech. Rep. UCB/CSD 87/381.
13. Tor E. Jeremiassen and Susan J. Eggers. Reducing False Sharing on Shared Memory Multiprocessors through Compile Time Data Transformations. *The fifth Symposium on Principles and Practice of Parallel Programming*, July 1995.
14. Monica S. Lam, Edward E. Rothberg, and Michael E. Wolf. The Cache Performance and Optimization of Blocked Algorithms. *Proceedings of the Fourth International Conference on Architectural Support for Programming Languages and Operating Systems*, April 1991.
15. Qi Ning, Van Dongen Vincent, and Guang R. Gao. Automatic Decomposition in EPPP Compiler. *CASCON '94 conference*, pages 283–291, November 1994.
16. M. J. Serrano. *Performance Tradeoffs in Multistreamed Superscalar Architectures.* PhD thesis, University of California at Santa Barbara, March 1994.
17. Ben Verghese, Scott Devine, Anoop Gupta, and Mendel Rosenblum. Operating System Support for Improving Data Locality on CC-NUMA Computer Servers . *The seventh International Conference on Architectural Support for Programming Languages and Operating Systems*, October 1996.
18. Michael E. Wolf and Monica S. Lam. A Data Locality Optimization Algorithm. *Proceedings of the ACM SIGPLAN Symposium on Programming Language Design and Implementation*, pages 30–44, June 1991.

Data Distribution and Loop Parallelization for Shared-Memory Multiprocessors *

Eduard Ayguadé, Jordi Garcia, M. Luz Grande and Jesús Labarta

Computer Architecture Department, Polytechnic University of Catalunya
cr. Gran Capità s/núm, Mòdul D6, 08034 - Barcelona, Spain

Abstract. Shared-memory multiprocessor systems can achieve high performance levels when appropriate work parallelization and data distribution are performed. These two actions are not independent and decisions have to be taken in a unified way trying to minimize execution time and data movement costs. The first goal is achieved by parallelizing loops (the main components suitable for parallel execution in scientific codes) and assign work to processors having in mind a good load balancing. The second goal is achieved when data is stored in the cache memories of processors minimizing both true and false sharing of cache lines. This paper describes the main features of our automatic parallelization and data distribution research tool and shows the performance of the parallelization strategies generated. The tool (named PDDT) accepts programs written in Fortran77 and generates directives of shared memory programming models (like Power Fortran from SGI or Exemplar from Convex).
Keywords: High Performance Compilers, Loop Parallelization, Static and Dynamic Data Mappings, Cache Behavior, Shared Memory Multiprocessors

1 Introduction

Parallelization and data distribution are two topics closely related when parallelizing loops for cache-coherent shared-memory parallel systems. In these systems, cache miss penalties can be significantly large and false sharing, invalidations and excessive data replication can have negative effects in performance. In some cases, these effects can easily offset any gain due to parallel execution.

Most current shared-memory compilers choose a loop in each nest for parallelization, and it is interchanged as far out as data dependence analysis allows. Inner loops are strip-mined and blocked to exploit all possible data reuse in the processor cache. Iterations in each parallel loop are distributed across the parallel threads according to a fixed scheme. Some compilers also ensure that each major data structure in the program is aligned on a cache line boundary and make the contiguous dimension of an array (i.e., the first dimension in Fortran) an integer multiple of a cache line. This is useful to avoid false sharing of cache lines so that each processor works with complete cache lines.

* This research has been supported by the Ministry of Education of Spain under contract TIC-429/95 and by the CEPBA (European Center for Parallelism of Barcelona).

Some researchers [AL93] have focussed on better determining which loop to parallelize with the purpose of obtaining maximum parallelism while minimizing sharing of cache lines (true sharing). They analyze data and computation decomposition without regard to the original layout of the data structures. A more recent work [AAL95] proposes to enhance spatial locality, reduce false sharing (access to different data items co-located on the same cache line) and conflict misses among accesses to the set of data assigned to each processor. This is done by applying some data transformations making data accessed by each processor contiguous in the shared address space. [JE95] have also proposed algorithms to transform data layouts to improve memory performance; they analyze per-process shared data accesses in parallel programs, identify data structures that are susceptible to false sharing and choose an appropriate layout transformation to reduce the number of false sharing misses. These data layout transformations require that all accesses to the arrays in the entire program use the new layout; programming languages (such as Fortran) can make these transformations difficult and the compiler has to guarantee that all possible accesses are updated accordingly and optimized.

In the past years, other researchers have targeted their efforts to automatic data distribution for distributed-memory multiprocessors [BCG+95, AGG+95, KK95, SSGC95], according to the array access patterns and parallel execution of operations within computationally intensive phases. The objective is to specify the mapping for the arrays used in these computational phases, and it can be either static or dynamic. In a static mapping, the layout of the arrays does not change during the execution of the program; in a dynamic mapping, remapping operations are performed in order to change the layout of arrays in different computational phases.

A basic observation of this paper is that this technology developed for distributed memory compilers is useful for shared memory architectures in which each processor has access to a high-capacity private cache (for instance, 4 Mbyte in each processor of a R8000 SGI Power Challenge or between 512 Kbyte and 16 Mbyte in each processor of a R10000 SGI Power Challenge architecture [SGI96]). In these systems, the cache behaves as an attraction local memory that stores data referenced by the processor. Trying to minimize true and false sharing reduces data motion through the interconnection network. The techniques we have developed represent the application of the owner computes rule, frequently used in distributed-memory systems, to shared-memory machines.

In a parallel loop, a chuck of iterations is assigned to each processor. The execution of this chunk will bring any remote data to its cache. Notice that data remapping is implicitly done by the caching mechanism itself. We propose to parallelize loops taking into account the data that is stored in the private cache of each processor, either because it has been previously computed or fetched in other loops, or that needs to be stored in the cache because it will be useful in the following loops. PDDT keeps track of the array sections that are accessed during the execution of the different computational phases in an application in order to decide, with a global view, the parallelization strategy for each loop. This is done by analyzing the reference patterns inside computational phases and predicting the cache behavior that different parallelizations would imply. The generation of code for the target shared-memory programming models makes intensive use of well known techniques, such as loop tiling and loop limit adaptation to partition the iteration space, loop interchange to reduce the overhead of parallel thread creation and improve spatial locality, and parallel synchronized execution of dependent loops to minimize execution time.

In cache-coherent shared-memory systems, false sharing might also introduce additional data motion. Since data is transferred in cache lines (for instance, 128 bytes long in SGI Power Challenge multiprocessors), different processors may share the same cache line and never access to the same data items. Every time a processor writes a data item in the line, other copies of the same line are invalidated. When another processor re-uses a data item (col-located on the same cache line), the item may no longer be in its cache due to the access by the other processor. Therefore, spatial locality may be lost and additional data movement may happen. PDDT also addresses the problem of minimizing false sharing by synchronizing the access to cache lines shared by different processors in parallel loops. In addition to that, PDDT also pads the contiguous dimension of arrays to make it multiple of cache line size and aligns major data structures to cache line boundaries.

Other techniques oriented to the optimization of code for uniprocessor cache performance are left to the native compiler of the target parallel machine and they are out of the scope of this paper.

PDDT is a research tool in the sense that it is flexible to specify machine dependent characteristics and to specify different compilation options and strategies. In addition to automatic parallelization, PDDT is also a performance prediction tool that may help the user in the task of writing parallel code for the target machine; it accepts directives in the source program which narrows the search space of solutions and provides the user with information about the behavior of the program.

The paper is organized as follows. Section 2 shows the main aspects that are considered in PDDT to generate parallelization strategies based on data distributions. Section 3 summarizes the main modules in PDDT that perform the parallelization process. More details about specific modules can be found elsewhere [AGG+94, AGG+95]. Section 4 evaluates the parallelization strategies explored by PDDT and compares them against the ones generated by a commercial compiler. Finally, Section 5 states our conclusions and summarizes future work.

2 Parallelization for Coherent Caches

In this section we show the feasibility of using information about data distribution to drive the parallelization process of a program in a coherent cache-based multiprocessor system. Keeping track of data motion among the caches in the system is useful to decide parallelization strategies in which both computation time and data movement costs are minimized. We also show further optimizations to reduce the negative effect caused by dependences and false sharing. In this section, we use an excerpt of the Alternate Direction Implicit (ADI) integration kernel[2]. The full kernel is evaluated in Section 4.

2.1 Using Data Mappings

The behavior of coherent caches is modeled when flowing from one computational phase to another within the execution of a procedure and inter-procedurally. We can model either distributed network caches (like in the Globally Shared Memory Convex SPP systems [Con94]) or private caches in bus based symmetric multiprocessor systems (like the Power Challenge SGI systems [SGI96]). To perform this modeling, we assume that capacity and conflict misses never happen[3].

In this section we analyze the two phases ($P4$ and $P7$) shown in Figure 1.a, and assume for each of them a parallelization strategy: the i loop in phase $P4$ and the j loop in phase $P7$ are fully parallelized. Figure 1.b shows the elements of the arrays that will be stored in the private cache of one of the processors (assuming 4 processors). Notice that, due to the parallelization of the inner i loop in phase $P4$, a set of consecutive rows of arrays a, b and x will be stored in the cache of each processor. Since arrays b and x are written, these elements will be owned by it and other copies will be invalidated, if existed. In phase $P7$, the outer j loop is parallelized. After executing this phase, each processor will own a set of columns of arrays b and x (since the rows that it owned have been invalidated by the other processors) and will have in its cache a set of rows and columns of array a. When these phases are executed again (because of the outer iterative $iter$ loop), processors either have a set of rows or columns of arrays b and x, and a set of rows and columns of array a.

The parallelization strategies that we consider lead to cache contents that can be characterized in terms of HPF-like array alignments and distributions. So for instance, for phase $P4$ and the first iteration of the $iter$ loop, one could say that arrays a, b and x are perfectly aligned and distributed across the caches in a $(BLOCK, *)$ way. In phase $P7$ and for arrays b and x, a $(*, BLOCK)$ distribution characterizes the contents of the cache. However, for array a the contents of the cache can not be characterized with a single distribution function; instead, one could say that it is the union of two distribution functions: $(BLOCK, *) \cup (*, BLOCK)$.

To estimate data movement costs, PDDT detects that the three arrays are moved when transitioning from phase $P4$ to phase $P7$ in the first iteration. After that, and for the rest of iterations, only arrays b and x are moved when alternating between these two phases; array a is not moved because each processor holds the rows and columns it needs to perform the computations.

---

[2] We use two different data sets: small (NUM=64 and MAXITER=1000) and large (NUM=256 and MAXITER=100).

[3] This assumption holds along the paper; some comments about handling these misses and including them in the parallelization process are given in Section 5.

```
      program adi
        double precision x(NUM,NUM)
        double precision a(NUM,NUM), b(NUM,NUM)

        do 10 iter = 1, MAXITER
           do 4 j = 2, NUM                                      Phase P4
             do 4 i = 1, NUM
               x(i, j) = x(i, j) - x(i, j - 1) * a(i, j) / b(i, j - 1)
               b(i, j) = b(i, j) - a(i, j) * a(i, j) / b(i, j - 1)
4          continue

           do 7 j = 1, NUM                                      Phase P7
             do 7 i = 2, NUM
               x(i, j) = x(i, j) - x(i - 1, j) * a(i, j) / b(i - 1, j)
               b(i, j) = b(i, j) - a(i, j) * a(i, j) / b(i - 1, j)
7          continue
10      continue
      end
```

(a)

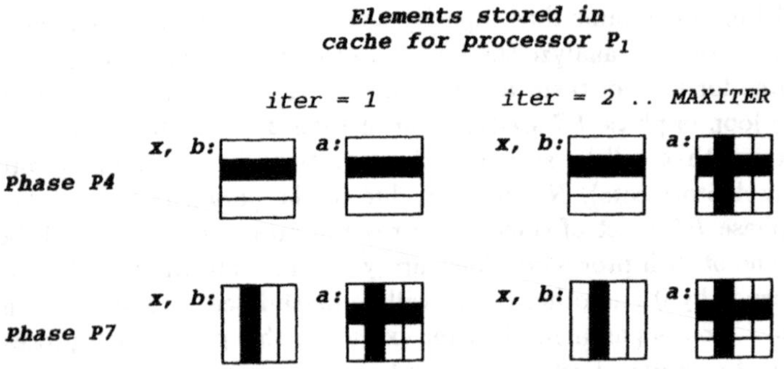

(b)

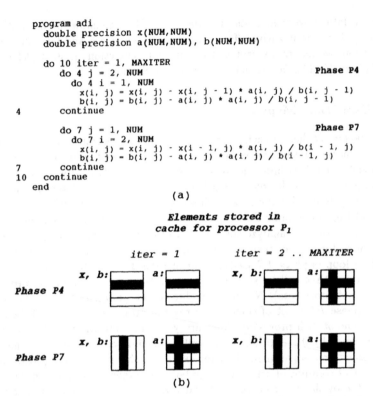

Fig. 1. (a) Excerpt of the ADI kernel. (b) Cache contents after executing phases $P4$ and $P7$.

For these two phases two other parallelization strategies would be possible: to execute phase $P4$ sequentially (because of data dependences) and phase $P7$ in parallel, or vice versa. If a single processor executes the sequential phase, then this processor will perform additional data movements and invalidations with the associated overhead. In the next section it is shown how PDDT minimizes the effect of this movement. Table 1 compares the execution time for the three parallelization strategies and for different number of processors (P). Notice that in this case, it is better to execute both phases in parallel.

	NUM=64			NUM=256		
	P=2	P=4	P=8	P=2	P=4	P=8
$P4_{par}$ and $P7_{par}$	3.89	2.10	2.71	6.18	3.32	1.74
$P4_{par}$ and $P7_{seq}$	6.02	5.06	6.16	9.45	8.11	7.50
$P4_{seq}$ and $P7_{par}$	5.94	5.04	4.70	9.45	8.10	7.49
$P4_{seq}$ and $P7_{seq}$	6.57			10.61		

Table 1. Phases $P4$ and $P7$ - Execution time on a Power Challenge of different parallelization strategies and sequential execution time.

Parallelization strategies where chunks of iterations are cyclically assigned to processors lead to data distributions that can be modeled using the *CYCLIC* or *BLOCK_CYCLIC* attribute in the HPF distribution directive.

2.2 Iteration Space Partitioning

In most commercial compilers, the iteration space of each parallel loop is partitioned in equally sized chunks trying to obtain a good load balancing. We propose to partition the iteration space of each loop in a sequence of phases so that each processor executes chunks of iterations that access the same array sections (when possible). This is useful to partition the iteration space when the bounds of the iteration space change from a phase to another, when offsets are used in array subscript expressions, or when we have a sequential loop that accesses distributed data. In all these cases, an adequate assignment of iterations to processors might reduce or eliminate data movements. The compiler has to insert code so that each processor computes its lower and upper bound of the iteration space that it has to execute. The owner computes rule is used to drive this iteration partitioning; this rule states that the owner of a piece of data is the responsible for its update along program execution. The ownership can change dynamically if considered profitable. We name this feature chunk affinity partitioning. The compiler has to detect if this partitioning lead to a loss of load balancing and decide an intermediate solution.

	NUM=64			NUM=256		
	P=2	P=4	P=8	P=2	P=4	P=8
$P4_{par}$ and $P7_{seq}$	6.02	5.06	6.16	9.45	8.11	7.50
$P4_{par}$ and $P7_{chunk}$	5.28	4.82	7.36	8.14	6.91	6.58

Table 2. Phases *P*4 and *P*7 - Execution time on a Power Challenge with static row distribution.

For instance, assume that we execute phases *P*4 and *P*7 in ADI with a static row distribution $(BLOCK, *)$. In this case, and due to data dependences, phase *P*4 can be executed fully in parallel and phase *P*7 must be executed sequentially. In most programming models, sequential phases are executed by a single processor; if so, additional data movement and invalidation overheads have to be paid in order to change the ownership of the data being computed and to bring to its cache all data needed to perform the sequential computation. To avoid these overheads, PDDT partitions the iteration space and inserts synchronization to preserve data dependences. In this way, each processor works with data it owns but it does not start execution until the previous processor completes its execution. The effects of this partitioning are shown in Table 2 and they reflect the trade off between synchronization and data movement; the first row shows the execution time when phase *P*7 is executed sequentially by a single processor; the second row shows the execution time when this phase is executed in parallel ensuring that a processor does not start execution until the previous one has finished. The decrease in the execution time is due to the overhead of data movements and invalidations that are avoided[4], and it is more noticeable when the arrays that are moved are bigger.

2.3 Pipelined Computation

In this section we show how parallelization strategies can benefit from pipelined computations. In a pipelined computation, a processor cannot begin execution until its predecessor has partially finished its computation. For instance, this is useful to reduce the negative effects of data dependences. Although pipelined computations are well known, most of the currently available compilers do not apply them. In this section we also show how pipelined computations are useful to minimize overheads due to false sharing of cache lines.

In the previous section we have noticed the benefits of executing phase $P7$ in a synchronized way preserving data dependences. However, there exists room to improve the performance of the execution if we pipeline the execution of the loop. In this case, once a processor finishes the computation of a chunk of iterations of the j loop, the next processor can start its computation using data previously computed. The size of the chunk determines the amount of overlap and the overhead of synchronization incurred due to the pipelined execution. Figure 2 shows the execution time of this phase for different sizes of the chunk. Notice that with small chunks we are obtaining near optimal performance; this means that the synchronization overhead we are paying compensates the negative effect of the sequential execution. In addition, this model of computation also reduces the overheads due to data motion, since they are overlapped with computation.

We also propose to use pipelined computations to minimize the overheads introduced by false sharing. For ADI, false sharing appears when we use the data set with NUM=64 and P=8. In the Power Challenge, cache lines are 128 bytes long; therefore each cache line holds 16 elements of the arrays if they are double precision. So notice that when we distribute the arrays in a $(BLOCK,*)$ way, each cache line is shared by two processors. Figure 3.a shows the distribution of cache lines among processors. Therefore, additional movement and invalidation happen due to false sharing. The negative effect of false sharing can be observed in Table 1 for the two parallelizations strategies that execute phase $P4$ in parallel; notice that the execution time with P=8 is greater than with P=4. The same effects can be observed in the first plot in Figure 2, where one can see that the execution time of the phase has an anomalous behavior for P=8.

The main idea behind the pipelined execution is that a processor starts using a set of cache lines when another conflicting processor finishes using them. To reduce the overheads of false sharing, we propose to independently pipeline the computation of all the processors that share cache lines. This synchronized execution model also allows PDDT to perform an estimation of the additional

[4] The experiment with NUM=64 and P=8 shows a performance degradation due to the false sharing; this situation is considered in the next section.

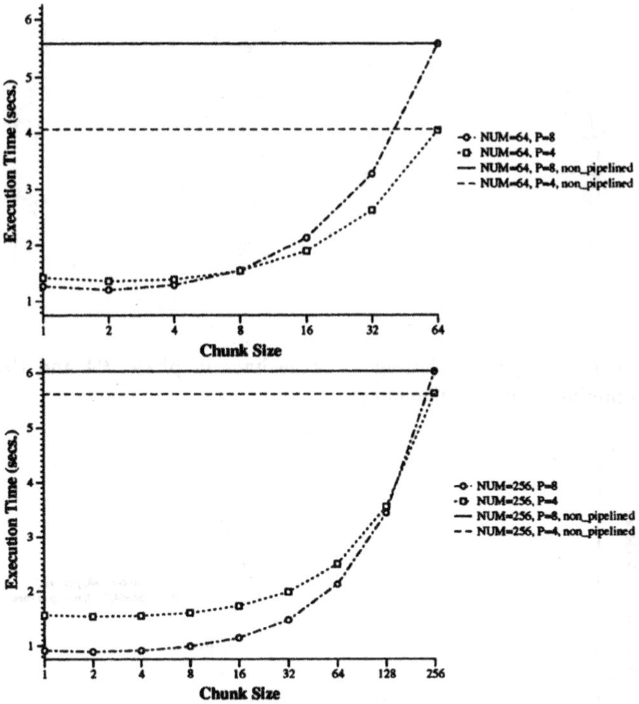

Fig. 2. Phase *P*7 - Using pipelined computations to minimize the negative effect of dependences on the execution time.

data movement that appears due to false sharing; if the execution is not synchronized, the additional costs become unpredictable at compile time. So for instance, in the previous case, PDDT would decide to pipeline the execution of processors 0 and 1, 2 and 3, and so on, as shown in Figure 3.b. Figure 4 shows the execution time of phase *P*4 for different sizes of the chunk. Again, notice that the overhead introduced by synchronization and the reduction of parallel execution in the pipelined model clearly compensates the negative effect of false sharing. For chunks smaller than 32, the pipelined execution improves over the fully parallel execution. However, for chunks bigger than 16 the sequentialization of the execution is worse than the negative effect of false sharing.

Table 3 shows the execution time of phases *P*4 and *P*7, when pipelining is used to minimize the negative effects of dependences and false sharing. In cases where false sharing does not occur (NUM=256 and P=8), pipelining reduces performance; the overheads introduced by synchronization and the loss of parallelism in the pipelined model are the causes of this degradation. However, when false sharing happens (for NUM=64 and P=8) these overheads compensate the additional data movement costs. Figure 5 shows the code generated by PDDT for phases *P*4 and *P*7; loops have been parallelized and pipelined (chunk size 4) for a static $(BLOCK, *)$ distribution.

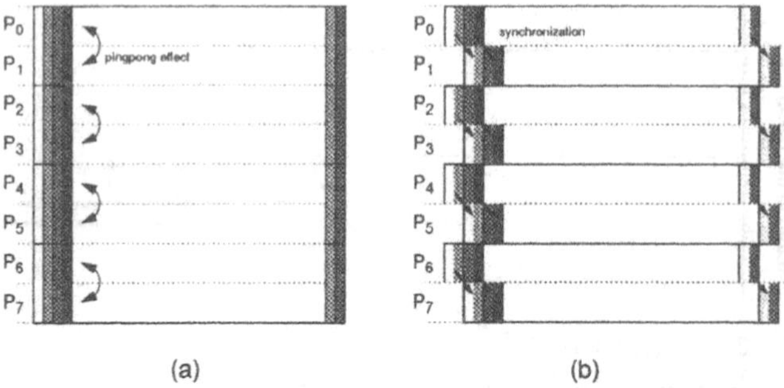

Fig. 3. Phase *P4* - (a) False sharing of cache lines in phase *P4* and (b) Pipelined execution to minimize its negative effects.

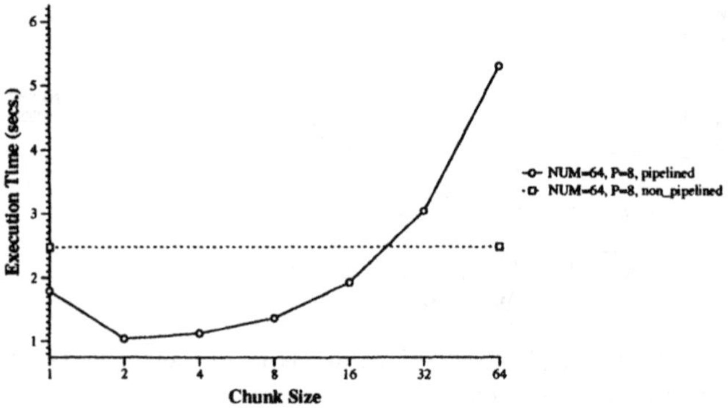

Fig. 4. Phase *P4* - Using pipelined computations to minimize the negative effects of false sharing on the execution time.

In order to reduce false sharing in the access to synchronization objects, they are padded to the size of the cache line and aligned to cache line boundaries. If not done, several elements of the synchronizing object are located on the same cache line; when a processor writes to one of these elements, the other elements co-located on the same cache line are invalidated and new invalidation misses appear when the waiting processors re-read their status.

3 Parallelization and Data Distribution Process in PDDT

Our research tool (PDDT - Parallelization and Data Distribution Tool) analyzes Fortran77 programs and annotates them with directives and executable statements of shared memory (Convex Exemplar, SGI Power Fortran) programming models. The structure of loop nests may be changed in order to minimize data motion, improve locality of references and minimize false sharing. These decisions are done so that the amount of remote accesses is reduced as much as possible, while maximizing the parallelism achieved.

	NUM=64	NUM=256
$P4_{par}$ and $P7_{par}$	2.71	1.74
$P4_{pipe}$ and $P7_{par}$	1.61	1.93
$P4_{par}$ and $P7_{pipe}$	3.28	1.57
$P4_{pipe}$ and $P7_{pipe}$	2.25	1.75

Table 3. Phases $P4$ and $P7$ - Execution time on a Power Challenge (P=8) using pipelined computation in phase $P4$ to minimize false sharing and in phase $P7$ to minimize the effect of dependences (chunk size 2). Rows 1 and 2 correspond to the dynamic solution; rows 3 and 4 correspond to static $(BLOCK, *)$ distribution.

```
      do 10 iter = 1, MAXITER
         do jj = 1, NUM, 2
            token(jj) = NUM/2
            token(jj+1) = 0
         enddo
C$PAR PARALLEL DO LOCAL(i, j, jj, my$p, lb$i, ub$i, next$p)
         do my$p = 0, 7                                    Phase P4
            lb$i = max((my$p * NUM / 8) + 1, 1)
            ub$i = min((my$p + 1) * (NUM / 8), NUM)
            next$p = 1
            do jj = 2, NUM, 4
444            if (next$p .gt. token(my$p+1)) goto 444
               do 4 j = jj, min(jj + 3, NUM)
                  do 4 i = lb$i, ub$i
                  ...
4              continue
               token(my$p + 1) = token(my$p + 1) + 1
               next$p = next$p + 1
            enddo
         enddo
         do jj = 1, NUM
            token(jj) = 0
         enddo
C$PAR PARALLEL DO LOCAL(i, j, jj, my$p, lb$i, ub$i)
         do my$p = 0, 7                                    Phase P7
            lb$i = max((my$p * NUM / 8) + 1, 2)
            ub$i = min((my$p + 1) * (NUM / 8), NUM)
            do jj = 1, NUM, 4
777            if (token(jj) .ne. my$p) goto 777
               do 7 j = jj, min(jj + 3, NUM)
                  do 7 i = lb$i, ub$i
                  ...
7              continue
               token(jj) = token(jj) + 1
            enddo
         enddo
10    continue
```

Fig. 5. Transformed code for phases $P4$ and $P7$ according to $(BLOCK, *)$ distribution; phase $P4$ has been parallelized with pipelining to minimize false sharing. Phase $P7$ has been parallelized for chunk affinity and pipelined to minimize the sequentilization due to dependences. Chunk size is 4 in both phases.

PDDT is targeted to generic Non-Uniform Memory Access Architectures (NUMA) with local and remote memory accesses. Each processor has its own memory hierarchy and can access the memories in other processors through the interconnection network. Data movement costs are estimated as the number of cache lines that need to be transferred multiplied by the remote access time. Given a parallelization strategy, computation costs are estimated from a profile of the sequential execution on a workstation based on the same processor and with the same memory hierarchy than the parallel machine (which is a common fact in most of the hardware vendor product lines).

All cost estimations in PDDT are done numerically assuming some problem and machine specific parameters. Profiling the sequential execution of the original Fortran 77 program is required in order to obtain these problem specific parameters, such as array sizes, the number of iterations for the loops and their execution time, and the probabilities of the different branches in conditional statements. A configuration file allows the user to specify some machine specific parameters (number of processors, overhead of parallel thread creation, local and remote memory access costs, ...), to restrict the kind of solutions explored by PDDT (number of distributed dimensions and loops to parallelize, static or dynamic solutions, number of candidate mappings for the phases and procedures, ...), and to specify the target programming model.

PDDT has evolved from our automatic data distribution tool (DDT) targeted to distributed-memory machines. Details about its implementation can be found elsewhere [AGG+94, AGG+95]. The main steps of the parallelization process performed by PDDT are outlined below:

- Detection of phases or computationally intensive portions of code, which mainly correspond to nested loops and calls to procedures. Phases are considered at this level as portions of code that modify the contents of the cache. The definition of phase by [KK95] is used.
- Selection of candidate solutions for the previously detected phases and estimation of their cost. Each solution represents a particular distribution of the elements of the arrays across the private caches and a parallelization strategy. For each phase, PDDT decides which loops to parallelize, which loops must be executed sequentially, and which ones benefit from pipelining. Detection of false sharing and minimization of its effects using pipelining are done at this stage of the parallelization process. The decisions are done based on an estimation of the computation and movement costs, which are both affected by the chunk size selected when the pipelined execution model is used. To do that, an analysis of the reference patterns and data dependences within the scope of phases is done.
- Analysis of compatibility among phases, and selection of solutions for each of them. This selection is done by exploring a search space composed of the different candidate solutions for each phase and estimating the data movement costs due to the remapping of arrays between phases. This analysis is done by characterizing cache contents in terms of HPF-like data mappings; in a cache-based system more than one mapping function may be needed to

characterize it after the execution of a phase. The phase control flow graph drives the process and identifies the different sequences of phases that might appear during the execution of a procedure.

- Code restructuring: generation of shared-memory parallelization directives that specify loops that are run sequentially or in parallel. In addition to that, PDDT also specifies the partitioning of the iteration space for the loops, changes in the structure of loop nests to improve spatial locality and introduces synchronization to guarantee the correct behavior of the program and to minimize false sharing. In this step, some changes in the declaration of data structures are also performed: (i) dummy arrays are inserted in order to guarantee that all major data structures are aligned on cache line boundaries; (ii) if the first dimension of an array is distributed, it is padded with "unused" elements in order to have an integral number of cache lines allocated to this dimension.

The process described above is done under control of the inter-procedural analysis module; this module builds the call graph for the entire program and records information about call sites and actual arguments. Once built, a bottom-up pass over the call graph decides the order in which procedures are analyzed, analyzes them and records information into the PDDT inter-procedural database.

The native compiler for the target machine is used to translate the annotated Fortran77 code generated by PDDT into an efficient code, taking care of all the aspects related to scalar optimizations, further locality exploitation and proper storage of the arrays.

4 Experimental Results

PDDT can be used either as a parallelizing tool or as a prediction tool able to help the user in writing parallel programs for cache-coherent shared-memory multiprocessors. In both cases, PDDT hides all the main architectural features of the target machine and guides the user during the parallelization process, showing him the sources of inefficiency. Given a (partial or complete) parallelization strategy for the program, PDDT estimates the cost of executing the program on the target machine, both in terms of computation and data motion costs. If the parallelization strategy is not complete, PDDT parallelizes those loops not specified by the user according to the user supplied parallelization for the rest of the loops.

In this section we analyze two programs: the Alternate Direction Implicit integration kernel *ADI*, and *swm* from the SPEC92 benchmark set. For the first one, we will show how PDDT generates parallelization strategies that are better than the ones generated by compilers that perform the parallelization process without caring about data distribution. In particular, we compare with the *pfa* compiler for the Power Challenge SGI architecture. For the second one, we will analyze the accuracy of the performance estimations performed by PDDT.

4.1 Alternate Direction Implicit ADI

The ADI kernel has a two-dimensional data space and has a set of computational phases that perform forward and backward sweeps along rows and columns of the data space. Three different array distribution strategies are evaluated (static row $(BLOCK, *)$, static column $(*, BLOCK)$ and dynamic in which some phases are executed with row distribution and some other phases with column distribution); for each of these strategies, different optimizations are turned on in order to evaluate their impact on performance (chunk affinity and pipelined computation to minimize dependences and false sharing). Table 4 shows the speed up obtained over the sequential execution on a single processor. The target architecture is a Silicon Graphics Power Challenge with eight R8000 processors, and 4 Mbyte of private cache per processor.

w/o Chunk Affinity and w/o Pipelined Execution						
	NUM=64			**NUM=256**		
	P=2	**P=4**	**P=8**	**P=2**	**P=4**	**P=8**
(BLOCK, *)	1.18	1.37	1.12	1.18	1.39	1.52
(*, BLOCK)	1.18	1.38	1.50	1.18	1.39	1.51
Dynamic	1.77	3.30	2.49	1.79	3.40	6.50
w/ Chunk Affinity and w/o Pipelined Execution						
	NUM=64			**NUM=256**		
	P=2	**P=4**	**P=8**	**P=2**	**P=4**	**P=8**
(BLOCK, *)	1.24	1.33	0.87	1.30	1.52	1.60
(*, BLOCK)	1.30	1.52	1.59	1.32	1.58	1.72
Dynamic	1.77	3.30	2.49	1.79	3.40	6.50
w/ Chunk Affinity and w/ Pipelined Execution						
	NUM=64			**NUM=256**		
	P=2	**P=4**	**P=8**	**P=2**	**P=4**	**P=8**
(BLOCK, *)	1.75	2.94	3.22	1.92	3.66	6.51
(*, BLOCK)	1.80	3.03	4.50	1.94	3.71	6.70
Dynamic	1.77	3.30	4.47	1.79	3.40	6.50

Table 4. ADI - Speed up for different program sizes and number of processors. Three data distributions are evaluated: static row, static column and dynamic distribution. Chunk affinity and pipelined computation are turned on and off to show their effect on performance.

The following conclusions can be drawn from the figures in Table 4. First of all one can see that in the static solutions it is important to partition the iteration space so that data are re-used by the same processor as much as possible; in particular for this code, to execute sequential phases using the processors that at the time are the owners of the distributed arrays. In general, the speed up of row distribution is worse than column distribution since the amount of data moved around in the first one is bigger (less elements in each cache line moved are useful). In addition, the row distribution suffers from false sharing, which even degrades more performance.

We can also observe that using pipelined computations to reduce the negative effect of dependences and false sharing reduces the performance gap between the dynamic and static solutions. Depending on the problem size and number of processors, static column distribution or dynamic distribution are automatically selected by PDDT. This is not the case for the native SGI compiler, which always selects the dynamic solution and does not perform pipelining to control false sharing.

4.2 Swm Benchmark

Finally we show the accuracy of PDDT in the performance prediction of the automatically parallelized programs. For this purpose we use one of the programs in the SPEC benchmark set. The program has been parallelized using PDDT configured with the architectural parameters of a Power Challenge Silicon Graphics multiprocessor system. The parallelized program, annotated with PFA directives, is fed into the native Fortran compiler.

Table 5 shows the actual and predicted speed-ups of the parallelized program using 2, 4, or 8 processors and two different problem sizes: 64 and 512. Notice that the accuracy of the prediction is enough to validate the data mappings and parallelization strategies suggested for this code.

	size=64		size=512	
Number of CPUs	Predicted	Measured	Predicted	Measured
2	1.9115	1.9126	1.9979	2.0246
4	3.6491	3.5064	3.9870	4.0289
8	6.6888	6.2407	7.3879	7.9543

Table 5. Predicted and measured speed-ups for swm on the Power Challenge SGI.

5 Conclusions and Future Work

PDDT is a flexible parallelizing compiler for cache-based shared-memory multiprocessors. It can automatically parallelize loops and change their structure based on tracking the dynamic placement of data along program execution. In these architectures a number of CPUs can simultaneously access data anywhere in the system. However, the non-uniformity of the memory accesses is an important issue to consider and may require a higher programming effort in order to achieve performance; trying to access those levels in the hierarchy closer to the processor may increase execution efficiency.

In this paper we have presented the set of features included in PDDT that most influence the selection of parallelization strategies for the loops in numerical programs: partitioning of the iteration space, and pipelined computation to minimize sequentialization and false sharing. The process relies on technology previously developed for automatic data distribution for distributed-memory systems. We have evaluated the quality of the solutions generated by PDDT by comparing the performance of the solutions suggested against the performance of solutions generated by the native compiler of a SGI Power Challenge system. We have also shown how the predicted speed-ups are close to the actual ones obtained when then program is executed. PDDT handles partially annotated Fortran 77 programs with directives that specify parallelization strategies; in this case PDDT is useful as a support tool for the developer of parallel codes in estimating the effect of user selected parallelization strategies in the final performance of the parallel program.

In this paper we have assumed that conflict misses never happen. This is not true in real systems with finite caches. Although this has not a severe impact for the programs we have evaluated (because of the size of the data sets and the size of each private cache in the SGI Power Challenge - 4 Mbyte), this is a topic of current research. The same technology can be used to perform a software controlled data prefetching and preflushing between computational phases.

References

[AAL95] J.M. Anderson, S.P. Amarasinghe, and M.S. Lam. Data and computation transformations for multiprocessors. In *Principles and Practice of Parallel Programming*, pages 166–178. ACM SIGPLAN, June 1995.

[AGG+94] E. Ayguadé, J. Garcia, M. Gironès, J. Labarta, J. Torres, and M. Valero. Detecting and Using Affinity in an Automatic Data Distribution Tool. In K. Pingali et al., editor, *Proceedings of the 7th Annual Workshop on Languages and Compilers for Parallel Computing*, pages 61–75, Ithaca, NY, August 1994. Lecture Notes in Computer Science vol. 892, Springer-Verlag.

[AGG+95] E. Ayguadé, J. Garcia, M. Gironès, M.L. Grande, and J Labarta. Data Redistribution in an Automatic Data Distribution Tool. In C.-H. Huang et al., editor, *Proceedings of the 8th Annual Workshop on Languages and Compilers for Parallel Computing*, pages 407–421, Columbus, Ohio, August 1995. Lecture Notes in Computer Science vol. 1033, Springer -Verlag.

[AL93] J.M. Anderson and M.S. Lam. Global optimizations for parallelism and locality on scalable parallel machines. In *Conference on Programming Language Design and Implementation*, pages 112–125. ACM SIGPLAN, June 1993.

[BCG+95] P. Banerjee, J.A. Chandy, M. Gupta, E.W. Hodges IV, J.G. Holm, A. Lain, D.J. Palermo, S. Ramaswamy, and E. Su. The Paradigm Compiler for Distributed-Memory Multicomputers. *IEEE Computer*, 28(10):37–47, October October 1995.

[Con94] Convex. *SPP1000 Systems Overview*. Convex Computer Corporation, 1994.

[JE95] T.E. Jeremiassen and S.J. Eggers. Reducing false sharing on shared memory multiprocessors through compile time data transformations. In *Principles and Practice of Parallel Programming*, pages 179–188. ACM, June 1995.

[KK95] K. Kennedy and U. Kremer. Automatic Data Layout for High Performance Fortran. In *Supercomputing'95, San Diego, CA*, December 1995.

[SGI96] Silicon Graphics Computer Systems SGI. *Power Challenge Technical Report*, 1996.

[SSGC95] T.J. Scheffler, R. Schreiber, J.R. Gilbert, and S. Chatterjee. Aligning Parallel Arrays to Reduce Communication. In *Frontiers95: The 5th Symposium on the Frontiers of Massively Parallel Computation*, pages 324–331, February 1995.

Data Localization Using Loop Aligned Decomposition for Macro-Dataflow Processing

Akimasa Yoshida and Hironori Kasahara

Department of Electrical, Electronics and Computer Engineering
Waseda University
3-4-1 Ohkubo, Shinjuku-Ku, Tokyo 169, Japan
{yoshida,kasahara}@oscar.elec.waseda.ac.jp

Abstract. This paper proposes a data-localization compilation scheme for Fortran macro-dataflow processing on a multiprocessor system with local memory and centralized shared memory. The data-localization scheme minimizes data transfer overhead for passing shared data among coarse-grain tasks composed of Doall loops and sequential loops by using local memory on each processor effectively. In this scheme, a compiler firstly partitions coarse-grain tasks like loops having data dependences among them and their data into multiple groups by a *loop aligned decomposition* so that data transfer among groups can be minimum. Secondly it generates dynamic scheduling routine which assigns decomposed tasks in a group to the same processor at run-time. Thirdly it generates parallel machine code to pass shared data inside the group through local memory. This compiler has been implemented for an multiprocessor system OSCAR having centralized shared memory and distributed shared memory in addition to local memory on each processor. Performance evaluation on OSCAR shows that macro-dataflow processing with the proposed data-localization scheme can reduce the execution time by 10% to 20% in average compared with macro-dataflow processing without data-localization.

1 Introduction

In parallel processing of Fortran programs on multiprocessor systems, loop parallelization techniques such as Doall and Doacross[1, 2] have been widely used. Currently, many types of Do-loops can be parallelized with support of strong data dependence analysis techniques[3, 4, 5, 6, 7]. There still exist, however, sequential loops which cannot be parallelized efficiently because of complex loop-carried data dependences and conditional branches to the outside loops. Also, parallelism outside Do-loops, for example, coarse grain parallelism among loops, subroutines and basic blocks, and (near) fine grain parallelism[8] inside a basic block[9] or a sequential loop, has not been effectively exploited by automatic compilers for multiprocessor systems.

Therefore, in order to improve the effective performance of multiprocessor systems, it is important to exploit the coarse grain parallelism[10] and also the (near) fine grain parallelism inside a sequential loops or a basic block[8], in addition to the medium grain parallelism among loop iterations exploited by the conventional loop parallelization. The coarse grain parallel processing on a multiprocessor system is also called the macro-dataflow processing[10, 11, 12, 13, 14, 15]. The macro-dataflow processing can be efficiently combined with the loop parallelization and the near fine grain parallel processing hierarchically as a multigrain parallel processing scheme[15, 16, 17].

In parallel processing schemes like macro-dataflow processing where coarse grain tasks (macrotasks) are dynamically scheduled to processors (PEs) or processor clusters (PCs), shared data among macrotasks are generally allocated onto centralized shared memory (or ordinary common memory) and data transfer among macrotasks are performed via centralized shared memory. However, data transfer via centralized shared memory causes large overhead. Therefore, in order to reduce data transfer overhead, it is necessary that a compiler automatically decomposes data and computation and allocates them to local memory on each processor so that data transfer overhead can be minimum.

To this end, Tu and Padua[18], Eigenmann[19], Li[20] proposed Array Privatization method, in which temporal array variables in a loop are allocated to local memory to reduce data transfer overhead. However, it can be applied only inside a loop.

Another popular approach for data decomposition and assignment on distributed memory multiprocessor systems is that user specifies distribution of data by using extended Fortran such as High Performance Fortran (HPF)[21][22] and Fortran D[23]. However, it is difficult for ordinary users to optimize both parallelism and data locality.

Recently, many researches have been performed on automatic data partitioning. Li and Chen[24] showed how explicit communication can be synthesized and how communication costs are estimated by analyzing reference patterns in the source program. Ramanujam and Sadayappan[25] focused on partitioning a nested Doall loop so that the partitioned loops can be executed without interprocessor communication. Chen and Sheu[26] also presented communication-free partitions for a nested loop. Agarwal et al.[27] presented a method for deriving an optimal hyperparallelepiped tiling of iteration spaces for minimal communication in a Doall loop. However, these methods can be applied only to a nested loop. Meanwhile, Gupta and Banerjee[28] proposed automatic data decomposition for a whole program. Palermo and Banerjee[29] showed where data redistribution is performed to reduce execution time of a program. Anderson and Lam[30] proposed automatic data and computation decomposition among loops when a compiler can allocate data and computation to processor using a linear transformation matrix. However, these schemes cannot be applied to a processing scheme in which computation and data are allocated dynamically, such as macro-dataflow processing.

Considering the above fact, this paper proposes a data-localization scheme to transfer data via local memory among macrotasks composed of Doall and sequential loops in macro-dataflow processing. The proposed scheme decomposes loops by *loop aligned decomposition* method considering data dependence among iterations over different loops. Then the compiler groups the decomposed loops into multiple groups to which data localization using task fusion or partial static task assignment technique is applied. Next, the compiler generates dynamic scheduling routine to assign the decomposed loops inside a group to the same processor and generates parallel machine codes in which shared data among the decomposed loops scheduled to the same processor are transferred via local memory. A compiler has been implemented and its performance is evaluated on a multiprocessor system OSCAR(Optimally SCheduled Advanced multiprocessoR)[8].

The rest of this paper is structured as follows. Section 2 states the macro-dataflow processing for a Fortran program. Section 3 proposes data-localization scheme. Section 4 evaluates performance of the proposed data-localization scheme on OSCAR. Section 5 concludes the paper.

2 Macro-Dataflow Processing

The macro-dataflow compilation scheme [10, 13, 14, 15, 17, 31, 32, 33, 34, 35] mainly consists of the following four parts.

2.1 Generation of Macrotasks (MTs)

In the macro-dataflow processing, a Fortran program is decomposed into three kinds of macrotasks (*MT*s), such as a Block of Pseudo Assignment statements (*BPA*), a Repetition Block (*RB*) and a Subroutine Block (*SB*)[10, 13, 15, 16, 17].

A BPA is composed of a basic block or multiple basic blocks. A BPA composed of multiple basic blocks is generated by fusing small basic blocks. To the contrary, BPAs are also defined by decomposing a basic block into several blocks if a basic block has independent data dependence graphs inside. A RB is a Do-loop or a loop generated by a backward branch, namely, an outermost natural loop[9]. RBs are restructured by the proposed *loop aligned decomposition* method mentioned in Sect.3.1. As to subroutines, the compiler defines subroutines to which the in-line expansion technique cannot efficiently be applied as SBs.

2.2 Generation of Macro Flow Graph (MFG)

Before detection of parallelism among macrotasks, control flow and data flow among macrotasks are analyzed and are represented by *Macro-Flow-Graph* (*MFG*)[10, 13, 14, 17] as shown in Fig.1. MFG is generally a directed acyclic graph since RBs contain all back edges inside them. In MFG, a node represents a macrotasks, a small circle inside a node shows a conditional branch, and a solid edge and a dotted edge represent data flow and control flow respectively.

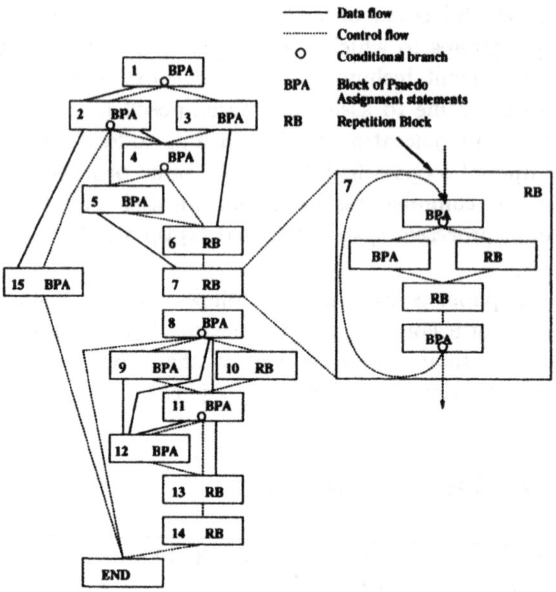

Fig. 1. MFG of a sample program

2.3 Generation of Macrotask Graph (MTG)

The MFG explicitly represents control flow and data flow among macrotasks though it does not show any parallelism among macrotasks. Generally, the control dependence graph, or the program dependence graph[36], represents maximum parallelism if there are not data dependences among macrotasks[37]. However, in practice, there exist data dependences among macrotasks. Therefore, in order to effectively extract parallelism among macrotasks from a macro-flow-graph, control dependences and data dependences should be analyzed together.

In this paper, an *earliest-executable-condition* [10, 13, 17, 15] analysis of each macrotask is used to find the maximum parallelism among macrotasks considering control dependences and data dependences. The earliest-executable-condition of a macrotask i (MT_i) is a condition on which MT_i may begin its execution earliest after data and control dependences are satisfied. For example, an earliest-executable-condition of MT_6 in Fig.1 is "MT_3 completes execution OR MT_2 branches to MT_4" as shown in Table 1.

Girkar and Polychronopoulos [38, 39] modified the original earliest executable condition analysis[10, 13, 17] assuming a conditional branch inside a macrotask is executed in the end of the macrotask.

The earliest-executable-conditions of macrotasks are represented by a directed acyclic graph called *MacroTask-Graph* (MTG) [10, 13, 17, 14] as shown in Fig.2.

Table 1. Earliest executable conditions of a sample program

Macrotask	Earliest executable condition
MT_1	
MT_2	1_2
MT_3	$(1)_3$
MT_4	$2_4 \vee (1)_3$
MT_5	$(4)_5 \wedge (2_4 \vee (1)_3)$
MT_6	$3 \vee (2)_4$
MT_7	$5 \vee (4)_6$
MT_8	$(2)_4 \vee (1)_3$
MT_9	$(8)_9$
MT_{10}	$(8)_{10}$
MT_{11}	$8_9 \vee 8_{10}$
MT_{12}	$11_{12} \wedge (9 \vee (8)_{10})$
MT_{13}	$11_{13} \vee 11_{12}$
MT_{14}	$(8)_9 \vee (8)_{10}$
MT_{15}	2_{15}

i : MT_i completes execution.
$(i)_j$: MT_i branches to MT_j.
i_j : MT_i branches to MT_j, and MT_i completes execution.

2.4 Generation of Dynamic Scheduling Routine

Next, the compiler generates a dynamic scheduling routine to assign macrotasks onto processors (PEs) or processor clusters (PCs) at run-time. Dynamic scheduling is adopted to cope with runtime uncertainties, such as conditional branches among macrotasks and a variation of macrotask execution time. As a dynamic scheduling algorithm, Dynamic-CP algorithm[17], which uses scheduling priority based on estimation of longest path length from each node to the exit node on MTG, is applied.

3 Data Localization Scheme

This section proposes a data-localization scheme to reduce data transfer overhead among macrotasks composed of Doall and sequential loops. In this paper, data-localization means to decompose multiple loops, or array data, and to assign them to processors (PEs) so that shared data among the macrotasks can be transferred through local memory on the PEs.

This compilation method consists of the following three steps: *loop aligned decomposition* which decomposes loop indices and arrays to minimize data transfer among processors, *generation of dynamic scheduling routine* to assign a set of decomposed loops, among which large data transfer may occur, onto the same PE and *generation of parallel machine code* to transfer data via local memory among the decomposed loops assigned onto the same PE.

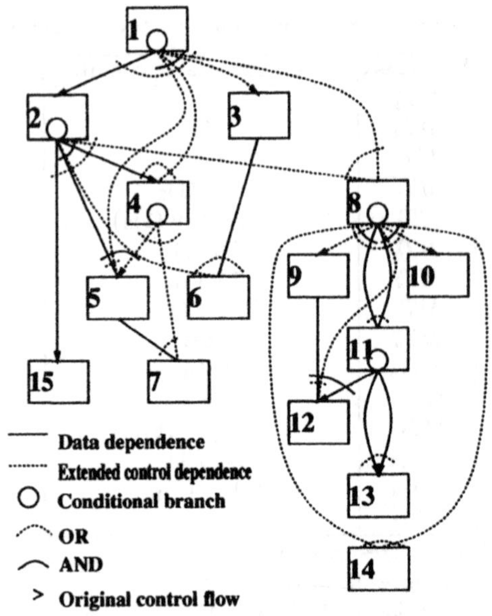

Fig. 2. MTG of a sample program

3.1 Loop Aligned Decomposition

In the previous definition of RB in Sect.2.1, a Doall loop is defined as a macrotask and is assigned to a single processor. To prevent this situation and to fully exploit parallelism of a Doall loop, the compiler decomposes the Doall loop into n small Doall loops (or macrotasks), where n is the multiple numbers of PEs in general. However, if the compiler decomposes Doall loops without consideration of data dependences among them independently, local memory will not be used effectively for data transfer among the decomposed loops.

Considering this fact, this paper proposes *loop-aligned-decomposition* method. In this method, for example, when RBs in Fig.3(a) are executed on two PEs, RB_1 in Fig.3(a) is decomposed into RB_1^1, $RB_1^{<1,2>}$ and RB_1^2 in Fig.4(b), also RB_2 in Fig.3(a) is decomposed into RB_2^1, $RB_2^{<1,2>}$ and RB_2^2 in Fig.4(b), and RB_3 into RB_3^1 and RB_3^2. In this case, array data inside a group composed of RB_1^1, RB_2^1 and RB_3^1 in Fig.4(b) and a group composed of RB_1^2, RB_2^2 and RB_3^2 in Fig.4(b) are passed through local memory. This loop aligned decomposition method can also be applied to multiple loops including a sequential loop such as Fig.5(a), where the loops are decomposed into partial loops as shown in Fig.5(b) when they three PEs are used. The following subsections describe this loop aligned decomposition method in detail.

Detection of Target-Loop-Group for Loop Aligned Decomposition. First, we find a set of RBs, or *Target-Loop-Group* (TLG), to which *loop aligned*

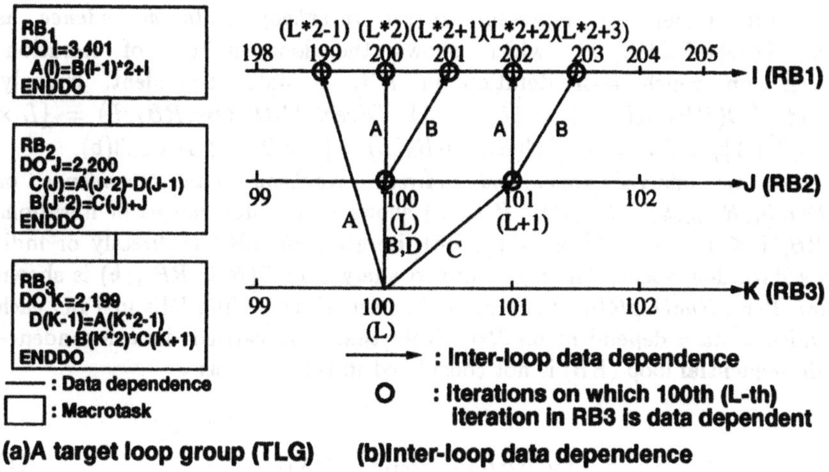

Fig. 3. Doall loops connected by a data dependence edge on MTG

decomposition is applied. A set of RB_1, RB_2 and RB_3 in Fig.3(a) and a set of RB_1, RB_2 and RB_3 in Fig.5(a) are examples of TLG. TLG is composed of RBs satisfying the following conditions:

(i)Adjacent two RBs are connected by a single data dependence edge on MTG. Here, a data dependence edge from a BPA which initializes scalar variables used in RB may exist in addition to the edge between RBs.

(ii) Each RB (Outermost loop) is a Doall loop, a reduction loop, or a sequential loop (with loop carried data dependence or with conditional branch outside the loop). Also, it is assumed that each RB has been normalized to have stride 1.

(iii) Subscript of array to be localized in TLG is expressed by a linear function of a loop index variable. That is, if a TLG includes an array whose subscript is not expressed by a linear function of a loop index variable such as array D in Fig.5(a), data localization is not applied to only the array.

In these conditions, it is also assumed that suitable loop restructuring techniques[2, 40] such as loop interchange, loop fusion, loop distribution and so on have been applied to each RB before this TLG detection phase.

Interloop Data Dependence Analysis. For each TLG composed of "m" RBs, or $RB_i (1 \le i \le m)$, the compiler analyzes data dependence among iterations over different RBs. For example, in a TLG of Fig.3(a), L-th iteration of RB_3 (e.g. 100th iteration) is data dependent on L-th (e.g. 100th) and $(L+1)$-th (e.g. 101st) iterations of RB_2 by array B, D, C as shown in Fig.3(b). Furthermore, L-th (e.g. 100th) iteration of RB_2 is data dependent on $(L \times 2)$-th (e.g. 200th) and $(L \times 2 + 1)$-th (e.g. 201st) iterations of RB_1 by array A, B. Also, L-th (e.g. 100th) iteration of RB_3 is data dependent on $(L \times 2 - 1)$-th (e.g. 199th) iteration of RB_1 by array A.

In this paper, we represent *Direct InterLoop Data dependence* as $Direct\_ILD(RB_i, RB_j, k)$, which shows the loop indices of iterations in RB_i on which k-th iteration in RB_j is data dependent. Namely, $Direct\_ILD(RB_2, RB_3, L) = \{L, L+1\}$, $Direct\_ILD(RB_1, RB_2, L) = \{L \times 2, L \times 2 + 1\}$, and $Direct\_ILD(RB_1, RB_3, L) = \{L \times 2 - 1\}$ in Fig.3(b).

Next, we analyze *direct and indirect InterLoop Data dependence*, or $ILD(RB_i, RB_m, k)$. $ILD(RB_i, RB_m, k)$ shows loop index ranges of iterations in $RB_i (1 \leq i \leq m-1)$ on which k-th iteration of RB_m is directly or indirectly data dependent. The algorithm to analyze $ILD(RB_i, RB_m, k)$ is shown below. Here, $SucDepRB(RB_i)$ represents a set of succeeding RBs in TLG each of which is data dependent on RB_i. Note that loop carried data dependence inside sequential loop (RB) is not considered in this analysis.

$$ILD(RB_m, RB_m, k) = \{k\}. \tag{1}$$

for $i := m-1$ *to* 1 *do*

$$ILD(RB_i, RB_m, k) = \bigcup_{RB_j \in SucDepRB(RB_i)} \left(\bigcup_{t \in ILD(RB_j, RB_m, k)} Direct\_ILD(RB_i, RB_j, t) \right). \tag{2}$$

$ILD(RB_i, RB_3, k)$ $(1 \leq i \leq 3)$ in Fig.3(a) are analyzed as follows; $ILD(RB_3, RB_3, L) = \{L\}$, $ILD(RB_2, RB_3, L) = \bigcup_{t \in ILD(RB_3, RB_3, L)} Direct\_ILD(RB_2, RB_3, t) = \{L, L+1\}$, and $ILD(RB_1, RB_3, L) = (\bigcup_{t \in ILD(RB_2, RB_3, L)} Direct\_ILD(RB_1, RB_2, t)) \cup (\bigcup_{t \in ILD(RB_3, RB_3, L)} Direct\_ILD(RB_1, RB_3, t)) = \{L \times 2 - 1, L \times 2, L \times 2 + 1, L \times 2 + 2, L \times 2 + 3\}$. Namely, L-th (e.g.100th) iteration of RB_3 is data dependent on L-th and $(L+1)$-th (e.g. 100th and 101st) iterations of RB_2 and on $(L \times 2 - 1)$-th through $(L \times 2 + 3)$-th (e.g. 199th through 203rd) iterations of RB_1 as shown in Fig.3(b).

In the calculation of $Direct\_ILD$ and ILD, a set of elements in $Direct\_ILD$ and ILD are expressed by lower-bound and upper-bound of elements to reduce calculation time. Also, if several iterations of RB_i exist between $ILD(RB_i, RB_m, k)$ and $ILD(RB_i, RB_m, k+1)$, those iterations are joined into $ILD(RB_i, RB_m, k)$.

Calculation of Group-Converted-Index-Range in Target-Loop-Group. Next, the compiler calculates *Group-Converted-Index-Range* ($GCIR$), which represents index range of array used (or defined) in $RB_i (1 \leq i \leq m)$ as a loop index range of RB_m.

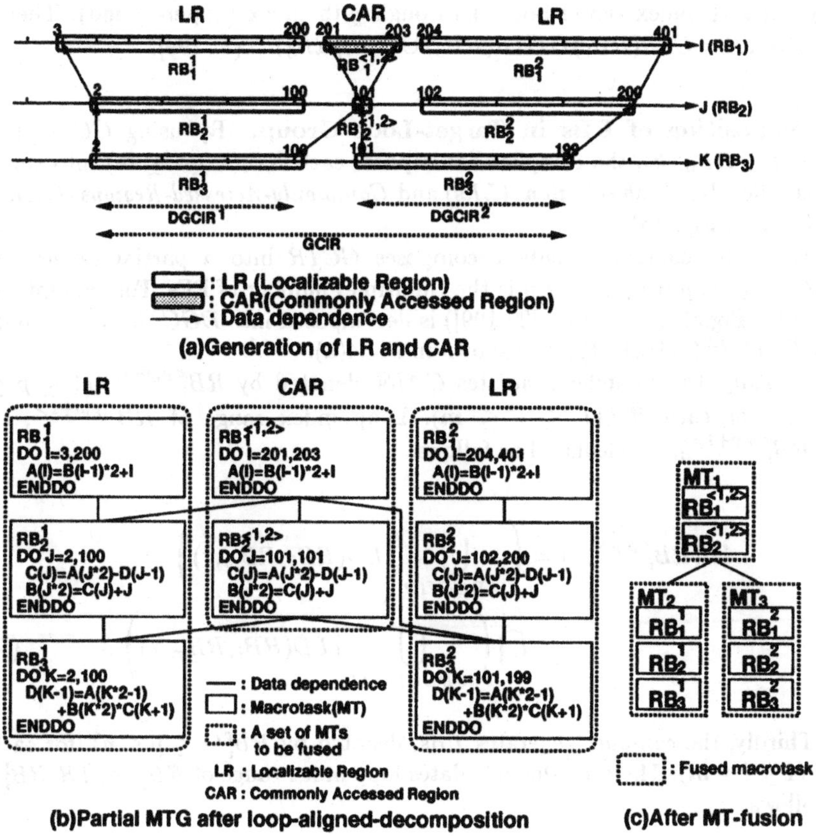

Fig. 4. Loop aligned decomposition

To do so, the compiler firstly converts index range of $RB_i (1 \leq i \leq m)$, or $IR(RB_i)$, into index range of the RB_m, or *Converted-Index-Range* ($CIR(RB_i)$). This $CIR(RB_i)$ is a set of indices to satisfy the following equation.

$$IR(RB_i) = \bigcup_{t \in CIR(RB_i)} ILD(RB_i, RB_m, t). \tag{3}$$

Secondly, the compiler calculates $GCIR$ as follows;

$$GCIR = \bigcup_{1 \leq i \leq m} CIR(RB_i). \tag{4}$$

For example, in the case of Fig.3(a), $CIR(RB_1) = CIR(RB_2) = CIR(RB_3) = [2 : 199]$ as shown in Fig.4(a), where $[x : y]$ denotes the range of x-th index (lower-bound) through y-th index (upper-bound). Therefore, $GCIR = CIR(RB_1) \cup CIR(RB_2) \cup CIR(RB_3) = [2:199]$.

Decomposition of RBs in Target-Loop-Group. By using $GCIR$ and $ILD(RB_i, RB_m, k)$, the compiler decomposes each $RB_i (1 \leq i \leq m)$ into small loops called *Localizable-Regions* (LRs) and *Commonly-Accessed-Regions* ($CARs$) as shown in Fig.4(a).

First, the compiler evenly decomposes $GCIR$ into n partial ranges, or $DGCIR^p (1 \leq p \leq n)$, where n is the (multiple) number of PEs. For example, if $n = 2$ for Fig.3(a), $GCIR(= [2:199])$ is decomposed into $DGCIR^1(= [2:100])$ and $DGCIR^2(= [101:199])$ as shown in Fig.4(a).

Secondly, the compiler generates $CARs$, denoted by $RB_i^{<p,p+1>}$ $(1 \leq p \leq n-1)$, for each $RB_i (1 \leq i \leq m)$. Loop index range of $RB_i^{<p,p+1>}$, or $IR(RB_i^{<p,p+1>})$, is calculated as follows.

$$IR(RB_i^{<p,p+1>}) = \left(\bigcup_{t \in DGCIR^p} ILD(RB_i, RB_m, t) \right) \cap \left(\bigcup_{t \in DGCIR^{p+1}} ILD(RB_i, RB_m, t) \right). \tag{5}$$

Thirdly, the compiler generates LRs, denoted by $RB_i^p (1 \leq p \leq n)$, for each $RB_i (1 \leq i \leq m)$. The compiler calculates loop index range of RB_i^p, or $IR(RB_i^p)$ as follows.

$$IR(RB_i^p) = \left(\bigcup_{t \in DGCIR^p} ILD(RB_i, RB_m, t) \right) - IR(RB_i^{<p-1,p>}) - IR(RB_i^{<p,p+1>}). \tag{6}$$

Here compiler initializes $IR(RB_i^{<0,1>}) = \emptyset$, $IR(RB_i^{<n,n+1>}) = \emptyset$ in advance.

Fourthly, the compiler examines whether loop index range of each decomposed RB (e.g. $IR(RB_i^p)$ or $IR(RB_i^{<p,p+1>})$) is included in loop index range of RB_i. If $IR(RB_i^p)$ or $IR(RB_i^{<p,p+1>})$ (the decomposed RB for RB_i) includes iterations outside $IR(RB_i)$, these iterations are removed from the index range of the decomposed RB.

Consider the example in Fig.4(a). Iterations of RB_1 (or RB_2) on which both a set of iterations of a partial RB_3 ($DGCIR^1$ in Fig.4(a)) and a set of iterations of the other partial RB_3 ($DGCIR^2$) are commonly data dependent are defined as *Commonly-Accessed-Region* $RB_1^{<1,2>}$ (or $RB_2^{<1,2>}$) respectively. Next, *Localizable-Region* RB_1^1, RB_2^1 and RB_3^1 are generated by using $DGCIR^1$ and RB_1^2, RB_2^2 and RB_3^2 are generated by using $DGCIR^2$. Loop index ranges of each decomposed RB are shown in Fig.4(b). Also, *TLG* with Doall and sequential loops in Fig.5(a) is decomposed into *LRs* in Fig.5(b) when the number of PEs is three. Here each *CAR* is fused into an adjacent *LR* described in Sect.3.2.

3.2 Dynamic Scheduling for Data Localization

In macro-dataflow processing, coarse-grain tasks are assinged to PEs at run-time by using dynamic scheduling routine generated by the compiler. The scheduling routine uses Dynamic-CP algorithm[15][34] described in Sect.2.4. This section describes two methods using macrotask fusion and using partial static task assignment to assign macrotasks inside a *LR*(Localizable-Region) to the same PE under dynamic scheduling environment.

Dynamic Scheduling with Macrotask Fusion. After loop aligned decomposition, a set of macrotasks in a *LR*(Localizable-Region), among which a large amount of data transfers are required, should be scheduled to the same PE at run-time. One approach to do so is that the compiler fuses a set of macrotasks in a *LR* into a macrotask to assign them to the same PE. This fused macrotask is scheduled to a PE by the dynamic scheduler at run-time. Note that this macrotask fusion is applied when all RBs inside *TLG*(Target-Loop-Group) are Doall loops. Also, in order to reduce dynamic scheduling overhead, a set of macrotasks in a *CAR* are fused into a macrotask.

For example, in a target loop group in Fig.4(b), decomposed RBs (a set of macrotasks in a *LR*, a set of macrotasks in a *CAR*) surrounded by broken line are fused, and MTG after macrotask-fusion is shown in Fig.4(c). Among loops inside a fused macrotask, array data are passed through local memory as mentioned later.

Dynamic Scheduling with Partial Static Task Assignment. If *TLG* consists of Doall loops and sequential loops as shown in Fig.5(a) or if *TLG* includes an array whose subscript is not expressed by a linear function of a loop index variable such as array *D* in Fig.5(a), each *LR* in Fig.5(b) after loop aligned decomposition can not be fused by the method in Sect.3.2 because decomposed loops require synchronization with other decomposed loops. Therefore, dynamic scheduling with partial static task assignment[41] is adopted for the *LR* with Doall and sequential loops as follows. When this partial static task assignment is used, a *CAR*(Commonly-Accessed-Region) is fused into an adjacent *LR* considering dynamic scheduling overhead as shown in Fig.5(b)[41].

The execution order of macrotasks in each *LR* is decided by data dependence among them uniquely. Therefore, in this partial static task assignment method, after entrance macrotask ($MT_{(d,entrance)}$) in a LR_d is scheduled to a processor PE_p at run-time, the dynamic scheduler assigns the other macrotasks ($MT_{(d,i\neq entrance)}$) in the LR_d to the same PE_p when $MT_{(d,i\neq entrance)}$ is executable. In implementation of this method, when the compiler generates a dynamic scheduling routine, it specifies succeeding $MT_{(d,i\neq entrance)}$ should be

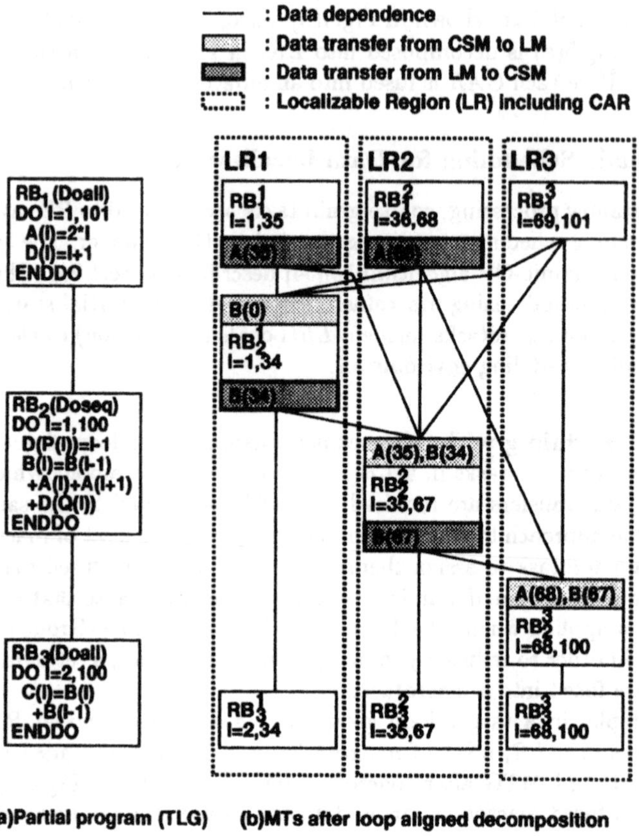

Fig. 5. Loop aligned decomposition considering sequential loops

scheduled to the same PE with $MT_{(d,entrance)}$. We call this scheme partial static task assignment.

In this approach, to avoid load unbalance among PEs, the dynamic scheduler assigns $MT_{(d,entrance)}$ in LR to a PE having smallest load. Here, load of each PE is estimated considering processing time for both a running macrotask on the PE and macrotasks in LR to be scheduled to the PE. In current implementation, it takes about 90 clocks to schedule a macrotask to a PE by using the proposed dynamic scheduling routine with partial static task assignment. Namely, the overhead of dynamic scheduling with partial static task assignment is very small.

3.3 Generation of Data-Transfer Code for Data Localization

This section generates parallel machine code to transfer data among macrotasks assigned to the same PE via local memory.

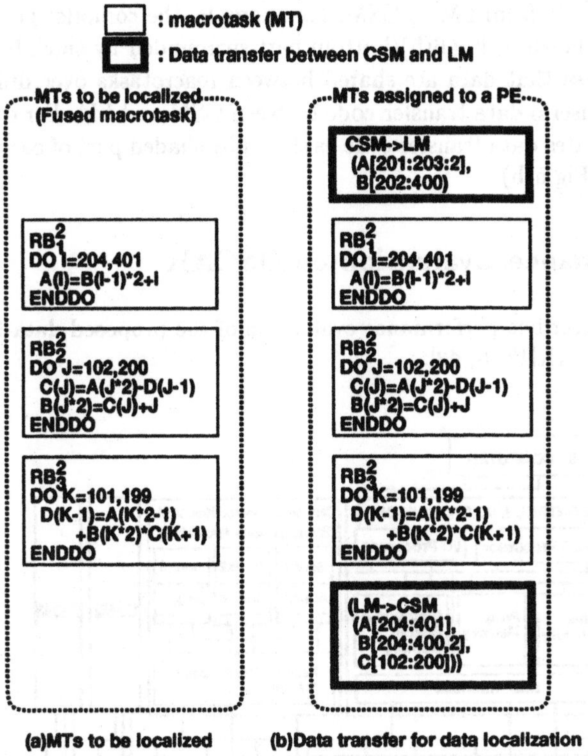

Fig. 6. Data transfer in fused macrotask

Detection of Array to Be Localized. In this code generation step, first, the compiler calculates data transfer time via LM(Local Memory), $t^X_{localize}$, and data transfer time via CSM(Centralized Shared Memory), t^X_{CSM}, for each array X which are used or defined in fused macrotask or in LR to which partial static task assignment is applied.

Secondly, for array X satisfying $t^X_{localize} < t^X_{CSM}$, the compiler generates data transfer code using LM, namely, store or load instructions to LM on PE. Meanwhile, for array X not satisfying $t^X_{localize} < t^X_{CSM}$, the compiler generates data transfer code via CSM.

Data Transfer between CSM and LM. The compiler generates machine code to transfer shared data among macrotasks between CSM(Centralized Shared Memory) and LM(Local Memory). For example, when data-localization is applied to array A, B, C in the fused macrotask (Fig.6(a), which is the same as MT_3 in Fig.4(c)), data transfer code from CSM to LM is generated as shown in Fig.6(b) (top part surrounded by thick line). Also, when data defined on LM in fused macrotask are used outside fused macrotask, the compiler inserts data transfer code from LM to CSM. For example, the compiler generates data transfer code shown in Fig.6(b)(bottom part surrounded by thick line).

Next, in case that data are shared between macrotasks over different *LRs*, the compiler inserts data transfer code between CSM and LM. For example, the compiler generates data transfer code as shown by shaded part of each macrotask inside *LRs* in Fig.5(b).

4 Performance Evaluation on OSCAR

This section describes performance evaluation of the proposed data-localization scheme on OSCAR[17, 8, 42].

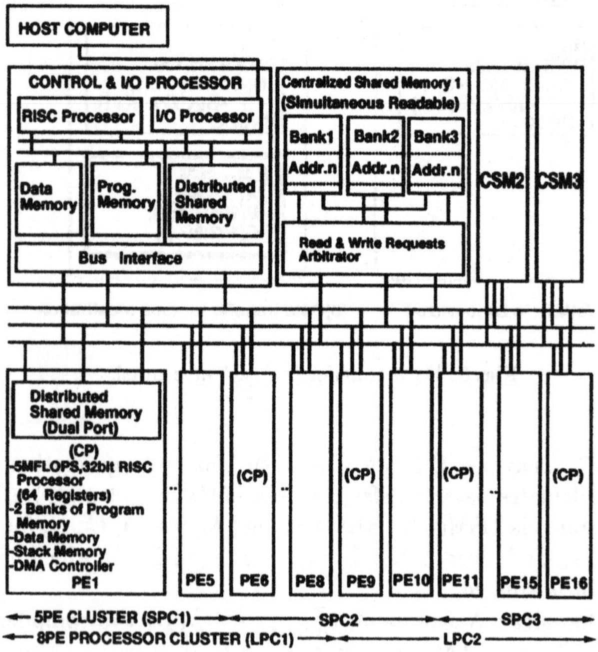

Fig. 7. OSCAR's architecture

4.1 OSCAR's Architecture

OSCAR was developed in 1987 by the authors and Fuji Facom Corp.. It is a multiprocessor system having centralized and distributed shared memories in addition to local program and data memories as shown in Fig.7. Its processor elements (PEs) and a Control and I/O processors are uniformly connected to centralized shared memory (CSM) through three buses. Each PE has a custom-made 32 bit RISC processor, distributed shared memory (DSM) and local memory (LM). On OSCAR, it takes 4 clocks to store (or load) one word data to CSM or DSM on the other PE, and 1 clock to store (or load) to LM or DSM inside PE.

4.2 Performance Evaluation Using Conjugate-Gradient Program

First, we evaluate the proposed scheme with task fusion by using a main convergent loop of Conjugate-Gradient (CG) method. This main loop is composed of 4 Doall loops, 2 reduction loops (i.e. loop to calculate summation), 5 Basic blocks.

Table 2. Performance evaluation using Conjugate-Gradient program

PEs	Processing schemes	Processing time[s]	Speed up
1	Sequential processing	4.793	1.00
3	Macro-dataflow	1.742	2.75
3	Macro-dataflow with data-localization	1.493	3.17
6	Macro-dataflow	1.002	4.78
6	Macro-dataflow with data-localization	0.805	5.95

The execution time on OSCAR is shown in Table 2. The sequential execution time of this program is 4.793[s]. In this case, all array data are initially allocated onto centralized shared memory because array data size is larger than local memory size on 1 PE. Ordinary macro-dataflow processing reduces execution time to 1.742[s] (1/2.75) for 3 PEs and to 1.002[s] (1/4.78) for 6 PEs. Furthermore, macro-dataflow processing with the proposed data-localization reduces execution time to 1.493[s] (1/3.17) for 3 PEs and to 0.805[s] (1/5.95) for 6 PEs. From these results, it can be confirmed that proposed data localization scheme reduces data transfer overhead remarkably.

4.3 Performance Evaluation Using Spline-Interpolation Program

Next, to evaluate the data-localization with partial static task assignment, a Fortran program for Spline Interpolation having 9 Doall loops, 2 sequential loops with loop carried data dependence and 3 basic blocks is used. Table 3 shows the execution result of this program on OSCAR.

Conventional Doall processing reduces execution time from 632[ms] for 1 PE to 284[ms] (1/2.23) for 3 PEs and to 218[ms] (1/2.90) for 6 PEs. On the other hand, macro-dataflow processing without data-localization reduces execution time to 246[ms] (1/2.57) for 3 PEs and to 188[ms] (1/3.36) for 6 PEs because

Table 3. Performance evaluation using Spline Interpolation program

PEs	Processing schemes	Processing time[ms]	Speed up
1	Sequential processing	632	1.00
3	Doall processing	284	2.23
3	Macro-dataflow	246	2.57
3	Macro-dataflow with data-localization	187	3.38
6	Doall processing	218	2.90
6	Macro-dataflow	188	3.36
6	Macro-dataflow with data-localization	152	4.16

coarse-grain parallelism among sequential loops and the other macrotasks can be exploited.

Furthermore, when the proposed data-localization method is applied, execution time is reduced to 187[ms] (1/3.38) for 3 PEs and to 152[ms] (1/4.16) for 6 PEs. In other words, speedup of 34% for 3 PEs and 30% for 6 PEs are obtained by the data-localization compared with conventional Doall processing.

In the above evaluation, OSCAR needs only 4 clocks to access CSM and 1 clock to access LM. However, since ratio of CSM access time to LM access time on multiprocessor system available in the market is larger than that on OSCAR, the proposed data-localization scheme may be more effective on these machines.

Currently, the authors are rewriting the prototype compiler to a practical version which can compile large scale application programs and generate parallelized program written in VPP Fortran, KSR Fortran, MPI etc. in addition to OSCAR parallel machine code.

5 Conclusions

This paper proposes the data-localization scheme for macro-dataflow processing on multiprocessor system OSCAR having distributed and centralized shared memories in addition to local memory. The data-localization scheme is composed of loop aligned decomposition, dynamic scheduling for data-localization with task fusion and partial static task assignment and generation of machine code to pass shared data among loops through local memory.

Performance evaluations on OSCAR showed that macro-dataflow processing with data-localization could reduce execution time by 19% for Conjugate Gradient program and 23% for Spline Interpolation program compared with macro-dataflow processing without data-localization. From these results, effectiveness of the proposed data-localization scheme was confirmed.

Currently, the authors are researching on combination of data-localization technique and data pre-loading / data post-storing technique to hide data transfer overhead by overlapping processing and data transfer for macro-dataflow processing.

Acknowledgements

This research was partly supported by the Education Ministry Grant-in-Aid for Scientific Research No.(C)07680372 and the Waseda University Grant for Special Research Project No.96B–033.

References

1. D.A. Padua and M.J. Wolfe. Advanced compiler optimizations for super computers. *Commun. ACM*, 29(12):1184–1201, 1986.
2. M. Wolfe. Optimizing supercompilers for supercomputers. *MIT press*, 1989.
3. U. Banerjee, R. Eigenmann, A. Nicolau, and D.A. Padua. Automatic program parallelization. *Proc. of IEEE*, 81(2):211–243, Feb. 1993.
4. D.A. Padua, D.J. Kuck, and D.H. Lawrie. High-speed multiprocessor and compilation techniques. *IEEE Trans. Comput.*, C-29(9):763–776, 1980.
5. M. Wolfe. High performance compilers for parallel computing. *Addison-Wesley Publishing Company*, 1996.
6. U. Banerjee. Dependence analysis for supercomputing. *Kluwer Academic Pub.*, 1988.
7. U. Banerjee. Loop parallelization. *Kluwer Academic Pub.*, 1994.
8. H. Kasahara, H. Honda, and S. Narita. Parallel processing of near fine grain tasks using static scheduling on OSCAR. *IEEE ACM Supercomputing'90*, 1990.
9. A.V. Aho, R. Sethi, and J.D. Ullman. Compilers (principles, techniques, and tools). *Addison Wesley*, 1988.
10. H. Honda, M. Iwata, and H. Kasahara. Coarse grain parallelism detection scheme of Fortran programs. *Trans. IEICE(in Japanese)*, J73-D-I(12):951–960, 1990.
11. D. Gajski, D. Kuck, D. Lawrie, and A. Sameh. Cedar. *Report UIUCDCS-R-83-1123, Dept. of Computer Sci., Univ. Illinois at Urbana-Champaign*, Feb. 1983.
12. D.D. Gajski, D.J. Kuck, and D.A. Padua. Dependence driven computation. *Proc. of COMPCON 81 Sprint Computer Conf.*, pages 168–172, 1981.
13. H. Kasahara, H. Honda, M. Iwata, and M. Hirota. A compilation scheme for macro-dataflow computation on hierarchical multiprocessor systems. *Proc. Int. Conf. on Parallel Processing*, 1990.
14. H. Honda, K. Aida, M. Okamoto, A. Yoshida, W. Ogata, and H. Kasahara. Fortran macro-dataflow compiler. *Proceedings of Fourth Workshop on Compilers for Parallel Computers*, pages 415–425, Dec. 1993.
15. H. Kasahara. Parallel processing technology. *Corona Pub. in Japan*, 1991.
16. H. Kasahara, H. Honda, K. Aida, M. Okamoto, and S. Narita. OSCAR Fortran compiler. *Proc. Workshop on Compilation of (Symbolic) Languages for Parallel Computers in 1991 Int. Logic Programming Symposium*, 1991.
17. H. Kasahara, H. Honda, A. Mogi, A. Ogura, K.Fujiwara, and S.Narita. Multi-grain parallelizing compilation scheme for OSCAR. *4th Workshop on Language and Compilers for Parallel Computing*, 1991.
18. P. Tu and D. Padua. Automatic array privatization. *6th Annual Workshop on Languages and Compilers for Parallel Computing*, 1993.
19. R. Eigenmann. Toward a methodology of optimizing programs for high-performance computers. *Proc. of ACM International Conference on Supercomputing'93*, pages 27–36, Jul. 1993.

20. Z. Li. Array privatization for parallel execution of loops. *Proc. of the 1992 ACM Int. Conf. on Supercomputing*, pages 313–322, 1992.
21. High Performance Fortran Forum. High performance Fortran language specification draft ver.1.0. *High Performance Fortran Forum*, 1993.
22. B. Chapman, P. Mehrotra, and H. Zima. Extending HPF for advanced data parallel applications. *Proceedings of Fifth Workshop on Compilers for Parallel Computers*, Jun. 1995.
23. S. Hiranandani, K. Kennedy, C. Koelbel, U. Kremer, and C.-W. Tseng. An overview of the Fortran D programming system. *Proc. 4th Workshop on Languages and Compilers for Parallel Computing*, 1991.
24. J. Li and M. Chen. Compiling communication-efficient programs for massively parallel machines. *IEEE Trans. on Parallel and Distributed System*, 2(3):361–376, 1991.
25. J. Ramanujam and P. Sadayappan. Compile-time techniques for data distribution in distributed memory machines. *IEEE trans. on parallel and distributed systems*, 2(4), 1991.
26. T.-S. Chen and J.-P. Sheu. Communication-free data allocation techniques for parallelizing compilers on multicomputers. *IEEE trans. on parallel and distributed systems*, 5(9), 1994.
27. A. Agarwal, D. A. Kranz, and V. Natarajan. Automatic partitioning of parallel loops and data arrays for distributed shared-memory multiprocessors. *IEEE Trans. on Parallel and Distributed System*, 6(9):943–962, 1995.
28. M. Gupta and P. Banerjee. Demonstration of automatic data partitioning techniques for parallelizing compilers on multicomputers. *IEEE Trans. on Parallel and Distributed System*, 3(2):179–193, 1992.
29. D. J. Palermo and P. Banerjee. Automatic selection of dynamic data partitioning schemes for distributed-memory multicomputers. *Proc. 8th Workshop on Languages and Compilers for Parallel Computing*, 1995.
30. J.M. Anderson and M.S. Lam. Global optimizations for parallelism and locality on scalable parallel machines. *Proc. of the SIGPLAN '93 Conference on Programming Language Design and Implementation*, pages 112–125, 1993.
31. L. Bic, A. Nicolau, and M.Sato (ed). Parallel language and compiler research in japan. *Kluwer Academic Pub.*, 1995.
32. K. Aida, K. Iwasaki, H. Kasahara, and S. Narita. Performance evaluation of macro-dataflow computation on shared memory multiprocessors. *Proceedings of IEEE Pacific Rim Conference on Communications, Computers, and Signal Processing*, 1995.
33. M. Okamoto, K. Yamashita, H. Kasahara, and S. Narita. Hierarchical macro-dataflow computation scheme on a multiprocessor system OSCAR. *Proceedings of IEEE Pacific Rim Conference on Communications, Computers, and Signal Processing*, 1995.
34. H. Honda, K. Aida, M. Okamoto, and H. Kasahara. Coarse grain parallel execution scheme of a Fortran program on OSCAR. *Trans. IEICE(in Japanese)*, J75-D-I(8):526–535, 1992.
35. H. Kasahara, H. Honda, and S. Narita. A multi-grain parallelizing compilation scheme for OSCAR. *Proc. 4th Workshop on Language and Compilers for Parallel Computing*, 1991.
36. J. Ferrante, K.J. Ottenstein, and J.D. Warren. The program dependence graph and its use in optimization. *ACM Trans. on Prog. Lang. and Syst.*, 9(3):319–349, 1987.

37. F. Allen, M. Burke, R. Cytron, J. Ferrante, W. Hsieh, and V. Sarkar. A framework for determining useful parallelism. *Proc. 2nd ACM Int. Conf. on Supercomputing*, 1988.
38. M. Girkar and C.D. Polychronopoulos. Optimization of data/control conditions in task graphs. *Proc. 4th Workshop on Languages and Compilers for Parallel Computing*, 1991.
39. M. Girkar and C.D. Polychronopoulos. Automatic extraction of functional parallelism from ordinary programs. *IEEE Trans. on Parallel and Distributed System*, 3(2):166–178, 1992.
40. U. Banerjee. Loop transformations for restructuring compilers. *Kluwer Academic Pub.*, 1993.
41. A. Yoshida, K. Koshizuka, and H. Kasahara. Data-localization for fortran macro-dataflow computation using partial static task assignment. *Proceedings of 10th ACM International Conference on Supercomputing*, pages 61–68, May. 1996.
42. W. Ogata, K. Fujimoto, M. Oota, and H. Kasahara. Compilation scheme for near fine grain parallel processing on a multiprocessor system without explicit synchronization. *Proceedings of IEEE Pacific Rim Conference on Communications, Computers, and Signal Processing*, 1995.

Exploiting Monotone Convergence Functions in Parallel Programs

William Pugh, Evan Rosser, and Tatiana Shpeisman

Department of Computer Science
University of Maryland
{pugh,ejr,murka}@cs.umd.edu

Abstract. Scientific codes which use iterative methods are often difficult to parallelize well. Such codes usually contain `while` loops which iterate until they converge upon the solution. Problems arise since the number of iterations cannot be determined at compile time, and tests for termination usually require a global reduction and an associated barrier. We present a method which allows us avoid performing global barriers and exploit pipelined parallelism when processors can detect non-convergence from local information.

1 Introduction

Many scientific programs solve problems iteratively; that is, they compute an approximation to a solution, check if the approximation is sufficiently accurate (check for convergence), and conditionally perform another iteration.

In most instances, the loops inside the `while` are parallel, with data only needing to be communicated from one iteration to the next. However, the convergence test requires a global reduction and barrier, which can impose substantial performance penalties on some systems.

In a few cases, such as when a natural ordering is used in a relaxation algorithm, the inner loops carry dependencies and cannot be run in parallel. To exploit parallelism in these loops, a number of researchers [1,4,5,2,7,3] have proposed *speculative execution*: a wavefront technique is used to execute the program in parallel, despite the fact that all loops carry dependences. Since this ignores the termination condition of the `while` loop, iterations of the `while` loop are executed speculatively until each iteration is completely executed and it can be determined that the loop will continue past that iteration.

For both of these situations, we propose that we recognize and exploit a common pattern: that the convergence condition depends monotonically on looking at more and more data: if, from looking at a subset of the data we can determine that the while loop has not terminated, looking at more data will not change that decision.

In particular, each processor can check to see it can determine that a while loop continues just from looking at local data. If so, it can start on the next iteration without waiting for the global reduction to complete. Figure 1 shows the advantages conferred by eliminating this dependency. In programs where the body of the while loop can be executed in parallel, this allows us to avoid the penalties imposed by a global barrier. In the case where the body of the while loop contains dependences, this can often allow us to obtain doacross/pipelined parallelism.

If this idea is to be exploited, it is important that it be provided or supported by the compiler. Unless the program is written in explicitly parallel form, there is no way for a user to write a program that computes a reduction on just all local data, and then goes on to compute a global reduction if needed.

No cross-processor dependences within an iteration of the while loop | Cross-processor dependences within an iteration of the while loop

Waiting for global reduction

Able to continue without waiting for global reduction

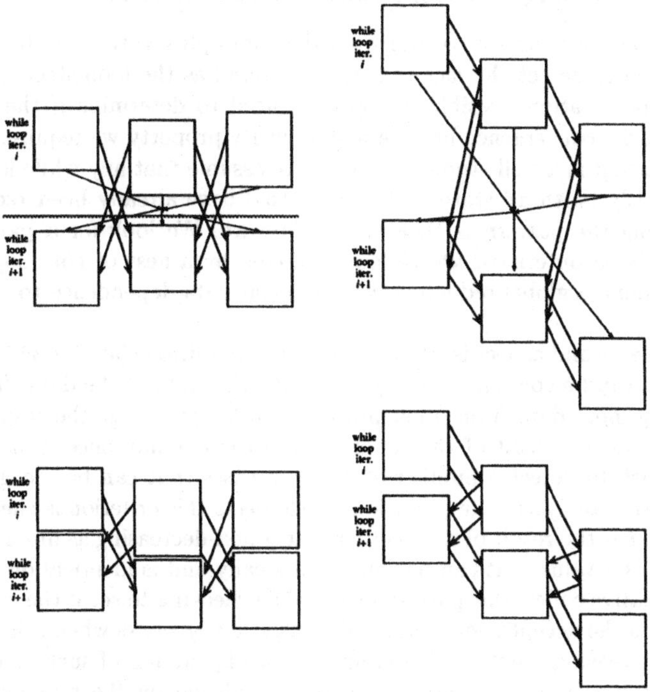

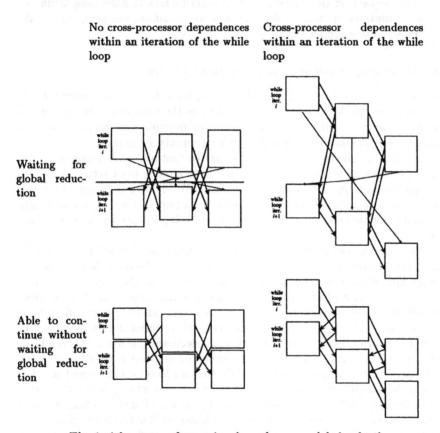

Fig. 1. Advantages of removing dependency on global reduction

In this paper, we discuss:

- What is required to recognize such patterns
- What code must be generated to exploit such patterns
- Experimental studies for the benchmarks SOR with Chebyshev acceleration and `tomcatv`.

2 Exploiting local information

In checking for convergence, the costs involved are the wait incurred by all processors while the result is computed, and that of the communication and synchronization associated with the reduction. To avoid these costs, we would like to do as much computation as possible on the local processor, and we would like to determine as quickly as possible the outcome of the convergence check. Specifically, if any processor could determine locally that the computation would not converge at this iteration, it could continue execution without fear that results could not be used. In this section, we first describe how to detect opportunities for this optimization; then we describe how we transform the program to take advantage of these properties.

2.1 Detecting monotone convergence functions

There are two aspects to detecting when our optimization can be applied. First, we need to detect the fact that the program has the loop structure that makes our optimization possible. Second, we need to determine if the function that checks for convergence has the monotonicity property we require.

Since it is a well-studied problem, we assume that any while loops that exist implicitly (with `if` statements and `goto`s) have already been recognized. Recognizing the pattern is then straightforward. We look for a pattern in which there is an outermost `while` loop, followed by a nest of `for` loops, and finally containing a global reduction, with a scalar data dependence to the `while` loop test.

The second aspect is detecting that the condition checking `while` loop termination can be computed locally with only a portion of the data. In other words, adding more data from other processors will not change the result of the function, and the result of the condition will change only once, from false to true. We wish to detect a number of common cases that can be recognized without extensive analysis. One condition which meets this criterion is checking if $x \geq y$, where x is the result of a reduction that is non-decreasing as more data is added, and y is a value that can be computed locally and is identical on all processors. In iterative codes, this pattern exists when checking to see if the current solution exceeds the acceptable error. Analogously, $x \leq y$ works when x is the result of a non-increasing function. A conjunction or disjunction of such conditions is also acceptable, as is a conjunction with a condition on the maximum number of iterations to perform (or any other scalar condition that can be computed on each processor from local data). Since this pattern is common in iterative codes, recognizing this pattern is sufficient for a number of programs.

Now we must characterize functions which are non-decreasing or non-increasing:

- Sum of non-negative numbers (as from absolute value or square)
- Maximum reductions

Non-increasing:

- Minimum reductions

If x_1, x_2 are results of non-decreasing (non-increasing) functions, the following are non-decreasing (non-increasing):

- $\sqrt{x_1}$, if x_1 is known to be positive
- $x_1 * x_2$, if x_1 and x_2 both positive (negative)
- $x_1 * y$ or x_1/y, where y is non-negative and invariant in the while loop

As an example, here are three commonly-used non-decreasing norms that fall into this category:

- $||x||_\infty$ (infinity norm) : $max_{i=1}^n |x_i|$
- $||x||_2$ (second norm) : $\sqrt{\sum_{i=1}^n x_i^2}$
- $||x||_1$ (first norm) : $\sum_{i=1}^n |x_i|$

It is feasible to detect these patterns in many real codes. In more complicated codes, a user directive might be useful to inform the compiler that the optimization is possible.

2.2 Changes to the code

In this section, we describe how the modified program will proceed on each processor.

New variables In order to take advantage of partial information about convergence, we need to keep track of several quantities in addition to the original program variables. These variables fall into two categories: first, those that record progress on the each processor, and those that record progress across all processors. One processor is designated as the master processor, which will handle the global reduction.

Each processor must keep track of how many iterations w of the while loop it has executed. This is necessary in order to provide the basis for processors to compare their relative progress through the program.

The master processor handles the remaining variables. First, it must record information about the global progress. If it is known that iteration w of the while loop will be executed, then it follows that all iterations $w' < w$ will also be executed. Therefore, the designated processor only need to know the number of w_{max}, the last iteration that is known not to converge. Each local processor keeps a local copy of this variable, $local\_w_{max}$.

The master processor must also combine partial reduction results. For iteration w_{max}, some processors may have completed their portion of the computation, but found that their portion of the reduction was not enough to prove non-convergence. The master processor accumulates results from each processor that has completed iteration w_{max}, to determine if a combination of individual contributions can prove non-convergence. In addition, on the last iteration, the accumulation represents the result of the global reduction once all processors have finished.

```
for(n = 1; n<= MAXITS; n++)
  rnorm = 0.0;
  jsw = 1;
  for(ipass=1; ipass<=2; ipass++)
    lsw = jsw;
    for(j = 2; j < jmax; j++)
      for(l = lsw+1; l<jmax; l+=2)
        resid=...
        rnorm += fabs(resid);
        u[j][l] -= omega*resid/-4;
      lsw=3-lsw;
    jsw = 3-jsw;
    omega=...;
  if(rnorm < EPS) return;
```

```
for(n = 1; n<= MAXITS; n++)
  local_rnorm = 0.0;
  jsw = 1;
  for(ipass=1; ipass<=2; ipass++)
    lsw = jsw;
    for(j = 2; j < jmax; j++)
      for(l = local_min+lsw+1;
          l<local_max;
          l+=2)
        resid=...
        local_rnorm += fabs(resid);
        u[j][l] -= omega*resid/-4;
      lsw=3-lsw;
    jsw = 3-jsw;
    omega=...;
  // Check termination locally.
  w = n;
  if(! w < local_w_max)
    send(master_proc, w, local_rnorm)
    if (! local_rnorm < EPS)
      // Can't proceed on local
      // information
      receive(master_proc, new_w);
      if (new_w == TERMINATE)
        return;
      else
        local_w_max = new_w;
```

Fig. 2. Pseudo-code for SOR with Chebyshev acceleration, before and after transformation

Checking non-convergence In this section, we describe how an individual processor decides whether it can safely proceed to the next iteration without waiting for the result of the global reduction.

Each processor p can proceed without waiting if $local\_w_{max} > w_p + 1$; that is, another processor has already detected non-convergence at iteration w, and that information was sent to p in a previous iteration.

Otherwise, the processor performs its local portion of the reduction. If it indicates non-convergence, it sends a pair of values (w, *local_reduction*) to the master processor, and continues to the next `while` iteration.

If the local reduction does not allow p to continue, it sends the values as above, and waits for a reply from the master processor. The reply will be either an iteration number, indicating that it is safe to go on, or a message that the program should terminate. If the response indicates non-convergence, the processor p saves the iteration number into $local\_w_{max}$, allowing it to avoid checking again until $w_p = local\_w_{max}$.

The master processor operates as follows. Upon receiving a pair of values $(w_p, reduction_p)$ from a processor p, it checks the global progress as indicated by w_{max}. If $w_p < w_{max}$, this message does not help prove more progress through the program. If $reduction_p$ shows that p was not able to prove non-convergence by itself, p must be waiting for a reply, and w_{max} is returned; $reduction_p$ is discarded as unnecessary. If $w_p = w_{max}$, then the $reduction_p$ portion is added into the growing global reduction. If the most recent contribution is enough to detect non-convergence, then the master processor sets w_{max} to $w_p + 1$, and sends it to all waiting processors to indicate that they can proceed (including p if $reduction_p$ was not sufficient by itself to prove this fact). Finally, if the master processor still cannot tell that the loop will continue after w_{max}, it adds p to the list of waiting processors and waits for more data.

If p is the last processor to report, and the master processor finds that the computation has converged, the master processor sends a message indicating termination to all processors. The partial reduction now contains the value for the global reduction.

An improvement to this scheme is to delay performing reduction communication between the worker processors and the master processor until at least one processor needs help in proving non-convergence. At that point, the processor in question sends a request to the master, which instructs all other processors to begin sending reduction messages. At each iteration, a processor probes to see if such a message from the master processor has arrived.

Communication between individual processors is not affected by this optimization.

An example of the transformed code appears in Figure 2. The code is adapted from [8].

3 Example: SOR

In this section we present an example program that can be parallelized using our method.

The major program class arises from solving partial differential equation (PDE) boundary value problems using finite-difference methods [8,6]. For example, consider solving a partial differential equation of the following form:

$$f_1(x,y) \cdot \partial u^2/\partial x^2 + f_2(x,y) \cdot \partial u^2/\partial y^2 + f_3(x,y) \cdot \partial u/\partial x + f_4(x,y) \cdot \partial u/\partial y + f_5(x,y) \cdot u(x,y) = f_0(x,y) \tag{1}$$

Given the open region Ω in $\mathcal{R}^2$ and a function $g(x,y)$, the problem is to find such a function u that is continuous on the closure of Ω, satisfies Equation 1 in Ω, and equals g on the boundary.

Discretizing this problem on the $N \times N$ mesh using finite-difference method leads to the following discrete problem:

$$a_{j,l} \cdot u_{j+1,l} + b_{j,l} \cdot u_{j-1,l} + c_{j,l} \cdot u_{j,l+1} + d_{j,l} \cdot u_{j,l-1} + e_{j,l} \cdot u_{j,l} + f_{j,l} = 0,$$
$$\text{for } j = 2, N-1 \text{ and } l = 2, N-1$$
$$u_{j,l} = g_{j,l}, \tag{2}$$
$$\text{for } j = 1 \text{ or } j = N \text{ or } l = 1 \text{ or } l = N$$

As a particular example of PDE boundary value problem we shall consider solving Laplace's equation $\partial u^2/\partial x^2 + \partial u^2/\partial y^2 = 0$ on the region $\Omega = \{(x, y) : 0 < x < 1, 0 < y < 1\}$ with the Dirichlet boundary conditions defined by function $g(x, y) = \sinh(3\pi y) \cdot \sinh(3\pi y) * 10^{-3}$ [6].

```
// Set the initial guess for u_{j,l}
for l = 1 to N do
    for j = 1 to N do
        if j = 1 or j = N or l = 1 or l = N
            then
                u_{j,l} = g((j-1)/N, (l-1)/N)
            else
                u_{j,l} = 0
    endfor
endfor
// Iterate until the convergence criteria is met
for i = 1 to MAXITS do
    rnorm = 0
    // Update values of u_{j,l} using red-black ordering
    jsw = 1
    for ipass = 1 to 2 do
        lsw = jsw
        for j = 2 to N - 1 do
            for l = lsw + 1 to N - 1 by 2 do
                r_{j,l} = u_{j+1,l} + u_{j-1,l} + u_{j,l+1} + u_{j,l-1} - 4u_{j,l}
                rnorm = rnorm + fabs(r_{j,l})
                u_{j,l} = u_{j,l} - ω * r_{j,l}/ - 4
            endfor
            lsw = 3 - lsw
        endfor
        jsw = 3 - jsw
        // adjust over-relaxation parameter ω
        ω = adjust(ω)
    endfor
    if rnorm < ε then return
endfor
error ("Iteration number limit exceeded")
```

Fig. 3. Algorithm for solving Dirichlet problem using SOR

After discretization we get a discrete problem of type 2 with the coefficients $a_{j,l} = b_{j,l} = c_{j,l} = d_{j,l} = 1, e_{j,l} = -4$ and $f_{j,l} = 0$.

This problem can be solved iteratively using one of the relaxation methods. We shall consider solving it using Successive Over-relaxation (SOR) with Chebyshev acceleration [8]. The algorithm is shown in Figure 3.

At each iteration the new values $u^{i+1}_{j,l}$ are computed from the old values $u^i_{j,l}, u^i_{j+1,l}, u^i_{j-1,l}, u^i_{j,l+1}$ and $u^i_{j,l-1}$. The values $u_{j,l}$ are updated in so called black-red order, when, first all $u_{j,l}$ s.t. $j + l$ is even ("black squares of the checkerboard") are processed, and then all $u_{j,l}$ s.t. $j + l$ is odd ("red squares") are processed.

The algorithm stops when the 1-norm of the residual r becomes sufficiently small: $\|r^i\|_1 \leq \varepsilon$.

4 Results

We performed experiments on several example codes to determine the effectiveness of this technique. We collected statistics based on uniprocessor runs to determine how often the technique may be useful, and we applied the technique by hand to two programs.

We ran an instrumented version of the SOR sample program on a uniprocessor machine to examine its convergence behavior. We assumed a data distribution that distributes columns of the u array over 16 processors. We modified the global reduction to perform each of the 16 reductions that would take place on local processors, then examined how useful the information would be in determining non-convergence locally.

We found that for the normal ordering, the sample code converged in 1141 iterations of the `while` loop. For the first 906 iterations, or 79.4%, all 16 processors were able to detect that the computation had not yet converged from purely local information. A majority of processors could determine this for the first 1026 iterations, or 89.3% of the total iterations.

For the red-black ordering, the sample code converged in 1028 iterations, and all processors could determine non-convergence locally for the first 902 iterations, or 87.7%. A majority of the processors could detect non-convergence for 937 iterations, or 91.1%.

So, for the greatest part of the computation, our optimization allows the program to avoid 90% of the global reductions (and the barriers associated with them). Furthermore, on the normal ordering, the optimization would allow us to use doacross-style parallelism for most of the program, where little parallelism was previously available.

We also examined the benchmark program `tomcatv` from the SPEC benchmarks. This program computes the infinity norm over two arrays, and exits when the norm falls below a value `eps`. The code does not converge given the test data, and runs for 100 iterations; thus, running it demonstrates the maximum potential gain from avoiding the reduction, and does not measure performance for the portion of computation closer to convergence.

#Processors	IP		User space	
	Optimized	Unoptimized	Optimized	Unoptimized
2	189	181	212	180
4	97	95	130	96
8	53	57	66	49
12	40	55	43	33
16	37	73	36	25

Table 1. Execution times in seconds for `tomcatv` (size 1025) on the SP2

We implemented a straightforward message-passing version of `tomcatv`, plus several latency-tolerating transformations, to produce a baseline version. We then applied our transformation to that program, and compared the two.

Experiments were performed on a 16-processor IBM SP2, using the `MPIF` library for communications. We first examined which processors could determine non-convergence in isolation. For a problem size of n=257, using any number of processors up to 16, all processors can determine convergence in every iteration. For a problem size of n=513, running on 16 processors, the last processor cannot detect non-convergence in iterations 36 - 100, and must communicate.

Table 1 shows results of running `tomcatv` with problem size 1025 under two different communications libraries on the SP2. Using the IP protocol for communication, which has a higher latency and overhead, the transformation improved performance, particularly on larger numbers of processors. Under the faster user space (US) protocol, however, the transformed code ran slower than the original. Contrary to our expectations, using looser synchronization to permit overlap resulted in worse performance than using barriers: when we inserted a barrier in the transformed code, it removed any opportunity for overlap, but improved performance. We speculated on the cause of this behavior, but were not able to conclusively determine the cause. Since the transformation is predicated on the assumption that removing barriers increases performance, it should not be used on systems where that assumption does not hold.

We also implemented a message-passing parallel version of SOR. The results are displayed in Figure 4. The best speedup on 15 processors (including a server process) was 5.8. The last portion of the computation, where reduction communication is required, is at least partially sequentialized. To examine the effect of that portion of the computation, we ran versions of the program that terminate after 1000 iterations, before any processor has to request assistance from the server (labeled as 1k on the graph). That version showed speedups to 7.7 on 15 processors. Since the version which computes until convergence comes reasonably close to the performance of the version which performs no reductions, improvements in performance are likely to come in areas unrelated to the reduction and convergence computation.

We also examined some more complicated applications to see what would be required to apply the transformation. We looked at the serial version of `bt`, one of the sample applications from the NAS Parallel Benchmarks. In this code,

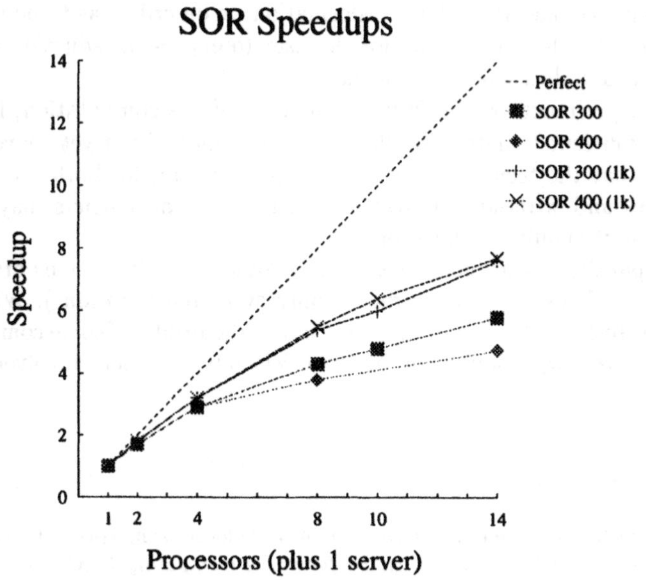

Fig. 4. Speedups for SOR on 16-processor SP2

in the badi subroutine, a vector of five norms is computed, and convergence is based upon all five meeting the convergence criteria. In addition, the computation of the norms takes place across a number of procedures. In order to be effective as an automatic transformation on this code, it would probably be necessary to both recognize more complicated convergence functions, and use interprocedural analysis to determine both possibility and profitability of applying the optimization; alternatively, users could supply directives to request it.

5 Conclusion

We have presented a method for reducing global reductions and increasing opportunities for doacross-style parallelism in certain kinds of iterative programs. The situation we have described, a monotone convergence test, arises frequently in real numerical applications. The techniques we have described allow us to avoid the cost of a barrier synchronization for most of the computation, until global information is necessary to determine if the computation has converged.

Our technique also allows us to provide efficient doacross/pipelined parallelism when the body of a while loop contains cross-processor dependencies. We believe the technique we propose is more practical than speculative execution [1,4,5,2,7,3].

In a language like HPF, the transformation we describe has to be performed by the compiler; there is no way for the user to express a reduction over local data and make a decision based on that.

In the experiments we performed, for most of the computation, local data alone was sufficient to determine that the algorithm had not yet converged. We also found that the technique can improve performance for both the case with dependences and without. On systems where removing barriers may decrease performance, it should not be applied.

In computations with convergence tests, other transformations are possible (for example, checking for convergence only every ten iterations). While these transformations may be useful, they can change the results of some computations and we believe they should not be done without the users involvement and concurrence.

References

1. J.-F. Collard. Space-time transformation of while-loops using speculative execution. In *Proc. of the 1994 Scalable High Performance Computing Conf.*, pages 429–436, Knoxville, TN, May 1994. IEEE.
2. J.-F. Collard. Automatic parallelization of while-loops using speculative execution. *Int. J. of Parallel Programming*, 23(2):191–219, April 1995.
3. M. Griebl and J.-F. Collard. Generation of synchronous code for automatic parallelization of while loops. In N.N., editor, *EuroPar 95*, Lecture Notes in Computer Science. Springer-Verlag, 1995.
4. M. Griebl and C. Lengauer. On scanning space-time mapped **while** loops. In B. Buchberger and J. Volkert, editors, *Parallel Processing: CONPAR 94 - VAPP VI*, Lecture Notes in Computer Science 854, pages 677–688. Springer-Verlag, 1994.
5. M. Griebl and C. Lengauer. On the space-time mapping of WHILE-loops. *Parallel Processing Letters*, 4(3):221–232, September 1994.
6. David Kincaid and Ward Cheney. *Numerical Analysis*. Brooks/Cole Publishing Company, 1991.
7. C. Lengauer and M. Griebl. On the parallelization of loop nests containing while loops. In N. N. Mirenkov, Q.-P. Gu, S. Peng, and S. Sedukhin, editors, *Proc. 1st Aizu Int. Symp. on Parallel Algorithm/Architecture Synthesis (pAs'95)*, pages 10–18. IEEE Computer Society Press, 1995.
8. William H. Press, Saul A. Teukolsky, William T. Vetterling, and Brian P. Flannery. *Numerical Recipes in C: The Art of Scientific Computing*. Cambridge University Press, second edition, 1992.

Exact versus Approximate Array Region Analyses

Béatrice CREUSILLET and François IRIGOIN*
Centre de Recherche en Informatique, École des mines de Paris
35, rue Saint-Honoré, F-77305 FONTAINEBLEAU Cedex FRANCE

Abstract. Advanced program optimizations, such as array privatization, require precise array data flow analyses, usually relying on conservative over- (or *may*) and under- (or *must*) approximations of array element sets [25, 33, 21]. In a recent study [13], we proposed to compute *exact* sets whenever possible. But the advantages of this approach were still an open issue which is discussed in this paper.
It is first recalled that must array region analyses cannot be defined on lattices. It implies that there exists no *better* solution for such data flow problems, and that ad-hoc solutions must be defined.
For that purpose, it is suggested to perform under- and over-approximate analyses at the same time, and to enhance the results of must analyses with those of may analyses, when the latter can be proved exact according to an *exactness criterion*. This is equivalent to our previous approach, and is more effective than using only existing techniques such as widening and narrowing operators which may fail to expose exact solutions even though their computability is decidable. This method is very general and could be applied to other types of analyses.
Keywords: Array region analysis, semantical analysis, exactness.

1 Introduction

Several studies [17, 4] have highlighted the need for advanced program optimizations to deal with memory management issues when compiling programs for massively parallel machines or hierarchical memory systems. For instance, BLUME and EIGENMANN [4] have shown that array privatization could greatly enhance the amount of potential parallelism in sequential programs. This technique basically aims at discovering array sections that are used as temporaries in loops, and can thus be replaced by local copies on each processor. An array section is said to be privatizable in a loop if each read of an array element is preceded by a write in the same iteration, and several different iterations may access each privatized array element [25, 34]. Solving such problems requires a precise intra- and inter-procedural analysis of array data flow.

Several algorithms for array privatization or array expansion (a similar technique for shared memory machines) have already been proposed [15, 26, 25, 34, 22, 13], based on different types of array data flow analyses. The first approach [15, 26] performs an *exact* analysis of array data flow, but for a restricted source language[2]. Most of the other methods use conservative approximations

* E-mail: `{creusillet,irigoin}@cri.ensmp.fr`
[2] monoprocedural, static control language.

of array element sets, such as *MayBeDefined* and *MustBeDefined* sets. In fact, may sets are over-approximations of exact solutions, while must sets are under-approximations, according to a predefined approximation ordering. On the contrary, the last approach [13] tries to compute exact solutions whenever possible, switching to conservative approximations only when exactness cannot be preserved anymore. However, except for specific applications [7, 8] requiring the knowledge of exactness, the advantages of our approach were still an open issue, which is discussed in this paper.

Traditionally, semantical analyses are defined on lattices. This ensures that they be precisely defined even in case of recursive semantical equations, which appear whenever the source language contains looping constructs. For instance, exact solutions of array region analyses belong to the lattice $(\wp(\mathbb{Z}^n), \varnothing, \mathbb{Z}^n, \cup, \cap)$. Over-approximate analyses of array regions are also defined on lattices: Lattice of convex polyhedra in PIPS [24] (our interprocedural parallelizer of scientific programs), or regular section lattice in the case of RSDs [6] for instance. However, as will be shown in Section 2.3, under-approximate solutions do not belong to a predefined lattice. This is due to the fact that, given an exact array region, no *best* under-approximation can be defined. This is illustrated in Figure 1 where several possible under-approximations of an array region are provided for two different representations. In this case, BOURDONCLE [5] suggests to approximate fixed points by decreasing under-approximate iterations[3], using a *narrowing operator*[4]. However, this approach may fail to compute under-approximations equal to the corresponding exact solutions while the computation of the latter is decidable, which is possible as shown in [13].

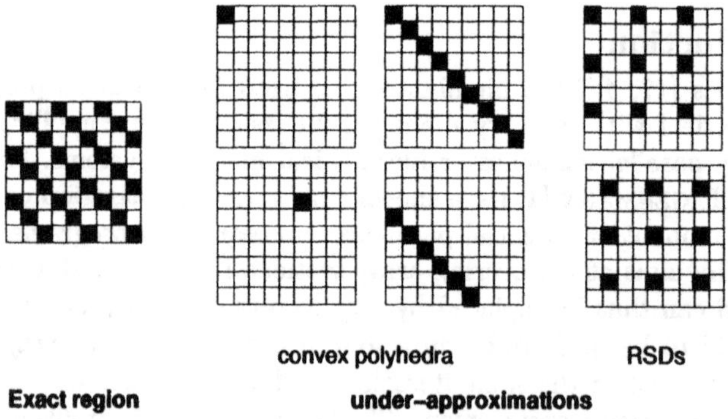

Fig. 1. Possible under-approximations

We thus propose another approach, based on our previous experience of exact array dataflow analyses [13, 14]: We suggest to perform under- and over-approximate analyses at the same time, and to enhance the results of must anal-

[3] He also proposes a more precise technique called *dynamic partitioning*, but its complexity would be too high in the case of array region computations.

[4] More precisely the dual of his *widening* operator.

yses with those of may analyses, when the latter can be proved exact according to a *computable exactness criterion*.

The paper is organized as follows. Section 2 presents the semantical analysis framework, and shows that some analysis solutions may not belong to a predefined lattice; existing ad-hoc solutions are also presented. Our solution and the *exactness criterion* are presented in Section 3. Section 4 finally discusses how existing approaches for under-approximate array region analyses fit into our framework.

2 Semantical Analysis Frameworks

The semantical analysis of a program aims at statically discovering its properties, or the properties of the objects it uses (variables, ...). However, semantical equations may not have solutions computable in finite time; this is the case of recursive functions in an infinite height lattice for instance. Moreover, exactly describing the behavior of any program written in a given language may happen to be impossible, or at least of an overwhelming complexity; most languages have I/O instructions whose effects are not completely foreseeable; representing all types of expressions, particularly real expressions, is also generally considered too complex for an average compiler. Facing these obstacles, the solution is either to restrict the input language (as in [15, 16, 29, 26]), or to perform conservative approximate analyses [9].

This section describes some usual characteristics of exact and approximate semantical analysis frameworks. It is then shown that some analyses do not respect these properties. Usual solutions are finally presented in the last subsection, and their limitations are discussed.

2.1 Sets and domains

Traditionally, mathematical spaces used for the denotation of programming constructs are called *semantical domains* and are *complete partial orders* or *lattices*.

Definition 1. A *complete partial order* (or cpo) is a set E partially ordered by a relation $\sqsubseteq_E$; it has a least element $\perp_E$ (E is *inductive*); and every countable increasing sequence $e_0 \sqsubseteq \cdots \sqsubseteq e_n \sqsubseteq \ldots$ has a limit in E, denoted by $\bigsqcup_i e_i$.

Examples of basic domains are boolean values, natural integers N, or relative integers $\mathbb{Z}$ (all of them augmented with an undefined element $\perp$). More complex domains are powerset domains, product domains, sum domains or continuous function domains[5].

Definition 2. A *lattice* is a cpo in which any two elements x and y have a greatest lower bound ($x \vee y$) and a least upper bound ($x \wedge y$).

The advantage of using cpo's as semantical domains is that the semantics of any recursive continuous semantical equation $f : D \longrightarrow E$ can be defined as the *least fixed point* of a continuous functional $\Phi : (D \longrightarrow E) \longrightarrow (D \longrightarrow E)$.

[5] For a more complete description see [27, 20].

Definition 3. Given cpo's $\boldsymbol{D}$ and $\boldsymbol{E}$, and a function $g : \boldsymbol{D} \longrightarrow \boldsymbol{E}$,
g is *monotone* if $x \sqsubseteq_{\boldsymbol{D}} y \implies g(x) \sqsubseteq_{\boldsymbol{E}} g(y)$.
g is *continuous* if $\forall\, e_0 \sqsubseteq \cdots \sqsubseteq e_n \sqsubseteq \ldots \quad g(\bigsqcup_i e_i) = \bigsqcup_i g(e_i)$.

Definition 4. Let $\boldsymbol{D}$ be a cpo, and $g : \boldsymbol{D} \longrightarrow \boldsymbol{D}$ a continuous function.
$d \in \boldsymbol{D}$ is called a *fixed point* of g if $g(d) = d$. Moreover, d is called the *least fixed point* of g if $\forall\, d',\ g(d') = d' \implies d \sqsubseteq_{\boldsymbol{D}} d'$.

Theorem 5. *Let $\boldsymbol{D}$ be a cpo, and $g : \boldsymbol{D} \longrightarrow \boldsymbol{D}$ a continuous function. Then g has a least fixed point* $\mathrm{lfp}(g) = \bigsqcup_{i>0} g^i(\bot)$.

In our framework, we require that exact semantical equations be continuous functions. This ensures that the exact semantics of the analysis be precisely defined. However, approximate semantical equations are not required to be continuous functions. This might be rather cumbersome in case of recursive definitions (which are usually needed to handle loops), since the existence of a fixed point is not guaranteed anymore. When the functions meet the weaker condition of monotonicity, Graham and Wegman [18] define an *acceptable* solution. However, as will be shown in Subsection 2.3, some approximate analysis solutions do not belong to predefined lattices, and recursive functions may not even be monotone.

2.2 Semantical functions

Since we are interested in the semantical analysis of program properties, semantical functions share the same pattern. Let $\mathcal{A}$ be an exact semantical analysis of a program written in a programming language $\mathcal{L}$. $\mathcal{A}$ is generally a function from a subset $\tilde{\mathcal{L}}$ of $\mathcal{L}$ to another set, usually a function set:

$$\begin{aligned} \mathcal{A} : \tilde{\mathcal{L}} &\longrightarrow (\boldsymbol{D} \longrightarrow \boldsymbol{A}) \\ l &\longrightarrow \mathcal{A}[\![l]\!] \end{aligned}$$

For instance, the exact semantics of array region analysis is described by a function $\mathcal{R} : \tilde{\mathcal{L}} \longrightarrow (\boldsymbol{\Sigma} \longrightarrow \wp(\mathbb{Z}^n))$, where $\boldsymbol{\Sigma}$ is the set of memory stores.

As stated in the introduction of this section, the solutions defined by $\mathcal{A}$ may be extremely difficult, indeed impossible, to compute. Hence the idea to replace $\mathcal{A}$ by approximate analyses, comparable to $\mathcal{A}$ by a partial order $\sqsubseteq$:

$$\overline{\mathcal{A}} \text{ is an over-approximation of } \mathcal{A} \iff \mathcal{A} \sqsubseteq \overline{\mathcal{A}}$$
$$\underline{\mathcal{A}} \text{ is an under-approximation of } \mathcal{A} \iff \underline{\mathcal{A}} \sqsubseteq \mathcal{A}$$

This *approximation ordering* [11] is a logical ordering, and is not necessarily related to a partial ordering between semantical values. However, since $\mathcal{A}$, $\overline{\mathcal{A}}$ and $\underline{\mathcal{A}}$ are defined on the same sub-domain of $\mathcal{L}$, it is equivalent to an ordering of the solution functions: $\mathcal{A} \sqsubseteq \overline{\mathcal{A}} \iff \forall\, l \in \tilde{\mathcal{L}} \quad \mathcal{A}[\![l]\!] \sqsubseteq \overline{\mathcal{A}}[\![l]\!]$.

Given this approximation ordering, a semantical analysis $\mathcal{A}$ can be surrounded by two new, and hopefully computable, approximate analyses: an over-approximation, denoted by $\overline{\mathcal{A}}$; and an under-approximation, denoted by $\underline{\mathcal{A}}$. The target sets of $\underline{\mathcal{A}}$ and $\overline{\mathcal{A}}$ are not necessarily the same as the target set of $\mathcal{A}$.

For instance, array element index sets are parts of $\mathbb{Z}^n$. Due to the complexity of being able to represent any part of $\mathbb{Z}^n$, several compact representations have been defined: convex polyhedra [30], RSD [6], DAD [2], ...

The approximate analyses we are interested in are then such that:

$$\overline{\mathcal{A}} : \tilde{\mathcal{L}} \longrightarrow (D \longrightarrow A') \quad \text{and} \quad \underline{\mathcal{A}} : \tilde{\mathcal{L}} \longrightarrow (D \longrightarrow A'')$$

2.3 Non-lattice frameworks: Why?

A natural question that arises is why we may need non-continuous, or even non-monotone functions, while very friendly data-flow frameworks have been so carefully designed for years. The answer is that, in some cases, it is not possible to define interesting approximations otherwise.

For instance, let us consider exact array region analysis:

$$\mathcal{R} : \tilde{\mathcal{L}} \longrightarrow (\Sigma \longrightarrow \wp(\mathbb{Z}^n))$$

Being able to represent any possible part of $\mathbb{Z}^n$ is generally considered too complex, and the representation is often limited to particular parts of $\mathbb{Z}^n$ (convex polyhedra, RSDs, DADs, lists of convex polyhedra with a maximum length, ...).

In the case of convex polyhedra ($\wp_{\text{convex}}(\mathbb{Z}^n)$), an over-approximate analysis framework can be obtained from the lattice $(\wp(\mathbb{Z}^n), \varnothing, \mathbb{Z}^n, \cup, \cap)$ by a simple upper closure[6] $\overline{\alpha} = \lambda x.\text{convex\_hull}(x)$ (see Figure 2). This ensures that the approximate semantical equations derived from their exact counterparts using $\overline{\alpha}$ are continuous functions.

However, there exists no interesting lower closure $\underline{\alpha}$ (that is to say $\underline{\alpha} \neq \lambda x.\varnothing$ and $\underline{\alpha} \neq \lambda x.x$) from $(\wp(\mathbb{Z}^n), \varnothing, \mathbb{Z}^n, \cup, \cap)$ to $\wp_{\text{convex}}(\mathbb{Z}^n)$. If such a closure existed, $(\wp_{\text{convex}}(\mathbb{Z}^n), \varnothing, \mathbb{Z}^n, \cup, \lambda xy.\underline{\alpha}(x \cap y))$ would be a complete lattice (see [9], Corollary 2.3.0.5); this is not possible, because $\wp_{\text{convex}}(\mathbb{Z}^n)$ is not closed under $\cup$.

The same conclusion holds for RSDs, DADs, and lists of convex polyhedra with a maximum length. It intuitively corresponds to the fact that the greatest convex polyhedron or RSD contained into any array region is not uniquely defined. An ad-hoc computable under-approximation must then be chosen. Some possible choices have already been described in [5]. This is the subject of the next subsection.

---

[6] An upper closure $\overline{\alpha}$ is an internal operator, which is monotone ($x \sqsubseteq y \Longrightarrow \overline{\alpha}(x) \sqsubseteq \overline{\alpha}(y)$), extensive ($\lambda x.x \sqsubseteq \overline{\alpha}$), and idempotent ($\overline{\alpha} \circ \overline{\alpha} = \overline{\alpha}$). A lower closure is reductive ($\underline{\alpha} \sqsubseteq \lambda x.x$). The monotonicity property ensures that inclusion relations are preserved.

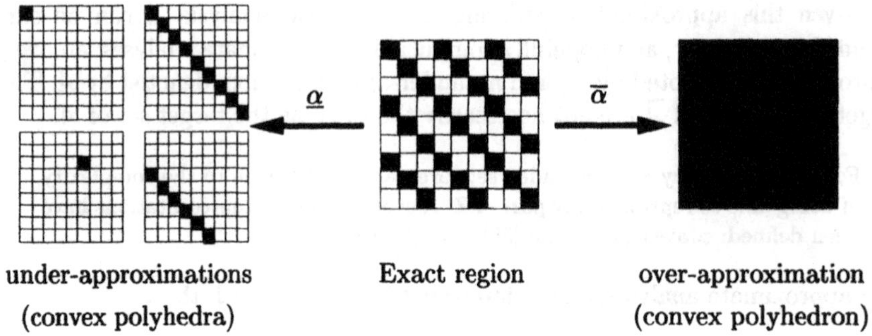

Fig. 2. Upper and under closures

2.4 Usual ad-hoc solutions

When the approximate solution space A'' is a lattice or cpo, its relations with the exact solution space A can be described by a GALOIS connection [3, 10], which defines two monotone functions: An *abstraction* function $\alpha : A \longrightarrow A''$, and a *concretization* or *meaning* function $\gamma : A'' \longrightarrow A$ (see Figure 3). The image of an exact continuous recursive function by α is then still continuous; its least fixed point is well defined, though its computability is not even decidable. COUSOT has shown that least fixed points can then be safely approximated by successive iterations relying on sequences of *narrowing* operators [10, 9].

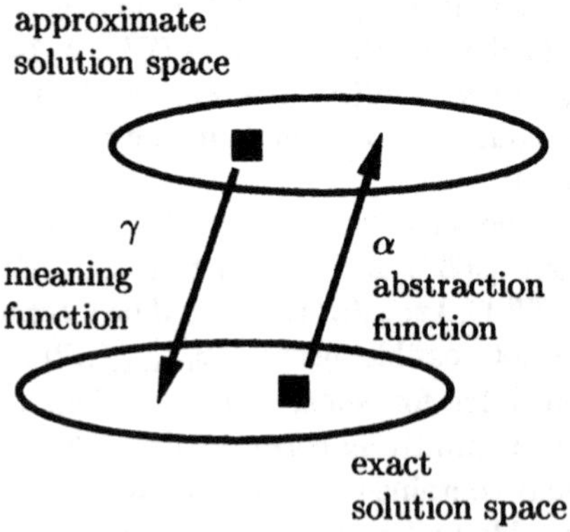

Fig. 3. GALOIS Connection

To handle cases where the approximate solution space is not a lattice or a cpo, but a mere partial order, BOURDONCLE [5] generalizes the traditional approach of GALOIS connections by defining *representations*, in which α is not required to be a monotone function. In this framework, least fixed points of exact continuous recursive functions are safely approximated by sequences of narrowing operators, even if their image by α is not continuous (see Appendix A).

Let us see on an contrived example how this technique performs for under-approximate array region analysis on trivial loops. We assume that the decreasing sequence of narrowing operators has only one iteration: Its result is the region corresponding to the first iteration of the loop.
In the innermost loop body of the contrived example in Figure 4, the sole ele-

```
do I = 1,5
   do J = 1,5
      A(I) =  ...
   enddo
enddo
```

Fig. 4. A small contrived example

ment A(I) is referenced. From our previous definition of the iterative process, we deduce that the summary region corresponding to the innermost loop is the set of array elements referenced at iteration $J = 1$, that is to say {A(I)}. It exactly describes the set of array elements read by the five iterations of the J loop. Repeating the process for the outermost loop, we obtain the set {A(1)}, which is far from the set of array elements actually referenced by the loop nest!

The previous example has been chosen for its simplicity, and it could be objected that the sequence of operators could be greatly enhanced. For instance, more iterations could be allowed; in our previous example, merging the sets of array elements during five iterations would give the exact result. But what if the loop upper bound is so great (`do I = 1,10000`) that the number of iterations would be overwhelming; or if it is unknown (`do I = 1,N`)? However, in all these cases, the exact set of array elements referenced within the previous loop nest is *computable* and *known* to be computable [14]. This is the basis for the solution we propose in the next section.

3 Approximations and Exactness

The previous section has just shown that existing under-approximate analyses may fail to expose interesting results, even in trivial cases, where the expected result is computable. This section describes a method to alleviate this problem, based on our previous experience of array region analyses [14]. It relies on the use of a *computable exactness criterion* which is introduced in a first subsection. Its optimality and applications are then discussed in Section 3.2.

3.1 Exactness of approximate analyses

From the definition of $\overline{\mathcal{A}}$ and $\underline{\mathcal{A}}$, we already know that:

$$\forall l \in \tilde{\mathcal{L}}, \quad \underline{\mathcal{A}}[l] \sqsubseteq \mathcal{A}[l] \sqsubseteq \overline{\mathcal{A}}[l]$$

An immediate consequence is: $(\underline{\mathcal{A}}[\![l]\!] \equiv \overline{\mathcal{A}}[\![l]\!]) \implies (\underline{\mathcal{A}}[\![l]\!] \equiv \mathcal{A}[\![l]\!] \equiv \overline{\mathcal{A}}[\![l]\!])$.

Hence, if the over-approximation is equal to the under-approximation, then both solutions are equal to the exact solution. However, the converse is not true:

$$(\overline{\mathcal{A}}[\![l]\!] \equiv \mathcal{A}[\![l]\!]) \not\Rightarrow (\underline{\mathcal{A}}[\![l]\!] \equiv \mathcal{A}[\![l]\!])$$

In the following simple counter-example, it is not possible to have $\overline{\mathcal{A}}[\![l]\!] \equiv \underline{\mathcal{A}}[\![l]\!]$:

$$\overline{\mathcal{A}} : l \longrightarrow (D \longrightarrow \top)$$
$$\underline{\mathcal{A}} : l \longrightarrow (D \longrightarrow \bot)$$

Thus a trivial way to check if the result of an approximation is exact is to verify that it is equal to the opposite approximation. A question that arises is whether this is the best possible criterion.

3.2 Optimality of the Exactness Criterion

The next theorem shows that if proving that $\overline{\mathcal{A}}[\![l]\!] \equiv \underline{\mathcal{A}}[\![l]\!]$ is not the best known criterion for checking the exactness of $\overline{\mathcal{A}}[\![l]\!]$ and $\underline{\mathcal{A}}[\![l]\!]$, then two other computable analyses $\overline{\mathcal{A}}'$ and $\underline{\mathcal{A}}'$ can be defined, which are better approximations of $\mathcal{A}$ than $\overline{\mathcal{A}}$ and $\underline{\mathcal{A}}$. A constructive proof is then given, which shows how to build $\overline{\mathcal{A}}'$ and $\underline{\mathcal{A}}'$ from $\overline{\mathcal{A}}$ and $\underline{\mathcal{A}}$. The consequences of this theorem are discussed afterwards.

Theorem 6. *If there exists a* computable *criterion* $C_{\underline{\mathcal{A}} \equiv \overline{\mathcal{A}}}$ *such that:*

$$\forall l \in \tilde{\mathcal{L}},\ C_{\underline{\mathcal{A}} \equiv \overline{\mathcal{A}}}(l) \implies \overline{\mathcal{A}}[\![l]\!] \equiv \underline{\mathcal{A}}[\![l]\!]$$

then any computable criterion $C_{\overline{\mathcal{A}} \equiv \mathcal{A}}$ *or* $C_{\underline{\mathcal{A}} \equiv \mathcal{A}}$ *such that:*

$$\forall l \in \tilde{\mathcal{L}},\ C_{\overline{\mathcal{A}} \equiv \mathcal{A}}(l) \implies \overline{\mathcal{A}}[\![l]\!] \equiv \mathcal{A}[\![l]\!]$$
$$\forall l \in \tilde{\mathcal{L}},\ C_{\underline{\mathcal{A}} \equiv \mathcal{A}}(l) \implies \underline{\mathcal{A}}[\![l]\!] \equiv \mathcal{A}[\![l]\!]$$

is equivalent to $C_{\underline{\mathcal{A}} \equiv \overline{\mathcal{A}}}$, *or there exists two* computable *approximations* $\overline{\mathcal{A}}'$ *and* $\underline{\mathcal{A}}'$ *such that* $\underline{\mathcal{A}} \sqsubseteq \underline{\mathcal{A}}' \sqsubseteq \mathcal{A} \sqsubseteq \overline{\mathcal{A}}' \sqsubseteq \overline{\mathcal{A}}$ *and* $C_{\underline{\mathcal{A}}' \equiv \mathcal{A}} \iff C_{\underline{\mathcal{A}}' \equiv \overline{\mathcal{A}}'} \iff C_{\overline{\mathcal{A}}' \equiv \mathcal{A}}$.

Proof

- If $C_{\underline{\mathcal{A}} \equiv \overline{\mathcal{A}}}(l)$ is true then $\overline{\mathcal{A}}[\![l]\!] \equiv \underline{\mathcal{A}}[\![l]\!] \equiv \mathcal{A}[\![l]\!]$. It implies that $C_{\overline{\mathcal{A}} \equiv \mathcal{A}}(l)$ and $C_{\underline{\mathcal{A}} \equiv \mathcal{A}}(l)$ are also true.
- On the contrary, let us assume that there exists $l \in \tilde{\mathcal{L}}$ such that $C_{\overline{\mathcal{A}} \equiv \mathcal{A}}(l)$ is true and $C_{\underline{\mathcal{A}} \equiv \overline{\mathcal{A}}}(l)$ is false (this implies that $C_{\underline{\mathcal{A}} \equiv \mathcal{A}}(l) = \mathit{false}$).

  $C_{\overline{\mathcal{A}} \equiv \mathcal{A}}(l)$ implies that $\mathcal{A}[\![l]\!]$ is computable and is equal to $\overline{\mathcal{A}}[\![l]\!]$. Then, we can define a new approximation of $\mathcal{A}$, $\underline{\mathcal{A}}'$ by:

$$\underline{\mathcal{A}}' : \tilde{\mathcal{L}} \longrightarrow (D \longrightarrow A' \cup A'')$$
$$l \longrightarrow \textbf{if } C_{\overline{\mathcal{A}} \equiv \mathcal{A}}(l) \textbf{ then } \overline{\mathcal{A}}[\![l]\!] \textbf{ else } \underline{\mathcal{A}}[\![l]\!]$$

And the exactness criteria $C_{\underline{A'}\equiv A}$ and $C_{\underline{A'}\equiv\overline{A}}$ are defined by:

$$\forall l \in \tilde{\mathcal{L}},\ C_{\underline{A'}\equiv A}(l) = \text{if } C_{\overline{A}\equiv A}(l) \text{ then } \mathit{true} \text{ else } C_{\underline{A}\equiv A}(l)$$
$$\forall l \in \tilde{\mathcal{L}},\ C_{\underline{A'}\equiv\overline{A}}(l) = \text{if } C_{\overline{A}\equiv A}(l) \text{ then } \mathit{true} \text{ else } C_{\underline{A}\equiv\overline{A}}(l)$$

Since $C_{\underline{A}\equiv A}(l) = C_{\underline{A}\equiv\overline{A}}(l) = \mathit{false}$, $C_{\underline{A'}\equiv\overline{A}}(l) = C_{\underline{A'}\equiv A}(l) = C_{\overline{A}\equiv A}(l)$.
The previous assumption that $\exists l : C_{\overline{A}\equiv A}(l) \wedge \neg C_{\underline{A}\equiv\overline{A}}(l)$ implies that for at least one element l of $\mathcal{L}$ we know that $\overline{A}[l] \equiv A[l] \equiv \underline{A'}[l]$, but we do not know whether $\underline{A}[l] \equiv A[l]$ or not. A consequence is that $\underline{A'}$ is either identical to $\underline{A}$ or more accurate ($\underline{A} \sqsubseteq \underline{A'} \sqsubseteq A$).
Thus, we have shown that either $C_{\overline{A}\equiv A} \iff C_{\underline{A}\equiv\overline{A}}$ or there exists a computable under-approximation $\underline{A'}$ of A, more accurate than $\underline{A}$, and such that $C_{\underline{A'}\equiv\overline{A}} \iff C_{\underline{A'}\equiv A} \iff C_{\overline{A}\equiv A}$.

The proof is identical for $C_{\underline{A}\equiv A}$ and $C_{\underline{A}\equiv\overline{A}}$. □

Figure 5 summarizes the relations between the different criteria of exactness, and the actual exactness of the approximate analyses. To sum up, if $C_{\underline{A}\equiv\overline{A}}$ is

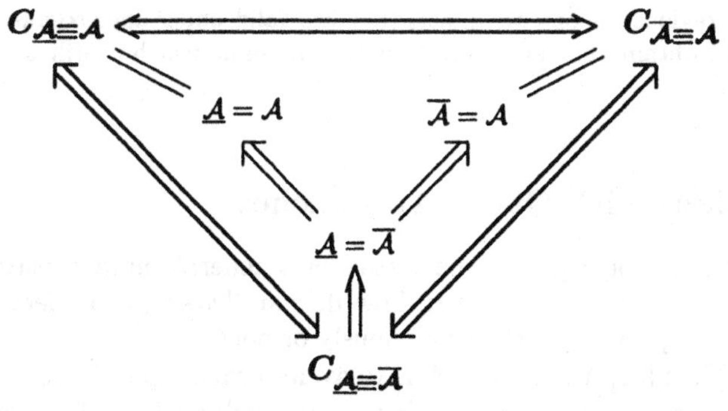

Fig. 5. Relations between approximations

not the best possible criterion for checking exactness, it is possible to define two other approximations, which are more accurate than the original ones. The new criterion $C_{\underline{A'}\equiv\overline{A'}}$ is then the best possible computable criterion (relatively to the available information about the program behavior). Moreover, from the previous proof, computing and testing the exactness of the new approximations is not more expensive than with the original solution.

Theorem 6 has two more consequences:

1. It may not always be useful to compute both $\overline{A}$ and $\underline{A}$; but we may well want to check the exactness of the chosen analysis, say $\overline{A}$. However, it may sometimes be difficult to find a computable exactness criterion $C_{\overline{A}\equiv A}$: it may

depend on $\mathcal{A}$, which is not computable! The above theorem gives a solution. If an opposite approximation $\underline{\mathcal{A}}$ is sufficiently well defined, $C_{\underline{\mathcal{A}}\equiv\overline{\mathcal{A}}}$ is the best possible exactness criterion for $\overline{\mathcal{A}}$. Thus, it is sufficient to define $\underline{\mathcal{A}}$, deduce the exactness criterion $C_{\underline{\mathcal{A}}\equiv\overline{\mathcal{A}}}$ and use it as $C_{\overline{\mathcal{A}}\equiv\mathcal{A}}$. It is not even necessary to explicitly compute $\underline{\mathcal{A}}$.

2. As shown in the previous section, defining an interesting approximation analysis is not always an easy task and general solutions may be disappointing. In this case, if a computable exactness criterion for the opposite analysis ($C_{\overline{\mathcal{A}}\equiv\mathcal{A}}$) is available, then $\underline{\mathcal{A}}$ can be refined by using $\overline{\mathcal{A}}$ whenever $C_{\overline{\mathcal{A}}\equiv\mathcal{A}}$ is true.

   Let us consider the example of Figure 4 to illustrate this. We assume that array regions are represented by convex polyhedra. For the loop body, the regions are exactly represented by $\{\Phi_1 : \Phi_1 = i\}$, Φ_1 being the descriptor of the first dimension of array A.
   An over-approximation for the innermost loop nest is readily obtained by adding the loop bound constraints to the above polyhedron, and eliminating the loop index j: $\{\Phi_1 : \Phi_1 = i \wedge 1 \leq j \leq 5\} \leadsto \{\Phi_1 : \Phi_1 = i\}$. This operation is exact because the loop bounds are affine, and the projection is exact according to [1, 28].
   For the outermost loop, an over-approximation is: $\{\Phi_1 : 1 \leq \Phi_1 \leq 5\}$ Again, the loop bounds are affine, and the elimination of i is exact. Since the previous regions are exact, they are valid under-approximations. We would obtain the same results with non-numerical but still affine loop bounds.

4 Relations with Other Approaches

Since the absence of a predefined lattice is a general characteristic of under-approximate array region analyses, how do parallelizing compilers other than PIPS handle the problem, either consciously or not?

In **Fiat/Suif** [21], the approach is to avoid inexact operations[7]. This is supported by an infinite representation, lists of polyhedra, which allows exact unions by simply appending regions to the list. For do loops with affine bounds, the loop index is merely replaced by a dummy variable, which is also an exact operation. For general loops, classical iterative techniques are used, but the underlying domain is the semi-lattice $(\wp_{\text{convex}}(\mathbb{Z}^n), \varnothing, \cap)$. This ensures safe approximations of fixed points, without having to use costly techniques such as dynamic partitioning. However, this may often result in coarse approximations, such as the empty set. And this prevents taking context information into account, since they are often exclusive in the several branches reaching join nodes of the control flow graph.

In **Polaris** [32], a similar approach is adopted, but applied to lists of RSDs. The main difference lies in the choice of the meet operator, which is called a *gated intersection*, but seems to be a guarded union, which matches the intrinsic

[7] This can be viewed as a *preventive* exactness criterion.

nature of the corresponding exact operation. How exponential growth of lists of regions is avoided is not specified.

In **Panorama** [19], lists of guarded RSDs are used to represent array regions. This allows to avoid inexact union and to handle do loops accurately. If during an operation a guard or RSD component cannot be computed, it is replaced by an unknown value, Ω. In fact, this is equivalent to compute exact regions whenever possible, and flag them as inexact otherwise. In this case, Ω can be interpreted as $\top$ or $\perp$ depending on the desired approximation (respectively *may* and *must*)[8]. For general loops, conservative approximations are performed. In particular, for loops with premature exits, an intersection operation is performed, as in Fiat/Suif.

To summarize, most under-approximate array region analyses are based on implicit exactness criteria, to avoid inexact operations. Infinite representations are used to handle sequences of instruction, for which union operations are involved. For do loops, ad-hoc solutions are used to compute exact solutions without using iterative techniques. But general loops for which fixed points would be required are conservatively handled, by switching to another lattice based on the same representation but associated with the intersection operator.

5 Conclusion

Due to a considerable amount of efforts over the last ten years, over-approximate array regions analyses are now well-known techniques, even if debates about the choice of the representation are still alive: Time and space complexity *versus* accuracy is the main issue, but usefulness is widely acknowledged [31, 4, 23, 21, 14].

The need for under-approximations appeared only recently [33, 25, 21], mainly for locality analysis, to allow advanced program transformations such as array privatization. But no study of the underlying semantical analysis framework had been made, thus missing its inherent problems due to the fact that under-approximate solutions of array region analyses do not belong to predefined lattices, as over-approximations do. We show that existing ad-hoc solutions based on iterative techniques do not bring interesting results, even though problems can be lessened by more accurate representations and more complex approximations of fixed points.

We thus propose a method based on our previous experience of array region analyses [13, 14]. The idea is to perform corresponding may and must analyses at the same time, and to enhance the results of must analyses with those of may analyses according to an *exactness criterion*. In our implementation, whose results are already used in PIPS for privatizing array regions [12], must regions are not even computed; instead, may regions are flagged as exact whenever the exactness criterion is true; under-approximations are thus always equal to the empty set, unless they are exact and equal to the corresponding over-approximations.

[8] This is very similar to the use of the *unknown* variable proposed by WONNACOTT in his thesis [35]

Less drastic solutions, combining our approach and iterative methods would certainly give better under-approximations; but their practical interest has to be demonstrated.

The method presented in this paper, though primarily introduced for array region analyses, is not solely restricted to them. It can be useful for every type of analysis where one of the approximation is not defined on a predefined lattice. But also when exact results are required for specific applications [7, 8]. Indeed, we show how to obtain an optimal *exactness criterion* valid for both may and must analyses. Finally, and from a theoretical point of view, being able to detect the exactness of an analysis gives a partial answer to a still unresolved question from COUSOT's thesis [9], about the distance between an approximation and its corresponding exact solution.

Acknowledgments

We are very thankful to François BOURDONCLE and Pierre JOUVELOT for insightful discussions about semantical analyses, and to Denis BARTHOU, Fabien COELHO and the referees for their helpful comments.

A Appendix

This appendix more formally describes the generalization of GALOIS connections proposed by BOURDONCLE in his thesis [5].

Definition 7 (Under-representation). Let $(\boldsymbol{A}, \perp, \sqsubseteq)$ be a cpo, $\boldsymbol{A}''$ a set, and $\gamma : \boldsymbol{A}'' \longrightarrow \boldsymbol{A}$ a *meaning* function. $(\boldsymbol{A}'', \preceq, \gamma, \underline{\Delta} = (\underline{\Delta}_i)_{i\in\mathrm{N}})$ is an *under-representation* of $\boldsymbol{A}$ if:

1. $(\boldsymbol{A}'', \perp, \preceq)$ is a partial order.
2. γ, the *meaning* or *concretization* function, is monotone.
3. Each element $a \in \boldsymbol{A}$ can be safely under-approximated by $\alpha(a) \in \boldsymbol{A}''$, that is to say $\gamma(\alpha(a)) \sqsubseteq a$.
4. $\underline{\Delta}$ is a sequence of operators $\underline{\Delta}_i : \boldsymbol{A}'' \times \boldsymbol{A}'' \longrightarrow \boldsymbol{A}''$, such that:
   - $\forall\, \underline{\Delta}_i \in \underline{\Delta},\ \forall\, a, a' \in \boldsymbol{A}'',\ \begin{cases} a\, \underline{\Delta}_i\, a' \preceq a \\ \gamma(a\, \underline{\Delta}_i\, a') \sqsubseteq \gamma(a') \end{cases}$
   - $\forall\, (a_i)_{i\in\mathrm{N}} \in \boldsymbol{A}''$, the sequence $(a'_i)_{i\in\mathrm{N}}$ defined by:

$$\begin{cases} a'_0 &= a_0 \\ a'_{i+1} &= a'_i\, \underline{\Delta}_i\, a_{i+1} \end{cases}$$

   has a lower bound.

BOURDONCLE then shows that if $\Phi : \boldsymbol{A} \longrightarrow \boldsymbol{A}$ is a continuous recursive function, and if $\underline{\Phi} : \boldsymbol{A}'' \longrightarrow \boldsymbol{A}''$ is a safe under-approximation of Φ ($\gamma \circ \underline{\Phi} \sqsubseteq \Phi \circ \gamma$), then the sequence

$$\begin{cases} a_0 &= \perp \\ a_{i+1} &= a_i\, \underline{\Delta}_i\, \underline{\Phi}(a_i) \end{cases}$$

is a decreasing sequence whose limit is a safe under-approximation of the least fixed point of Φ.

This method does not give the ***best solution*** but ***one*** possible solution. The following example shows its limitations. Our purpose is to show that the solution built using $\underline{\Phi}$ as the under-approximation of the least fixed point of Φ can lead to disappointing approximations, whereas the exact solution is known to be computable.

Example We consider array region analysis, and approximate array element sets by convex polyhedra. With the notations of Definition 7, we have: $(\boldsymbol{A}, \bot, \sqsubseteq) = (\boldsymbol{\Sigma} \longrightarrow \wp(\mathbb{Z}^n), \lambda x\sigma.\varnothing, \subseteq)$ and $(\boldsymbol{A}'', \bot, \preceq) = (\boldsymbol{\Sigma} \longrightarrow \wp_{\text{convex}}(\mathbb{Z}^n), \lambda x\sigma.\varnothing, \subseteq)$. γ is trivially defined by $\gamma = \lambda x.x$. And $\underline{\Delta}$ by:

$$\forall\, a, a' \in \boldsymbol{A}'', \quad \begin{cases} a \,\underline{\Delta}_0\, a' = a' \\ a \,\underline{\Delta}_i\, a' = a', \ \forall\, i > 0 \end{cases}$$

Thus the under-approximation of the least fixed point of any continuous recursive function is reached in exactly one iteration and is equal to $\underline{\Phi}(\varnothing)$.

For `while` loops the semantics of write regions is defined by:

$$\begin{aligned} \mathcal{R}[\![\texttt{while}(C)\ \ S]\!] &= (\mathcal{R}[\![\texttt{while}(C)\ \ S]\!] \circ \mathcal{T}[\![S]\!] \cup \mathcal{R}[\![S]\!]) \circ \mathcal{E}_c[\![C]\!] \\ &= \Phi(\mathcal{R}[\![\texttt{while}(C)\ \ S]\!]) \end{aligned}$$

which must be interpreted as: If the evaluation of the condition $\mathcal{E}_c[\![C]\!]$ is true, then the element written by S ($\mathcal{R}[\![S]\!]$) belong to the result, as well as the elements written by the next iteration (including the evaluation of the condition), but in the memory store modified by S, $\mathcal{T}[\![S]\!]$.

Φ can be under-approximated by:

$$\underline{\Phi} = \lambda f\sigma.(f \circ \mathcal{T}[\![S]\!] \,\underline{\cup}\, \underline{\mathcal{R}}[\![S]\!]) \circ \mathcal{E}_c[\![C]\!]\sigma$$

where $\underline{\cup}$ is an under-approximation of $\cup$ defined by:

$$x \,\underline{\cup}\, y = \textbf{if } x \cup y \in \boldsymbol{\Sigma} \longrightarrow \wp_{\text{convex}}(\mathbb{Z}^n) \textbf{ then } x \cup y \textbf{ else } \lambda\sigma.\varnothing$$

For the sake of simplicity, we assume that $\mathcal{E}_c$, $\mathcal{T}$, and $\circ$ do not need to be approximated. Given the previous definition of $\underline{\Delta}$, an under-approximation of $\text{lfp}(\Phi)$ is:

$$\underline{\Phi}(\lambda\sigma.\varnothing) = \underline{\mathcal{R}}[\![S]\!] \circ \mathcal{E}_c[\![C]\!]$$

This is the under-approximation of the region corresponding to the first iteration of the loop, after the evaluation of the condition, which is always true if the loop has at least one iteration.

Now let us consider the loop nest of Figure 4. In the innermost loop body, the sole element `A(I)` is referenced. It can be exactly represented, and thus under-approximated, by the convex polyhedron $\{\phi_1 = \texttt{I}\}$. The under-approximation obtained using $\underline{\Phi}$ for the innermost loop is the set of elements read during the first iteration, and is thus $\{\phi_1 = \texttt{I}\}$. It exactly describes the set of array elements read by the five iterations of the `J` loop. Repeating the process for the outermost loop, we then obtain $\{\phi_1 = 1\}$, which is far from the set of array elements actually referenced by the loop nest: $\{1 \leq \phi_1 \leq 5\}$.

References

1. Corinne Ancourt and François Irigoin. Scanning polyhedra with DO loops. In *Symposium on Principles and Practice of Parallel Programming*, pages 39–50, April 1991.
2. V. Balasundaram and K. Kennedy. A technique for summarizing data access and its use in parallelism enhancing transformations. In *International Conference on Programming Language Design and Implementation*, pages 41–53, June 1989.
3. Garrett Birkhoff. *Lattice Theory*, volume XXV of *AMS Colloqium Publications*. American Mathematical Society, Providence, Rhode Island, third edition, 1967.
4. W. Blume and R. Eigenmann. Performance analysis of parallelizing compilers on the Perfect Benchmarks programs. *IEEE Transactions on Parallel and Distributed Systems*, 3(6):643–656, November 1992.
5. François Bourdoncle. *Sémantique des Langages Impératifs d'Ordre Supérieur et Interprétation Abstraite.* PhD thesis, École Polytechnique, November 1992.
6. D. Callahan and K. Kennedy. Analysis of interprocedural side effects in a parallel programming environment. *Journal of Parallel and Distributed Computing*, 5:517–550, 1988.
7. Fabien Coelho. Compilation of I/O communications for HPF. In *Frontiers'95*, pages 102–109, February 1995. Available via `http://www.cri.ensmp.fr/~coelho`.
8. Fabien Coelho and Corinne Ancourt. Optimal compilation of HPF remappings. Technical Report A-277-CRI, CRI, École des Mines de Paris, October 1995. To appear in JPDC in 1996.
9. Patrick Cousot. *Méthodes Itératives de Construction et d'Approximation de Points Fixes d'Opérateurs Monotones sur un Treillis, Analyse Sémantique des Programmes.* PhD thesis, Institut National Polytechnique de Grenoble, March 1978.
10. Patrick Cousot and Radhia Cousot. Abstract interpretation : a unified lattice model for static analysis of programs by construction or approximation of fixpoints. In *Symposium on Principles of Programming Languages*, pages 238–252, 1977.
11. Patrick Cousot and Radhia Cousot. Higher-order abstract interpretation (and application to comportment analysis generalizing strictness, termination, projection and PER analysis of functional languages). In *International Conference on Computer Languages, IEEE Computer Socitey Press*, pages 95–112, May 1994.
12. Béatrice Creusillet. Array regions for interprocedural parallelization and array privatization. Report A-279, CRI, École des Mines de Paris, November 1995. Available at `http://www.cri.ensmp.fr/~creusil`.
13. Béatrice Creusillet and François Irigoin. Interprocedural array region analyses. In *Languages and Compilers for Parallel Computing*, number 1033 in Lecture Notes in Computer Science, pages 46–60. Springer-Verlag, August 1995.
14. Béatrice Creusillet and François Irigoin. Interprocedural array region analyses. *To appear in International Journal of Parallel Programming (special issue on LCPC)*, 24(6), 1996. Extended version of [13].
15. Paul Feautrier. Array expansion. In *International Conference on Supercomputing*, pages 429–441, July 1988.
16. Paul Feautrier. Dataflow analysis of array and scalar references. *International Journal of Parallel Programming*, 20(1):23–53, September 1991.
17. Kyle Gallivan, William Jalby, and Dennis Gannon. On the problem of optimizing data transfers for complex memory systems. In *International Conference on Supercomputing*, pages 238–253, July 1988.

18. S. Graham and M. Wegman. Fast and usually linear algorithm for global flow analysis. *Journal of the ACM*, 23(1):172–202, January 1976.
19. Jungie Gu, Zhiyuan Li, and Gyungho Lee. Symbolic array dataflow analysis for array privatization and program parallelization. In *Supercomputing*, December 1995.
20. C. Gunter and D. Scott. Denotational semantics. In Jan van Leeuwen, editor, *Theoretical Computer Science*, volume B, chapter 12. Elsevier Science Publisher, 1990.
21. Mary Hall, Saman Amarasinghe, Brian Murphy, Shih-Wei Liao, and Monica Lam. Detecting coarse-grain parallelism using an interprocedural parallelizing compiler. In *Supercomputing*, December 1995.
22. Mary Hall, Brian Murphy, Saman Amarasinghe, Shih-Wei Liao, and Monica Lam. Interprocedural analysis for parallelization. In *Languages and Compilers for Parallel Computing*, Lecture Notes in Computer Science, pages 61–80. Springer-Verlag, August 1995.
23. Michael Hind, Michael Burke, Paul Carini, and Sam Midkiff. An empirical study of precise interprocedural array analysis. *Scientific Programming*, 3(3):255–271, May 1994.
24. François Irigoin, Pierre Jouvelot, and Rémi Triolet. Semantical interprocedural parallelization: An overview of the PIPS project. In *International Conference on Supercomputing*, pages 144–151, June 1991.
25. Zhiyuan Li. Array privatization for parallel execution of loops. In *International Conference on Supercomputing*, pages 313–322, July 1992.
26. Dror E. Maydan, Saman P. Amarasinghe, and Monica S. Lam. Array data-flow analysis and its use in array privatization. In *Symposium on Principles of Programming Languages*, January 1993.
27. Peter Mosses. Denotational semantics. In Jan van Leeuwen, editor, *Theoretical Computer Science*, volume B, chapter 11. Elsevier Science Publisher, 1990.
28. William Pugh. A practical algorithm for exact array dependence analysis. *Communications of the ACM*, 35(8):102–114, August 1992.
29. Peiyi Tang. Exact side effects for interprocedural dependence analysis. In *International Conference on Supercomputing*, pages 137–146, July 1993.
30. Rémi Triolet. *Contribution à la parallélisation automatique de programmes Fortran comportant des appels de procédures.* PhD thesis, Paris VI University, 1984.
31. Rémi Triolet, Paul Feautrier, and François Irigoin. Direct parallelization of call statements. In *ACM SIGPLAN Symposium on Compiler Construction*, pages 176–185, 1986.
32. Peng Tu. *Automatic Array Privatization and Demand-Driven Symbolic Analysis.* PhD thesis, University of Illinois at Urbana-Champaign, 1995.
33. Peng Tu and David Padua. Array privatization for shared and distributed memory machines (extended abstract). In *Workshop on Languages and Compilers for Distributed Memory Machines*, pages 64–67, 1992.
34. Peng Tu and David Padua. Automatic array privatization. In *Languages and Compilers for Parallel Computing*, August 1993.
35. David Wonnacott. *Constraint-Based Array Dependence Analysis.* PhD thesis, University of Maryland, College Park, August 1995.

Context-Sensitive Interprocedural Analysis in the Presence of Dynamic Aliasing

Patrick W. Sathyanathan and Monica S. Lam

Computer Systems Laboratory
Stanford University
Stanford CA 94305

Abstract. Context-sensitive interprocedural data-flow analysis, for problems where the flow value is a mapping from symbols to values from an abstract domain, requires solutions to be computed for differing aliasing conditions existing at distinct calling contexts. This paper presents an approach for computing context-sensitive solutions to forward, monotone data-flow problems for statically allocated scalar variables that does not require reanalysis of procedures. The algorithm handles dynamic aliasing, due to non-recursive pointer types, and recursion. This paper applies the technique to constant propagation for statically allocated scalars.
We propose an elimination-style approach that computes a single *canonical transfer function* for a procedure, under the assumption that no aliases hold between its arguments (including both explicitly and implicitly passed globals) on entry. The canonical transfer functions are expressed as a set of parameterised data flow mappings, augmented with *sequence tokens* and *alias assertions*. The sequence tokens and alias assertions succinctly capture sufficient control-flow and alias conditions, respectively, so that accurate solutions in the presence of aliasing can be computed from the canonical one. The information represented by the sequence tokens allows approximations that yield conservative solutions, with varying levels of flow and context sensitivity.

1 Introduction

Interprocedural data-flow analysis (IPA) algorithms may be classified based on whether they have the following two characteristics:

1. Flow-sensitivity: an IPA algorithm is said to be *flow-sensitive* if the intra-procedural control flow is considered in analysing a procedure (i.e. in propagating flow values to a procedure's callees). Flow-sensitive algorithms yield more precise information compared to their flow-insensitive counterparts.
2. Context-sensitivity: an IPA algorithm is said to be context-sensitive if the solutions for a procedure include some notion of its calling context, allowing information from different calling contexts to be distinguished.

Context information may be explicitly encoded as *call-strings* [SP81] and are coupled with the data flow values. In the presence of recursion, call-strings become unbounded and some approximating scheme, such as *k-limiting*, that yields a solution with reasonable efficiency is adopted. The invocation graph [EGH94] explicitly encodes context in its structure, and is equivalent to using call-strings that are approximated only within recursive parts of the program call graph. This approach faces a potential exponential growth in the size of the invocation graph and a corresponding increase in

This research was supported in part by the Air Force Material Command and DARPA under the contract F30602-95-C-0098 and an NSF Young Investigator award.

analysis time due to independent analysis of each instance of a procedure. Memoization of transfer functions for reuse between different calling contexts is proposed as an approach to reducing the expected complexity [Ghi95].

The disadvantage of call-strings based approach, such as k-limited call-strings, is that they depend solely on the control flow structure of the program, and the context sensitivity they exhibit (which is a function of the approximation scheme) does not depend on the different input data contexts under which the procedure may actually be called. A second approach to context sensitivity [WL95] seeks to exploit similarity across calling contexts. It computes one or more parameterised partial transfer functions (PTFs) for a procedure to characterise its effect under different calling contexts. Parameterisation, which generalises a PTF, combined with proper selection of only the "relevant" portion of the context data to form the domain of the PTF, increases the probability that it may be applicable at calling contexts other than the one for which it was constructed. However, as for the previous approach, this method can experience exponential complexity in the worst case.

The method we propose replaces the potentially expensive computation of multiple transfer functions for a procedure by constructing a single *canonical transfer function* (*CTF*) for each procedure. Given a forward, monotone data-flow problem on non-pointer variables within a procedure, this approach allows us to derive an interprocedural context-sensitive analysis that handles dynamic aliasing due to non-recursive pointer data types. The technique is applicable to strongly-typed, imperative programs, with recursion and no indirect function calls. The algorithm consists of two phases, the first computes the CTFs, and the second applies them at calling contexts to compute the solution with the desired degree of context-sensitivity. The *primary* data flow analysis of interest — the example used is constant propagation — is performed concurrently with a store-based alias analysis.

The difficulty in computing precise transfer functions lies in the handling of aliases. In our approach, each CTF is computed under the assumption that no aliases exist between any actual arguments on entry. However, when computing the CTF, we do not perform any operations that would otherwise lose precision, but capture the necessary information succinctly in the form of *alias assertions* and *sequence tokens* so that they can be performed at the time the CTF is applied to a particular calling context.

Alias assertions express aliasing information relevant to increasing the applicability of *strong updates*. They enable an elegant generalization of *Must points-to* and *May points-to* relationships through the use of *possibly-strong* data-flow values (Section [5]). The *possibly-strong* values also enable the expression of the previously distinct concepts of *strong* and *weak* updates, as special cases of a *possibly-strong* update (Section [5.3]). Data-flow values, generated by assignments to two locations, assumed to be distinct as a result of the no-alias assumption, will need to be combined in a flow-sensitive manner, if the locations are aliased at a calling context. Sequence tokens capture the control-flow information required to derive flow-sensitive results in the presence of aliasing. Sequence tokens may be compactly represented, and they allow solutions to be computed with varying levels of precision and context sensitivity.

The canonical transfer function is represented as a set of parameterised data-flow mappings augmented with alias assertions and sequence tokens. The alias assertions indicate the alias conditions for which the mapping is strong, and the sequence token indicates where the mapping is created. To apply a CTF, we use the known alias relationships to determine whether the updates are strong or weak. The alias information at a call-site is also used to group together all the mappings computed for the different aliases of the same variable. We then use their sequence tokens to combine the different mappings to arrive at the precise result. Since the cost of applying the CTF at a given context is less than the cost of reanalysing the procedure, we expect the approach to perform well in analysing large programs.

Interprocedural constant propagation [CCKT86, CH95], the primary data-flow problem considered here, attempts to identify and interprocedurally propagate initialization constants and constant assignments to program variables. It is a useful optimizing transformation that moves runtime computation of constant expressions to compile time. The information computed is useful for improving the precision and applicability of other program analyses/transformations. In particular it is especially useful for high-level program transforms to enhance parallelism and memory hierarchy performance. Discovery of constants in loop bound and array index expressions may convert an intractable analysis problem into one for which efficient solutions exist. Context sensitivity is required as these transforms may be applicable under one calling context and not in another. Another flow problem of interest is context-sensitive type analysis, where type information could form the basis for cloning decisions, and specialised versions of procedures with direct method invocations replacing indirect ones may be generated.

The contributions of this work are (1) the sequence token abstraction that captures sequencing information, (2) the lattice of *alias assertions* that generalise weak/strong updates, and increase the applicability of *strong updates*, and (3) their use in computing precise transfer functions under the no-alias assumption.

2 Overview

This section introduces some of the notation and concepts with the help of the example program in Figure (1). Sequence tokens are presented in Section [3] and alias assertions in Section [4]. Section [5] introduces data-flow values for the primary and the pointer data-flow problem. The interprocedural algorithm is discussed in Section [6]. Some proofs of correctness are presented in Section [7], followed by a discussion of related work, and finally our conclusions. The example shown in Figure (1) is a simple program with no recursion, containing a call to procedure `f` with aliased arguments, and is used as a running example to illustrate concepts as they are introduced.

We use *extended parameters* to symbolically represent initial values on entry to a procedure. Addresses of memory locations, and values passed to formals or accessible through formals, are given names that are derived from the corresponding formal name. The names are generated on demand, when the values or locations are referenced, and are derived by appending a small integer, whose value is one less than the number of indirections that must be made through the formal to access the location/value. For example the location (of type integer) accessed through the formal p (of type integer pointer) is represented by the extended parameter $p0$. $p0$ in turn has the symbolic initial value $p1$ of type integer. This naming scheme implicitly conforms to the no-alias assumption by generating distinct names for each extended parameter.

Data-flow values are represented by mappings of the form $x \Rightarrow v$. In the example above, the $\Rightarrow$ symbol is overloaded to indicate "points-to" if x is a pointer variable, and "has the value" otherwise. The example above shows only "must points-to" relationships — "may points-to" relationships could arise from weak updates, intra-procedural control flow, or a procedure call, and are discussed in Section [5]. Data-flow values are annotated by sequence tokens, $S = \{p_1, p_2, ..., p_n\}$, where each p_i represents a program point within a procedure (Section [3]) at which the mapping came into effect.

In the interprocedural algorithm, the data-flow values of interest occur at two locations in the control flow graph (CFG) of a procedure: (1) the values at the *Exit* node, which contribute to the canonical transfer function, and (2) the values at a call-site, called *Jump Functions* [CCKT86]. Both CTFs and Jump Functions are represented as a mapping from the flow values at the procedure entry, to the flow values at the exit node or call-site respectively. *MOD/REF* information may be used to reduce the number of non-pointer globals considered. In Figure (1), the data-flow values for the variables `x`, `y`, and `var`, constitute the jump-function at the call-site `call1`. Phase 1 of

Program	Data-flow Values
void f(int *a, int *b)	{<a ⇒ a0, {0}>, <b ⇒ b0, {0}>
0 {	<a0 ⇒ a1, {0}>, <b0 ⇒ b1, {0}>}
1 = *b;	
2 if (...) {	
3 *a = c1;	<a0 ⇒ c1, {3}>
4 *b = c2;	<b0 ⇒ c2, {4}>
} else {	
call2 g(a, b);	
}	<a0 ⇒ c1, {call2$_1$}>, <b0 ⇒ c2, {call2$_2$}>
5	
.. = *a;	<a0 ⇒ c1, {3, call2$_1$}>, <b0 ⇒ c2, {4, call2$_2$}>
6	
}	
void g(int *p, int *q)	{<p ⇒ p0, {0}>, <q ⇒ q0, {0}>,
0 {	<p0 ⇒ p1, {0}>, <q0 ⇒ q1, {0}> }
1 *p = c1;	<p0 ⇒ c1, {1}>
2 *q = c2;	<q0 ⇒ c2, {2}>
}	
void main()	
0 {	
int var, *x, *y;	{<var ⇒ top>, <x ⇒ top>, <y ⇒ top>}
1 x = &var;	<x ⇒ var>
2 y = &var;	<y ⇒ var>
call1 f(x, y);	<var ⇒ c2, call1$_2$>
}	

The integers to the left of each statement represent the program points. call1, and call2 represent call-sites.

Fig. 1. Example program

our algorithm analyses the strongly connected components of the program call-graph in reverse topological order, `g`, `f`, and `main`, to compute transfer functions and jump functions for each procedure/call-site respectively.

3 Sequence Tokens

Sequence tokens are subsets of intra-procedural program points. They annotate data-flow values generated within a procedure, and are used to determine the sequencing relation between the assignments of values to distinct names, which under actual aliasing conditions, may represent the same memory location.

3.1 Intraprocedural Paths

Definition 1. A set of program points, $S = \{p_1, p_2, ..., p_n\}$, is a sequence token if no element p_i is *post-dominated* by another:

$$\forall p_i \in S, \neg \exists p_j \in S, p_j \neq p_i \text{and } p_j \mathbf{PDOM}\ p_i \tag{1}$$

where **PDOM** represents the post-dominator relation in the control flow graph of the procedure.

We define a partial ordering on sequence tokens, with the intent that $S_1 < S_2$ at a given program point C, if every path in the procedure, from a point in S_1 to C, must pass through a point in S_2. We first consider only intraprocedural paths. $S_1 <_C S_2$ at a given program point C, if every intraprocedural path terminating at C contains $p \in S_1$ only if it also contains a succeeding $q \in S_2$. The *partial post-dominator relation* with respect to a given program point, that captures the above property, is defined as follows:

Definition 2. $p_1 \mathbf{PPDOM}_C p_2$ is said to hold at a program point C if every program path from p_2 to C also passes through p_1.

Definition 3. Given two sequence tokens, $S_1 = \{p_1, p_2, ..., p_n\}$, and $S_2 = \{q_1, q_2, ..., q_m\}$, and a program point C, we define

$$S_1 <_C S_2 \text{ iff } \forall p \in S_1 \exists q \in S_2 \text{ such that } q\mathbf{PPDOM}\ {}_C p$$

C is typically a call-site, or the procedure exit node, where the relation between S_1 and S_2 needs to be determined. We are particularly interested in the exit node of a procedure, thus whenever the context is clear, we simply use $S_1 < S_2$ to denote $S_1 <_{EXIT} S_2$. We say $S_1 = S_2$ if they contain an identical set of points. If neither $S_1 \leq S_2$ nor $S_2 \leq S_1$ holds, we say that they are not comparable, $S_1 <> S_2$.

The $\mathbf{PPDOM}_C$ relation may be computed using a variant of the bit-vector approach of [UH75], or the fast dominator algorithm [LT79]. The bit vector algorithm for computing $\mathbf{PPDOM}_C$ is presented in Appendix A. The set of sequence tokens consisting of points within a procedure, partially ordered by the $\leq$ relation, forms the semi-lattice $\mathcal{L}_{seq}$.

The meet operation of two sequence tokens S_1 and S_2, at program point C, is:

$$S_1 \wedge_C S_2 = Normalise(C, S_1 \cup S_2), \tag{2}$$

where $Normalise(C, S)$ filters out those program points in S that do not satisfy Definition (1).

$$Normalise(C, S) = \{p | p \in S \text{ and } \neg \exists q \in S, q\mathbf{PPDOM}_C p\} \tag{3}$$

A data-flow value, which is a mapping from a name to a value, is annotated with a sequence token. The program points in the sequence token represent those set of program points at which the association between the name and the value came into effect. This can occur in one of three ways — assignment statements, meet points where information from different control flow paths are combined, and, procedure calls.

3.2 Interprocedural paths

Since sequence tokens only consist of intraprocedural program points, we need a way of annotating data-flow values generated within a callee procedure. We use a special version of program-points, derived from the call-site, as sequence tokens for these data-flow values. Every distinct sequence token S, within a callee procedure, is assigned a unique sequence token in the caller, derived from the call-site C, by the function $GenToken_C(S)$.

To extend the definition of the ordering relation to interprocedural paths, we define the $<$ relation on program points derived from a call-site:

Definition 4. Let two program points,

$$C_1^P = GenToken_C(S_1^Q) \text{ and } C_2^P = GenToken_C(S_2^Q),$$

in procedure P be derived from the tokens S_1^Q and S_2^Q in procedure Q, at the call-site C in P calling Q. We say $C_1^P < C_2^P$ if every interprocedurally balanced path from C, passing through a point in S_1^Q, subsequently passes though a point in S_2^Q.

An interprocedurally balanced path is one where every call-edge to the entry of a procedure is matched by a return-edge to the call-site invoking it. Determining the ordering relation between sequence tokens containing program points derived from distinct call-sites in a procedure, requires only intraprocedural control flow information. To determine the sequencing relation between two tokens derived from the same call-site, the comparison needs to be done within the callee procedure, between the original tokens from which the compared tokens were derived. In the absence of recursion, this process of referencing callee procedures, which we call token *expansion*, will terminate. How recursion is handled is described in detail below.

Note that this scheme of generating sequence tokens at call-sites, and later expanding them for the purpose of determining the ordering, ensures that we only consider interprocedurally valid paths. In addition, the derived tokens effectively *summarise* those within callee procedures, and the token expansion needs to be performed only when two tokens derived from the same call-site need to be compared.

Recursion introduces cycles in the call-graph and it is possible that the expansion process for computing $S_1 < S_2$ becomes cyclic. An example program where this situation occurs is given in Figure (2).

For the above example program, applying the CTF (Section [6.2]) of the function `f` to the actual arguments at the call-site *call3*, yields the set of mappings

$$\{< x \Rightarrow \text{c1}, S_1 = \{call3_1\} >, < x \Rightarrow \text{c2}, S_2 = \{call3_2\} >\},$$

where

$$\{call3_1\} = GenToken_{call3}(\{2, call1_1\}) \text{ and } \{call3_2\} = GenToken_{call3}(\{3, call1_2\}).$$

Computing the aliased solution from these mappings requires finding the ordering relation between S_1 and S_2 at *call3*. The sequence tokens S_1 and S_2 expand in procedure `f`, into ${S^f}_1 = \{2, call1_1\}$, and $S_2^f = \{3, call1_2\}$ respectively. Since $2 < 3$ at the exit node of `f`, we need to determine if $call1_1 < call1_2$, where

$$\{call1_1\} = GenToken_{call1}(\{2, call2_1\}) \text{ and } \{call1_2\} = GenToken_{call1}(\{3, call2_2\}),$$

are derived from the same call-site, *call1*. This leads to the next level of expansion, which yields at the exit node of procedure `g`, the pair $S_1^g = \{2, call2_1\}$ and $S_2^g = \{3, call2_2\}$, where

$$\{call2_1\} = GenToken_{call2}(\{2, call1_1\}) \text{ and } \{call2_2\} = GenToken_{call2}(\{3, call1_2\}).$$

Program	Data-flow Values
void f(int *p, int *q)	{<p ⇒ p0, {0}>, <q ⇒ q0, {0}>,
0 {	<p0 ⇒ p1, {0}>, <q0 ⇒ q1, {0}>}
1 if (..) {	
2 *p = c1;	<p0 ⇒ c1, {2}>
3 *q = c2;	<q0 ⇒ c2, {3}>
} else	
call1 g(p, q);	<p0 ⇒ c3, {call1$_1$}>, <q0 ⇒ c2, {call1$_2$}>
4	
}	<p0 ⇒ c1, {2, call1$_1$}>, <q0 ⇒ c2, {3, call1$_2$}>
void g(int *a, int *b)	{<a ⇒ a0, {0}>, {b ⇒ b0, {0}>,
0 {	<a0 ⇒ a1, {0}>, <b0 ⇒ b1, {0}>}
1 if (...) {	
2 *a = c1;	<a0 ⇒ c1, {2}>
3 *b = c2;	<b0 ⇒ c2, {3}>
} else	
call2 f(a, b);	<a0 ⇒ c1, {call2$_1$}>, <b0 ⇒ c2, {call2$_2$}>
4	<a0 ⇒ c1, {2, call2$_1$}>, <b0 ⇒ c2, {3, call2$_2$}>
}	
void main()	
{	
int x;	
call3 f(&x, &x);	<x ⇒ c2, {call3$_2$}>
}	

Fig. 2. Example with recursion

Expanding the tokens derived from *call*2, again yields in procedure f, the original tokens $S_1^f = \{2, call1_1\}$ and $S_2^f = \{3, call1_2\}$.

Cycles in the expansion process occur within a set of recursive procedures $\{P_i, i \in 1:n\}$, each containing a call-site C_i calling the next procedure in the cycle. Let S_1^1 and S_2^1 be the original tokens in P_1 that need to be compared at the exit of P_1. The corresponding expanded tokens in procedure $P_i, i \in 2:n$ are denoted S_1^i, and S_2^i, respectively, and contain a program point derived from the call-site C_i. Let S'^i_1 and S'^i_2 denote the sequence tokens obtained from S_1^i and S_2^i, respectively, by deleting the program points derived from C_i.

Claim 1 *The expansion process is cyclic only if, for every procedure P_i, all non-call program points in S_1^i and S_2^i are strictly ordered.*

If there did exist a pair of non-call points from S_1^i and S_2^i which are not strictly ordered, that fact may be determined solely by intraprocedural control flow, and obviously $S_1^i <> S_2^i$ in P_i. Hence the expansion process stops in procedure P_i.

Lemma 1 *For the cyclic case described above, $S_1^1 < S_2^1$ if and only if $\forall i \in 1:n, S'^i_1 < S'^i_2$.*

Proof. Proof is by induction on m, the number of completed procedure calls in interprocedurally balanced paths, in invocations of the procedures P_i, from the call-sites C_i.

For $m = 0$, the only possible paths are those that do not include C_i, and $S_1^i < S_2^i$ iff $S'^i_1 < S'^i_2$.

Let the lemma be true for $m \leq k$. Let $I_k^l \subseteq P_i, i \in 1:n$, be the set of procedures that could be invoked in k invocations or less, from C_l. Then $S_1^l < S_2^l$ iff $\forall j$ such that $P_j \in I_k^l, S'^j_1 < S'^j_2$.

An interprocedurally balanced path with $k+1$ procedure invocations from C_l, must consist of one with $\leq k$ invocations, to some procedure P_m, followed by another with $\leq k$ invocations, from C_m. Such paths now include those intraprocedural paths in P_m that include the call-site C_m. By the induction hypothesis, on these paths, $S_1^m < S_2^m$ iff $\forall j$ such that $P_j \in I_k^m, S'^j_1 < S'^j_2$. It follows that $S_1^l < S_2^l$ iff $\forall j$ such that $P_j \in I_k^l \cup I_k^m, S'^j_1 < S'^j_2$.

For $m \geq n-1$, all procedures $P_i, i \in 1:n$ could be invoked. □

Lemma (1) allows us to handle recursive programs. In the above example, the lemma allows us to eliminate the call-sites in the recursive cycle from their corresponding sequence tokens. The modified tokens, containing only non-call program points, are now $S'^f_1 = \{2\}$, $S'^f_2 = \{3\}$, $S'^g_1 = \{2\}$, and $S'^g_2 = \{3\}$. The original problem may now be restated as follows: $S_1 < S_2$ iff $S'^f_1 < S'^f_2$ and $S'^g_1 < S'^g_2$. It is easily seen that $S_1 < S_2$ does indeed hold and allows us to deduce $< x \Rightarrow c2, \{call3_2\} >$ as the aliased solution from the set $\{< x \Rightarrow c1, \{call3_1\} >, < x \Rightarrow c2, \{call3_2\} >\}$

4 Alias Assertions

Aliasing occurs at a calling context when two or more extended parameters represent the same actual, which may be a pointer or a non-pointer variable. Computing the alias solution from the no-alias solution needs to account for the following effects for the flow values generated within a procedure:

- The simplest is due to direct assignments to two or more non-pointer extended parameters that may become aliased. For this case, the sequencing information is sufficient to compute the aliased solution by a process elaborated in Section [6.2].
- Another effect of the no-alias assumption, due to indirect assignments through formals/extended parameters, is illustrated by the code fragment in Figure (3). At program point 5, the pointer `local` points to both the extended parameters, $p0$ and $q0$, and the assignment generates a *weak update* (Section [5.3]). However, if at a calling context, $p0$ and $q0$ refer to the same location, the assignment would generate a strong update to the aliased location. We use a distinct form of data-flow value to represent the effect of such indirect assignments, called *possibly-strong* mappings, which includes the minimal external aliasing that must occur in order to generate a strong update. The intent of this form of mapping is to eliminate the loss of precision that would result from not using strong updates.

To handle the above situation, we conditionalise the mappings generated by assignment statements, using *Alias Assertions*. An alias assertion is a set of disjoint subsets of extended parameters of the same type. A member subset of an alias assertion is said to be *satisfied* if all its elements, with symbolic names replaced by actual values at a calling context, are identical. An alias assertion, A, is said to be *satisfied* if actual

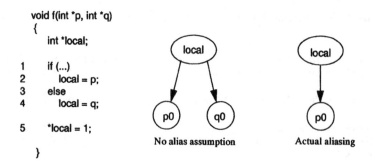

```
void f(int *p, int *q)
{
    int *local;

    if (...)
        local = p;
    else
        local = q;

    *local = 1;

}
```

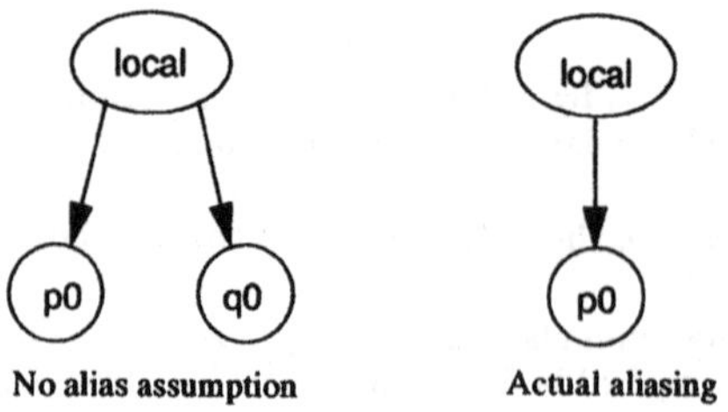

Fig. 3. Indirect assignments through formals/extended parameters

arguments at a calling context satisfy *every* member subset of A. An alias assertion is said to be *satisfiable* if it is possible for actual arguments at a calling context to satisfy it. Note that for a member subset of pointer type to be satisfiable, all its elements must be extended parameters, which may, at a call-site, represent the same memory location. Scalar type member subsets are satisfiable only if they contain at most one literal constant. An alias assertion containing an unsatisfiable member subset is denoted $\perp_{assert}$.

If the alias assertion, conditionalising a possibly-strong mapping (Section [5.3]), is satisfied, the mapping is changed to a strong one. A partial ordering on alias assertions, similar to that on sequence tokens, is defined as follows:

Definition 5. Given two alias assertions $A_1 = \{a_1, a_2, ..., a_n\}$ and $A_2 = \{b_1, b_2, ..., b_m\}$,

$$A_1 \leq A_2 \text{ iff } \forall b \in A_2 \exists a \in A_1 \text{ such that } b \subseteq a$$

The lattice of alias assertions, with $\perp_{assert}= false$ representing the impossible aliasing condition, and $\top_{assert} = true$, is denoted $\mathcal{L}_{assert}$.

5 Data-Flow values

Two distinct sets of data-flow values are computed, the first being the *Points-to* values representing the alias relationships, and the other being the environment, representing mappings from symbols to elements of the primary data-flow lattice, $\mathcal{L}_{pri}$. The primary data-flow lattice considered in this paper is the constant propagation lattice extended with symbolic initial values of formals and extended parameters.

5.1 Alias representation

Our alias analysis is a store-based one that uses the points-to representation of alias information. Points-to corresponds to storing edges between adjacent nodes of the abstract storage graph (ASG), and occurs in two flavours: *Must Points-to* and *May Points-to*, representing strong and weak edges, respectively. *Possibly-strong* mappings represent conditionally-strong edges in the graph. *Points-to* flow-values have the following three forms:

1. *Strong mappings* are represented as a single mapping $< x \Rightarrow v, S >$. This form represents a *Must Points-to* relationship between x and the location v.

2. *Possibly-strong mappings* represent mappings that could be strong, depending on the actual arguments at some calling context. For *Points-to* values, $< x \rightarrow v, A, S >$ represents a *Conditional Points-to* relationship between x and v, with A as the alias assertion. The semantics of this mapping is that if A is *satisfied* by the aliasing at a particular calling context, the mapping represents the strong one $< x \Rightarrow v, S >$. If A is not satisfied, the mapping is reduced to the weak one $< x \rightsquigarrow v, S >$.
3. *Weak mappings* are represented as $\{< x \rightsquigarrow v, S >$. For *Points-to* values, this form indicates that a *May Points-to* relationship holds for x, and that this relationship is not an artifact of the no-alias assumption.

5.2 Environment representation

For the constant propagation problem, the primary lattice is $\mathcal{L}_{const}$, which consists of the flat lattice of literal constants, augmented with symbolic values to represent the initial values of non-pointer type formals. The lattice for the primary data-flow problem is assumed to have a bottom element represented as $\bot_{pri}$. Weak mappings for the constant propagation problem arise as a result of possibly-strong mappings whose alias assertions are not satisfied.

1. *Strong mappings* are represented again as a single mapping $< x \Rightarrow v, S >$. They indicate that x *must have value* v; that is, the mapping is independent of the aliasing between extended parameters.
2. *Possibly-strong mappings* for the primary problem are represented as $< x \rightarrow v, A, S >$ where A is the alias assertion. The semantics of this mapping is that, if external aliasing causes A to be satisfied, the mapping is strong: $< x \Rightarrow v, S >$. If A is not satisfied, the resulting mapping is $< x \rightsquigarrow v, S >$.
3. *Weak mappings* are represented as $< x \rightsquigarrow v, S >$. For the primary problem, weak mappings arise as a result of possibly-strong mappings whose alias assertions are not satisfied by actuals at a call-site. If the actual values of the symbolic names were known at the point where the possibly-strong mappings are created, the node transfer function would have applied the meet operation — this meet operation is thus delayed until the symbolic names become bound to actual values at a call-site.

For constant propagation, each value v could be either a literal constant, or the symbolic initial value of a non-pointer extended parameter.

With the data-flow values conditionalised by elements of $\mathcal{L}_{assert}$, it is easy to see that strong and weak mappings are merely special cases of possibly-strong mappings. The strong mapping $< x \Rightarrow v, S >$ is identical to the possibly-strong mapping $< x \rightarrow v, \top_{assert}, S >$. Likewise, the weak mapping $< x \rightsquigarrow v, S >$ is equivalent to the possibly-strong mapping, $< x \rightarrow v, \bot_{assert}, S >$, as $\bot_{assert}$ represents impossible aliasing. Thus the alias assertion of a mapping is an indication of its "strength". Henceforth, we use $\mapsto$ as a placeholder to represent any of $\Rightarrow$, $\rightarrow$, or $\rightsquigarrow$.

The definition of the possibly-strong mapping reflects the basic idea behind deriving the alias solution from the no-alias one: delay the application of the meet operation until the actual values of the extended parameters are known.

5.3 Assignment statements

Assignment statements are of two forms, direct or indirect, depending on whether the location being assigned to is referenced directly by name or indirectly by a pointer dereference. Indirect assignments have different effects depending on whether the pointer being dereferenced has a strong, possibly-strong, or weak mapping, and also on the form of the value being assigned. The particular form of the mappings generated by indirect assignments may not be inferred from the assignment statement, and requires knowledge of the aliasing that exists when the transfer function is evaluated. The transfer function for an assignment statement annotates the generated mappings with a sequence token containing the current program point as its sole member.

We assume that dereferences involving multiple levels of indirections are decomposed into simple statements, each having at most one level of indirection. We elaborate the various cases for the assignment statement

```
p:        lhs = rhs;
```

where p is a program point.

1. *Strong updates:* Direct assignments, or assignments through pointers which have a *Must Points-to* value are referred to as strong updates. Consider the assignment statement $*x = y$, where x has the mapping $< x \Rightarrow v, S_{lhs} >$. Let *GEN* be the set of mappings generated from those for y as follows: for each $< y \rightarrow b, A, S >$, generate a mapping $< v \rightarrow b, A, \{p\} >$. The strong update replaces the mappings for v with *GEN*.
2. *Possibly-strong updates:* Indirect assignments, through a pointer with a possibly-strong mapping, are referred to as possibly-strong updates. Possibly-strong updates could eliminate the current mapping of the location being assigned to, depending on whether the actual aliasing satisfies the alias assertion of the possibly-strong mapping being dereferenced. Since the actual aliasing is unknown when the assignment is being processed, we defer the application of the update until such time as that information is available. Consider the assignment statement $*x = y$, where x has the possibly strong mapping $< x \rightarrow v, A, S >$. The current mappings of y generate a set of mappings, *GEN*, as follows: each $< y \rightarrow b, A', S' >$ generates $< v \rightarrow b, A \wedge A', \{p\} >$. If *IN* is the set of initial mappings for v, the result of the possibly-strong update is the meet of the two sets: $IN \wedge GEN$, which is defined to be *GEN* itself if $IN = \emptyset$.
3. *Weak Updates:* Indirect assignments through a pointer that has a weak mapping are referred to as weak updates. Weak updates have the property that they do not eliminate the current mapping of the location being assigned to — additional weak mappings are added. Consider the assignment statement $*x = y$, where x has a weak mapping $< x \rightarrow v, \perp_{assert}, S >$. Let *GEN* be the set of mappings generated from those for y as follows: for each $< y \rightarrow b, A, S >$, generate a mapping $< v \rightarrow b, \perp_{assert}, \{p\} >$. The weak update replaces the mappings for v with the meet of its current mappings *IN* with *GEN*.

As in the case of the data flow values, it is obvious that the possibly-strong update is the generalisation of the strong and weak updates. A strong update is just a possibly-strong update, where all current mappings are eliminated immediately, and the result is just the generated set of mappings, *GEN*. A weak update on the other hand, does not eliminate any existing mappings, and the result is the meet of all existing mappings with the generated ones.

5.4 Meet operation

The meet operation, applied at program point p, for both the data-flow problems, points-to and constant propagation, are modified to handle the meet of sequence tokens and alias assertions as follows:

$$< x \rightarrow v_1, A_1, S_1 > \wedge < x \rightarrow v_2, A_2, S_2 >=$$
$$\begin{cases} < x \rightarrow v, A_1 \wedge A_2, S_1 \wedge S_2 > & \text{if } v_1 = v_2 = v \\ < x \rightarrow v_1 \wedge v_2, A_1 \wedge A_2, \{p\} > & \text{else if both } v_1 \text{ and } v_2 \text{ are scalars and} \\ & \text{are not extended parameters} \\ \left. \begin{array}{l} < x \rightarrow v_1, A_1 \wedge \{\{v_1, v_2\}\}, S_1 > \\ < x \rightarrow v_2, A_2 \wedge \{\{v_1, v_2\}\}, S_2 > \end{array} \right\} & \text{otherwise} \end{cases} \quad (4)$$

Note that, of the three cases on the right-hand side of Equation (4), the second one does not apply to the points-to values. It applies only to the primary data-flow values and handles the meet of two distinct literal values. The intuition for the first case is that the meet operation does not *change* the values of the associated mapping, and hence, the single resulting mapping needs to be annotated with the meet of the two sequence tokens, which contains the "last" points where x was assigned the value v. The meet of the alias assertions represents the minimal aliasing for the resulting mapping to be strong. The last case handles the situation where both v_1 and v_2 are distinct extended parameters, which may become aliased at some calling context. To account for this possibility, we do a meet of the alias assertion $\{\{v_1, v_2\}\}$ with the existing alias assertions for the two mappings. This ensures that if v_1 and v_2 are different names for the same value, say v, for a calling context, the mappings are transformed to the pair $< x \rightarrow v, A_1, S_1 >$ and $< x \rightarrow v, A_2, S_2 >$, respectively. The meet operation is then applied to this pair at the call-site. Thus the alias assertions defer the application of strong updates to an extended parameter until the aliasing is known. Likewise, the sequence tokens defer the application of the meet operation for distinct extended parameters that may become aliased.

6 Interprocedural algorithm

The program call-graph, $PCG =< N_0, N, E >$, consists of a set of nodes N corresponding to procedures, where node N_p represents procedure p, and node N_0 is the node for the "main" procedure. E is the set of edges, and contains one edge between N_P and N_Q for each call-site in P calling Q. Phase I processes the call-graph in reverse topological order of the strongly connected components (SCCs), and requires that the SCC being analysed be present in memory, with the text and CFG for each procedure in it.

The overall structure of our algorithm is as follows:

- Compute the strongly connected components (SCCs) of the call graph.
- Phase 1: process the SCCs in reverse topological order, computing the canonical transfer function and jump functions for every procedure in each SCC.
- Phase 2: Traverse the call graph in forward topological order to determine the actual alias solution from the canonical transfer functions and jump functions.

Note that Phase 2 may *use* the CTFs to compute context-sensitive solutions to any desired degree of precision, cloning procedures if necessary. During Phase 2, we only need to store the CTF and jump functions, for each procedure in the program, allowing large programs to be analysed.

6.1 Computing canonical transfer functions

In processing an acyclic SCC containing a single procedure, the CTFs for all callee procedures have already been computed, and a single analysis of the procedure is sufficient to compute its CTF. However, in analysing a procedure in a recursive cycle, the above condition will not hold, and all the procedures in the cyclic SCC need to be analysed iteratively, until their CTFs reach a fix-point. While processing an SCC, procedures that contain exit paths are analysed first to obtain an initial approximation to the CTF. To conform with the no-alias assumption, strong mappings are generated for all referenced formals and extended parameters on entry to a procedure.

Algorithm ProcessSCC(*SCC*)
Compute the CTFs for all procedures in SCC

{

```
  Initialise the CTF of each procedure to ⊤_CTF;
  While (fix-point not reached) do
        For each procedure P in SCC do
            IntraproceduralAnalyse(P);
}
```

The following algorithm is an outline of the intraprocedural analysis method.

Algorithm IntraproceduralAnalyse(P)
Compute the CTF for procedure P

```
{
  Repeat until no changes to any jump-function/CTF (flow-value at exit node):
      Process each CFG node based on its type:
          Case assignment: Process assignment (Section [5.3]);
          Case meet: Do meet (Equation (4));
          Case call-site: Apply MapCall ; (Section [6.2])
                          Apply ApplyCTF ;
                          Apply UnmapCall ;
}
```

6.2 Applying CTFs

For the example program in Figure (1), given the aliasing of the actual arguments to function `f` at call-site `call1` within function `main`, a straight-forward mapping of the actual arguments to the canonical transfer function of function `f`, would yield the following mappings for `var` after the call: $\{< var \Rightarrow \text{c1}, \{call1_1\} >, < var \Rightarrow \text{c2}, \{call1_2\} >\}$. Once the mapping between the actuals and extended parameters has been established, the information required to compute the aliased solution is present in the alias assertions and the sequence tokens of the translated mappings.

The process of applying a CTF at a call-site consists of three stages: mapping the actual arguments to the extended parameters, computing the alias solution from the CTF, and unmapping the alias solution back to the actual arguments.

The mapping process associates actual arguments with extended parameters. The result of the mapping process is a set of *bindings*, denoted $[a, f, A]$, for each actual a, to the symbolic extended parameter f, conditionalised by an alias assertion A, indicating the aliasing condition under which the binding is *strong*. A binding is said to be strong if it is created by a strong mapping in the caller. Note that during Phase 1, the alias assertions are conditions that must exist in the caller procedure, and hence may contain extended parameters of the caller. During the Phase 2 propagation, the only possible alias assertions are either $\top_{assert}$ or $\bot_{assert}$, as actual argument values will be known. The abstract storage graph ASG (which is a DAG for our restricted domain of non-recursive pointer types) for the actual arguments may be considered to consist of levels, with globals and actuals passed at the call-site at the first level, and nodes at a level point*ing*-to nodes at the next lower level. *MapCall* processes the actual ASG level by level.

Algorithm MapCall(*actuals*, C)
Establish the mapping from actual arguments to extended parameters at call-site C. *Deref*(f) returns the name of the extended parameter obtained through dereferencing f, by incrementing the integer value suffixing f.

```
{
  Process the first level of the ASG:
  For each actual passed as an argument (explicitly or implicitly) do
      Create the binding [actual, formal, ⊤_assert];
```

For each level l of the ASG in increasing order do
    For each binding [*actual, formal, A*] at level l do
        If *Deref(formal)* was created in callee
            For each actual mapping $< actual \rightarrow v, A', S >$ in decreasing order of A' do
                Generate [v, *Deref(formal)*, $A \wedge A'$];
}

MapCall ensures that for each strong binding $[a, f, \top_{assert}]$, there exist paths, possibly empty, from one or more top-level nodes in the ASG, to a, consisting of only strong edges. Note that the bindings created by *MapCall* in Phase 1, may be conditionalised by extended parameters of the caller, as the only aliasing relationships that are known at this point are those that are *created* within the procedure. The following algorithm generates the set of alias assertions obtained by mapping the symbolic names in the alias assertion A to the actual arguments at the call-site C.

Algorithm MapAssert(*C, A*)
Generate the set of alias assertions obtained by replacing symbolic names in A with the actual arguments bound to them using the bindings computed by *MapCall*. The function *SatisfiableOrBot(set)* is used to test the satisfiability of *set*, a set of actual arguments. It returns an alias assertion containing *set* if it is satisfiable else $\perp_{assert}$. If B is a set of bindings, $B = \{[a_i, f_k, A_k] | k \in 1:m\}$, the function *Actuals*(B) returns the set $\{a_k | k \in 1:m\}$, and *Assert*(B) returns the meet of the component alias assertions, $\bigwedge_{k \in 1:m} A_k$ from B.

{
  Let $A = \{s_1, s_2, ..., s_m\}$;
  Let $s_i = \{f_{i_1}, f_{i_2}, ..., f_{i_n}\}$;
  Let $B(f_{i_j})$ be the set of bindings computed by *MapCall*(C) for extended parameter f_{i_j};
  $B(s_i) = \prod_{j=1}^{i_n} B(f_{i_j})$;
  $NewA(s_i) = \prod_{b \in B(s_i)} SatisfiableOrBot(Actuals(b)) \wedge Assert(b)$;
  return $\prod_{i=1}^{m} NewA(s_i)$;
}

The mappings in the CTF are now translated into mappings for the actual arguments using the bindings generated by *MapCall*. *ApplyCTF* calls *DeferredMeet* to perform the deferred meet operations on the translated mappings.

Algorithm ApplyCTF(*C*)
Apply the mappings in the CTF of the procedure called at C, to the actual arguments, using the bindings generated by algorithm *MapCall*. $GenToken_C(S)$ generates a unique sequence token derived from the call-site C, for each distinct sequence token S in the callee procedure.

{
  For each actual a at the call-site C with a mapping in the CTF do
      $M_a = \emptyset$;
      For each binding $[a, f, A_a]$ do
          For each mapping $< f \rightarrow v, A, S >$ in the CTF do
              For each $A' \in$ *MapAssert(C, A)* do
                  If v is an extended parameter then
                      For each binding $[b, v, A_b]$ do
                          $M_a = M_a \cup \{< a \rightarrow b, A_a \wedge A_b \wedge A', \{GenToken_C(S)\} >\}$;
                  Else
                      $M_a = M_a \cup \{< a \rightarrow v, A_a \wedge A', \{GenToken_C(S)\} >\}$;
      $AliasedSolution_a$ = **DeferredMeet**(M_a);
}

Note that the mappings generated within the callee procedure, when mapped back to the name space of the caller, are tagged with a sequence token containing just the call-site C. The aliased solution at a call-site C, computed by *ApplyCTF* , is then combined with the existing mappings for the actuals, by *UnMapCall*. This process treats the new mappings generated at the call-site as a strong update or a possibly-strong update, depending on the nature of the bindings for the actual.

Algorithm UnmapCall(C)
Combine the aliased solution, generated by algorithm *ApplyCTF* , expressed in terms of the callers name space, with the existing mappings at call-site C.

```
{
  For each indirectly passed actual a do
      Let Existing_a be the mappings for a at call-site C;
      If (every binding for a is strong) then
         Mappings for a after C is AliasedSolution_a;
      Else
         Mappings for a after C is Existing_a ∧ AliasedSolution_a;
}
```

The aliased solution for the variable **var** in Figure (1) depends on the ordering relation between the sequence tokens in two mappings, $M_1 =< var \Rightarrow$ c1, $\{call1_1\}>$ and $M_2 =< var \Rightarrow$ c2, $\{call1_2\}>$. Three cases may arise depending on the ordering relation that holds between the sequence tokens:

1. $\{\mathbf{call1_1}\} < \{\mathbf{call1_2}\}$: the aliased solution is M_2
2. $\{\mathbf{call1_2}\} < \{\mathbf{call1_1}\}$: the aliased solution is M_1
3. $\{\mathbf{call1_1}\} <> \{\mathbf{call1_2}\}$: the aliased solution is $M_1 \wedge M_2$

For the example shown, the first case holds and the solution is $< var \Rightarrow$ c2, $\{call1_2\}>$.

The sequencing information, contained in the sequence tokens, is used to combine a set of strong, possibly-strong, and weak mappings, generated by *ApplyCTF*. Strong mappings represent more precise information than possibly-strong and weak ones, and the meet of a strong mapping with a weak always results in a weak one. Hence for the general problem, it is desirable for the result of the combination to be a strong mapping. We use Algorithm *DeferredMeet* to first compute the resultant of the strong mappings, and then combine it with the set of possibly-strong and weak mappings.

Algorithm DeferredMeet(Mappings$_x$)
Compute aliased solution for x, from the set of no-alias mappings $Mappings_x = \{< x \rightarrow v_i, A_i, S_i > | i = 1 : n\}$. *MaximalElements*($M$) returns the set of maximal elements, with respect to sequence tokens, in M the set of mappings.

```
{
  Let M_s be the set of strong mappings in Mappings_x;
  Result = ∧_{M ∈ MaximalElements(M_s)} M;
  If (Result is strong) then
     Attempt to discard as many possibly-strong and weak mappings as possible:
     For each non-strong mapping M =< x → v, A, S > in Mappings_x do
         If (SequenceToken(M) < SequenceToken(Result))
            discard M;
  For each remaining mapping M do
     Result = Result ∧ M;
  Return Result;
}
```

7 Correctness and Approximations

Lemma (2) below establishes the fact that, for a calling context, our algorithm computes at least the same set of strong mappings as an iterative reanalysis of the called procedure. Thus, the aliased solution obtained by *ApplyCTF* at a calling context in Phase 2 is at least as precise as that obtained by reanalysing the procedure for the same calling context. During Phase 2, the only possible values for the alias assertion annotating a mapping are $\top_{assert}$ and $\bot_{assert}$. We assume that *MapCall* is used to obtain the mappings on entry to the procedure, before reanalysing it with an iterative algorithm, and that *UnmapCall* is used to combine the result of the reanalysis with the existing mappings at the call-site. We first consider only intraprocedural paths.

Lemma 2 *Let C be a call-site in procedure P, calling procedure Q. Let S be the set of strong mappings computed at some program point p within Q, by applying algorithm* ApplyCTF *to the actual aliasing at C, only considering intraprocedural paths in Q. Then S contains the strong mappings computed at p by an iterative reanalysis of intraprocedural paths of the procedure Q, for the same calling context.*

Proof. If the binding for an actual parameter, $[a, f, A]$, is strong, then there exists paths, possibly empty, from one or more top-level nodes in the ASG to a consisting of only strong edges. The proof is by induction on the number of indirections n, required to create the strong mapping.

$n = 0$: the only possible mappings are those created by direct assignments to formals.

If p is the entry node of Q, the lemma is trivially true, since the only mappings are those that exist at the call-site. Let $< f \Rightarrow v >$ be the strong mapping at point p computed by iterative style reanalysis. There are two cases to consider:

1. v was propagated to f from the entry of procedure Q to the set of direct assignments that created $< f \Rightarrow v >$. Then every intraprocedural path from the entry of Q to p must contain one or more assignments that propagate v to f. It can be shown, by induction on the number of operators in path expressions [Tar81] representing such paths, that *ApplyCTF* computes at least the set of strong mappings as iterative reanalysis for the target of each of these intervening assignments. It follows that, at the set of "last" such assignments to f that reach p, *ApplyCTF* computes the strong mapping $< f \Rightarrow v, S >$. S contains the program points of these "last" assignments to f that collectively partially post-dominate all other assignments to f with respect to p.
2. v was generated within Q and was propagated by some set of direct assignments to f. An argument similar to Case (1) can be used to show that *ApplyCTF* computes the mapping $< f \Rightarrow v, S >$. Again, S contains the program points of these "last" assignments to f that collectively partially post-dominate all other assignments to f with respect to p.

$n = k$: If the lemma is true for all $n \leq k$, strong mappings created by k or less indirections that *ApplyCTF* computes at p is a superset of those computed by iterative reanalysis at p.

Let $< a \Rightarrow v, S >$ be a strong mapping computed by iterative reanalysis at point p, that was created by $k+1$ indirections. The only way a strong mapping can be created with $k+1$ indirections is by some set of indirect assignments, $*x_i = y_i; i \in 1 : m$, where each x_i has the strong mapping $< x_i \Rightarrow a >$ at the assignment dereferencing it, and that mapping was created by k indirections. Every intraprocedural path from the entry of Q to p must contain at least one such assignment for $< f \Rightarrow v >$ to reach p. The mappings for the x_i were created by k indirections, and by the induction hypothesis, *ApplyCTF* computes the strong mappings $< x_i \Rightarrow a, S_i >$ at the assignments. In addition, for the mapping of a to v to be strong, every y_i must have the strong mapping $< y_i \Rightarrow v >$ at the assignment using it. Since the mappings for y_i must be created by $< k$ indirections, the induction hypothesis implies that *ApplyCTF* will compute the identical strong mapping for y_i at the assignment using it. It follows that *ApplyCTF* will compute $< a \Rightarrow v, S >$ at p, where S is the subset of the assignments $*x_i = y_i$ which collectively partially post-dominate all other assignments with respect to p. □

Theorem 1 *Let C be a call-site in procedure P, calling procedure Q, whose canonical transfer function is CTF_Q. The aliased solution at C for an indirectly passed actual a computed by* ApplyCTF*, is at least as precise as that obtained by an iterative reanalysis of the procedure Q.*

Proof. Follows from Lemma (2), by letting p be the exit point of procedure Q, and by induction on the number of procedure invocations in interprocedural paths originating in Q. □

There are different ways in which the ordering relation on sequence tokens may be approximated. The simplest approximation is to assume that every pair of sequence tokens in a procedure are incomparable, and the result is a flow-insensitive solution. Different levels of "callee" context sensitivity may be achieved by limiting the expansion of the tokens derived from call-sites within the program to some level k, and assuming them incomparable beyond that level. Since any approximation on $\mathcal{L}_{seq}$ can only increase the number of mappings whose meet is the aliased solution computed by *DeferredMeet* , the approximate aliased solution is conservative. Alias assertions may also be approximated; one obvious way is by k-limiting maximum size of an alias assertion. Assertions whose size increases beyond this limit may be approximated by $\perp_{assert}$. Approximations on $\mathcal{L}_{seq}$ reduce the flow-sensitivity, while approximations on $\mathcal{L}_{assert}$ lose the precision provided by strong updates.

8 Related Work

Landi and Ryder [LR92] present a flow-sensitive/context-insensitive pointer analysis algorithm for a C-like imperative language, with no type-casts and no indirect function calls. The alias representation used is *Conditional May-Alias* where the alias information is made conditional on sets of assumed aliases. Our use of *alias assertions* in the data-flow values differs in that they increase the applicability of strong updates, and hence the precision of the aliased solution.

The algorithm of Choi et al. [CBC93] is flow-sensitive and is applicable to the same domain as [LR92], but computes a more precise solution than that algorithm. They use an efficient representation for alias pairs using transitive reduction. An efficient flow-insensitive algorithm is also presented, which produces solutions with varying degrees of precision by using *ForwardKill* and *BackwardKill* information for each call-site, to eliminate aliases from the procedure entry to the call-site, and from the call-site to the procedure exit. The kill information is computed using dominator and post-dominator information.

Wilson and Lam [WL95] propose the partial transfer function (PTF) approach to context sensitivity and the algorithm presented there handles all features of the C language, including pointer arithmetic and indirect function calls. Experimental results on a subset of the SPEC benchmarks have found a maximum of 1.39 *PTF*'s computed per procedure. [Ghi95] uses the invocation graph and quotes a maximum invocation graph node count to call-site ratio of 2.4 for the set of 13 benchmarks studied. Programs that exhibit the worst case exponential complexity have also been encountered in practice. These results indicate that the benchmarks studied contain procedures that are analysed multiple number of times.

The flow-sensitive constant propagation of [CH95] computes flow-insensitive solutions which are used to handle cycles in the call-graph during the flow-sensitive analysis. The approximation in the presence of recursion yields less precise solutions, but has the advantage of analysing each procedure only once. Our technique also provides for approximations, but at several levels rather than only in recursive cycles.

Carini et al. [CSH95] propose a context-sensitive type analysis algorithm that is performed concurrently with an alias analysis algorithm. Our method can be adapted to the same problem by making the primary problem a type analysis.

The Sparse Evaluation Graph [CCF91] uses dominators to construct a sparse version of the CFG of a procedure for a given data flow problem. The nodes in the sparse graph are flow-value generators (either due to program statements or meet points) and incoming edges to nodes with constant transfer functions are eliminated. The sequence tokens, annotating the mappings in the CTF, are a sparse representation of the relevant control-flow information required to handle aliasing.

9 Conclusions

The proposed approach to context sensitivity is more efficient in the number of times a procedure is analysed at different calling contexts, especially in cases where a procedure is called with different "relevant" aliases. Reanalysis of procedures is replaced by the process of applying the CTFs. Since CTFs are parameterised by the use of symbolic extended parameters, it is possible to *reuse* the results of applying a CTF across different calling contexts with identical aliasing. The alias assertions in the data-flow values capture the aliasing that is relevant to applying strong updates, making the computed aliased solutions at least as precise as iterative style analysis. More importantly, sequence tokens are an abstraction that capture relevant control flow within a procedure and permit intra and interprocedural approximations that yield conservative solutions. The conservativeness is with respect to flow sensitivity and "callee" context sensitivity, which determines the levels of procedure calls are accurately expanded in analysing a given procedure, and provides a non-conventional notion of context sensitivity. The pointer analysis method may be extended to any finite abstraction of the abstract storage graph.

Acknowledgments We wish to thank Mary Hall and Bob Wilson for discussions on the subject, and the reviewers for their comments and suggestions.

References

[BCCH95] Michael Burke, Paul Carini, Jong-Deok Choi, and Michael Hind. Flow-insensitive interprocedural alias analysis in the presence of function pointers. In K. Pingali, U. Banerjee, D. Gelernter, A. Nicolau, and D. Padua, editors, *Lecture Notes in Computer Science, 892*, pages 234–250. Springer-Verlag, 1995. Proceedings from the *7th International Workshop on Languages and Compilers for Parallel Computing*. Extended version published as Research Report RC-19546, IBM T. J. Watson Research Center, September, 1994.

[CBC93] Jong-Deok Choi, Michael Burke, and Paul Carini. Efficient flow-sensitive interprocedural computation of pointer-induced aliases and side effects. In *Proceedings of the 20th Annual ACM Symposium on Principles of Programming Languages*, pages 232–245, January 1993.

[CCF91] Jong-Deok Choi, Ron Cytron, and Jeanne Ferrante. Automatic construction of sparse data flow evaluation graphs. In *Proceedings of the 18th Annual ACM Symposium on Principles of Programming Languages*, pages 55–66, January 1991.

[CCKT86] David Callahan, Keith D. Cooper, Ken Kennedy, and Linda Torczon. Interprocedural constant propagation. In *Proceedings of the ACM SIGPLAN'86 Symposium on Compiler Construction*, pages 152–161, July 1986.

[CH95] Paul R. Carini and Michael Hind. Flow-sensitive interprocedural constant propagation. Technical Report RC 20290, IBM Research Division, T.J. Watson Research Center, 1995.

[CSH95] Paul R. Carini, Harini Srinivasan, and Michael Hind. Flow-sensitive type analysis for c++. Technical Report RC 20267, IBM Research Division, T.J. Watson Research Center, 1995.

[EGH94] Maryam Emami, Rakesh Ghiya, and Laurie J. Hendren. Context-sensitive interprocedural points-to analysis in the presence of function pointers. In *Proceedings of the ACM SIGPLAN'94 Conference on Programming Language Design and Implementation*, pages 242–256, June 1994.

[Ghi95] Rakesh Ghiya. Practical techniques for interprocedural heap analysis. Master's thesis, School of Computer Science, McGill University, March 1995.

[LR92] William Landi and Barbara G. Ryder. A safe approximate algorithm for interprocedural pointer aliasing. In *Proceedings of the ACM SIGPLAN'92 Conference on Programming Language Design and Implementation*, pages 235–248, June 1992.

[LT79] Thomas Lengauer and Robert E. Tarjan. A fast algorithm for finding dominators in a flow-graph. *ACM Transactions on Programming Languages and Systems*, 1(1):121–141, July 1979.

[SP81] M. Sharir and A. Pnueli. Two approaches to interprocedural data-flow analyis. In S.S. Muchnick and N. D. Jones, editors, *Program Flow Analysis: Theory and Applications*, chapter 7, pages 189–234. Prentice-Hall, 1981.

[Tar81] Robert E. Tarjan. Fast algorithms for solving path problems. *Journal of the ACM*, 28(3):594–614, July 1981.

[UH75] J. D. Ullman and M. S. Hecht. A simple algorithm for global fata flow analysis. *SIAM J. Computing*, 4:519–532, 1975.

[WL95] Robert P. Wilson and Monica S. Lam. Efficient context-sensitive pointer analysis for C programs. In *Proceedings of the ACM SIGPLAN'95 Conference on Programming Language Design and Implementation*, pages 1–12, June 1995.

10 Appendix A : Computing Partial post-dominators

The bitvector algorithm for computing dominators due to Hecht and Ullman, may be easily modified to compute $PPDOM_C$, the partial post-dominator relation with respect to paths passing through the given program point C. It is based on the observation that a set of nodes D are the partial post-dominators of a node n, with respect to paths passing through C, only if D partially post-dominates every successor of n which has a path to C. Let $CFG =< N, E, Entry, Exit >$ be the CFG for a procedure, with entry node $Entry$ and some node $C \in N$.

Algorithm *ComputePPDOM$_C$(Compute partial post-dominators with respect to program point C.)*

{
Initialise $PPDOM(C) = \{C\}$, and $PPDOM(Exit) = \emptyset$;
For every other node $n \in N$ do
    Initialise $PPDOM(n) = N$;
While changes to some $PPDOM(N)$ occur, repeat
    For each $n \in N - \{C\}$ do
        Set $temp = \cap_{m \in succ(n)} PPDOM(m)$;
        Set $PPDOM(n) = \begin{cases} \{n\} \cup temp & \text{if } temp \neq \emptyset \\ \emptyset & \text{otherwise} \end{cases}$
}

Initial Results for Glacial Variable Analysis

Tito Autrey and Michael Wolfe

Department of Computer Science and Engineering
Oregon Graduate Institute of Science and Technology
P.O. Box 91000 Portland, Oregon 97291-1000, USA

Abstract. Run-time code generation that uses specific values to generate specialized code is called value-specific optimization. Variables which provide values for value-specific optimization are called candidate variables. They are modified much less frequently than they are referenced. In current systems that use run-time code generation, candidate variables are identified by programmer directives.
We describe a novel technique, *staging analysis*, for automatically identifying candidate variables. We refer to such variables as *glacial variables*. Glacial variables are excellent candidate variables.
Glacial Variable Analysis is an interprocedural analysis. We perform several experiments with glacial variable analysis to characterize the programs in the PERFECT benchmark suite. We explain the imprecision of our results due to procedure boundaries. We examine the structure of the programs to determine how often value-specific optimization might be applied.
We will explain how staging analysis relates to run-time code generation; briefly describe *Glacial Variable Analysis*; and, present some initial results.

1 Introduction

Specialization is tailoring general-purpose procedures to a specific invocation or set of invocations. Specialization takes advantage of specific values of parameters. Functional language compilers use partial evaluation to produce specialized versions of functions [3]. Imperative language compilers use procedure cloning for the same purpose [7]. Value-specific optimization (VSO) uses run-time code generation (RTCG) to produce specialized code at run-time instead of compile-time [11].

Value-specific optimization is effective when the total run-time of the program is reduced. The execution time savings must exceed the cost of RTCG. The cost is paid for when the $\# \ invocations * savings/invocation$ is high enough. Value-specific optimization uses slowly changing variables to ensure effectiveness. Keppel refers to these variables as *candidate variables* [10]. We call them *glacial variables* because they vary glacially.

A *staging transformation system* takes a source-language program and a set of transformation rules, and partitions a program into two stages. It moves computations from the *late* stage into the *early* one [13]. In classical work, the compiler is the first stage, and it evaluates expressions that use only compile-time values, such as constants. Consequently the cost of the first stage is treated as zero. The rules are syntax-based and are universally applied. We propose extending the partitioning to more than two stages and we insert an analysis phase, *staging analysis*, to guide the application of the transformation rules. With multiple stages, many of which are specialized at run-time, we believe that more powerful rules and a cost model to decide where the rules should be applied needs to be developed.

Current approaches to compiler-inserted RTCG require the programmer to insert directives into the program source code that identify candidate variables [1, 4, 5, 12]. We use a staging analysis, *Glacial Variable Analysis*, to automatically identify candidate variables from two pieces of information. One, it estimates the execution frequency of each block of code. Two, it labels each expression and subexpression with its estimated modification frequency. Glacial variables are modified infrequently compared to the frequency with which they are used. The *degree of glacialness* of an expression is a measure of the difference between its execution and modification frequencies.

A staging analysis labels stages by predicted execution frequency. A level i stage (indicated later by Stage-i) is predicted to be less frequently executed than a level $i+1$ stage. In a complete staging transformation system, RTCG is applied at the boundary between a level i stage and a level $i+1$ stage. Value-specific optimization generates a specialized version of the level $i+1$ stage using the values of candidate variables available at that point in level i stage. These variables aren't modified in a higher level stage. For example, if there is a subexpression at level $i+1$ that uses values only from level i then level i stage is extended with a call to a run-time code generator. The code generator evaluates the subexpression and generates code specialized with the *resulting values* of that evaluation. This code is a specialized version of level $i+1$ stage.

In Fig. 1a, each loop defines a stage. We give every basic block in the body of a loop a stage-level equal to the loop-nest depth of the containing loop. A level $i+1$ stage is a *sub-stage* of a level i stage if it is contained within that stage. Correspondingly, that level i stage is the *super-stage* of the level $i+1$ stage. Sub-stages execute more frequently than their super-stages. Each stage at a given level is composed of a sequence of basic blocks interspersed with sub-stages. We use loops to define stages because historically they are used as indicators of frequency of execution. Frequency of execution translates directly into reuse of values referenced by the stage body code and reuse of the code itself.

As an example, in Fig. 1b, a compiler can determine that `n` is constant; interprocedural constant propagation can determine that formal argument `i` in the subroutine `sub` also is constant, and that the first conditional is never taken. Glacial variable analysis determines that the variable `m` is written only once. It also determines that the second conditional in the subroutine is used inside a loop, the loop that encloses the procedure call, but does not vary within that loop. This makes the second conditional a candidate for VSO. The run-time code generator is invoked between the `read` statement and the start of the `k`-loop to

```
...                 Stage-1
do i1               Stage-1
  a[i1] = ...       Stage-1
  do i2             Stage-2
    b[i2] = ...     Stage-2
    do i3           Stage-3
      c[i3] = ...   Stage-3
    end             Stage-3
  end               Stage-2
  do i4             Stage-2
    d[i4] = ...     Stage-2
  end               Stage-2
end                 Stage-1
...                 Stage-0
```

(a)

```
program main
n = 5
read *,m
do k = 1,100
  call sub (n, m, x(k))
enddo
end
subroutine sub (i, j, x)
x = x + 1
if (i > 5) then
  x = x + 5
endif
if (j > 5) then
  x = x * 2
endif
end
```

(b)

Fig. 1. Examples of - a) computation stages; b) glacial variable analysis

produce a specialized version of **sub**[1].

The rest of the paper is organized as follows: in Section 2 we discuss Glacial variable analysis in more detail; in Section 3 we present some experiments to identify glacial variables; in Section 4 we present some initial results from applying glacial variable analysis to the PERFECT benchmark suite; in Section 5 we present related work; and in Section 5 we conclude.

2 Glacial Variable Analysis

Glacial variable analysis is a staging analysis composed of two parts. The first, *Global Recursion-Level Analysis* (GRLA[2]) identifies the stages inherent in the program and labels each stage with an element from the stage-level lattice shown in Fig. 2. This labeling is a partition of the computations in the program. The second, *Glacial Variable Propagation* (GVP) labels variable definitions and expressions, also with elements from the stage-level lattice. The labels generated by GRLA are called *code stage-levels* (CSLs) and those from GVP are called *variant stage-levels* (VSLs). Glacial variable propagation uses the results of GRLA so it must be executed subsequent to GRLA.

[1] The body will be either `x=x+1` or `x=2*x+2` depending on the value of `m`.

[2] Pronounced 'gorilla'.

2.1 Global Recursion-Level Analysis

The result of GRLA is to label each block of code with a CSL. The CSL is a measure of the block's frequency of execution. A higher CSL indicates code that is more frequently executed and therefore more important to optimize. A higher frequency of execution indicates a greater level of reuse when the code is specialized. Code that computes a constant is replaced by a value, consequently the *Constant* lattice element is never used for a CSL. Global recursion-level analysis is an interprocedural analysis. It uses the program's call graph and the control-flow graphs of each procedure.

Global recursion-level analysis partitions the program's computations into stages. A stage is a natural loop and its enclosed body. By definition, any two loops are either nested, one fully contained within the other, or disjoint, having no blocks of code in common. Following is summary of the full interprocedural GRLA:

1. Within each procedure, compute its natural loops and loop nest-levels.
2. Compute the complete call graph. We use Hall and Kennedy's algorithm [8].
3. Assign CSLs to each procedure. Each call site CSL is the procedure CSL plus the stage-level of the loop containing the call site.
   (a) For the main program, the procedure CSL is zero.
   (b) Otherwise, the procedure CSL it is the meet of the CSLs of the call sites to that procedure.
   (c) We handle recursive procedures in a manner similar to loops. Since the benchmark set is written in Fortran, without recursion, we skip the details of handling recursion in this paper.

The CSL is composed of two parts, a procedure CSL and a basic block CSL. This separation supports future work on procedure cloning and examining different meet-functions. Step 1, from above, describes a straightforward labeling within a single procedure.

We treat GRLA as forward data-flow problem. When there are no cycles in the graph, a demand-driven data-flow solver can label all procedures in a single pass over the call graph. We use MAX as our meet-function. This choice ensures that the deepest possible nesting of stages in the program is labeled with largest the CSL.

The procedure CSL is ambiguous if calls to a procedure appear at different stage-levels. In Fig. 2a, the main program has a CSL of zero. If the only call to a subroutine appears at a CSL of one, the subroutine would be assigned a CSL of one. In this case, we assign subroutine `sub` a CSL of $MAX(0,1) = 1$. With this choice, information that the `i`-loop in `sub` is executed more frequently than the `k`-loop in `main` is retained.

2.2 Glacial Variable Propagation

The result of glacial variable propagation is to label each variable definition and expression with a variant stage-level. The VSL is a measure of how frequently the value changes.

```
program main
do k ...
  call sub (n, m, y[k])
enddo
call sub (n, m, x[0])
end
subroutine sub (n, m, x)
do i ...
  ...
enddo
end
```

(a)

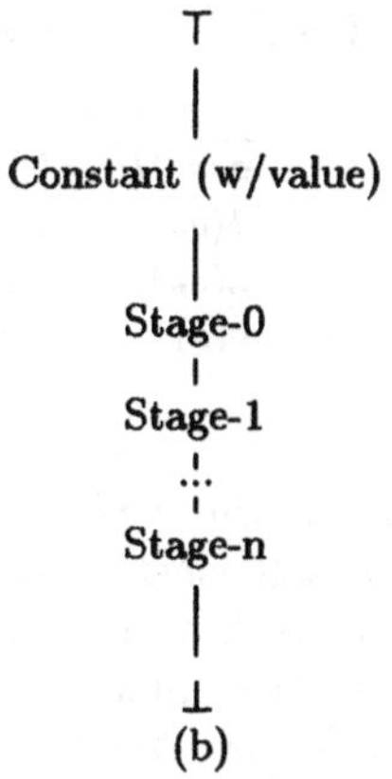

(b)

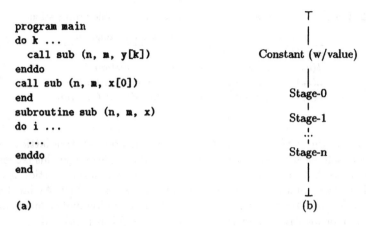

Fig. 2. a) Ambiguous procedure code stage-levels; b) Stage-level lattice

We have a Static Single-Assignment (SSA) graph in our intermediate representation. The VSL is set by assignments and pseudo-assignments. Assignments are labeled with the meet of the stage-level lattice elements of the right-hand side expression after operator folding. ϕ-functions are labeled with the VSL corresponding to the CSL of their containing block. Our SSA form is extended with μ- and η-functions in the manner of Gated Single Assignment (GSA) [2, 9]. μ-functions are ϕ-functions at loop headers. The VSL of a μ-function is labeled equivalently to a ϕ-function. The μ-function captures the stage-level for variables modified within a loop. At each loop exit there is an η-function capturing the final value of a variable modified within the loop. Consequently, it is in the super-stage and has a lower stage-level than the corresponding μ-function[3]. If the meet of the right-hand side of a pseudo-assignment function is *Constant* then that is the left-hand side, otherwise the left-hand side is the CSL of the code block where the pseudo-assignment was placed.

Table 1. Glacial variable propagation meet-function

Meet	Result
$Constant(v_1) \cap Constant(v_2)$	$Constant(v_1)$ if $v_1 = v_2$, CSL (ϕ) otherwise
$Constant \cap X$	X
Stage-i ∩ Stage-j	$Stage - MAX(i, j)$

Glacial variable propagation is a minor modification of Wegman and Zadeck's sparse conditional constant propagation algorithm (WZ) [15]. We use a taller

[3] GOTO statements in or out of loops may require constructing code blocks at particular stage-levels for η-functions or the analysis may be abandoned for such procedures or programs.

Table 2. Equations for variable definitions in glacial variable propagation

IR-node	Glacial Variable Propagation Equation
$a = f(a_n)$	$\bigcap VSL(a_n)$
$\phi(b_n)$	Stage-j | $j = CSL(\phi)$, or *Constant*
$\mu(c_n)$	Stage-i | $i = CSL(\mu(c_i))$, or *Constant*
$\eta(d)$	Stage-$(i-1)$ | $i = CSL(\mu(d))$, or *Constant*

lattice, as shown in Fig. 2b. The standard constant propagation lattice has elements for each constant and one for run-time values. We extend this lattice with Stage-i elements to represent computation stages. The meet function is shown in Table 1. The equations for variable definitions are in Table 2. We label arrays as well as scalars. Arrays are treated as whole units; individual elements are not labeled independently. Otherwise the structure of WZ is preserved.

We use an interprocedural constant propagation algorithm that has been extended to use the stage-level lattice. Global recursion-level analysis already uses the call graph, so using an interprocedural propagator increases the precision of GVP for free.

The time-complexity of WZ is retained, $O(|E| + |S|)$, where E is the set of edges in the control flow graph and S is the set of edges in the SSA graph. Global recursion-level analysis has complexity $O(|C|)$, where C is the set of edges in the call graph. Interprocedural constant propagation has complexity $O(MAX(Length(binding - graph - chains)))$, but in practice it takes much less time than WZ. Since the two main algorithms in GVA are both linear-time algorithms, it is efficient.

3 Experiments

We describe a series of experiments that use glacial variable analysis to discover the opportunities for applying RTCG. The experiments are applied to the PERFECT benchmark suite. There are 13 programs in the suite, however 3 of them have ENTRY statements[4]. Our compiler, Nascent, cannot handle them, so they are left out of the experiment. This set of benchmarks is not particularly favorable for RTCG. The programs are example scientific programs selected to test the capabilities of parallelizing compilers. The code tends to be heavily hand-optimized with minimal opportunities for a scalar compiler. We chose this set of programs precisely because they are mature programs not specifically suited for RTCG.

3.1 Stage or Code Stage-Level Characterization

Our global recursion-level analysis partitions a program into stages. We would like to understand what the structure of the partitioning is and the relationships

[4] The programs are: TRACK (mts.f), DYFESM (sds.f), FLO52Q (tfs.f).

that arise between stages. This gives us insight into and further justification for the choice of loops as stages. We perform the following experiments:

1. Count how many stages there are at each level in a program. Also count the number of sub-stages per stage per CSL. This gives us an idea of how bushy the stage hierarchy tree is.
2. Perform this experiment as if procedures had been cloned, one for each CSL of call sites to the procedure. Cloning in this manner represents the worst case for code explosion at run-time if no inlining is performed.
3. Also perform this experiment by simulating a completely inlined program. This allows us to see how much information about stages is lost due to procedures. The CSL counting experiment in the previous subsection does not uncover information that is as complete, however it is a cheaper analysis.

3.2 Variant Stage-Level Characterization

Our glacial variable propagation algorithm labels all expressions with their VSL. We would like to understand how many values are produced at each stage-level. This gives us some insight into which source program stage-levels are large in terms of values generated. Large expressions may have been broken down into assignments to temporaries which makes stages appear to generate more values than have uses beyond the stage. Copy propagation eliminates some intrastage definitions, and dead store elimination eliminates some interstage definitions. We have not yet implemented these optimizations. We perform the following experiments:

1. Count the number of scalar definitions at each variant stage-level. Separate if-statements, assignments, ϕ-, μ- and η-functions.
2. Count the number of array definitions at each variant stage-level. Separate if-statements, assignments, ϕ-, μ- and η-functions. Scalars are simpler to embed in specialized code than arrays, but arrays are bigger so the potential payoff is larger. So we count the two classes separately.

3.3 RTCG Opportunity Characterization

The goal of glacial variable analysis is labeling variables with useful properties to aid selection of cost-effective value-specific optimization. It determines, abstractly, the modification frequency of variables and the execution frequency of code. More work is needed to analyze how much code and how many values are control-dependent on a given fork in the control-flow graph.

1. Compare the VSLs and CSLs of scalar uses. Compute the breakdown of difference in levels. A larger difference indicates more potential invocations to specialized code.
2. Do the same for arrays. As noted earlier, scalars are easier to optimize around than arrays.

4 Initial Results

The Nascent compiler generated the results presented in this section. It builds a complete call graph of the program and it assumes that code for all routines is present. Builtin functions are treated differently from user procedures. A leaf procedure is one that has no calls to user procedures. A procedure with calls to missing or present user procedures is a nonleaf procedure. We distinguish between leaf and nonleaf procedures because noninterprocedural compilers can perform more sophisticated optimizations on leaf procedures. The results are normalized across all the programs, except where noted.

4.1 Stage or Code Stage-Level Characterization

Table 3. Distribution of sub-stages per stage, no compile-time specialization

Stage #	# Sub-stages in a super-stage										
	0	1	2	3	4	5	6	7	8	9	10
0	.80%	1.34%	.36%	.19%	.19%	.17%	.18%	.02%	.06%	.02%	-
1	6.40%	5.17%	2.09%	.41%	.12%	.10%	.07%	.06%	.05%	-	.01%
2	9.95%	8.17%	1.13%	.38%	.22%	.08%	.05%	.01%	.01%	.01%	-
3	11.64%	6.09%	.95%	.58%	.10%	.11%	.07%	.04%	.03%	.04%	.02%
4	11.05%	3.50%	.36%	.24%	.03%	.07%	.14%	-	.04%	-	.02%
5	7.55%	3.28%	.20%	.01%	.06%	.05%	-	-	.02%	-	-
6	6.66%	1.76%	.11%	.05%	-	.03%	.02%	-	-	-	-
7	2.17%	1.00%	.10%	.01%	-	.05%	-	-	-	-	-
8	1.19%	.52%	.16%	.01%	-	-	-	-	-	-	-
9	.82%	.10%	.06%	-	-	-	-	-	-	-	-
10	.18%	.15%	.05%	-	-	-	-	-	-	-	-

We show here the number of inner loops contained within each loop, averaged over our 10 programs. Table 3 shows the results for the programs as written. Table 4 shows the results if we were to clone procedures based on the code stage-levels from which they are called. So if a procedure were called from Stage-i and Stage-$(i + 2)$ then there would be two versions of the procedure. A procedure's code will not be regenerated more frequently than its CSL. Cloning based on the CSL of the call site represents different versions based on changing *all* parameter values. Table 5 shows the results if the program were to be fully inlined, i.e. all procedure calls are removed and replaced with the body of the invoked procedures. Full inlining represents the complete set of stages executed over the course of program run-time. The experiments are intended to show how bushy the stage hierarchy is. The tables have been shortened to make them fit on a page, but there are nonzero entries out to Stage-15 in both directions.

The first column lists the percentages of innermost loops at a given stage-level. Roughly 57% of all loops are innermost loops. With cloning it goes up to

Table 4. Distribution of sub-stages per stage, procedure cloning, one per call site CSL

Stage #	# Sub-stages in a super-stage										
	0	1	2	3	4	5	6	7	8	9	10
0	.84%	1.66%	.63%	.27%	.15%	.14%	.14%	.02%	.04%	.01%	-
1	6.33%	5.14%	2.16%	.49%	.16%	.11%	.07%	.03%	.04%	-	.01%
2	10.65%	6.97%	1.05%	.43%	.22%	.12%	.04%	.03%	.01%	.03%	.01%
3	12.22%	5.88%	.81%	.51%	.10%	.09%	.11%	.02%	.05%	.02%	.02%
4	10.30%	4.11%	.39%	.19%	.05%	.05%	.08%	-	.04%	-	.01%
5	7.21%	3.49%	.29%	.02%	.03%	.05%	.01%	-	.01%	-	-
6	6.22%	2.13%	.19%	.05%	-	.01%	.01%	-	-	-	-
7	2.47%	.90%	.17%	.01%	-	.04%	-	-	-	-	-
8	1.37%	.33%	.19%	.01%	-	-	-	-	-	-	-
9	.70%	.11%	.08%	-	-	-	-	-	-	-	-
10	.23%	.11%	.04%	-	-	-	-	-	-	-	-

Table 5. Distribution of sub-stages per stage, complete procedure inlining

Stage #	# Sub-stages in a super-stage										
	0	1	2	3	4	5	6	7	8	9	10
0	.49%	1.27%	.44%	.19%	.09%	.10%	.11%	.01%	.02%	.00%	-
1	4.70%	4.39%	2.04%	.23%	.11%	.05%	.04%	.00%	.01%	-	-
2	9.17%	5.86%	.95%	.72%	.11%	.04%	.01%	.01%	-	.23%	.00%
3	12.14%	5.93%	.62%	.47%	.05%	.02%	.02%	.01%	.01%	.13%	.00%
4	8.30%	4.62%	.47%	.27%	.01%	.03%	.01%	-	.01%	-	.00%
5	6.55%	5.10%	.34%	.04%	.01%	.04%	.00%	-	.00%	-	-
6	7.00%	3.50%	.23%	.09%	-	.00%	.00%	-	-	-	-
7	4.57%	1.40%	.19%	.03%	-	.01%	-	-	-	-	-
8	2.77%	.50%	.16%	.01%	-	-	-	-	-	-	-
9	1.30%	.47%	.09%	-	-	-	-	-	-	-	-
10	.72%	.11%	.01%	-	-	-	-	-	-	-	-

about 58% and with inlining it stays at about 58%. The second column lists the contribution of loops with only one inner loop. This is not the same as a perfectly nested loop. Roughly 27% of all loops have only 1 inner loop. With cloning this goes up to 31% and with inlining to almost 34%.

This result also shows how many opportunities there might be for refining sub-stages of a single stage at run-time. The refinement would be based on earlier sub-stage results. Innermost loops, and those with only 1 sub-stage obviously cannot be split.

4.2 Variant Stage-Level Characterization

The experiments in the previous section showed the hierarchy of execution frequencies. These experiments show the modification-frequency distribution. Each entry in the table is the number of that intermediate-representation node type found at that stage-level divided by the sum of all types over all stage-levels. Only

Table 6. Percentage of scalar definitions by type and stage-level

	Definition Stage-Level										
Definition Type	0	1	2	3	4	5	6	7	8	9	10
Predicates	.11%	.33%	.23%	.29%	.25%	.18%	.07%	.03%	.02%	.00%	.05%
Assignments	1.97%	4.25%	3.93%	3.25%	1.37%	1.36%	.78%	.30%	.31%	.02%	.05%
ϕ-functions	4.85%	8.46%	3.61%	2.04%	1.92%	1.39%	.79%	.13%	.21%	.05%	.11%
μ-functions	-	2.96%	6.91%	6.08%	3.84%	2.86%	3.08%	1.50%	.33%	.11%	.10%
η-functions	3.35%	7.15%	6.56%	4.07%	2.98%	3.14%	1.53%	.34%	.13%	.09%	.04%

Table 7. Percentage of array definitions by type and stage-level

	Definition Stage-Level										
Definition Type	0	1	2	3	4	5	6	7	8	9	10
Assignments	3.46%	6.96%	5.81%	6.65%	3.66%	2.55%	2.63%	1.81%	.84%	.53%	.46%
ϕ-functions	4.13%	5.61%	2.63%	1.82%	.94%	1.34%	.91%	.13%	.08%	.04%	.14%
μ-functions	-	2.90%	5.27%	5.56%	3.53%	2.30%	1.71%	.86%	.46%	.19%	.05%
η-functions	3.09%	5.50%	5.95%	3.63%	2.34%	1.73%	.86%	.46%	.19%	.05%	.04%

the array vs. scalar attribute is distinguished. Predicates means if-statements, and the result is always a scalar, even if two array elements are compared. That row does not account for loop-statements.

The percentages decrease fairly quickly after Stage-6. They drop not quite so quickly from Stage-1 to Stage-6. It is important to remember that the stage-level is effectively on a log-scale. The tiny percentages in the Stage-8 column are huge if they are multiplied by 10^8.

The variant stage-levels of uses will be shown in subsection 4.5.

4.3 RTCG Opportunity Characterization

This experiment shows the potential for VSO based on glacial variables. Figures 3 and 4 show the glacial scalars and arrays, respectively, for BDNA. The code stage-level of the use goes from low (left) to high (right) along the X-axis. Higher means it executes more frequently. The difference between the variant nest-level of the reaching definition and the code stage-level is the Z-axis. The difference goes from low (back) to high (front). A higher number means the use is more glacial with respect to the definition. The row of values with a difference of zero has been left off to make the graph more distinct, but the number of such values is accounted for in the percentages. The left graphs show the absolute count and the right graphs show the percentages of uses with the indicated degree of glacialness. The percentages sum to 100 along the Z-axis if the uses with a 0 degrees of glacialness are included. In Fig. 4, notice the very high percentage, 35%, of uses across all Stage-2s that have 1 degree of glacialness. And in Fig. 3, notice the high percentage, 20%, of uses across all Stage-6s that have 2 degrees of glacialness. Scalars and arrays are graphed separately because it is

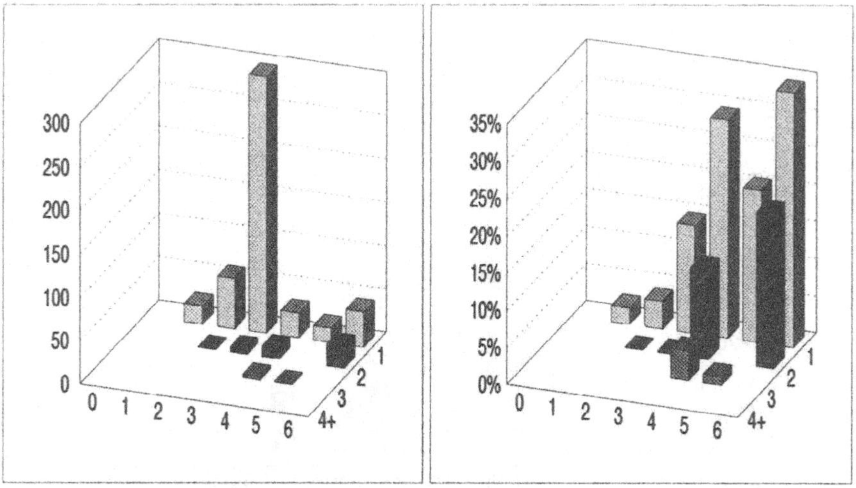

Fig. 3. Degrees of glacialness (Z-axis) by stage-level (X-axis) for BDNA/nas.f (scalars)

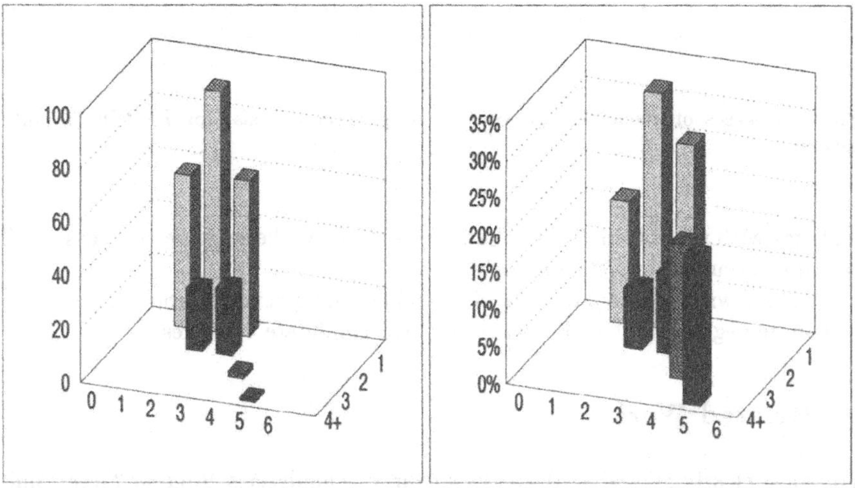

Fig. 4. Degrees of glacialness (Z-axis) by stage-level (X-axis) for BDNA/nas.f (arrays)

much easier to see how to take efficient advantage of a glacial scalar variable than a glacial array.

Figure 6 shows the results of the same analysis for scalars averaged over the 10 programs from thee PERFECT benchmark suite. Recall that to prevent larger applications from dominating the results, the percentages have been normalized for each application and then averaged together. Figure 6 shows the results for arrays. They were calculated the same as for the scalars. Compare these per-

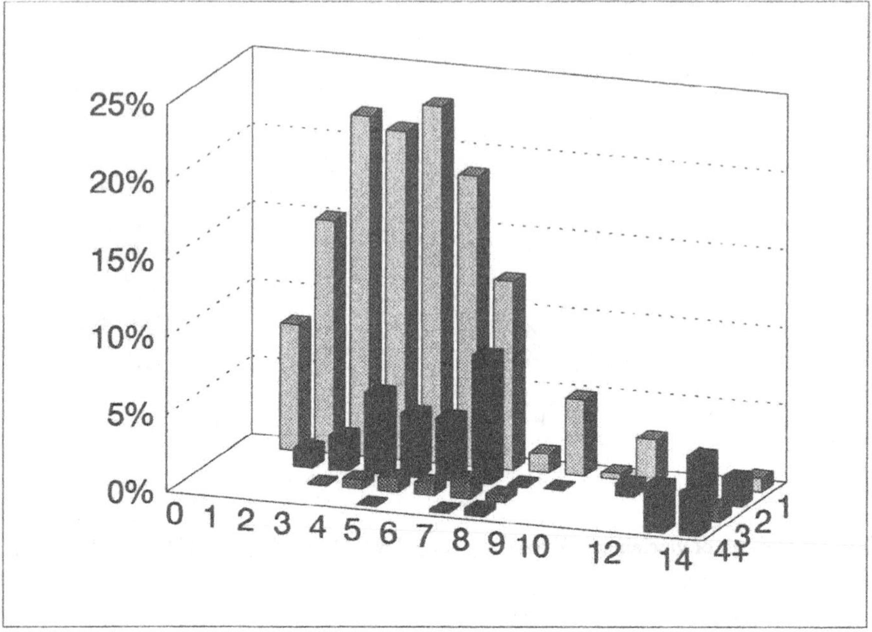

Fig. 5. Degrees of glacialness (Z-axis) by stage-level (X-axis) for PERFECT suite (scalars)

centages with those from Tables 7 and 6 which show the total percentages of all defs that occur at a given stage-level.

All uses with non-zero degrees of glacialness are glacial variables. Those with 2 or more degrees of glacialness are excellent candidate variables.

5 Related Work

The most closely related work to glacial variable analysis is *Binding Time Analysis* (BTA) which is used by offline partial evaluation. Binding time analysis takes an annotation of the inputs to a program with the lattice elements *Static* and *Dynamic*. The analysis proceeds to annotate every expression with *Static* or *Dynamic*. The annotated program is then passed to a partial evaluator, along with a set of values for the static inputs, and it produces a *residual* program where all static expressions have been evaluated and replaced with their value. Staging analysis is more powerful because it doesn't require that the inputs be annotated. It can identify the computation stages by examining the control flow structure of the program.

Staging transformations are syntactic rules used to move computations from

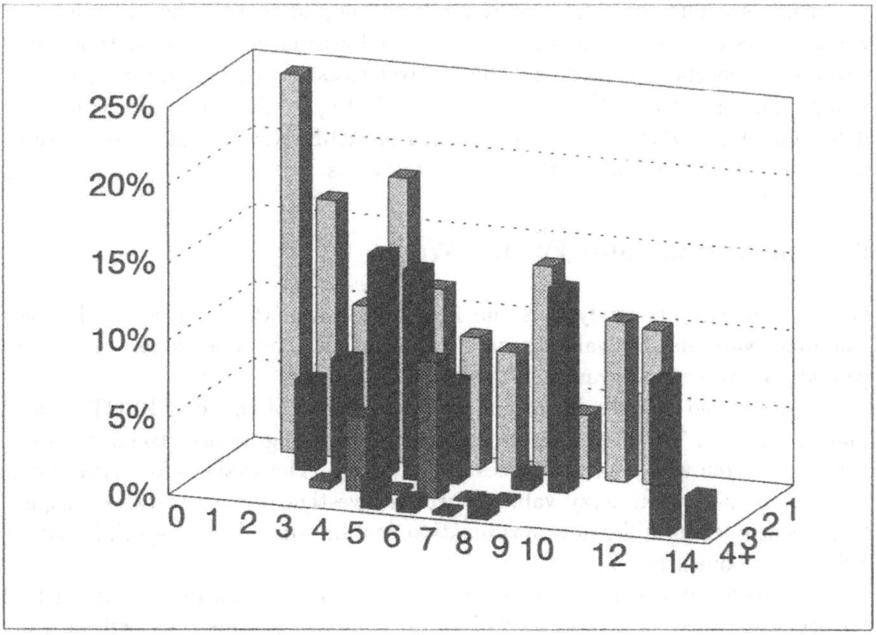

Fig. 6. Degrees of glacialness (Z-axis) by stage-level (X-axis) for PERFECT suite (arrays)

run-time to compile-time [13]. This is very similar to partial evaluation. In fact, Ershov shows that what is traditionally called partial evaluation is a subset of what Jorring and Scherlis call staging transformations [6]. One of our results is that it is useful to separate the transformation rules from the decision of where to apply them. We call the combination of the *where* analysis and the *what-to-do* rule set, a staging transformation system. Early work consists only of the rules, and we add the supporting analysis.

There are several compiler-supported RTCG systems [1, 4, 5, 12]. All of them rely on programmer annotations to identify candidate variables for VSO. Leone and Lee's Fabius system [12] is the first RTCG system to identify staging transformations as a more powerful technique than partial evaluation, but they have not yet implemented staging transformations. The programmer separates the arguments into an early-tuple and a late-tuple. The compiler inserts calls to the run-time code generator that use the early-tuple to generate a specialized version of the function that takes the late-tuple as its argument. With a staging analysis the programmer wouldn't have to do the argument partitioning herself. Programmer annotations are prone to errors, both incorrect application and forgotten application can lead to less than best possible results.

SELF is a pure object-oriented programming language. The compiler and run-time system monitor method invocations for receiver classes. Method invocations are specialized based on the receiver class in order to improve performance. This is not a VSO, but it is RTCG. A staging analysis could be used to determine where RTCG should be applied in SELF. However, it would have to work on *glacial types* rather than glacial variables.

6 Conclusions and Future Work

Our glacial variable analysis is the first fully automatic analysis to discover candidate variables for value-specific optimization. The analysis is fully interprocedural, and no programmer assistance is required.

We presented the results of our analysis on ten of the PERFECT benchmark programs. The initial results are quite promising: many glacial variables are found, often with several degrees of glacialness. The analysis for arrays hints that specialization on array values is worth investigating; for instance, inspector/executor communication optimization can be viewed as a special case of VSO on the index array.

Our future work will include experimenting with modifications to the GRLA, for routines called at several levels and for recursive routines. We will also integrate our glacial variable analysis with a RTCG system to experiment with cost/benefit analyses, as well as studying opportunities for new optimizations based on VSO.

7 Acknowledgements

We would like to acknowledge Robert Prouty for his thoughtful review that greatly aided the comprehension of the paper and the anonymous reviewers for their suggested improvements.

References

1. J. Auslander, M. Philipose, C. Chambers, S. J. Eggers, and B. N. Bershad. Fast, effective dynamic compilation. In PLDI96 [14], pages 149–159.
2. R. A. Ballance, A. B. Maccabe, and K. J. Ottenstein. The Program Dependence Web: A representation supporting control-, data-, and demand-driven interpretation of imperative languages. In *Proc. ACM SIGPLAN '90 Conf. on Programming Language Design and Implementation*, pages 257–271, White Plains, NY, June 1990.
3. C. Consel and O. Danvy. Tutorial notes on partial evaluation. In *Conf. Record 20th Annual ACM Symp. Principles of Programming Languages*, pages 493–501, Charleston, SC, Jan. 1993.
4. C. Consel and F. Noël. A general approach to run-time specialization and its application to C. In *Conf. Record 23rd Annual ACM Symp. Principles of Programming Languages*, pages 145–156, St Petersburg, FL, Jan. 1996.

5. D. R. Engler. Vcode: A retargetable, extensible, very fast dynamic code generation system. In PLDI96 [14], pages 160–170.
6. A. Ershov. Mixed computation: The potential applications and problems for study. *Theoretical Computer Science*, 18:41–67, 1982.
7. M. Hall. *Managing Interprocedural Optimization*. PhD thesis, Department of Computer Science, Rice University, 1991.
8. M. Hall and K. Kennedy. Efficient call graph analysis. *Letters on Programming Languages and Systems*, 1(3):227–242, September 1992.
9. P. Havlak. Construction of Thinned Gated Single-Assignment form. In U. Banerjee, D. Gelernter, A. Nicolau, and D. A. Padua, editors, *Languages and Compilers for Parallel Computing*, number 768 in Lecture Notes in Computer Science, pages 477 – 499. Springer-Verlag, 1993.
10. D. Keppel. *Runtime Code Generation*. PhD thesis, University of Washington Department of Computer Science and Engineering, Mar. 1996.
11. D. Keppel, S. Eggers, and R. Henry. Evaluating runtime-compiled value-specific optimizations. Technical Report UWCSE 93-11-02, University of Washington Department of Computer Science and Engineering, November 1993.
12. P. Lee and M. Leone. Optimizing ML with run-time code generation. In PLDI96 [14], pages 137–148.
13. U. Jørring and W. L. Scherlis. Compilers and staging transformations. In *Conf. Record 13th Annual ACM Symp. on Principles of Programming Languages*, pages 86–96, St. Petersburg Beach, Jan. 1986.
14. *Proceedings ACM SIGPLAN '96 Conf. on Programming Language Design and Implementation*, Philadelphia, PA, May 1996.
15. M. N. Wegman and F. K. Zadeck. Constant propagation with conditional branches. *ACM Trans. on Programming Languages and Systems*, 13(2):181–210, Apr. 1991.

Compiler Algorithms on If-Conversion, Speculative Predicates Assignment and Predicated Code Optimizations

Jesse Z Fang

Microcomputer Research Lab
Intel Corporation
jfang@gomez.sc.intel.com

Abstract. Instruction level parallelism has become more and more important in today's microprocessor design. These microprocessors have multiple function units, which can execute more than one instruction at the same machine cycle to enhance the uniprocessor performance. Since the function units are usually pipelined in such microprocessors, branch misprediction penalty tremendously degrades the CPU performance. In order to reduce the branch misprediction penalty, predicated operation has been introduced in such microprocessor design as one of the new architectural features, which allows compilers to remove branches from programs.

The compiler converts programs with conditional branch to predicated code on these microprocessors with predicate operation support by using comparison instructions to set up Boolean predicates corresponding to branch conditions. Instructions previously guarded by a branch are guarded by a predicate. Predicates guard execution by either executing or nullifying the instruction according to the predicate's value.

In this report we present an algorithm to convert a control flow graph into predicated code. The algorithm shown in this report not only minimizes the number of predicates used for basic blocks in the control flow, but also moves the predicate assignments as early as possible to relax dependence constrains introduced by the if-conversion for the later phases of compiler such as the instruction scheduler and register allocator. The algorithm doesn't simply assign the predicate associated with a basic block to the instructions in the basic block. It assigns the predicate associated with the "farthest" dominator basic block to an instruction, to which the instruction can be speculatively moved without introducing compensation code in the instruction scheduling.

An optimization algorithm for if-converted code is discussed in the report as well. The algorithm is specially developed for predicated code optimization, which is different from the traditional optimizations. Common subexpression hoisting and sinking employs flow analysis, that extends the traditional common subexpression elimination technique. This algorithm requires traditional flow analysis information such as dominate and post-dominate relationship. Actually, the algorithm can be generalized on predicated code after if-conversion, which is particularly beneficial for single assignment DAG representation of the predicated code.

1 Introduction

In recent years, instruction level parallelism has become more and more important in microprocessor design. For instance, multiple data paths and function units are provided in today's superscalar microprocessor to improve uniprocessor performance. The multiple resources can be used by concurrently executing independent instructions in the instruction-stream. Great efforts have been devoted to developing compiler technologies to exploit the instruction level parallelism for such microprocessors. Most of the instruction level parallel compiler concepts underlying the Multiflow Trace compiler[1,2] and the Cydra 5 compiler[3,4] are based on static scheduling at compile time. Conditional branches are the difficult problem for the instruction scheduler at such compilers to make vulnerable choices in terms of the direction of the branches. Profiling information on the branch probability is very useful to predict the branch outcome, and the execution of instructions along the likely paths of the control flow can be overlapped to enhance the performance[1,5]. Another approach to correctly predict branch outcome without profiling information is to identify the regular program structure in the application programs such as the innermost loops. Dependence analysis helps the compiler to organize software pipelines, which overlap executions of instructions in the contiguous iterations to achieve the nearly maximal performance for such processors[3,4,6]. If branch prediction is correct, the code generated by the compiler based on instruction level parallelism is executed perfectly. However, if the branch prediction is wrong, the misprediction penalty tremendously degrades the execution performance. The branch misprediction can reduce superscalar performance from two to more than ten times in recent study[7,8].

Hardware predicated execution has been introduced in today's high performance microprocessor design as an effective means to reduce the branch misprediction penalty[9,10]. Predicated execution is a special hardware feature, which refers to the conditional execution of an instruction relying on the value of a boolean operand. A predicated instruction has an additional boolean predicate source operand, which enables the instruction to execute if it is true. The instruction with predicate is fetched regardless of value of its predicate. The instruction whose predicate is false will be nullified; the instruction whose predicate is true will be executed normally. The instruction with false predicate will not modify any processor state. This architecture feature is a little similar to the mask register in a vector machine, and it was implemented in Cydra 5 Departmental Supercomputer[3,4]. Predicated execution allows compilers to eliminate conditional branches from the control flow. The compiler converts conditional branches into predicated code in such a way that the condition comparison instruction sets up the boolean predicates, and the instructions along the alternative paths of the branch are converted into predicated instructions that are guarded by the predicates set by the comparison instruction. At run time, the execution of the instructions previously guarded by the branch are guarded by the predicates. The simple conditional branch conversion algorithm is similar to if-conversion in a vectorized compiler[11,12], which converts the control dependence to data dependence.

This new architecture feature, predicated execution, gives compiler designers many new challenges. The obvious challenge to use predicated execution is that merging multiple execution paths of control flow at compile time to eliminate conditional branches may extremely reduce the ratio of effective instructions vs. the number of instructions fetched by the processor. For instance, a microprocessor may issue four instructions guarded by four different predicates after if-conversion. Maybe only one of them is executed normally, while all the others are nullified. Furthermore, these nullified instructions will degrade the memory bandwidth from I-cache. This challenge brings a problem which conditional branches does compiler decide to convert into predicated code? or which region of control flow does the compiler select to convert into predicated code? The solution depends on application programs, and some hueristics are being developed to select a profitable region of control flow for if-conversion. We will not discuss the heuristics how to select the region for if-conversion in this paper. We concentrate on another challenge after selecting the right region: how to optimally convert the conditional branches in the selected region into predicated code, and how to optimize the predicated code in the selected region to maximize the performance gain.

In this report we first present an algorithm to convert the control flow graph of the selected region into predicated code. The region may be the loop body of an innermost loop that will be software pipelined at the compiler backend, or a single-entry multiple-exit interval, in which most of conditional branches have nearly 50% branch probability. The conversion algorithm shown in this report not only minimizes the number of predicates used for basic blocks in the control flow region, but also moves the predicate assignments as early as possible to relax dependence constrains introduced by the if-conversion for the later phases of compiler such as instruction scheduler and register allocator. It doesn't simply assign the predicate associated with a basic block to the instructions in the basic block. The algorithm assigns to each instruction the predicate associated with the earlest basic block to which that instruction can be speculatively moved without introducing compensation code.

Optimization for if-converted code is presented in the report as well. The optimization is specially designed for predicated code, which is different from the traditional optimizations in [13]. Common subexpression hoisting and sinking employs flow analysis, that globally move the common subexpression up or down in the control flow of the selected region, and finalize the value of the modified subexpression for the code outside of the region. The optimization extends the traditional common subexpression elimination technique, and eliminates redundant code as much as possible for the if-converted code in the selected region. The optimizations can be implemented even at the later phases of compiler. A more powerful version of the algorithm can be developed in a single assignment DAG at the instruction scheduling phase. This algorithm uses one instruction to represent two exclusively predicated instructions in the if-converted code of the selected control flow region.

The rest of the report is organized as follows. In section 2, the architectural support for predicated execution is described. In section 3, the algorithm to convert conditional branches into predicated code and assign predicate to each statement is presented. In section 4, a common subexpression hoisting and sinking algorithm is presented, which is implemented on the traditional control flow before converting conditional branches into predicated code. The modified version of the algorithm is briefly discussed in section 4 as well, which are implemented on predicated code after if-conversion. In section 5, we conclude our discussion and compare our research with related work.

2 Predicated Execution

Predicated execution refers to the conditional execution of instructions based on a boolean value of an additional predicate input operand for the instructions. If the boolean predicate input operand is true, it enables the instruction's execution. If the predicate is false, it disenables the instruction's execution. The functionality of predicated execution is similar to the mask register in vector machine[11], or to the nullification bit in some microprocessor today[14]. Syntactically, the additional predicate boolean operand is specified in Assembly language by an **if clause** before the instruction as shown below:

if p_{in}: r_1=**add**(r_2,r_3)

If an instruction is executed unconditionally, its predicate input operand is set up as the constant TRUE **T**. The instruction is

if T: r_1=**add**(r_2,r_3), that is equivalent to r_1=**add**(r_2,r_3).

Values of the boolean predicates can be set up by comparison instructions. The comparison instructions are just like regular one with greater than, equal to, and less than functions. In order to simplify the description of the algorithms in the report, we assume that the comparison instructions have two outputs. Both of them are boolean predicates. If the result of the compare is true, the first result predicate is true, and the second result predicate is false. If the result of the compare is false, the first predicate is false, and the second predicate is true. More interesting is that the comparison instructions can be predicated also. If the predicate which guards the compare is false, the comparison instruction isn't permitted to modify the state of the processor, including its outputs – the two predicates. The comparison instruction is in the Assembly form as below:

if p_{in}: (p_1,p_2)=**cmp-type**(r_1,r_2), where **type** is one of (**gt,eq,lt,...**).

This instruction assigns boolean value to predicates p_1 and p_2 according to the comparison of r_1 and r_2 specified by **type** in the instruction. The comparison **type** is equal(eq), not equal(ne), greater than(gt), less than(lt), etc. It is assumed that the special predicate p_0 represents boolean constant value **True**, which is similar to the special global register r_0 always representing constant integer value **0**. Therefore, the unconditionally executed instruction **if T:** r_1=**add**(r_2,r_3) can be in the equivalent form **if** p_0: r_1=**add**(r_2,r_3).

A comparison instruction may only have one output predicate p_1. The value of the predicate p_1 is **True** if the compare is success and is **False** if the compare is failure. The second predicate output is totally ignored. The boolean constant predicate p_0 can be used as the second output predicate. The comparison instruction has the format like:

if p_{in}**: (**p_1**,**p_0**)=cmp-type(**r_1**,**r_2**)**, or in the form **if** p_{in}**: (**p_1**,**T**)=cmp-type(**r_1**,**r_2**)**.

A comparison instruction may also only have one output predicate p_2. The value of the predicate p_2 is **True** if the compare is failure and is **False** if the compare is success. The first predicate output is totally ignored. In that case, the boolean constant predicate p_0 can be used as the first output predicate. The single output comparison instruction is like:

if p_{in}**: (**p_0**,**p_2**)=cmp-type(**r_1**,**r_2**)**, or in the form **if** p_{in}**: (**T**,**p_2**)=cmp-type(**r_1**,**r_2**)**.

To simplify our discussion and focus on compiler algorithms of predicated code, we don't introduce the complicated predicate boolean operations in this report. It is assumed that all predicates are initialized before they are used. In general, the initialization resets all the predicates to **False**. The truth table of the simple comparison instruction is shown in Table 1.

Input p_{in}	Comparison	First Output p_1	Second Output p_2
false	true	unchanged	unchanged
false	false	unchanged	unchanged
true	true	true	false
true	false	false	true

Table 1: Truth Table of Comparison Instruction

```
real exmp(a,b,q,r,s)
real a, b;
real *q, *r, *s;
{
    real x, y;
    y = a*b;
    if (y < 0.0)
        x = *q + y;
    else
        if (y==0.0)
            x = *r + y;
        else
            x = *s + y;
    return x;
}
```

Figure 1(a):
Source Code

```
L0:  y=fmul(a,b)
     p1=cmp-fge(y,0.0)
     branch(L1) if p1
     t1=fld(q)
     x=fadd(y,t1)
     branch(L3)
L1:  p2=cmp-fne(y,0.0)
     branch(L2) if p2
     t2=fld(r)
     x=fadd(y,t2)
     branch(L3)
L2   t3=fld(s)
     x=fadd(y,t3)
L3   return(x)
```

Figure 1(b):
Assembly Code

```
if T:   y=fmul(a,b)
if T:   (p1,p4)=cm p-flt(y,0.0)
if p4:  (p 2,p3)=cmp-feq(y,0.0)
if p1:  t1=fld(q)
if p2:  t2=fld( r)
if p3:  t3=fld(s)
if p1:  x=fadd(y,t1)
if p2:  x= fadd(y,t2)
if p3:  x=fadd(y,t3)
if T:   ret urn(x)
```

Figure 1(c):
If-Converted Code

The detailed design of predicated execution including predicate boolean operations has been described in [3,4,9,10]. Figure 1 contains a simple example to illustrate predicated execution.

In Figure 1(a), a routine **example** in C returns the summation of **a** × **b** and another value which is either ***q**, or ***r**, or ***s** depending on whether the product of **a** and **b** is less than, equal to, or greater than **0**. The assembly code for the routine is shown in Figure 1(b), which contains two conditional branches that potentionaly bring serious branch misprediction penalty at the execution time. Figure 1(c) shows the if-converted code for the routine using predicated instructions. The predicated code contains two comparison instructions that set up predicates p_1, p_2 and p_3, and then eleminate all conditional branches in the routine. It may cause some nullified operations at execution time. For instance, two of the three **floating load** instructions and two of the three **floating add** instructions are nullified by the predicates. It may degrade the execution performance. However, if the microprocessor can issue enough instructions per cycle and branch misprediction is expensive, predicated execution is able to achieve better performance when an intelligent heuristic selects a region of control flow which can profitably be converted into predicated code.

3 If-Conversion Algorithm

As we have mentioned in the Introduction Section, the new architectural feature, predicated execution, brought a big challenge for compiler designers. An intelligent hueristic is necessary to develop to select the "just right" control flow region for if-conversion. Careful performance fine-turning will be very important for compiler developers on such microprocessors with predicated execution. Clearly, it is not easy to select a good control flow region such that the if-conversion algorithm can achieve the optimal performance. However, on the other hand, some regular program structures with conditional branches are definitely benefited by predicated execution, which include the loop body with conditional branches of the innermost loops or the simple hammock structure containing branches with uncertain branch probability. The approach to select the optimal region of control flow for if-conversion into predicated code is not the topic in this report. In this report, we concentrate on algorithms of how to effectively convert the conditional branches in the selected flow region into predicated code, and how to optimize the if-converted code. The former is presented in this section, and the latter will be discussed in the next section.

An optimal algorithm for if-conversion has very similar nature to the program dependence analysis in [15]. It is to determine control conditions to assign a predicate for each basic block. The algorithm is required not only to minimize the number of predicates used for the selected control flow region, but also to find the earlest points to assign these predicates. The early assignments of predicates can relax the data dependence constrains introduced by the if-conversion. It will be beneficial for instruction scheduling and register allocation. Our algorithm of if-conversion employs a similar concept to program dependence, but doesn't build a program dependence graph like the method presented in [12].

The input of the if-conversion algorithm is a control flow region. In order to simplify our discussion in the paper, it is assumed that the control flow region doesn't have backedges, but that it has a single entry and may have multiple exits. In practical compiler design, backedge can be viewed as a loop, and the loop-body of the innermost loop can be handled as a flow region, that is to be if-converted into predicated code. The representation of the region consists of **bblock-list** – a sequence of basic blocks, **head** – the entry basic block, and **exit-list** – a list of the multiple exit basic blocks. Each basic block is composed of a series of instructions in the block and the block information. The block information contains a list of its **predecessor**, a list of its **successors** in the control flow region. Some standard concepts of flow analysis [13] in our algorithm are presented below:

- **Dominators:** we say a basic block bb_1 of a flow graph *dominates* another basic block bb_2, written bb_1 **dom** bb_2, if every path from the entry basic block **head** of the flow graph to bb_2 through bb_1.
- **Post-Dominators:** we say a basic block bb_1 of a flow graph *post-dominates* another basic block bb_2, written bb_1 **pdom** bb_2 , if every path from bb_2 to any exit basic block in the **exit-list** of the flow graph through bb_1.
- **Breadth First Order:** braedth first search assigns numbers to basic blocks in a selected control flow region in such a way, that the numbers assigned to **predecessors** of a given block are always less than the number assigned to the block; meanwhile the numbers assigned to the **successors** of a given block are always greater than the number assigned to the block.

The standard algorithm to calculate all dominators and post-dominators for a given basic block can be found in [13]. We assume that each basic block of the input control flow region contains **dominator-list** and **post-dominator-list**.

Our if-conversion algorithm consists of two parts. The first part assigns predicates to basic blocks in the input flow region. An example of the first part is shown in Figure 2(a), and the algorithm is presented in Figure 3(a). The second part of the algorithm assigns predicates associated with basic blocks to instructions in such a way that helps an instruction scheduler speculatively move the instructions across basic block boundaries without introducing compensation code, which is shown in Figure 3(b).

Three new attributes are added to each basic block needed by the first part of our if-conversion algorithm:

1. **predicate** is used to save the predicate that the algorithm assigns to the basic block.
2. **if-true-list** is a list of predicates, which need to be set up when the comparison instruction in the basic block is success.
3. **if-false-list** is a list of predicates, which need to be set up when the comparison instruction in the basic block is failure.

An internal data structure required by the algorithm is **check-pdom-set**, which contains a set of basic blocks of the region to check whether they are post-dominated by the given basic block. The first part of if-conversion algorithm goes forward through the *bblock-list* with breadth first order. For each basic block *ccur-bb*, it steps backward from the basic block to the *head*. If *ccur-bb* doesn't post-dominate a basic block in the backward order, the algorithm assigns a predicate to *ccur-bb* and puts it into the corresponding *if-true-list* or *if-false-list* of the basic block according to *ccur-bb* is in the true branch or false branch. If *ccur-bb* post-dominates a basic block in the backward order and the basic block dominates *ccur-bb*, they should have the same predicate. If *ccur-bb* post-dominates a basic block and the basic block doesn't dominate *ccur-bb*, the algorithm continues the process and backward steps to previous basic block in *bblock-list*.

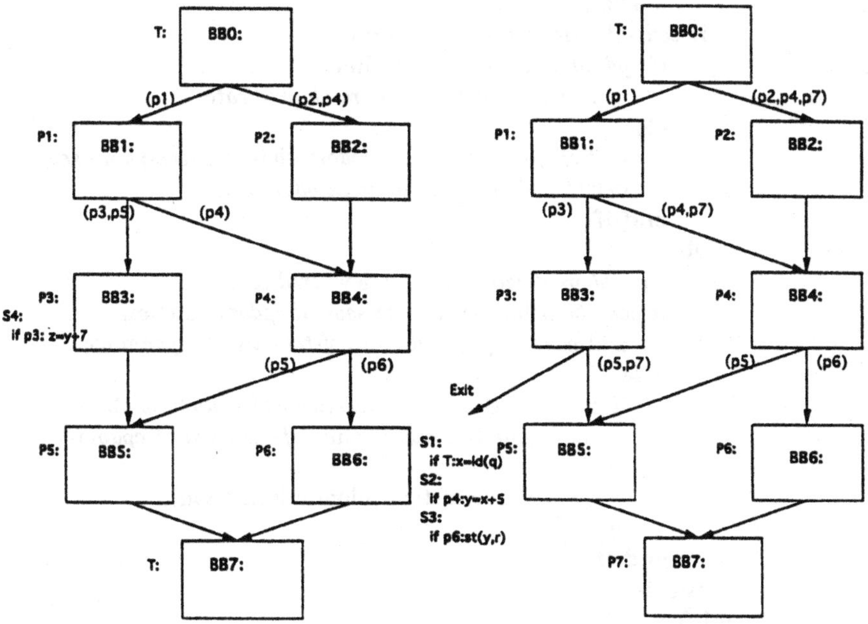

- *Input:* A control flow region **G** with information described above.[1]
- *Output:* Predicates assigned to each basic block and predicate lists assigned to **if-true-list** and **if-false-list** of each basic block.

```
Algorithm to assign predicates to basic blocks in a region G
    procedure assign-predicate-basic-block(G)
    rearrange bblock-list of G in Breadth First Order;
    assign predicate T to head block with order number 0;
    create a set of basic blocks: check-pdom-set;
    for each basic block ccur-bb in forward order of bblock-list do begin
        empty check-pdom-set;
        add all predecessors of ccur-bb into check-pdom-set;
        for each basic block cpdom-bb in backward order of
            bblock-list from ccur-bb to head do begin
            if cpdom-bb is not in check-pdom-set then
                continue;
            if ccur-bb pdom cpdom-bb then
                if cpdom-bb dom ccur-bb then
                    ccur-bb.predicate = cpdom-bb.predicate
                else
                    add all predecessors of cpdom-bb into check-pdom-set;
                    delete cpdom-bb from check-pdom-set;
                end-if
            else
                curr-bb.predicate = create new predicate;
                if ccur-bb pdom true-successor of cpdom-bb then
                    add ccur-bb.predicate into if-true-list of cpdom-bb;
                else
                    if ccur-bb pdom false-successor of cpdom-bb then
                        add ccur-bb.predicate into if-false-list of cpdom-bb;
                    else
                        error(inconsistent pdom information);
                    end-if
                end-if
            end-if
        end-for
    end-for
```

Figure 3(a): Algorithm 3.1 to Assign Predicate into Basic Blocks

An example of the algorithm is given in Figure 2(a). In the example, we start from basic block BB_0. Since it is the *head* block, the predicate assigned to it

[1] The algorithms 3.1 and 3.2 was based on the code originally developed by Ping Sheng Tseng, who was working at HP Lab from July 1992 to Argust 1993.

is always true **T**. Then the algorithm steps to BB_1. Since BB_1 doesn't post-dominate its predecessor BB_0, a new predicate p_1 is assigned to BB_1 and is put in *if-false-list* of BB_0. For the same reason, BB_2 is assigned a new predicate p_2, which is kept in the *if-true-list* of BB_0. BB_1 dominates BB_3, so the new predicate p_3 assigned to BB_3 is kept in *if-false-list* of BB_1. BB_4 has two predecessors. It doesn't post-dominate BB_1, so the predicate p_4 assigned to BB_4 is kept in *if-true-list* of BB_1. Another predecessor BB_2 is post-dominated by BB_4, so check its predecessor BB_0 and keep p_4 into *if-true-list* of BB_0. Similarly, BB_5 post-dominates BB_3, predicate p_5 is assigned to BB_5 and kept in *if-false-list* of BB_4 and in *if-false-list* of BB_1. Since BB_6 is dominated by BB_4, the algorithm puts predicate p_6 in *if-true-list* of BB_4. Finally, BB_7 post-dominates its predecessors, the algorithm checks their predecessors. BB_7 post-dominates all the predecessors of its predecessors BB_3 and BB_4, therefore it checks their predecessors again BB_1 and BB_2. It post-dominates them, so moves to their predecessor. Because BB_7 post-dominates BB_0 and BB_0 dominates BB_5, they should have the same predicate **T**.

From the example, it can be seen that the predicate assignments are moved as early as possible in our algorithm. It relaxes the data dependence constrains introduced by the if-conversion. For instance, if execution of the example takes the false branch from BB_0, any instruction in BB_5 predicated by p_5 can be executed with instructions in BB_3, assuming the critical path of the given flow region is in BB_3 and the latency of assignments of p_5 including **cmp** instructions in BB_1 and BB_4 is shorter than the latency in BB_3.

Algorithm 3.1 also works very well for multiple exit region. Figure 2(b) shows a similar example with multiple exits. Every step of Algorithm 3.1 is the same as one in Figure 2(a) until it steps to BB_5. Since BB_3 has an exit, and it is no longer post-dominated by BB_5. Therefore, predicate p_5 assigned to BB_5 is kept in *if-true-list* of BB_3 rather than in *if-false-list* of BB_1 as it happend in Figure 2(a). BB_7 post-dominates BB_2, BB_4, BB_5 and BB_6, but it doesn't post-dominate BB_3. Therefore, *if-true-list* of BB_1 and *if-true-list* of BB_3 keeps the predicate p_7 for BB_7.

After assigning predicates to basic blocks in the given flow region, we need to develop the second part of our if-conversion algorithm that assigns a predicate to each instruction. Instead of simply assigning an instruction the predicate associated with its home basic block, our algorithm assigns the predicate associated with the "earliest" basic block, that dominates the home basic block, to the instruction without causing any compensation code. The traditional flow analysis concepts in [13] such as *def*, *kill* and *used* are used in the algorithm.

For a basic block **bb**, **bb.used** represents a set of variables, which are used in the basic block before they may be redefined in the block and **bb.def** is a set of variables which are defined in the basic block. Two more attributes are added for each basic block. They are **bb.in** and **bb.out**. In Algorithm 3.2, **bb.out** is used to keep all variables which will be used after the basic block in the control flow, and **bb.in** contains all variables which will be used, but not killed after the starting point of the basic block. In other words,

bb.in = bb.used ∪ (bb.out − bb.def).

Algorithm to assign predicates to instructions in the region *G*.

```
procedure assign-predicate-instruction(G)
for each basic block bb in bblock-list do begin
    calculate bb.used and bb.def;
end-for
for each basic block bb in backward order of bblock-list do begin
    for each successor succ-bb of bb in G do begin
        bb.out = bb.out ∪ succ-bb.in;
    end-for
    bb.in = bb.used ∪ (bb.out − bb.def);
end-for
create check-dom-set and doms-list;
for each basic block ccur-bb in forward order of bblock-list do begin
    empty check-dom-set and doms-list;
    add ccur-bb into check-dom-set;
    {** Find dominator list for ccur block **}
    for each basic block cdom-bb in backward order of
        bblock-list from ccur-bb to head do begin
        if cdom-bb is not in check-dom-set then
            continue;
        if cdom-bb dom ccur-bb then
            add cdom-bb into doms-list;
        add all predecessors of cdom-bb into check-dom-set;
    end-for
    {** Now assign predicate to each instruction in the ccur block **}
    for each instruction instr in ccur-bb do begin
        if instru is cmp or store then
            instru.predicate = ccur-bb.predicate;
            continue;
        end-if
        for each dom-bb in reverse order of doms-list do begin
            if output of instru is not in dom-bb.out then
                instru.predicate = dom-bb.predicate;
            break;
        end-for
    end-for
end-for
```

Figure 3(b): Algorithm 3.2 to Assign Predicate to Instruction

It is assumed that the variables used outside of the selected region are saved by **bb.out** of the basic blocks in **exit-list**, and **bb.out** of all the other basic blocks and all the **bb.in** are initially reset. Two internal data structures are required in the algorithm. A set of basic blocks, **check-dom-set**, is used to contain basic blocks to check whether they are dominated by a given basic block. Its role is the same as **check-pdom-set** in Algorithm 3.1. A list of dominator **doms-list** is used to find the "earliest" dominated block for a given basic block.

An example of the second part in the if-conversion algorithm is given in Figure 2(a). There are three instructions S_1: *x=ld(q)*, S_2: *y=add(x,5)* and S_3: *st(y,r)* in BB_6. Assuming that there is no instruction in other basic blocks using the variable x, and there is an instruction S_4: *z=add(y,7)* in BB_3. Since both BB_0 and BB_4 dominate BB_6 and no basic block uses variable x, predicate T associated with BB_0 can be assigned to S_1: *if T: x=ld(q)*. Because the output y of S_2 is used by S_4: *z=add(y,7)* in BB_3, we have S_2: *if* p_4: *y=add(x,5)*. S_3 is a store operation that cannot be speculatively moved out of its home basic block, so S_3: *if* p_6: *st(y,r)*.

It is trivial to generate predicated code after Algorithm 3.2. The comparison instructions for conditional branches are simply modified to generate predicates using information in *if-true-list* and *if-false-list*. After that, the instructions in the selected flow region just need to be concatenated in Breadth First Order of the basic blocks.

4 Optimization for Predicated Execution

4.1 Compiler Strategy for If-Conversion

Predicated execution allows a compiler to eliminate conditional branches in a given control flow region, and thereby reduce the branch misprediction penalty at the execution time. As a tradeoff, it may convert "too many" instructions into predicated code, and then degrades the performance by carrying out "too many" useless instructions. An intelligent hueristic is required to select a "just right" control flow region for if-conversion. Careful performance tuning is very important for such compilers on microprocessors with predicated execution. A simple heuristic is to use the regular programming structures with conditional branches as a right candidate for if-conversion, which includes the loop body of innermost loops and hammock structure containing conditional branches with uncertain branch probability. The approach to select the right region of control flow for if-conversion is beyond the topic of this report. We are interested in how to optimize the predicated code after if-conversion.

In general, an if-conversion phase of a compiler consists of the following components:

1. *A heuristic* to select the right control flow region for if-conversion.
2. *A pre-optimizer* to implement some special optimizations on the selected control region. These optimizations will be particularly beneficial for predicated code using traditional flow analysis before if-conversion.
3. *An if-converter* to assign predicates to basic blocks and instructions in the given flow region. The algorithms described in section 3 can be used here.

4. *A post-optimizer* to further optimize the predicated code in directed acyclic graph in single assignment form, which can be used in a later compiler phase also such as instruction scheduler and register allocator.

In this section, we concentrate on an optimization technique used in *pre-optimizer*, which is different from the traditional optimizations in [13]. This technique may be not beneficial for compilers on processors without predicated execution support. The optimization, that we present in this paper, is called "Common Subexpression Hoisting and Sinking". This algorithm uses traditional control flow analysis before if-conversion. We will have a little discussion on the optimizations after the next subsection also in the next section.

4.2 Common Subexpression Hoisting and Sinking

To reduce the number of useless instructions at execution time, an aggressive redundant code elimination strategy is necessary for if-conversion. A common subexpression hoisting and sinking algorithm speculatively moves the common subexpressions up or down in the selected flow region, although there may exist some paths from the entry block to exits that don't contain the subexpressions. The algorithm is required to finalize the value of the modified subexpressions for the code outside of the region. It extends the traditional common subexpression elimination technique.

If a common subexpressions exit in two basic blocks, there may be a path from the entry block to some exit block without passing any of them. In such a case, a traditional **cse**(common subexpression elimination) will not be applied, because the hoisted subexpression may happen in a critical path of the given region, and then degrades the execution performance. On a processor with predicated execution, we hoist the common subexpressions from the basic blocks up to their "latest" dominator or sink them from the basic blocks down to their "earlest" post-dominator according to whether the subexpressions contain common output. Since the consumers of the subexpressions will be predicated and the subexpressions are speculatively moved, the optimization benefits if-converted code in most of the applications having a resource bottleneck in the instruction scheduling.

The input of the common subexpression hoisting or sinking algorithm is the same as a selected control flow region in Section 3. To simplify our discussion in this section, it is assumed that the control flow region doesn't have backedges. It has single entry and may have multiple exits. In practical compiler design, a backedge can be viewed as defining a loop. The representation of the selected flow region is the same as in Section 3. It consists of **bblock-list**, **head** and **exit-list**. The same internal data structure in Algorithm 3.2 of Section 3 is used in the common subexpression hoist and sink algorithms. For each basic block **bb**, there are two attributs **bb.out** and **bb.in**. The former is used to keep all variables which will be used after the basic block in the control flow, and the latter contains all variables which will be used, but not killed after the starting point of the basic block. Two internal data structures are used in the following common subexpression hoist algorithm. Instructions in the flow region are **hoistable** if it has *written* part and *read* part. Most of the regular instructions such as *load*, *add*, *mult*, are hoistable. Store instructions are not hoistable.

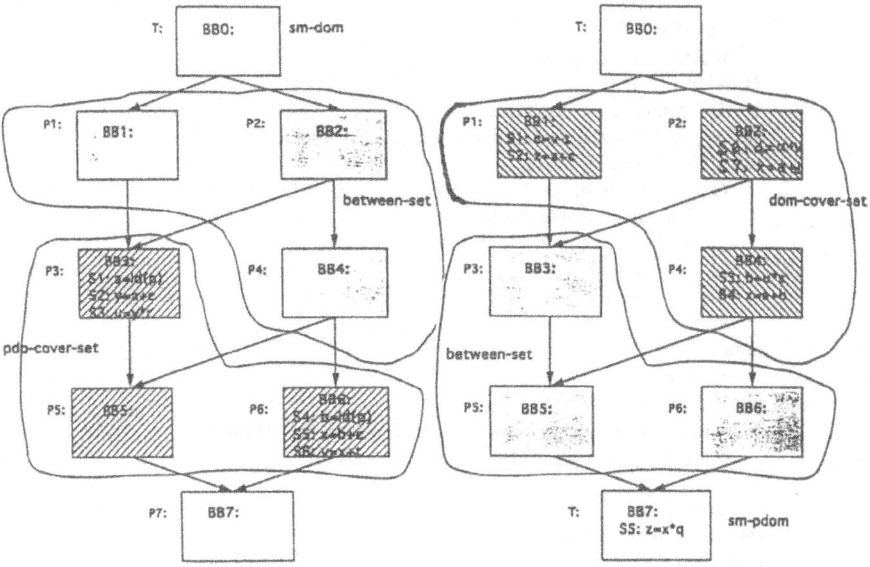

Several new definitions are introduced in our common subexpression hoist algorithm. For any given two basic blocks, **sm-dom** represents their "latest" common dominator, which dominates both of the basic blocks and there is no other common dominator of the two blocks dominated by the **sm-dom**. For the two basic blocks and their **sm-dom**, **pdom-cover-set** is a minimum set of basic blocks which contains the two blocks, but not any their predecessors. The set has the following property that any path from **sm-dom** to exit should go through one and only one of the basic blocks in the set. The **pdom-cover-set** actually post-dominates **sm-dom** in the given flow region. The set of all basic blocks between **sm-dom** and **pdom-cover-set** is defined as **between-set**. A recursive subroutine *find-between* is in Figure 5 to calculate **between-set** for two given basic blocks and their **sm-dom**.

Algorithm Hoist Common Subexpressions in Selected Control Flow Region *G*.

```
procedure common-subexpression-hoisting(G)
rearrange bblock-list of G in Breadth First Order;
calculate bb.used,bb.def,predecessors and successors for each basic block bb in bblock-list;
for each basic block bb in backward order of bblock-list do begin
    bb.out = bb.out ∪ succ.in for all successors succ of bb;
    bb.in = bb.used ∪ (bb.out − bb.def) ;
end-for
do begin
    for each basic block bb1 in forward order of bblock-list do begin
        reset pdom-cover-set and between-set empty;
        reset a boolean variable found = FALSE;
        for each hoistable instruction instr1 in bb1 do begin
            for each basic block bb2 in forward order of bblock-list from bb1 do begin
                if found an instruction instr2 with the same read as instr1 then
                    found = TRUE;
                    break;
            end-for
            if found then break;
        end-for
        if NOT found then continue;
        add bb1 and bb2 into between-set and pdom-cover-set;
        if bb1 NOT dom bb2 then
            for each basic block bb in backward order of bblock-list
                from bb1 to head do begin
                if bb dom both bb1 and bb2 then
                    sm-dom = bb;
                    break;
            end-for
        else
            sm-dom = bb1;
        add sm-dom into between-set;
        if found-between(between-set,sm-dom,sm-dom, bb2) then
            delete sm-dom, bb1 and bb2 from between-set;
        else
            break;
        reset a boolean variable flag = FALSE;
        if bb1 NOT dom bb2 then
            for each basic block bb in forward order
                of bblock-list from sm-dom do begin
                if sm-dom NOT dom bb then continue;
                if bb is in between-set then continue;
                if all predecessors of bb are in between-set or
```

```
            pdom-cover-set, or are sm-dom then
            if at least one of predecessor of bb is in between-set then
                add bb into pdom-cover-set;
        end-for
        for each bb in pdom-cover-set do begin
            if any written of instr1 or instr2 is in bb.in then
                flag = TRUE;
                break;
        end-for
    end-if
    if flag break;
    for each bb in between-set do begin
        if any read of instr1 or instr2 is in bb.def then
            flag = TRUE;
            break;
    end-for
    if flag break;
    add instr1 into sm-dom and delete instr1 from bb1;
    relace written of instr2 by written of instr1 in all successors of bb2;
    if written of instr2 is in some bb.out of exit-list then
        add copy instructionwritten of instr2 = written of instr1 in bb;
    delete instr2 from bb2;
  end-for
end-do until nothing changed

boolean found-between(between-set,bb,sm-dom,bb2)
  if bb is in exit-list or is not in between sm-dom and bb2 then
      return FALSE;
  if bb is in between-set then
      return TRUE;
  for each successor succ of bb do begin
      if found-between(between-set,succ,sm-dom ,bb2) then
          add succ into between-set;
          return TRUE;
  end-for
  return FALSE;
end
```

Figure 5: Algorithm to Hoist Common Subexpression in Region.

An example of our common subexpression hoisting algorithm is given in Figure 4(a). There are three instructions S_1*: a=ld(p)*, S_2*: y=a+c* and S_3*: u= y*r* in BB_3 and three instructions S_4*: b=ld(p)*, S_5*: x=b+c* and S_6*: v=x+t* in BB_6. It is assumed that variables *c* and *p* are invariant in the flow region, and no instruction uses variables *x*, *y*, *a* and *b* in basic blocks BB_5 and BB_7. The "closest" common dominator *sm-dom* of BB_3 and BB_6 is BB_0. The *pdom-cover-set* contains BB_3, BB_5 and BB_6 and the *between-set* contains BB_1, BB_2 and BB_4. The algorithm hoists S_1 and S_4 to BB_0, and changes S_5 to S_5: *x=a+c*. Then in the second iteration of the **do-unil** loop, it hoists S_2 and S_5 to BB_0, and changes S_6 to S_6: *v=y+t*.

Our common subexpression sinking algorithm is very similar to the common subexpression hoisting shown in Figure 5. Assuming that there are several two-input instructions in the control flow region, which have the same output variable and at least one common input variable. If the set of their home basic blocks is a "cover" for their common post-dominator block, the sinking algorithm can move them down to the "closest" common post-dominator block, and then reduce the redundant instructions in the flow region. Similar internal definitions are used for our common subexpression sinking algorithm. For a set of basic blocks, **sm-pdom** represents their "closest" common post-dominator, which post-dominates all of the basic blocks and there is no other common post-dominator of these blocks post-dominated by the **sm-pdom**. For the basic blocks and their **sm-pdom**, **dom-cover-set** is a minimum set of basic blocks which contains these blocks, but not any of their successors. The set of all basic blocks between **dom-cover-set** and **sm-dom** is defined as **between-set**. One more condition in common subexpression sinking algorithm is to check whether all basic blocks in *dom-cover-set* contain the common subexpression. Since the two algorithms are very similar, we don't describe the latter in the report.

An example of common subexpression sinking algorithm is given in Figure 4(b). There are instructions S_1: *c=v-t* and S_2: *x=a+c* in BB_1, S_6: *d=v+u* and S_7: *x=d+a* in BB_2, and S_3: *b=u*s* and S_2: *x=a+b* in BB_4. It is assumed that varibale *a* is constant in the flow region, and no instruction uses variables *x*, *b*, *c* and *d* in BB_3, BB_5 and BB_6. The *sm-pdom* in the example is BB_7, while *dom-cover-set* contains BB_1, BB_2 and BB_4 and *between-set* contains BB_3, BB_5 and BB_6. The common subexpression sinking algorithm moves S_2 and S_4 down into BB_7, and changes S_6 to S_6: *c=v+u* in BB_2 and S_3 to S_3: *c=u*s* in BB_4 respectively.

Notice that when the algorithm sinks **store** instructions, there are more conditions to be satisfied. The store operation to the same memory location should be in every basic block in *dom-cover-set* and they must not have memory dependence with any load instructions in *between-set*.

Optimizations after if-conversion may have less constrains than pre-optimizer in if-conversion. For instance, if there is an instruction S_0: *p=p+5* in BB_1 of example Figure 4(a), common subexpression hoisting algorithm in Figure 5 cannot hoist S_1: *a=ld(p)* and S_4: *b=ld(p)* to BB_0 because value of variable *p* may be modified in BB_1. Then the two almost exactly same instructions S_1 and S_4 will appear in the if-converted code with different predicates. After if-conversion, the instruction S_1: *if* p_1: *a=ld(p)* and S_2: *if* p_1: *y=a+c* can be merged into one instruction. The following is a brief description of the post-optimization algorithm that eliminates redundant code for predicated code.

1. Create new instruction S_{11}: p_{11}=p_1 *OR* p_6 if hardware provides the logic operations for predicates, and insert the instruction at the beginning of instructions in BB_6.
2. Instructions S_1: *if* p_1: *a=ld(p)* and S_2: *if* p_1: *y=a+c* are eliminated from the predicated code.
3. Instructions S_4: *if* p_6: *b=ld(p)* and S_5: *if* p_6: *x=b+c* is changed into S_{11}: *if* p_6: *b=ld(p)* and S_5: *if* p_{11}: *x=b+c* and follow the new instruction S_{11}: p_{11} = p_1 *OR* p_6.
4. Instruction S_3: p_1: *u=y*r* is changed to S_3: p_1: *u=x*r* and set up data dependence from S_5 to S_3.

More research results on post-optimizations for predicated code are coming soon. The detailed discussion on the post-optimization can be seen in our next technical report.

5 Conclusions

Predicated execution provides an effective method to reduce conditional branch misprediction penalty. This new architectural feature brings a big challenge to compiler research and development. In this report, we briefly describe one way how compiler might implement if-conversion using predicated execution. The optimization technique to hoist or sink common subexpressions in a given control flow region is presented in detail. The optimization may not be beneficial for compilers on regular processors without predicated execution, but it is helpful to reduce redundant code after converting a control flow region into predicated code.

The algorithm shown in this report is just one example of a series of optimizations for if-converted code. More research activities are in progress to develop advanced optimizations for predicated code. Future research work includes investigating new algorithms to optimize the predicated code without flow analysis, which should be more direct and more effective than the method presented in this report.

The strategy to select a profitable piece of control flow for if-conversion is another important and challenging research topic. Besides intelligent hueristic by performance tuning the compiler, more theoritical research on programming structure is demanded by the new architectural feature.

References

[1] J.A.Fisher, "Trace scheduling: A technique for global microcode compaction," *IEEE Transactions on Computers*, vol. c-30, pp.478-490, July 1981.

[2] P.G. Lowney, S.M. Freudenberger, T.J. Karzes, W.D. Lichtenstein, R.P. Nix, J.S. O'Donnell, and J.C. Ruttenberg, "The Multiflow trace scheduling compiler", *The Journal of Supercomputing*, 1992.

[3] B.R.Rau,D.W.L.Yen,W.Yen,and R.A.Towle,"The Cydra 5 departmental supercomputer," *IEEE Computer*, pp.12-35, January 1989.

[4] J.C.Dehnert and R.A.Towle,"Compiling for the Cydra 5", *The Journal of Supercomputing*, 1992.

[5] P.P.Chang, S.A.Mahlke, W.Y.Chen, N.J.Warter, and W.W.Hwu, "IMPACT: an architectural framework for multiple-instruction-issue processors", *In Proceedings 18th Annual International Symposium on Computer Architecture*, Toronto, Canada, pp.266-275, May 1991.

[6] A.Nicolau, "Percolation scheduling: a parallel compilation technique", *Technical Report TR 85-678*, Department of Computer Science, Cornell, 1985.

[7] D.W.Wall,"Limits of instruction-level parallelism", *Proceedings of the 4th International Conference on Architectural Support for Programming Languages and Operating Systems*, pp.176-188, April 1991.

[8] M.Butler,T.Y.Yeh,Y.Patt,M.Alsup,H.Scales,and M.Shebanow,"Single instruction stream parallelism is greater than two",*Proceedings of the 18th International Symposium on Computer Architecture*, pp.276-286, May 1991.

[9] S.Mahlke, R.Hank, R.Bringmann, J.Gyllenhaal, D.Gallagher, and W.M.Hwu, "Predicated Execution Support for Superscalar Processor', to be appear.

[10] P.Tirumalai, M.Lee, and M.S.Schlansker, "Parallelization of loops with exits on pipelined architectures", *In Proceedings Supercomputing '90*, pp.200-212, November 1990.

[11] J.R.Allen,K.Kennedy,C.Porterfield,and J.Warren,"Conversion of control dependence to data dependence", *in Proceedings of the 10th ACM Symposium on Principles of Programming Languages*, pp.177-189, January 1983.

[12] J.C.H.Park and M.Schlansker,"On Predicated Execution",*Tech. Rep. HPL-91-58*, Hewlett-Packard Software System Laboratory, May 1991.

[13] A.Aho,R.Sethi, and J.Ullman,"Compilers:Principles,Techniques,and Tools", Reading *MA: Addison-Wesley*, 1988.

[14] Hewlett-Packard Co. *PA-RISC 1.1 Architecture and Instruction Set Reference Manual*, Cupertino, CA: Hewlett-Packard Co. 1990.

[15] J.Ferrante,K.J.Ottenstein, and J.D.Warren,"The program dependence graph and its use in optimization", *ACM Transactions on Programming Languages and Systems*, vol.9, pp.319-349, July 1987.

[16] N.Water, et al, "Enhanced modulo scheduling for loops with conditional branches", *Proceedings of the 25th Annual International Symposium on Microarchitecture*, Portland, Oregon, 1992.

Determining Asynchronous Pipeline Execution Times

Val Donaldson and Jeanne Ferrante

University of California, San Diego

Abstract. *Asynchronous pipelining* is a form of parallelism in which processors execute different loop tasks (loop statements) as opposed to different loop iterations. An asynchronous pipeline schedule for a loop is an assignment of loop tasks to processors, plus an order on instances of tasks assigned to the same processor. This variant of pipelining is particularly relevant in distributed memory systems (since pipeline control may be distributed across processors), but may also be used in shared memory systems.

Accurate estimation of the execution time of a pipeline schedule is needed to determine if pipelining is appropriate for a loop, and to compare alternative schedules. Pipeline execution of n iterations of a loop requires time at most $a + bn$, for some constants a and b. The coefficient b is the *iteration interval* of the pipeline schedule, and is the primary measure of the performance of a schedule. The *startup time* a is a secondary performance measure.

We generalize previous work on determining if a pipeline schedule will deadlock, and generalize Reiter's well-known formula [19] for determining the iteration interval b of a deadlock-free schedule, to account for nonzero communication times (easy) and the assignment of multiple tasks to processors (nontrivial). Two key components of our generalization are the use of pipeline scheduling edges, and the notion of negative data dependence distances (in a single unnested loop). We also discuss implementation of an asynchronous pipeline schedule at runtime; derive bounds on the startup time a; and discuss evaluation of the iteration interval formula, including development of a new algorithm.

1 Introduction

Pipelining is an "assembly line" form of parallelism in which instances of subcomputations or *tasks* of a repeated computation, such as statements in a loop body, are executed concurrently. Pipeline parallelism exploits concurrency both within and across loop iterations, complementing other forms of parallelism. A computation which can not be parallelized using *doall* parallelism [17], which assigns different loop iterations to different processors, or noniterative task (or DAG) parallelism [20, 22], may permit pipeline parallelization. Figure 2 in Sect. 3 is an example of pipeline execution.

Under the broad umbrella of pipeline parallelism, there are a number of variants which make different assumptions, or focus on different aspects of the computation which is being pipelined. Examples include instruction and vector pipelining in hardware [12], and *software pipelining* on sequential, VLIW, or superscalar processors [1, 14]. Our focus is on a form of pipelining which we call *asynchronous pipelining*, where application program loops are pipelined on multiprocessors or multicomputers, and pipeline tasks are scheduled as soon as processor and data resources are available. This form of pipelining has been studied particularly in the context of digital signal processing algorithms [2, 10], although it has been considered in other contexts as well [21]. Tasks may be of arbitrary size, from simple statements to complex compound statements or subroutine calls. Task execution times may vary from iteration to iteration, although we assume that there is an expected execution time for each task.

We are particularly interested in pipeline execution on distributed memory architectures. This emphasis has several consequences. First, nonzero communication times between tasks on different processors must be taken into account. Second, we assume that tasks are assigned statically to processors, and all instances of a task are executed on the same processor. Third, pipeline control should be local to each processor, to avoid the bottleneck of global control. Based on these requirements, an asynchronous pipeline schedule is an assignment of pipeline tasks to processors, plus specification of when instances of tasks assigned to the same processor execute, relative to each other. Although our focus is on pipelining in distributed memory systems, our results are also applicable to shared memory systems. We formalize our basic pipeline model in Sect. 2, and refine it in Sect. 4.

For any form of pipelining, it is important to be able to predict the execution time of a pipeline schedule, to determine whether or not pipelining is an appropriate implementation strategy for a loop, as well as choosing between alternative pipeline schedules. The pipeline execution time of n iterations of a loop requires time at most $a + bn$, where a and b are constants. The coefficient b is the *iteration interval* of the pipeline schedule, which is the average time between completion of successive iterations, and is the primary measure of the performance of a schedule. The term a is the *startup time* of the schedule, and is a secondary performance measure. Previous asynchronous pipeline scheduling algorithms targeting distributed memory systems [2, 10, 21] use conservative estimates of the pipeline iteration interval as their performance measure, derived in part from Reiter's well-known iteration interval formula [19]. Reiter's formula assumes that intertask communication times are zero, and each task is assigned to a distinct processor.

The primary contributions of this paper are a generalization of previous work on determining if a pipeline schedule will deadlock, and generalization of Reiter's formula for determining the iteration interval b. Our generalizations of these results incorporate nonzero communication times (easy), and account for the assignment of multiple tasks to processors (nontrivial). A key component of our approach is the use of scheduling edges with potentially negative data dependence distances, which generalizes the use of scheduling edges in noniterative task graphs [22]. We also explicitly discuss the specification of an asynchronous pipeline schedule in terms of schedule subcomponents; describe a simple mechanism for implementing a pipeline schedule at runtime; derive bounds on the startup time a; and discuss evaluation of the iteration interval formula, including the design of a new algorithm.

The paper is organized as follows. Section 2 formalizes our loop and basic pipeline execution models. Section 3 summarizes previous results on characterizing deadlock and determining pipeline execution times, including Reiter's formula. Section 4 includes a short discussion of the effect of nonzero communication times, and extends our pipeline execution model to permit multiple tasks to execute on the same processor. Section 5 discusses data dependence distances in detail, including negative dependence distances. Section 6 presents our generalized results on deadlock characterization and iteration interval determination. Section 7 discusses evaluation of the iteration interval formula, including design of a new algorithm, and derives bounds on the startup time a. We summarize our conclusions in Sect. 8.

2 Loop and Pipeline Execution Models

Pipeline scheduling and analysis may be performed on a multiply weighted directed multigraph, variations of which have been given a wide variety of names in the literature, including ***computation graph*** [19], ***marked directed graph*** [4], ***dataflow graph*** [13, 14], ***dependence graph*** [8], ***flow graph*** [10], ***signal flow graph*** [2], ***iterative task graph*** [21], ***collapsed-constraint graph*** [3], and ***semisystolic network*** [16], among others. Alternative models such as variations of Petri nets [18] have also been analyzed. Although the large choice of names and model variations is perhaps confusing, it also illustrates that pipelining is useful in a variety of contexts. Variants of this data structure have been extensively studied in the optimizing compiler literature under the name ***data dependence graph*** [17], which is the name we will use.

Definition 1. A *data dependence graph* (DDG) is a weighted directed multigraph $G = (V, E, f_{\text{vtime}}, f_{\text{etime}}, f_{\text{dist}})$, where:

- V is a set of vertices or *tasks*. We use v to denote $|V|$.
- E is a multiset of $e = |E|$ directed edges between tasks in V, where $(X, Y) \in E$ denotes that task Y is *data dependent* on task X.
- f_{vtime} is a function from V to the nonnegative reals denoting the execution time of tasks. For a task $X \in V$, we use $X.time$ to denote $f_{\text{vtime}}(X)$.
- f_{etime} is a function from E to the nonnegative reals denoting the communication time of data from task X to task Y. We use $(X, Y).time$ to denote $f_{\text{etime}}((X, Y))$. This definition of communication time abstracts away details such as communication startup times, and the volume of data transmitted.
- f_{dist} is a function from E to the integers which gives the *dependence distance* of an edge. We use $(X, Y).dist$ to denote $f_{\text{dist}}((X, Y))$. If $(X, Y).dist = d$, then iteration $k + d$ of task Y is dependent on iteration k of task X. □

```
for i := 1 to n do
  A[i] := f1(A[i],D[i-2]);
  B[i] := f2(A[i],E[i-2]);
  C[i] := f3(A[i],E[i-2]);
  D[i] := f4(C[i],B[i-1]);
  E[i] := f5(E[i],B[i]);
endfor
```

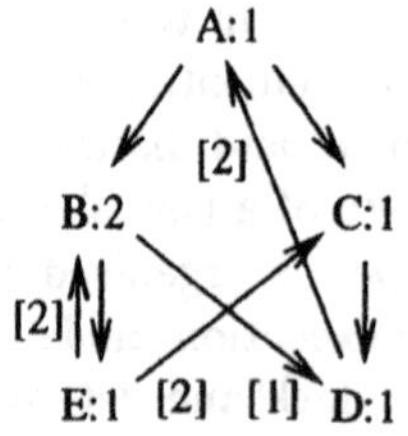

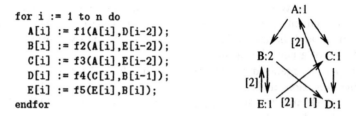

Fig. 1. An example loop and statement level DDG from [8]. Tasks are named for the array which is defined. Unbracketed numbers in the DDG are execution times, and bracketed numbers are dependence distances. Omitted values are assumed to be zero.

Figure 1 is an example loop from [8] with the corresponding statement level DDG. As notational conventions, we use uppercase letters for task names, unbracketed numbers for task and edge times, and bracketed numbers for dependence distances. For example, "A:1" denotes a task A with an execution time of 1 time unit. Communication times and dependence distances which are omitted are assumed to be zero. In Fig. 1, all communication times and four dependence distances are zero.

In Definition 1, we require task execution and data communication times to be fixed, invariant times, but we expect variances in component execution times to typically translate to similar magnitude variances in pipeline execution times [21]. Much of the literature on pipeline scheduling, particularly outside compiler research, uses the term "delay" as a synonym for what we refer to as dependence distance. Literature on systolic and semisystolic networks uses the term "register."

Our DDG definition is different from prior definitions in one significant respect: we allow dependence distances to be negative, as well as nonnegative. To get the usual definition, which is useful for presenting previous results, we can restrict dependence distances to be nonnegative. Dependence distances are discussed in more detail in Sect. 5.

Definition 2. A *nonnegative DDG* is a DDG in which all edges have nonnegative dependence distances. □

Asynchronous pipeline execution is a form of macro-dataflow execution [20]. Task execution is atomic. An instance of a task may not begin execution until all input data is available. Once a task instance begins execution, it executes without interruption to completion, and any output data becomes available for communication to other tasks only when execution of the task instance is complete. We assume that all iterations of a task execute on the same processor. An iteration of a task begins execution at the earliest time that two constraints are met:

1. *Processor availability* — Previously scheduled iterations of tasks assigned to the same processor, including previous iterations of the task itself, must be complete.

2. *Data availability* — Current iteration input data from DDG predecessors must be available, taking into account dependence distances and communication times.

When each task in a DDG is executed on its own distinct processor, this is often referred to as execution on an unbounded, or infinite number of processors. "Unbounded" or "infinite" in this case actually equates to v, the number of tasks in the DDG. Borrowing and expanding on terminology from [2], when a processor has multiple tasks assigned to it, we say it is a ***shared processor***, and any task assigned to a shared processor is a ***sharing task***. We will use the phrase "execution without processor sharing" to refer to the case where each task executes on a distinct processor.

When asynchronous pipeline execution of a DDG G does not deadlock, we use the notation $G.time_n$ to denote the execution time of n iterations of G. We can then define constants a and b such that $G.time_n \leq a + bn$ for all $n \geq 1$, and $G.time_n = a + bn$ for at least one value of n, as follows.

Definition 3. Let G be a DDG with finite pipeline execution times $G.time_n$ for all $n \geq 1$. Then the ***iteration interval*** b and ***startup time*** a for pipeline execution of G are

$$b = \lim_{n \to \infty} \frac{G.time_n}{n}$$

$$a = \max\{G.time_n - bn | n \geq 1\}$$

□

This definition of the iteration interval b, and a proof of the existence of the limit can be found in [18] (see also [19]). The iteration interval is the average time between completion of successive iterations of the DDG, and is the primary measure of the performance of a pipeline schedule. We will show how to find b for any pipeline schedule which does not deadlock.

Our definition of the startup time a, which is a secondary measure of the performance of a pipeline schedule, is based in part on results from [19]. In Sect. 7.3 we will show that the set in this definition is finite and therefore has a maximum, so a is well-defined. We will also show how to find a conservative approximation a^* of a such that $G.time_n \leq a^* + bn$ for all n, although $G.time_n$ may be strictly less than $a^* + bn$ for all n.

One additional quantity associated with a DDG G is $G.vmax$, the largest execution time of any task in G, defined as $G.vmax = \max_X\{X.time\}$.

3 Related Work

Previous work on determining pipeline execution times restricts the generality of the DDG which is analyzed, or assumes that tasks do not share processors. The algorithm in [6] assumes that the DDG is a *task graph*, which is a DDG in which all dependence distances are uniformly zero, and also assumes that processors are not shared. This algorithm, however, is unique in that it finds the exact execution time $G.time_n$ in $O(e+v)$ time for any value of n, rather than an approximation.

One important consideration in the analysis of pipeline execution of a DDG is the possibility of deadlock. The following constraint is the key to deadlock characterization. A cycle in a DDG is a closed path which starts and ends at the same task. A simple cycle is a cycle in which each task is the source of exactly one cycle edge (and the sink of exactly one cycle edge).

Definition 4. A DDG satisfies the *positive cycle constraint* if the sum of dependence distances in any simple cycle is positive. □

If a DDG is a nonnegative DDG, the only way that the positive cycle constraint may be violated is for a cycle to consist solely of edges with dependence distances of zero. Some authors implicitly assume the following theorem on deadlock; explicit discussion and a proof can be found in [4] (see also [13]).

Theorem 5. *Pipeline execution of a nonnegative DDG G with zero communication times and without processor sharing is free of deadlock iff G satisfies the positive cycle constraint.* □

This result can be recast as stating that under the given restrictions, if a nonnegative DDG satisfies the positive cycle constraint, then the pipeline execution time of $n \geq 1$ iterations of the DDG is finite. If the DDG violates the positive cycle constraint, then the pipeline execution time of n iterations ($n=1$ iteration in particular) of the DDG is infinite. We will generalize this result to remove the restrictions on G, and to allow processor sharing.

Beyond deadlock considerations, the primary result in determining the pipeline execution time of a DDG is Reiter's formula [19] for determining the iteration interval b of a nonnegative DDG, when all data communication times are zero, and processors are not shared. To motivate this formula, consider the DDG in Fig. 2, which is a simple cycle of tasks. Figure 2 also shows a Gantt chart for eight iterations of the DDG, where each task executes on its own unshared processor. As illustrated by the Gantt chart, the pattern is completion of 2 "steady-state" iterations every 5 time units, for an average of one completion every $5/2 = 2.5$ time units, i.e., the iteration interval of the DDG is $b = 2.5$. Since the interval between completion of successive iterations is nonuniform, this example also illustrates why it is not possible to simply define the iteration interval as the time between completion of successive iterations.

As suggested by this example, Reiter showed that for any cycle in a DDG, the iteration interval b could not be less than the sum of all computation in the cycle, divided by the sum of all dependence distances in the cycle. Therefore, the maximum such ratio over all cycles is a lower bound on b. Further, this lower bound can be achieved, except when $G.vmax$ (the largest task time in G) is greater than this bound. This result (Theorem 7 below) has been analyzed by a

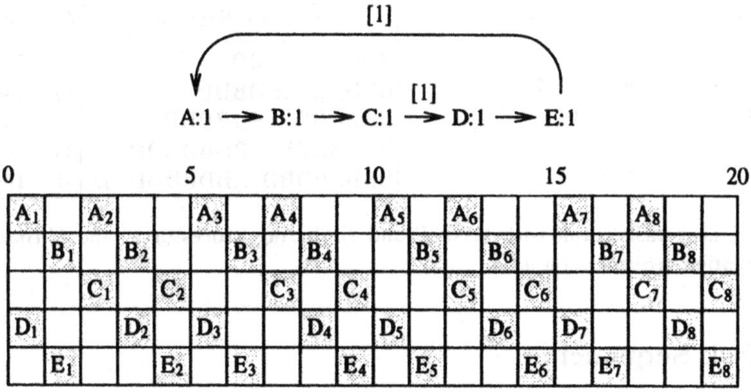

Fig. 2. A DDG which is a simple cycle, and a Gantt chart for eight iterations of the DDG. Each row represents execution of instances of a task on a processor dedicated to that task. The DDG has an iteration interval $b = 2.5$, and $G.time_n \leq 0.5 + 2.5n$.

number of authors in addition to Reiter, including [4, 10, 13, 18]. Our statement of the result borrows from the discussion in several of these papers.

In anticipation of our later generalization of Theorem 7, we state the theorem in terms of the following definition, which incorporates a communication term which in the immediate case is zero. This definition could be phrased in terms of arbitrary cycles rather than simple cycles, but this is unnecessary since indexing over simple cycles is equivalent to indexing over arbitrary cycles [13]. For any cycle c in a DDG, V_c is the set of tasks in c, and E_c is the set of edges in c.

Definition 6. Let G be a DDG satisfying the positive cycle constraint, and let C be the set of all simple cycles in G. If $C \neq \phi$, the *maximum cycle ratio* of G is

$$\max_{c \in C} \left\{ \frac{\sum_{X \in V_c} X.time + \sum_{(X,Y) \in E_c} (X,Y).time}{\sum_{(X,Y) \in E_c} (X,Y).dist} \right\}$$

If $C = \phi$, the maximum cycle ratio of G is 0. □

Theorem 7 [Reiter]. *Let G be a nonnegative DDG with zero communication times satisfying the positive cycle constraint. Then the iteration interval b for pipeline execution of G without processor sharing is the maximum of $G.vmax$ and the maximum cycle ratio of G.* □

As an example of the application of Theorem 7, the iteration interval for pipeline execution of the DDG in Fig. 1 is 1.5, which corresponds to the three cycles (A, B, E, C, D), (A, C, D), and (B, E).

$$A{:}10 \xrightarrow{1} B^{q}{:}1 \xrightarrow{4} C{:}10 \xrightarrow{4} D^{q}{:}9$$

Execution Sequence	$G.time_n$
BDBD...BDBD	$11 + 28n$
BBDBD...BDBDD	$25 + 14n$
BBBDBD...BDBDDD	$29 + 10n$
BBBBDBD...BDBDDDD	$38 + 10n$
BBBBBDBD...BDBDDDDD	$47 + 10n$

Fig. 3. Linear task graph with tasks B and D sharing processor q, and $G.time_n$ for five execution sequences on q.

4 Task Sequencing

Our primary goal is to generalize Theorems 5 and 7 to allow nonzero communication times and processor sharing. Accounting for nonzero communication times is straightforward. Theorems 5 and 7 are still true if the phrase "with zero communication times" is deleted. The basic idea of the proof of these generalizations is to insert new tasks on edges of a DDG which have nonzero communication times. Full proofs can be found in [7].

Accounting for the possibility that tasks may share processors is more difficult. We must first consider how a pipeline schedule may be specified when processors are shared. An asynchronous pipeline schedule for a DDG has two components. The first component is a ***processor assignment***: an assignment of tasks to processors. The second component is a ***task sequence***, which is an order on ***instances*** of tasks assigned to the same processor. The only fundamental restriction on a task sequence is that data dependence constraints must not be violated.

As a motivating example, consider the linear DDG in Fig. 3, which is to be pipelined on three processors. Tasks B and D share processor q, and tasks A and C execute on unshared processors. As notational conventions, processor assignments are indicated by lowercase superscripts, and tasks without explicit processor assignments are assumed to execute on distinct, unnamed processors (and recall that the unbracked edge weights are communication times; the omitted dependence distances are zero).

A solution to the task sequencing problem for processor q must specify an order for executing instances of tasks B and D. The only constraint is that for any iteration i, B_i, the ith instance of B, must execute before D_i, the ith instance of D. A sequence which satisfies this constraint is to alternate execution of the two tasks, to get the sequence $BDBD \ldots BDBD$. With this sequence, task instance B_2 must wait on completion of D_1, which in turn must wait on completion of C_1, so B_2 may only start after the sequence $B_1C_1D_1$ (including intervening communication times) completes. Similarly, B_3 must then wait for $B_2C_2D_2$, and so on, so the iteration interval is $1+4+10+4+9 = 28$ time units.

An alternative is to execute B_2 before executing D_1, to get the sequence $BBDBD \ldots BDBDD$, which results in an iteration interval of 14, which is a significant improvement over the previous sequence. B_3 may also be executed before D_1, to get the sequence $BBBDBD \ldots BDBDDD$. In this case, execution of task B will get far enough "ahead" of execution of task D, so that once processor q starts executing the first instance of D, it will never idle waiting for input from task C. The iteration interval in this case is 10, which is optimal for this example. The table in Fig. 3 gives $G.time_n$ values for five different execution sequences for tasks B and D of the example.

As mentioned, the only fundamental restriction on task sequences is that data dependence constraints must not be violated. However, it is useful to further restrict task sequences to those which are easily implemented at runtime, and are also easier to analyze. Informally, we want task sequences to exhibit regular "steady-state" behavior. Except for the initial and terminal phases of pipeline execution, each processor should execute instances of all tasks assigned to it in some invariant order.

We can specify such a *regular* task execution sequence by specifying the task sequence component of the pipeline schedule in terms of two subcomponents. The first subcomponent is a *task order* on tasks (rather than task instances) sharing the same processor. This task order is the steady-state execution order for task instances. The second task sequencing subcomponent is a mapping from tasks to integers called a *stage assignment*, which for a task X is denoted as $X.stage$. Stage assignments guide sequencing in the initial and terminal phases of pipeline execution. In the initial phase, some tasks may execute multiple times before other tasks begin execution, and in the terminal phase, some tasks may complete while other tasks still have multiple task instances to execute. For basic scheduling purposes, only sharing tasks require stage assignments. However, to simplify our exposition, we also require that nonsharing tasks have stage assignments. For any processor, the combined effect of specifying an order on tasks sharing the processor (a degenerate "order" on one task if the processor is not shared), plus a stage assignment for the tasks, is the specification of a task sequence. If for each processor q we define $q.min\_stage$ and $q.max\_stage$ to be the smallest and largest stage assignments of tasks sharing q, then the tasks on q may be executed in sequence (at runtime) by executing the generic control code in Fig. 4. The code in Fig. 4 assumes that loop iterations are indexed from 1 to n, but may be modified to permit arbitrary lower and upper loop bounds.

A convenient way to textually specify sequencing information is to list the tasks assigned to each processor in task order, with the associated stage assignments. To get the task sequence $BBBDBD \ldots BDBDDD$ on a processor q, we can use the *task sequence specification* $q : \langle D : 3, B : 0 \rangle$, which means that the order of tasks on processor q is $\langle D, B \rangle$, and the stage assignments are $D.stage = 3$ and $B.stage = 0$. For an unshared processor executing a task A, a sequence specification $\langle A : s \rangle$ may be used, where s is any integer value ($s = 0$ might be used in the absence of any other choice).

Task orders and stage assignments are not unique; different task sequence specifications may represent the same sequence. The specification $q : \langle B : 0, D : 2 \rangle$ also produces the sequence $BBBDBD \ldots BDBDDD$, which can be verified by stepping through the code in Fig. 4. In general, the first task in a task order

```
for i := q.min_stage + 1 to q.max_stage + n do
   for each task X on q in task order do
      j := i - X.stage
      if j ≥ 1 and j ≤ n then
         • receive/read X's jth iteration input (if any)
         • execute X_j
         • send/write X's jth iteration output (if any)
      endif
   endfor
endfor
```

Fig. 4. Pipeline control code for sequencing tasks for n iterations of a loop on a processor q, with iterations indexed from 1 to n.

may be shifted to the last position by subtracting one from its stage assignment, and the last task may be moved to the first position by adding one to its stage assignment, without changing the generated task sequence. These cyclic shifting operations change the position that a task is executed in the inner `for` loop relative to other tasks, but compensate by shifting the interval of outer loop iterations for which the task satisfies the `if` condition. As an extension of these shifting operations, uniformly adding or subtracting a constant value to or from the stage assignments of all tasks sharing a processor does not change the task sequence. This changes the range of values which the outer loop index i takes, but the sequence of values assigned to j in the inner loop will be unchanged. Task sequence specification is discussed in more detail in [7].

Pipeline scheduling algorithms from the literature specify schedules in terms specific to a particular algorithm. In our terminology, the pipeline scheduling algorithms in [2, 10] assign all tasks sharing the same processor to the same stage, which can therefore be assigned any arbitrary value (either zero or the "current" stage number are logical choices). The order in which tasks are assigned to a processor is the corresponding task order. The scheduling algorithm of [8] generates a noniterative task graph schedule "σ_a" which provides a processor assignment and a task order for each processor. Stage assignments are given by the "μ" function. The algorithm in [21] is a generalization of the algorithm in [8]. The processor assignment and task order for each processor are again provided by a task graph schedule, the schedule of the "kernel graph," while the ith task is assigned to stage "DIV(α_i, β_f)."

5 Negative Dependence Distances

Given a DDG and task sequence specifications for all processors, we would like to add edges to the DDG to ensure that tasks are sequenced in accordance with the sequence specifications. To do this, we need to consider negative dependence distances.

Figure 5a illustrates normal sequential execution on a single processor of $n = 5$ iterations of a DDG with two tasks A and B, with B dependent on A with a dependence distance of 2. Solid edges represent data dependences, and dashed edges represent sequential execution order. Time progresses from left to right in the figure. The processor executes a single loop which encompasses both A and B, alternating execution of instances of A and B. All tasks in one iteration are completed before any task in the next iteration is executed. Execution of a DDG with a nonnegative dependence distance d from a task A to a task B on a single processor can be interpreted as follows.

- The values produced by task A in the first $n-d$ iterations of the loop will be used d iterations later in the loop by task B. The values produced by task A in the last d iterations will not be used by task B.
- The values used by task B in the first d iterations of the loop are not defined in the loop. The values used by task B in the last $n-d$ iterations are defined d iterations earlier in the loop by task A.

The DDG in Fig. 5a can also be executed using pipeline parallelism by assigning each task to a different processor. Figure 5b illustrates execution of $n = 5$ iterations of the same DDG, where each task executes on its own processor. In this case, the loop is distributed into two distinct loops, one for each processor. When executing for n iterations on distinct processors, a nonnegative dependence distance of d from a task A to a task B can be interpreted as follows. For this example, we use "processor A" to denote the processor executing task A, and similarly for task B.

- The first $n-d$ values produced by task A must be communicated to processor B. The last d values produced by task A need not be communicated to processor B.
- The first d iterations of task B may execute independent of input from processor A. The last $n-d$ iterations of task B require input from processor A.

In Fig. 5c, if we attempt to execute a DDG with a negative dependence distance of -2 on one processor, with all tasks in one iteration executing before any task in the next iteration executes as in normal sequential loop execution, we find that this is impossible. An instance of a statement can not use a value which will be defined in a later iteration. However, in Fig. 5d which considers execution of the same DDG on two processors, execution is possible by virtue of the distribution of the single sequential loop into two loops which execute on different processors. In this case, executing n iterations of a DDG containing a dependence edge (A, B) with a negative dependence distance $-d$ ($d > 0$) can be interpreted as follows.

- The first d values produced by task A need not be communicated to processor B. The last $n-d$ values produced by task A must be communicated to processor B.

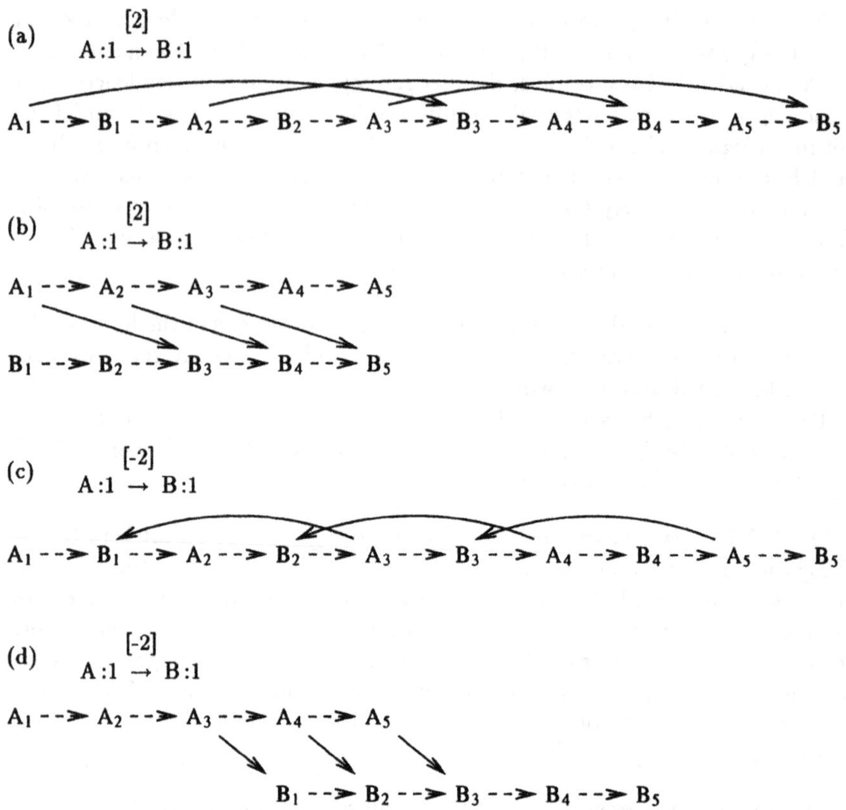

Fig. 5. Sequential and parallel execution of $n = 5$ iterations of simple DDG's with positive and negative dependence distances. Solid edges represent data communication edges, and dashed edges represent execution order on a processor. (a) Sequential execution of a DDG with a positive dependence distance. (b) Parallel execution of a DDG with a positive dependence distance. (c) Sequential execution of a DDG with a negative dependence distance; this execution will deadlock. (d) Parallel execution of a DDG with a negative dependence distance.

- The first $n - d$ iterations of task B require input from processor A. The last d iterations of task B may execute independent of input from processor A.

With parallel execution on two processors as in Fig. 5d, a dependence distance of -2 forces task A to finish three iterations before task B may execute its first iteration. Although it is impossible to execute instances of A and B in this sequence by executing a simple loop on a single processor, it is possible to execute this DDG on a single processor if we remove the requirement that all tasks in one iteration must execute before any task in the next iteration executes. This is exactly the behavior we want when sequencing multiple tasks on a processor as discussed in Sect. 4, and can be realized using the control code in Fig. 4. We will add edges with potentially negative dependence distances to a DDG, to enforce execution of a particular task sequence on a processor. Which edges to add, and the choice of dependence distances for these edges, is determined by the task sequence specification for a processor.

6 Pipeline Execution with Processor Sharing

We now have the necessary background to present our generalizations of the deadlock characterization and iteration interval determination results which account for processor sharing. The key idea is to add scheduling edges with potentially negative dependence distances to a DDG, to enforce execution of a particular task sequence. Scheduling edges allow the problem of analyzing pipeline execution of a graph when processors are shared to be reduced to a problem where processors are not shared. This is a generalization of the use of scheduling edges in noniterative task graph scheduling [22].

From Sect. 4, a regular asynchronous pipeline schedule for a DDG G has three components: a processor assignment, and for each processor, a task order and stage assignment. Information for sequencing $k \geq 1$ tasks on a processor q, in a form which can be implemented at runtime by executing the generic control code in Fig. 4, is specified as $q : \langle X_1 : s_1, X_2 : s_2, \ldots, X_k : s_k \rangle$. We use this sequence specification to add ***scheduling edges*** to G as follows. For each $i \in [1, k-1]$, create a scheduling edge (X_i, X_{i+1}), with $(X_i, X_{i+1}).dist = s_i - s_{i+1}$. Also create a scheduling edge (X_k, X_1), with $(X_k, X_1).dist = s_k - s_1 + 1$. All scheduling edges are given communication times of zero. The set of scheduling edges for a processor forms a simple cycle, called a ***scheduling cycle***. By construction, the sum of dependence distances in any scheduling cycle is 1. For nonsharing tasks, the scheduling cycle is a single scheduling edge from the task to itself, with a dependence distance of 1.

Definition 8. A *scheduled DDG* is a DDG in which each task is contained in exactly one scheduling cycle. □

Figure 6 shows a scheduled DDG for the "unscheduled" DDG from Fig. 1. "Original" DDG edges are shown as solid edges, and scheduling edges are shown as dashed edges.

To simplify our exposition, Definition 8 requires that nonsharing as well as sharing tasks be contained in scheduling cycles in a scheduled DDG. Theorem 10 below may be modified to remove this requirement, by explicitly accounting for $G.vmax$ as in Theorem 7 above. We also nominally assume that all scheduling edges are "new" edges added to an unscheduled DDG. It is also possible to allow original DDG edges to perform the role of scheduling edges (the scheduling edge (C, D) in Fig. 6 is redundant).

Execution of a scheduled DDG without processor sharing is very similar to execution of the corresponding unscheduled DDG with processor sharing. This idea is the basis of the following two theorems, which generalize Theorems 5 and 7, and are our primary results. When G is a scheduled DDG with p scheduling

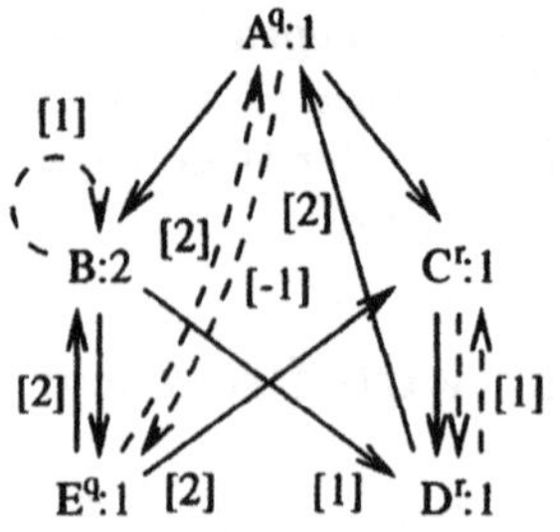

Fig. 6. The DDG from Fig. 1 scheduled for execution on three processors using the sequence specifications $q : \langle A:0, E:1\rangle$ and $r : \langle C:0, D:0\rangle$. Scheduling edges are shown as dashed edges.

cycles, the phrase "execution of G on p processors" implies the obvious processor assignment: all tasks in a scheduling cycle are assigned to the same processor, and tasks in different scheduling cycles are assigned to different processors. Further, this phrase implies that instances of tasks sharing the same processor are executed in a sequence which is compatible with the edges in the corresponding scheduling cycle. When all tasks in a scheduling cycle are executed on the same processor using the control code in Fig. 4, this task sequence is unique; there is a one-to-one correspondence between scheduling cycles and task sequences generated by the code in Fig. 4 (a proof of this can be found in [7]).

There is one subtle point regarding deadlock which deserves mention. Based on the discussion of dependence distances in Sect. 5, when the total number of iterations that a DDG is executed is not larger than the absolute value of a dependence distance, the dependence edge may be ignored. For example, if the DDG in Fig. 5a (or Fig. 5c) is executed for $n = 1$ or $n = 2$ iterations, then there is no dependence between tasks A and B in the loop. Therefore, a DDG which deadlocks when executed for a larger number of iterations may not necessarily deadlock when executed for a smaller number of iterations. Note that this was not an issue in Theorem 5, since execution of a nonnegative DDG will only deadlock if all dependence distances in some cycle are zero, and such a DDG will deadlock even for $n = 1$ iteration. Rather than explicitly accounting for this in Theorem 9, to simplify our exposition we simply assume that deadlock claims apply when the iteration count is "large enough," or equivalently, that a DDG may only be considered to be free of deadlock if it will not deadlock for *any* iteration count n.

Theorem 9. *Let G be a scheduled DDG with p scheduling cycles. Then pipeline execution of G on p processors is free of deadlock iff G satisfies the positive cycle constraint.*

Proof. See [7]. □

Theorem 9 may be used to determine if a given schedule for a DDG will deadlock. It may also be used to show that a scheduling algorithm always produces schedules which are free of deadlock.

Theorem 10. *Let G be a scheduled DDG with p scheduling cycles, satisfying the positive cycle constraint. Then the iteration interval b for pipeline execution of G on p processors is the maximum cycle ratio of G.*

Proof. See [7]. □

Note that because Theorem 10 assumes that every task in G is contained in a scheduling cycle (from Definition 8), and the sum of dependence distances in any scheduling cycle is one, the maximum cycle ratio of G is at least as large as $G.vmax$, so no explicit reference to $G.vmax$ is necessary. As an example of the application of Theorem 10, execution of the DDG in Fig. 6 on 3 processors has an iteration interval of 2 time units, from the cycles (A, E), (B), (C, D), (C, D), and (A, B, E). Theorem 10 may be applied to obtain exact iteration interval values for examples from the literature. For example, the iteration interval of the schedule in [21, Fig. 1d] is 80, rather than the reported conservative estimate of 90.

7 Iteration Interval Formula Evaluation

Theorem 10 states that the iteration interval of a scheduled DDG is equal to the maximum cycle ratio of the DDG. A natural question to ask is: If a DDG contains cycles, can the maximum cycle ratio be computed efficiently?

A straightforward approach, used in [10], is to enumerate all simple cycles, and explicitly calculate the value of the maximum cycle ratio. All $|C|$ simple cycles in a graph can be enumerated in $O(|C|(e+v))$ time [11], but there may be more than 2^v cycles in a DDG, so this technique is only feasible if it is known that the DDG has only a few cycles.

7.1 Binary Search Algorithm

Lawler [15, Sect. 3.13] describes a technique for computing the maximum cycle ratio of a DDG G by looking for positive cycles in a family of derivative graphs with edge weights. If the maximum cycle ratio of G is b, then the ratio for any cycle is no greater than b, and there must be some cycle for which the ratio equals b. Therefore, referring to Definition 6, for any cycle c,

$$\sum_{X \in V_c} X.time + \sum_{(X,Y) \in E_c} (X,Y).time - b \sum_{(X,Y) \in E_c} (X,Y).dist \leq 0$$

and this inequality must be an equality for at least one cycle. Let b^* be a candidate guess for the value of b, and for every edge (X, Y) define

$$(X,Y).weight_{b^*} = X.time + (X,Y).time - b^*(X,Y).dist$$

Let $G_{b^*} = (V, E, f_{\text{weight}_{b^*}})$ be the directed graph consisting of the tasks and edges in G with edge weights $(X,Y).weight_{b^*}$. If G_{b^*} does not contain any positive weight cycles, then $b^* \geq b$, and if G_{b^*} does contain one or more positive weight cycles, then $b^* < b$. In particular, b is the smallest b^* value such that G_{b^*} does not contain any positive weight cycles (this graph will contain at least one zero weight cycle).

Longest paths between vertices in a graph are not well-defined if the graph contains a positive weight cycle, so general single-source longest path algorithms such as the $O(ev)$ Bellman-Ford algorithm [5], detect the existence of positive cycles as a necessary precondition or side-effect of the search for longest paths. (Bellman-Ford and other longest path algorithms are usually referred to as shortest path algorithms, but are equally applicable as longest path algorithms.) Therefore, any given value of b^* can be compared to b by running a longest path algorithm on G_{b^*} and checking for positive cycles.

Two questions remain. The first question concerns the choice of candidate b^* values to use in the search for b. Lawler discusses both monotonic and binary searches for this purpose, but favors a binary search. If $G.vtime$ and $G.etime$ are the sum of all task and edge times in G, respectively, then a binary search can be performed on the interval $[0, G.vtime + G.etime]$. However, the lower interval bound can be increased to $G.pmax$, the largest sum of task times on any processor, and if a pipeline schedule is only considered if its execution time is no more than the sequential execution time of G, then $G.vtime$ can be used as an upper bound, resulting in a smaller search interval $[G.pmax, G.vtime]$.

The second question concerns search termination: How can it be determined that the current smallest b^* value such that G_{b^*} has no positive cycles is the actual value of b? One solution is to settle for a conservative approximation of b. In [8], the search is confined to integral values, and b is approximated as $\lceil b \rceil$. Using the Bellman-Ford algorithm as a subroutine, the resulting binary search algorithm runs in $O(ev \log G.vtime)$ time. This same general approach is also used in [21], but with the accuracy specified by a parameter ϵ, i.e., b is approximated as $\epsilon\lceil \frac{b}{\epsilon} \rceil$ (0.5 is used as an example value for ϵ). Additionally, since b is only approximated, an approximate longest path algorithm can be used, and the approximation of b can be found in $O(e\sqrt{v} \log^2 \frac{vG.vmax}{\epsilon})$ time.

7.2 Monotonic Search Algorithm

There are two drawbacks to the binary search algorithm. First, only a conservative approximation of b is found. Second, the best case execution time of the binary search is equivalent to the worst case time. If the first guess for b^* is correct, i.e. the first value of b^* is b (or its nearest approximation), it is still necessary to check other b^* values before concluding that the original guessed value was correct.

Both of these problems can be addressed by using a monotonic search with an initial guess $b^* = G.pmax$ (the lower bound of the search interval), with a simple technique for terminating the search or choosing the next value of b^* to check. If G_{b^*} has no positive cycles, then b is exactly b^*, and the search process terminates.

# Tasks/ DDG	# of b^* Trials			Exec. Time (secs)		
	Mean	Med	Max	Mean	Med	Max
4–10	1.2	1	4	.0001	.0001	.0012
11–50	2.4	2	7	.0038	.0022	.0444
51–100	3.1	3	8	.0271	.0210	.2898
101–200	3.3	3	9	.1314	.1014	.7065

Table 1. Monotonic search algorithm statistics. Each row summarizes algorithm execution for 2,916 random DDG's on a Sparc 10 workstation.

If G_{b^*} has one or more positive cycles, an augmented version of the Bellman-Ford algorithm can be used to find one. When longest paths are well-defined, the Bellman-Ford algorithm can explicitly enumerate the vertices in a longest path by constructing a *predecessor subgraph* [5]. The same technique can be used to explicitly identify a positive cycle, by following predecessor links until a cycle is found in $O(v)$ time. The ratio for this cycle can then be calculated in $O(v)$ time, and this value can be used as the next value of b^*. As a heuristic, we can start the search for a positive cycle at the task which has the largest "relaxation delta" [5] in the cycle checking pass. Additional discussion on implementation of this algorithm can be found in [7].

The primary question with this approach is: How many b^* trial values must be checked before b is found? To address this question, we implemented the monotonic search algorithm using the $O(ev)$ Bellman-Ford algorithm as the longest path subalgorithm. Statistics for finding the iteration intervals of 11,664 randomly generated DDG's are shown in Table 1. Each row of the table summarizes algorithm execution for a set of 2,916 random DDG's, grouped by the number of tasks in each DDG, as listed in the first column. DDG's in each group have a variety of task and edge times and dependence distances, as well as numbers of cycles. Each DDG is scheduled on some choice of from 2 to 20 processors using a simple pipeline scheduling algorithm which attempts to minimize $G.pmax$ (and hopefully b) by balancing the task load on each processor. The second set of columns lists the mean, median, and maximum number of b^* candidate trials required to determine b for DDG's in the group. The final set of columns gives the wall clock times for execution of the algorithm on a Sparc 10 workstation.

It is worth noting that if a pipeline schedule for a DDG is not known a priori to be free of deadlock, deadlock detection is easily incorporated in the monotonic search algorithm. When a graph G_{b^*} associated with a candidate b^* value is found to have a positive cycle, part of the calculation for determining the next candidate b^* value involves finding the sum of dependence distances in a cycle. If this sum is nonpositive, the pipeline schedule will deadlock. Similar detection of deadlock is often possible with other algorithms, avoiding the necessity of independently checking for deadlock. In the binary search algorithm, if a schedule deadlocks, the graph associated with the upper bound value of the binary search range will have a positive cycle.

In addition to the binary and monotonic search algorithms, there are other algorithms which may be used to calculate the maximum cycle ratio of a DDG as required by Theorems 7 and 10. Burns [3] and Hartmann and Orlin [9] describe competitive alternative algorithms, and also provide references for additional algorithms. Some algorithms require that the DDG be a nonnegative DDG. A technique for transforming a general DDG into a nonnegative DDG with an equivalent maximum cycle ratio in $O(ev)$ time is discussed in [7]. The choice of which algorithm to use depends on both the theoretical and practical characteristics of each algorithm, including computational complexity considerations and ease of implementation. Application specific considerations such as a requirement to find "earliest starting times" as discussed in the next section, may also influence algorithm choice.

7.3 Bounds on the Startup Time a

We conclude this section with a discussion of bounds on the startup time a, and with a justification of our definition of a in Definition 3. With the exception of [6], which restricts the form of a DDG and does not allow processor sharing, previous work has not addressed the issue of determining a value for a, in part because the iteration interval b was not known.

Let $G_b = (V, E, f_{\text{weight}_b})$ be the weighted graph defined in Sect. 7.1 using the actual iteration interval value b. For each task X, define $X.est$, the *earliest starting time* of X, to be the largest sum of edge weights in any path from any task to X in G_b, including the path from X to itself. By definition, the path from X to itself has weight zero, so $X.est$ is nonnegative. Since G_b has no positive cycles, this value is well-defined. This definition of the earliest starting time of a task in a DDG is a generalization of the same notion in noniterative task graphs. These values are automatically found for all tasks as a side-effect of using a longest path algorithm to determine b (or given b, may be found in $O(ev)$ time with a single longest path calculation). Reiter [19] showed that with reference to a global clock, the ith iteration of task X could legally start at time $X.est + b(i-1)$. With asynchronous execution, this value is an upper bound on when the ith iteration of X will begin execution. We can therefore set

$$a^* = \max_X\{X.est + X.time\} - b$$

and for any n, $G.time_n \leq a^* + bn$. Note that a^* (and a) may be negative. In Fig. 2, if we set $(E, A).time = 15$, $(E, A).dist = 2$, and $(C, D).dist = 0$, then $a^* = a = -5$, and $G.time_n \leq -5 + 10n$.

To measure how accurate this bound on a is, we simulated pipeline execution of the 11,664 random DDG's from Table 1 to get actual values of $G.time_n$ for $n \in [1900, 2000]$. For 45% of these DDG's, a^* was equal to a for this range, i.e., one or more actual $G.time_n$ values were equal to the computed bound $a^* + bn$. Of the remaining 55% of the DDG's, a^* overestimated a by an average of $2.9b$ time units, with a maximum difference of $142b$ time units. DDG's for which a^*

overestimated a by a larger multiple of b were all small granularity DDG's, with large communication to computation ratios, so that the time required to produce the first pipeline result was much larger than b. It might be possible to borrow techniques from [6] to get a more accurate value for a^*.

$a^* + bn$ is an upper bound on $G.time_n$, the execution time of n iterations of a DDG G. To justify the definition of a in Definition 3, we can derive a lower bound on $G.time_n$, which can be used to show that the actual value of a will be chosen from a finite number of potential choices. Let G be a DDG with maximum cycle ratio b. Let c be any cycle in G with cycle ratio $b = t/d$, where t is the sum of task execution and data communication times in c, and d is the sum of dependence distances in c. c must have at least one edge with a positive dependence distance, and may have one or more edges with negative dependence distances. If c does *not* have any edges with negative dependence distances, define D to be the largest positive dependence distance of any edge in c. If c *does* have edges with negative dependence distances, define D to be the largest positive dependence distance in c, plus the absolute value of the most negative dependence distance in c. D is an upper bound on the number of iterations of G in which edges of c with nonzero dependence distances may be ignored, as discussed in Sect. 6. For any iteration count n, cycle c will execute for at least $\lfloor (n - D)/d \rfloor$ complete traversals. The execution time of this many traversals of c is $\lfloor (n - D)/d \rfloor t \geq (n - D - d)t/d = -b(d + D) + bn$. We therefore have

$$-b(d + D) + bn \leq G.time_n \leq a^* + bn$$

so a is in the finite range $[-b(d + D), a^*]$. Since there are only a finite number of (nonnegative) task execution and data communication times in G, there are only a finite number of distinct sums of these component times which may be added to the lower bound $-b(d + D)$ without exceeding the upper bound a^*. The set used to define a in Definition 3 is therefore finite, which implies that it has a maximum, so a is well-defined.

8 Conclusion

Asynchronous pipelining is a form of pipeline parallelism which is particularly relevant in distributed memory environments, since it allows pipeline control to be distributed across processors using the generic control code in Fig. 4. We have generalized previous results on deadlock characterization and iteration interval determination for asynchronous pipeline schedules, to include nonzero communication times, and to allow multiple tasks to be assigned to the same processor. Theorem 9 (deadlock characterization) may be applied to show that a pipeline scheduling algorithm produces schedules which are free of deadlock. Theorem 10 (iteration interval determination) may be applied to precisely determine the iteration interval of schedules derived from existing scheduling algorithms [2, 10, 21]. We have also discussed specification of a pipeline schedule in terms of its components; execution of a schedule at runtime; algorithms for evaluating the iteration interval formula for a schedule; and bounds on the startup time of a pipeline. The monotonic search algorithm we described for deriving the iteration interval of a schedule is a middle ground between implementation simplicity and execution efficiency, while providing an exact solution of the formula. A more detailed treatment of these topics, including proofs of Theorems 9 and 10, and several additional results such as a technique for transforming an arbitrary DDG into a nonnegative DDG with the same maximum cycle ratio, and a technique for efficiently simulating execution of a pipeline schedule on a sequential processor, may be found in [7].

Several ideas that we discussed may be of interest in other contexts, such as the notion of negative dependence distances in a single unnested loop. The addition of scheduling edges to a DDG, and the definition of earliest starting times for tasks in a DDG in Sect. 7.3 are generalizations of the corresponding notions in noniterative task graph scheduling.

While the focus of the paper has been on determining the execution time of a pipeline schedule, we expect that a precise characterization of the factors which determine the execution time of a schedule will be useful in improving existing asynchronous pipeline scheduling algorithms, and may also suggest ideas for new scheduling algorithms.

Acknowledgments

This work was supported in part by an IBM Cooperative Fellowship. We would also like to thank Larry Carter, Rich Wolski, and other members of the Parallel Computation Lab at UCSD for their comments on earlier versions of this paper.

References

1. Alexander Aiken and Alexandru Nicolau. Optimal loop parallelization. *Proc. SIGPLAN '88 Conference on Programming Language Design and Implementation*, Atlanta, GA, June 1988, pp. 308–317.
2. Sati Banerjee, Takeo Hamada, Paul M. Chau, and Ronald D. Fellman. Macro pipelining based scheduling on high performance heterogeneous multiprocessor systems. *IEEE Transactions on Signal Processing* 43:8 (June 1995), pp. 1468–1484.
3. Steven M. Burns. *Performance analysis and optimization of asynchronous circuits.* Ph.D. Thesis, California Institute of Technology, Pasadena, California, 1991.
4. F. Commoner, A. W. Holt, S. Even, and A. Pnueli. Marked directed graphs. *Journal of Computer and System Sciences* 5:5 (October 1971), pp. 511–523.
5. Thomas H. Cormen, Charles E. Leiserson, and Ronald L. Rivest. *Introduction to Algorithms.* MIT Press, Cambridge, MA, 1990.
6. Val Donaldson and Jeanne Ferrante. Determining asynchronous acyclic pipeline execution times. *Proc. 10th International Parallel Processing Symposium*, Honolulu, HI, April 1996, pp. 568–572.
7. Val Donaldson and Jeanne Ferrante. *Determining asynchronous pipeline execution times.* Technical Report CS96-481, Computer Science and Engineering Dept., University of California, San Diego, La Jolla, CA, April 1996.

8. Franco Gasperoni and Uwe Schwiegelshohn. Scheduling loops on parallel processors: a simple algorithm with close to optimum performance. *Second Joint International Conference on Vector and Parallel Processing (Parallel Processing: CONPAR 92-VAPP V)*, Lyon, France, September 1992, pp. 625–636.
9. Mark Hartmann and James B. Orlin. Finding minimum cost to time ratio cycles with small integral transit times. *Networks* 23:6 (September 1993), pp. 567–74.
10. Phu D. Hoang and Jan M. Rabaey. Scheduling of DSP programs onto multiprocessors for maximum throughput. *IEEE Transactions on Signal Processing* 41:6 (June 1993), pp. 2225–2235.
11. Donald B. Johnson. Finding all the elementary circuits of a directed graph. *SIAM Journal on Computing* 4:1 (March 1975), pp. 77–84.
12. Peter M. Kogge. *The Architecture of Pipelined Computers*. Hemisphere Publishing, New York, 1981.
13. S. Y. Kung, P. S. Lewis, and S. C. Lo. Performance analysis and optimization of VLSI dataflow arrays. *Journal of Parallel and Distributed Computing* 4:6 (December 1987), pp. 592–618.
14. Monica Lam. Software pipelining: an effective scheduling technique for VLIW machines. *Proc. SIGPLAN '88 Conference on Programming Language Design and Implementation*, Atlanta, GA, June 1988, pp. 318–328.
15. Eugene L. Lawler. *Combinatorial Optimization: Networks and Matroids*. Holt, Rinehart, and Winston, New York, 1976.
16. F. Thomson Leighton. *Introduction to Parallel Algorithms and Architectures: Arrays, Trees, Hypercubes*. Morgan Kaufmann, San Mateo, CA, 1992.
17. David A. Padua and Michael J. Wolfe. Advanced compiler optimizations for supercomputers. *Communications of the ACM* 29:12 (December 1986), pp. 1184–1201.
18. C. V. Ramamoorthy and Gary S. Ho. Performance evaluation of asynchronous concurrent systems using Petri nets. *IEEE Transactions on Software Engineering* SE-6:5 (September 1980), pp. 440–449.
19. Raymond Reiter. Scheduling parallel computations. *Journal of the ACM* 15:4 (October 1968), pp. 590–599.
20. Vivek Sarkar. *Partitioning and Scheduling Parallel Programs for Multiprocessors*. MIT Press, Cambridge, MA, 1989.
21. Tao Yang, Cong Fu, Apostolos Gerasoulis, and Vivek Sarkar. Mapping iterative task graphs on distributed memory machines. *Proc. 24th International Conference on Parallel Processing*, Oconomowoc, WI, August 1995, Vol II, pp. 151–158.
22. Tao Yang and Apostolos Gerasoulis. DSC: scheduling parallel tasks on an unbounded number of processors. *IEEE Transactions on Parallel and Distributed Systems* 5:9 (September 1994), pp. 951–967.

Compiler Techniques for Concurrent Multithreading with Hardware Speculation Support *

Zhiyuan Li, Jenn-Yuan Tsai†, Xin Wang, Pen-Chung Yew, and Bess Zheng

Department of Computer Science
University of Minnesota
Minneapolis, MN 55455

†Department of Computer Science
University of Illinois
Urbana, IL 61801

Abstract. Recently proposed concurrent multithreading architectures employ sophisticated hardware to support speculation on control and data dependences as well as run-time data dependence check, which enables parallelization of program regions such as while-loops which previously were ignored. The new architectures demand compilers to put more emphasis on the formation and selection of parallel threads. Compilers also play an important role in reducing the cost of run-time data dependence check. This paper discusses these new issues.

1 Introduction

Increasing density of VISI microprocessors not only continues to shorten the circuit latency but also provides more transistors on a single chip. Each new generation of microprocessors introduces more sophisticated mechanisms to support instruction-level parallelism. Future microprocessors will soon be able to issue and execute more than a dozen instructions per machine cycle. How to extract sufficient independent instructions per machine cycle from an ordinary program has become an increasingly difficult challenge. The currently predominant superscalar architectures adopt a single thread of control flow. Parallelism can be extracted only from within a relatively narrow window of consecutive instructions. Although independent instructions can be statically reordered and packed into a window, such code motion is constrained by programs' control structures. Growing evidences suggest that future processors need to take advantage of multiple threads of execution in order to find sufficient parallel operations [11]. Allowing multiple threads of execution is similar to, but not exactly like, placing multiprocessors on a single chip or on a multichip-module (MCM) [10].

* This work was supported in part by NSF CAREER Award CCR-9502541, NSF Grant MIP 9496320, a gift from Intel Corporation, and by the U.S. Army Intelligence Center and Fort Huachuca under Contract DABT63-95-C-0127 and ARPA order no. D 346. The views and conclusions contained herein are those of the authors and should not be interpreted as necessarily representing the official policies or endorsements, either expressed or implied, of the U. S. Army Intelligence Center and Fort Huachuca, or the U.S. Government.

This approach avoids some difficulties in traditional multiprocessor, such as high overhead in scheduling and synchronization.

Much of the responsibility of forming and scheduling parallel threads to execute on multiprocessors traditionally rests on compilers. There are several aspects to this responsibility:

- identifying independent operations;
- selecting and scheduling threads whose parallel execution could result in the shortest possible execution time; and
- inserting synchronization instructions to observe the dependences, if any, among parallel threads.

For traditional multiprocessors, control dependences greatly limit the compiler's ability to create parallel threads. For example, a compiler normally does not know how many iterations of a while-loop will be executed at run time and hence it cannot safely generate multiple threads to execute different loop iterations simultaneously. Recently, several hardware mechanisms have been proposed to allow speculative execution of multiple threads [3, 11, 2, 12]. A thread, whose execution may depend on run-time conditions, is allowed to execute before those conditions are resolved. Once those conditions are resolved, a correctly speculated thread can then write its results to the memory. On the other hand, an incorrectly speculated thread is squashed. Such *concurrent multithreading* architectures may also provide hardware for run-time data dependence check [11, 12]. These new hardware features create new parallelization opportunities to the compiler, which may result in a myriad of potential parallel threads. The selection and scheduling of parallel threads is expected to have a great impact on the program's performance.

In this paper, we discuss several issues regarding compiler optimizations for concurrent multithreading architectures with hardware support for speculative execution and for run-time data dependence check. We use two particular designs, namely *multiscalar*[11] and *superthreaded processors*[12], as examples to show the implications of such hardware on compiler techniques. In the next section, we describe these two microarchitectures and their execution models. In Section 3, we examine how data dependence analysis can be applied to while-loops and how the removal of loop-carried data dependences can improve the effectiveness of speculative execution of while-loops. In Section 4, we discuss how static data dependence analysis can reduce the need for synchronization and the frequency of incorrect speculation. In Section 5, we explore the issue of parallel threads selection. In Section 6, we describe our current experimentation effort. We summarize our discussion in Section 7.

2 Speculative Concurrent Multithreaded Architectures

2.1 Multiscalar architecture

The multiscalar paradigm [3, 11] exploits thread-level parallelism with aggressive hardware support for both control and data speculation. The compiler for the multiscalar processor must partition the control flow graph of a program into threads, each to be executed by a processing unit at run-time. The control and data flow information between threads is stored in *thread descriptors*. With the help of the thread descriptors, the hardware of the multiscalar processor can rapidly traverse the control flow graph of a program and assign threads to processing units on the fly.

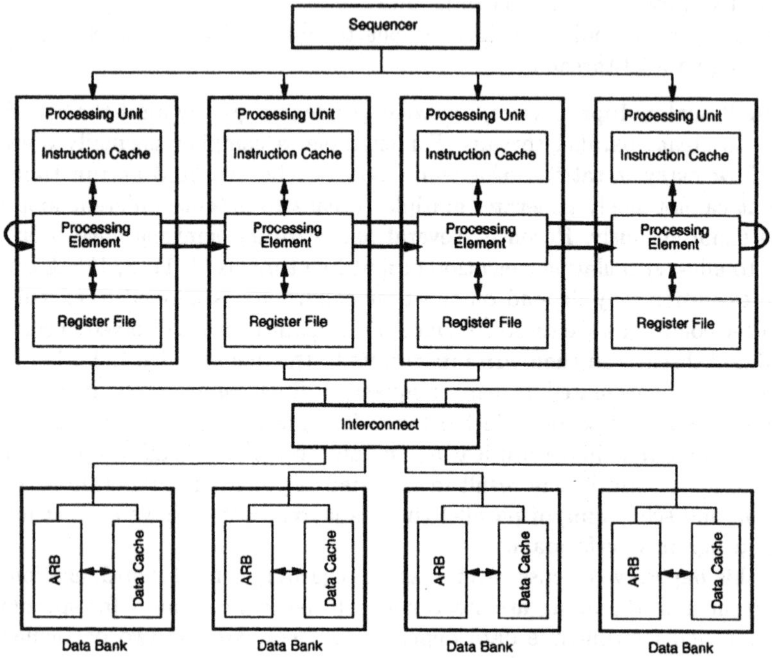

Fig. 1. The microarchitecture of the multiscalar processor [8]

Figure 1 shows the general microarchitecture of a multiscalar processor. The processor consists of multiple processing units, which are connected to each other with a unidirectional ring. Each processing unit has its own register file and functional units. A processing unit can pass register data to its down-stream processing units via the unidirectional ring connection. The sequencer reads information from the thread descriptors and assigns the threads to the processing units in the sequential order of the original program.

To exploit more potential parallelism between the threads, the multiscalar processor allows multiple threads to be executed in parallel with speculation on both control dependences and data dependences. For control speculation, the sequencer predicts which thread should be executed next according to the control flow and assigns that thread to the next processing unit down-stream. If the control speculation later turns out to be incorrect, the processor will squash the speculative thread and its following threads, and resume the correct thread sequence. For data speculation, a thread can load data from a memory location with the expectation that the concurrent predecessor threads will not store a value to the same memory location later. However, if any predecessor thread executes a store operation to the memory location, i.e., if a data dependence is violated, the later thread must be squashed and re-started from the beginning of the thread.

The multiscalar processor uses an *Address Resolution Buffer* (or ARB) to hold the results of the speculative memory operations by the currently active threads and to detect violations of data dependences. The store data held in the ARB can be written back to the data cache only when the thread that executes the store operation becomes a non-speculative thread. The ARB also keeps track of all load and store operations performed by each active thread. A data dependence violation is detected if a thread writes to a memory location whose corresponding ARB entry records an earlier load operation by a successor thread.

2.2 Superthreaded architecture

The superthreaded processor [12] is similar to the multiscalar processor, but it does not speculate on data dependences. Instead, the superthreaded processor performs run-time data dependence checking for load operations. If a load operation is detected to be flow dependent on a store operation by a predecessor thread, it waits for the stored data from the predecessor thread. Checking and enforcing data dependences at run-time can avoid squashing caused by data dependence violations as in the multiscalar, and it can reduce the hardware complexity of detecting memory dependence violation.

Figure 2 shows the microarchitecture of a superthreaded processor. Like a multiscalar processor, the multiple processing units are connected with a unidirectional ring. Each processing unit can forward the addresses and the data of its store operations to the down-stream units via the unidirectional ring connection. Each processing unit has its own memory buffer to keep the addresses and the data of its own store operations as well as those sent by the up-stream units.

The superthreaded processor uses a thread pipelining execution model to initiate new threads and to enforce data dependences between concurrent threads. As shown in Figure 3, the execution of a thread is partitioned into *continuation stage*, *target-store-address-generation (TSAG) stage*, *computation stage*, and *write-back stage*. The continuation stage is responsible for computing recurrence variables, such as loop index variables, and forking the next thread. A thread can fork a successor thread with speculation on the control flow. The TSAG stage computes the addresses of store operations upon which the successor threads could be data dependent. Those addresses are called *target store addresses* and are forwarded to the memory buffers of the successor threads for run-time dependence checking. To guarantee the correctness of run-time dependence checking, a thread cannot perform any load operation that may be

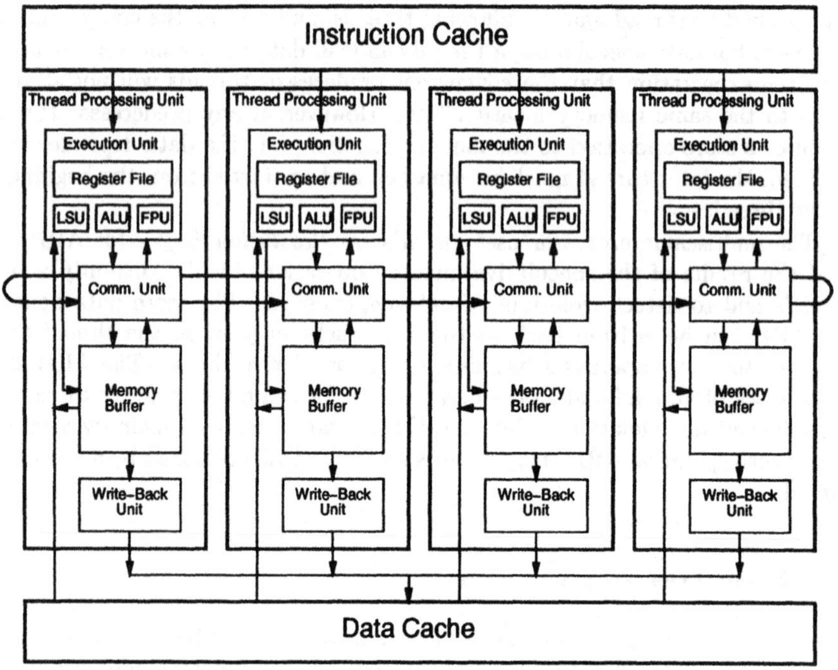

Fig. 2. The microarchitecture of the superthreaded processor

dependent on its predecessor threads until the predecessor threads complete the TSAG stage.

The computation stage performs the remaining computation of the thread. When a thread executes a load operation whose address matches that of a target store entry in the memory buffer, the thread either reads the data from that entry if it is available or waits until the data is received by the thread's processing unit. The write-back stage is performed by the write-back unit automatically after a thread completes its execution. All the data written by the thread to the buffer are to be written back to the data cache at this stage. The write-back stages of contiguous threads are performed in the program sequential order to preserve the non-speculative memory state and to honor the output and anti-dependences between the threads.

3 Analyzing and Removing Loop-Carried Data Dependences in While-Loops

Multiscalar and superthreaded architectures automatically squash an incorrectly speculated thread. As a result, the compiler can focus on loop-carried data dependences when analyzing the parallelism, leaving the loop-carried control dependence to the speculation hardware. Loop-carried data dependences penalize

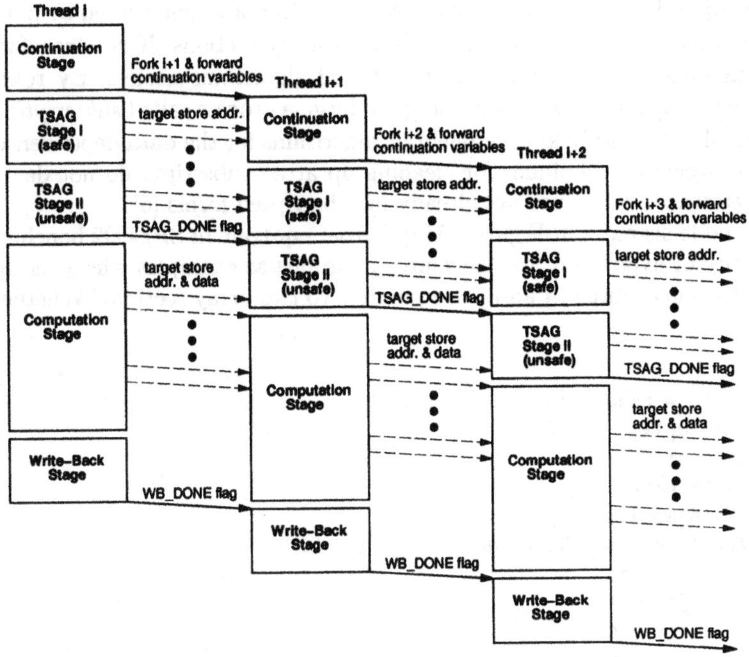

Fig. 3. The pipelined execution of the superthreaded architecture

the speculative execution of while-loops mainly in two ways. The true dependences, i.e., flow dependences between loop iterations, reduce the degree of overlap between parallel threads. No hardware mechanisms alone can eliminate such a performance bottleneck. The output and anti-dependences also penalize the performance of such architectures, because the multiple copies of the same variable at different processing units must be written back to the data cache in the sequential order, which is a potential performance bottleneck.

In this section, we first present a technique for pointer arithmetics removal which enables data dependence analysis on variables referenced through pointer arithmetics. At the same time, this technique also removes loop-carried data dependences due to such pointer arithmetics. We then discuss the removal of output and anti-dependences via variable privatization, an issue not examined previously in the context of while-loops. In this paper, a while-loop refers to any loop whose iteration count is not determined before the loop exit condition is tested true.

3.1 Pointered arrays subscriptization

A central issue in identifying parallel threads is the analysis of loop-carried data dependences. Traditional data dependence analysis assumes that arrays are indexed by subscripts. In C programs, most often array references are not indexed by well-formed linear subscripts, but rather are represented by pointers. Pointer arithmetic is used to index through array sections. If not transformed, such references would render the traditional algorithms useless. By rewriting pointered array references in a subscripted form, a process called ***subscriptization***, the compiler can apply known algebraic algorithms for the data dependence test [1]. The previous techniques for cleaning up array subscripts do not deal with array references which are *not* already in subscripted forms [5].

The code segment in Figure 3.1(a) is from `eqntott` in SPEC92 benchmarks. For clarity of exposition, we use source programs as examples whenever appropriate. In this example, i and j are pointers to two array sections. Whether the

```
for (j = lo = base; (lo += qsz) < hi;)
   if ((*qcmp)(j, lo) > 0)
      j = lo;
   if (j != base)
   {   /* swap j into place */
      for (i = base, hi = base + qsz; i < hi;)
      {    c = *j;
          *j++ = *i;
          *i++ = c;
      }
   }
```

(a)

```
for (arr_j = lo = base; (lo += qsz) < hi;)
   if ((*qcmp)(arr_j, lo) > 0)
     arr_j = lo;
  if (arr_j != base)
  {  for (inew = 0; inew < qsz; inew++)
     {  c = arr_j[inew];
        arr_j[inew] = arr_i[inew];
        arr_i[inew] = c;
     }
  }
```

(b)

Fig. 4. Transforming a code segment from `eqntott`.

same array elements are modified and used in different loop iterations determines whether parallel threads should be created to execute different iterations. For this case, we first perform symbolic and predicate analysis to determine that, within the second for-loop, the two array sections addressed by i and j are separate, because their beginning positions are apart by at least the value of qsz. We then create two new array names, arr_i and arr_j, to represent these two sections. In order to apply traditional data dependence test algorithms, we transform the code segment as shown in Figure 3.1(b). Note that, if the compiler cannot determine whether array sections addressed by different pointers overlap, the above transformation is still valid. However, arr_i and arr_j will be potential aliases in this case. Since we have determined that arr_i and arr_j are separate, we can safely apply traditional data dependence test algorithms to these two arrays separately, which show that the array references do not cause loop-carried data dependences.

Pointer arithmetics removal also serves as one way, among others, to eliminate artificial loop-carried flow dependences caused by updates to pointer values. Such pointer updates may severely decrease the parallel overlap between successive loop iterations. In the example given above, the increments of i and j create loop-carried flow dependences which reduce the parallel overlap of successive iterations. The increment of i in particular nearly sequentializes the loop because the i value is used for comparison with hi in every iteration. After we transform the array references to subscripted forms, the updates to i and j are removed. The values of i and j are dead after the second for-loop. So, their last values need not be saved. After c is privatized (*c.f. next subsection*), $inew++$ becomes the only sequential portion of the second for-loop.

Both multiscalar and superthreaded processors provide run-time data dependence check to guarantee safe computation. Moreover, their synchronization hardware allows parallel threads to have loop-carried data dependences. The degree of parallelism is the main concern. Hence, even if certain loop-carried data dependences due to *array* references do exist, pointer arithmetics removal may still contribute to the elimination of sequential bottlenecks.

Our general strategy for the elimination of pointer arithmetics is as follows:

1. Identify pointers whose values are incremented or decremented in the loop body.
2. Analyze the address range of these pointers for their degree of overlap, which affects the profitability of the transformation.
3. Designate a primary induction variable, say i, whose initial value is 0.
4. Apply induction variable recognition algorithms to the pointers identified above to see whether they are induction variables whose values can be written in closed forms in terms of i.
5. If the last step succeeds and the transformation is estimated as profitable, a new array name is created for each pointer variable identified above. Each pointer dereference in the loop body is replaced by array references indexed by the closed forms computed above.
6. Insert code after the loop to save last values of pointers if they are live.

3.2 Variable privatization

If a variable's updated value in one iteration of the while-loop can never reach a later iteration, then a distinct copy of the variable can be created for each processing unit, either by register allocation or by renaming. Loop-carried output and anti-dependences can thus be eliminated. Both multiscalar and superthreaded hardware dynamically rename variables in their buffers, i.e., the

memory buffer in the superthreaded processor and the ***address resolution buffer (ARB)*** in the multiscalar. Hence, unlike traditional multiprocessors, loop-carried output and anti-dependences do not require explicit synchronization on superthreaded and multiscalar architectures.

Nonetheless, variable privatization by compilers is still desirable for both architectures. When a compiler privatizes a variable, it can be stored in a register instead of in the ARB or the memory buffer with a much faster access time. In order to simplify the hardware for run-time dependence check, the buffer sizes should be kept small. However, too small a buffer size will incur too frequent buffer overflows. When a buffer overflow occurs, the thread must be stalled until all early threads are completed because the run-time dependence check will no longer function properly. Therefore, the less demand on memory buffer or ARB, the less frequently the buffer will overflow. Moreover, any data that are updated in the buffer must eventually be written back to the memory. This write-back by different threads is sequentialized to guarantee program correctness. In order to reduce the write-back overhead, we also need to keep the size of the memory buffer and the ARB small. By allocating the private variables to registers, the buffer size can be reduced.

The following code segment is from program `eqntott` in SPEC92.

```
int cmppt (a, b)
PTERM *a[], *b[];
     register int i, aa, bb;

     for (i = 0; i < ninputs; i++) {
       aa = a[0]->ptand[i];
       bb = b[0]->ptand[i];
          if (aa == 2)
            aa = 0;
          if (bb == 2)
            bb = 0;
          if (aa != bb) {
             if (aa < bb) {
               return (-1);
             }
             else {
               return (1);
             }
          }
     }
     return (0);
}
```

The above for-loop contains premature exits, which is considered as a while-loop in this paper. By speculating on `aa != bb` being false, both the superthreaded processor and the multiscalar can create parallel threads to execute the loop iterations. The variables *aa* and *bb* are privatizable and, hence, they can be allocated to registers on different processing units.

If the compiler allocates a privatized variable to a register, it must examine whether the variable is live after the termination of the while-loop. If so, then the last value must be written back to the memory location. If the variable is unconditionally updated in every iteration, then the last thread, which aborts all successive speculated threads, is responsible for the store. The store instruction can be inserted in the beginning of the branch which is executed when the exit condition is tested true.

If the variable is conditionally updated in each iteration, then it is better not to privatize the variable. The following code segment from program compress in SPEC95 shows such an example. Variable p is not suitable for privatization, although it is only involved in output dependences.

```
char * rindex(s, c)
register char *s, c;
{
char *p;
for (p = NULL; *s; s++)
    if (*s == c)
                p = s;
return(p);
}
```

4 Reducing Synchronization and Misspeculation Penalties

In the superthreaded processor, data synchronization is done by forwarding *target store* addresses to succeeding threads in the *target-store-address-generation* stage. If a succeeding thread issues a read reference whose address matches a forwarded target store address, then the thread must wait until data is forwarded or until the preceding thread is completed. If the preceding thread updates the data more than once, only the last updated value needs to be forwarded. Here we see two potential sources of performance penalties due to synchronization. One is the cost of forwarding target store addresses and the other is the data waiting time. However, if the succeeding threads do not have matches of the target store addresses at run-time, then no data waiting penalty will occur.

On the multiscalar, data synchronization for flow dependences between threads can be done in two forms, either by waiting at ARB or by register forwarding. There are no synchronization instructions to force a thread to wait. Instead, the ARB hardware can speculate, based on memory reference history, that a flow dependence may occur at a particular memory address [9]. The hardware then forces the thread which may be the sink of the dependence to wait for a flag associated with that memory address. As soon as a preceding thread stores data to that address, the flag is raised, which permits the waiting thread to proceed.

Note that if a preceding thread must store the data several times to the memory address, the flag may be raised before the last store is completed. The ARB will detect the violation of flow dependence and the processing unit will squash the thread which is the sink of the dependence. Also note that if the ARB speculates a synchronization incorrectly, the waiting thread will wait until its preceding thread finishes execution and is released. Both incorrect speculations and premature flag-raising can potentially be costly.

Synchronization can also be done via register forwarding. On the multiscalar, each processing unit has its own register file. Each register's content is forwarded from one processing unit to the next, using the same register number. Each register has a bit which is automatically set and tested by the hardware to indicate the availability of the forwarded value. These bits are transparent to the software. The registers of a processing unit can be dynamically configured at the thread creation time, with *creation masks*, as *filtered* and *nonfiltered* registers. A filtered register is forwarded when the register is written within the current thread. A nonfiltered register is forwarded without being modified. The compiler can use the register files to satisfy a loop-carried flow dependence as follows. The thread which writes a variable which is to be read by a later thread writes the value to a filtered register, say $r4$. The thread that uses that value then reads $r4$ instead of reading from the ARB. If the threads which execute the source and the sink are not immediately adjacent to each other, those threads in between should mark $r4$ as nonfiltered. Using this form of synchronization, the compiler must precisely analyze the loop-carried flow dependence, and the dependence distance must be calculated. Also, if the variable causing the dependence can potentially be updated several times before it is read by the dependence sink, then the register should not be forwarded before the last update is done.

The problem of identifying last writes for the purpose of synchronization has previously been discussed [8, 6]. Analysis of last writes has also been proposed to support array privatization and other optimizations [7] When it is not clear which writes are last writes, the compiler needs to find a program point that ***post-dominates*** all potential last writes in order to safely forward the data. The following code segment serves as an example.

```
for (i = 0; i++) {
     if (!c1]) break;
     ...
     c1 = ...
     ...
     if (c2) c1 = ...
     /* place to forward c1 */
     ...
}
```

For the superthreaded processor, the general compiler strategy for data forwarding is as follows:

1. Identify stores that are potential sources of loop-carried flow dependences between threads. Mark them as target stores.
2. Group those stores which access the same location.
3. For each group, identify the program point for forwarding the data.
4. Insert code in the target-store-address-generation stage to forward target store addresses.
5. Insert code to forward target store data at the selected program points.

In the example above, there are two target stores to cl. The address of cl is a target store address that should be forwarded in the target-store-address-generation stage. The data of cl is forwarded at the marked program point.

For the multiscalar, the general compiler strategy for data forwarding is as follows:

1. Identify stores that are potential sources of loop-carried flow dependences between threads.
2. Group those stores which access the same location.
3. For each group, allocate a register and mark it as filtered.
4. For that group, identify and mark the program point for forwarding the data.
5. Insert code to write the data to the filtered register at the marked forwarding program point.
6. Insert code to read the forwarded register value.

In the example above, at the marked forwarding point, an instruction should be inserted to write cl to a filtered register, say $r4$. The read of cl in the if-statement is then replaced by a read from $r4$.

5 Partitioning Parallel Threads

By combining multiple processing units with hardware speculation, concurrent multithreading architectures provide many opportunities for parallel execution which are unavailable to superscalar processors and traditional multiprocessors. Particularly important is their highly efficient thread creation. Starting a new thread can take as few as a couple of instructions, which makes it profitable to execute fine-grain threads. The low thread start-up overhead also makes loop-carried data dependences more tolerable. Loops with a modest amount of overlap among the iterations may still be speeded up by having the iterations executed in parallel. Still, in order to maximize the performance, it is important that processing units spend less time on synchronization. Moreover, it is essential that the idle time of the processing units is minimized. A processing unit becomes idle if its current thread is forced to wait for the completion of the previous thread. Such waiting may be either due to a buffer overflow, the presence of flow dependences between threads, or load unbalancing between threads. On the multiscalar, when the hardware detects that two threads violate data dependences, the succeeding thread must be squashed, which increases the unit's idle time.

Clearly, the partitioning and scheduling of parallel threads will have an impact on both the synchronization overhead and the idle time of processing units.

In order to explore this issue further, we review the thread creation models of the multiscalar and superthreaded processors.

On the superthreaded processor, each thread is created by an explicit *fork* *<address>* instruction. Correspondingly, an explicit *abort* instruction squashes all future threads. This instruction is inserted by the compiler at the program points where branching decisions are made and an incorrect speculation can be detected. On the multiscalar, a *task tag* is inserted at the program point where a thread may begin its execution. A task tag contains several control targets which the current program point may potentially lead to. At run time, the sequencer, using a prediction table, picks one of the targets at which it starts a new thread. Figure 5 shows an example, in which thread 1 and thread 2 will run in parallel, but which branch becomes thread 2 is determined by hardware using execution history as a guide. Thread squashing is also done by the sequencer when it finds a branch prediction is incorrect. In Figure 5, suppose target *t1* was speculated but *t2* is actually the branch target, then the sequencer automatically squashes thread 2 starting at *t1*.

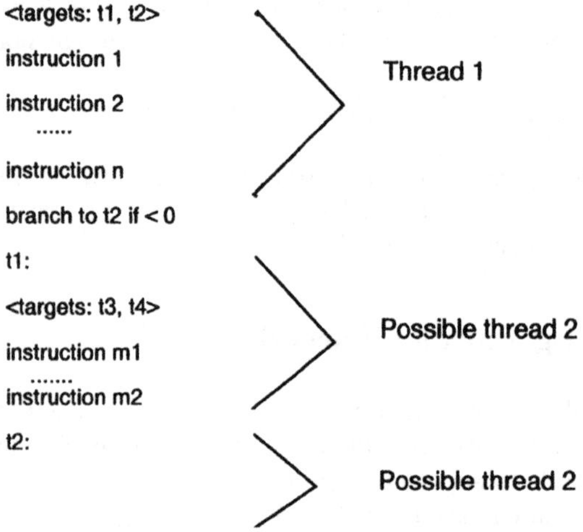

Fig. 5. Multiple potential thread targets on the multiscalar processor

From the above, it is clear that for the superthreaded processor, the compiler is responsible for both thread partitioning and thread speculation, while for the multiscalar, the compiler is responsible only for thread partitioning. Insertion of target tags is straightforward once the thread boundaries are identified.

On both multiscalar and superthreaded processor, each thread can fork only one successor thread during its lifetime. This restriction, a clear distinction from traditional multiprocessing models, is imposed so that the speculation hardware can be implemented efficiently. Due to the speculation support, virtually any kinds of program segments can be executed as individual threads, subject to the *single successor rule* mentioned above. The followings are several common examples:

- parallel sections;
- loop iterations, including while-loops; and
- function calls.

In the above, parallel sections can take a variety of forms. A section can be as small as a basic block, or as large as a function call or a whole loop. A section can also be one branch of a conditional statement.

The single successor rule, however, has a few important implications:

- A thread cannot simultaneously speculate both branches of a branch instruction.
- For a nested loop, once an outer loop iteration forks a new thread from the outer loop, it will not fork new threads to execute inner loop iterations.
- For a loop which contains function calls, once a loop iteration forks a new thread to execute the next iteration, it cannot fork a new thread to execute any section of the loop body, e.g. a function call.
- If threads are forked to execute function calls, then these threads cannot fork new threads to execute loops which may be recognized as parallel.

These restrictions are imposed as a tradeoff for efficient thread start-up and speculation. Due to these restrictions, how threads are partitioned may have a significant impact on a program's performance. For example, if the compiler knows that the inner loop has more parallelism than the outer loop, then threads should be created for the inner loop instead of the outer loop, and vice versa. Thread partitioning is perhaps the most complex issue in compilation for the multiscalar and superthreaded processors as in multiprocessors. Currently we are pursuing the following studies:

- Estimating the working set size of a thread to allow the working set to fit in the memory buffer or the ARB;
- Estimating the amount of parallelism based on the data dependence graph;
- Constructing a hierarchical task graph [4] which reflects speculation possibilities;
- Affirming the existence of data dependences in addition to affirming data independences, which is important for parallelism estimate and for avoiding excessive incorrect data speculation on the multiscalar.
- Interprocedural analysis to support the above studies.

6 An Integrated Compiler for Experimentation

Since concurrent multithreaded processors, such as the multiscalar and the superthreaded processors, are basically microprocessors which allow a large number of instructions issued per machine cycle, it is important to compare their performance against superscalars and VLIW architectures. Interestingly, the multiscalar and superthreaded architectures also have a strong resemblance to a small-scale, tightly-coupled multiprocessor with additional support for thread-level speculation. Hence, many traditional compilation techniques for both superscalars, VLIW and multiprocessors could be used for such architectures as well.

In general, traditional compilation techniques for superscalars and VLIW focus primarily on exploiting instruction-level parallelism in the back end compilers. On the other hand, traditional compilation techniques for multiprocessors focus primarily on exploiting loop-iteration level parallelism in the front end parallelizing compilers. To allow both loop-iteration level and instruction-level parallelism to be exploited on concurrent multithreaded architectures, we need an integrated compiler that has at least the capability of both the front end parallelizing compilers and the back end compilers that deal with the instruction-level parallelism.

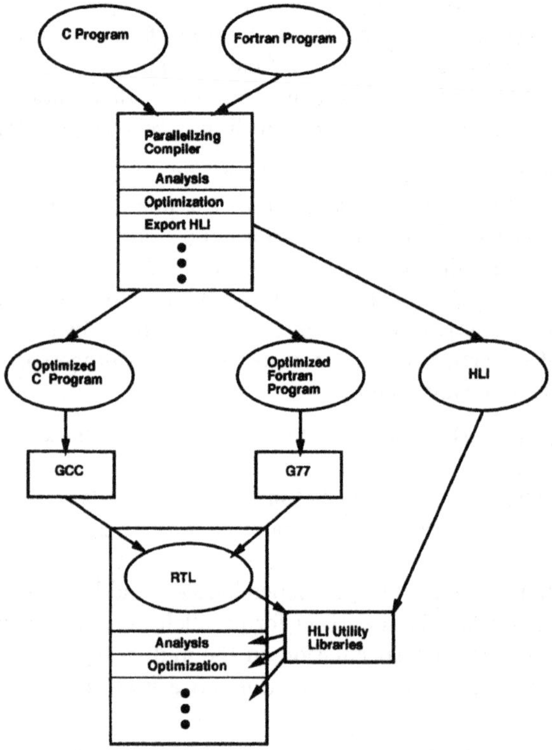

Fig. 6. The Agassiz compiler system

Because it is a major effort, and also very time consuming, to develop such an integrated compiler from scratch that can match today's state-of-the-art parallelizing compilers and back end compilers, we instead leverage existing compilers for our purpose. The Agassiz compiler project is an effort to integrate state-of-the-art parallelizing compilers to back end compilers. A data structure that can store high-level information (HLI) is developed which allows the results of elaborate program analysis in the front end parallelizing compiler to be exported and used in the back end compiler to exploit instruction-level parallelism and machine-specific optimizations.

The current Agassiz prototype (Figure 6) targets both Fortran and C. It leverages gcc/g77 common back ends and a parallelizing compiler that can deal with both C and Fortran. The HLI data structure includes loop-carried data dependences, array dataflow information, and alias information for high-level program structures such as loops and procedures. It can be easily exported from any parallelizing compilers and imported into the gcc/g77 back end compiler.

The front end parallelizing compiler and the gcc/g77 back end compiler are modified to include compiler techniques specific to the multiscalar and superthreaded architectures as described earlier.

7 Conclusion

The multiscalar and superthreaded architectures provide hardware speculation support for concurrent multithreading. The multiscalar relies more on hardware for data dependence check and for thread speculation, while the superthreaded processor relies more on compiler information. The followings are a list of compiler techniques which can benefit both architectures.

- Pointered array subscriptization to convert pointered arrays to subscripted arrays.
- Pointer arithmetics removal to reduce loop-carried data dependences.
- Variable privatization to reduce buffer overflow and write-backs.
- Last-write identification for efficient data forwarding between successive threads.
- Program parallelism and workload analysis to assist thread partitioning.

Since the superthreaded architecture does not rely on hardware to speculate on data dependences, it requires more compiler analysis on data dependences for synchronization. A more precise data dependence analysis at compile time will also allow more parallel threads to be created. On the other hand, the multiscalar aggressively speculates on data dependences and thus aggressively creates parallel threads. A more precise data dependence analysis at compile time can lead to better thread partitioning and reduced thread squashing.

Lastly, several of the compiler techniques presented in this paper can potentially benefit superscalar processors. It is interesting to compare the impact of these techniques on concurrent multithreading versus superscalars.

References

1. Randy Allen and Steve Johnson. Compiler C for vectorization, parallelization, and inline expansion. In *Prof. of SIGPLAN '88 Conference on Programming Language Design and Implementation*, pages 241–249, June 1988.

2. Pradeep K. Dubey, Kevin O'Brien, Kathryn O'Brien, and Charles Barton. Single-program speculative multithreading (SPSM) architecture: Compiler-assisted fine-grained multithreading. In *Proceedings of the IFIP WG 10.3 Working Conference on Parallel Architectures and Compilation Techniques, PACT '95*, pages 109–121, June 27–29, 1995.
3. Manoj Franklin and Gurindar S. Sohi. The expandable split window paradigm for exploiting fine-grained parallelism. In *Proceedings of the 19th Annual International Symposium on Computer Architecture*, pages 58–67, May 19–21, 1992.
4. M. Girkar and C. Polychronopoulos. The HTG: An intermediate representation for programs based on control and data dependences. CSRD Technical Report No. 1046, Univ. of Illinois at Urbana-Champaign, 1991.
5. Justiani and L. J. Hendren. Supporting array dependence testing for an optimizing/parallelizing c compiler. In *Proc. of the 1994 International Conference on Compiler Construction. Volume 749 of Lecture Notes in Computer Science.* Springer Verlag, April 1994.
6. Z. Li. Compiler algorithms for event variable synchronization. In *Proc. of the Fifth International Conference on Supercomputing (ACM)*, June 1991.
7. D.E. Maydan, S.P. Amarasinghe, and M.S. Lam. Array data-flow analysis and its use in array privatization. In *Proc. of the 20th ACM Symp. on Principles of Programming Languages*, pages 2–15, January 1993.
8. S. P. Midkiff and D. A. Padua. Compiler algorithms for synchronization. *IEEE Transactions on Computers*, C-36(12):1485–1495, December 1987.
9. Andreas I. Moshovos, Scott E. Breach, T. N. Vijaykumar, and Guri. S. Sohi. Submitted for a blind review to a conference.
10. B. A. Nayfeh and K. Olukotun. Exploring the design space for a shared-cache multiprocessor. In *Proceedings of the 21st Annual International Symposium on Computer Architecture*, pages 166–175, April 1994.
11. Gurindar S. Sohi, Scott E. Breach, and T. N. Vijaykumar. Multiscalar processors. In *Proceedings of the 22nd Annual International Symposium on Computer Architecture*, pages 414–425, June 22–24, 1995.
12. Jenn-Yuan Tsai and Pen-Chung Yew. The superthreaded architecture: Thread pipelining with run-time data dependence checking and control speculation. In *Proceedings of International Conference on Parallel Architectures and Compilation Techniques, PACT '96*, October 1996.

Resource-*Directed* Loop Pipelining *

Steven Novack and Alexandru Nicolau

Department of Information and Computer Science
University of California, Irvine, CA 92717

Abstract. Resource-*Directed* Loop Pipelining (RDLP) is a new approach to loop pipelining that allows the availability of target resource to in some sense *guide* the parallelization process. One of the key features of RDLP is the separation of control heuristics from transformations that allows the loop pipelining to be as general as the underlying system of code motion transformations. This paper presents results that show that RDLP is capable of "adapting" to target resources, exposing just enough parallelism (i.e., incurring a minimum of code explosion) to effectively utilize the resources of the specific target.

1 Introduction

Exploiting more than trivial amounts of parallelism at the instruction-level requires loop pipelining (i.e., overlapping the execution of successive iterations of a loop), and literally dozens of pipelining techniques have been proposed over the last several years. So, why do we need "yet another one"? The answer is that Resource-*Directed* Loop Pipelining is not "yet another one", since it differs from virtually all other loop pipelining techniques in one important way: RDLP does not rely on the built-in, systemic constraints (i.e., built-in heuristics) traditionally used to control the pipelining process. Instead, RDLP makes heuristics explicit, precisely defined, and *tunable* for different application domains and target architectures. In this paper we highlight the ability of RDLP to "adapt" to different target architectures by exposing just the right amount of parallelism to effectively utilize their resources.

Heuristics are essential to dealing with NP-hard problems such as resource-constrained scheduling. However, by encoding important aspects of these heuristics directly within the pipelining algorithm itself, conventional approaches arbitrarily, and sometimes severely, limit the performance of both the compiled code and the compiler. For example, Modulo Scheduling[13], arguably the most widely used pipelining technique, also has some of the strictest systemic constraints: conditionals must be *if-converted*,[2] and each (minor) iteration from the original loop within the final pipelined loop (major iteration) must have exactly the same schedule (i.e., the same operations scheduled at the same time relative to the beginning of each minor iteration). Both of these constraints can severely limit the possible schedules produced by Modulo Scheduling.

* This work was supported in part by ONR grant N00014-93-1-1348.

[2] I.e., replace conditional structures with predicated operations.

Conceptually, the general loop pipelining problem consists of three main tasks: exposing code to parallelize using loop transformations (e.g., unrolling), parallelizing that code using scheduling transformations (e.g., list scheduling, percolation scheduling, etc.), and finally determining when to stop pipelining, or "converge" on a final schedule. In order to recognize/force convergence of loop pipelining, virtually all loop pipelining techniques solve a simplified abstraction of the general loop pipelining problem that places constraints on how code is exposed, how it is parallelized, or more typically, both. For example, the problem abstraction used by Modulo Scheduling introduces the "fixed iteration" requirement that constrains both how code is exposed (i.e., only expose the fixed iteration) and how it is parallelized (i.e., the minor iteration schedule must remain fixed — the only scheduling allowed is in finding the initiation interval, or starting over with a new fixed iteration).

Resource-*Directed* Loop Pipelining adopts a "back to basics" approach to loop pipelining in which we try to solve the problem of maximizing performance directly, without relying on simplifying abstractions. For any target architecture, maximizing performance equates to maximizing the effective utilization of the highly parallel, specialized, and/or irregular resources of the specific target. RDLP attempts to accomplish this using a completely general system of parallelism exposing and parallelizing transformations. Unlike other techniques that use built-in constraints (i.e., built-in heuristics) to determine how much parallelism is exposed or how it is exploited, RDLP places no *a priori* restrictions on either, relying instead on a separate suite of heuristics to control the process that can be tuned for different target architectures, application domains and cost vs. performance trade-offs.

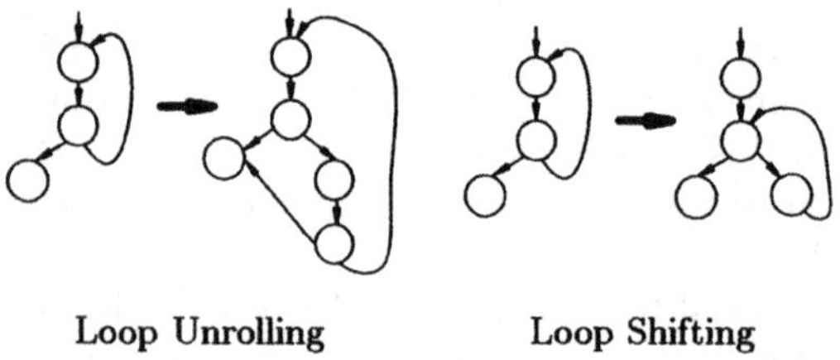

Fig. 1. Exposing parallelism within loops

RDLP works by repeatedly exposing and exploiting parallelism within a loop until resource dependencies or loop carried (i.e., cyclic) data dependencies prevent further parallelization, or a specified cost vs. performance goal is achieved. Parallelism is *exposed* using loop unrolling and loop shifting,[3] both

[3] Loop shifting refers to "unwinding" a loop so that its loop head becomes a true successor of each of its predecessors (i.e., the successor(s) of the head become the new loop head(s) and the original head becomes the last instruction in the loop), thus exposing operations from succeeding iterations to be scheduled in parallel with preceding iterations.

of which are illustrated in Figure 1. After each unroll or shift transformation, parallelism is *exploited* by parallelizing (i.e., *compacting*) the current loop body using a provably complete system of Trailblazing Percolation Scheduling (TiPS) transformations[12].

Both unrolling and shifting have the effect of exposing code from succeeding iterations for parallelization. The key difference between the two is that whereas loop unrolling exposes a new iteration in its entirety, thus increasing the *amount* of code to parallelize, loop shifting simply restructures the loop, essentially "moving" operations across the backedge, without increasing the overall amount of code within the loop body.

The goal of RDLP, when allowed by cost vs. performance trade-offs, is to expose just enough parallelism to maximally utilize the available resources of the target architecture. Resources are "maximally" utilized if there exists a kind of resource (e.g., alu, falu, etc.) for which utilization is 100% over the entire loop,[4] or loop carried dependencies prevent any further parallelization.

If the loop body does not contain enough operations to maximally exploit the available resources, then loop unrolling is used to increase the number of operations in the loop until resources *can be* maximally utilized by the exposed parallelism, or cost vs. performance goals are achieved. Unrolling and then parallelizing or *compacting* the loop body has the effect of overlapping the execution of the unrolled iterations, but can not in general guarantee maximal utilization of target resources due to sequentiality imposed at the end-points of the new "multi-iteration" loop body — even though there may be enough operations in the loop to maximally utilize resources, the "structure" of the loop may prevent that parallelism from actually being exploited. For instance, if the loop body consists of $k \geq 1$[5] compacted iterations of the original loop, then there is still no overlap between iterations k and $k+1$, which may yet be possible, and necessary if resources are to be maximally utilized. In this case, RDLP restructures the loop, using loop shifting, to remove whatever sequentiality may exist at the end-points of the (possibly unrolled) loop body. Loop shifting (and compacting) continues until resources *are* maximally utilized, or cost vs. performance goals are achieved.

1.1 An Example

Figure 2 shows the progression of RDLP for Livermore Kernel 1 in the form graphical representations of the code obtained from the Visual Interface for Scheduling Transformation and Analysis (VISTA)[10], a visualization/parallelization

[4] I.e., Resource dependencies prevent further parallelization since 100% utilization for some resource R within the loop implies that if the throughput of the loop is k iterations every n cycles, then, due to resource dependencies on R, unrolling and scheduling another iteration (from the original loop) would increase the length of the loop schedule by at least $\lceil n/k \rceil$ cycles, resulting in a throughput of at most $(k+1)/(n+\lceil n/k \rceil)$ which is less than or equal to the throughput before the unrolling, k/n; and shifting and scheduling would simply retain the same k/n throughput.

[5] $k = 1$ means only the original loop body is compacted, without any unrolling.

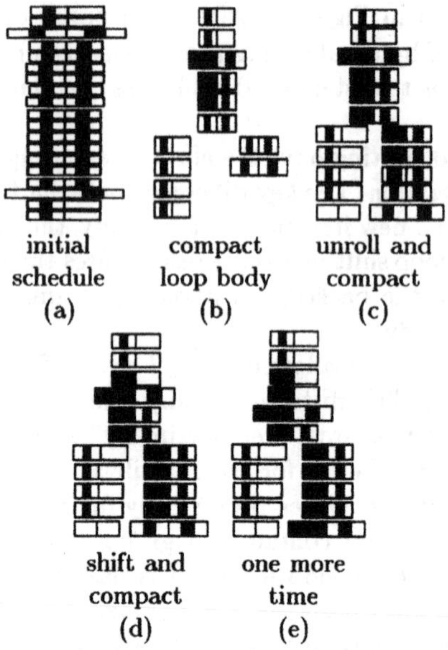

Fig. 2. RDLP Example: Livermore Kernel 1

tool that is part of the EVE Mutation Scheduling compiler (see Section 4). Figure 2 consists of five snapshots, labelled (a) through (e), that, as described below, show the resource utilization of the loop at each stage of the pipelining process, by "shading" instructions in proportion to their resource utilization. In each snapshot, the outermost rectangles represent VLIW instructions, in this case for a VLIW architecture with four general purpose functional units (capable of executing arbitrary arithmetic and logical operations), and two conditional branch units.[6] The execution semantics for instructions are modelled after the IBM VLIW architecture[3]. Notice that the graphical representation of each instruction is divided into two segments. For each instruction, the left segment is shaded in proportion to the functional unit utilization at that node. For instance, in snapshot (a), the code has not been parallelized yet, so each VLIW instruction contains only one operation or conditional branch, and therefore, the left segment of each instruction (except for the instruction containing the loop control conditional) is shaded in by 25% (i.e., only 1 out of a possible 4 operations have been scheduled in the instruction). The shading in the righthand segment is simply used to indicate which instructions are part of the loop — if the right segment is shaded for an instruction, then that instruction is part of the loop. Note that the loop head and tail instructions of the loop are graphically designated by slightly wider rectangles in each of the snapshots (the relative widths

[6] To make this example as simple as possible, we choose a loop with no conditional control flow (other than the loop control conditional), and we use a simple, unicycle target architecture.

```
instr(16):
   [0] (fgetmem $f0.1  (iadd $3.2 0))

instr(17):
   [0] (fmul $f2.1 $f8.1 $f0.1)

instr(18):
   [0] (fgetmem $f0.2  (iadd $4.2 0))

instr(19):
   [0] (fmul $f0.3 $f6.1 $f0.2)

instr(20):
   [0] (fadd $f2.2 $f2.1 $f0.3)

instr(21):
   [0] (fgetmem $f0.4  (iadd $2.2 -8104))

instr(22):
   [0] (fmul $f2.3 $f2.2 $f0.4)

instr(23):
   [0] (fadd $f0.5 $f4.1 $f2.3)

instr(24):
   [0] (fputmem $mf1.1 $f0.5  (iadd $2.2 -4096))

instr(25):
   [0] (iadd $4.3 $4.2 4)

instr(26):
   [0] (iadd $3.3 $3.2 4)

instr(27):
   [0] (iadd $2.3 $2.2 4)

instr(28):
   [0] (iadd $5.3 $5.2 1)

instr(29):
   [0] (ile $cc0.1  (isub $5.3 400))

instr(30):
   [0] (if $cc0.1 -- 0 exit-loop)
```

Before RDLP: Code for Fig. 2 snapshot (a) executes 1 iteration every 15 time steps.

```
instr(20):
 [0] (ile $cc0.1 (isub $5.3 400) )
 [0] (fgetmem $f0.4 (iadd $2.2 -8104))
 [0] (fadd $f2.2 $f2.1 $f0.3)
 [1] (iadd $4.4 $4.3 4)

instr(21):
 [0] (if $cc0.1 -- 0 exit-loop)
 [0] (fmul $f2.3 $f2.2 $f0.4)
 [1] (fgetmem $f0.6 (iadd $4.3 0))
 [1] (fgetmem $f0.7 (iadd $3.3 0))
 [1] (iadd $3.4 $3.3 4)

instr(40):
 [0] (fadd $f0.5 $f4.1 $f2.3)
 [1] (iadd $2.4 $2.3 4)
 [1] (fmul $f0.8 $f6.1 $f0.6)
 [1] (fmul $f2.4 $f8.1 $f0.7)

instr(38):
 [0] (fputmem $mf1.1 $f0.5 (iadd $2.2 -4096))
 [1] (fgetmem $f0.9 (iadd $2.3 -8104))
 [1] (iadd $5.4 $5.3 1)
 [1] (fadd $f2.5 $f2.4 $f0.8)

instr(51):
 [1] (fmul $f2.6 $f2.5 $f0.9)
 [1] (ile $cc0.2 (isub $5.4 400) )
 [2] (iadd $3.6 $3.4 4)
 [2] (iadd $4.6 $4.4 4)

instr(50):
 [1] (fadd $f0.10 $f4.1 $f2.6)
 [1] (if $cc0.2 -- 0 exit-loop)
 [2] (iadd $2.6 $2.4 4)
 [2] (fgetmem $f0.13 (iadd $4.4 0))
 [2] (fgetmem $f0.14 (iadd $3.4 0))

instr(48):
 [1] (fputmem $mf1.3 $f0.10 (iadd $2.3 -4096))
 [2] (iadd $5.6 $5.4 1)
 [2] (fmul $f0.16 $f6.1 $f0.13)
 [2] (fmul $f2.8 $f8.1 $f0.14)
```

After RDLP: Code for Fig. 2 snapshot (e) executes 2 iterations every 7 time steps.

Fig. 3. Code before and after RDLP

of the outer rectangles does *not* signify a larger number of resources for these instructions).

To help in understanding the snapshots shown in Figure 2, the actual N-addr code corresponding to the initial and final snapshots is shown in Figure 3. The N-addr code is in SSA form[2] and its opcodes are essentially those of the MIPS architecture. Note that for brevity only the loop body is shown, without loop control or phi functions.

Figure 2, snapshot (a) shows the loop before pipelining. The loop contains 14 operations and one conditional jump (for loop control), initially scheduled one per instruction. Snapshot (b) shows the loop after the original loop body has been compacted. Notice that the loop control conditional has "moved up" from the bottom of the loop a couple of instructions, thus causing the bifurcation in the control flow (the left branch is the loop exit, as indicated by the absence of shading in the righthand segment of those instructions). The shading in the lefthand side of the loop instructions in snapshot (b) indicates that functional unit utilization is 100% in the first two instructions, and then tapers off until the end of the loop. At this point, RDLP attempts to determine if there are enough operations currently in the loop body to maximally utilize the resources, or whether a loop carried dependence prevents further utilization. Only trivial loop carried dependencies on induction variables exist for this loop, so making this determination essentially involves determining whether or not the number of operations competing for the most heavily used type of resource is evenly divided by the number of available resources of that type. In this case, the most heavily utilized resource type is the generic functional unit (as opposed to the conditional branch units), so given that 14 operations / 4 functional units = 3.5, no matter how well loop shifting might overlap these operations, it is not yet possible for the functional units within the loop to be fully utilized. Assuming that the performance goal is 100% utilization and that cost constraints (e.g., code size, compile time) allow it, RDLP would then unroll the loop in order to increase the number of operations in the loop body. Snapshot (c) shows the loop after it has been unrolled once and compacted. Notice that resources are now almost completely utilized within the loop. Moreover, the loop now has 28 operations,[7] which is evenly divided by the 4 available functional units, so no further unrolling is needed. At this point, RDLP uses loop shifting to fill the few remaining unutilized resources at the bottom of the loop. Snapshot (d) shows the loop after being shifted one instruction and compacted. Notice that resource utilization has increased, as indicated by the darker shading in the lefthand segment. However, resources are not yet fully utilized, so more shifting is indicated. Snapshot (e) shows that one more loop shift and compaction is enough to completely utilize the resources for this loop on this target architecture.

Notice that RDLP places no *a priori* limitations on how much parallelism is exposed, or how it is exploited — the amount of unrolling/shifting and the aggressiveness of the parallelization is determined entirely by a separate set of heuristics that depend on the application domain, target architecture, and cost vs. performance trade-offs.

The remainder of this paper is organized as follows: Section 2 describes the related work that motivates RDLP, Section 3 describes the RDLP algorithm, and finally Section 4 describes an implementation of RDLP and results showing its effectiveness.

2 Related Work

Resource-*Directed* Loop Pipelining (RDLP) is motivated by three other well-known pipelining techniques: Modulo Scheduling[13], Resource-Constrained Software Pipelining (RCSP)[1], and Enhanced Pipelined Percolation Scheduling (EPPS)[4]. Each of these techniques has been proven to have theoretical and/or practical advantages; nevertheless, all three rely on built-in, systemic constraints that limit their efficiency and/or performance. Below we describe each of these techniques in turn, with emphasis on their strengths, which we try to retain in RDLP, and their weaknesses, which we try to avoid.

[7] In this example, unrolling and compacting one more iteration resulted in exactly 14 more operations for a total of 28; however, in general, the incremental increase in the number of operations after compaction need not equal the number of operations in the original loop body since one of the strengths of RDLP is that other code transformations and optimizations that can change the number of operations, like load-after-store elimination, redundant operation removal, constant folding, etc. can be integrated as part of the parallelization process. See [11] for a discussion of how this can be done elegantly and uniformly and why it is important.

2.1 Modulo Scheduling

Modulo Scheduling is by far the most widely used of these techniques and has proven itself to be very useful in practice. The basic algorithm consists of scheduling one operation at a time, such that if an operation from iteration zero is scheduled at time t, then for each subsequent iteration i, the same operation from iteration i, is scheduled at time $t + is$, where s is a fixed value, called the *initiation interval*, that depends on the resource- and data-dependence structure of the loop body. In effect, Modulo Scheduling schedules a single iteration, and then repeats it every "initiation interval" time steps until resource constraints prevent any further overlapping of iterations.

The advantages of Modulo Scheduling are that it is simple, efficient, and in some sense "guided" by target resources (i.e., it continues to "unroll" the fixed iteration until resource constraints prevent any further overlap). The disadvantages of Modulo Scheduling are twofold. First, if the loop contains conditional control flow, then it must be *if-converted*, whereby operations are replaced by guarded operations that depend on the predicates of the conditionals that control their execution, and the conditionals themselves are deleted. In this way, control dependencies are replaced by data dependencies, at the cost of forcing operations from disjoint control paths to compete for the same resources, even though in the final schedule they would never be executed simultaneously. The second disadvantage of Modulo Scheduling is simply the requirement that each iteration (from the original loop) in the pipelined loop have exactly the same schedule. This is not only a completely arbitrary restriction on the possible code motions, but also complicates or prevents the application of other transformations or optimizations that may be exposed during pipelining (e.g., load-after-store elimination, redundant operation removal, constant folding, copy propagation, etc.).

2.2 Resource-Constrained Software Pipelining (RCSP)

Resource-Constrained Software Pipelining (RCSP)[1] is one of the more aggressive pipelining techniques and provides a foundation for discussing software pipelining in the presence of resource constraints. The algorithm consists of repeatedly unrolling and scheduling a loop until a repeating scheduling pattern emerges. This repeating pattern is then made the new (pipelined) loop body, and everything before and after it becomes pre- and post-loop code, respectively. In order to ensure that a repeating pattern will form, RCSP requires that operations from each unrolled iteration be the same, and scheduled in the same order (though, the resulting schedules for each unrolled iteration need not be the same).

The main advantages of RCSP are that it gracefully handles conditional control flow within the loop body (e.g., *if-conversion* is not necessary) and it is "guided" by target resources in the sense that the degree of parallelism in the loop increases (via unrolling) until a repeating scheduling pattern forms. In fact, with respect to full unrolling of the loop, and its own self-imposed scheduling constraints (i.e., each iteration has the same operations scheduled in the same order), RCSP is provably optimal.[8] The principal disadvantage of RCSP is that the built-in, systemic constraint of unrolling and scheduling until a pattern repeats, often causes the loop to be unrolled many more times than is needed to fully utilize the available resources. Another disadvantage of RCSP is that the requirement that each iteration have exactly the same operations scheduled in the same order, though less severe than for Modulo Scheduling, still arbitrarily limits the kinds of transformations and optimizations that can be performed during scheduling.

2.3 Enhanced Pipelined Percolation Scheduling (EPPS)

Enhanced Pipelined Percolation Scheduling (EPPS)[4] adopts a very different approach to pipelining than Modulo Scheduling and RCSP. Like the others, EPPS is resource-constrained, however unlike the others, it is not *guided* by resources. Whereas, Modulo Scheduling and RCSP are both capable of increasing the degree of parallelism of the loop (via unrolling) in response to resource availability, EPPS relies exclusively on loop "shifting" (essentially moving operations across the backedge), thus exposing operations from successive iterations to be scheduled in parallel, but limiting the total pipelined loop body to a single iteration (of the original loop). EPPS continues to shift the loop until each instruction from the original loop body has been shifted.

The advantages of EPPS are that it is simple, efficient, gracefully handles conditional control flow, and places no restrictions whatsoever on the transformations and optimizations that can be performed within the loop body. The main disadvantage of EPPS is that it arbitrarily limits the degree of parallelism to what is available in a single iteration of the original loop, regardless of how well or poorly it utilizes the available resources. Another disadvantage is that the termination condition is completely arbitrary, thus potentially causing more code explosion than necessary if too much shifting is done, or less performance than possible if too little shifting is done.

2.4 How RDLP Relates

The Resource-*Directed* Loop Pipelining (RDLP) technique presented in this paper attempts to retain the advantages of all three of the abovementioned techniques, while avoiding the limitations of any of them. Like Modulo Scheduling and RCSP, RDLP is "guided" by target resources, so that the degree of parallelism can grow in proportion to available resources; like RCSP and EPPS, RDLP gracefully handles conditional control flow; and, like EPPS, RDLP places no restrictions at all on what transformations and optimizations can be performed within the loop body. By explicitly separating the parallelism exposing and parallelizing transformations from each other and from the heuristics that control them, RDLP does not suffer from any of the built-in, systemic constraints

[8] Of course, optimal with respect to full unrolling is not the same as absolute optimality; however, given the NP-hard nature of the problem and the results of [14], in practice, optimality with respect to unrolling may be the strongest form possible for general loop pipelining algorithms.

on functionality inherent to the other techniques. Note that RDLP is no more or less heuristic-based than any other (tractable) loop pipelining technique — the difference is that RDLP makes the heuristics explicit and tunable, rather than fixed and hidden within the mechanics of the algorithm.

3 The Algorithm

This section describes the general RDLP technique, a specific implementation of which is then described in Section 4.

```
procedure RDLP(loop L)
    compact(L)
    while not done-unrolling(L)
        unroll(L)
        compact(L)
    while not done-shifting(L)
        shift(L)
        compact(L)
end procedure

function done-unrolling(loop L)
    return enough-operations-in-loop(L)
        or unroll-cost-constraints-reached(L)
end function
function done-shifting(loop L)
    return maximal-resource-utilization(L)
        or shift-cost-constraints-reached(L)
end function
```

Fig. 4. The RDLP Algorithm

Figure 4 shows the RDLP algorithm. RDLP starts by compacting the initial loop body, and then repeatedly refining that schedule until a desired cost vs. performance goal is achieved, first by unrolling and compacting to increase the degree of parallelism within the loop, when needed, and then by shifting and compacting to eliminate any sequentiality that may still exist at the end-points of the loop.

Compaction (i.e., parallelization) of the loop body at each stage of the pipelining process is done using the COMPACT routine. One of the advantages of RDLP is that the method used for compacting the code is orthogonal to the pipelining algorithm itself — any technique can be used, including any of [5, 8, 7]. In the implementation of RDLP described in Section 4, we use Trailblazing Percolation Scheduling (TiPS)[12], a completely general and provably complete system of parallelizing transformations.

3.1 The UNROLL/COMPACT cycle

The UNROLL/COMPACT cycle is used to increase the number of operations in the loop, if needed, until resources *can be* maximally utilized by the available operations, or cost constraints are reached. The UNROLL routine is responsible for making a copy of the original (compacted) loop body at the end of the current partially pipelined loop (which may already contain multiple iterations from previous unrollings). Because we allow arbitrary optimizations to occur during compaction, possibly including very aggressive code transformations (e.g., mutations[11]), it is not possible to determine *a priori* how much unrolling will be needed. Therefore, the UNROLL/COMPACT cycle is done incrementally and terminates when DONE-UNROLLING returns `true`.

DONE-UNROLLING is responsible for determining when enough operations have been exposed for parallelization to maximally utilize the available resources, or cost constraints have been reached. ENOUGH-OPERATIONS-IN-LOOP determines whether or not resources *can be* maximally utilized by the operations currently in the loop body.[9] Specifically, ENOUGH-OPERATIONS-IN-LOOP behaves as follows:

Let k = the number of different kinds of resource (e.g., alu, falu, etc.)

$\text{ops}^n = \langle \text{ops}_1, \ldots, \text{ops}_k \rangle$
where ops_i = the number of operations scheduled at instruction n that use resource i

$\text{ops}^p = \sum_{n \in p} \text{ops}^n$
where p is a path of instructions through the loop

$\text{avail} = \langle \text{avail}_1, \ldots, \text{avail}_k \rangle$
where avail_i = the total number of resources of kind i

$\text{height}^p = \lceil \text{ops}^p / \text{avail} \rceil$
i.e., height_i is the minimum number of instructions necessary to accommodate ops_i^p

Then ENOUGH-OPERATIONS-IN-LOOP returns `true` if for all paths p in the loop at least one of the following holds:

1. $\exists i \; \forall j \; \text{height}_i^p \geq \text{height}_j^p \wedge \text{height}_i^p * \text{avail}_i = \text{ops}_i^p$
   i.e., there are enough operations on this path to fully utilize the most heavily used resource.
2. $\forall i \; \text{height}_i^p \leq \text{longest-cyclic-dep}^p$ i.e., the length of the longest cyclic dependency (i.e., loop carried dependency) on path p ($\text{longest-cyclic-dep}^p$) is longer than the best schedule that could be obtained even if resources could be fully utilized on p.

Note that in terms of resource-constraints, multi-cycle operations are handled as in [1], by treating each k-cycle operation as a sequence of k 1-cycle (stage-level) operations, and similarly treating each k-cycle functional unit as k 1-cycle functional units (pipeline stages).

Even if ENOUGH-OPERATIONS-IN-LOOP returns `false`, DONE-UNROLLING can still return `true` if UNROLL-COST-CONSTRAINTS-ARE-REACHED returns `true`. This routine, in conjunction with SHIFT-COST-CONSTRAINTS-ARE-REACHED and the heuristics used by COMPACT, are what allow RDLP to be explicitly tuned for different application domains, target architectures, and cost vs. performance trade-offs.

Since the heuristics that control RDLP depend on the context in which it is used, we will not attempt to give an exhaustive list of the possibilities. Rather,

[9] Recall that resources *are* maximally utilized if resource utilization for some resource type is 100%, or loop carried dependencies prevent further parallelization.

in this section, we will simply describe the three principle kinds of heuristics, and then in Section 4, we will describe one particular instantiation. For UNROLL-COST-CONSTRAINTS-ARE-REACHED, the following three classes of heuristics are applicable to most target architectures and application domains:

- Code size constraints: stop unrolling if the resulting code size would exceed a certain amount. The "cut-off" size can be fixed for all loops or dependent on the characteristics of specific loops, such as loop bounds (possibly obtained via analysis or assertions) or the relative importance of the loop (obtained via profiling, assertions, or analysis).
- Compile time constraints: only spend a certain amount of time unrolling. As for size constraints, this amount can be fixed for all loops or dependent on the characteristics of specific loops.
- Performance threshold constraints: stop unrolling after a certain goal resource utilization can be achieved (like testing for the ability to maximally utilize resources, but instead of testing for 100% utilization, check for some utilization $X < 100\%$). The performance threshold can be fixed, or can depend on the relative importance of the loop, as for the previous constraints, or can change dynamically depending on the total cost accrued so far (e.g., initially try for maximal utilization, but then periodically decrease the goal utilization after a certain amount of code explosion and/or compile time).

3.2 The SHIFT/COMPACT cycle

The shift/compact cycle is used to schedule operations from successive iterations in parallel with preceding iterations, without increasing the number of iterations in the loop, until resources are maximally utilized or cost constraints have been reached. As for the UNROLL/COMPACT cycle, there is no way to tell beforehand how much shifting will be necessary since COMPACT has the freedom to perform other transformations and optimizations to the loop body that may have nothing to do (directly) with loop pipelining (e.g., load-after-store elimination). Therefore, the SHIFT/COMPACT cycle continues until DONE-SHIFTING returns `true`.

DONE-SHIFTING is responsible for determining when resources are maximally utilized (using MAXIMAL-RESOURCE-UTILIZATION), or cost constraints have been reached (SHIFT-COST-CONSTRAINTS-ARE-REACHED). Using the same notation as above, MAXIMAL-RESOURCE-UTILIZATION returns `true` if for all paths p in the loop, at least one of the following is true:

1. $\exists i\ \text{ops}_i^p/|p| = \text{avail}_i$ i.e., some resource is fully utilized
2. $|p| = \text{longest-cyclic-dep}^p$ i.e., a loop carried dependence prevents further parallelization

where $|p|$ is the number of instructions on path p.

SHIFT-COST-CONSTRAINTS-ARE-REACHED mirrors UNROLL-COST-CONSTRAINTS-ARE-REACHED. The only difference is that shifting, rather than unrolling is constrained.

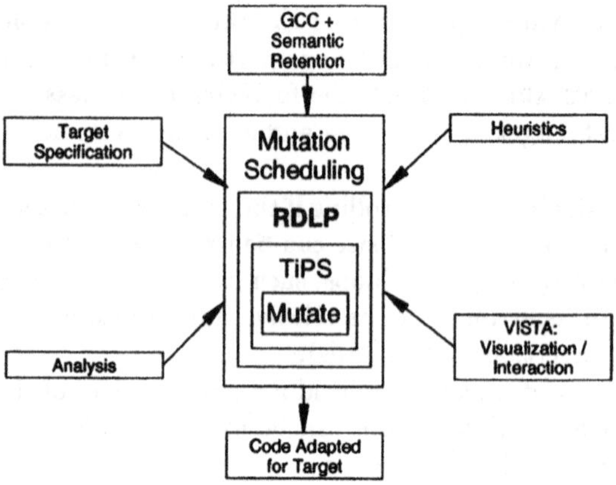

Fig. 5. Structural Overview of the EVE Compiler

4 Implementation and Results

Resource-*Directed* Loop Pipelining (RDLP) is a general loop pipelining technique that could be implemented as part of most compilers for fine-grain parallel architectures. This section describes one such implementation, as part of the EVE Mutation Scheduling compiler being developed at UCI,[10] and presents results that highlight the ability of RDLP to expose just enough parallelism to maximally utilize resources.

Figure 5 shows a structural overview of the EVE compiler. One of the main objectives of the EVE compiler is to provide a completely general and powerful system of transformations, controlled by an independent suite of heuristics that can be tuned for different application domains, target architectures and cost vs. performance trade-offs. RDLP is at the highest level of this system of "Mutation Scheduling" transformations, followed next by Trailblazing Percolation Scheduling (TiPS)[12], a non-incremental system of code motion transformations that schedules operations within a hierarchical representation of the control flow graph, called the Hierarchical Task Graph[6], and finally by the Mutate transformation[11], a mechanism that allows the expression used in computing any value to change "on the fly" during scheduling in response to changing resource constraints and availability. Mutation Scheduling effectively integrates code selection, register allocation and instruction scheduling into a unitifed framework in which context sensitive trade-offs can be made between the functional, register, and memory bandwidth resources of the target architecture. Indeed one of the main strengths of RDLP is that it allows arbitrary optimizations and transformations to be performed during the pipelining process,

[10] The main features of the EVE compiler are described separately in [11, 12, 9, 10]. An overview of the system as a whole can be found on the world wide web at http://www.ics.uci.edu/~snovack/EVE.

including very aggressive transformations such as code mutation, thus allowing RDLP to take advantage of opportunities for optimizations/transformations that are exposed by loop unrolling and/or shifting.[11]

In order to highlight the ability of RDLP to expose just enough parallelism to maximally exploit the resources of fine-grain parallel architectures, we present the results of six experiments in which we compare the performance (in terms of speedup[12]) and the cost (in terms of the number of unroll and shift transformations) of RDLP against results that are optimal with respect to the capabilities of the underlying system of code motion transformations. The "optimal" results were produced as follows. We choose a maximum amount of unrolling to try, say U, and a maximum amount of shifting, say S, and then maximally compact the code for each possible combination of unroll and shift transformations within these limits (i.e., for each $(x, y) \in \{0 \ldots U\} \times \{0 \ldots S\}$, unroll and compact x times, and then shift and compact y times). We try progressively larger values of U and S until performance ceases to improve. For the experiments presented in this paper, this happened at U <= 10 and S <= 20.

Figure 6 shows the results of our experiments. This figure contains three graphs that compare performance, in terms of average speedup, and cost, in terms of the amounts of unrolling and shifting, of RDLP against those of the "optimal" algorithm for each of six different target architectures with varying numbers and kinds of functional unit. For each target architecture, the average speedup and amounts of unrolling and shifting are over 14 benchmarks taken from the Livermore Kernels: hydro, diffprod, firstdiff, ICCG, matrixmul, planckdist, 2dhydro, innerprod, BLE, tridiag, recurrence, eqofstate, ADI, and integrate. The target architectures used in all six experiments are simulated, unicycle VLIW's with 3-way branching (i.e. up to two conditional branches per instruction), and 32 integer and 32 floating point registers. Each target uses the same instruction set, which is essentially that of the MIPS architecture. The first three targets listed in each graph has 2, 3, or 4, resp. of each kind of heterogeneous functional unit (FU): ALU, SHIFT, FALU, FMUL, FDIV, and MEM. The last three targets listed in each graph has 2, 4, or 8 homogeneous FU's, resp. (i.e., each FU is capable of executing any operation).

The current implementation of RDLP within EVE uses a few very simple cost constraints controlled by the following parameters, read as inputs by EVE: UNROLL_LIMIT specifies the maximum amount of unrolling for any loop, SHIFT_LIMIT specifies the maximum number of shift transformations to be applied to any loop, and SHIFT_TRY_LIMIT specifies the maximum number of shift transformations to be applied without improving the schedule (i.e., as long as shifting improves the schedule at least once each SHIFT_TRY_LIMIT shift transformations, RDLP will continue shifting until resources are maximally uti-

[11] A good example is load-after-store elimination which is often enabled by both unrolling and shifting, as when a load from iteration i simply reads a value that was stored in iteration $i - 1$ — in this case the load can usually be eliminated and each use of it can be replaced by a use of the value that was stored.

[12] i.e., the ratio of sequential to parallel cycles observed during execution

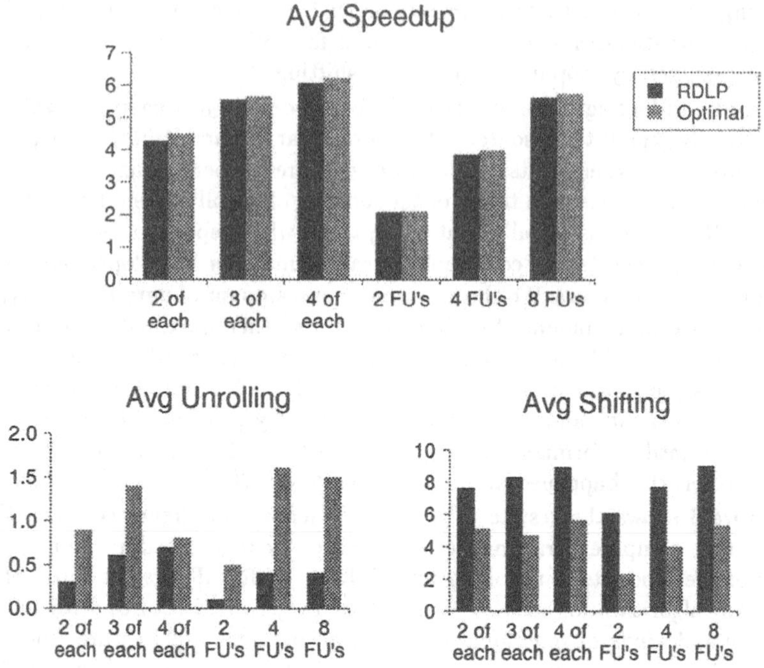

Fig. 6. RDLP vs. Optimal

lized or the SHIFT_LIMIT is reached, whichever comes first). Obviously, better heuristics are possible (e.g., making the cost constraints on a per loop basis and dependent on context), but as shown in the tables, these very simple cost constraints yield significant results. For both experiments the following largely arbitrary control parameters were used: UNROLL_LIMIT = 20, SHIFT_LIMIT = 40, and SHIFT_TRY_LIMIT = 4. Note that in these experiments RDLP was able to expose "enough" operations with at most 3 unrollings and 14 shifts, so any UNROLL_LIMIT >= 3 and SHIFT_LIMIT >= 14 would have yielded the same results.

For the optimal results, the amount of unrolling and shifting is the minimum amount for which the performance was maximized. Notice that on average RDLP achieves within 3% of the optimal speedup, and can achieve this with approximately one third of the unrolling that would be required for achieving maximum performance. RDLP does however require more shifting, but in general this is not very significant since each shift transformation only increases the code size by one instruction. Note that even though the six target architectures used in these experiments have very different numbers/kinds of resources, there is little deviation between the ratios of RDLP performance (and cost) to the optimal performance (and cost): for all six experiments, RDLP achieves within

1% (the "2 FU's" experiment) and 5% ("2 of each") of the optimal speedup, usually with significantly less code explosion than would be required to achieve the last few percent in performance. This fact highlights two key features of RDLP: its ability to adapt to different target architectures and to expose enough, but no more, parallelism than is necessary to effectively utilize the resources of the specific target.

References

1. A. Aiken, A. Nicolau, and S. Novack. Resource-constrained software pipelining. *TOPADS*, 6(12), December 1995.
2. R. Cytron, J. Ferrante, B. Rosen, M. Wegman, and K. Zadeck. An efficient method of computing static single assignment form. In *Proceedings of the 16th Annual Symposium on the Principles of Programming Languages*, Austin, TX, January 1989.
3. K. Ebcioglu. Some design ideas for a vliw architecture for sequential-natured software. In *IFIP Proceedings*, 1988.
4. K. Ebcioglu and T. Nakatani. A new compilation technique for parallelizing loops with unpredictable branches on a vliw architecture. In *Proceedings of the 2nd Workshop on Programming Languages and Compilers for Parallel Computing*, Urbana, IL, 1989.
5. K. Ebcioglu and A. Nicolau. A *global* resource-constrained parallelization technique. In *ICS*, Crete, Greece, June 1989.
6. M. Girkar and C.D. Polychronopoulos. Automatic extraction of functional parallelism from ordinary programs. *TOPADS*, 3(2):166–178, March 1992.
7. Wen mei W. Hwu, Scott A. Mahlke, William Y. Chen, Pohua P. Chang, Nancy J. Warter, Roger A. Bringmann, Roland G. Ouellette, Richard E. Hank, Tokuzo Kiyohara, Grant E. Haab, John G. Holm, and Daniel M. Lavery. The superblock: An effective technique for VLIW and superscalar compilation. *The Journal of Supercomputing*, 7:229–248, 1993.
8. S. Moon and K. Ebcioglu. An efficient resource constrained global scheduling technique for superscalar and vliw processors. In *MICRO*, Portland, OR, December 1992.
9. S. Novack, J. Hummel, and A. Nicolau. A simple mechanism for improving the accuracy and efficiency of instruction-level disambiguation. In *Lang. and Compilers for Par. Comp.* Springer, 1995.
10. S. Novack and A. Nicolau. Vista: The visual interface for scheduling transformations and analysis. In *Lang. and Compilers for Par. Comp.* Springer-Verlag, 1993.
11. S. Novack and A. Nicolau. Mutation scheduling: A unified approach to compiling for fine-grain parallelism. In *Lang. and Compilers for Par. Comp.* Springer-Verlag, 1994.
12. S. Novack and A. Nicolau. A hierarchical approach to instruction-level parallelization. *International Journal of Parallel Programming*, 23(1), February 1995.
13. B.R. Rau and C.D. Glaeser. Efficient code generation for horizontal architectures: Compiler techniques and architectural support. In *Symp. on Comp. Arch.*, April 1982.
14. U. Schwiegelshohn, F. Gasperoni, and K. Ebcioglu. An optimal parallelization of arbitrary loops. *Journal of Parallel and Distributed Computing*, 11(2):130–134, [2] 1991.

Integrating Program Optimizations and Transformations with the Scheduling of Instruction Level Parallelism*

David A. Berson[1] Pohua Chang[1] Rajiv Gupta[2] Mary Lou Soffa[2]

[1] Intel Corporation, Santa Clara, CA 95052
[2] University of Pittsburgh, Pittsburgh, PA 15260

Abstract. Code optimizations and restructuring transformations are typically applied before scheduling to improve the quality of generated code. However, in some cases, the optimizations and transformations do not lead to a better schedule or may even adversely affect the schedule. In particular, optimizations for redundancy elimination and restructuring transformations for increasing parallelism are often accompanied with an increase in register pressure. Therefore their application in situations where register pressure is already too high may result in the generation of additional spill code. In this paper we present an integrated approach to scheduling that enables the selective application of optimizations and restructuring transformations by the scheduler when it determines their application to be beneficial. The integration is necessary because information that is used to determine the effects of optimizations and transformations on the schedule is only available during instruction scheduling. Our integrated scheduling approach is applicable to various types of global scheduling techniques; in this paper we present an integrated algorithm for scheduling superblocks.

1 Introduction

Compilers for multiple-issue architectures, such as superscalar and very long instruction word (VLIW) architectures, are typically divided into phases, with code optimizations, scheduling and register allocation being the latter phases. The importance of integrating these latter phases is growing with the recognition that the quality of code produced for parallel systems can be greatly improved through the sharing of information. Integration of register allocation and instruction scheduling has been recently studied by various researchers [1, 14, 13]. However, the integration of optimizations and transformations with schedulers has not been fully addressed.

In the optimization phase, optimizations are applied to improve the quality of code while restructuring transformations are applied to increase the instruction level parallelism (ILP). Since optimizations and transformations may increase the requirements for registers and functional units beyond the numbers supported by the architecture, their application may adversely affect the quality of code generated.

* Partially supported by National Science Foundation PYI Award CCR-9157371 and a grant from Intel Corporation to the University of Pittsburgh.

In the scheduling phase, both local and global techniques are used to exploit ILP. Global scheduling techniques uncover and exploit ILP across basic blocks [5, 8, 6, 1]. The program is divided into scheduling units (such as traces, superblocks, and control dependence regions) composed of a collection of basic blocks. The scheduling units are processed one at a time by a scheduler and are represented using directed acyclic graphs (*DAG*) to assist in the scheduling process. ILP is uncovered by restructuring the code within a scheduling unit. If enough parallelism is not found within the unit, code is propagated from adjacent scheduling units. Code is moved across units using code duplication, speculative execution [9], and predicated execution [7].

The separation of the optimization and scheduling phases is problematic in that the applications of optimizations and transformations are performed without knowing if the scheduler will be able to utilize their effects. For example, DAG restructuring transformations can be applied to increase parallelism within a superblock as well as reduce critical path length within a superblock. However, the optimizer cannot apply these transformations unless it is aware of the superblocks that will be constructed during instruction scheduling. Thus, the usefulness of these transformations cannot be known until scheduling actually begins. Also, when a choice of restructuring opportunities is available, the scheduler has the best information to determine which choice would produce the best schedule. Code that is moved by the scheduler can create opportunities for further optimizations. For example, hoisting of partially redundant code can result in fully redundant code. Such opportunities can only be exploited by integrating the redundancy elimination optimization with instruction scheduling.

In this paper, we present an approach to scheduling with the goal of integrating selected code transformations and optimizations into the scheduler. We present simple guidelines that enable the identification of optimizations that should be integrated with instruction scheduling and those that may be performed prior to instruction scheduling. The decision to apply an optimization or transformation duing scheduling is based upon information that is only available during instruction scheduling. Such information includes the effect of optimizations and transformations upon (1) the availability of registers, (2) the availability of functional units, and (3) the schedulability of instructions in an idle slot of a schedule in progress. The integrated approach utilizes measures of the resources required, including both functional units and registers, that are maintained and used by the scheduling algorithm. By reorganizing code within a block in a manner that keeps register pressure in check, we attempt to minimize the generation of spill code. Furthermore, resource utilization levels also guide the selection of code statements for code motion between blocks.

The remainder of the paper is organized as follows. In section 2 we identify the optimizations that should be integrated with instruction scheduling. In section 3 we briefly outline the relationship between resource requirements and global code motion. In section 4 we present an integrated schedule driven algorithm using superblocks [8].

2 Optimizations and Instruction Scheduling

While the integration of optimizations with instruction scheduling may improve their effectiveness, it also increases the complexity of the instruction scheduling algorithm. Therefore it is important to examine the interactions between various optimizations and the instruction scheduler to identify the optimizations that should be integrated. The optimizations that do not significantly interact with the instruction scheduling may be applied in a separate optimization phase that precedes scheduling.

Three main characteristics of optimizations that determine whether or not an optimization should be integrated with the instruction scheduler are:

Opportunity: If all of the opportunities for applying an optimization can be determined prior to scheduling, then the optimizations can be carried out independently of the scheduler. On the other hand, if scheduling actions create additional opportunities for optimization, these opportunities can only be exploited by applying optimizations during scheduling.

Usefulness: If the optimization is always considered to be useful, it need not be integrated. If the usefulness of an optimization requires information that is typically available during instruction scheduling, such as the availability of registers, then the optimization should be integrated with scheduling.

Reversability: An optimization may be generally useful, but harmful in some situations. Furthermore, the latter situations may only become apparent during instruction scheduling. This type of optimization may be applied prior to scheduling and selectively reversed during instruction scheduling if it is determined that the application of the optimization was indeed harmful and, in fact, the optimization can be reversed.

According to the above criteria, there are a number of traditional optimizations that can be applied prior to instruction scheduling. The optimizations of constant propagation, loop invariant code motion, induction variable elimination, strength reduction, and dead code elimination can be applied prior to scheduling. The opportunities for these optimizations are not created during scheduling, they are generally useful, and their reversal is not required. Copy propagation can also be applied prior to scheduling. However, in some situations creation of copies may facilitate code reordering. In these situations copy creation can be carried out during scheduling. Partial dead code is another optimization which is useful in most situations and therefore can be performed prior to scheduling. In some situations it may be beneficial to reverse this optimization. However, this can be easily achieved by the scheduler through global code motion.

The above criteria also suggest that some optimizations should be integrated with instruction scheduling. These include the redundancy elimination optimization and DAG restructuring transformations. Opportunities of redundancy elimination can be created by code motion, its usefulness cannot be fully estimated prior to scheduling due to its influence on register pressure, and it cannot always be reversed during scheduling. The usefulness of DAG restructuring cannot always be determined prior to scheduling. In the remainder of this section we discuss the integration of above optimizations with instruction scheduling.

2.1 Redundancy Elimination

The scope over which the redundancy elimination optimization is applied is important in determining its integration with instruction scheduling. The application of this optimization to individual basic blocks can be applied prior to instruction scheduling because the effect of local optimization on register pressure is expected to be minimal. In rare situations where the effect is significant, local optimization can be easily reversed during instruction scheduling using rematerialization. On the other hand, global redundancy elimination can significantly increase register pressure. Furthermore, in general, the reversal of this optimization during scheduling is not possible due to code that is already scheduled. Finally opportunities for redundancy elimination may be created due to code motion performed during instruction scheduling. Therefore global redundancy elimination should be integrated with instruction scheduling.

Let us consider instruction scheduling based upon superblocks. Elimination of global redundancy within a superblock can be performed immediately preceding its scheduling. This redundancy may arise due to multiple evaluations of an expression within the superblock or due to the availability of an expression at the entry of the superblock. The former opportunities can be exploited in much the same way as local redundancy elimination. The exploitation of latter opportunities increases the register pressure for other parts of the program and also may require the introduction of copy statements to save the value of the expression in a specific location. However, if the superblocks processed earlier are more important than those processed later, then the application of redundancy elimination improves the quality of code for the current superblock at the expense of the quality of code for superblocks processed later.

The application of redundancy elimination to a superblock requires the computation of available expressions at the entry point of the superblock. Since new available expressions may be generated during code motion performed by the instruction scheduler, the expressions available at the entry to the superblock currently being scheduled must be computed immediately preceding the optimization of the superblock. Only the expressions computed inside the superblock prior to the redefinition of variables used in the expressions can be potentially optimized. Given such an expression, the demand driven algorithm presented in Figure 1 determines whether or not the expression is available at the superblock's entry.

Starting from the entry of the superblock, the algorithm searches backwards through the flow graph of a predecessor superblock for the evaluations of the expression. If such evaluations are found, a temporary variable T is created into which the value of the expression is copied so that it is available at the entry of the superblock in T. It should be noted that during the search for an expression, parts of the program that have already been scheduled may also be encountered. Since scheduled parts correspond to more important superblocks, we should not introduce a copy instruction within the schedule since it would increase the schedule's length. Instead we ensure that an expression evaluated in a scheduled superblock is only considered available at one of its exits if the value of the expression is available in a register at the exit.

Our algorithm maintains a worklist that contains points in the program at which availability of the expression is required to ensure that the expression is available at the superblock's entry. Each member of the worklist is a query of the form $(n, regs)$ indicating that we need to determine whether the expression is available at n's exit. The set $regs$ is used during traversal through scheduled portions of the code to track the identities of registers whose current values are available at a superblock exit. Thus, if the expression being searched for is computed into one of the registers in $regs$, then it will be available at the exit. On the other hand, if the scheduled code computes the expression into registers that are overwritten prior to exiting the superblock, then the expression is not available. If the algorithm finds available evaluations of the expressions along all paths, the worklist becomes empty and the search terminates. The introduction of copies into T makes this value available at the superblock entry.

```
Available(exp, SB_entry)
 Worklist = {(n, REGS)_exp : n ∈ Pred(SB_entry) and n is scheduled}
          ∪{(n, φ)_exp : n ∈ Pred(SB_entry) and n is unscheduled};
 success = true;
 while Worklist ≠ empty and success do
  get a query (m, regs)_exp from Worklist;
  if m computes exp then
   if (m is scheduled and it writes to a register R ∈ regs) or (m is unscheduled)
   then Add m to expression evaluation set Eval endif
  elseif (m defines variables used in exp) or (m is the dummy start node of cfg)
  then success = false
  else - propagate query
   Worklist = Worklist
    ∪{(p, φ)_exp : p ∈ Pred(m) and p is unscheduled}
    ∪{(p, regs − {R})_exp : p ∈ Pred(m), p and m are scheduled and m writes to R}
    ∪{(p, REGS)_exp : p ∈ Pred(m), p is scheduled and m is unscheduled}
  endif
 endwhile
 if success then
  create a new temporary T;
  for each instruction/statement ∈ Eval do
   move value of expression from register/variable to T
  endfor
  return(T)
 else return() endif
```

Fig. 1. Demand Driven Determination of the Availability of expression exp at superblock SB_{entry}.

From the above discussion it is clear that our algorithm exploits only those opportunities that benefit superblocks scheduled earlier at expense of superblocks scheduled later. That is, the register pressure is only increased for superblocks that are yet to be scheduled. Also, our approach allows the exploitation of new opportunities for redundancy elimination that arise due to code motion performed by the instruction scheduler.

In our discussion so far we have not considered the elimination of partial redundancy elimination [10]. This is because the application of tail duplication that is performed prior to superblock construction, converts partial redundancy to full redundancy. On the other hand, if trace scheduling is being used, then prior to scheduling a trace, we must also perform partial redundancy elimination using a similar integrated technique.

2.2 DAG Restructuring Transformations

As in the case of redundancy elimination, the scope over which DAG restructuring transformations are applied is relevant to their integration with instruction scheduling. The transformations of individual basic blocks can be carried out prior to instruction scheduling since their application is typically beneficial. However, the transformations over a larger scope, such as within a superblock and across superblocks, cannot be applied prior to instruction scheduling. This is due to two main reasons. First, the superblocks are identified during instruction scheduling. Only after one superblock is identified and scheduled is another superblock constructed. This is because the scheduling of a superblock is followed by introduction of compensation code which must be considered prior to constructing future superblocks. Second, the application of DAG restructuring transformations are typically accompanied with an increase in register and functional unit requirements. Therefore the application of these transformations over large segments of code, such as those that form a superblock, may significantly increase register pressure and hence the potential for spill code generation. Thus, this class of transformations, when performed over a scope larger than a basic block, is best left for the instruction scheduler to perform.

During instruction scheduling, DAG restructuring transformations are used in two types of situations. First, if a superblock contains insufficient parallelism, then restructuring of a DAG can be performed to increase the amount of parallelism within the block. Note that the transformation of a superblock may require global code motion. Second, if restructuring of the DAG is not enough to create sufficient parallelism in a superblock, then the DAGs of adjacent unscheduled basic blocks can be restructured to facilitate the propagation of operations from an adjacent basic block to the superblock with insufficient parallelism.

There are two types of transformations that we consider for DAG restructuring. The first type of transformation, shown in Figure 2, exploits the presence of *constant operands* to reduce the height of a DAG and increase ILP. The second type of transformation, shown in Figure 3, exploits *algebraic properties* of the operators to restructure the DAG. The situations under which the transformations are applicable and the conditions under which they are useful during the restructuring of a DAG are also given in the figures. In the discussion of these transformations we assume that the DAG corresponds to a superblock. Thus, it should be noted that the application of DAG restructuring transformations involves global code motion and thus may require the introduction of compensation code. To emphasize this fact, we assume that the nodes in the figures come from two different basic blocks which are indicated by shaded and unshaded nodes. A change in the shading of a node indicates that the node has been moved using global code motion.

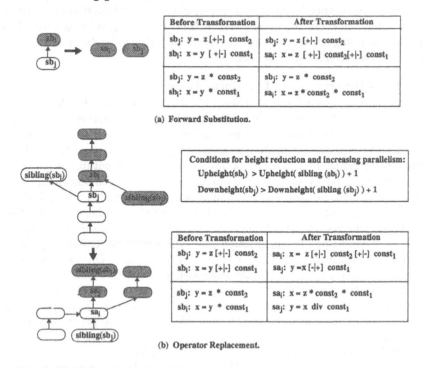

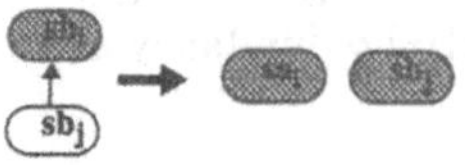

Before Transformation	After Transformation
sb_j: y = z [+|-] $const_2$ sb_i: x = y [+|-] $const_1$	sb_j: y = z [+|-] $const_2$ sa_i: x = z [+|-] $const_2$[+|-] $const_1$
sb_j: y = z * $const_2$ sb_i: x = y * $const_1$	sb_j: y = z * $const_2$ sa_i: x = z * $const_2$ * $const_1$

(a) Forward Substitution.

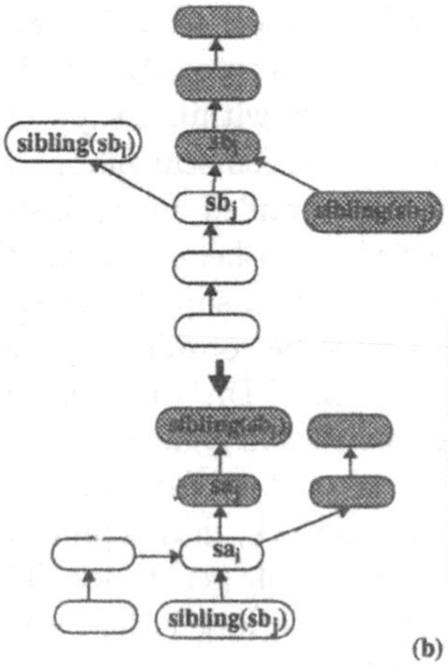

Conditions for height reduction and increasing parallelism:
Upheight(sb_i) > Upheight(sibling (sb_i)) + 1
Downheight(sb_j) > Downheight(sibling (sb_j)) + 1

Before Transformation	After Transformation
sb_j: y = z [+|-] $const_2$ sb_i: x = y [+|-] $const_1$	sa_i: x = z [+|-] $const_2$ [+|-] $const_1$ sa_j: y = x [-|+] $const_1$
sb_j: y = z * $const_2$ sb_i: x = y * $const_1$	sa_i: x = z * $const_2$ * $const_1$ sa_j: y = x div $const_1$

(b) Operator Replacement.

Fig. 2. Exploiting Constant Operands.

Forward substitution in the presence of constant operands eliminates a data dependency between operations (see Figure 2(a)). As can be seen in the Figure 2(a), whenever a dependency exists between two nodes that have constant operands and have no other dependencies, height reduction and increased parallelism always occurs when we eliminate the dependency through forward substitution. Therefore, there are no conditions needed for applying this transformation. Before the application of the transformations the two nodes are in different basic blocks. However, after the transformation, they belong to the same basic block.

We can sometimes apply a transformation to reduce the height and increase parallelism even when there are other dependencies involved in expressions with constant operands. *Operator replacement* is the transformation used to reorder a pair of data dependent operations, enabling height reduction and parallelism under certain conditions. In Figure 2(b) a node *sibling*(sb_i) is dependent on sb_j, and sb_i depends on *sibling*(sb_j) (e.g., output dependency). In order to create more parallelism, we ideally would like to have the bottom node and sibling of sb_j, which have no dependencies, execute in parallel. Since one of sb_i's dependencies would have then been computed, by using the operator replacement transformation, we can compute sb_i before sb_j. We then compute sb_j and its dependent node. This transformation enables the bottom part of the DAG and the top part of the DAG to execute in parallel with the computation of the dependent section. However, in order for this transformation to be beneficial, we must ensure that the transformed path that computes sb_i and sb_j does not increase such that it takes longer to execute than the bottom part of the DAG or the top part of the DAG. Thus conditions are given to ensure that the height of the DAG from sb_i to the top (*Upheight*(sb_i)) is greater by more than one than the height of the sibling of sb_i to the top of the DAG. It is this portion of the graph that would execute in parallel with the top part of the DAG. A similar check is needed for the bottom of the DAG, using the function *Downheight*(sb_j) since the sb_j and the sibling sb_j would execute in parallel with the bottom part of the DAG. The shading of nodes indicates that the application of this transformation requires global code motion.

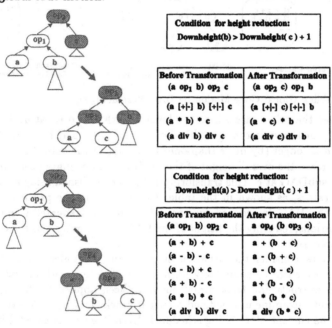

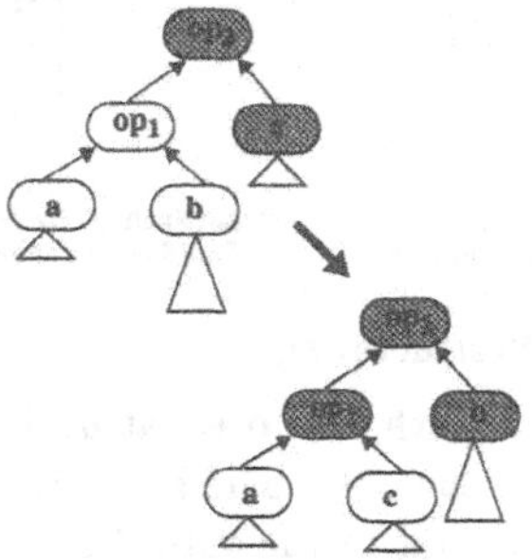

Condition for height reduction:
Downheight(b) > Downheight(c) + 1

Before Transformation (a op_1 b) op_2 c	After Transformation (a op_2 c) op_1 b
(a [+|-] b) [+|-] c	(a [+|-] c) [+|-] b
(a * b) * c	(a * c) * b
(a div b) div c	(a div c) div b

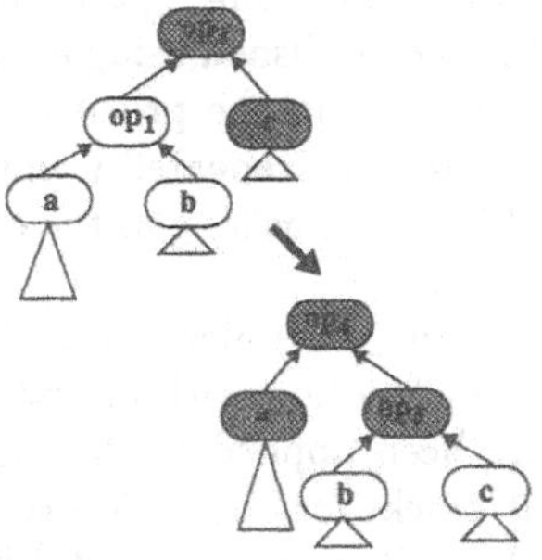

Condition for height reduction:
Downheight(a) > Downheight(c) + 1

Before Transformation (a op_1 b) op_2 c	After Transformation a op_4 (b op_3 c)
(a + b) + c	a + (b + c)
(a - b) - c	a - (b + c)
(a - b) + c	a - (b - c)
(a + b) - c	a + (b - c)
(a * b) * c	a * (b * c)
(a div b) div c	a div (b * c)

Fig. 3. Exploiting Algebraic Properties of Operators.

In expressions that do not necessarily involve constant operands, we may be able to exploit the algebraic properties of *associativity* and *commutativity* of operators to perform restructing of a DAG to reduce its height, enabling more parallelism. The general idea is to reduce the height of a DAG by shortening a path in the DAG that is longer than other paths. By using appropriate conditions on the length of paths involved, transformations will reduce the height of a DAG by reducing the length of a longer path in the DAG and lengthening a shorter path in the DAG. Consider the DAGs and two transformations shown in Figure 3. The first transformation handles the case where the length of the path from the bottom of the DAG to *b* is longer that the length of the path from the bottom to *c*. The transformation is to swap the subDAGs of *b* and *c*, using commutativity and associativity properties of operators. This transformation is applied when the height of the subDAG rooted at *b* is at least one greater than the height of the subDAG rooted at *c*. The transformation shortens the overall height of the DAG by one. As in the case of earlier DAG transformations, this transformation may also require global code motion.

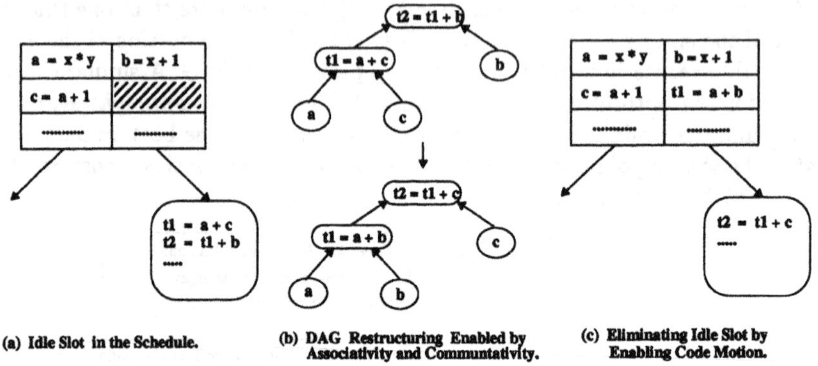
a = x*y
b=x+1
c= a+1
t1 = a+c
t2 = t1+b
t2=t1+b
t1=a+c
a
c
b
t2=t1+c
t1=a+b
a
b
c
a = x*y
b=x+1
c= a+1
t1 = a+b
t2 = t1+c
(a) Idle Slot in the Schedule.
(b) DAG Restructuring Enabled by Associativity and Communtativity.
(c) Eliminating Idle Slot by Enabling Code Motion.

Fig. 4. Enabling Global Code Motion by DAG Restructuring.

Consider the other case where the longest path is rooted at *a*. The second transformation shown in the figure handles this case. If the height of the subDAG rooted at *a* is longer (by more than one) than that of the subDAG rooted at *c*, we can decrease the overall height of the DAG by interchanging the subDAG at *a* with the subDAG at *c*. This transformation is accomplished using associativity of the operators, as shown in the table. As was true in the previous case, the height of the DAG is reduced by one. Thus, we can repeatedly apply these transformations, reducing the height of the DAG by one as long as the conditions continue to exist.

Let us now consider the situation in which the scheduler is unable to find sufficient parallelism to completely fill a long instruction with operations even after DAG restructuring transformations have been applied to the superblock. Thus, we must examine unscheduled adjacent blocks for operations that can be moved to the current block being scheduled. Even if we are successful in finding operations that can be propagated, the propagation of operations may not always be useful. It is only beneficial to propagate operations that are immediately schedulable. However, if such operations are not immediately apparent in an unscheduled adjacent block, then we may be able to expose such operations by restructuring the DAG of the adjacent block. If the unscheduled adjacent block is a successor (predecessor) of the block with insufficient parallelism, then the leaves (roots) of the adjacent block must be considered for transformation.

The scheduled block in Figure 4(a) contains an idle slot and Figure 4(b) represents the portion of the DAG for an unscheduled adjacent block. We would like to propagate operations from that DAG to the scheduled block to eliminate the idle slot. The values of *a*, *b* and *c* are computed in the scheduled block and used by the adjacent block. Since the operation that computes the value of *c* has not been scheduled prior to the instruction with the idle slot, the statement $t1 = a + c$ cannot be propagated and scheduled in the position of the idle slot. On the other hand since the values of a and b have already been computed, we can restructure the DAG as shown in Figure 4(b) and propagate the operation $t1 = a + b$ to the position of the idle slot. Thus, depending upon the availability of operand values we may choose between the equivalent DAGs shown in Figure 4(b). As we can see from this situation, the appropriate DAG can only be selected by the scheduler.

Another example in Figure 5(a) shows a schedule with two idle slots. These idle slots may be created due to a long latency of the multiplication operator. As shown in Figure 5(b) one of the idle slots can be eliminated by propagating a statement from the adjacent block. However, if the DAG for the adjacent block is restructured using forward substitution, then both idle slots can be eliminated (see Figure 5(c)).

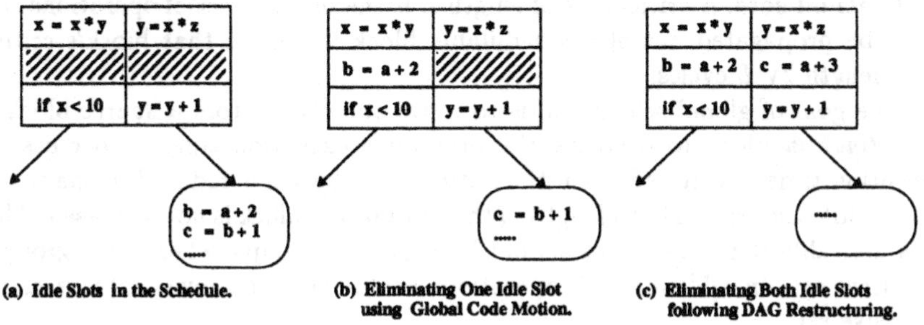
x = x*y
y=x*z
if x<10
y=y+1
b = a+2
c = b+1
x = x*y
y=x*z
b = a+2
if x<10
y=y+1
c = b+1
x = x*y
y=x*z
b = a+2
c = a+3
if x<10
y=y+1
(a) Idle Slots in the Schedule.
(b) Eliminating One Idle Slot using Global Code Motion.
(c) Eliminating Both Idle Slots following DAG Restructuring.

Fig. 5. Increasing Global Code Motion by Exposing Parallelism.

3 Resource Requirements and Global Code Motion

The scheduling of operations is driven by the requirement levels of resources, which includes both functional units and registers. We have developed a resource conscious scheduling technique that integrates register allocation and scheduling. The technique consists of identifying sections of a program that underutilize registers and functional units and sections that require more of these resources than are available. The scheduler is guided by the resource requirements at each point in the block being scheduled and the critical paths through the block. The scheduler tries to move code from the overutilized sections to underutilized sections. The technique first measures the requirements of resources at each program point. This information is then used by the scheduler to determine where code motion should occur, taking into account the resource requirements of both resources simultaneously [1].

To measure the resource requirements, we first create a special type of DAG for each resource that reflects the resource requirements for the code in a block. For each resource, the precedence and usage information in a block is used to construct a partial ordering of the operations indicating which pairs of operations temporally share a single instance of the resource under any allowable schedule. Details of computing usage information for registers is described elsewhere [2]. For each resource R, a $Reuse_R$ DAG is constructed to represent the partial order. Sets of operations in the $Reuse_R$ DAG that are fully ordered are called ***allocation chains***, since by definition of the partial order, they can all safely be allocated a single instance of R. The maximum number of resources required to exploit all exposed parallelism is given by the minimum number of allocation chains that cover the $Reuse_R$ DAG.

The technique requires identification of the following sets:

Excessive sets: A block may have areas where the ILP exceeds the resources provided by the architecture. We call sets of operations that can execute in parallel and would require too many resources ***excessive sets***. While the number of allocation chains covering a schedulable block indicates if there are any excessive sets, it is desirable to know exactly which operations are in excessive sets. Excessive sets are computed by finding the sections of the schedulable block where there are portions of an excessive number of allocation chains, which is performed in graph linear time [2].

Critical sets: A critical set of length L is the minimal set of operations that must be propagated out of a schedulable block to reduce that block's critical path length by L cycles.

The goal of global scheduling is to move operations from a ***source*** block to a ***destination*** block to decrease the program's execution time. A decrease in execution time is achieved when the critical path length is reduced in the source block while the critical path length of the destination block is not increased. Thus it is desirable that operations should be moved in groups, where each group is a critical set. In addition, the operations should not be moved into or create excessive sets.

As an example, consider the block of code shown in Figure 6(a), which uses only integer functional units and registers. Since a single type of functional unit is used, the $Reuse_{FU}$ DAG is the same as the program DAG. The partial schedule for functional units is shown in Figure 6(b). Each column represents one allocation chain, so three functional units are required to exploit all exposed ILP. Similarly, a $Reuse_{Reg}$ DAG and partial schedule can be constructed for registers by considering their usage characteristics.

Assume that the architecture has two functional units available. Then the sets {`C, D, E`}, {`C, D, G`}, and {`C, F, G`} are all functional unit excessive sets. For scheduling, only a summary set of all nodes that are in at least one excessive set for a resource is needed, and can be computed in graph linear time. The summary excessive set for functional units is {`C, D, E, F, G`}. Now assume that global code motion is being performed on the DAG in Figure 6(a) to move operations from the top of the block to some other location. The first critical set is {`B`}, as that will reduce the height of the block by one operation. Now operations `C`, `D`, and `E` can be moved. However, moving `C` at this time will not affect the block's height, so the next critical set is {`D, E`}.

Consider the construction of a final schedule for the DAG in Figure 6(a). `C` is in an excessive set but there are no idle slots in the other two allocation chains. That is, the scheduling of `C` would require an increase in the execution time of the block. However `E` is a candidate for the forward substitution transformation

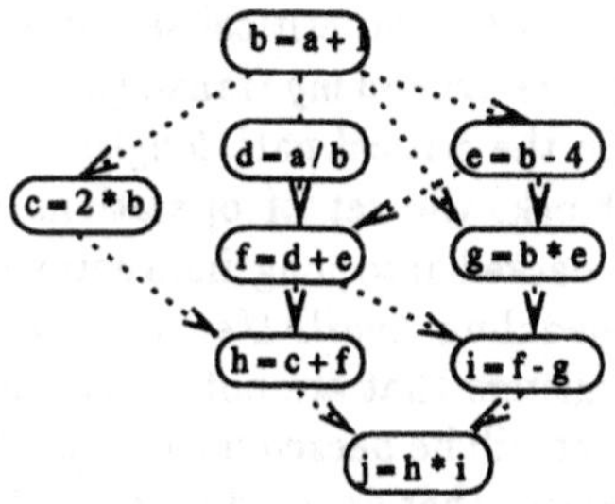

(a) $Reuse_{FU}$ DAG.

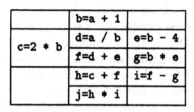

	b=a + 1	
c=2 * b	d=a / b	e=b - 4
	f=d + e	g=b * e
	h=c + f	i=f - g
	j=h * i	

(b) Functional Unit Partial Schedule.

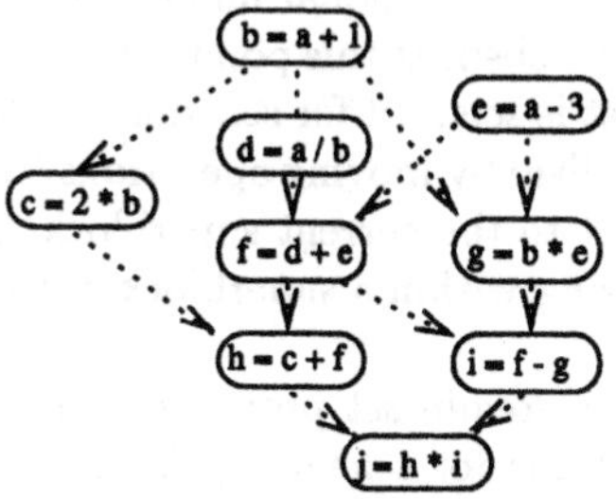

(c) Post $Reuse_{FU}$ DAG.

b=a + 1	e=a - 3
d=a / b	c=2 * b
f=d + e	g=b * e
h=c + f	i=f - g
j=h * i	

(d) Functional Unit Final Schedule.

Fig. 6. *Reuse* DAGs and Schedules.

discussed in Section 2.2. After performing the transformation, B and E can be scheduled in parallel, as shown in Figure 6(c). Application of the transformation allows C to be scheduled in the slot previously used by E, eliminating all excessive sets. The transformation also enables E to be moved out of the region by global code motion, decreasing the critical path length of the region by one instruction.

This scheduling technique is integrated with optimizations and transformations (including using a common DAG) to produce our final scheduler. The algorithm for this scheduler is given in the next section.

4 An Integrated Superblock Scheduling Algorithm

In this section we present a scheduling algorithm for superblocks that integrates the optimizations and restructuring transformations described in the previous sections with the resource conscious scheduling algorithm of the preceding section. A superblock is a loop free sequence of basic blocks which has a single entry point and possibly multiple exit points. Thus, a superblock can pass through several splits in the control flow graph but it cannot include a join in the flow graph. In order to create large superblocks our algorithm first carries out *tail duplication* which duplicates code following a join in the flow graph. Superblocks are constructed one at a time using profiling information and scheduled using the integrated scheduling and optimization algorithm.

Using the available expression information, a superblock is examined for redundancy elimination prior to scheduling. The DAG for the superblock is constructed, and using the analysis summarized in the previous section, the register and functional unit requirements, the excessive sets, and critical sets in the superblock are identified. We then perform *DAG restructuring* transformations to increase parallelism, if so required, and reduce the critical path length.

During the scheduling of a given superblock, the set of operations ready for scheduling are repeatedly identified and packed into long instructions of a VLIW machine. At any given point during scheduling *AvailFUs* and *AvailRegs* denote the number of functional units and registers that are not in use and are therefore available for use by the operations that will be packed into the next long instruction. Let *Ready* denote the set of operations that are ready for scheduling. There are two possibilities at this point. Either the *Ready* set is large enough and therefore provides enough parallelism to keep all functional units busy during the next instruction or there is insufficient parallelism at this point. In the former case a subset of operations from the *Ready* set is selected for scheduling while in the latter case we must find additional parallelism by moving operations from as yet unscheduled superblocks that are adjacent to the current superblock. Thus, our algorithm not only performs code reordering within a superblock but it also performs code motion between superblocks.

Let us consider the situation in which the *Ready* set provides sufficient or excessive parallelism. The selection of operations for scheduling is based upon several criteria. First, we should give preference to operations which belong to a critical path in the superblock. Second, we should also keep register pressure in check so that scheduling of operations can continue unhindered through the rest of the superblock. By keeping a balance between operations requiring new registers and operations freeing up registers we attempt to keep register pressure below a preset threshold. An operation frees a register if it represents the last use of the register's value. If enough operations that free registers are not available we may also consider generating spill code. If a register contains a value that is not used for the remainder of the superblock, we can consider spilling the value into memory. Therefore, the operations scheduled in the current long instruction may contain operations from the *Ready* set and some additional spill code (*Spill*).

If the *Ready* set provides insufficient parallelism for filling the next long instruction we proceed as follows. We examine basic blocks that are as yet unscheduled and are adjacent to the superblock being currently scheduled. Operations from these adjacent blocks are moved into the current block to increase the number of operations available for scheduling. Our goal during the propagation of operations is not only to create sufficient parallelism in the current superblock but also to increase the potential of obtaining shorter schedules for the adjacent block being considered. If the adjacent block contains excessive functional unit sets, then we should propagate operations from these sets. On the other hand, if the adjacent block contains insufficient parallelism, then we must attempt to propagate operations from critical sets in order to reduce the critical path length of the adjacent block. Finally, if the operations that can be found for propagation cannot be immediately scheduled in the current block, then we apply DAG restructuring transformations to expose operations for propagation that can be immediately scheduled in the current block. Thus, in this situation operations

```
IntegratedScheduling() {
 Perform tail duplication to create larger superblocks.
 Apply all of the scheduling-independent optimizations.
 Compute available expressions information.
 while unscheduled code remains do
     Construct the next superblock, SB, using profile information.
     Compute available expression information for SB.
     Eliminate fully redundant expressions within SB including
       those that may be created by duplication of partially redundant expressions.
     Compute resource usage, excessive sets, and critical sets for SB.
     Initialize AvailFUs and AvailRegs by examining usage of resources
       at the end of each already scheduled superblock whose execution
       immediately precedes the execution of SB.
     Apply DAG restructuring transformations to SB for
       increasing parallelism, if required, and reducing critical path length.
     while operations in SB remain unscheduled do
         Ready ← { I: operation I is ready to be scheduled }
         if |Ready ≥ AvailFUs| then
           Identify operations for scheduling Select ⊆ Ready using following criteria:
             • Reduce critical path length: give preference to operations
               that are a part of a critical path in the superblock.
             • Control register pressure and spilling: balance selection of operations
               requiring additional registers with operations that free registers and
               spill registers if register pressure is too high.
           Let Sched = Select ∪ Spill be the set of operations scheduled.
         else -|Ready < AvailFUs|
           Propagate set of operations Prop from unscheduled basic blocks
             adjacent to SB using the following criteria:
             • Redistribute excessive ILP: Move operations from
               an adjacent block that belong to functional unit excessive sets.
             • Reduce critical path length: Move operations that are in a critical set
               of an adjacent block to reduce critical path length for the adjacent block.
             • Transform and propagate: Apply DAG restructuring transformations to
               an adjacent block to enable propagation of operations.
           Let Sched = Ready ∪ Prop be the set of operations scheduled.
         endif
         Mark operations in Sched as scheduled.
         Update AvailFUs and AvailRegs.
     endwhile
 endwhile
}
```

Fig. 7. An Integrated Scheduling Algorithm.

from the *Ready* set and also operations that are propagated from neighboring blocks (*Prop*) are scheduled in the current long instruction. The steps of the algorithm are summarized in Figure 7.

We presented an algorithm using the integrated approach for scheduling superblocks. However, this technique is also applicable to other global scheduling techniques such as those based upon control dependence regions.

The research most closely related to our work is the mutation scheduling technique proposed by Novack and Nicolau [12] which integrates a number of DAG transformations into the instruction scheduler. In most architectures certain functions can be performed through a number of alternative instruction sequences. Mutation scheduling selects the appropriate alternative based upon availability of resources. DAG transformations which exploit constant operands are also used. In other related work Ebcioglu et al. and Chang et al. consider the removal of partially dead code during instruction scheduling [4, 3].

References

1. D. Berson, R. Gupta and M.L. Soffa, "Resource Spackling: A framework for integrating register allocation in local and global schedulers," In *Proc. of Intl. Conf. on Parallel Architectures and Compilation Techniques*, pages 135-146, 1994.
2. D. Berson, R. Gupta and M.L. Soffa, "GURRR: A global unified resource requirements representation," In *ACM SIGPLAN Workshop on Intermediate Representations, Sigplan Notices*, vol. 30, pages 23-34, April 1995.
3. P.P. Chang, S.A. Mahlke, and W-M. Hwu, "Using profile information to assist classic code optimizations," *Software-Practice and Experience*, 21(12):1301–1321, Dec. 1991.
4. K. Ebcioglu, R.D. Groves, K-C. Kim, G. Silberman, and I. Ziv, "VLIW compilation techniques in a superscalar environment," In *Proc. of Sigplan Conf. on Prog. Language Design and Implementation*, pages 36-48, 1994.
5. J.A. Fisher, "Trace scheduling: a technique for global microcode compaction," *IEEE Trans. on Computers*, C-30(7):478-490, 1981.
6. R. Gupta and M.L. Soffa, "Region scheduling: an approach for detecting and redistributing parallelism," *IEEE Trans. on Software Engineering*, 16(4):421-431, 1990.
7. P. Hsu and E. Davidson, "Highly concurrent scalar processing," In *Proc. of 13th Annual International Symposium on Computer Architecture*, pages 386-395, 1986.
8. W-M. Hwu et al., "The superblock: an effective technique for VLIW and superscalar compilation," In *The Journal of Supercomputing* vol. A, pages 229-248, 1993.
9. W-M. Hwu and Y. Patt, "Checkpoint repair for out-of-order execution machines," In *Proc. of 14th Annual Intl. Symp. on Comp. Architecture*, pages 18-26, 1987.
10. J. Knoop, O. Ruthing and B. Steffen, "Optimal code motion: theory and practice," In *ACM Trans. on Programming Languages and Systems*, 16(4):1117-1155, 1994.
11. J. Knoop, O. Ruthing, B. Steffen, "Partial dead code elimination," In *Proc. of Sigplan Conf. on Prog. Language Design and Implementation*, pages 147-158, 1994.
12. S. Novack and A. Nicolau, "Mutation scheduling: a unified approach to compiling for fine-grain parallelism," *Proc. Languages and Compilers for Parallel Computing*, LNCS 892, 1994.
13. C. Norris and L. Pollock, "A scheduler-sensitive global register allocator," In *Proc. of Supercomputing*, pages 804-813, 1993.
14. S. Pinter, "Register allocation with instruction scheduling: a new approach," In *Proc. of Sigplan Conf. on Prog. Lang. Design and Impl.*, pages 248-257, 1993.

Bidirectional Scheduling: A New Global Code Scheduling Approach

Pohua Chang
Dong-yuan Chen
Yong-fong Lee
Youfeng Wu
Utpal Banerjee

Intel Corporation
M/S RN6-18
2200 Mission College Blvd.
Santa Clara, CA 95052-8119
Corresponding Author: Pohua Chang
E-Mail: pohua@gomez.sc.intel.com
Phone: (408) 765-6423

Abstract

Instruction scheduling is an important compiler code transformation step for generating code for pipelined and VLIW processors. Dependencies among instructions need to be enforced. In this paper, we describe a global code scheduling algorithm that moves instructions upward and downward in the control flow graph. Downward code motion is first applied. The purpose of downward code motion is to move store instructions and other instructions on the tail portion of critical paths to later basic blocks. This allows for better code compaction. After downward code motion is applied, upward code motion and code compaction are applied. Upward code motion moves instructions on the beginning portion of critical paths to preceding basic blocks. This allows for better code compaction. In our algorithm, we integrate some instruction-level parallelization techniques with upward code motion to permit more code motion freedom.

1. Introduction

In a VLIW processor, dependence checking logic is often very simple. For example, upon the detection of a register dependence, the instruction issue unit would stall. Therefore, compile-time code scheduling is essential to ensure that independent instructions are scheduled together and dependent instructions are scheduled apart.

In this paper, we describe a global code scheduling algorithm that are unique in two aspects. First, downward code motion is applied. Traditional code scheduler often moves instructions only in the upward direction. Second, instruction-level parallelization techniques are integrated with the upward code motion algorithm. This allows more code motion freedom.

1.1. Related Work

Local code scheduling algorithms apply to instructions within a basic block. The most popular algorithm is List Scheduling [C76]. List Scheduling is refined to become Level Scheduling [BRG87] and Refined Level Scheduling [B88]. It has been noted that list scheduling tends to schedule many short-latency leaf nodes too soon. These nodes can be used to fill delay slots. The solution is to delay scheduling decision [BRG89]. A successful commercial compiler code scheduler is described in [C89]. An integrated code scheduling and register allocation algorithm is described in [GH88]. A two-pass scheduling algorithm is described in [HC88].

Global code scheduling algorithms apply to instructions in multiple basic blocks. Superblock code scheduling is a popular code generation method [HMC93]. Hyperblock code scheduling is an extension of superblock code scheduling for handling predicated instructions [MLC92]. Trace scheduling is a code scheduling algorithm that works on a sequence of basic blocks that are likely to be executed in series [F81][E85]. Bernstein described a global code scheduling algorithm that is implemented in the IBM XL Compiler [BCLR92]. Moon and Ebcioglu described a VLIW code scheduling algorithm [ME92].

1.2. Organization Of This Paper

Section 2 describes the high-level algorithm. Section 3 describes how we determine upward or downward code motion of an instruction. Section 4 gives the downward code motion algorithm Section 5 gives the upward code motion algorithm. Section 6 shows some experimental data. Finally, Section 7 offers some concluding remarks.

2. Algorithm

The algorithm works on a region at a time. A region is a single entry, multiple exit control flow subgraph. There is a basic block that dominates all other basic blocks in the region. The overall code scheduling algorithm is as follows.

```
for (each region) {
        Apply Path-Based Motion Estimation;
        Apply Downward Code Motion;
        Apply Upward Code Motion;
}
```

Path-Based Motion Estimation:

There can be one or more basic block sequences from the dominating basic block of the region. Each basic block sequence is called a path. We look at the instructions in a path and schedule them according to data dependencies, ignoring control dependencies. From the schedule, we know if we like to move an instruction to a preceding basic block or to a later basic block.

Downward Code Motion:

For instructions that are identified to be candidates of downward code motion according to path-based motion estimation, we predicate the execution of such instructions and move the instructions to later basic blocks. It is important to predicate (conditional execution) the execution of downward moving instructions because there can be multiple control flow paths that reach the destination block to which the instructions are moved to. For an example,

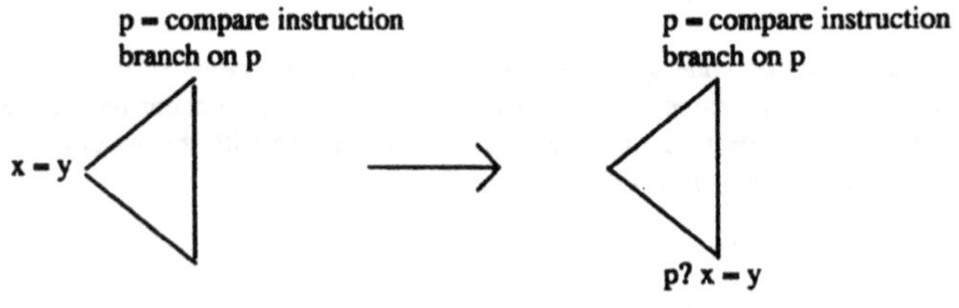

Upward Code Motion:

We schedule basic blocks from the bottom of the region towards the dominating basic block. When we schedule a basic block, we first apply instruction-level parallelization techniques (such as renaming destination register operand) to increase the freedom of code scheduling. Then, we schedule the basic block according to the machine model. We schedule instructions as late as possible without increasing the longest critical path in the basic block, so that instructions are packed near the bottom of the basic block. Then we move instructions at the upper portion of the compacted basic block where there are less parallelism to previous basic block. When we move instructions to preceding basic blocks, we apply partial redundancy elimination.

We define a function weight(basic block) to be the estimated execution count of the basic block. For a control flow edge e, we define src(e) to be the source basic block and dst(e) to be the destination basic block. A control flow edge is said to be a no-cross-over edge if one of the following conditions apply:

weight(src(e)) / weight(dst(e)) > 3

.OR.

weight(dst(e)) / weight(src(e)) > 3

We do not wish to perform code motion across a no-cross-over edge because the overhead introduced by code motion may be too large. We add control dependence edges between instructions to the branch instruction that represents a no-cross-over edge.

3. Path-Based Motion Estimation

For each instruction in a region, we like to know to which basic blocks it is to be moved to. We propose a path-based motion estimation approach. For each control flow path in the region, we apply List Scheduling, ignoring the control dependencies (except between branch instructions). This means that branch instructions can be moved above data computation instructions. The result of scheduling is critical paths that are spread out in the control flow graph.

For each path that we List Schedule, each instruction has a destination basic block. If the destination basic block is different than the source basic block, we record (source-block, destination-block, path) in the instruction. We use this information in the downward code motion algorithm.

We do not consider moving instructions downward, whose source operands and destination operands overlap. We also do not consider moving serialization instructions downward. Therefore, we add control dependence edges between aforementioned instruction types to later branch instructions.

4. Downward Code Motion

```
For each instruction that we want to move downward (i.e. destination-block is a successor of source-block)
{
    For each path that the instruction is to be moved downward
        (i.e. destination-block <> source-block for all paths)
    {
        p - a new predicate register;
        if (source-block is not the dominating basic block of the region)
        {
            Insert a "p - FALSE" in the dominating basic block;
        }
        if (source-block does not end with a branch instruction)
        {
            Insert a "p - TRUE" in the source-block;
        }
        In the path, generate additional instructions so that p is TRUE only if control flow
            goes from source-block to destination-block along the path;
        Generate a copy of the instruction in destination-block predicated by p;
    }
    Delete the instruction;
}
```

For example, in the below example, we want to move instruction x down along three paths.

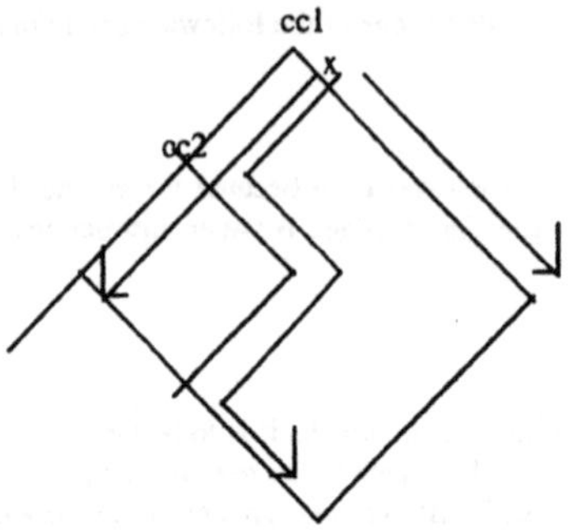

By applying our algorithm, we get

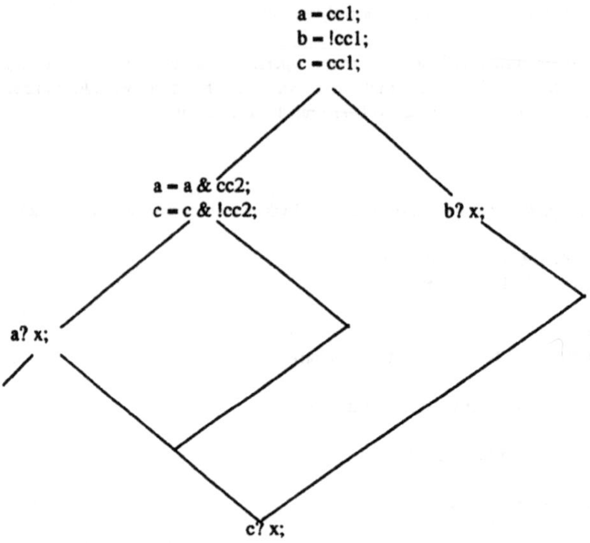

After applying scheduling, we want to apply predicate register coalescing to reduce the number of predicate registers used in the downward code motion algorithm.

5. Upward Code Motion

Algorithm Global-Code-Scheduling
  Order extended blocks in a region by the level information; the lower level
    blocks show up first on the sorted list;
  for (each extended block EB in the sorted list) {
    Remove redundant and dead instructions from extended block;
    Apply ILP-Transformations on extended block;

```
        Apply local code scheduling to extended block;
        Determine instructions to be moved forward;
        if (there are instructions to be moved upward) {
                Move those instructions upward;
        }
    Apply register coalescing;
    Apply predication;
    Apply local code scheduling to each extended block;
```

ILP-Transformations:

```
        Operation Combining;
        Constant Combining;
        RHS Split;
        Combining Induction Variables;
        Forward Substitution;
```

Operation Combining:

```
        for (p=first_instruction; p!=NULL; p=p->next) {
                for (q=p->next; q!=NULL; q=q->next) {
                        if ((q is more critical than p) and
                           ({p,q} can be replaced by {r,q',p}) and
                           (r can be computed very early)) {
                                // For example,
                                //      p:      j = j - disp;
                                //      q:      t = htab[j + hsize_reg];
                                // becomes
                                //      r:      offset = hsize_reg - disp;
                                //      q:      t = htab[j + offset];
                                //      p:      j = j - disp;
                                change {p,q} to {r,q',p};
                        }
                }
        }
```

Constant Combining:

```
        for (p=first_instruction; p!=NULL; p=p->next) {
                for (q=p->next; q!=NULL; q=q->next) {
                        if ((q can absorb p) and (q can be moved to before p) and
                           (q is more critical than p)) {
                                // For example,
                                //      p:      r0 = r0 + 1;
                                //      ...
                                //      q:      r1 = mem[r0 + 4];
                                move q to before p;
                                modify q so that {p,q} and {q',p} are equivalent;
                        }
                }
        }
```

RHS Split:

```
        for (p=first_instruction; p!=NULL; p=p->next) {
                if ((p is a critical instruction) and
                   (p cannot be moved above a previous branch instruction because the
                    destination operand of p is live on exit of the branch)) {
                        convert p to a pair of instructions {p1,p2} such that
```

```
                p1: tmp = p.RHS;
                p2: p.LHS = tmp;
        }
}
```

Combining Induction Variables:

```
for (p=first_instruction; p!=NULL; p=p->next) {
        for (q=p->next; q!=NULL; q=q->next) {
                if ((p and q are computation on the same induction variable) and
                   (there is no instruction between p and q use or modify p.LHS))
        {
                        remove p;
                        modify q so that {p,q} is equivalent to {q'};
                }
        }
}
```

Forward Substitution:

```
for (p=first_instruction; p!=NULL; p=p->next) {
        for (q=p->next; q!=NULL; q=q->next) {
                if ((q can absorb p) and
                   (source operands of p are not modified between p and q)) {
                        // For example,
                        //      p:      r0 = r1;
                        //      q:      if (r0 > 0) goto L0;
                        modify q so that the RHS of q uses source operands of p;
                }
        }
}
```

Our local code scheduler is a typical List Scheduler. For each instruction, we first calculate the earliesst issue time, according to the available time of the source operands and the latency of previous instructions. Then, we calculate the latest issue time of each instruction that the overall schedule will not be prolonged. The instruction priority is set according to the latest issue time of each instruction and the instruction latency of each instruction. Once the instruction priorities are calculated, we apply the List Scheduling algorithm. We prefer to generate a as-late-as-possible schedule, in that instructions are scheduled as late as possible without increasing the overall schedule. This allows critical instructions (that need to be moved to previous basic blocks) to be exposed.

Once we have the local code schedule, we can divide each extended block into two parts. The upper half is the non-saturating region and the bottom half is the saturating region. We use a heuristic to decide the deviding line. The instructions in the non-saturating region are to be moved to previous extended blocks.

An instruction can be moved to a previous extended block if all the of following conditions are true.
(1) the instruction does not modify the source operand of the branch instruction of the previous extended block.
(2) the instruction does not modify a value that is live on exit of the branch instruction of the previous extended block.
(3) the instruction is safe (non-trapping). (we assume that the hardware has special control speculation support).
The above conditions are also used to determined the dividing line of the non-saturating and saturating regions.

Note that we need to be aware of the effect of long latency instructions on subsequent extended blocks. For example, if there is a LOAD instruction that is scheduled in cycle 1 of a basic block that is compressed to a single cycle of execution, and the value of the LOAD is used immediately in a subsequent extended block, we want to mark the LOAD instruction as an instruction that need to be moved forward.

A heuristic that we can use to determine the dividing line between the non-saturating region and the saturating region is to define an AVG parallelism measure. After local code scheduling, we mark each cycle of the schedule as satisfactory or non-satisfactory depending if there are enough number of instructions in each cycle (more than AVG). Starting from the last cycle of the schedule, we look at each preceding cycle of the schedule until a non-satisfactory cycle is found. Everything from that non-satisfactory cycle and above are candidates for upward code motion.

We start from the bottom extended blocks (that have no successors in the DAG) and process extended blocks up towards the root extended block. For each extended block, we check if some of the candidate instructions can be moved to the preceding extended blocks, according to the safety and dataflow conditions. We sort all control edges by their estimated execution frequency. We traverse backward following the control flow edges with higher frequencies first.

There are some special cases that we detect. For one, if extended block A goes to extended blocks B and C. After moving instructions from B to A, we want to move some instructions from C to A. It may be the case that we want to move the same set of instructions from C to A, as from B to A. That can be caused due to code duplication when we moved instructions from D to both B and C. We need to detect this special case and allow code motion to occur between C and A.

Redundancy can be introduced by global code motion. In the original program, for each instruction, we create an EQUIV set containing that instruction. As instructions are duplicated, they are added to the corresponding EQUIV sets. An instruction p is redundant, and can be removed from the corresponding EQUIV set, if
(1) there is another instruction q in the EQUIV set that dominates p, and
(2) the source operands of q are not modified on any path from q to p.

An instruction p is dead if its result is not used anywhere. Detecting dead instructions in an extended block is a trivial task, given that the register-IN/OUT information are available.

Register Coalescing:

RHS Split transformation can introduce register copy instructions. After code scheduling, we can apply register coalescing to remove some register copy instructions.

Predication:

For a branch instruction that is unlikely to be predicted correctly, if there are many empty instruction slots between the compare instruction and the branch instruction, we can predicate and then move instructions from the subsequent extended blocks to fill the empty slots. Note that this may means copying instructions from off-trace paths into the middle of some extended blocks.

6. Experiment

We have profiled the SPEC95 CINT benchmark programs and extracted the most time consuming near leaf-level procedures. In the below tables, the Benchmark column shows the benchmark function, the IPC column shows the average number of instructions issued per cycle, and the Speedup column shows the speedup of our proposed algorithm over Hyperblock Scheduling [MLC92]. For each benchmark program, we select up to the top three procedures. We assume a 10-issue VLIW architecture, with a load latency equaling to 2 cycles. We assume that compare instructions and the dependent branch instructions can be scheduled in the same cycle. We assume a perfect cache system.

[BRG87] D. Bernstein, M. Rodeh, and I. Gertner, "Approximation algorithms for scheduling arithmetic expressions on pipelined machines," TR-88.227, IBM Haifa Scientific Center, July 1987.

[BRG89] D. Bernstein, M. Rodeh, and I. Gertner, "On the complexity of scheduling problems for parallel/pipelined machines," IEEE Trans. on Computers, vol. 38, no. 9, Sep. 1989.

[C76] E. G. Coffman, Computer and job-shop scheduling theory, John Wiley and Sons, New York, 1976.

[C89] P. Chow, The MIPS-X RISC Microprocessor, Kluwer Academic Publishers, 1989.

[E85] J. R. Ellis, Bulldog: A Compiler for VLIW Architecture, Ph.D. Thesis, Yale Univ. DCS RR-364, Yale Univ. Feb. 1985.

[F81] J. Fisher, "Trace scheduling: a technique for global microcode compaction," IEEE Trans. on Computers, vol. c-30, no. 7, July 1981.

[GH88] J. R. Goodman and W.-C. Hsu, "Code scheduling and register allocation in large basic blocks," in Proc. of the IEEE-ACM Supercomputing Conf., 1988.

[HC88] W. Hwu and P. Chang, "Exploiting parallel microprocessor microarchitectures with a compiler code generator," in Proc. of the 15th Annual Intl. Symp. on Computer Architecture, May 1988.

[HMC93] W. Hwu, et. al., "The superblock: an effective technique for VLIW and superscalar compilation, " in J. of Supercomputing, Jan. 1993.

[ME92] S.-M. Moon and K. Ebcioglu, "An efficient resource-constrained global scheduling technique for superscalar and VLIW processors," in Proc. of the 25th Annual Intl. Symp. on Microarchitecture, Dec. 1992, pp. 55-71.

[MLC92] S. Mahlke, D. Lin, W. Chen, R. Hank, and R. Bringmann, "Effective compiler support for predicated execution using the hyperblock," in Proc. of Intl. Symp. on Microarchitecture, pp. 45-54, Dec. 1992.

Parametric Computation of Margins and of Minimum Cumulative Register Lifetime Dates

Benoît Dupont de Dinechin*
bd3@cs.mcgill.ca

ACAPS Laboratory, School of Computer Science, McGill University

Abstract. We present simple and efficient algorithms for solving three basic problems which occur while modulo scheduling loops: a) computing the minimum initiation interval which satisfies the recurrence constraints, and exposing the most constraining recurrence cycle; b) computing and maintaining, as scheduling proceeds, the earliest and latest possible schedule dates (the margins) of the not yet scheduled instructions; c) computing and maintaining the tentative schedule dates of the not yet scheduled instructions which minimize the cumulative lifetimes of the registers. In addition, these problems are solved parametrically with the initiation interval.

Introduction

The purpose of the techniques presented in this paper is to enable simple and efficient lifetime-sensitive scheduling in graph-based modulo schedulers. By graph-based modulo schedulers, we mean those which use the scheduling graph[1] as the primary data-structure for scheduling. This includes early non-backtracking schedulers by Rau [16], Lam [12], backtracking schedulers by Huff [10], Rau [17], Cydrome [4], Silicon Graphics [18], insertion schedulers by Dinechin [7], and optimal schedulers using explicit enumeration of schedules by Altman [1].

All these modulo schedulers solve the following problems:

- Compute the lower bound λ_{rec} on the Initiation Interval (II), which make scheduling possible as far as recurrence constraints are concerned. This bound, and the lower bound λ_{res} on the II set by the resource constraints, provide together the initial value $\max(\lambda_{rec}, \lambda_{res})$ of the II (throughout the paper, the current value of the II is denoted λ).
- Schedule the instructions one after the other, subjected to: a) the modulo resource constraints at λ must not be violated; b) each instruction must be scheduled within its *margins*, that is, its current earliest and latest possible schedule dates (called Estart and Lstart by Huff [10]).

* On leave from the CEA CEL-V, 94195 Villeneuve St Georges cedex France. Part of this research was funded by the DGA grant ERE/SC N° 95-1137/A000/DRET/DS/SR.

[1] A dependence graph which includes register, memory, and control, dependences.

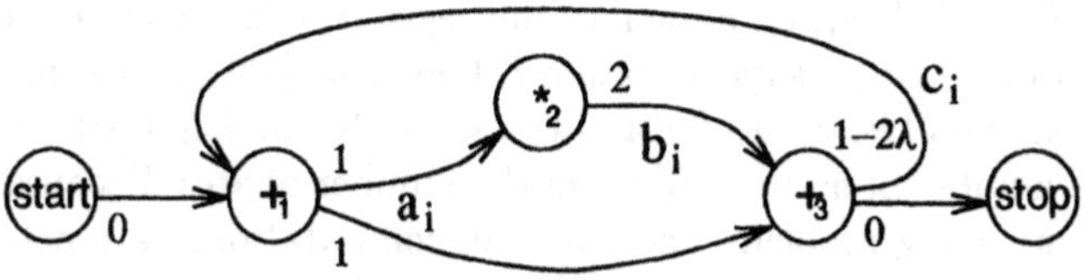

DO I=1, N
  A(I) = X+C(I-2)
  B(I) = A(I)*F
  C(I) = A(I)+B(I)
END DO

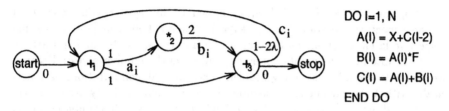

Fig. 1. The sample scheduling graph and its source code.

Either all the instructions can be scheduled this way, and we end up with the *local schedule* of the software pipeline. From this local schedule, the complete software pipeline code is easily constructed [8]. Or a *failure condition* is detected because the current instruction modulo resource conflicts, for all dates within its margins, with the already scheduled instructions.

The varieties of graph-based modulo schedulers mainly differ by the way they handle failure conditions at the current II. Non-backtracking modulo schedulers simply increase the II, and start all over again. Backtracking modulo schedulers unschedule some scheduled instructions, and reschedule them several times at the current II, before giving up and restarting at a higher II. Insertion schedulers enlarge the modulo issue table to make room for the conflicting instruction, thus increasing the II. Optimal modulo schedulers enumerate all the interesting schedules at a given II, before trying to schedule at a higher II.

Regardless of the technique used, the following problems must be solved efficiently: a) computing the lower bound on the II set by the recurrence constraints; b) maintaining the margins of the not yet scheduled instructions as instructions are scheduled, or unscheduled; c) when scheduling an instruction, select among the possible schedule dates one which is likely to reduce register requirements.

Our first contribution is to present a parametric version of the "Dynamic Breadth-First Search" algorithm by Goldfarb, Hao and Kai [9], which is further extended with network simplex techniques, in order to solve problems a) and b) more efficiently than what was proposed before. In addition to being very efficient, this algorithm is more general because we carry all the computations parametrically with λ the II. The algorithm also reports what is the most constraining recurrence cycle in the scheduling graph, an information which is useful for optimizing further the loop before scheduling.

Our second contribution is to present a new formulation of the minimum cumulative register lifetimes / minimum "buffers" [15] problems, which is also solved by the algorithm above. Solving this formulation allows us to maintain, for all the not yet scheduled instructions, a tentative schedule date which minimizes the sum of the register lifetimes in the schedule. Cumulative register lifetime minimization has been shown to be very effective in reducing the register requirements of modulo schedules [1, 10, 13]. It has also been observed [18] that minimizing buffers helps producing schedules with a shorter span.

Throughout the paper, we shall take as example the scheduling graph used by Ning & Gao in [15]. The graph is displayed in figure 1, along with its corresponding source code. The labels a_i, b_i, c_i denote the register values computed by the respective operations $+_1$, $*_2$, $+_3$ at iteration i. Following [15], we assume respective latencies of one and two cycles for additions, and for multiplications.

We denote by n the number of nodes, and by m the number of arcs. Because we deal with modulo scheduling problem, and carry all computations parametrically with λ the current II, we assume that the *length* v_k of any arc $[i_k, j_k, v_k]$ is expressed as: $v_k \stackrel{\text{def}}{=} \alpha_k - \lambda\beta_k$. The α_k and β_k values, which are non negative, are called respectively *delay* and *distance* of the arc. Likewise, any *potential* π_i of a node i, such as a schedule date or a margin, is expressed as: $\pi_i \stackrel{\text{def}}{=} \mu_i + \lambda\nu_i$.

The paper is organized as follows. In section 1, we present the algorithm we use to compute λ_{rec}, and to track the most constraining recurrence cycle. Then we introduce the new formulations of the margins problems, and of the Minimum Cumulative Register Lifetimes (MCRL) / minimum buffers problems, which makes them easily solvable as maximum-cost network flow problems.

In section 2, we describe a practical way of solving such network flow problems, by means of an adapted version of the primal network simplex algorithm. We then describe how these algorithms are used in a industrial-strength modulo scheduler, and report the efficiency of our implementation.

1 Formulation and Comparison to Earlier Work

1.1 Computing the Recurrence II

Traditionally, computing the recurrence II λ_{rec} on a scheduling graph is achieved with either of the following techniques [16, 10, 17]:

- Enumerate all the cycles of the graph using Tiernan's algorithm [20], and for each of them compute the so-called *date inequality* [16]. This method is interesting because one does not have to guess the value of λ_{rec} before running the algorithm. However the number of cycles is not polynomially bounded by the size of the graph.
- Find the lowest value of λ such that the all-pairs longest path problem on the scheduling graph has a solution. Solving the all-pairs longest path problem using Floyd's algorithm takes $O(n^3)$ time. This solution is interesting because the all-pairs longest paths can be used to maintain the margins (see §1.2).

Finding the lowest value of λ such that a longest path problem has solutions typically involves a binary search among the λ values [17], so the longest path algorithm is run possibly many times. Another solution is to use a parametric longest path algorithm. While existing parametric longest path algorithms run in $O(nm \log n)$ [11] and $O(nm + n^2 \log n)$ [21] time, they assume that the β values are 0 or 1. Clearly, collision distances greater than 1 are important in modulo scheduling problems, as shown by our example.

The solution we propose is based on a parametric version of the recent "Dynamic Breadth-First Search" (DBFS) label-correcting algorithm by Goldfarb,

Hao and Kai [9], named the Parametric Label Correcting (PLC) algorithm. The DBFS algorithm actually comes in two variants: one which is similar to the Bellman–Ford–Moore (BFM) algorithm, but runs typically in 85% of the time taken by BFM without giving up the $O(mn)$ worst-case time complexity; the other variant of DBFS, called DBFS Simplex, has a $O(mn^2)$ worst-case time complexity, but is on average only 10% slower than BFM [9].

The performances reported above assume that no positive-valued directed cycles exist in the graph. When it comes to detect such cycles, the DBFS Simplex is "clearly the best performing algorithm", being 13 times faster on average than BFM [9]. Since detecting such cycles is a main issue in scheduling problems, we selected the DBFS Simplex variant as the basis for our PLC algorithm. Another argument for DBFS Simplex is that it builds the data-structures required by our network flow algorithms. These algorithms are used later for maintaining the margins, and for minimizing the cumulative register lifetimes.

The pseudo-code for the PLC algorithm is displayed in figure 2. Longest-path algorithms build a longest-path spanning tree, which is materialized here by the **edge** array. Indexing this array by a node l yields the edge (that is, an arc q such that either orig[q] = l or dest[q] = l) which connects l to its parent in the tree. For the sake of speed, cached information is maintained at the nodes thanks to the **next**, **prev**, and **depth** arrays. The **next** and **prev** arrays return for each node its successor and predecessor in a preorder traversal of the tree. The **depth** array returns the current depth of each node in the tree. We refer to [9] for the high-level explanations on how this algorithm works.

Since maintaining the **next**, **prev** and **depth** arrays in parallel with the tree **edges** is a classic technique in network algorithms [3], the original point of the PLC algorithm is the way the date inequalities are collected. Following [19], the only place in a label correcting algorithm where a critical directed cycle might appear is when the tree update **edge**[l] $\leftarrow$ q is performed, in the case where $l \in \text{pred}^+(k) : \text{pred} \stackrel{\text{def}}{=} \lambda x.\text{orig}[\text{edge}[x]]$ already holds. Thus the only place we need to check for date inequalities is when we encounter such directed cycles. This is precisely what CDC does.

From the way the PLC algorithm works, it is also apparent that the last cycle processed by CDC before PLC terminates which is responsible for an increase of λ, is precisely the most constraining recurrence cycle of the scheduling graph.

1.2 Maintaining the Margins

Computing the margins before scheduling at the current II, and updating them as scheduling proceeds, is traditionally achieved in two steps [10, 17]:

1. Solve the all-pairs longest path problem at the current II, in order to compute the MinDist information for any pair of nodes in the scheduling graph. Then start with the following values:

$$\begin{cases} \text{Estart}(x) = \text{MinDist}(\text{start}, x) \\ \text{Lstart}(x) = \text{Lstart}(\text{stop}) - \text{MinDist}(x, \text{stop}) \end{cases}$$

```
procedure PLC(node root)
    integer flag ← 0
    prev[root], next[root] ← root, root
    flag[root], depth[root] ← flag, flag
    μ[root], ν[root] ← 0, 0
    foreach node k ∈ nodes() − { root }
        edge[k] ← null
    end foreach
    sequence c1, c2 ← [ root ], [ ]
    do
        do while ¬c1.empty()
            node k ← c1.top()
            if depth[k] = flag
                foreach arc q ∈ outarcs(k)
                    node l ← dest[q]
                    if edge[l] = null
                        GST(q, k, l)
                        c2.put(l)
                        flag[l] ← flag+1
                    else
                        integer newlabel ← μ[k] + α[q] + λ(ν[k] − β[q])
                        integer oldlabel ← μ[l] + λν[l]
                        if newlabel ≥ oldlabel ∧ flag[l] ≠ flag+1
                            c2.put(l)
                            flag[l] ← flag+1
                        end if
                        if newlabel > oldlabel ∧ ¬CDC(q, k, l)
                            RST(q, k, l, l)
                        end if
                    end if
                end foreach
            end if
            c1.pop()
        end do
        c1 ↔ c2
        flag ← flag+1
        exit if c1.empty()
    end do
end procedure PLC

procedure GST(arc q, node k, l)
    edge[l], depth[l] ← q, depth[k] + 1
    μ[l], ν[l] ← μ[k] + α[q], ν[k] − β[q]
    node n ← next[k]
    next[l], prev[n] ← n, l
    next[k], prev[l] ← l, k
end procedure GST

boolean function CDC(arc q, node k, l)
    node a ← k
    integer α, β ← α[q], β[q]
    do while depth[a] > depth[l]
        arc e ← edge[a]
        α, β ← α + α[e], β + β[e]
        a ← orig[e]
    end do
    λ ← max(λ, ⌈α/β⌉) if a = l
    return a = l
end function CDC

procedure RST(arc q, node k, l, j)
    arc e ← edge[l]
    node z, a, b ← l, l, l
    node x, r ← next[a], prev[a]
    integer depth ← depth[k] − depth[l] + 1
    integer μ ← μ[k] − μ[l]
    integer ν ← ν[k] − ν[l]
    μ, ν ← μ + α[q], ν − β[q] if orig[q] = k
    μ, ν ← μ − α[q], ν + β[q] if orig[q] ≠ k
    b ← if orig[e] ≠ b then orig[e] else dest[e]
    do
        do while depth[x] > depth[a]
            depth[x] ← depth[x] + depth
            μ[x], ν[x] ← μ[x] + μ, ν[x] + ν
            z, x ← x, next[x]
        end do
        depth[a] ← depth[a] + depth
        μ[a], ν[a] ← μ[a] + μ, ν[a] + ν
        exit if a = j
        next[r], prev[x] ← x, r
        x, r ← next[b], prev[b]
        next[z], prev[b] ← b, z
        z, a ← b, b
        depth ← depth + 2
        edge[a] ↔ e
        b ← if orig[e] ≠ b then orig[e] else dest[e]
    end do
    node n ← next[k]
    if n ≠ j
        next[r], prev[x] ← x, r
        next[z], prev[n] ← n, z
    end if
    next[k], prev[l] ← l, k
    edge[l] ← q
end procedure RST
```

Fig. 2. The Parametric Label Correcting algorithm.

2. Whenever an instruction y is scheduled at date t, iterate the following system of distance equations, for all not yet scheduled x, until it stabilizes:

$$\begin{cases} \mathsf{Estart}(\mathsf{x}) = \max(\mathsf{Estart}(\mathsf{x}), t + \mathsf{MinDist}(\mathsf{y}, \mathsf{x})) \\ \mathsf{Lstart}(\mathsf{x}) = \min(\mathsf{Lstart}(\mathsf{x}), t - \mathsf{MinDist}(\mathsf{x}, \mathsf{y})) \end{cases}$$

In our opinion, the above method exhibits two drawbacks. First, it requires the all-pairs longest-path problem to be solved at every II. Second, the method falls short to recover Estart(x) and Lstart(x) after an instruction is unscheduled, since iterating distance equations can only increase Estart(x), or decrease

Lstart(x). Recovering the margins after unscheduling actually involves a search of the graph which can be slow [10].

Conceptually, computing and updating the left margins Estart(x) boils down to maintaining the single-source longest paths on the scheduling graph, rooted form node start. Likewise, the right margins are obtained from MinDist(x, stop), using any value Lstart(stop) ≥ Estart(stop), such as Lstart(stop) $\stackrel{\text{def}}{=} \lambda\lceil \frac{\text{Estart(stop)}}{\lambda} \rceil$ [10], or Lstart(stop) $\stackrel{\text{def}}{=}$ Estart(stop) $+ \lambda - 1$ [1]. The MinDist(x, stop) values are in turn the longest-paths on the reversed scheduling graph, rooted from node stop.

Our solution is to formulate the margin problems as a (trivial) maximum-cost network flow problem. Indeed the single-source longest-path problem is solved on a network by maximizing the cost of a flow supplied with capacity $n-1$ at the root node, and demanded with capacity -1 at the other nodes [2]. This is efficient in practice (see §2.3), because the bulk of the work of margins maintenance is performed by the PLC algorithm in the initialization step (§2.1), while general network flow solver steps are only needed after an instruction is scheduled, or unscheduled[2], in the course of building the local schedule.

Another advantage of this solution is that it only requires the algorithms we already need for solving the minimum cumulative register lifetimes problem.

1.3 The Minimum Cumulative Register Lifetimes Problem

Let us first illustrate the concept of a register lifetime on our sample scheduling problem. The value of a register lifetime is the time elapsed between the update of a register, and the last use of the updated value. We assume here that the registers are statically single-assigned in the loop body, and that the target architecture is such that the life of a register value starts at the time the instruction which produces it is issued.

Taking our example, let $\vec{t}$ be the variables associated with the schedule dates of $+_1, *_2, +_3$ respectively, and let $\vec{l}$ be the lifetimes of the register values produced by these instructions. Then we have the following system of inequalities:

$$\begin{pmatrix}\textit{dependence}\\ \textit{inequalities}\end{pmatrix}\begin{cases} t_2 - t_1 \geq 1 \\ t_3 - t_1 \geq 1 \\ t_3 - t_2 \geq 2 \\ t_1 - t_3 \geq 1 - 2\lambda \end{cases} \qquad \begin{pmatrix}\textit{lifetime}\\ \textit{inequalities}\end{pmatrix}\begin{cases} l_1 \geq t_2 - t_1 \\ l_1 \geq t_3 - t_1 \\ l_2 \geq t_3 - t_2 \\ l_3 \geq t_1 + 2\lambda - t_3 \end{cases}$$

These are the equations described by Dinechin [5], and the Minimum Cumulative Register Lifetimes (MCRL) problem is defined by setting the goal to $\min \sum_i l_i$. It is interesting to compare these equations to those of the minimum buffers problem, as defined by Ning & Gao. In the minimum buffers problem, the buffer variables are $\vec{b}$, and the objective function is $\sum_i b_i$. From [15]:

$$\begin{pmatrix}\textit{dependence}\\ \textit{inequalities}\end{pmatrix}\begin{cases} t_2 - t_1 \geq 1 \\ t_3 - t_1 \geq 1 \\ t_3 - t_2 \geq 2 \\ t_1 - t_3 \geq 1 - 2\lambda \end{cases} \qquad \begin{pmatrix}\textit{buffer}\\ \textit{inequalities}\end{pmatrix}\begin{cases} \lambda b_1 \geq t_2 - t_1 \\ \lambda b_1 \geq t_3 - t_1 \\ \lambda b_2 \geq t_3 - t_2 \\ \lambda b_3 \geq t_1 - t_3 + 3\lambda - 1 \end{cases}$$

[2] Or λ is increased, in the case of Insertion Scheduling.

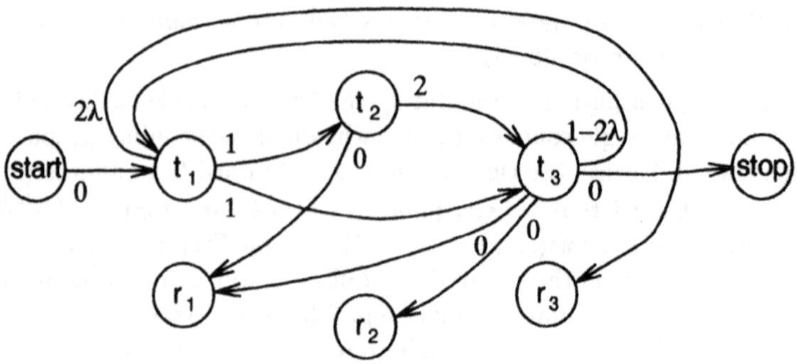

Fig. 3. The augmented scheduling graph for minimizing the lifetimes.

Obviously, the dependence equations are the same, while buffer and lifetime equations are different, although related. To make the buffers problem easier to solve, Ning & Gao make the change of variables $\lambda b_i \stackrel{\text{def}}{=} b'_i \ \forall i$, so the left-hand side of the buffer inequalities become identical to the left-hand side of the lifetime inequalities. Using different techniques, Ning & Gao [15], and Dinechin [5], make the proof that the constraint matrices of the resulting linear programs (after variable substitution in the buffer case) are totally unimodular, hence the MCRL / minimum buffers problems can be solved in polynomial time.

When it comes to solving these problems in practice, Dinechin uses a lexico-parametric simplex algorithm [5], while Ning & Gao describe a reduction to a minimum-cost network flow problem [15]. However, the Ning–Gao reduction is not better than a simplex algorithm, since a network flow problem is obtained only after a complex sequence of transformations is applied to the dual of the minimum buffers problem. Actually, buffer minimization was implemented and tested in MOST [1] using a vanilla simplex algorithm.

We now describe how a new transformation of the MCRL / minimum buffers problems makes them solvable in a simple and efficient way as a maximum-cost network flow problem. Basically, we introduce the variables $\vec{r}$ and make the change $l_i + t_i \stackrel{\text{def}}{=} r_i$ in the lifetime case, or $\lambda b_i + t_i \stackrel{\text{def}}{=} r_i$ in the buffer case. On our example and in the lifetime case, we get:

$$\left(\begin{array}{c}\textit{dependence}\\ \textit{inequalities}\end{array}\right)\begin{cases} t_2 - t_1 \geq 1 \\ t_3 - t_1 \geq 1 \\ t_3 - t_2 \geq 2 \\ t_1 - t_3 \geq 1 - 2\lambda \end{cases} \qquad \left(\begin{array}{c}\textit{reduced}\\ \textit{lifetime}\\ \textit{inequalities}\end{array}\right)\begin{cases} r_1 - t_2 \geq 0 \\ r_1 - t_3 \geq 0 \\ r_2 - t_3 \geq 0 \\ r_3 - t_1 \geq 2\lambda \end{cases}$$

This new system of inequalities obviously defines an "augmented" scheduling graph, which is derived from the original scheduling graph as follows: any register value "producer" node is paired with a "lifetime" node, and for any lifetime arc between the producer node and a "consumer" node, we add an arc from the consumer node to the lifetime node associated with the producer node. The process is illustrated in figure 3 for our sample scheduling graph. Since $l_i + t_i \stackrel{\text{def}}{=} r_i \ \forall i$, the objective function $\min \sum_i l_i$ becomes $\min \sum_i r_i - t_i$.

Theorem 1 [6, 15]. *The minimum cumulative lifetimes problem and the minimum buffers problem can be solved in polynomial time.*

Proof: The constraint matrix of the associated linear program after the change of variables $l_i + t_i \stackrel{\text{def}}{=} r_i \ \forall i$ (in the lifetime case), or $\lambda b_i + t_i \stackrel{\text{def}}{=} r_i \ \forall i$ (in the buffer case), is a graph arc-node incidence matrix, which is totally unimodular. □

To solve the MCRL problem in practice, we only need to consider the dual of the associated linear program. To simplify the presentation, we assume below that all the arcs of the scheduling graph carry a lifetime. Then, if U denotes the arc-node incidence matrix of the original scheduling graph, we have the following primal–dual relationships:

$$\left.\begin{array}{c} \min \begin{pmatrix} -\vec{1} \\ \vec{1} \end{pmatrix}^{\mathrm{T}} \begin{pmatrix} \vec{t} \\ \vec{r} \end{pmatrix} \\ \begin{bmatrix} U & 0 \\ 0 & -U \end{bmatrix} \begin{pmatrix} \vec{t} \\ \vec{r} \end{pmatrix} \geq \begin{pmatrix} \vec{\alpha} - \lambda\vec{\beta} \\ \lambda\vec{\beta} \end{pmatrix} \\ \vec{t},\ \vec{r} \text{ unrestricted in sign} \end{array}\right\} \rightleftharpoons \left\{\begin{array}{c} \max \begin{pmatrix} \vec{\alpha} - \lambda\vec{\beta} \\ \lambda\vec{\beta} \end{pmatrix}^{\mathrm{T}} \begin{pmatrix} \vec{x} \\ \vec{y} \end{pmatrix} \\ \begin{bmatrix} U^{\mathrm{T}} & 0 \\ 0 & -U^{\mathrm{T}} \end{bmatrix} \begin{pmatrix} \vec{x} \\ \vec{y} \end{pmatrix} = \begin{pmatrix} -\vec{1} \\ \vec{1} \end{pmatrix} \\ \vec{x} \geq \vec{0},\ \vec{y} \geq \vec{0} \end{array}\right.$$

Here the linear program associated with the MCRL problem appears on the left, and the dual on the right. Now if we negate both sides of the equal sign in the dual linear program, we get a maximum-cost network flow problem on the scheduling graph augmented with the lifetime nodes, where each producer node supplies unit flow, and where each lifetime node demands unit flow. In the sequel the amount of flow supply or demand of a node is referred to as its flow *requirement*, which is positive for supply nodes, and negative for demand nodes.

A nice property of network flow problems is that their dual variables $\vec{\pi}$ are readily available from the network (see §2.1), so we get MCRL schedule dates $\vec{t}$ (and $\vec{r}$) even though we are actually solving the dual of the MCRL problem. Thus the technique presented here is quite different from the one proposed by Ning & Gao in [15], where the relationships between the solutions of the final network flow problem, and the schedule dates, are not apparent. In fact, making the Ning–Gao reduction work is even more complicated than described [14].

2 Application to Modulo Scheduling

2.1 Solving the Network Flow Problems

In a network flow problem, the primal variables are the flows along the arcs. Like in the regular simplex algorithm, interesting solutions are described by a *basis*, that is, a subset of the primal variables with values which together identify a vertex of the solution space. In the case of network flow problems, any basis happens to be completely described by the arcs of a spanning tree of the network [2]. From a basis spanning tree, the dual variables of a network flow problem, traditionally called the node *potentials*, are computed as follows: assuming that

```
procedure CEF(node root)
    node j ← prev[root]
    do while j ≠ root
        temp[j], j ← require[j], prev[j]
    end do
    j ← prev[j]
    do while j ≠ root
        arc p ← edge[j]
        if orig[p] ≠ j
            node i ← orig[p]
            flow[p] ← −temp[j]
            temp[i] ← temp[i] + temp[j]
        else
            node i ← dest[p]
            flow[p] ← temp[j]
            temp[i] ← temp[i] + temp[j]
        end if
        j ← prev[j]
    end do
end procedure CEF
```

```
node, node, node function FLE(arc q)
    integer δ ← +∞
    arc u, v ← null, null
    node a, b ← orig[q], dest[q]
    do while a ≠ b
        if depth[a] ≥ depth[b]
            arc e ← edge[a]
            δ, u ← flow[e], e if orig[e] = a ∧ flow[e] ≤ δ
            a ← if orig[e] ≠ a then orig[e] else dest[a]
        else
            arc f ← edge[b]
            δ, v ← flow[f], f if dest[f] = b ∧ flow[f] < δ
            b ← if dest[f] ≠ b then dest[f] else orig[f]
        end if
    end do
    return dest[q], orig[q], orig[u] if v = null
    return orig[q], dest[q], dest[v] if u = null
    return dest[q], orig[q], orig[u] if flow[u] ≤ flow[v]
    return orig[q], dest[q], dest[v]
end function FLE
```

Fig. 4. Computing the initial edge flows, and finding the leaving edge.

node i is the father of node j in the tree, if arc $[i, j, v_{ij}]$ is the tree edge then $\pi_j \stackrel{\text{def}}{=} \pi_i + v_{ij}$ else the tree edge is an arc $[j, i, v_{ji}]$ and $\pi_j \stackrel{\text{def}}{=} \pi_i - v_{ji}$.

Using these equations, the node potentials are easily computed in $O(n)$ by a preorder traversal of the basis tree using the next values [2]. In our case however, the node potentials are automatically maintained by GST and RST, so we do not need extra code. Likewise, the flows on the tree edges are computed in $O(n)$ from the node flow requirements by a reverse preorder traversal of the basis tree using the prev values (non-tree arcs carry zero flow), as illustrated in figure 4 by the Compute Edge Flows (CEF) procedure.

The network simplex algorithm is a popular method for solving minimum-cost network flow problems [3]. When properly implemented, it is also one of the most efficient [2] (it is used in CPLEX to solve network problems). The version we present is adapted to solve maximum-cost network flow problems parametrically with λ, and is simplified by the fact that arc flows have no upper bounds. Like in a regular primal simplex algorithm, the problem is solved as follows:

Phase I Find an initial primal-feasible solution. Here, the PLC algorithm followed by a call to CEF directly provides an initial solution in the case of the margin problems. In the case of the MCRL problem, we start from the spanning tree already built by PLC for the margins, then we extend this tree by calling GST to insert a dummy tree edge with length $-\infty$ between any producer node, and its associated lifetime node. The initial flows are likewise computed by calling CEF.

Phase II Do while the current solution is not optimal:

1. Find an arc q which violates the optimality criterion to enter the basis. This criterion is quite simple: any non-basic arc $\mathsf{q} \stackrel{\text{def}}{=} [k, l, v_{kl}]$ such that $\pi_l < \pi_k + v_{kl}$ (that is, the dependence implied by q is violated) is eligible to enter the basis. Dantzig's entering arc selection rule is to select the arc whose $\pi_k + v_{kl} - \pi_l > 0$ is maximum.

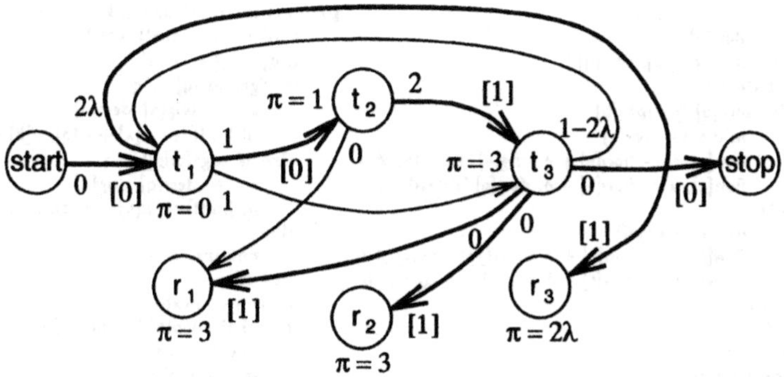

Fig. 5. An optimal basis tree and the associated node potentials and edge flows.

2. Find an arc p to leave the basis. The choice of the leaving arc is performed by the function Find Leaving Edge (FLE) listed in figure 4, which also implements Cunningham's anti-cycling rule [2]. Let k, l, j be the three nodes returned by FLE. By construction, p $\stackrel{\text{def}}{=}$ **edge**[j] is the leaving edge.

3. Do the (p, q)-pivot step. To perform the pivot operation, we first update the flows by calling UEF(q, j) (figure 6), then we reorder the basis tree by calling RST(q, k, l, j).

Moreover, this implementation maintains *strongly feasible* basis trees, a property which together with Dantzig's entering arc selection rule make our network simplex a polynomial-time method [2]. On our example, the spanning tree after MCRL is solved appears in figure 5 (bold arcs), along with the associated node potentials, and the tree edge flows (within brackets).

2.2 Lifetime-Sensitive Modulo Scheduling

In this section, we describe how the network flows algorithms are actually used in a software pipeliner we developed for the DEC Alpha 21064. This software pipeliner is currently part of a pre-release compiler for the Cray T3E massively parallel supercomputer, and has been extensively tested as such. Although our software pipeliner is based on the Insertion Scheduling technique [7], using these network flows algorithms in the setting of another modulo scheduler would be similar. In the description below, we also rely on the fact that solving the MCRL problem actually yields *leftmost* (that is, earliest) MCRL schedule dates.

To achieve lifetime-sensitive modulo scheduling in presence of resource constraints, we maintain three network flow problems in parallel: the original scheduling graph augmented with the lifetime nodes **mcrldates** for the MCRL dates, the original scheduling graph **earlydates** for the left margins, and the reversed scheduling graph **latedates** for the right margins. The **mcrldates** graph is the main data-structure, as it is used after the local schedule is built to rename (modulo expand) and assign registers. The **earlydates** and **latedates** are temporary data-structures, which are discarded after the local schedule is built.

```
procedure UEF(arc q, p)
    int δ ← flow[p]
    node a, b ← orig[q], dest[q]
    do while a ≠ b
        if depth[a] ≥ depth[b]
            arc e ← edge[a]
            flow[e], a ← flow[e] + δ, orig[e] if orig[e] ≠ a
            flow[e], a ← flow[e] − δ, dest[e] if dest[e] ≠ a
        else
            arc f ← edge[b]
            flow[f], b ← flow[f] + δ, dest[f] if dest[f] ≠ b
            flow[f], b ← flow[f] − δ, orig[f] if orig[f] ≠ b
        end if
    end do
    flow[q] ← δ
end procedure UEF

procedure freeze(node n, int τ, ϕ)
    int α, β ← τ, −ϕ
    arc arc1, arc2 ← pair1[n], pair2[n]
    UNP(arc1, α, β) if α[arc1] ≠ α ∨ β[arc1] ≠ β
    UNP(arc2, −α, −β) if α[arc2] ≠ −α ∨ β[arc2] ≠ −β
end procedure freeze

procedure UNP(arc q, int α, β)
    node k, l ← null, null
    α[q], β[q] ← α, β
    if edge[dest[q]] = q
        k, l ← orig[q], dest[q]
        μ[l], ν[l] ← μ[k] + α[q], ν[k] − β[q]
    else if edge[orig]] = q
        k, l ← dest[q], orig[q]
        μ[l], ν[l] ← μ[k] − α[q], ν[k] + β[q]
    else
        return
    end if
    node j ← next[l]
    do while depth[j] > depth[l]
        arc p ← edge[j]
        if orig[p] ≠ j
            node i ← orig[p]
            μ[j], ν[j] ← μ[i] + α[p], ν[i] − β[p]
        else
            node i ← dest[p]
            μ[j], ν[j] ← μ[i] − α[p], ν[i] + β[p]
        end if
        j ← next[j]
    end do
end procedure UNP
```

Fig. 6. Procedures for updating the edge flows, and the node potentials.

Modulo scheduling starts by setting λ the II to λ_{res}, and by running PLC on **mcrldates** without its lifetime nodes. This sets λ to $\max(\lambda_{res}, \lambda_{rec})$, and also yields the critical recurrence cycle if $\lambda_{rec} > \lambda_{res}$. We add the lifetime nodes and the related arcs, call CEF, and then run network simplex phase II. This returns a solved problem for the **mcrldates** graph. Then we run PLC followed by CEF on the **latedates** graph, and on the **earlydates** graph. Because λ does not increase during those calls to PLC, there is no need to run the network simplex phase II, as the flow problem is guaranteed to be solved for these graphs.

Now the instructions are scheduled for resources one after the other, following a heuristic order which may or may not be a topological sort of the scheduling graph minus its loop-carried dependences. List schedulers require such an order, while backtracking schedulers [18], and insertion schedulers [7], are not so constrained. Scheduling an instruction entails assigning to it a date within its margins which does not create modulo resource conflicts with the previously scheduled instructions. Because the modulo resource conflicts have a period of λ, in practice λ consecutive dates must be considered at most.

To be more precise, let e_i, l_i, m_i be the left margin, right margin, and current MCRL schedule date of the instruction i selected for scheduling. We define two numbers $a_i \stackrel{\text{def}}{=} \min(l_i - m_i, \lambda - 1)$ and $b_i \stackrel{\text{def}}{=} \min(m_i - e_i, \lambda - 1 - a_i)$. We check all the dates $s_i \in [m_i, m_i + a_i]$ in increasing order, then all the dates $s_i \in [m_i - b_i, m_i[$ in decreasing order, looking for the first s_i which does not create modulo resource conflicts[3]. The way we define a_i and b_i guarantees that at most λ schedule dates are considered, and that s_i is among the MCRL dates when possible. Indeed the

[3] In the setting of Insertion Scheduling, we actually look for a date where inserting the instruction in the modulo issue table would entail a minimum increase of the II.

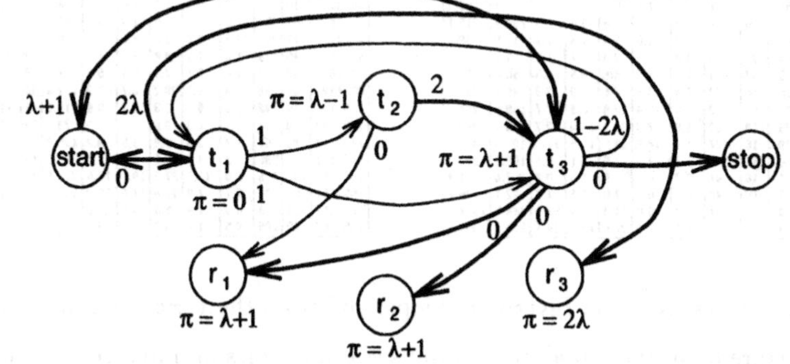

Fig. 7. The new optimal MCRL solution after nodes t_1 and t_3 are scheduled.

dates which are at the right of the leftmost MCRL date m_i are scanned first.

The fact that an instruction i is to be scheduled at a particular date s_i is mirrored in the graphs **mcrldates**, **latedates**, and **earlydates**, exactly the same way: a pair of arcs [start, i, s_i], [i, start, $-s_i$] is added, in order to enforce the constraints $t_i \geq s_i \wedge -t_i \geq -s_i \Leftrightarrow t_i = s_i$. In practice, we call freeze(i, τ_i, ϕ_i) (figure 6), where $\tau_i \stackrel{\text{def}}{=} s_i \bmod \lambda$, and $\phi_i \stackrel{\text{def}}{=} s_i \div \lambda$. If unscheduling a previously scheduled instruction j were required[4], the associated pair of arcs [start, j, s_j], [j, start, $-s_j$] would be reversed to [start, j, 0], [j, start, $-\infty$], with the node potentials updated accordingly. In any case, optimality of the flows in the graphs is restored by running the network simplex phase II.

In figure 7, we display the network of the solved MCRL problem after the nodes t_1 and t_3 are scheduled at dates $s_1 = 0$ and $s_3 = 1 + \lambda$ respectively, assuming $\lambda = 3$ (arc pairs are displayed as bi-directional edges). As shown by the node potentials, the leftmost date for t_2 which minimizes the cumulative lifetimes is $\lambda - 1$, so t_2 is kept as close to t_3 as possible. The r_i values are also of interest, since they maintain by definition the date of the last use of the register value produced by the associated t_i nodes. For instance, value c_i, which is produced by node t_3 at date $\lambda + 1 = 4$, is last used at date $2\lambda = 6$ by node t_1.

2.3 Experimentations

Using a Cray C90 vector computer to run our software pipeliner for the Cray T3E machine, we collected compile-time statistics for the 14 Livernore loops, and for the 14 most important loops in the `tomcatv.f` program of the SPEC benchmark. These codes have been compiled with the `-Ounroll2` command line option (automatic unrolling enabled), in order to create larger loop bodies. The results are presented in figure 8. The first column lists the name of the loop, or gives its line position in the source code (`tomcatv.f` program). The n and m columns display the number of nodes and arcs of the original scheduling graph.

---

[4] Insertion Scheduling does not require unscheduling, however some previously scheduled instruction might be *moved* if the modulo issue table happens to be enlarged. Moving instructions is also achieved by calling freeze.

Loop	n	m	PLC	Solve	mcrl	late	early	Insert	Total
lll01	40	111	0.6	1.4	5.2	3.3	2.9	32.2	85.4
lll02	86	251	1.2	8.6	20.8	9.8	6.9	108.2	215.1
lll03	22	59	0.3	1.0	2.0	1.4	1.1	11.5	30.9
lll04	22	59	0.3	1.0	2.0	1.4	1.1	11.4	31.2
lll05	67	194	1.4	3.2	4.6	3.8	2.8	50.0	712.2
lll06	66	203	1.4	3.3	4.6	3.9	2.8	49.4	1496.5
lll07	91	292	1.8	12.4	22.0	8.8	7.7	109.9	294.2
lll08	110	369	1.9	17.3	39.3	13.4	12.7	184.4	362.3
lll09	118	427	1.7	14.7	32.0	15.5	11.3	199.9	445.3
lll10	64	199	1.2	2.5	11.5	8.1	6.6	107.9	292.4
lll11	18	47	0.3	0.6	0.9	1.0	0.6	7.6	61.4
lll12	19	48	0.3	0.5	2.0	1.6	1.4	12.1	26.2
lll13	128	2037	14.0	20.8	73.3	56.4	58.5	484.9	1327.1
lll14	92	653	4.4	7.8	22.4	15.4	14.4	154.8	393.6

Loop	n	m	PLC	Solve	mcrl	late	early	Insert	Total
30–30	18	53	0.2	0.5	1.1	1.0	0.7	8.5	18.9
33–39	51	484	1.9	3.4	13.9	12.9	10.3	87.2	762.2
41–41	42	201	1.3	2.8	7.0	4.6	4.4	40.3	101.7
44–46	45	178	1.0	2.0	8.8	5.2	4.2	48.5	135.8
44–46	49	184	1.4	2.4	7.9	5.6	5.3	57.2	193.9
88–112	83	294	1.4	9.5	28.2	8.7	9.2	127.4	303.4
139–140	19	48	0.3	0.5	1.3	1.2	0.9	13.1	31.4
143–147	68	284	1.1	4.3	9.6	4.7	3.9	78.4	590.2
143–147	86	257	1.4	3.6	9.4	5.5	4.2	105.3	239.8
149–151	63	236	1.3	4.7	14.1	7.6	6.5	93.2	192.2
155–157	103	448	2.0	13.3	37.2	19.1	14.5	214.5	373.0
155–157	85	370	2.1	7.9	21.8	11.6	10.2	149.7	395.2
165–167	33	128	0.5	1.4	5.3	4.0	3.0	43.5	104.2
165–167	40	105	0.5	1.2	6.0	5.2	4.2	57.5	114.8

Fig. 8. Data from the Livermore loops, and from the `tomcatv.f` program.

In figure 8, all the remaining columns contain times in milliseconds. Column PLC lists the times spent by each call to PLC. Column Solve gives the times taken by the network simplex phase II to compute an initial solution for the **mcrldates** graph. Columns mcrl, late, and early, report the cumulated times spent by the network algorithms in the respective graphs **mcrldates**, **latedates**, and **earlydates**. Column Insert summarizes the times spent doing Insertion Scheduling, and Total displays the total times taken by the software pipeliner.

A first general observation is that the network algorithms are quite efficient. On average they account for less than 35% of the time taken by Insertion Scheduling, which is already a very fast technique. Lifetime-sensitive scheduling does not increase scheduling times significantly, as the time spent in the **mcrldates** graph is typically lower than the cumulated time spent in the **latedates** and **earlydates** graphs. Also apparent is the surprising efficiency of the PLC algorithm, which consistently takes a linear time with m (the number of arcs).

To expose the linear behavior of the PLC algorithm, we compared it on a logarithmic scale to the number of arcs (figure 9). Actually, a precise estimator of the time taken by PLC is $0.005\,m$ milliseconds. In figure 9, we also plotted the total times spent in the graphs **mcrldates**, **latedates**, **earlydates**, and doing Insertion Scheduling, each divided by n (the number of nodes). The resulting curves also match the m curve, a clear indication that these algorithms behave in $O(mn)$ ($\simeq 0.0025\,mn$ for the total time spent in the network algorithms).

Furthermore, it appears that the total time spent per node in any of the graphs is one order of magnitude lower than the time taken by PLC, a fact which clearly support our claim (§1.2) that reoptimizing the flows using network simplex algorithms is faster that recomputing a solution from scratch.

Conclusions

In this paper, we demonstrate that using network flows to maintain the margins, and the MCRL (Minimum Cumulative Register Lifetime) schedule dates, yields efficient, and easy to program, algorithms. Besides using network flows, our techniques are unique because they carry all the computations parametrically with λ the software pipeline initiation interval. In the case of the MCRL problem, we

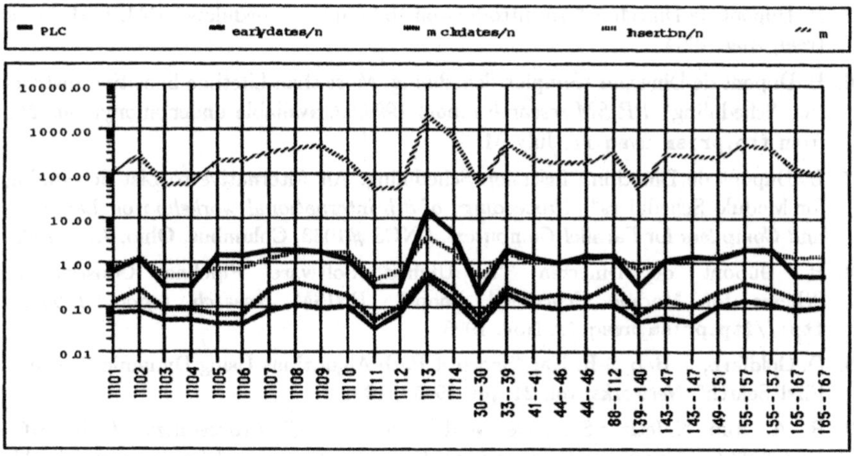

Fig. 9. $O(m)$ behavior of PLC, and $O(mn)$ behavior of network simplex.

are able to use network flows, thanks to a new transformation which is much simpler than the reduction described by Ning & Gao to minimize buffers [15].

Unlike Huff's technique [10], ours does not fail to move whole regions of not yet scheduled instructions in order to minimize cumulative lifetimes. Unlike techniques by Llosa et al. [13], our solution has clean mathematical foundations, and is easily understood. Unlike Dinechin's Simplex Scheduling [5], we do not need to maintain a simplex tableau in addition to the scheduling graph. Unlike Ning & Gao [15], we do not assume resource-free scheduling problems.

The techniques described have been implemented, and extensively tested, in a software pipeliner based on Insertion Scheduling [7], which is part of a pre-release compiler for the Cray T3E. The Cray T3E is a massively parallel supercomputer based on DEC Alpha 21164 (4× superscalar) microprocessors, but as far as software pipelining is concerned, this system remains close to a single processor machine (tasking is performed at the middle-end level). We invite anyone to try our algorithms, which are not patented, and whose implementation in C (less than 500 lines) is available from the author upon simple request.

References

1. E. R. Altman "Optimal Software Pipelining with Function Unit and Register Constraints" *Ph.D. thesis*, ACAPS laboratory, McGill university, Montreal, Oct. 1995.
2. R. K. Ahuja, T. L. Magnanti, J. B. Orlin "Network Flows" *Optimization*, G. L. Nemhauser, A. H. G. Rinnooy Kan, M. J. Todd editors, North-Holland 1989.
3. A. Ali, R. Helgason, J. Kennington, H. Lall "Primal Simplex Network Codes: State-of-the-Art Implementation Technology" *Networks*, vol. 8, pp. 315–339, 1978.
4. J. C. Dehnert, R. A. Towle "Compiling for Cydra 5" *Journal of Supercomputing*, vol. 7, pp. 181–227, May 1993.

5. B. Dupont de Dinechin "An Introduction to Simplex Scheduling" PACT'94, Montreal, Aug. 1994.
6. B. Dupont de Dinechin "Simplex Scheduling: More than Lifetime-Sensitive Instruction Scheduling" *PRISM research report 1994.22*, available under anonymous `ftp` from `ftp.prism.uvsq.fr`, July 94.
7. B. Dupont de Dinechin "Insertion Scheduling: An Alternative to List Scheduling for Modulo Schedulers", *Proceedings of 8th international workshop on Language and Compilers for Parallel Computers*, LNCS #1033, Columbus, Ohio, Aug. 1995.
8. B. Dupont de Dinechin "A Unified Software Pipeline Construction Scheme for Modulo Scheduled Loops", *PRISM research report 1996.xx*, `ftp://ftp.prism.uvsq.fr`, Nov. 1996.
9. D. Goldfarb, J. Hao, S-R. Kai "Shortest Path Algorithms Using Dynamic Breadth-First Search" *Networks*, vol. 21, pp. 29–50, 1991.
10. R. A. Huff "Lifetime-Sensitive Modulo Scheduling" *Proceedings of the SIGPLAN'93 Conference on Programming Language Design and Implementation*, Albuquerque, June 1993.
11. R. M. Karp, J. B. Orlin "Parametric Shortest Path Algorithms with an Application to Cyclic Staffing" *Discrete Applied Mathematics*, vol. 3, pp. 37–45, 1981.
12. M. Lam "Software Pipelining: An Effective Scheduling Technique for VLIW Machines" *Proceedings of the SIGPLAN'88 Conference on Programming Language Design and Implementation*, 1988.
13. J. Llosa, M. Valero, E. Ayguade, A. Gonzalez "Hypernode Reduction Modulo Scheduling" *Proceedings of the IEEE / ACM Annual Symposium on Microarchitecture / MICRO-28*, 1995.
14. Q. Ning "Re: Question about the POPL paper", private communication, Feb. 1996.
15. Q. Ning, G. R. Gao "A Novel Framework of Register Allocation for Software Pipelining" *Proceedings of the ACM SIGPLAN'93 Symposium on Principles of Programming Languages*, Jan. 1993.
16. B. R. Rau, C. D. Glaeser "Some Scheduling Techniques and an Easily Schedulable Horizontal Architecture for High Performance Scientific Computing" *IEEE / ACM 14th Annual Microprogramming Workshop*, Oct. 1981.
17. B. R. Rau "Iterative Modulo Scheduling: An Algorithm for Software Pipelining Loops" *IEEE / ACM 27th Annual Microprogramming Workshop*, San Jose, California, Nov. 1994.
18. J. Ruttenberg, G. R. Gao, A. Stoutchinin, W. Lichtenstein "Software Pipelining Showdown: Optimal vs. Heuristic Methods in a Production Compiler" *Proceedings of the SIGPLAN'96 Conference on Programming Language Design and Implementation*, Philadelphia, May 1996.
19. R. E. Tarjan "Data Structures and Network Algorithms" *CBMS-NSF Regional Conference Series in Applied Mathematics*, no. 44, 1983.
20. J. C. Tiernan "An Efficient Search Algorithm to Find the Elementary Circuits of a Graph" *Communications of the ACM*, vol. 13, no. 12, Dec. 1970.
21. N. E. Young, R. E. Tarjan, J. B. Orlin "Faster Parametric Shortest Path and Minimum-Balance Algorithms" *Networks*, vol. 21, pp. 205–221, 1991.

Global Register Allocation Based on Graph Fusion

Guei-Yuan Lueh[3], Thomas Gross[1,2], and Ali-Reza Adl-Tabatabai[1]

[1]School of Computer Science [2]Institut für Computer Systeme [3]ECE Department
Carnegie Mellon University ETH Zürich Carnegie Mellon University
Pittsburgh, PA 15213 CH 8092 Zürich Pittsburgh, PA 15213

Abstract. A register allocator must effectively deal with three issues: live range splitting, live range spilling, and register assignment. This paper presents a new coloring-based global register allocation algorithm that addresses all three issues in an integrated way: the algorithm starts with an interference graph for each region of the program, where a region can be a basic block, a loop nest, a superblock, a trace, or another combination of basic blocks. Region formation is orthogonal to register allocation in this framework. Then the interference graphs for adjacent regions are fused to build up the complete interference graph. The algorithm delays decisions on splitting, spilling, and register assignment, and therefore, the register allocation may be better than what is obtained by a Chatin-style allocator. This algorithm uses execution probabilities, derived from either profiles or static estimates, to guide fusing interference graphs, allowing an easy integration of this register allocator into a region-based compiler.

1 Introduction

Graph coloring is a well established approach to register allocation and a crucial component of many optimizing compilers. However, recent developments in compiler design and processor technology warrant a new look at global register allocation. Modern compilers include aggressive transformations (e.g, function inlining or loop unrolling) to exploit instruction level parallelism well beyond a single basic block. These transformations, together with global instruction scheduling, create two challenges: (i) the register pressure increases, since there are more values that may be allocated to a register; and (ii), the register allocator should be sensitive to the other compiler optimizations, i.e., if a compiler heavily optimizes one region of the program, then the register allocator should consider this information when deciding when and where to insert spill code.

We developed a register allocation framework that addresses these two concerns, and Figure 1 illustrates the benefits that can be obtained using this new approach for the `alvinn` program from the SPEC suite. This figure shows the total number of data movement operations executed that are due to register allocation (i.e., operations to save or restore a register, and register copies). All functions called by the main loop of this program are inlined. On the left, we see the number of data movement operations for an enhanced Chaitin-style register allocator [5]. In the middle, we see the results for the approach described in this paper which removes about 50 % of the data movement operations compared to a Chaitin-style register allocator. A simple enhancement, based on the observation that using caller-saved or callee-saved registers implies different costs, improves the results further and reduces the data movement overhead by 80%, as shown on the right.

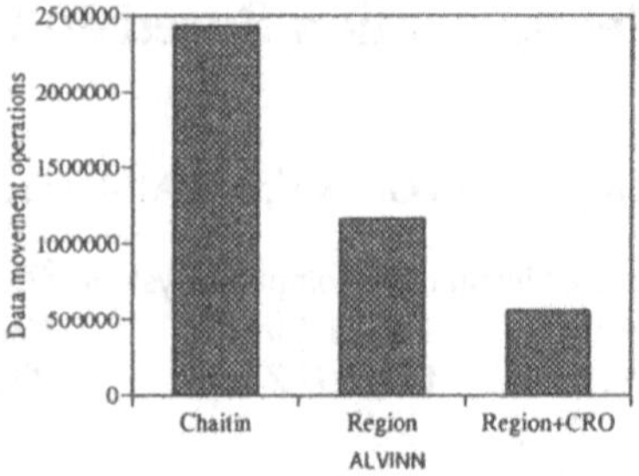

Fig. 1. Impact of different register allocation strategies.

The framework presented in this paper is *region-based* [10]: the register allocator operates on groups of basic blocks formed using either profile information or static analysis. The register allocator does not dictate how these regions are formed and thus provides a general and flexible approach to register allocation; form and priorities of regions are parameters to our algorithm. Regions can be individual basic blocks, traces [14], superblocks [11], or any other grouping used in the compiler (e.g., the loop structure). This framework fits nicely into code generators that take a similar approach to instruction scheduling [14, 6]: the register allocator now uses the same units of compilation and the same execution probability estimates as the instruction scheduler. This framework allows us to model a number of different approaches to register allocation [4, 9, 15], including the classical Chaitin-style register allocation [5] if a region is a function.

The key idea of our approach is to incrementally build up the interference graph. Consider the task of allocating registers for a compilation unit, e.g., a function. Instead of building an interference graph for the function and then cutting it down to make it colorable, we start with the interference graphs of smaller units and then build up towards the interference graph of the complete function. This approach allows the register allocator to delay decisions like which live range to spill or where to split, until more parts of a program have been analyzed. The order in which parts of a program are analyzed determines where overhead operations are placed. That's how the register allocator takes the priorities of regions into account when making spilling and splitting decisions: Live ranges are split only when necessary and then at boundaries to lower priority regions, thus minimizing the cost of additional data movement code. Spilling and splitting are well integrated: only those segments of a live range that have low spill cost but span regions of high priority and high register pressure are spilled. The base of our register allocator is a powerful *fusion* operator: the interference graphs of regions are fused to build up the complete interference graph.

A major benefit of the region-based approach is that the register allocator can custom-tailor the use of caller-saved and callee-saved registers. Many discussions of register allocation do not pay attention to the common practice of designating some registers as callee-saved and others as caller-saved. This register allocator can split a live range L so that those parts of L that cross frequent function calls are isolated.

1.1 Terminology

A common approach is to model the register allocation problem as a graph coloring problem by assigning colors (physical registers) to nodes (live ranges of virtual registers) in some heuristic order. This process blocks when either all vertices have degree greater than N (the number of registers) [5] or when no legal color exists for a node [7, 3]. When coloring blocks, the compiler must somehow lower the maximum degree of the vertices in the interference graph to allow coloring to proceed. Two major techniques have been developed to lower the degree of the interference graph:

Splitting: Live range splitting segments a long live range $lr(x)$ into smaller live ranges $lr_i(x)$. *Shuffle* code is then needed to move the data value x when control passes from a segment lr_1 to another segment lr_2. Splitting does not reduce register pressure, but rather reduces the degree of the interference graph. The expectation is that each $lr_i(x)$ has a lower degree than $lr(x)$ and that the new graph can then be colored.

Spilling: A live range L is assigned a location in memory, and all references to L are done by memory accesses (loads/stores), which are referred to as *spill code*. A spilled live range is removed from the interference graph since it is no longer a register assignment candidate, thus lowering the register pressure.

The *spill cost* or *split cost* is then the execution cost of the spill or shuffle code. These two basic techniques still leave the compiler with a wide range of options, and the compiler's decisions influence the quality of the code. Among the decision that a compiler must make are:

- How to order the live ranges considering them for coloring.
- Whether to spill or split when coloring fails, which live ranges to spill or split, and in the case of splitting, where to place the shuffle code.
- Whether to assign a callee-save or caller-save register to a live range.

Our register allocator isolates these three aspects and thereby allows a compiler to pick the heuristic or strategy that is most in line with the rest of the compiler design.

2 Background and prior work

A frequently employed technique is to first allocate a *virtual register* from an infinite pool of registers to each register allocation candidate. Candidates can be user variables, constants, or compiler generated temporaries, depending on the strategy chosen [7]. Then, liveness analysis and reaching analysis determine the live range for each virtual register. Live ranges that are constructed in this manner, however, may be comprised of disjoint segments, resulting in an unnecessarily high number of conflicts for a live range. Renumbering [5] and web analysis [12] are two techniques to construct concise live ranges, which result in interference graphs of potentially lower degree. Virtual registers are mapped to physical registers by the register allocator, and spill or shuffle code is added to the program, as necessary.

2.1 Chaitin-style register allocation

Chaitin's algorithm is based on the observation that if a vertex V has degree $< N$, then V can be trivially colored since no matter what colors are assigned to V's neighbors, a legal color will remain for V. Such a vertex with degree less than N is called *unconstrained*. Given an interference graph, Chaitin's algorithm proceeds by successively removing unconstrained vertices from the graph. Each time a vertex V is removed, the edges that are incident upon V are also removed, and the degrees of V's neighbors are decremented. This process is known as *simplification*. Once all vertices have been removed, colors can be assigned to vertices in the *reverse order* in which they were removed. Simplification blocks when all remaining vertices have degree $\geq N$ and at this time a live range is picked to be spilled based on a heuristic cost function. This cost function is based on the spill cost of a live range as well as the benefit of removing the live range from the interference graph (the degree of the live range). Since registers must also be assigned to spill code, the process of building the interference graph and performing simplification is repeated until no more spilling is necessary.

Several refinements to this basic algorithm have been implemented. The coloring based register allocation algorithm used in the RS/6000 compiler [1] improves on this basic algorithm in two ways. First, the interference graph is colored three times, each time using a variation of the cost function, and the coloring with the least resulting total spill cost is selected. Second, when a live range L is selected for spilling, instead of inserting a load before each use and a store after each definition of L, an attempt is made to insert at most a single load and store inside each basic block. In effect, L is split into segments that span at most a basic block.

Simplification is a heuristic approach to coloring, and as such may miss legal coloring opportunities. Optimistic coloring [3] improves simplification by attempting to assign colors to live ranges that would have been spilled by the basic algorithm. Optimistic coloring delays spill decisions until the register assignment phase. As in the basic algorithm, a *spill candidate* L is chosen when simplification blocks, but rather than deciding to spill L, this live range is removed from the graph and added to the set of live ranges that will be assigned colors. Spill decisions are made during the register assignment phase: when no legal color exists for the next live range to be colored, this live range is spilled.

The Chatin-style approach is simple and fast, and produces good results for programs with colorable interference graphs. However, when an interference graph cannot be colored using simplification, this approach makes spilling decisions that are all-or-nothing: *all* definitions and uses of a spilled live range go through memory even though some parts of the live range could have been allocated a register. It is more beneficial to spill only the troublesome segments of a live range (i.e., segments that contain few or no references and span regions of high register pressure), while keeping in registers those segments that have references in regions of high execution frequency. Besides, despite all the attempts to improve spill code, in practice there are situations where splitting produces better results [2].

It is difficult to adopt live range splitting into Chaitin's approach. Since the interference graph does not encode information about the program control flow structure and reference patterns of live ranges, this graph cannot be used to guide partitioning of live ranges. Moreover, it is difficult to make splitting decisions when simplification blocks, for several reasons. First, it is difficult to decide how to partition a live range in a manner that not only allows registers to be assigned in the most critical regions of code and minimizes split cost but also allows simplification to proceed. Second, the interference graph must be *rebuilt* each time live ranges are split. This is in contrast to spilling where simplification can *resume* after a spilled live range is removed from the interference graph. Third, it is difficult to decide between spilling and splitting, i.e., it is difficult to distinguish between cases of high register pressure where spilling is absolutely necessary, and cases where the interference graph has high degree and splitting can reduce the interference graph's degree.

2.2 Splitting live ranges before coloring

Several recent approaches have tried to fit live range splitting into Chaitin's coloring framework by splitting live ranges prior to coloring. The motivation is to reduce the degree of the interference graph and to allow the spilling of only those live range segments that span program regions of high register pressure. Aggressive live range splitting [2] uses the Static Single Assignment (SSA) representation of a program to determine split points. A live range is split at a ϕ node when the incoming values to the ϕ node result from distinct assignments. The approach also splits all live ranges that span a loop by splitting these live ranges immediately before and after the loop. Kolte and Harrold [13] partition a live range at a finer granularity by considering the ranges of instructions between loads and stores of a virtual register.

These approaches to splitting live ranges before coloring have several drawbacks. First, decisions regarding which live ranges to split and where to split them are made prematurely. Thus, live ranges are split unnecessarily, resulting in a performance degradation due to unnecessary shuffle code. Various heuristics have been developed to eliminate shuffle code by increasing the chance that the same color is given to partner live ranges, e.g., biased-coloring or conservative coalescing [2]. Rather than determining the critical regions where splitting and spilling are beneficial, these approaches split live ranges arbitrarily and greedily, with the hopes that later heuristical steps will clean up unnecessary splits. Second, the points in the program where live ranges are split by these approaches are not necessarily points of low execution probability. Although these approaches may use execution probabilities to determine the points to split live ranges, there is no guarantee that the resulting live ranges will fit into registers without spilling. That is, the register allocator runs the risk of either splitting too much (leading to unnecessary shuffle code), or not enough (with the consequence that high-frequency live ranges are spilled).

2.3 Priority-based coloring

The priority-based coloring [7] approach is an alternative framework that allows splitting decisions to be delayed until coloring blocks. In contrast to Chaitin's approach, where the register allocator assigns physical registers to virtual registers, this approach begins with each live range assigned a home location in memory. In effect, the algorithm begins with all live ranges spilled to memory. Coloring greedily assigns colors to live ranges in a heuristic order determined by a priority function. The priority function captures the savings in memory accesses from assigning a register to a live range rather than keeping the live range in memory. This priority function can be based on either profile information or static estimates, e.g., live ranges that have references within deeply nested-loops can be given high priority [7]. Before colors are assigned, unconstrained live ranges are removed from the interference graph, since unconstrained live ranges can always be assigned a legal color, after colors have been assigned to other live ranges. Unlike simplification, the degree of nodes neighboring the removed unconstrained nodes are not decremented.

Color assignment blocks when no legal color exists for the next live range L to be colored, i.e., when all N colors have been taken up by L's neighbors. At this point, L is split. To facilitate splitting, the live range for a candidate V is defined as a collection of *live units*, where each live unit is a basic block within which V is live. Splitting forms a new live range L' by starting from a seed live unit and incrementally adding live units to the new live range until adding one more live unit renders L' uncolorable. In [7], live units are added in a breadth-first traversal of the control flow graph, preferably starting from a live unit where the first reference to V is a definition. A live range is spilled (i.e., remains in its home location) when no live units that comprise the live range can be given a register.

An important consideration in live range splitting is selecting the points where shuffle code is inserted. To reduce split cost, shuffle code should be placed at points of low execution probability. The priority based approach does not take execution frequency into account when inserting shuffle code, and there is no guarantee that split points do not end up along frequently executed edges. Shuffle code induced by a split may end up, e.g., on a loop back arc. Code motion techniques are used after register assignment, to optimize placement of shuffle code [7].

2.4 Program structure based approaches

Several more recent approaches to register allocation attempt to make graph coloring sensitive to program structure by dividing a program into regions and prioritizing the regions according to execution probabilities. The register allocator than colors regions in order of their priorities, and shuffle is code is inserted at the boundaries of these regions. Representative program structure based approaches include the Tera [4], Multiflow [9] and RAG [15] compilers.

The Tera compiler (as described in [4]) constructs a tile tree for a program; this tree corresponds to the control-flow hierarchy of the program. Register allocation colors the tiles in two phases. The first phase traverses the tile tree from the bottom up and allocates pseudo registers to the live ranges in each tile using graph coloring. Pseudo registers capture the constraint that two virtual registers are to be allocated to the same physical register. Once two variables in a tile are assigned to the same pseudo register, the parents of the tile must adhere to this decision. The second phase walks through the tile tree top-down and binds pseudo registers to physical registers. Biased-coloring is used to avoid unnecessary shuffle code at tile boundaries. As coloring is performed hierarchically, shuffle code tends to be outside of the innermost loops. The requirement

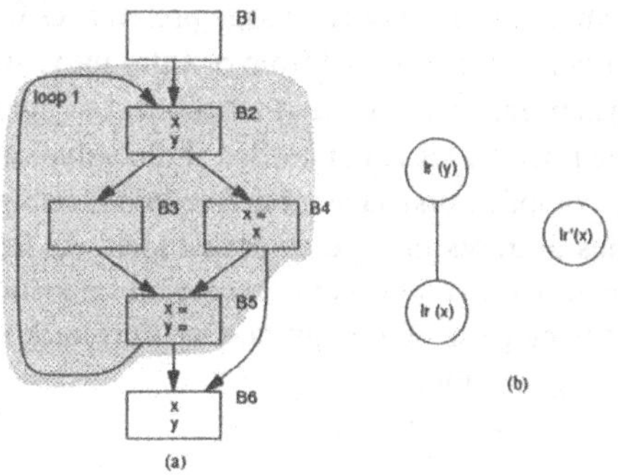

Fig. 2. Premature coloring decision with $N = 2$.

to observe the lower-level coloring imposes more and more constraints as coloring moves toward the root of the tile tree.

Figure 2 illustrates unnecessary constraints imposed on the register allocation by premature coloring decisions. The code in Figure 2(a) consists of two tiles, one for the loop (the shaded region) and one for blocks B_1 and B_6. The loop region is colored first. The interference graph *for this region* is depicted in Figure 2(b). Inside this region, the live range $lr(y)$ is live in B_2 and B_5. There are two live ranges for x, $lr(x)$ and $lr'(x)$, in the loop. The live range $lr(x)$ is live in B_2 and B_5, and $lr'(x)$ is live in B_4. Coloring the graph with two registers, $lr'(x)$ is placed into the same pseudo register as $lr(x)$ or into the same pseudo register as $lr(y)$. Based on the information inside the loop region, both choices are reasonable. However, if $lr'(x)$ and $lr(y)$ use the same pseudo register, a shuffle move is inevitable either on $\langle B_4, B_6 \rangle$ or on $\langle B_5, B_6 \rangle$, since $lr(x)$ and $lr'(x)$ merge in B_6. If $lr'(x)$ and $lr(x)$ use the same pseudo register, no shuffle code is required, but that this mapping is beneficial can only be determined when dealing with B_6. This paper presents an approach to address this deficiency by delaying binding decisions. In contrast to [4], our algorithm takes a lazy approach to color assignment so as to avoid premature coloring decisions.

Instead of a tile tree, the RAG compiler colors the region nodes in a function's Program Dependence Graph (PDG), proceeding in a hierarchical manner from the leaves to the root [15]. Chaitin's algorithm is used at each region node. The coloring decision made for a region is preserved by the parent nodes of the region. This may prevent graph coloring from finding the best solution and affects live range splitting as well. A live range is split when that live range is spilled in the parent region; such a live range is split at the boundaries of the parent region and all subregions in which the live range is live. All live ranges that are determined to be in the same register in the subregions are considered as one node in the parent region and therefore interfere with the union of the live ranges with which the individual live ranges interfere.

The Multiflow compiler employs trace scheduling as a framework for both register allocation and scheduling [9]. The trace scheduler picks a trace and then passes it to the code scheduler; the code scheduler then performs register allocation and scheduling together. The code scheduler records register usage preferences for the scheduled trace; this information is maintained for each exit from or entry into a trace. This information is subsequently used when translating traces that connect to these exit or entry points and shuffle code between two traces is not needed if the value can be kept in the same register. Traces that are compiled first have more freedom in using registers, and shuffle code ends up boundaries to traces that are compiled later. As long as the trace picker presents the traces in an order that reflects the execution frequency, this scheme favors the most frequently executed parts of a program. One drawback of the approach is that coloring is not used for register allocation.

3 Overview of register allocation based on graph fusion

The key idea is to *build up* the interference graph, starting off with live ranges that extend at most a single region. Each region initially has its own interference graph. A region can be as small as a single basic block, or as large as a whole function (in which case the algorithm is identical to Chaitin-style register allocation). Regions are connected via control-flow edges, which are prioritized. These edges are then considered in priority order, and the interference graphs of two regions connected by an edge are merged by *fusing* the interference graphs. This fusion operator coalesces live ranges that span the control flow edge and maintains the invariant that the resulting merged interference graph is colorable, if necessary by splitting (suppressing the coalescing) of a live range. Thus the fusion operator makes spilling and splitting decisions when it becomes clear that it is impossible or unprofitable to keep all live ranges in registers. After all control flow edges have been considered, a single colorable interference graph remains.

There are four phases in this framework: *region formation*, *graph simplification*, *graph merging*, and *register assignment*. In the *region formation phase*, regions are formed using any number of possible techniques. For example, a region can be a single basic block, a trace [14], a superblock [11], a region as defined in [10], the blocks at a particular static loop nesting level [4], or the blocks within a PDG region node [15]. Control flow edges that lie outside of regions are then ordered according to some priority function consistent with the region formation approach, e.g., edges entering innermost loop regions are ordered before those entering outermost loop regions. One particularly attractive priority function is the use of execution probabilities. These can be derived either from profile information [8, 16], from static estimates such as loop nesting depth [7], or from static branch estimates [14]. The choice of edge ordering is orthogonal to register allocation but of course impacts the quality of the code, as our register allocation framework is edge order sensitive: shuffle code is less likely to end up on edges that are ordered first, and spilling decisions are delayed until later edges are processed.

During region formation, an interference graph G_R is built for each region R. Given a virtual register x, the segment of x's live range $lr(x)$ that extends block B_i is denoted by $lr_i(x)$, and there is one or more segment for every region R where x is live and reaching.

The objective of the *graph simplification phase* is to determine how many live ranges must be spilled within each region. If an interference graph G_R can be simplified, then no spill code is necessary within region R. But if G_R cannot be simplified, then from R's perspective the cheapest live ranges to spill within R are those that are *transparent*, i.e., live ranges $lr(y)$ that span R with no definition or use of y in R. From a global perspective, the choice of *which* live ranges are the best ones to spill cannot be determined at this point in the algorithm. Thus the decision on which live range to spill is delayed until more global knowledge of reference patterns is available; this phase determines only *how many* transparent live ranges need to be spilled within each region. The next phase, graph merging, determines *which* live ranges are the best ones to spill. This technique is referred to as *delayed spilling* and is discussed in more detail in Section 4.3. There, we also describe what to do if the compiler must spill more live ranges than there are transparent ones.

The *graph merging phase* takes the sequence of control flow edges determined by the region formation phase and fuses interference graphs along each edge. Graph merging is based on a powerful *fusion* operator that maintains the invariant that the resulting interference graph is simplifiable (i.e., can be simplified). Live range splitting decisions are made by the fusion operator: if fusing two graphs G_1 and G_2 along an edge E results in an interference graph that cannot be simplified, then one or more live ranges that span E are split. Only the live ranges that span E need to be considered, because in the worst case, splitting all such live ranges partitions the graph $G_1 \cup G_2$ back to the two original graphs, G_1 and G_2, both of which are simplifiable. At the end of the graph merging phase, we are left with one simplifiable interference graph; we know how many live ranges to spill for each region and where to place the shuffle code, but no physical registers are committed to any live range. The invariant is the lazy approach which allows us to avoid making any coloring decisions prematurely during the graph merging phase. Therefore there is no coloring assignment decision to any live range while graphs of the loop region are fused in Figure 2. All we know is that the interference graph of the loop region is colorable. The actual coloring decision is deferred till the register assignment phase.

As more graphs are fused, the delayed spilling mechanism gradually spills live ranges. The net effect of combining splitting with delayed spilling is that the register allocator may spill only those segments of a virtual register's live range that do not contain references but span regions of high register pressure.

In the *register assignment phase*, physical registers are assigned to live ranges and shuffle code is generated. The simplifiability invariant guarantees that once all interference graphs have been fused, the resulting interference graph is colorable and spilling or splitting decisions have already been made. Shuffle code is inserted at an edge $E = \langle B_1, B_2 \rangle$ for those live ranges that extend across E but have different storage locations in B_1 and B_2. Shuffle code is either a load, store or register to register move; shuffling between memory locations is not necessary as all live ranges of a virtual register x are spilled to the same location in memory. This straight forward insertion of shuffle code may result in partial redundancies among the shuffle code. While a general partial redundancy elimination algorithm could be used to optimize the shuffle code, a simple technique is effective in practice, details of which are discussed in Section 5. There exist further opportunities for improving the code in this phase: biased coloring [2] may eliminate shuffle code, optimistic coloring [3] may assign registers to live ranges that have been spilled by simplification, and if we notice that a live range gets a caller-saved register in a region with high call frequency, then the register assigner may decide to spill this live range nevertheless.

	$lr_2(x)$		
$lr_1(x)$	Spilled	Transparent	Non-transparent
Spilled	Spilled	Spill (Section 4.3)	Split (Section 4.3)
Transparent		Coalesced, transparent	Coalesced, non-transparent
Non-transparent			Coalesced, non-transparent

Fig. 3. Different possibilities when coalescing $lr_1(x)$ and $lr_2(x)$.

4 Fusing two interference graphs

Consider two basic blocks B_1 and B_2 that are in two regions R_1 and R_2, and connected by an edge $E = \langle B_1, B_2 \rangle$ in the control flow graph. Let x be a virtual register that is live along edge E. Each of these live range segments lr_i can be in one of these three states: it has been spilled, it is represented in G_{R_i} and transparent, or it is represented in G_{R_i} and non-transparent (i.e., there is a reference). The fusion operation attempts to coalesce the live range segments $lr_1(x)$ and $lr_2(x)$ range in the interference graph $G_{R_1 \cup R_2}$ so that no shuffle code is needed for x along E. If both segments are spilled, no shuffle code is needed. If one is spilled and the other is transparent, we spill the combined live range in $R_1 \cup R_2$ and thereby reduce the register pressure, since the live range is already spilled in one region and there are no references to it in the other. If one is spilled and the other non-transparent, we have a split point. Otherwise the segments are coalesced, although if the new interference graph is not simplifiable, coalescing may be suppressed (i.e., a split). Figure 3 enumerates these cases.[1]

Each live range has three attributes that are propagated during graph fusion: *caller-save cost*, *spill-cost* and *has-def*. The *caller-save cost* attribute is the estimated cost of assigning a caller-saved register to the live range. This cost is the number of saves and restores that must be executed around function calls if this live range is assigned a caller-saved register. The *spill-cost* attribute is the estimated spill cost of a live range. The *caller-save cost* and *spill-cost* properties are used during register assignment to decide whether a live range is assigned a callee-save register, a caller-save register, or whether it is more profitable to spill the live range. The *has-def* property is true for a live range $lr(x)$, if there is a definition of x within $lr(x)$. This information indicates whether x's value needs to be stored to memory at exits from $lr(x)$; if a live range does to modify the value of a virtual register, then no stores are required at exits from the live range.

For each basic block B, two data flow sets are maintained: *ReachIn*(B) and *LiveOut*(B). Given a virtual register x, $x \in$ *ReachIn*(B) if a definition of x reaches the entry of B, and $x \in$ *LiveOut*(B) if x is live at the exit of B. The *ReachIn* and *LiveOut* sets indicate which live ranges span edge E.

The fusion operator ensures that the simplifiability invariant holds by performing simplification on $G_{R_1 \cup R_2}$. If simplification of $G_{R_1 \cup R_2}$ blocks, then a coalesced live range

[1] Empty entries in this table are symmetric cases.

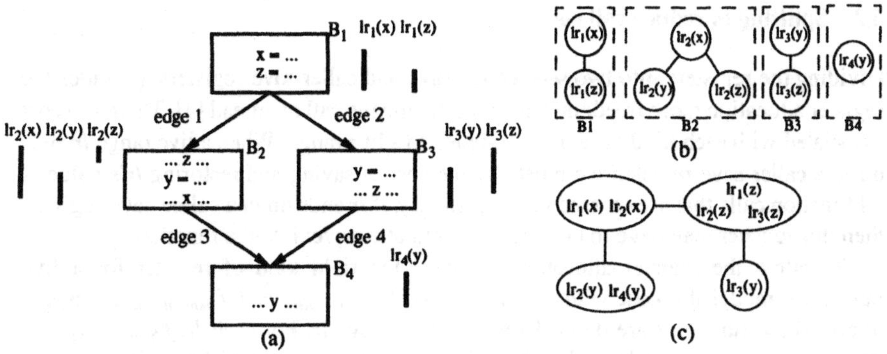

Fig. 4. Simple code fragment for a world with $N = 2$.

$lr(x)$ is chosen for splitting from among the set of remaining constrained nodes. $lr(x)$ will be split along E back into $lr_1(x)$ and $lr_2(x)$. After splitting a live range, the degree of the interference graph may be lowered, allowing the simplification to proceed from the point where it blocked. If the simplification blocks again, additional live ranges are split. Since the original graphs G_{R_1} and G_{R_2} are simplifiable, then at worst all live ranges that span E are split.

As graph merging proceeds further, more interference graphs are fused, resulting in denser interference graphs. Thus, the earlier an edge is considered by the fusion process, the less likely it is that live ranges are split along that edge. This provides a nice property: if we don't want shuffle code on a particular edge, we can fuse the interference graphs along that edge first. Consequently, the decision of *where* to split is prioritized according to the edge ordering, and shuffle code ends up on less frequently executed edges.

4.1 Example

We illustrate the above steps with an example. Consider assigning registers to the program fragment shown in Figure 4(a). Assume we have only two physical registers ($N = 2$) and that regions are basic blocks. There are three virtual registers (x, y and z) in this program with initial live ranges indicated by the vertical bars. The interference graph of each basic block prior to fusion is depicted in Figure 4 (b). Suppose edges 1 and 3 form the most frequently executed path and edges are fused in the order 1, 3, 2, 4. After we fuse along edges 1, 3 and 2, we obtain the interference graph of Figure 4 (c) (interference graph nodes list live ranges that have been fused). If we now fuse the interference graphs along edge 4, $lr_3(y)$ and $lr_4(y)$ are combined, since the only live range spanning edge 4 is $lr(y)$. However, fusing along edge 4 makes the graph unsimplifiable (clique of size 3), so the algorithm undoes combining $lr_3(y)$ and $lr_4(y)$. $lr(y)$ is effectively split at the less frequently executed point in this control flow graph. The result is that all values can be kept in registers with an additional register move instruction at the end of block B_3.

4.2 Splitting to reduce call cost

Dividing the registers into two sets, callee-save and caller-save registers, provides the register allocation more freedom when minimizing the call overhead [7]. There is a cost associated with each kind of register assigned to a live range. When a live range *lr* ends up in a caller-save register, we must pay the cost of saving and restoring *lr*'s value at all function calls that are crossed by *lr*. Similarly, if *lr* ends up in a callee-save register, then this register may have to be saved/restored at entry/exit to the function.

To allow the register allocator to choose the right kind of register for a live range, we model the cost with two functions, $f_{benefit\_caller}$ and $f_{benefit\_callee}$, respectively. These functions are defined for each live range *lr*. For each *lr*, $f_{benefit\_caller}(lr)$ (resp. $f_{benefit\_callee}(lr)$) is defined as the weighted reference counts of the spill code minus the weighted caller-save (resp. callee-save) cost. That is, these two functions indicate the estimated number of loads and stores that are eliminated if a caller-save (or callee-save) register is assigned to *lr*. During the register assignment phase, the selection of the kind of register to use is based on these two functions. If $f_{benefit\_callee}(lr) > f_{benefit\_caller}(lr)$, finding an available *callee-save* register for *lr* is attempted prior to finding an available caller-save register. If $f_{benefit\_callee}(lr) \leq f_{benefit\_caller}(lr)$, it is preferable to put *lr* into a *caller-save* over using a callee-save register. However, sometimes *not* using a register (i.e., spilling a live range) is better than using the wrong kind of register. For example, the spill-cost may be less than the caller-save cost. In such a case, the whole live range is spilled to reduce the overall load/store counts even though there is an available register, since this register is of the wrong kind.

Fusing two interference graphs tends to grow live ranges aggressively to reduce the shuffle cost as long as the colorability invariant is maintained. One improvement to the algorithm sketched above is to limit the growth of live ranges that cross function calls, by constraining coalescing. In this manner, the (smaller) live range has a chance to get the best kind of register or be spilled (at lower spill-cost), thus reducing the overall load/store counts. Even though the graph is colorable, it may be better if the live range is split at infrequently executed edges; then we pay the *lower* shuffle cost (along these edges) instead of the *higher* caller-save cost at all call sites. When applied to the `alvinn` program, this improvement results in the 80% reduction in data movement operations shown in Figure 1.

The heuristic we use to constrain coalescing is based on two functions: $f_{threshold}$ and f_{split}. $f_{threshold}$ is a threshold function that determines good candidates for splitting, and f_{split} is a function that determines whether splitting would result in savings. Consider two live ranges $lr_1(x)$ in region R_1 and $lr_2(x)$ in R_2. R_1 and R_2 are joined by edge E. $f_{threshold}(lr_1, lr_2, E)$ is a function of the edge E's execution frequency, the number of registers available for assignment, and the weighted reference counts of $lr_1(x)$ and $lr_2(x)$. If $f_{threshold}(lr_1, lr_2, E)$ decides that edge E is a good place to suppress the coalescing of lr_1 and lr_2, $f_{split}(lr_1, lr_2, E)$ judges whether this decision could drive down the number of data movement operations. This function tests if one live range has a caller-save cost less than its spill-cost and the other live range has a caller-save cost greater than its spill cost plus the shuffle-cost along E. If that is the case, then the two live ranges are not coalesced since adding $lr_1 \cup lr_2$ to the interference graph is likely to hurt performance if $lr_1 \cup lr_2$ ends up in a caller-save register.

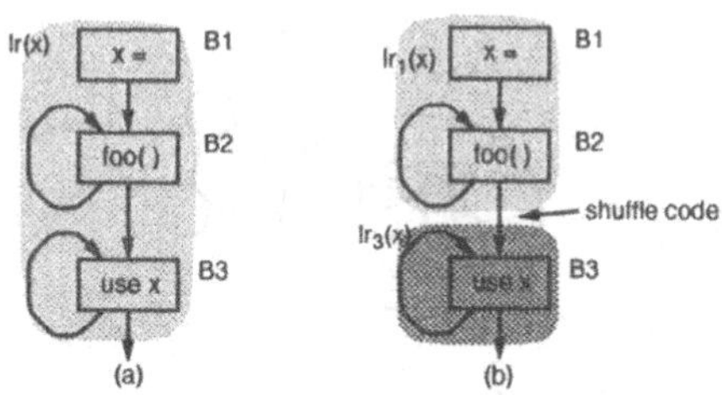

Fig. 5. Eliminating caller-save cost by splitting.

Figure 5 depicts an example of how caller-save cost is reduced by splitting. In this example, the live range x is live through out the whole program. Assume $lr(x)$ is not split, i.e. x occupies one register in Figure 5 (a). If this register is a caller-save register , $lr(x)$ pays a high caller cost (saving and restoring x around function `foo`). It is much cheaper to split the live range of x into $lr_1(x)$ and $lr_3(x)$ along the edge $\langle B_2, B_3 \rangle$, as illustrated by Figure 5 (b). Now $lr_1(x)$ can either reside in memory, or a callee-save register (if the callee-save cost is low).

4.3 Delayed spilling

When a region R needs M physical registers to be colored, and $M > N$, then $M - N$ live ranges must be spilled. Considering only local spill costs inside R, the best spill choice is a transparent live range L_t, since L_t has a high degree in the interference graph, and the cost of spilling L_t is zero inside R. If we assume that there are T transparent live ranges in region R, then there are three cases that must be considered:

$M - N < T$: In this case, the number of transparent live ranges is more than the number of live ranges that must be spilled. However, choosing the transparent live ranges for spilling should be delayed until the compiler obtains more global information about the reference patterns of the transparent live ranges. Searching the region's immediate neighbors does not solve the problem because transparent live ranges may be transparent across many basic blocks. *Delayed spilling* deals nicely with this case, as explained below. A large number of transparent live ranges is common while processing the first, high-priority edges.

$M - N = T$: In this case, the spill needs are satisfied by spilling all transparent live ranges.

$M - N > T$: In this case, all transparent live ranges, as well as $M - N - T$ live ranges with a reference inside R, are spilled.

We note that spill decisions may not be globally optimal. Although spilling a transparent live range is very attractive, we can construe flow graphs for which this decision is not optimal. And if $M - N > T$, we must spill some non-transparent live ranges, which are selected by a heuristic based on spill cost, area, and the degrees in the interference graph [1].

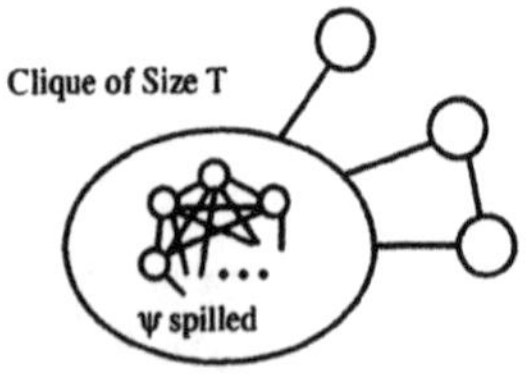

Fig. 6. Clique summary node.

We now describe in more detail the delayed spilling technique used to handle the case where $M - N < T$. Since all transparent live ranges conflict with each other, these live ranges form a clique in a region's interference graph. The transparent live ranges are therefore collected into a single *clique summary node* C in the interference graph, as depicted in Figure 6. This node C contains an edge to all other nodes in the graph, since the transparent live ranges interfere with all other live ranges in a region. The clique summary node is annotated with the number of transparent live ranges that it represents, i.e., $T(C)$. We record that $\psi(C) = M - N$ of the T transparent live ranges must be spilled, without specifying which ones. The actual size of the clique is thus $T(C) - \psi(C)$. The clique is dealt with as a single unit; eventually $\psi(C)$ live ranges will be spilled. By keeping a summary node in the graph, we can keep more live ranges in the interference graph than there are registers, and we delay the decision on *which* range(s) to spill until more information is available.

Given an edge $E = \langle B_1, B_2 \rangle$, the live ranges that span across E are merged. When a live range lr_1 is merged with lr_2, and one of the two is transparent, there are three cases to consider:

1. If lr_1 is a spilled live range, lr_2 is in a clique C (transparent): lr_2 is removed from C and spilled. Both $T(C)$ and $\psi(C)$ are decremented by one. This decision grows a spilled live range, thereby allowing the compiler to avoid shuffle code (a contiguous range of spilled or non-spilled live range segments does not incur shuffle code; only a transition from spill to non-spilled or vice versa requires shuffle code).
2. If lr_1 is a non-transparent live range, lr_2 is in a clique C: lr_2 is removed from C, but not spilled. Only $T(C)$ is decremented. This decision enlarges a non-spilled live range; since this live range is in a register in an adjacent region, the compiler favors it over the other live ranges in the clique.
3. If lr_1 is in clique C_1 and lr_2 is in clique C_2 : lr_1 and lr_2 are coalesced and added to a new clique, $C = C_1 \cap C_2$. After processing all live ranges across E, there are three cliques C, C'_1 and C'_2, where $C'_1 = C_1 - C$ and $C'_2 = C_2 - C$. $\psi(C)$ establishes how many ranges of C must be spilled and is computed as a function of $\psi(C_1)$ and $\psi(C_2)$.

If $T(C) = \psi(C)$ for a clique C at any time during this phase, then this means that all live ranges of C must be spilled. At that point, C is removed from the interference graph.

5 Placement of shuffle code

After the register assignment (coloring) phase is done, shuffle code is inserted as necessary along edges. At an edge $E = \langle B_1, B_2 \rangle$, shuffle code is inserted for a virtual register x that has been split at E, i.e., if $lr_1(x)$ and $lr_2(x)$ have not been assigned the same storage location. Shuffle code can be of three types: register-to-register ($lr_1(x)$ and $lr_2(x)$ are assigned to different registers, so a move operation is required), register-to-memory ($lr_1(x)$ is assigned to a register and *has-def* is set, and $lr_2(x)$ is spilled), or memory-to-register ($lr_1(x)$ is spilled and $lr_2(x)$ is assigned to a register). There is no need for memory-to-memory shuffle code, because all live ranges belonging to the same virtual register x are spilled to a single location in memory (i.e., $lr_1(x)$ and $lr_2(x)$ are spilled to the same memory location).

The insertion of shuffle code is simple and straight forward, but this step may result in partial redundancies in the code. For instance, the has-def property of a live range $lr(x)$ determines whether shuffle stores of x are needed on the exit edges of $lr(x)$. When the definitions of x are in less frequently executed blocks, and the exit edges (splitting points) are more frequently executed than the definitions, the shuffle stores are executed more often than necessary. Based on the estimated costs of *def-cost* and the estimated costs of the shuffle move (register-to-register), store (register-to-memory) and load (memory-to-register) operations, a simple technique is used to optimize the shuffle stores. For each live range, the costs of the shuffle move, store and load can easily be obtained since each edge is annotated with the estimated execution frequency (either static or profile). The def-cost of a live range is the estimated (weighted) number of definition within the live range. If the sum of the def-cost plus the cost of shuffle moves, which move values into the live range, is less than the cost of shuffle store, then all shuffle stores are eliminated by inserting a new shuffle store right after each definition and the shuffle moves. In other words, for each definition (which includes the shuffle moves), there is a store writing the new value back to the memory location of the live range so as to keep the value in memory up-to-date.

The technique is quite effective in practice. The reason is that the code motion step of the global optimization phase moves loop-invariant common subexpressions out of loops, which the definitions of those common subexpressions are less frequently executed, and they may be spilled inside part of the loops due to the high register pressure. Figure 7 depicts the optimized placement of the shuffle code. The live range x is defined in B_0 and live through out the whole program. x is spilled within the loop, as indicated by the shaded region. The shuffle code is highlighted in bold face. The straight forward shuffle code insertion requires two shuffle code, depicted in Figure 7(a), one shuffle store on Edge 1 (from B_1 to the spilled region) and one shuffle load on Edge 2 (from the spilled region to B_2). The shuffle store is executed on every loop iteration in despite of the fact that x is never modified in B_1 and B_2. Since x is defined in B_0, which is less frequently executed than Edge 1 is traversed, the placement of the shuffle store can be optimized by eliminating the shuffle store on Edge 1 and inserting a new shuffle store immediately after the definition of x (depicted in Figure 7(b)).

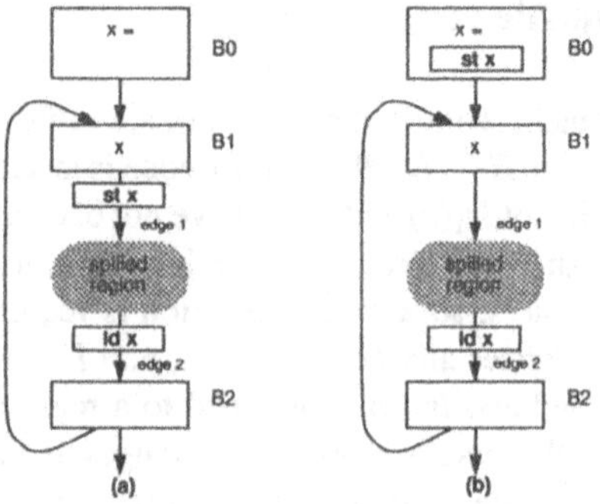

Fig. 7. Placement of shuffle store.

6 Evaluation

The framework is implemented in the *cmcc* compiler, an optimizing retargetable compiler developed at CMU. Our data are based on the code generator for the MIPS; dynamic numbers have been obtained on a DECStation 5000. The runtime cost of our algorithm is moderate. A version of `cmcc` that has been compiled with debug support on (`-g`, i.e., without optimizations), runs 2 – 4 times slower than the native C compiler[2].

We measured the impact of this register allocation strategy for various SPEC programs (`li`, `alvinn`, `espresso`, `compress`, `eqntott`, `ear`, `sc`, `matrix300`, `doduc`, `spice`, `nasa7` and `fpppp`). We first contrast our baseline algorithm (i.e., without the improvement of Section 4.2) with results using the well-known (enhanced) Chaitin-style approach. We use all registers on the MIPS, adhering to the standard calling convention. We start with the smallest region size, one basic block, and grow these until we have the interference graph for the function. All functions within the main loop of `alvinn` are inlined.

For both approaches, we run two experiments. First, we use only static information to guide the register allocation. That is, we use loop depth to estimate the execution frequency of a block. In our region-based approach, when considering the basic blocks inside a loop, we use breath-first order to select edges for fusing. In a second experiment, we use profile information from a prior execution.

6.1 All available registers

As expected, for programs with many small functions, Chaitin's algorithm works fairly well, and our approach produces identical results. For most of these programs, use of

[2] This figure is to be taken as preliminary. `cmcc` has not been tuned at all. Since the compiler used to compile `cmcc` does not support debugging of optimized code, we are forced to use the `-g` flag, since `cmcc` is still undergoing active development. Finally, `cmcc` is implemented in C++, and we cannot assess if this choice of language implies a performance penalty relative to the native compiler.

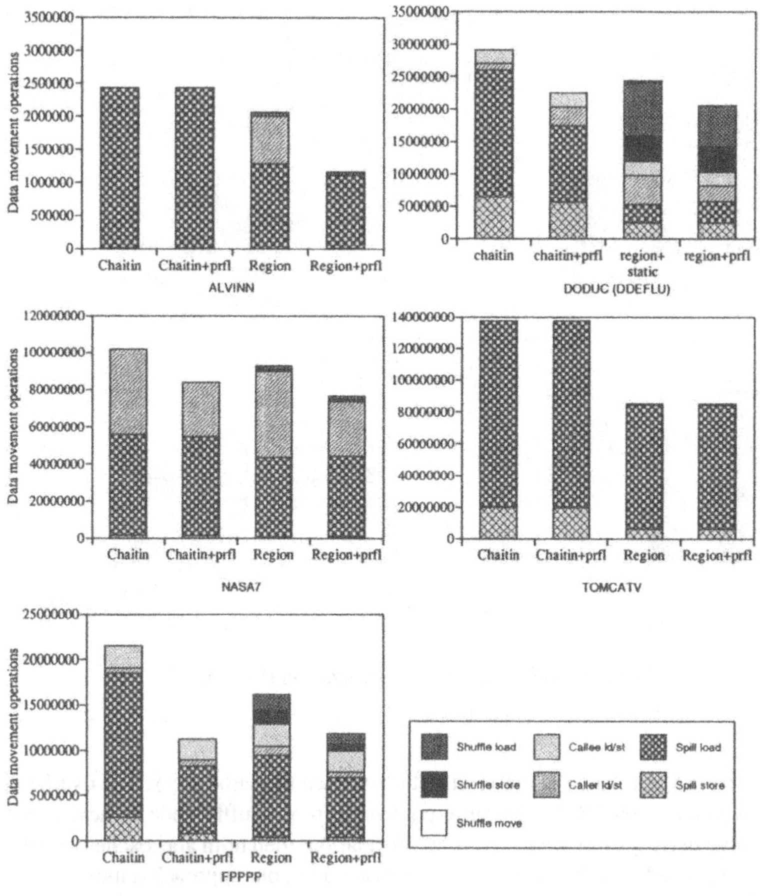

Fig. 8. All available registers (26 int, 16 double).

profile information improves the result, independent of the register allocation strategy. We therefore turn our attention to programs with significant register pressure.

`alvinn`, `nasa7`, `tomcatv`, `doduc` and `fpppp` are the programs with high register pressure, and here we see the limitations of the all-or-nothing approach to spilling that is the foundation of Chaitin-style register allocation. Figure 8 shows register allocation based on graph fusion is able to split live ranges properly and thereby cuts for `alvinn` nearly 52 % of the overhead required by Chaitin-style allocation. Chaitin-style allocation finds the "best" complete live ranges to put into registers, therefore, the result is not improved by using profile information. Our approach breaks live ranges, as can be seen by the lower number of spill loads. And profile information provides a better cost function for the register assignment phase (when deciding if a live range should go into a caller-save register or be spilled), resulting in a further improvement. Looking

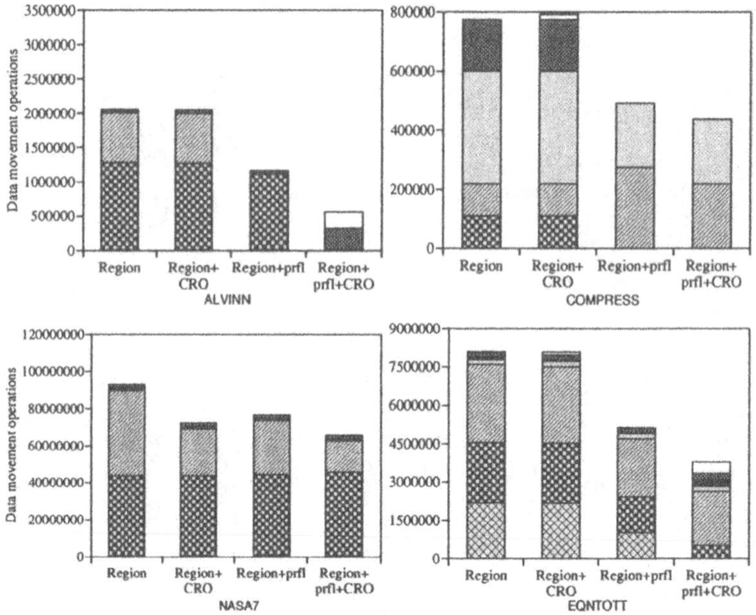

Fig. 9. Impact of call cost optimization (CRO).

at the results for `fpppp` using static information, we see the same story. The overhead of `fpppp` is reduced by 28 %; the large contribution of shuffle code indicates that live ranges have been split. If we use profile information, then both approaches find the "right" live ranges and give the same result. For `tomcatv`, our approach removes 40 % of the overhead operations. Because the estimated static information provides a good estimation, the profile information does not help in this case. There are 3 big functions in `doduc`: `subb`, `supp` and `ddeflu`. These three account for the majority of data movement operations. `subb` and `supp` consist of only one big block. For those types of functions, our register allocator produces the same amount of data movement operations as a Chaitin-style allocator, since the sole basic block is the complete compilation unit. One simple way to deal with such blocks is to partition the big block into smaller blocks so that our approach can be applied to make better spilling and splitting decisions. We show in Figure 8 the result for `ddeflu`, where large portions of the spill loads and stores are replaced by shuffle code (17 % reduction for edge ordering based on static information and 30 % reduction for profile-based edge ordering).

6.2 Call cost optimization

Given the importance of getting the right kind of register in a last experiment, we take positive action to limit the growth of live ranges, as described in Section 4.2. Figure 9 presents the results for `alvinn`, `compress`, and `eqntott` for this call cost optimization. Without profile information, the differences are negligible. (This is not surprising given the definition of the threshold and cost functions.)

Recall that a live range that is assigned a caller-save register but has high caller-save cost and low spill cost is spilled to memory during the register assignment phase, even though there are enough registers to hold the live range. Once a live range is picked to be spilled at this stage, no splitting is attempted. In other words, all references go through memory. The effect of such a decision is to increase the amount of spill code to reduce loads and stores of the caller-saved registers. The spill code that we see in Figure 9 (i.e., for `alvinn` and `eqntott`) is due to such live ranges that we spilled during register assignment. The call cost optimization of Section 4.2 suppresses coalescing of two live range segments lr_1 and lr_2 if one of them (say lr_2) has high caller-save cost (because the coalesced live range has high caller-save cost as well). Without coalescing, lr_1(with low caller-save cost) gets the desired caller-save register; lr_2 ends up in a memory or in a callee-saved register. If lr_2 is in memory, extra shuffle loads and stores are required. If lr_2 is in a callee-save register instead, no shuffle loads and stores are needed, but shuffle *moves* must be inserted. However, on most modern machines, moves are cheaper than loads/stores.

The results shown in Figure 9 illustrate the benefits nicely. This optimization succeed in isolating high caller-save cost regions at less frequently executed edges. Consequently, the register assignment phase spills fewer live ranges to memory. In the case of `alvinn`, about half of all overhead operations are shuffle moves. For `eqntott`, there are more shuffle moves than shuffle loads or stores.

Overall, in the case of `alvinn`, our approach of dealing with spilling and splitting, including call cost optimization, reduces total data movement overhead by 80 % compared to a Chaitin-style allocator.

7 Conclusion

In this paper we presented a new approach to register allocation. Our algorithm produces good results in those situations where a conventional Chaitin-style allocator breaks down. We have measured a reduction of the runtime cost of register allocation by up to 80 %. Of course, there are programs without significant register pressure. However, as aggressive compiler transformations become more common, even those simple programs are turned into challenges for a global register allocator. This algorithm is therefore especially attractive for compilers that look in regions beyond basic blocks for optimization opportunities or perform global scheduling. For those compilers, our register allocator presents an effective way to deal with programs that exhibit high register pressure.

Acknowledgements

We appreciate comments and feedback by D. Bernstein, IBM Israel, F. Chow, Silicon Graphics/MIPS, S. Freudenberger, HP Laboratories, and J. Ruttenberg, Silicon Graphics/MIPS.

References

1. D. Bernstein, D. Q. Goldin, M. C. Golumbic, H. Krawczyk, Y. Mansour, I. Nahshon, and R. Y. Pinter. Spill code minimization techniques for optimizing compilers. In *Proc. ACM SIGPLAN '89 Conf. on Prog. Language Design and Implementation*, pages 258–263. ACM, July 1989.
2. P. Briggs. *Register Allocation via Graph Coloring*. PhD thesis, Rice University, April 1992.
3. P. Briggs, K. D. Cooper, K. Kennedy, and L. Torczon. Coloring heuristics for register allocation. In *Proc. ACM SIGPLAN'89 Conf. on Prog. Language Design and Implementation*, pages 275–284. ACM, July 1989.
4. D. Callahan and B. Koblenz. Register allocation via hierarchical graph coloring. In *Proc. ACM SIGPLAN'91 Conf. on Prog. Language Design and Implementation*, pages 192–203, Toronto, June 1991. ACM.
5. G. J. Chaitin, M. A. Auslander, A. K. Chandra, J. Cocke, M. E. Hopkins, and P. W. Markstein. Register allocation by coloring. Research Report 8395, IBM Watson Research Center, 1981.
6. P. P. Chang, S. A. Mahlke, W. Y. Chen, N. J. Warter, and W. W. Hwu. Impact: An architectural framework for multiple-instruction-issue processors. In *Proc. 18th Intl. Symp. on Computer Architecture*, pages 266–275. ACM/IEEE, May 1991.
7. F. C. Chow and J. L. Hennessy. A priority-based coloring approach to register allocation. *ACM Trans. on Prog. Lang. Syst.*, 12:501–535, Oct. 1990.
8. J. A. Fisher and S. M. Freudenberger. Predicting conditional branch direction from previous runs of a program. In *Proc. Fifth Intl. Conf. on Architectural Support for Prog. Languages and Operating Systems (ASPLOS V)*, pages 85–97. ACM, October 1992.
9. S. Freudenberger and J. Ruttenberg. Phase ordering of register allocation and instruction scheduling. In R. Giegerich and S. L. Graham, editors, *Code Generation - Concepts, Tools, Techniques*, pages 146–170. Springer Verlag, 1992.
10. R. Hank, W. Hwu, and B. Rau. Region-based compilation: An introduction and motivation. In *Proc. 28th Annual ACM/IEEE Intl. Symp. on Microarchitecture*, pages 158–168, Ann Arbor, Nov 1995. ACM/IEEE.
11. W. W. Hwu, S. A. Mahlke, W. Y. Chen, P. P. Chang, N. J. Warter, R. A. Bringmann, R. O. Ouellette, R. E. Hank, T. Kiyohara, G. E. Haab, J. G. Holm, and D. M. Lavery. The superblock: An effective technique for vliw and superscalar compilation. *Journal of Supercomputing*, 7(1,2):229–248, March 1993.
12. M. S. Johnson and T. C. Miller. Effectiveness of a machine-level global optimizer. In *Proc. ACM SIGPLAN '86 Symp. on Compler Construction*, pages 99–108. ACM, July 1986.
13. P. Kolte and M. J. Harrold. Load/store range analysis for global register allocation. In *Proc. ACM SIGPLAN '93 Conf. on Prog. Language Design and Implementation*, pages 268–277. ACM, June 1993.
14. P. G. Lowney, S. M. Freudenberger, T. J. Karzes, W. D. Lichtenstein, R. P. Nix, J. O'Donnell, and J. C. Ruttenberg. The multiflow trace scheduling compiler. *Journal of Supercomputing*, 7(1,2):51–142, March 1993.
15. C. Norris and L. L. Pollock. Register allocation over the program dependence graph. In *Proc. ACM SIGPLAN '94 Conf. on Prog. Language Design and Implementation*, pages 266–277. ACM, June 1994.
16. D. Wall. Predicting program behavior using real or estimated profiles. In *Proc. ACM SIGPLAN '91 Conf. on Compiler Construction*, pages 59–70. ACM, June 1991.

Automatic Parallelization for Non-cache Coherent Multiprocessors *

Yunheung Paek David A. Padua

Department of Computer Science
University of Illinois at Urbana-Champaign,
1304 West Springfield Avenue,
Urbana, IL 61801, USA
{paek,padua}@csrd.uiuc.edu

Abstract

Although much work has been done on parallelizing compilers for cache coherent shared memory multiprocessors and message-passing multiprocessors, there is relatively little research on parallelizing compilers for noncache coherent multiprocessors with global address space. In this paper, we present a preliminary study on automatic parallelization for the Cray T3D, a commercial scalable machine with a global memory space and noncoherent caches.

1 Introduction

Of the three main classes of today's parallel computers, namely, message-passing multiprocessors, cache coherent multiprocessors, and noncoherent cache multiprocessors with a global address space, parallelizing compilers [2, 9, 11, 12] have been extensively studied for only the first two. In this paper, we present a preliminary study on the automatic parallelization of Fortran programs for the third class machine. Our translation algorithms were implemented in the Polaris restructurer [2], which was developed by the authors and others at Illinois. Important advances in automatic parallelization for cache coherent multiprocessors have been demonstrated recently with the Polaris restructurer. For the work reported in this paper, we have extended Polaris to generate code for the Cray T3D, the only noncoherent cache machine commercially available today. Our current implementation does a straightforward translation involving only a few optimizations beyond parallelism detection. However, our long-term objective is to develop more sophisticated techniques, such as those necessary for loop scheduling, data distribution, and communication minimization.

*The research described is supported by Army contract #DABT63-95-C-0097. This work is not necessarily representative of the positions or policies of the Army or the Government.

This paper is organized as follows. In Section 2, we briefly introduce the Polaris restructurer. The Cray T3D and CRAFT, the target language of our code generator, are discussed in Section 3. In Section 4, we discuss the compiler techniques we have implemented. In Section 5, we present the results of applying these techniques to ten programs from the SPEC and Perfect Benchmarks. We also discuss some of the factors that limit the performance of the target programs. In Section 6 we discuss a few advanced techniques we plan to implement in the near future to deal with these factors.

2 Polaris

The main objective of the Polaris project [2, 7] is to develop and implement effective parallelization techniques for scientific programs. One important characteristic of Polaris is its powerful internal representation [1]. It includes an extensive collection of program manipulation operations to facilitate the implementation of compiler transformations. After a program is converted into Polaris' internal form, it is analyzed and transformed by a sequence of compiler passes which add annotations to identify the parallelism detected by the compiler. Passes currently implemented in Polaris include: symbolic dependence analysis, inlining, induction variable substitution, reduction recognition, and privatization [3, 5, 8]. To support data dependence analysis, Polaris applies range propagation techniques based on symbolic program analysis [10]. After the input program is restructured into the internally-represented parallel program, a final pass or *backend* applies machine-specific transformations and outputs the target parallel program. As mentioned above, we have implemented two backends in Polaris: one for shared-memory multiprocessors, and one for the Cray T3D which is discussed in this work.

Our main focus during the past two years has been on accurately identifying parallelism. Very little effort has been devoted to the backend. However, even without a sophisticated code generation algorithm, Polaris has been quite successful. On an extensive collection of programs gathered from the Perfect Benchmarks, SPEC, and other sources, Polaris substantially outperforms the native parallelizer of the SGI multiprocessor. Work on parallelism detection continues on several fronts, including the study of efficient interprocedural analysis techniques, the parallelization of loops containing complex recurrences, and run-time dependence analysis [16].

3 The Cray T3D and CRAFT

While the lack of cache coherence in the Cray T3D helps make the machine affordable and scalable, it also introduces some difficulties in the development of efficient programs [18]. The experimental results presented in this paper give us hope that these programming difficulties can be overcome with effective compiler techniques. In this section, we very briefly describe the Cray T3D and CRAFT.

More detailed descriptions of the machine can be found in [14, 15, 21].

The Cray T3D was designed mainly for large-scale parallel scientific applications. It consists of up to 1024 processing nodes, each containing 2 processing elements(PE) and a local memory. The PEs are 150 MHz DEC Alpha 21064 microprocessors. The interconnection network is a 3-D torus network with high throughput and low latency. Remote memory latency on the T3D ranges from 90 to 130 cycles [33]. Local memory latency is 22 cycles. The T3D also contains a special tree-like network for global barrier synchronization. Various communication primitives, including single-sided communication primitives such as GET and PUT, are supported in hardware. The local memory is logically partitioned into private and shared address spaces. The shared memory in the T3D is no more than the collection of the shared address portions of all local memories. Every shared memory access is manipulated by off-chip components before sending the request to the appropriate module. This off-chip manipulation requires 20-30 cycles. The T3D has a first level on-chip cache which is used only for data in the private address space of the local memory.

There are implementations of the PVM and MPI message passing libraries for the Cray T3D. The machine is often programmed using these primitives to facilitate portability to other scalable multiprocessors. However, programming and compiling for the T3D following the shared-memory model is simpler for most problems and is, therefore, the approach we followed in our work. This can be done using CRAFT, an extension of Fortran for the T3D which has several features in common with other languages for distributed shared-memory machines [19, 25, 28]. CRAFT follows the Single-Program Multiple-Data(SPMD) model and contains a shared address space. In our experiments, each CRAFT process was allocated to a separate physical processor. Data objects can be declared as shared or private. Shared data can be distributed across memory using directives similar to those made popular by High Performance Fortran, Vienna Fortran and other similar languages [4, 6, 13, 20]. CRAFT uses `:block` for block distribution and `:block(`N`)` for block-cyclic distribution.

The `do shared` directive of CRAFT is used to mark parallel loops. To illustrate its semantics, consider the loop

```
cdir$ shared A(:block(1)), B(:block)
cdir$ do shared (I) on A(I)
      do I = 1, N
         A(I) = B(I)
      enddo
```

Its I-th iteration is executed by the PE that owns `A(`I`)` in its local memory. Since the elements of `A` are local to the PE accessing them, the compiler enables the caching of `A`. The elements of `B`, on the other hand, are not cached because some of them may be accessed remotely. Therefore, due to the `on` clause, CRAFT users can partition the computation according to the data distribution and thereby enable the caching of some shared data structures. In the example, the computation happens to be distributed according to the owner computes rule, as is done in HPF; however, other distributions could also have been used.

Table 1 summarizes the differences between CRAFT and HPF, as discussed in [14].

	CRAFT	HPF
Memory Classes	shared/private	implicitly all shared
Data Distribution	*W*:block(*N*)	block/cyclic/align
Computation Distribution	programmer-controlled	owner-computes rule
Redistribute statement	NO	YES
Explicit Communication and Synchronization	YES	NO

Table 1: Comparison of CRAFT and HPF

Although the machine-supported shared memory model facilitates programming on the T3D, inefficiencies could arise if the program is not carefully designed for the following reasons:

- Unlike cache coherent machines, a remote memory access to a single array element does not take advantage of spatial locality.
- Shared data objects are not cached, even when they are accessed from local memory. Therefore, shared data objects have to be fetched from the remote location every time the program references them. This significantly increases average memory latency and network contention.

To avoid these inefficiencies it is necessary to explicitly control caching and data transfer. We plan to do so in future versions of the translator. To this end we will use the SHMEM [21, 22] communication library which contains various single-sided communication primitives, such as PUT and GET, and explicit cache control routines. For example, SHMEM enables message aggregation which is not possible in ordinary CRAFT programs. The PUT/GET communication [19] allows asynchronous non-blocking access to any memory location. This means that with the SHMEM primitives, the whole memory either private or shared can be shared by all processors. Therefore, all data can be cached without losing the ability to share it. Furthermore, the SHMEM library can be used in programs containing shared data, whereas conventional message passing libraries, such as PVM and MPI, assume all data to be private. SHMEM is more efficient than current implementations of other message-passing models. In fact, in experiments conducted on a 16-processor partition [17], the latency of a SHMEM PUT operation was measured at 2 μsec and the peak throughput was measured at 116.8 MB/s, while the equivalent figures for PVM send/receive operations are 63 μsec and 26 MB/s respectively.

4 The Cray T3D backend

In this section, we describe the transformations applied by the Cray T3D backend module of Polaris. The backend applies four classes of transformations which we describe in separate subsections below.

Before invoking the backend, Polaris marks all loops it identifies as parallel. It also marks all the induction variables and reductions that have to be substituted, as well as the variables that have to be privatized to make the loop parallel.

4.1 Translation into SPMD form following the master/slave model

The first step of the T3D backend is to translate the parallelized Fortran program into SPMD form. We follow a relatively simple approach. One of the processes, designated as the master, executes a program that, outside parallel loops, is identical to the original sequential Fortran program. The master and slave processes cooperate in the execution of parallel regions, while the slaves do not participate in the execution of sequential regions.

We use barriers to enforce synchronization in the master/slave model. Barriers are inserted around parallel loops and calls to subprograms containing parallel regions. Barriers are also needed for some other statements that read or initialize privatized, and therefore replicated, variables.

Barriers do not have a significant impact on overall program execution time in the T3D. One reason is the efficient hardware implementation of barriers in the machine. Table 2 shows the performance of the T3D barrier [33].

PEs	Barrier Time(μsec)
4	1.73
32	1.81
256	1.90

Table 2: Barrier Performance. Times are the average of 5000 barrier executions.

Furthermore, in the experiments reported in Section 5, barriers are executed infrequently. The execution time increases by less than 1% due to barriers in all cases. For instance, in FLO52, the dynamic counts of barrier calls are about 50,000. The total overhead due to barriers is approximately 0.1 sec on a 64-processor partition, which is less than 0.2 % of the overall execution time of FLO52.

We, therefore, apply only a few simple techniques to minimize barrier overhead. One of techniques is to identify the places where *implicit* barriers are inserted by CRAFT and avoid placing *explicit* barriers there. For instance, CRAFT automatically places a barrier at the entrance and exit of shared subprograms in order to synchronize allocation and deallocation of shared data and data redistribution. As a consequence, our code generation algorithm does not need to insert explicit barriers at the boundaries of shared routines. Also, we eliminate the in-between barriers when parallel regions are adjacent. We found that Polaris' strategy of preferring outer loops for parallelization further contributes to reducing barriers.

4.2 Work partitioning

This transformation uses the on clause to partition the iteration space of a parallel loop across processors. We currently use the same code generation algorithm for the T3D as we use for cache coherent machines. Thus, parallel triangular loops are given cyclic schedules and square loops are given block schedules. Only one loop in a nest is parallelized. If several loops in a nest are parallel, then the outermost loop is parallelized unless its number of iterations is small relative to the number of processors. In this case, loop interchanging will be applied to move more practical inner loops to the outer level so that an inner loop can be parallelized.

For the case of loops containing reductions, it was necessary to modify the simple strategy applied by Polaris for cache coherent machines with a few processors. Consider, for example, the loop

```
do J = 1, M
   do I = 1, N
      ...
      A(I) = A(I) + ...
      ...
   enddo
enddo
```

Loops such as this arise frequently in real codes. Assuming that the loop is parallel except for the reduction on **A**, the backend for cache coherent machines generates the loop

```
cdir$ preamble
      A_priv(1:N) = 0.0
cdir$ parallel loop(J)
      do J = b*my_PE+1,(my_PE+1)*b
        do I =1, N
          ...
          A_priv(I) = A_priv(I) + ...
          ...
        enddo
      enddo
cdir$ postamble
      call set_lock(lock)
      A(1:N) = A(1:N)+A_priv(1:N)
      call clear_lock(lock)
```

Here, `A_priv` is a private array of the same size and type as `A`, and `b` is a block size; that is, M/P, where P is the number of processors. The `preamble` and `postamble` code segments are executed once by each processor cooperating in the execution of the loop. The `loop(J)` code is strip-mined to distribute computation across the processors.

This parallel version of the loop has the disadvantage that the `postamble` is executed serially because it is in a critical section. This works well for a few processors, but a different strategy is needed for a large number of processors. In our current implementation, **A_priv** is divided into P sections within each processor. The postamble consists of two phases. First, for $1 \leq i \leq P$, the i-th section of all processors is copied into the i-th processor. Then all processors add the P sections copied into them. As expected, this approach of parallelizing the postamble has an important impact on performance. This is illustrated in Figure 3.

PEs	Preamble	Middle Loop	Serial Postamble	Parallel Postamble
2	0.014	260	0.39	0.1
64	0.017	11	2.7	0.129

Table 3: Times for parallel version of loop INTERF_do1000 in MDG

4.3 Data Distribution and Privatization

In the T3D, if a variable is declared **shared**, it is not cached even when the reference is to a local memory module. In fact, performance difference between the best and worst distributions in a loop of the form

```
cdir$ shared A(distribution descriptor)
      do I = 1, N
         ... A(f(I)) ...
      enddo
```

is only a factor of 2 on 16 processors. On the other hand, declaring data as **private** has an important impact on performance since private data is cached: approximately one order of magnitude.

Our implementation of the T3D backend follows a simple strategy. Polaris identifies loop-private data using the existing privatization algorithm. Furthermore, the T3D backend marks as procedure-private those scalar variables local to a procedure and never used in parallel loops, and other temporal variables exclusively used by individual processors. Both the loop level and the procedure level privatizable variables are declared as **private** in the target program. All other variables are declared **shared** and are given **:block** distribution in all their dimensions.

```
cdir$ private(procedure-level privatizable variables)
      X = 3
          :
      do I = L, U
cdir$ private(loop-level privatizable variables)
          :
      enddo
```

The implementation of this simple strategy involves some complex issues. For example in CRAFT, the **private/shared** attribute of formal arguments has to be explicit and match that of the actual arguments. This is discussed in more detail in Section 4.4.

In future implementations, the local sections of logically shared arrays will be privatized to enable the use of the cache. Routines from the SHMEM library could be used to fetch and store remote sections of these logically shared arrays.

4.4 Compatibility problems between Fortran and CRAFT

Many MPP Fortran extensions, such as CRAFT and HPF [20], help the user attain high performance through distribution of data and other directives, while maintaining some degree of compatibility with conventional Fortran 77. However, total compatibility has not been achieved because these languages impose several restrictions in the name of performance. The following list shows the major restrictions imposed by CRAFT:

- Fortran's sequence and storage association rules [23] do not apply to shared data.
- Shared data may not be in `EQUIVALENCE` or blank `COMMON`.
- Shared data may not be of type `CHARACTER`.
- The dimension size of shared arrays must be a power of two[1].
- Shared formal parameters may not be associated with private actual parameters, and their size and shape must match those of the corresponding actual parameters.

We have endeavored to develop translation techniques to overcome these limitations. Three of these techniques are discussed below.

4.4.1 Renaming

Aliasing has always been an important issue in program analysis in general, and in automatic parallelization in particular [32]. Aliasing is also one of the most difficult problems in automatic parallelization for the T3D. Consider, for example, the following segment extracted from HYDRO2D:

```
subroutine X1
real A, B, C, D, E, F
common /SCRA/ A, B, C, D, E, F
    :
subroutine X2
real G(5)
integer I
common /SCRA/ I, G
```

[1] In the Cray T3E, this restriction is no longer imposed.

CRAFT cannot distribute a shared data object if it is aliased to other objects with different shape or type. In the code above, the shared variables within `SCRA` cannot be distributed because of the aliasing of `A` and `I`. In order to address this problem, we interprocedurally check the life times associated with each variable and apply renaming. In the previous example, it can be proven that the life time of the values of `SCRA` in `X1` and in `X2` are disjoint. As a result, we could rename either occurrence of the common block without affecting the outcome of the program.

4.4.2 Linearization

Variable linearization and renaming are the most common techniques used to solve problems related to storage association rules. For example, linearization is needed to inline a subroutine call when an actual parameter differs in shape from the corresponding formal parameter.

We use linearization to deal with array equivalences because of the restriction that the size of all shared array dimensions must be a power of 2. When two arrays of different shapes are equivalenced, we linearize the array before dimension expansion. Linearization also helps to save memory. For example, a shared array `A(9,9,9)` is expanded to `A(16,16,16)` without linearization, and `A(1024)` with linearization. Linearization, in this case, saves 3K words. However, we do not want to apply linearization to all multidimensional arrays because linearization makes the program less readable and program analysis more difficult due to the complex subscript expressions.

4.4.3 Array Reshaping and Procedure Cloning

The following code, where we assume that `A` and `B` are shared arrays, illustrates one important difference between Fortran 77 and CRAFT:

```
real A(8,8)
call foo(A(1,7))
    :

subroutine foo(B)
real B(4,4)
... B(2,2)
```

If interpreted as Fortran 77, `B(2,2)` in this code is aliased with `A(6,7)`; but, if interpreted as CRAFT, it is aliased with `A(2,8)`. This is because, in CRAFT, aliasing between shared arrays takes place at the submatrix level, whereas in Fortran, a linear storage sequence is often assumed for parameter aliasing. Many real Fortran codes rely on such association rules.

We address this problem by changing the subscript expressions within the subroutine to conform to the CRAFT semantics. *Procedure cloning* is applied whenever the same routine is called with different submatrices as actual parameters.

For example, our algorithms would translate codes like the previous one using the following transformation pattern:

real A($L_1:U_1$,...,$L_n:U_n$) call foo(A(f_1,...,f_n))		real A($L_1:U_1$,...,$L_n:U_n$) call foo_clone(A)
⋮	$\Rightarrow$	⋮
subroutine foo(B) real B($L'_1:U'_1$,...,$L'_m:U'_m$) ... B(g_1,...,g_m)		subroutine foo_clone(B) real B($L_1:U_1$,...,$L_n:U_n$) ... B(h_1,...,h_n)

Notice that in the resulting code the origin of the parameter array is passed to the subroutine rather than the address of one of its elements. The actual and formal parameter arrays are forced to have the same size and shape. Let X be the offset of A(f_1,...,f_n) from the first address of A, and X' be that of B(g_1,...,g_m). Then, the array index h_k is defined as

$$h_k = X_k \bmod N_k + L_k$$

where $N_k = U_k + L_k + 1$, $X_1 = X + X'$ and $X_i = \lfloor X_{i-1}/N_{i-1} \rfloor$ for $i > 1$.

Our experiments show that cloning does not increase the size of the original programs by more than a factor of 2. This is the case because actual and formal parameters usually have the same shape, size and dimension.

5 Preliminary Results

Figure 1 presents the speedups obtained by Polaris on the T3D for five programs from the Perfect Benchmarks (ARC2D, BDNA, FLO52, MDG, and TRFD), and five programs from the SPEC collection (APPSP, HYDRO2D, SU2COR, SWIM, and TOMCATV).

We report speedups for processor numbers that are powers of two between 1 and 64. During the sequential execution of an original program, we measured the percentage of overall running time of the program for each loop, and added the percentages of each parallelizable loop to obtain the total sum. We call this total sum *parallel coverage* [2]. Two dotted lines in Figure 1 plot the ideal speedups for programs with parallel coverage of 99% and 90% respectively. The ideal speedup, S, is calculated by using the Amdahl's equality: $S = 1/(c/P + 1 - c)$ where P is the number of processors and c is a parallel coverage.

After all ten analyzed programs were transformed by Polaris, their parallel coverages were between 90 and 99%. Therefore, the speedup curves for these programs should, under ideal conditions, lie between the two dotted lines. Real program speedups are much lower than the ideal for several reasons, including synchronization and scheduling overhead, communication costs, and shared data bypassing the cache. These speedups should improve once we implement in Polaris optimizations to deal with these issues.

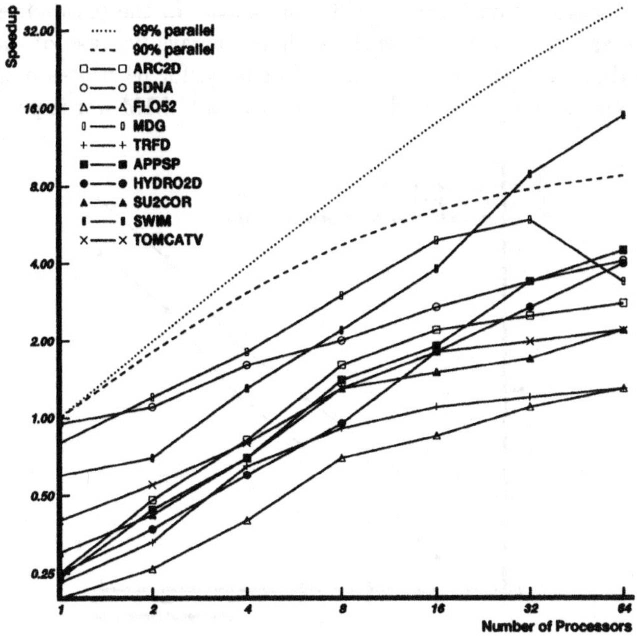

Figure 1: Preliminary Results for the Perfect and SPEC Benchmarks

The effect of bypassing the cache, which we call *cache bypassing penalty*, is reflected in the speedups for one PE, where the speedup is below one in all cases, as shown in Figure 1. The largest values are 0.9 for BDNA and 0.8 for MDG. This occurs because both programs use several large privatized reduction arrays and, thus, have very few accesses to shared data. To the contrary, FLO52 and TRFD have lowest speedups for one PE because they repeatedly access large sections of shared arrays in the loops.

In addition to the cache bypassing penalty, as we increase the number of processors, other factors become significant, such as communication, amount of parallelism, and the number of iterations of parallel loops. Such factors tend to decrease the efficiency as the number of processors grow. In this paper, *efficiency* is defined as the ratio between speedup and the ideal speedup made possible by the parallel coverage of the program. For example, the efficiency of TRFD, whose parallel coverage is 90%, goes from 0.23 to 0.13 as the number of processors grows from 1 to 64.

In the rest of this section, we discuss the behavior of three of the ten programs presented in Figure 1: SWIM, MDG, and TRFD.

5.1 SWIM

SWIM is a finite difference solver of the shallow water equation on a 512x512 grid. Its serial execution time on the T3D is 2378 seconds. SWIM performs most of its operations on fourteen 513x513 arrays. In the parallelized version, these arrays are expanded to 1024x1024 shared arrays because of the CRAFT restrictions discussed in Section 4.4. Fortunately, for 64 processors, the total amount of extra memory required is relatively small: 0.1M words per processor.

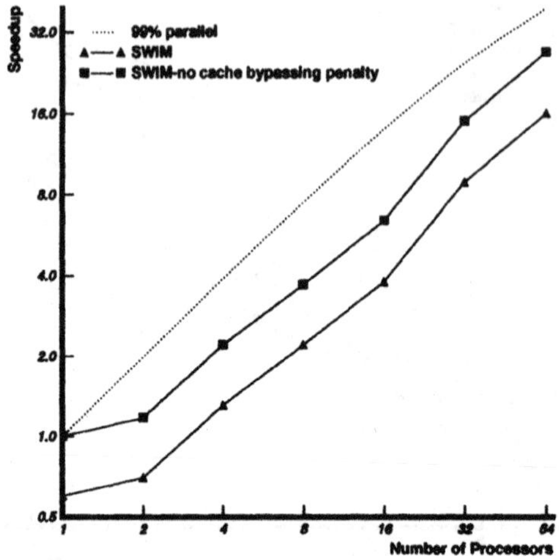

Figure 2: Speedup Analysis for SWIM

SWIM shows the best speedups in Figure 1. The main reason for these speedups is that Polaris parallelizes all the outermost loops, which results in a parallel coverage of almost 100%. Most parallel loops in SWIM are doubly-nested loops with 512x512 iterations. This is large enough to saturate 64 processors. Furthermore, each processor accesses different regions of the shared arrays in parallel loops, so there are few memory access collisions during the execution of the parallel loops. Above all, our simple block distribution policy happens to match computation distribution in SWIM, thus reducing a large amount of remote memory access overhead. As a result, we see that the speedup grows with the number of processors.

Despite the good characteristics of SWIM, we notice that the efficiency, for a single processor is still 0.55. As mentioned earler, this number mainly refects the impact of the cache-bypassing penalty in the T3D. In other words, if caching is allowed for shared data, we would get a speedup of $1.8(= 1/0.55)$. We plot this predicted speedup line in Figure 2. Therefore, we conclude that one of the major optimization efforts in SWIM should focus on increasing the fraction of cacheable data.

5.2 MDG

MDG is a molecular dynamics model of water. Its sequential execution time on the T3D is 330 seconds. The most important loop in MDG is `INTERF_do1000`, which accounts for 92% of sequential execution time. This loop is parallelized because of several advanced techniques applied by Polaris, including inlining, array privatization, induction variable recognition, and histogram reduction recognition. The parallel version of **INTERF_do1000** has many privatized reduction arrays instead of shared arrays. Figure 3 shows that the speedup will not grow significantly even after eliminating all the cache bypassing penalty for the parallel loops. Thus, the cache bypassing penalty is not as influential in MDG as it is in SWIM.

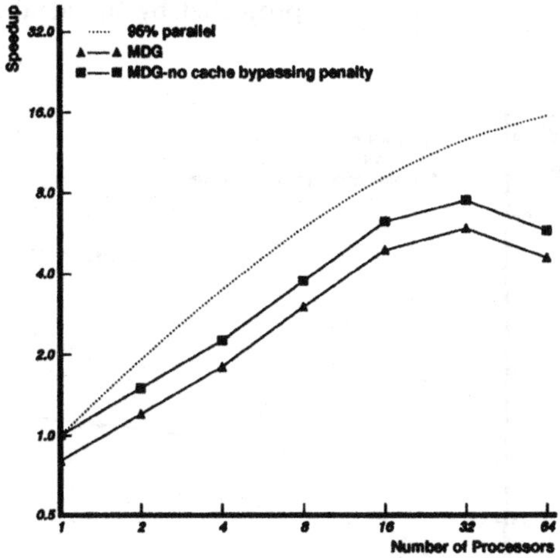

Figure 3: Speedup Analysis for MDG

The main cause of the drop in speedup is a doubly-nested sequential loop, **INTRAF_do1000**, which accounts for just 1% of sequential execution time. This loop accesses shared data and, when the number of processors grows, so does the execution time of this loop, as shown in Table 4. This shows that, in some cases, communication costs in a serial loop grow much faster than the same costs in a parallel loop. Hence, we need to reduce these costs in sequential loops even when their execution time is relatively small. In fact, the loop **INTRAF_do1000** is parallel and, thus, the speedup will improve when Polaris is extended to parallelize this loop.

PEs	INTERF_do1000 (sec)	INTRAF_do1000 (sec)
2	260	4.6
4	140	5.8
8	76	8.4
16	41	14
32	21	26
64	11	59

Table 4: INTERF_do1000 and INTRAF_do1000 on the T3D

5.3 TRFD

TRFD is a small kernel for quantum mechanics calculations. It has two major loops, `OLDA_do100` and `OLDA_do300`, both of which correspond to 90% of the sequential execution time. All the other parallel loops in TRFD take up less than 1% of sequential execution time. Judging from the case on a single processor in Figure 1, TRFD suffers from bypassing the cache for shared data more than SWIM and MDG. Removing such a penalty would drastically boost the performance by a factor of 4.6, as projected by the ideal speedup shown in Figure 4.

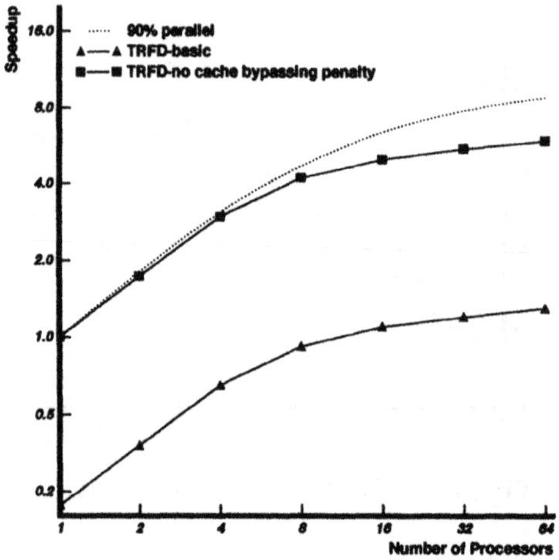

Figure 4: Speedup Analysis for TRFD

Even after we eliminate the cache bypassing penalty, the efficiency of TRFD would be too small still, as indicated in Figure 4. This is primarily due to the small data set size for TRFD [24, 26].

6 Program Optimizations and the Data Copying Strategy

From the discussion above, it is clear that the main factors influencing parallel performance are:

- the parallel coverage;
- the parallel loop structure of a program;
- the amount of shared data used in local computations; and,
- the data access pattern.

In [7], we discuss several on-going efforts in the Polaris project to increase the parallel coverage and, in Section 4, we briefly deal with the parallel loop structure of a program. In this section, we discuss the last two factors.

From the evaluation outlined in Section 5, we concluded that to subtantially improve performance it is necessary to privatize shared data. One strategy that we plan to explore, the *shared data copying scheme*, uses shared memory as a source/repository of values for private variables. In this strategy, most of the work is done on private variables. Before a program section starts, the processors copy all that is used in the computation from shared memory into private memory. At the end of the section, the processors copy the results back to shared memory so that all processors have access to the results. Shared memory coherence is maintained by explicit synchronization.

PUT/GET primitives will be used for data copying in our future work. One reason we have chosen to use PUT/GET is that these primitives match the shared-memory programming paradigm assumed by Polaris. Another reason is that PUT/GET is rapidly gaining widespread acceptance. In fact, several portable shared-memory programming models supporting PUT/GET are already implemented on ordinary message-passing machines, such as the IBM SP-1/2, Intel Paragon and TMC CM-5 [19, 25, 28]. Furthermore, several existing and newly proposed large-scale machines, such as the T3E, directly support these primitives in hardware [21, 27], which reduces the effect of the increased communication overhead resulting from the extra data copy operations.

Communication aggregation is useful in reducing the overhead. In most Fortran programs, the natural program section that organizes copying from/to global memory is the loop. The following code example shows how Polaris transforms the information about the range of arrays fetched and written by the loop into PUT/GET primitives.

```
cdir$ must_read (A(l1:u1:s1))        call polaris_get(A(l1:u1:s1),a(l1':u1':s1'))
cdir$ must_write (A(l2:u2:s2))       do I = l',u',s'
      do I = l,u,s               =>      access a
         access A                    enddo
      enddo                          call polaris_put(A(l2:u2:s2),a(l2':u2':s2'))
```

In the transformation, a shared array **A** is replaced by a private array **a**. The **must_read** directive indicates the shared data sections that *must* be used in the loop, and **must_write** indicates the shared data sections that *must* be updated in the loop. We generate PUT/GETs to move the data sections specified in these directives around each loop. In addition to the two directives, **may_read** and **may_write** can be generated to mark shared data sections that *may* be used and updated in a loop.

We implemented high level data transfer routines, **polaris_put/get**, which make use of the T3D's lower level single-sided communication primitives. Microbenchmarking experiments on a 16-processor partition show that the throughput of these routines is approximately 1.5 Mwords/sec with data over 1K words long. Table 5 shows the effect of our PUT/GET operations on the performance of loop **OLDA_do100** of TRFD. The sequential execution time of the loop is 23.6 sec.

PEs	No Data Copying (sec)	Data Copying (sec)	
		Loop	PUT/GET
2	65	13	0.2
4	38	6.3	0.6
8	26	3.2	0.7
16	23	1.5	1.1
32	21	0.76	1.4
64	20	0.40	1.8

Table 5: Reduction of Cache Bypassing Penalty by PUT/GET on TRFD: The total amount of data transferred at a time for the loop execution is about 1 Mwords with sizes varing from 0.1 to 600 Kwords

Even without using any other techniques, the effect of the work on loop OLDA_do100 increases the overall program speedup to 2. For the loop itself, with overhead ignored, the speedup is 59 on 64 processors. Although the PUT/GET overhead reduces the speedup to 11, this is still 9 times faster than the execution time before optimization. Another program that benefits from using PUT/GET is SWIM. Figure 5 shows the speedup obtained by hand on up to 64 processors. These and other test results have convinced us that the T3D's PUT/GET operations are efficient enough to improve performance across the board.

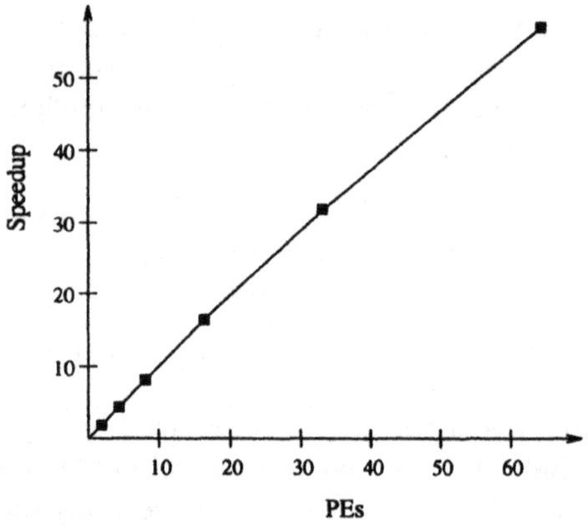

Figure 5: Hand-optimized SWIM using PUT/GET

An important strategy that can be used to complement shared data copying is prefetching and poststoring. Unlike cache memory, the data copied into private memory is fully software controllable; that is, the data would never be flushed out until explicitly done so by the program. Hence, as long as the local memory space is available, a processor can prefetch data anytime before it is needed and poststore it sometime after the computation. In [29], some other advantages of the compiler-directed communication over cache-coherence protocol driven communication on the non-cache coherent architecture are discussed.

The shared data copying scheme is especially useful when the data distribution requirements of a program are dynamic. The conventional technique for such a case is *data redistribution* [30]. Data redistibution usually moves much of the array across the distributed memories. Unless most elements of the array are fully used for a long time, this total data movement is inefficient. In contrast, PUT/GET operations enable us to avoid this inefficiency by making each processor copy only the portions of an array that are needed for its local computations.

Shared data distribution is another important issue that we will have to consider. In general, as discussed above, data distribution by itself did not significantly influence performance in our experiments. However, we found that it is important to distibute shared data in order to minimize data copy overhead in the shared data copying scheme. One way to reduce the copy overhead is to aggregate the data as much as possible, taking advantage of the T3D's high-bandwidth low-latency network. Most GET/PUT primitives support contiguous data streams with regular stride more effectively. For these reasons, we simply block distribute shared arrays in the shared data copying scheme. This also helps simplify the calculation of the owner of the target data before issuing PUT/GET calls. In TRFD, for example, the data sections needed by `OLDA_do100` change every time we encounter the loop and thus, no single data distribution can match this changing data access pattern. The simple block distribution always guarantees no more than P PUT/GET calls per data copy for a P-processor partition.

In any case, distributing data so that most target data are in local memory is our ultimate goal since local copy operations are faster than remote copy operations. We plan to investigate the possibility of improving data distribution for the data copying scheme.

7 Conclusion

We have reported some preliminary experience using the Polaris restructurer to parallelize Fortran codes for the Cray T3D. The strategy we used here was to extend the traditional parallelizing compiler techniques for cache coherent machines to deal with non-cache coherent multiprocessors. We discussed our translation algorithms and presented optimization techniques that should significantly improve the preliminary results once they are implemented. Our long-term objective is to develop and implement these advanced techniques in Polaris.

Acknowledgements

We would like to thank the Cray Research Inc. for generously granting machine time for the experiments reported in this paper. We are especially grateful to Thomas MacDonald for helping us access and understand the Cray T3D.

References

[1] K. Faigin, J. Hoeflinger, D. Padua, P. Petersen, S. Weatherford. The Polaris Internal Representation. *International Journal of Parallel Programming,* Vol. 22, No. 5, Oct. 1994, pp. 553–586

[2] B. Blume, et al., Polaris: Improving the Effectiveness of Parallelizing Compilers, *Proceedings of the Seventh Workshop on Languages and Compilers for Parallel Computing, OR. Lecture Note in Computer Science,* Aug. 1994, pp. 141-154

[3] B. Pottenger, R. Eigenmann, Idiom Recognition in the Polaris Parallelizing Compiler, *Proceedings of the 9th ACM International Conference on Supercomputing,* July 1995

[4] Z. Bokus, et al, Compiling Fortran 90D/HPF for Distributed Memory MIMD Computers, Journal of Parallel and Distributed Computing, Vol. 21, 1994, pp. 15-26

[5] J. Grout, Inline Expansion for the Polaris Research Compiler, Master's thesis, Univ. of Illinois at Urbana-Champaign, Cntr. for Supercomputing Res. & Dev., May 1995

[6] B. Chapman, P. Mehrota, H. Moritsch, H. Zima, Dynamic Data Distributions in Vienna Fortran, *Supercomputing '93 Proceedings,* 1993, pp. 284-293

[7] B. Blume, et al., Advanced Program Restructuring for High-Performance Computers with Polaris, Tech. Report, Univ. of Illinois at Urbana-Champaign, Cntr. for Supercomputing R & D, 1996, CSRD Report No. 1473

[8] P. Tu, D. Padua, Automatic array privatization, *Proc. 6th Workshop on Language and Compilers for Parallel Computing, OR. Lecture Note in Computer Science,* Aug. 1993, pp. 500-521

[9] C. Polychronopoulos, et al., The Structure of Parafrase-2: An Advanced Parallelizing Compiler for C and Fortran, *Languages and Compilers for Parallel Computing,* MIT Press, 1990

[10] W. Blume, R. Eigenmann, The Range Test: A Dependence Test for Symbolic Non-linear Expression, *SuperComputing '94 Proceedings,* Nov. 1994, pp. 643-656

[11] P.Banerjee, et al., The PARADIGM Compiler for Distributed-Memory Multicomputers, *IEEE Computer,* Vol. 28, No. 10, Oct. 1995, pp 37-47

[12] S. Amarasinghe, et al., An Overview of the SUIF Compiler for Scalable Parallel Machines, *Proceedings of the Seventh SIAM Conference on Parallel Processing for Scientific Computing,* Feb. 1995, pp. 662-667

[13] C. Tseng, An Optimizing Fortran D Compiler for MIMD Distributed-Memory Machines, PhD Thesis, Rice University, Jan. 1993

[14] W. Oed, The Cray Reseach Massively Parallel Processor System CRAY T3D, Cray Research, Nov 1993

[15] CRAY T3D System Architecture Overview, Cray Research, 1993

[16] L. Rauchwerger, D. Padua, The PRIVATIZING DOALL Test: A Run-Time Technique for DOALL Loop Identification and Array Privatization, *Proceedings of the 8th ACM International Conference on Supercomputing*, July 1994, pp. 33-43

[17] R. Marcelin, Message Passing on the CRAY T3D, Massively Parallel Computing Group, NERSC, 1995

[18] D. Bernstein, et al., Solutions and Debugging for Data Consistency in Multiprocessors with Noncoherent Caches, *International Journal of Parallel Programming*, Vol. 23, No. 1, 1995, pp. 83-103

[19] M. Snir, Proposal for MPI-2, MPI meetings, 1995

[20] High Performance Fortran Language Specification, High Performance Fortran Forum, May 1993

[21] CRAY MPP Fortran Reference Manual, Cray Research, 1993

[22] SHMEM Technical Note for Fortran, Cray Research, Oct. 1994

[23] Programming Language FORTRAN, American National Standards Institute, ANSI X3.9-1978 ISO 1539-1980

[24] J. Gustafson, Reevaluating Amdahls Law, *Communications of the ACM*, Vol. 31, No. 5, May 1988, pp. 532-533

[25] D. Culler, et al., Parallel Programming in Split-C,*Supercomputing '93 Proceedings*, 1993

[26] A. Grama, A. Gupta, V. Kumar, Isoefficiency: Measuring the Scalability of Parallel Algorithms and Architectures, *IEEE Parallel & Distributed Technology*, Aug. 1993, pp. 12-21

[27] K. Hayashi, et al., AP1000+: Architectural Support of PUT/GET Interface for Parallelizing Compiler. Proc. 6th International Conference on Architechtural Support for Programming Language and Operating Systems, Oct. 1994, pp. 196-207

[28] J. Nielocha, R. Harrison, R. Littlefield, Global Arrays: A Portable Shared-Memory Programming Model for Distributed Memory Computers, *Supercomputing '94 Proceedings*, 1994, pp.340-349

[29] J. R. Larus, Compiling for Shared-Memory and Message-Passing computer, *ACM Letters on Programming Languages and Systems*, 1996

[30] K. Kenney, Compiler Technology for Machine-Independent Parallel Programming, *International Journal of Parallel Programming*, Vol. 22, 1994, pp. 79-98

[31] R. Eigenmann, J. Hoeflinger, G. Jaxon, D. Padua, The Cedar Fortran Project, Tech. Report, Univ. of Illinois at Urbana-Champaign, Cntr. for Supercomputing R & D, Apr. 1992, CSRD Report No. 1262

[32] H. Zima, B. Chapman, Supercompilers for Parallel and Vector Computers, ACM Press, 1992

[33] R. Arpaci, et al., Empirical Evaluation of the CRAY-T3D: A Compiler Perspective, *Proceedings of ISCA*, 1995, pp.320-331

Lock Coarsening: Eliminating Lock Overhead in Automatically Parallelized Object-Based Programs

Pedro Diniz[†] and Martin Rinard[‡]

Department of Computer Science
University of California, Santa Barbara
Santa Barbara, CA 93106
{pedro,martin}@cs.ucsb.edu

Abstract. Atomic operations are a key primitive in parallel computing systems. The standard implementation mechanism for atomic operations uses mutual exclusion locks. In an object-based programming system the natural granularity is to give each object its own lock. Each operation can then make its execution atomic by acquiring and releasing the lock for the object that it accesses. But this fine lock granularity may have high synchronization overhead. To achieve good performance it may be necessary to reduce the overhead by coarsening the granularity at which the computation locks objects.
In this paper we describe a static analysis technique — lock coarsening — designed to automatically increase the lock granularity in object-based programs with atomic operations. We have implemented this technique in the context of a parallelizing compiler for irregular, object-based programs. Experiments show these algorithms to be effective in reducing the lock overhead to negligible levels.

1 Introduction

Atomic operations are an important primitive in the design and implementation of parallel systems. Operations are typically made atomic by associating mutual exclusion locks with the data that they access. An atomic operation first acquires the lock for the data that it manipulates, accesses the data, then releases the lock.

We have implemented a compiler designed to automatically parallelize object-based computations that manipulate irregular, pointer-based data structures. This compiler uses commutativity analysis [9] as its primary analysis paradigm. For the generated program to execute correctly, each operation in the generated parallel code must execute atomically. The automatically generated code therefore contains mutual exclusion locks and constructs that acquire and release these locks.

We have found that the granularity at which the generated parallel computation locks objects can have a significant impact on the overall performance.

[†] Sponsored by the PRAXIS XXI program administrated by Portugal's JNICT – Junta Nacional de Investigação Científica e Tecnológica, and holds a Fulbright travel grant.
[‡] Supported in part by an Alfred P. Sloan Research Fellowship.

The natural lock granularity is to give each object its own lock and generate code in which each operation acquires and releases the lock for the object that it accesses. Our experimental results indicate, however, that locking objects at this fine granularity may introduce enough overhead to significantly degrade the overall performance. To achieve good performance we have found it necessary to coarsen the lock granularity to reduce the amount of lock overhead.

This paper presents the analysis algorithms and program transformations that the compiler uses to automatically coarsen the lock granularity. We have implemented these algorithms in the context of a parallelizing compiler for object-based programs [9]. This paper also presents experimental results that characterize the performance impact of using the lock coarsening algorithms in the compiler.

The results show the algorithms to be effective in reducing the lock overhead to negligible levels. They also show that an overly aggressive lock coarsening algorithm can significantly impair the performance by artificially increasing lock contention (lock contention occurs when two processors attempt to acquire the same lock at the same time). A successful compiler must therefore negotiate a trade off between reducing lock overhead and increasing lock contention.

This paper makes the following contributions:

- It introduces two techniques for reducing lock overhead: data lock coarsening and computation lock coarsening.
- It presents novel and practical lock coarsening algorithms that a compiler can use to reduce the lock overhead.
- It presents experimental results that characterize the performance impact of the lock coarsening algorithms on several automatically parallelized applications. These performance results show that, for these applications, the algorithms can effectively reduce the lock overhead to negligible levels.

The rest of this paper is structured as follows. Section 3 presents an example that illustrates how coarsening the lock granularity can reduce the lock overhead. Section 4 describes the kinds of programs that the lock coarsening algorithms are designed to optimize. In Sections 5 and 6 we present the lock coarsening algorithms and transformations. In Section 7 we present experimental results that characterize the impact of the lock coarsening algorithms on the overall performance of two automatically parallelized applications.

2 Basic Issues in Lock Coarsening

The lock coarsening algorithms deal with two basic sources of performance loss: lock overhead and lock contention.

- **Lock Overhead:** Acquiring or releasing a lock generates overhead; the goal of the algorithms is to reduce this overhead by applying transformations that make the computation execute fewer acquire and release constructs.

- **Lock Contention:** Lock contention occurs whenever one processor attempts to acquire a lock held by another processor. In this case the first processor must wait until the second processor releases the lock; the first processor performs no useful computation during time it spends waiting for the lock to be released. Increased lock contention therefore reduces the amount of available parallelism.

All of the transformations that the algorithms apply to reduce the lock overhead have the potential to increase the lock contention. The algorithms must therefore negotiate a tradeoff between the lock overhead and the lock contention.

The algorithms apply two lock coarsening techniques: data lock coarsening and computation lock coarsening.

- **Data Lock Coarsening:** Data lock coarsening is a technique in which the compiler associates one lock with multiple objects that tend to be accessed together. The compiler then transforms computations that manipulate one or more of the objects. Each transformed computation acquires the lock, performs the manipulations, then releases the lock. The original computation, of course, acquired and released a lock every time it manipulated any one of the objects.
  Data lock coarsening may improve the computation in two ways. First, it may reduce the number of executed acquire and release constructs — it enables computations to access multiple objects with the overhead of only a single acquire construct and a single release construct. Second, it may reduce the number of locks that the computation requires to execute successfully — giving multiple objects the same lock may reduce the number of allocated locks.
  An overly aggressive data lock coarsening algorithm may introduce *false contention.* False contention occurs when two operations attempt to acquire the same lock even though they access different objects.
- **Computation Lock Coarsening:** Consider a computation that repeatedly acquires and releases the same lock. This may happen, for example, if a computation performs multiple operations on the same object or on objects that have all been given the same lock by the data lock coarsening algorithm. The computation lock coarsening algorithm analyzes the program to find such computations. It then transforms the computations to acquire the lock, perform the operations with no additional synchronization, then release the lock. This transformation may significantly reduce the number of executed acquire and release constructs.
  An overly aggressive computation lock coarsening algorithm may introduce *false exclusion.* False exclusion may occur when a computation holds a lock for an extended period of time during which it does not access one of the lock's objects. If another computation attempts to acquire the lock (so that it may access one of the lock's objects), it must wait for the first computation to release the lock even though the first computation is not actively accessing any of the lock's objects. False exclusion may therefore reduce the performance by decreasing the amount of available concurrency.

There is a potential interaction between lock coarsening and concurrency generation. To ensure that all of the operations within a given coarsened mutual exclusion region execute atomically with respect to each other, the algorithms require that the entire computation within the coarsened region execute sequentially. There are two options: refusing to apply the lock coarsening transformation if the coarsened region would contain a concurrency generation construct, or removing all of the concurrency generation constructs within the coarsened region. The current transformations apply the first option.

There may be a concern that the transformations will introduce deadlock. As explained in Sections 5 and 6, the lock coarsening transformations never cause a program to deadlock.

3 Example

In this section we provide an example, inspired by the Barnes-Hut application in Section 7, that illustrates both kinds of lock coarsening. The example computation manipulates an array of pointers to nodes; each node has a vector and a count. There is also a set of values stored in a binary search tree. The computation scales every node by all of the values in the tree that fall within a certain range. It finds all of these values by traversing the binary search tree.

Figure 1 contains the parallel C++ code for this example. Each class is augmented with a mutual exclusion lock; the parallel code uses this lock to make operations on objects of that class atomic. If an operation modifies its receiver object[1], it first acquires the receiver's lock, performs the modification, then releases the lock.

The computation starts at the nodeSet::scaleNodeSet method. This method invokes the node::traverse method in parallel for each node in the array; the parallel for loop makes the loop iterations execute concurrently. Note that all of the invocations of the node::traverse method may not be independent — if two array elements point to the same node, the corresponding loop iterations will modify the same node. The operations in the loop iterations must therefore execute atomically for the computation to execute correctly.

The node::traverse method traverses the binary search tree to find all of the values in the range [min,max]. Whenever it finds a value inside the range, it invokes the node::scaleNode method to scale the node by the value. The node::scaleNode method scales a node by incrementing the count of applied scale operations, then invoking the vector::scaleVector method to scale the vector stored in the node.

3.1 Data Lock Coarsening in the Example

An examination of the parallel code in Figure 1 reveals that the computation acquires and releases two locks every time it scales a node: the lock in the node

[1] Programs that use the object-based programming paradigm structure the computation as operations on objects. Each operation has a single receiver object; as described in Section 4 this object is the object that the operation manipulates.

```
const int NDIM 3;
class vector {
  lock mutex;
  double value[NDIM];
public:
  void scaleVector(double s){
    mutex.acquire();
    for(int i=0; i < NDIM; i++)
      value[i] *= s;
    mutex.release();
  }
};
class tree {
public:
  double x;
  tree *left;
  tree *right;
};
class node {
  lock mutex;
public:
  int count;
  vector value;
  void scaleNode(double s);
  void traverse(tree *t,
    double min, double max);
};
class nodeSet {
  int size;
  node **elements;
public:
  void scaleNodeSet(tree *t,
    double min, double max);
};
```

```
node::scaleNode(double s){
  mutex.acquire();
  count++;
  mutex.release();
  value.scaleVector(s);
}
node::traverse(tree *t,
    double min, double max){
  if((min ≤ t->x) && (t->x < max))
    scaleNode(t->x);
  if(min ≤ t->x)
    traverse(t->left,min,max);
  if(t->x ≤ max)
    traverse(t->right,min,max);
}
nodeSet::scaleNodeSet(tree *t,
    double min, double max){
  scaleNodeSet(t, min, max);
  wait();
}
nodeSet::scaleNodeSet(tree *t,
    double min, double max){
  parallel for(int i = 0; i < size; i++){
    elements[i]->traverse(t, min, max);
  }
}
```

Fig. 1. Parallel Node Scaling Example

object (the node::scaleNode method acquires and releases this lock) and the lock in the nested vector object inside the node object (the vector::scaleVector method acquires and releases this lock).

It is possible to eliminate the acquisition and release of the lock in the nested vector object by coarsening the lock granularity as follows. Instead of giving each nested vector object its own lock, the compiler can use the lock in the enclosing node object to make operations on the nested vector object atomic. Figure 2 contains the transformed code that locks the objects at this granularity. The compiler generates a new version of the vector::scaleVector method (this new version is called vector::syncFree_scaleVector) that does not acquire the lock. It invokes this new version from within the node::scaleNode method and transforms the code so that it holds the node's lock during the execution of the vector::syncFree_scaleVector method.

```
vector::syncFree_scaleVector(double s){
  for(int i=0; i < NDIM; i++)
    value[i] *= s;
}
node::scaleNode(double s){
  mutex.acquire();
  count++;
  vector.syncFree_scaleVector(s);
  mutex.release();
}
```

Fig. 2. Data Lock Coarsening Example

```
node::syncFree_scaleNode(double s){
  count++;
  vector.syncFree_scaleVector(s);
}
node::syncFree_traverse(tree *t,
  double min, double max){
  if((min ≤ t->x) && (t->x < max))
    syncFree_scaleNode(t->x);
  if(min ≤ t->x)
    syncFree_traverse(t->left,min,max);
  if(t->x ≤ max)
    syncFree_traverse(t->right,min,max);
}
node::traverse(tree *t,
    double min, double max){
  mutex.acquire();
  syncFree_traverse(t, min, max);
  mutex.release();
}
```

Fig. 3. Computation Lock Coarsening Example

To legally perform this transformation, the compiler must ensure that every thread that executes a vector operation acquires the corresponding node lock before it executes the operation. An examination of the code shows that it satisfies this constraint.

This transformation illustrates the utility of data lock coarsening. It reduces the number of executed locking constructs by a factor of two because it eliminates the acquire/release pair in the vector::scaleVector method. The compiler can also omit the mutual exclusion lock declaration in the vector class because none of the methods in the parallel computation acquire or release the lock.

3.2 Computation Lock Coarsening in the Example

The example also contains an opportunity for computation lock coarsening. Consider the subcomputation generated as a result of executing a node::traverse method. This subcomputation periodically executes node::scaleNode methods, which acquire and release the node's mutual exclusion lock. All of these executions acquire and release the same mutual exclusion lock. In fact, all of the operations in the entire subcomputation that acquire any lock acquire the same lock: the lock in the receiver object of the original node::traverse operation. It is therefore possible to coarsen the lock granularity by acquiring the lock once at the beginning of the subcomputation, then holding it until the subcomputation finishes. This transformation eliminates all of the lock constructs except the initial acquire and the final release. Figure 3 shows the transformed code.

This example also illustrates the potential for false exclusion. Consider the original program in Figure 1. This program only holds the node's lock when it is actually updating the node. The transformed code in Figure 3 holds the lock for the entire traversal. If two traversals on the same node seldom update the node, they can execute mostly in parallel in the original version of the code. In the coarsened version they will execute serially. As we will see in Section 7, this kind of serialization may significantly impair the performance of the parallel computation. The compiler must therefore ensure that its lock coarsening policy does not introduce a significant amount of false exclusion.

4 Model of Computation

Before presenting the lock coarsening algorithms, we discuss the kinds of programs that they are designed to optimize. First, the algorithms are designed for pure object-based programs. Such programs structure the computation as operations on objects. Each object implements its state using a set of instance variables. Each instance variable can be either a nested object or a primitive type from the underlying language such as an integer, a double, or a pointer to an object. Each object has a mutual exclusion lock that exports an acquire construct and a release construct. Once a processor has successfully executed an acquire construct on a given lock, all other processors that attempt to acquire that lock block until the first processor executes a release construct. Operations on the object use its lock to ensure that they execute atomically.

Programmers define operations by writing methods. Each operation corresponds to a method invocation: to execute an operation, the machine executes the code in the corresponding method. Each operation has a receiver object and several parameters. When an operation executes it can access the parameters, invoke other operations or access the instance variables of the receiver. There are several restrictions on instance variable access. An operation cannot directly access an instance variable of a nested object — it can only access the variable indirectly by invoking an operation that has the nested object as the receiver. If an instance variable is declared in a parent class from which the receiver's class inherits, the operation can not directly access the instance variable — it can only access the variable indirectly by invoking an operation whose receiver's class is the parent class.

The computation consists of a sequence of alternating serial and parallel phases. Within a parallel phase the computation uses constructs such as parallel loops to create operations that execute concurrently. The only synchronization consists of the mutual exclusion synchronization required to make the operations atomic and the barrier synchronization at the end of a parallel phase.

If an operation accesses an instance variable that may be modified during the parallel phase, it uses the lock in the instance variable's object to make its access atomic. Before the operation executes its first access to the instance variable, it acquires the object's lock. It releases the lock after it completes the last access.

We extend the model for read-only data as follows. If no operation in the parallel phase modifies an instance variable, any operation in the phase (including operations whose receiver is not the object containing the instance variable) can directly access the variable without synchronization.

There may be a concern that the model of computation imposes overhead in the form of excessive method invocations. We have found that inlined methods and the extension described in the previous paragraph eliminate virtually all of this overhead. The serial C++ versions of our two benchmark applications, for example, perform slightly better than the C versions from the SPLASH benchmark set running on one processor [9].

5 Data Lock Coarsening

The data lock coarsening algorithm starts with a computation in which each object has its own mutual exclusion lock. The basic idea is to increase the lock granularity by giving multiple objects the same lock. Before the computation accesses any one of these objects, it first acquires the lock. Once it has acquired the lock it can access any other object that has the same lock with no further synchronization.

The algorithm must first choose which objects should have the same lock. The current policy attempts to give nested objects the same lock as their enclosing object. The algorithm must then determine if it can transform the entire parallel computation to lock objects at the new granularity. The key issues are to determine statically the new lock that each operation must hold, to make sure that in the generated code each operation actually holds that lock, and to ensure that no part of the computation locks objects at the old granularity.

5.1 The Data Lock Coarsening Algorithm

The primary responsibility of the data lock coarsening algorithm is to ensure that every time the computation executes an operation on a nested object, it holds the lock in the nested object's enclosing object. The algorithm checks that the computation satisfies this constraint by computing the set of methods that may have a nested object as the receiver. It then verifies that all of these methods are invoked only from within methods that have the nested object's enclosing object as their receiver. In this case, the algorithm can generate code that holds the enclosing object's lock for the duration of all methods that execute on nested objects. Because the lock in the enclosing object ensures the atomic execution of all methods that execute with nested objects as the receiver, the compiler can eliminate the lock constructs in these methods. Figure 4 outlines this algorithm.

Primitive Operations:
receiverClass(*method m*) : the class that *m* is defined in.
methods(*class c*) : set of potentially invoked methods in the computation that have class *c* as receiver.
closed(*method m*) : true if the entire computation generated as a result of executing *m* only accesses the receiver object of *m* or nested objects of the receiver object of *m*. The compiler computes this by traversing the call graph.
invokedMethods(*method m*) : set of methods that may be directly or indirectly invoked as a result of executing *m*.
generatesConcurrency(*method m*) : true if *m* contains any constructs that generate parallel execution.
method set m_1 **dominates** *method set* m_2 : true if for every method $m \in ms_2$, every path from the root of the call graph to *m* contains a method in ms_1.
CoarsenGranularity(*method m*) : true if *m* satisfies the false exclusion policy in Section 6.

```
global lockClass;
void DataLockCoarseningClass(class c)
  ms1 = {m : m ∈ methods(c) and closed(m)};
  ms2 = ∪{invokedMethods(m) : m ∈ ms1} − ms1;
  ms3 = {m : m ∈ ms1 and invokedMethods(m) ⊆ ms2}
  cs  = {receiverClass(m) : m ∈ ms2};
  ms4 = ∪{methods(c') : c' ∈ cs};
  if(ms3 dominates ms4) then
    for all methods m ∈ ms3 ∪ ms4 do
      if(generatesConcurrency(m) or (not CoarsenGranularity(m))) return;
    for all methods m ∈ ms3 do
      Make the generated parallel version of m invoke the synchronization-free
      version of each method that it invokes. This synchronization-free version
      contains no lock constructs and invokes the synchronization-free version
      of all methods that it invokes. Also make the first statement of m
      acquire its receiver's lock and the last statement of m release the lock.
    for all methods m ∈ ms4 do
      lockClass[m] = c;
```

Fig. 4. Data Lock Coarsening Algorithm

The algorithm records the results of the data lock coarsening in the variable `lockClass`. Given a method *m*, `lockClass`[*m*] is the class whose lock ensures the atomic execution of *m*. The computation lock coarsening algorithm presented below in Section 6 uses `lockClass` to determine if can legally apply the computation lock coarsening transformation.

To generate code for the transformed computation, the compiler generates a new *synchronization-free* version of all methods whose receivers are nested objects — in other words, all of the methods in the set ms_4. The synchronization-free version is the same as the original version except that it omits any synchronization constructs present in the original version and invokes the synchronization-free version of all of the methods that it executes. The compiler also modifies all of the call sites of the methods in the set ms_3 to ensure that they invoke the synchronization-free version of each invoked method.

Finally, we briefly note that the data lock coarsening algorithm can never introduce deadlock. The model of computation in Section 4 ensures that the processor holds no locks when it enters the transformed version of one of the methods in ms_3. Because the entire computation of the transformed method only acquires and releases the lock in its receiver object, there is no possibility of deadlock.

6 Computation Lock Coarsening

The computation lock coarsening algorithm traverses the call graph, attempting to identify methods whose computation repeatedly acquires and releases the same lock. At each node of the program call graph the computation lock coarsening algorithm uses the **ComputationLockCoarseningMethod**(m) algorithm to determine if it should coarsen the granularity at the execution of the corresponding method m of the call graph node.

Figure 5 presents **ComputationLockCoarseningMethod**(m) algorithm. It first checks that m is closed. It then checks that none of the methods that m's computation may execute acquire and release different locks. It also checks to make sure that none of these methods contain any concurrency generation constructs. If m passes all of these tests, it is legal for the compiler to apply the computation lock coarsening transformation.

```
global lockClass;
void ComputationLockCoarseningMethod(method m)
  if(generatesConcurrency(m)) return;
  if(m is closed)
    c = receiverClass(m);
    for all m' ∈ invokedMethods(m) do
      if(lockClass[receiverClass(m)] ≠ c) or (generatesConcurrency(m)) return;
    if(CoarsenGranularity(m))
      Make the generated parallel version of m invoke the synchronization-free
      version of each method that it invokes. This synchronization-free version
      contains no lock constructs and invokes the synchronization-free version
      of all methods that it invokes. Also make the first statement of m
      acquire its receiver's lock and the last statement of m release the lock.
```

Fig. 5. Computation Lock Coarsening Algorithm

The remaining question is whether coarsening the granularity will generate an excessive amount of false exclusion. The compiler currently uses one of three policies to determine if it should apply the transformation:

- **Original:** Never apply the transformation — use the original granularity.
- **Bounded:** Increase the granularity only if the transformation will not cause the computation to hold a lock for a statically unbounded number of method executions. The compiler implements this policy by testing for cycles in the call graph of the set of methods that may execute while the computation holds the lock. It also checks to make sure that none of these methods contain loops that invoke methods. The idea is to limit the potential severity of any false exclusion by limiting the amount of time the computation holds any given lock.
- **Aggressive:** Always increase the granularity if it is legal to do so.

This policy choice is encapsulated inside the `CoarsenGranularity`(m) algorithm. If the algorithm determines that it should apply the transformation, the compiler generates code for m that acquires the lock, invokes the synchronization-free versions of all of the methods that it invokes, then releases the lock.

The computation lock coarsening algorithm can never introduce deadlock. It simply replaces computations that acquire and release the same lock with computations that acquire and release the lock only once. If the original version does not deadlock, the transformed version can not deadlock.

7 Experimental Results

We have implemented the lock coarsening algorithms described in Sections 5 and 6 and integrated them into a prototype compiler that uses commutativity analysis [9] as its primary analysis paradigm. In this section we present experimental results that characterize the performance impact of using the lock coarsening algorithms in a parallelizing compiler. We report performance results for two automatically parallelized scientific applications: the Barnes-Hut hierarchical N-body solver and the Water code [11].

7.1 Methodology

We implemented the three lock coarsening policies described in Section 6. We then built three versions of the prototype compiler. The versions are identical except that each uses a different lock coarsening policy. We then used the three versions of the compiler to automatically parallelize the benchmark applications. We obtained three automatically parallelized versions of each application — one from each version of the compiler. The generated code for each application differs only in the lock coarsening policy used to reduce the lock overhead. We evaluated the performance of each version by running it on a 32-processor Stanford DASH machine [6]. Because the prototype compiler is a source-to-source translator, we use a standard C++ compiler to generate object code for the automatically generated parallel programs.

7.2 Barnes-Hut

The Barnes-Hut application simulates the trajectories of a set of interacting bodies under Newtonian forces [1]. It uses a sophisticated pointer-based data structure: a space subdivision tree that dramatically improves the efficiency of a key phase in the algorithm. The application consists of approximately 1500 lines of serial C++ code. The compiler is able to automatically parallelize phases of the application that together account for over 95% of the execution time.

Figure 6 presents the speedup curves for this application. The speedups are calculated relative to the serial version of the code, which executes with no lock or parallelization overhead. All versions scale well, which indicates that the compiler was able to effectively parallelize the application. Although the absolute performance varies with the lock coarsening policy, the performance of the different parallel versions scales at approximately the same rate. This indicates that the lock coarsening algorithms introduced no significant contention.

7.3 Water

Water uses a $O(n^2)$ algorithm to simulate a set of n water molecules in the liquid state. The application consists of approximately 1850 lines of serial C++ code. The compiler is able to automatically parallelize phases of the application that together account for over 98% of the execution time.

Figure 7 presents the corresponding speedup curves. [2] The Original and Bounded versions initially perform well (the speedup over the sequential C++ version at sixteen processors is approximately 5.2). But both versions fail to scale beyond eight processors. The Aggressive version fails to scale well at all — the maximum speedup for this version is only 2.0.

A further investigation into the source of the lack of scalability reveals that the application suffers from high lock contention. For this application, the Bounded policy yields the best results and the corresponding parallel code attains respectable speedups. Although the Aggressive policy dramatically reduces the number of executed locking operations, the introduced lock contention almost completely serializes the execution.

8 Related Work

8.1 Automatically Parallelized Scientific Computations

Previous parallelizing compiler research in the area of synchronization optimization has focused almost exclusively on synchronization optimizations for parallel loops in scientific computations [8]. The natural implementation of a parallel

[2] The speedup curves are given relative to the sequential C++ version. We have also obtained sequential C and sequential Fortran versions of this application. The running times for these versions on an input size of 343 molecules are: 65 seconds (Fortran), 68 seconds (C) and 73 seconds (C++).

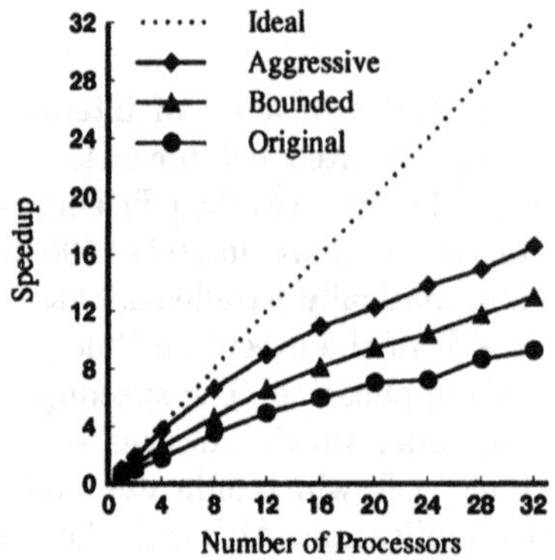

Fig. 6. Speedup for Barnes-Hut (16384 bodies)

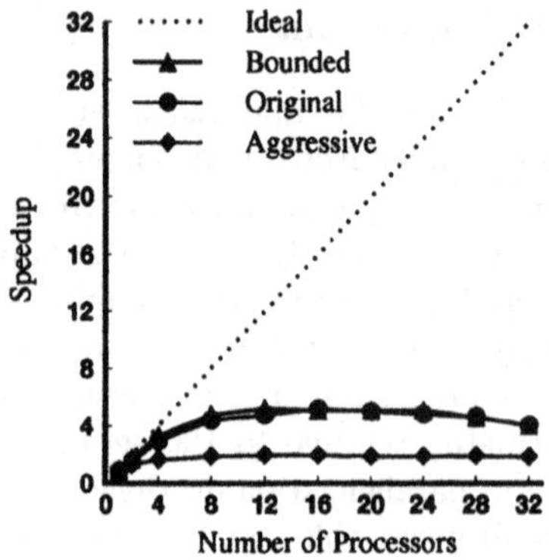

Fig. 7. Speedup for Water (512 molecules)

loop requires two synchronization constructs: an initiation construct to start all processors executing loop iterations, and a barrier construct at the end of the loop. The majority of synchronization optimization research has concentrated on removing barriers or converting barrier synchronization constructs to more efficient synchronization constructs such as counters [10]. Several researchers have also explored optimizations geared towards exploiting more fine grained concurrency available within loops [3]. These optimizations automatically insert one-way synchronization constructs such as post and wait to implement loop-carried data dependences.

The research presented in this paper investigates synchronization optimizations for a compiler designed to parallelize object-based programs, not loop nests that manipulate dense arrays using affine access functions. The problem that our compiler faces is the efficient implementation of atomic operations, not the efficient implementation of data dependence constraints.

8.2 Database Concurrency Control

A goal of research in the area of database concurrency control is to develop efficient locking algorithms for atomic transactions. This goal is similar to our goal of efficiently implementing atomic operations in parallel programs. In fact, database researchers have identified lock granularity as a key issue in the implementation of atomic transactions, and found that excessive lock overhead can be a significant problem if the lock granularity is too fine [2, 4].

The proposed solution to the problem of excessive lock overhead in the context of database concurrency control is to dynamically coarsen the lock granularity using a technique called lock escalation. The idea is that the lock manager (which is responsible for granting locks to transactions) may coarsen the lock granularity by dynamically locking a large section of the database on behalf of a given transaction. If the transaction requests a lock on any object in that section, the lock manager simply checks that the transaction holds the coarser granularity lock.

There are several key differences between the lock manager algorithm and the lock coarsening algorithms presented in this paper. The lock manager algorithm only attempts to increase the data lock granularity — there is no attempt to increase the computation lock granularity. This paper presents algorithms that coarsen both the data and the computation lock granularities.

Several other differences stem from the fact that the lock manager algorithm takes place dynamically, which means that it can not change the program generating the lock requests. The programs therefore continue to execute lock acquire and release constructs at the fine granularity of individual items in the database. The goal of the lock manager algorithm is to make it possible to implement the fine grain lock requests more efficiently in cases when the lock manager has granted the transaction a coarse grain lock on a section of the database, not to change the granularity of the lock requests themselves.

Because the transactions always generate lock requests at the granularity of items in the database, the lock manager must deal with the possibility that a transaction may attempt to lock an individual item even though it does not hold a lock on the section of the database that includes the item. The locking algorithm must therefore keep track of correspondence between different locks that control access to the same objects. Tracking this correspondence complicates the locking algorithm, which makes each individual lock acquire and release less efficient in cases when the lock manager has not already granted the transaction a coarse grain lock.

The lock coarsening algorithms presented in this paper, on the other hand, transform the program so that it always generates lock requests at the coarser granularity. The fine grain lock acquire and release operations are completely eliminated and generate no overhead whatsoever. Furthermore, computations that access the same object always execute acquire and release constructs on the same lock. This property makes it possible for the implementation to use an extremely efficient lock implementation. Modern processors have synchronization instructions that make it possible to implement the required lock acquire and release constructs efficiently [5].

8.3 Efficient Synchronization Algorithms

Other researchers have addressed the issue of synchronization overhead reduction. This work has concentrated on the development of more efficient implementations of synchronization primitives using various protocols and waiting mechanisms [7]. The research presented in this paper is orthogonal to and synergistic with this work. Lock coarsening reduces the lock overhead by reducing the frequency with which the generated parallel code acquires and releases locks, and not by providing a more efficient implementation of the locking constructs.

9 Conclusions

This paper addresses a fundamental issue in the implementation of atomic operations: the granularity at which the computation locks the data that atomic operations access. We have found that using the natural lock granularity for object-based programs (giving each object its own lock and having each operation lock the object that it accesses) may significantly degrade the performance. We have presented algorithms that can effectively reduce the lock overhead by automatically increasingly the granularity at which the computation locks data. We have implemented these algorithms and integrated them into a parallelizing compiler for object-based languages. We present experimental results that characterize the performance impact of using the lock coarsening algorithms in this context. These results show that the algorithms can effectively reduce the lock overhead to negligible levels.

References

1. J. Barnes and P. Hut. A hierarchical O(NlogN) force-calculation algorithm. *Nature*, pages 446–449, December 1976.
2. P. Bernstein, V. Hadzilacos, and N. Goodman. *Concurrency Control and Recovery in Database Systems*. Addison-Wesley, 1987.
3. R. Cytron. Doacross: Beyond vectorization for multiprocessors. In *Proceedings of the 1986 International Conference on Parallel Processing*, St. Charles, IL, August 1986.
4. U. Herrmann, P. Dadam, K. Kuspert, E. Roman, and G Schlageter. A lock technique for disjoint and non-disjoint complex objects. In *Proceedings of the International Conference on Extending Database Technology (EDBT'90)*, pages 219–235, Venice, Italy, March 1990.
5. G. Kane and J. Heinrich. *MIPS Risc Architecture*. Prentice-Hall, 1992.
6. D. Lenoski. *The Design and Analysis of DASH: A Scalable Directory-Based Multiprocessor*. PhD thesis, Stanford, CA, February 1992.
7. B-H. Lim and A. Agarwal. Reactive synchronization algorithms for multiprocessors. In *Proceedings of the Sixth International Conference on Architectural Support for Programming Languages and Operating Systems*, San Jose, CA, October 1994.
8. S. Midkiff and D. Padua. Compiler algorithms for synchronization. *IEEE Transactions on Computers*, 36(12):1485–1495, December 1987.
9. M. Rinard and P. Diniz. Commutativity analysis: A new analysis framework for parallelizing compilers. In *Proceedings of the SIGPLAN '96 Conference on Program Language Design and Implementation*, Philadelphia, PA, May 1996. (http://www.cs.ucsb.edu/~martin/pldi96.ps).
10. C. Tseng. Compiler optimizations for eliminating barrier synchronization. In *Proceedings of the Fifth ACM SIGPLAN Symposium on Principles and Practice of Parallel Programming*, pages 144–155, Santa Barbara, CA, July 1995.
11. S. Woo, M. Ohara, E. Torrie, J.P. Singh, and A. Gupta. The SPLASH-2 programs: Characterization and methodological considerations. In *Proceedings of the 22th International Symposium on Computer Architecture*, Santa Margherita Ligure, Italy, June 1995.

Are Parallel Workstations the Right Target for Parallelizing Compilers? *

Rudolf Eigenmann Insung Park Michael J. Voss

Purdue University, School of Electrical and Computer Engineering

Abstract. The growing popularity of multiprocessor workstations among general users calls for a more easy-to-understand approach to parallel programming. Providing standard, sequential languages with automatic translation tools would enable a seamless transition from uniprocessors to multiprocessor workstations. In this paper we study the success and limitations of such an approach. To this end, we have retargeted the Polaris parallelizing compiler at a 4-processor Sun SPARCstation 20 and measured the performance of parallel programs. Here, we present the results from six of the Perfect Benchmark programs along with our analysis of the performance and some of the issues brought up during the experiments. Our research will help answer some of the questions that have been posed by both users and manufacturers concerning the practicality and desirable characteristics of parallel programming in a workstation environment.

1 Introduction

From an end-user's point of view, parallelizing compilers are not yet consistently useful tools. There have been significant improvements of these tools over the past few years [BDE+96, HAA+96]. However, they are not yet in a state where users can write programs in standard sequential languages and expect good performance on most applications and parallel machines. To achieve such performance, programmers have to be willing to write in architecture-specific parallel languages. The user community of expensive high-performance computers often includes such expert programmers.

The situation is different on parallel workstations. The user community of these machines is more diverse and includes a majority of non-computer experts, who may not be able to invest the time in learning architecture-specific parallel languages. The burden, then, is on compilers, which face the challenge of translating programs written by a layman programmer into efficient machine code. For scientific and engineering applications we have measured the success rate of parallelizing compilers in meeting this challenge to be about one in two programs [BDE+96]. Therefore, given the fact that workstation manufacturers

* This work was supported in part by U. S. Army contract #DABT63-92-C-0033. This work is not necessarily representative of the positions or policies of the U. S. Army or the Government.

currently offer multiprocessors at a price that is only little over the base price of a uniprocessor system, we hypothesize that the availability of parallelizing compilers on such machines is of very practical value.

In this paper we test this hypothesis. Although it may seem straightforward to put parallelizing compilers into a toolbox of parallel workstation, there are a number of open questions: What performance can we expect of applications that have been successfully parallelized on other parallel machines? What are the reasons that the performance is the way it is? Do we need additional optimization techniques to compile for multiprocessor workstations? Are there architectural limitations that impede the performance of parallel or parallelized programs on this class of machines, and can we give recommendations to their manufacturers for removing these limitations?

In order to answer such questions, we have retargeted the Polaris parallelizing compiler at a 4-processor Sun SPARCstation 20 and we have measured the performance of parallel programs run on this system. Section 1.1 will give some details of the architecture of our target machine. Section 2 gives an overview of the Polaris compiler and describes the modifications that we have made so that it generates optimized code for the Sun multiprocessor. In Section 3 we present measurements of parallel programs run on our machine along with our analysis. In Section 3.3, we present open issues and ongoing work.

1.1 The Sun SPARC 20 Multiprocessor architecture

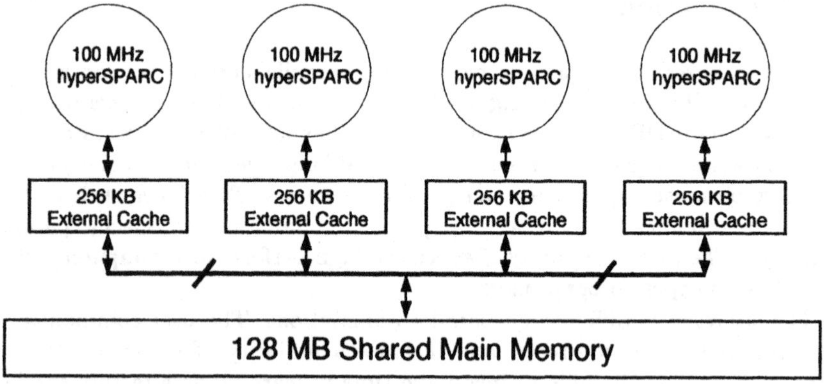

Fig. 1. The Sun SPARCstation20 architecture

Figure 1 shows the Sun Sparc20 workstation used in our experiments. It consists of four 100 MHz hyperSPARC processors that share a single global memory space [Sun96b]. Each processor has its own 256-KB external cache and an 8-KB on-chip instruction cache. Both write-through with no write allocate and copy-back with write allocate caching schemes are provided. The write-through scheme is used only for the block copy and fill operations provided in the hyperSPARC instruction set. In all other cases, the external cache uses the copy-back scheme, maintaining cache coherency through a high performance snoop mechanism. The copy-back scheme is preferred as it writes to main memory less often than a write through scheme, and therefore saves memory bandwidth for interprocessor communications through the shared global memory.

1.2 Expressing parallel programs on the SPARC20 MP

The Sun FORTRAN77 Compiler version 4.0 (SC4.0) [Sun96a, GL96] was chosen as the backend compiler for our study. This compiler is an early release of Sun Microsystem's Fortran compiler that supports language features for expressing parallelism in the form of parallel DO loops. All of the information required for specifying such loops are conveyed by two directives, **C$PAR DOSERIAL** and **C$PAR DOALL**.

C$PAR DOSERIAL : The DOSERIAL directive, when placed before a DO loop, specifies that the loop immediately following it is to be executed sequentially. By default, loops labeled with neither DOSERIAL nor DOALL will be serialized, and therefore this directive is optional.

C$PAR DOALL : The DOALL directive, when placed before a DO loop, specifies that the loop immediately following it is to be executed in parallel. In the case of a parallel loop, it is also required to classify variables within the loop as private, shared, or reduction variables. SC4.0 provides three subdirectives for this purpose, **SHARED()**, **PRIVATE()**, and **REDUCTION()**.

The **C$PAR DOALL PRIVATE(*variable_list*)** subdirective specifies variables within the loop body that are to be treated as private to each processor. By default, all scalar variables are assumed to be private.

The subdirective **C$PAR DOALL SHARED(*variable_list*)** specifies which variables within the loop body are to be treated as shared by all processors. By default, all arrays are assumed to be shared. We have also found that shared read-only scalar variables need not be declared as shared.

Finally, the subdirective **C$PAR DOALL REDUCTION(*variable_list*)** specifies which variables are used for reduction operations. The Sun compiler only allows *scalar reductions*, and therefore only scalars are included in the argument list. Scalar reduction operations are statements within a loop of the form `sum = sum + expr`, where `expr` is a loop-variant term and `sum` is the reduction variable. *Array reductions* are similar patterns, however, the reduction variable is an array with a loop-variant subscript. Array reductions are not supported by the directive language. Because of this, Polaris transforms them into fully parallel loops, as we will describe.

2 Retargeting Polaris at the SPARC20 Multiprocessor

2.1 Polaris overview

Polaris is a parallelizing compiler, originally developed at the University of Illinois. As illustrated in Figure 2, the compiler takes a Fortran77 program as input, transforms it so that it can run efficiently on a parallel computer, and outputs this program version in one of several possible parallel Fortran dialects.

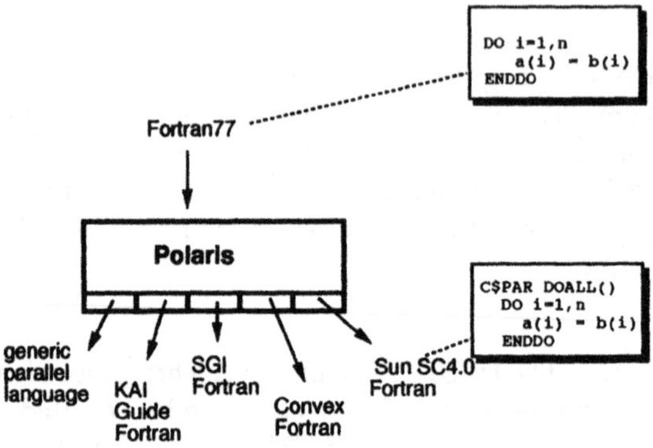

Fig. 2. Overview of the Polaris parallelizing compiler

The input language includes several directives, which allow the user of Polaris to specify parallelism explicitly in the source program. The output language of Polaris is typically in the form of Fortran77 plus parallel directives as well. For example, the *generic parallel language* includes the directives "CSRD$ PARALLEL" and "CSRD$ PRIVATE a,b", specifying that the iterations of the subsequent loop shall be executed concurrently and that the variables a and b shall be placed "private to the current loop". Figure 2 shows several other output languages that Polaris can generate, such as the directive language available on the SGI Challenge machine series and the Sun SC4.0 Fortran directive language introduced above.

Polaris performs its transformations in several *compilation passes.* In addition to many commonly known passes, Polaris includes advanced capabilities for array privatization, symbolic and nonlinear data dependence testing, idiom recognition, interprocedural analysis, and symbolic program analysis. An extensive set of optional switches allow the user and the developer of Polaris to experiment with the tool in a flexible way. An overview of the Polaris transformations is given in [BDE+96].

The implementation of Polaris consists of approximately 170,000 lines of C++ code. A basic infrastructure provides a hierarchy of C++ classes that the developers of the individual compilation passes can use for analyzing and manipulating the input program. This infrastructure is described in [FHP+94]. The Polaris

Developer's Document [Hoe96] gives a more thorough introduction for compiler writers.

Polaris is available as a general infrastructure for analyzing and manipulating Fortran programs. The use of this infrastructure as a parallelizing source-to-source restructurer is the main application. Another application is that of a program instrumentation tool. Currently, Polaris can instrument programs for gathering loop-by-loop profiles, iteration count informations, and for counting data references. We made use of these facilities in order to obtain the results described in this paper.

2.2 Polaris modifications and enhancements

The Sun SPARC20 multiprocessor is a shared-memory architecture, which is one of the classes of machines for which Polaris has been developed. Because of this, the initial movement of the compiler to this platform was fairly simple. Most of the additions to the code were localized to the final *output pass*, since it is here that the generic directives used in the internal representation are mapped to architecture-specific directives. The output pass is the last one in a series of compilation passes. It generates the Fortran-plus-directive output language from the internal representation.

Polaris internally provides to its output pass generic directives that distinguish between serial and parallel loops, shared and private variables, and reduction and non-reduction variables. These generic directives could be directly mapped to their corresponding Sun directives.

One issue that we had to resolve in the output pass for the Sun machine, was to provide an efficient means of identifying the current processor on which a particular loop iteration is executed. The next section describes why this is necessary. The Sun compiler provides a function that can return the current processor number at runtime. However, Polaris-generated programs read this number once or even several times per loop iteration, and so a subroutine call would cause too much overhead.

Another issue we had to deal with was due to a temporary problem with the Sun backend compiler, which did not allow multiple directive lines. Because of this, we had to shorten the directive lines as much as possible. We did this by leaving out variables from the private and shared lists that had the proper default attributes.

Array Reduction and Privatization Both reduction parallelization and array privatization are among the most important transformations of a parallelizing compiler [BDE+96, TP93, PE95]. As we have mentioned above, Polaris transforms array reductions into fully parallel loops.

Figure 3 gives an example array reduction in its serial and parallelized forms. Often, the number and indices of the array elements involved in an array reduction operation (array `A` in our example) cannot be determined at compile time. In the case of such reductions, Polaris provides a local copy of the array to each

```
DIMENSION A(M)
DO I=1,N
 A(B(I)) = A(B(I)) + X
ENDDO
```

(a) Serial Array Reduction

```
DIMENSION A(M),Aloc(M,number_of_processors)
PARALLEL DO I=1,M
 Aloc(I,my_proc_id()) = 0
ENDDO

PARALLEL DO I=1,N
 Aloc(B(I),my_proc_id()) =
  Aloc(B(I),my_proc_id()) + X
ENDDO

PARALLEL DO I=1,M
 DO J=1,number_of_processors
   A(I)=A(I)+Aloc(I,J)
 ENDDO
ENDO
```

(b). Parallel Array Reduction

Fig. 3. Array Reduction operation

processor, performs the accumulation operations of this array in the now fully parallel loop, and then recombines the local arrays after the loop is complete.

Array privatization likewise requires creation of local copies of an array for each processor. In cases that warrant privatization, an array is used as temporary storage for a given iteration. Data dependencies that may exist are a matter of storage reuse, and are not true flow dependencies [TP93]. Private arrays can be expressed in the Sun directive language by listing the arrays on the DOALL PRIVATE list. An array whose size is not known at compile time cannot be declared private in this way. Because of this, Polaris expands these arrays by a dimension equal to the number of processors, allocates them in shared space, and uses the processor identification as an index, as shown in Figure 4. Dynamic allocation of shared arrays is supported in the Sun Fortran dialect.

```
DO J=1,M
 DO I=1,N
   A(I) = ...
 ENDDO
 ...
 DO I=1,N
   ... = A(I)
 ENDDO
ENDDO
```

(a) Serial

```
PARALLEL DO J=1,M
 DO I=1,N
   A(I,my_proc_id())= ...
 ENDDO
 ...
 DO I=1,N
   ... = A(I,my_proc_id())
 ENDDO
ENDO
```

(b) Expanded array

Fig. 4. Array privatization through *expansion*

As mentioned above, there is no efficient way of getting the value **my_proc_id()** used in these transformations. Polaris resolves this problem by stripmining the loop with 4 (=**number_of_processors**) outer iterations and then using the outer loop index instead of the processor number. This is shown in Figure 5. We have used this transformation in both cases where the processor_id would be needed: parallel loops with reduction operations and private arrays.

```
PARALLEL DO J=1,M
   ... A(x,my_proc_id()) ...
ENDO
```

(a) With Function

```
PARALLEL DO proc = 1,number_of_processors
 DO J=proc,M,number_of_processors
   ... A(x,proc) ...
 ENDO
ENDDO
```

(b) Through Stripmining

Fig. 5. Identifying the current processor

3 Parallel program performance

3.1 The experiment

In our experiments, we have studied several programs in three forms: the serial version, the version produced by Polaris, and the version parallelized by SC4.0. The serial version is the original version instrumented with timing functions. In the first step of our experiments, we measured the execution time of the serial loops. We inserted the instrumentation functions at the beginning and end of each loop and ran the resulting code to generate the timing profile. In order to minimize perturbation, we then eliminated the instrumentation functions inserted for either insignificant loops or the loops that execute a large number of times. We did this based on the profile obtained previously. We ran the resulting program to obtain the final profile, which then served as the basis for performance comparisons. To ensure consistent results, we usually ran the programs several times under the same environment and checked the range of execution time before we obtained the timing measurement.

In some cases we had to hand-modify the Polaris-generated code in order to resolve compatibility problems between Polaris and the back-end compiler. Since the back-end compiler is a preliminary release of Sun's Fortran SC4.0 compiler, we expect these problems to be resolved in the next release.

The Fortran SC4.0 compiler also includes a capability to do automatic parallelization. We will compare the performance of programs parallelized by Polaris with the performance of this compiler. The comparison will be interesting because the SC4.0 compiler is a commercially-available optimizing compiler of the newest generation. Hence, it allows us to compare Polaris with the latest industrial state of technology.

During the experiments, we did not enforce a single-user mode, however, we reduced the load on the machine as much as possible, In this way, we were able to obtain consistent timing while maintaining an ordinary workstation environment.

3.2 Results

Overall Performance Results This section presents the experimental results obtained through various runs of the Perfect Benchmark programs BDNA, TRFD, ARC2D, FLO52, MDG, and OCEAN.

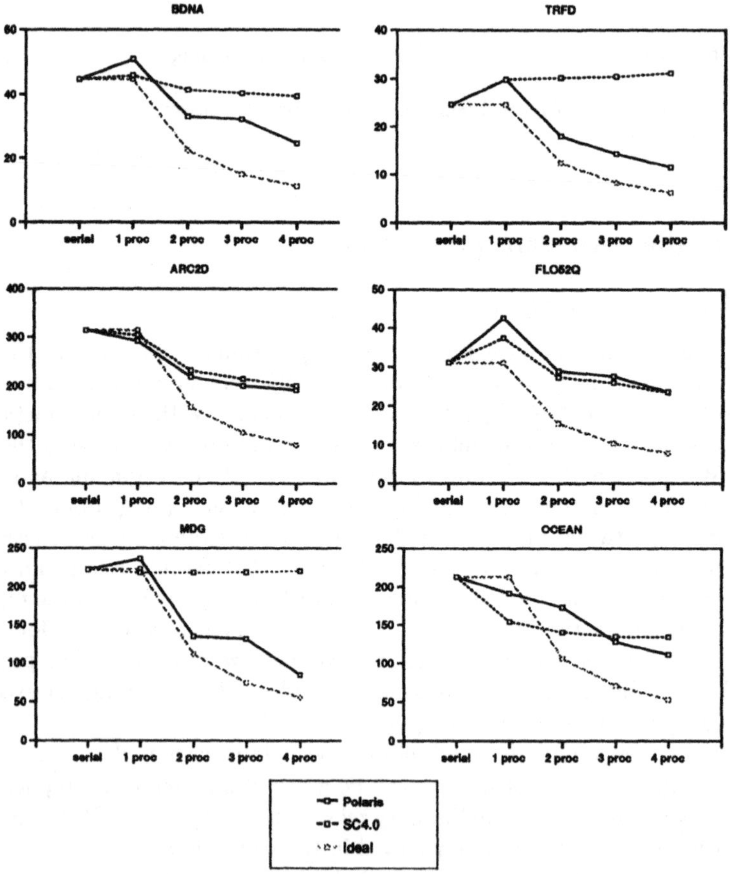

Fig. 6. Execution time of the programs parallelized with Polaris and SC4.0

Figure 6 shows the overall timing of the serial and 4-processor parallel execution of these programs. The curves correspond to programs parallelized with

Polaris and with the Sun parallelizing compiler, respectively. For comparison, the "ideal" curve shows $\frac{serial\_execution\_time}{number\_of\_processors}$.

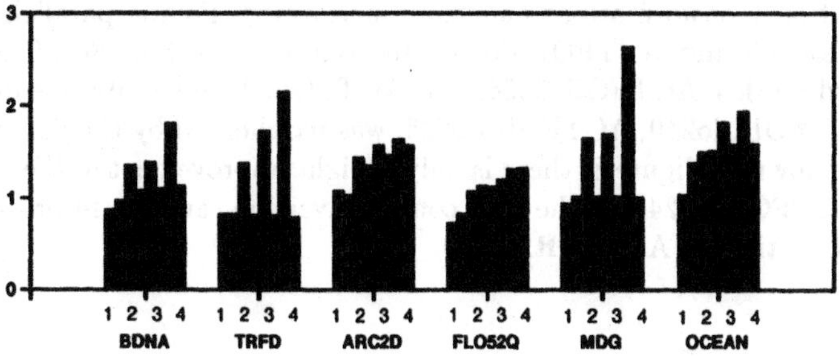

Fig. 7. Speedups of the test programs relative to the serial execution. (gray: Polaris; black: SC4.0)

Figure 7 shows the speedups of the 1 through 4-processor parallel versions of the programs, relative to the serial execution. The gray bars represent the speedups of the versions generated by Polaris and the black bars represent those of the versions generated through SC4.0 automatic parallelization.

The obtained 4-processor speedups range from 0.8 to 2.6. Parallel versions created by Polaris outperformed those by the Sun parallelizer, although, in the case of BDNA, FLO52, and MDG, the overhead of the Polaris version, when going from the serial to the 1-processor parallel version, is higher. We refer to this as the *parallelization overhead*. The Polaris versions of BDNA and MDG show a relatively small performance increase from 2 to 3 processors. This is due to our method of stripmining, which we will discuss in the next section.

Input/output loops in BDNA take up about 8 seconds of the execution time. These loops are not parallel. Since the total execution time of BDNA is about 45 seconds, Amdahl's law limits the speedup to 45 / (37 / 4 + 8) = 2.6. The number we get from our experimental results is 1.8. TRFD shows similar difference between the expected speedup and the experimental result. In MDG, the second most time-consuming loop, POTENG_do2000, could not be run in parallel due to a limitation of the back-end compiler, mentioned earlier. This restricts the speedup to 3.3 while the measured speedup was 2.6. We will discuss these results in more detail by looking at the performance of individual loops.

Performance results of individual loops The performance figures of individual loops give us more insight into the behavior of the programs and the machine architecture. We measured the total execution time of each loop accumulated over repetitive runs in the program as well as average execution time. In BDNA, the execution time of the entire program is dominated by three loops:

ACTFOR_do240[2] , ACTFOR_do500, and RESTAR_do15. Figure 8 shows the execution times and speedups of these loops, in the same terms as for Figure 6. RESTAR_do15 handles sequential file I/O and it is not parallelized. Note that this loop becomes dominant in the overall execution time, limiting the overall speedup. In order to parallelize the other two loops, array privatization and parallel reduction transformations had to be performed. Polaris parallelized both ACTFOR_do240 and ACTFOR_do500. In contrast, the Sun SC4.0 optimizer parallelized neither ACTFOR_do240 nor ACTFOR_do500. Only one inner loop within ACTFOR_do240, ACTFOR_do235, was parallelized by the Sun compiler. Hence, as shown in Figure 8, there is only a slight improvement in the execution time of ACTFOR_do240 in the Sun compiler version, and no improvement in the execution time of ACTFOR_do500.

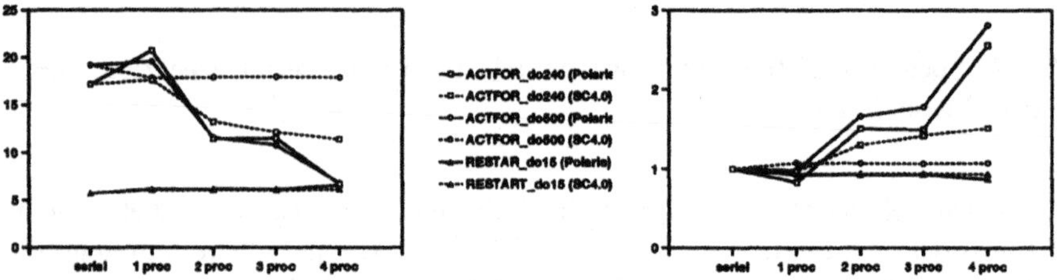

Fig. 8. Execution times and speedups of individual loops in BDNA

Both loops ACTFOR_do240 and ACTFOR_do500 perform reasonably well on our machine. However, there is no increase in performance from 2 to 3 processors. The reason for this is that the loops are stripmined (cf. Fig. 5), with the outer, parallel loop iterating four times. If we use three processors, one processor will have to do two iterations – the same as for two processors.

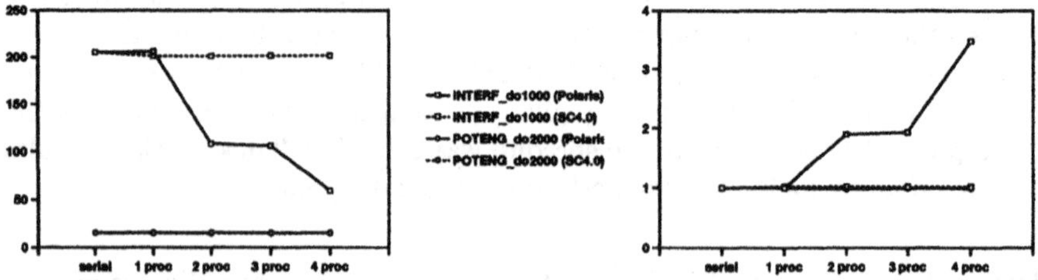

Fig. 9. Execution times and speedups of individual loops in MDG

[2] Our notation means the loop with label 240 in subroutine ACTFOR.

This effect is also visible in the experiment with MDG, as seen in Figure 9. The execution time of MDG is dominated by one loop, INTERF_do1000, which is stripmined in the same way. The 4-processor speedup of this loop shows an excellent 3.47. The loop POTENG_do2000 was not run in parallel because a problem in the back-end compiler, mentioned earlier. Polaris detected both loops as parallel. In contrast, the Sun parallelizer did not detect parallelism in either loop, resulting in no overall speedup.

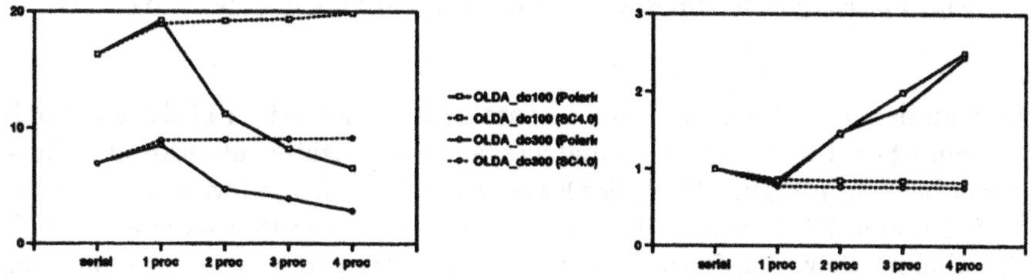

Fig. 10. Execution times and speedups of individual loops in TRFD

In TRFD, there are only two loops that have significant effects on the execution time: OLDA_do100 and OLDA_do300. Parallelization of these loops requires the substitution of generalized induction variables [PE95] and a dependence test on non-linear subscripts [BE94]. They were successfully parallelized by Polaris, but not by the Sun compiler. Instead, the Sun compiler parallelized several loops within these two loops. However, the execution times of these loops is so small that their parallelization is not profitable. The execution times and speedups are plotted in Figure 10.

Another code that we studied is ARC2D. The overall performance of ARC2D is less than that of BDNA, MDG, and TRFD. Moreover, the major loops parallelized by Polaris in BDNA and TRFD show good speedups while the loops in ARC2D, as presented in Figure 11, do not. Individual loop speedups are within the range of 1 to 2 times the serial version. Figure 11 shows the parallel execution times of a few of the most time-consuming loops. Unlike the above three programs, where there are only a few loops dominating the execution time, ARC2D has a large amount of smaller loops that contribute to the overall execution time. Almost all of these loops are easy for compilers to parallelize. In fact, in studies with previous parallelizing compilers, we have found that all loops of this code were almost fully parallelized [BE92]. Our performance curves show that fully parallel loops do not necessarily guarantee good speedup. We have identified the performance of the memory to be the primary bottleneckv6 . We have found that loops that access mostly private data can take advantage of the cache and perform well, whereas loops dominated by shared accesses usually perform significantly worse.

FLO52 is another program with plenty of parallelism. As for ARC2D, previ-

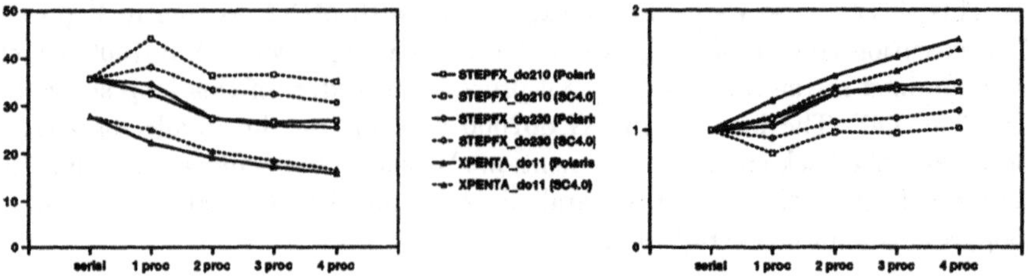

Fig. 11. Execution times and speedups of individual loops in ARC2D

ous compilers have been successful in parallelizing this code. FLO52 is the only program where the Sun compiler matches, and even slightly outperforms Polaris. As can be seen in Figure 12, major loops were all parallelized with speedups between 2.0 and 3.2, except CPLOT_do30, which is a loop that handles file I/O. Several loops showed differences in the optimizations performed by the two compilers, however the overall difference in execution time is insignificant.

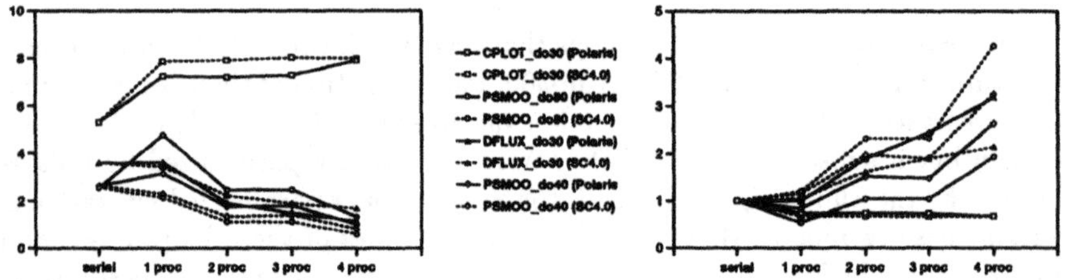

Fig. 12. Execution times and speedups of individual loops in FLO52

Finally, Figure 13 shows three of the most time-consuming loops in OCEAN. Polaris was not able to parallelize the most time-consuming loop, FTRVMT_do109. Instead, it parallelized three inner loops. The Sun compiler did not parallelize either of these loops, but the execution time was reduced by 20 seconds, nevertheless. Such "negative parallelization overheads" can be caused by the back-end compiler applying different scalar optimizations to the serial and parallel code. The same effect can be seen in the other two loops shown. Because of this, the Polaris version does not execute faster than the SC4.0 version until three or more processors are used, as can be seen in Figure 6. Notice also that the speedup for FTRVMT_do109 in the Polaris version is not as good as for the other two loops. However, it turns out that FTRVMT_do109 is parallel and its performance can be improved. A brief discussion on this will be presented in the next section.

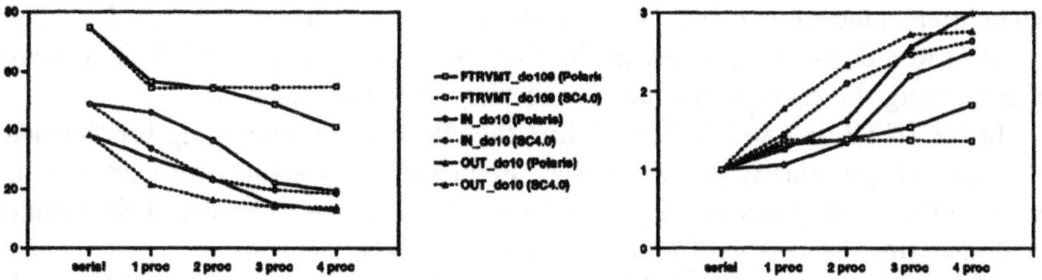

Fig. 13. Execution times and speedups of individual loops in OCEAN

3.3 Ongoing Work

In order to identify additional compiler transformations that could improve performance on our machine, we are currently hand tuning and studying the Polaris-generated codes. The most important such transformation, identified so far, is loop interchanging. Loop interchanging is a well-known technique [BENP93], but not yet applied by Polaris. The transformation was applicable in two distinct cases. The first case was to increase locality of reference by creating a stride of 1 in array accesses. The second case was to increase parallelism by exchanging an inner parallel loop with an outer serial loop (when such an exchange is legal). This increases granularity and allows more work to be done in parallel, reducing the total startup overhead of repeatedly starting the inner, parallel loop.

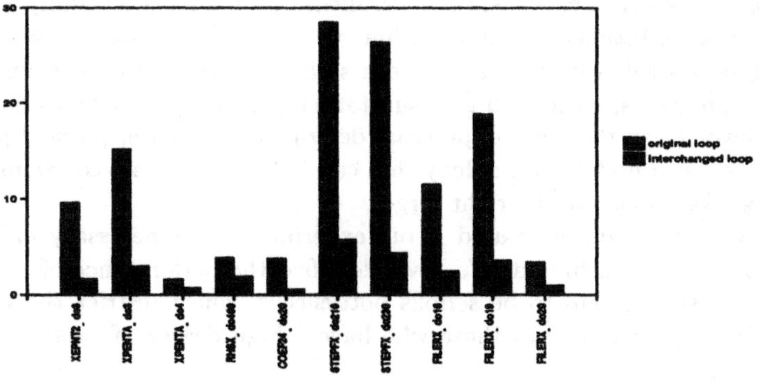

Fig. 14. Execution times of interchanged loops in ARC2D

Figure 14 presents the change in execution times for each of these modified loops. The loops STEPFX_do210 and STEPFX_do230, which were the two most time-consuming loops in the benchmark, greatly reduce their execution time due to the creation of stride 1 accesses. Their 4-processor execution times decreased by the factors 4.88 and 5.84, respectively. Both loops have an inner loop, which when interchanged enhances the spatial locality that each cache can exploit. This speedup would also be present in the 1-processor execution, since it is a result of improving the cache behavior of each individual processor.

In XPENT2_do3 and XPENTA_do3 the effect of interchanging for the sake of increased granularity can been seen. Reducing the startup overhead and increasing the total work done in parallel allows these loops to reduce their parallel execution time by factors 5.77 and 5.26, respectively.

After interchanging these 10 loops, the overall execution time of the code dropped from 192 seconds to 97 seconds, a speedup of 2. This increased the program speedup with respect to the original, serial version significantly, from 1.6 to 3.2. We are currently implementing a Polaris pass that determines where loop interchanging is profitable and then applies the transformation.

Another improvement was possible in OCEAN. The most time-consuming loop, FTRVMT_do109, consists of one loop enclosing three inner loops. As mentioned earlier, Polaris parallelized these three loops. We have found that the outer loop can be run in parallel as well, reducing the total execution time of FTRVMT_do109 down to 32 seconds. As the result, the overall speedup of OCEAN increased from 1.91 to 2.07. Recognizing this situations requires enhancements to the symbolic range propagation techniques of Polaris [BE95], which is another ongoing effort.

4 Conclusions

Our results show that compilers can parallelize programs successfully for multiprocessor workstations. Given a machine with balanced resources, we can expect a good return from investing into a small number of workstation CPUs. For many programs, a user can gain substantial performance without having to become involved in the parallel program design. In this sense, parallel processing has become a mature technology that can serve a wide user community and parallel workstations are the right target.

However, in the machine used in our experiments, the necessary balance of resources is not yet achieved. We have identified the performance of the memory and the I/O system to be serious bottlenecks, which restrict the range of well-performing programs to those who have a high degree of locality and insignificant disk traffic.

In the past, parallel programming has not been very popular among workstation users. Because of this, there is a lack of information on how well parallel programs perform, and what languages, compilers, and tools we need. Our study has tried to fill this very void. More such data is necessary. It will enable a field that is perhaps the first really practical application of parallel computing.

References

[BDE+96] William Blume, Ramon Doallo, Rudolf Eigenmann, John Grout, Jay Hoeflinger, Thomas Lawrence, Jaejin Lee, David Padua, Yunheung Paek, Bill Pottenger, Lawrence Rauchwerger, and Peng Tu. Advanced program restructuring for high-performance computers with Polaris. *IEEE Computer*, December 1996.

[BE92] William Blume and Rudolf Eigenmann. Performance Analysis of Parallelizing Compilers on the Perfect Benchmarks Programs. *IEEE Transactions of Parallel and Distributed Systems*, 3(6):643–656, November 1992.

[BE94] William Blume and Rudolf Eigenmann. The Range Test: A Dependence Test for Symbolic, Non-linear Expressions. *Proceedings of Supercomputing '94, Washington D.C.*, pages 528–537, November 1994.

[BE95] William Blume and Rudolf Eigenmann. Symbolic Range Propagation. *Proceedings of the 9th International Parallel Processing Symposium*, pages 357–363, April 1995.

[BENP93] Utpal Banerjee, Rudolf Eigenmann, Alexandru Nicolau, and David Padua. Automatic Program Parallelization. *Proceedings of the IEEE*, 81(2):211–243, February 1993.

[FHP+94] Keith A. Faigin, Jay P. Hoeflinger, David A. Padua, Paul M. Petersen, and Stephen A. Weatherford. The Polaris Internal Representation. *International Journal of Parallel Programming*, 22(5):553–586, October 1994.

[GL96] Vinod Grover and Michael Lai. Directives for SC4.0 Fortran and Fortran MP. Technical report, Sun Microsystems, Inc., 1996.

[HAA+96] M. W. Hall, J. M. Anderson, S. P. Amarasinghe, B. R. Murphy, S.-W. Liao, E. Bugnion, and M. S. Lam. Getting performance out of multiprocessors with the SUIF compiler. *IEEE Computer*, December 1996.

[Hoe96] Jay Hoeflinger. Polaris developer's document. Technical report, Univ. of Illinois at Urbana-Champaign, Center for Supercomp. R&D, 1996. http://www.csrd.uiuc.edu/polaris/polaris_developer/polaris_developer.html.

[PE95] Bill Pottenger and Rudolf Eigenmann. Idiom Recognition in the Polaris Parallelizing Compiler. *Proceedings of the 9th ACM International Conference on Supercomputing*, pages 444–448, 95.

[Sun96a] Sun Microrsystems, Inc., Mountain View, CA. *FORTRAN 4.0 User's Guide*, 1996.

[Sun96b] Sun Microsystems, Inc. *SPARCstation 20 Series with SuperSPARC and SuperSPARC-II Processors*, 1996. http://www.sun.com:80/products-n-solutions/hw/wstns/jtf_ss20.html.

[TP93] Peng Tu and David Padua. Automatic Array Privatization. In Utpal BanerjeeDavid GelernterAlex NicolauDavid Padua, editor, *Proc. Sixth Workshop on Languages and Compilers for Parallel Computing, Portland, OR. Lecture Notes in Computer Science.*, volume 768, pages 500–521, August 12-14, 1993.

Optimal Reordering and Mapping of a Class of Nested-Loops for Parallel Execution

Chi-Chung Lam*, P. Sadayappan*, and Rephael Wenger

Department of Computer and Information Science
The Ohio State University
Columbus, OH 43210
e-mail: {clam, saday, wenger}@cis.ohio-state.edu

Abstract

This paper addresses the compile-time optimization of a class of nested-loop computations that arise in some computational physics applications. The computations involve summations over products of array terms in order to compute multi-dimensional surface and volume integrals. Reordering additions and multiplications and applying the distributive law can significantly reduce the number of operations required in evaluating these summations. In a multiprocessor environment, proper distribution of the arrays among processors will reduce the inter-processor communication time. We present a formal description of the operation minimization problem, a proof of its NP-completeness, and a pruning strategy for finding the optimal solution in small cases. We also give an algorithm for determining the optimal distribution of the arrays among processors in a multiprocessor environment.

1 Introduction

This paper addresses the problem of compile-time optimization of a particular form of nested loop computations that arise in the calculation of multi-dimensional surface and volume integrals in some computational physics applications. In addition to the issue of mapping of data and computations to optimize performance, there is also a need to optimize the total number of arithmetic operations by judicious application of the distributive law of multiplication over addition. The following example is used to explain the problem being addressed (assume array S is pre-initialized to zeros):

```
for i = 1 to N_i do
    for j = 1 to N_j do
        for k = 1 to N_k do
            for t = 1 to N_t do
                S[t] = S[t] + A[i,j,t] × B[j,k,t]
            endfor
        endfor
    endfor
endfor
```

* Supported in part by NSF grant DMR-9520319.

Execution of this program fragment involves $N_iN_jN_kN_t$ floating point multiplications and an equal number of floating point additions, making a total of $2N_iN_jN_kN_t$ floating point operations. It computes the discrete function (for simplicity, we use $\sum_i$ to denote $\sum_{i=1}^{N_i}$):

$$f(t) = S[t] = \sum_i \sum_j \sum_k (A[i,j,t] \times B[j,k,t])$$

If the above loop were input to an optimizing compiler, it would perform dependence analysis [10] on the loop and determine that the innermost (t-loop) was an independent loop and that the other three loops involved dependences due to reductions. Although the loop could be parallelized, no attempt would be made by the compiler to reduce the number of arithmetic operations involved. As shown below, considerable reduction in the number of operations is in fact possible for this computation, through application of algebraic properties.

Since addition and multiplication can both be considered associative and commutative, and multiplication distributes over addition, we have:

1. $\sum_i \sum_j X = \sum_j \sum_i X$

2. If term X does not depend on i, then $\sum_i (X \times Y) = X \times \sum_i Y$

The first rule allows us to switch the positions of any number of consecutive summations while the second rule permits the extraction of an expression independent of a summation index out of that summation. By application of the algebraic properties, we can rewrite the function as:

$$f(t) = S[t] = \sum_j \left(\sum_i A[i,j,t] \times \sum_k B[j,k,t] \right)$$

This form of the expression can be transformed into the program fragment below:

```
for t = 1 to Nt do
    for j = 1 to Nj do
        Temp1 = 0
        for i = 1 to Ni do
            Temp1 = Temp1 + A[i,j,t]
        endfor
        Temp2 = 0
        for k = 1 to Nk do
            Temp2 = Temp2 + B[j,k,t]
        endfor
        S[t] = S[t] + Temp1 × Temp2
    endfor
endfor
```

The new program fragment requires only N_jN_t floating point multiplications and $N_iN_jN_t + N_jN_kN_t + N_jN_t$ floating point additions. The total number of floating point operations, which is $N_iN_jN_t + N_jN_kN_t + 2N_jN_t$, is an order of magnitude less than that of the original program fragment. The temporary storage required is only for two scalar variables, *Temp*1 and *Temp*2, and hence is very efficient.

The above example is simple enough to be able to manually seek the optimal reordering and application of the distributive law to minimize the number of operations. However, the complex sequence of such summations that arise in some computational physics applications are not easily hand-optimized. In addition to minimizing the number of operations, the effective mapping of the computations and the data onto a parallel machine also needs to be addressed. Thus, automatic compile-time support for operation minimization and mapping onto a parallel machine is desirable. These issues are addressed in this paper.

Reduction of arithmetic operation has been traditionally done by compilers using the technique of common subexpression elimination [1,8]. Other approaches to reduce operation count can be found in [6,7,9]. Loop transformations that improve locality and parallelism have been studied extensively in recent years [3,4,10,11]. However, we are not aware of any framework that considers loop transformation together with the application of the distributive law in order to minimize the amount of computation in nested loops.

Section 2 formalizes the operation minimization problem in terms of a sequence of function definitions that compute the same result as the original function. Section 3 proves that the problem of operation minimization is NP-complete. A search procedure for determining the optimal form that minimizes the number of operations is developed in Section 4. Section 5 analyzes the amount of data movement incurred in implementing a sequence of formulae on parallel computers. An algorithm to determine the optimal data partitioning is presented. Section 6 touches upon work in progress and provides conclusions.

2 Formalization of the Optimization Problem

Generalizing from the first example of the previous section, we consider optimization of perfectly nested loops of the form, with a single reduction statement as its loop body:

```
for i1 = 1 to N1 do
   for i2 = 1 to N2 do
       ...
      for ik = 1 to Nk do
          A0[I0] = A0[I0] + A1[I1] ×A2[I2] × ...
      endfor
          ...
   endfor
endfor
```

where N_j are positive integers and I_j represents the indices of A_j and is a list of distinct indices from the set $\{i_1, i_2, ..., i_k\}$. Note that 1) the arrays A_j are distinct, 2) the loop indices have constant upper and lower bounds, and 3) array entries are directly referenced by a list of loop indices. Thus, for example, we do not consider a loop such as the following, which violates all three of these conditions:

```
for i1 = 1 to N1 do
    for i2 = 1 to i1 do
        A0[i1] = A0[i1] + A1[i1,i1] × A2[i1] ×A2[i1-i2]
    endfor
endfor
```

Such examples do arise in practice and will be considered in future work.

We wish to reduce the number of arithmetic operations in evaluating nested loops by reordering operations and applying the distributive law. However, we do not consider more complicated strategies such as the transformation of the standard matrix multiplication into Strassen's algorithm [9]. Hence we first have to define more precisely the space of equivalent programs that are to be searched amongst. We formalize this space as a set of function sequences. Each function in a function sequence is either:

- a multiplication formula of the form: $f_r[...] = X[...] \times Y[...]$, or
- a summation formula of the form: $f_r[...] = \sum_i X[...]$

where $X[...]$ and $Y[...]$ is either an initial array $A_j[...]$ or a previously defined function $f_s[...]$. Let IX, IY and If_r be the sets of indices in $X[...]$, $Y[...]$ and $f_r[...]$ respectively. For a formula to be well-formed, every index in $X[...]$ and $Y[...]$, except the summation index in the second form, must appear inside $f_r[...]$, that is, $IX \cup IY = If_r$ for a multiplication formula and $IX - \{i\} = If_r$ for a summation formula. Each formula in a sequence computes a partial result of the function and the last formula produces the final result desired. Such a sequence of formulae fully specifies the multiplications and additions to be performed to compute the result.

For example, the function $S[t] = \sum_i \sum_j \sum_k (A[i,j,t] \times B[j,k,t])$ can be represented by the formula sequence below:

$$f_1[i,j,k,t] = A[i,j,t] \times B[j,k,t]$$

$$f_2[i,j,t] = \sum_k f_1[i,j,k,t]$$

$$f_3[i,t] = \sum_j f_2[i,j,t]$$

$$S[t] = f_4[t] = \sum_i f_3[i,t]$$

whereas the optimized form $S[t] = \sum_j \left(\sum_i A[i,j,t] \times \sum_k B[j,k,t] \right)$ corresponds to the sequence:

$$f_1[j,t] = \sum_i A[i,j,t]$$

$$f_2[j,t] = \sum_k B[j,k,t]$$

$$f_3[j,t] = f_1[j,t] \times f_2[j,t]$$

$$S[t] = f_4[t] = \sum_j f_3[j,t]$$

The cost, or total number of floating point operations, of a formula sequence is the sum of the costs of the individual formulae in the sequence, which can be obtained as below:

- For a multiplication formula of the form $f_r[...] = X[...] \times Y[...]$, the cost is $\prod_{h \in IX \cup IY} N_h$. For instance, the formula $f_1[i,j,k,t] = A[i,j,t] \times B[j,k,t]$ has a cost of $N_i N_j N_k N_t$.
- For a summation formula of the form $f_r[...] = \sum_i X[...]$, the cost is $(N_i - 1) \times \prod_{h \in IX - \{i\}} N_h$. The term $N_i - 1$ arises because adding N_i numbers requires $N_i - 1$ additions. For example, the formula $f_2[i,j,t] = \sum_k f_1[i,j,k,t]$ has a cost of $(N_k - 1) N_i N_j N_t$.

A formula sequence can be represented graphically as a binary tree to show the hierarchical structure of the computation more clearly. In the binary tree, the leaves are the arrays A_j's and the internal nodes are the functions $f_r[...]$ defined by the formulae, with the last defined function at the root. An internal node may either be a multiplication node or a summation node. A multiplication node corresponds to a multiplication formula and has two children which are the terms being multiplied together. A summation node corresponds to a summation formula and has only one child, the term on which summation is performed. As an example, the binary tree that represents the above formula sequence is shown in Fig. 1.

3 NP-Completeness of the Operation Minimization Problem

The operation minimization problem is: Given a formula of the form $S[I_0] = \sum_{i_1=1}^{N_1} \sum_{i_2=1}^{N_2} \cdots \sum_{i_k=1}^{N_k} (A_1[I_1] \times A_2[I_2] \times \ldots)$, $I_j \subseteq \{i_1, i_2, \ldots, i_k\}$, construct a

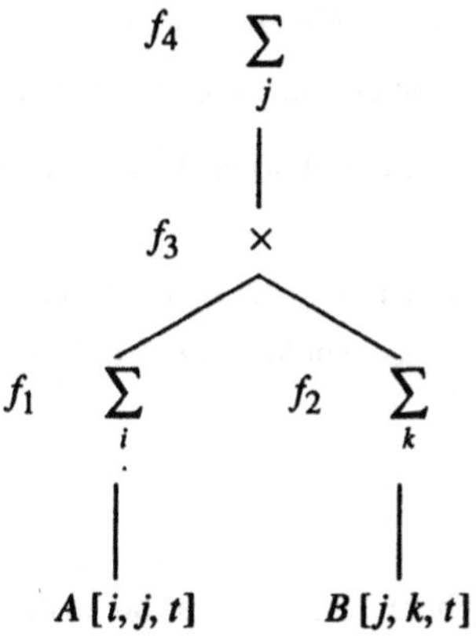

Fig. 1. A binary tree representation

sequence of multiplication and summation formulae which compute the array S using the fewest arithmetic operations. In this section, we prove that this problem is NP-Complete. To show this, we identify a simpler sub-problem: the multiplication sub-problem. Proving this sub-problem to be NP-complete will prove the operation minimization problem to be NP-complete.

The multiplication sub-problem is one where no summation indices are present at all. Given a set of array variables, they are to be multiplied together in some order so as to minimize the total multiplication cost. Note that multiplication in this context is commutative and the variables can be rearranged and grouped in any order. Thus the polynomial time dynamic programming algorithm for matrix-chain multiplication problem does not generalize to our problem.

To illustrate the multiplication subproblem, let us consider the example $A[i] \times B[j] \times C[i,k] \times D[j,k]$, where $N_i = N_j = 10$ and $N_k = 20$. One way to perform the multiplications is $((A[i] \times B[j]) \times C[i,k]) \times D[j,k]$, which requires $N_iN_j + 2N_iN_jN_k = 4100$ arithmetic operations. However, this is not optimal; the optimal order of multiplication is $(A[i] \times C[i,k]) \times (B[j] \times D[j,k])$, which requires only $N_iN_k + N_jN_k + N_iN_jN_k = 2400$ arithmetic operations. Note that the cost of each node in the binary tree representing the order of multiplication is equal to the product of the sizes of the indices of the matrix represented at that node. The multiplication cost of the root in the binary tree is fixed and independent of the order of multiplication.

We prove the NP-completeness of the multiplication subproblem in two steps. First, we reduce a known NP-complete problem, the Subset Product problem, to a new problem we call the Product Partition problem. Next, we reduce the Product Partition Problem to the multiplication subproblem. This proves NP-completeness of the multiplication subproblem as well as the operation minimization problem.

The Subset Product problem is: Given a finite set A, a size $s(a) \in Z^+$ for each $a \in A$, and a positive integer y, determine whether there exists a subset $A' \subseteq A$ such that $\prod_{a \in A'} s(a) = y$. This problem is known to be NP-complete [2]. The Product Partition problem is similar. Given a finite set B and a size $s'(b) \in Z^+$ for each $b \in B$, the Product Partition problem asks whether there exists a subset $B' \subseteq B$ such that $\prod_{b \in B'} s'(b) = \prod_{b \in B - B'} s'(b)$.

Let x equal $\prod_{a \in A} s(a)$ where $\langle A, s, y\rangle$ is an instance of the Subset Product problem. Note that if $2x/y$ is not an integer, then there is no solution to this instance. Otherwise, reduce the Subset Product problem to the Product Partition problem by adding two new elements of sizes $2x/y$ and $2y$ to the set A. Formally, for each Subset Product problem instance $\langle A, s, y\rangle$, form a Product Partition problem instance $\langle B, s'\rangle$ where $B = A \cup \{b', b''\}$, $s'(a) = s(a)$ for all $a \in A$, $b' \notin A$, $b'' \notin A$, $s'(b') = 2x/y$, $s'(b'') = 2y$, and $x = \prod_{a \in A} s(a)$. If the Subset Product problem instance $\langle A, s, y\rangle$ has a solution A', then $B' = A' \cup \{b'\}$ is a solution to the Product Partition problem instance $\langle B, s'\rangle$ since $\prod_{b \in B'} s'(b) = \prod_{b \in B - B'} s'(b) = 2x$. Conversely, if the Product Partition problem instance $\langle B, s'\rangle$ has a solution B', then either one of b' or b'' (but not both) must belong to B' because $b'b'' = 4x$ is greater than $\prod_{b \in B'} s'(b) = \sqrt{\prod_{b \in B} s'(b)} = 2x$. In this way, either $A' = B - B' - \{b'\}$ or $A' = B' - \{b'\}$ would be a solution to the Subset Problem instance $\langle A, s, y\rangle$. Since this reduction can be performed in polynomial time, it follows that the Product Partition problem is NP-complete.

Given a Product Partition problem instance $\langle B, s'\rangle$, we construct a multiplication subproblem instance whose optimal solution has equal costs on the two nodes at the second level in the binary tree representation if and only if the Product Partition problem instance $\langle B, s'\rangle$ has a solution. As before, let $x = \prod_{b \in B} s'(b)$ and note that if $\sqrt{x}$ is not an integer, then the instance has no solution. Otherwise, reduce the Product Partition problem to the multiplication subproblem as follows. First, for each $b \in B$, form a single-dimensional matrix $M_b[i_b]$ where $N_{i_b} = s'(b)$. Then, add two more

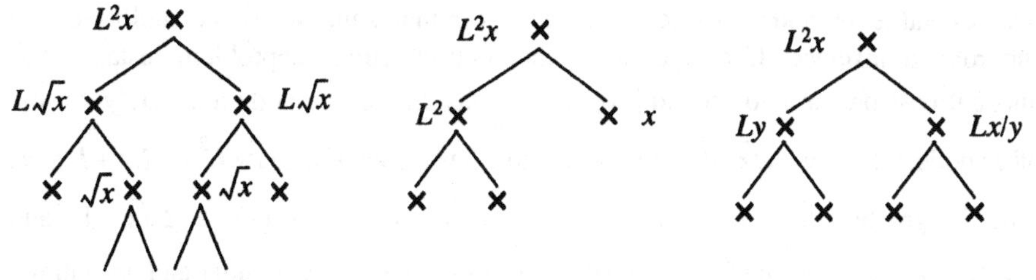

(a) (b) (c)

Fig. 2. Different binary trees for a multiplication subproblem instance

matrices $M_{b'}[i_{b'}]$ and $M_{b''}[i_{b''}]$ where $N_{i_{b'}} = N_{i_{b''}} = L = (n+1)\sqrt{x}$, $n = |B|$, and $x = \prod_{b \in B} s'(b)$. This reduction can be done in polynomial time. These n+2 matrices, namely $M_{b'}$, $M_{b''}$ and M_b for each $b \in B$, define the multiplication subproblem instance. Matrices $M_{b'}$ and $M_{b''}$ are so large that their relative position in the binary tree becomes very significant.

We use two facts about the multiplication subproblem. First, the cost of the root is node is the same in all solutions and is the product of the sizes of all indices, in this case L^2x. Second, the cost at any node is bounded by the cost of any of its ancestors. Thus the cost of any solution is bounded by $(n+1)L^2x$.

If an optimal solution to the multiplication subproblem instance has equal cost at the two second-level nodes, then those two nodes must cost $L\sqrt{x}$ each (see Fig. 2(a)). Since the n+2 matrices require n+1 multiplications, there are $n+1-3 = n-2$ multiplication nodes below the second level in the binary tree. Thus, the binary tree has a cost of at most $L^2x + 2L\sqrt{x} + (n-2)\sqrt{x}$. If $M_{b'}$ and $M_{b''}$ are not split at the second level, the binary tree would have a cost of at least $L^2x + L^2 + x$ which is greater than $L^2x + 2L\sqrt{x} + (n-2)\sqrt{x}$ (see Fig. 2(b)). Therefore, $M_{b'}$ and $M_{b''}$ must each belong to a different node at the second level of the binary tree. Removing $M_{b'}$ and $M_{b''}$ from these two nodes gives us a solution to the Product Partition problem instance <B, s'>.

Conversely, if the Product Partition problem instance <B, s'> has a solution, then a binary tree for the multiplication subproblem instance can be constructed so that the two nodes at the second level have equal cost $L\sqrt{x}$. We show that equal cost on the two second-level nodes is necessary in an optimal solution to the multiplication subproblem instance. If a solution to the multiplication subproblem instance has unequal cost on the two second-level nodes, say Ly on one node and Lx/y on the other node, where $y \neq \sqrt{x}$, then the binary tree has a cost of at least $L^2x + Ly + Lx/y$. This is greater than $L^2x + 2L\sqrt{x} + (n-2)\sqrt{x}$, since $y + x/y \geq 2\sqrt{x} + 1$ and $L > (n-2)\sqrt{x}$ (see Fig. 2(c)). So, such a solution cannot be optimal and an optimal solution must have equal cost on the two second-level nodes.

If the multiplication subproblem can be solved in polynomial time, we can look at the second level of the optimal binary tree to see if the two nodes have equal cost and thus solve the Product Partition problem in polynomial time. But, the Product Partition problem has been shown above to be NP-complete. It follows that the multiplication subproblem is NP-complete. Since every instance of the multiplication subproblem is an instance of the operation minimization problem, the latter problem is also NP-complete.

4 A Search Procedure for the Minimal-Cost Sequence

Since the operation minimization problem has been shown to be NP-Complete, it is impractical to seek a polynomial-time algorithm for it. We have to resort either to heuristics or use exponential-time searches for the optima. For the kind of loops that arise in practice, the number of nested loops and the number of array variables is typically less than ten. Thus a well-pruned search procedure should be practically feasible. Hence we pursue such an approach here.

Our objective is to find the formula sequence that computes the desired function and incurs the least cost, i.e. requires the minimum number of floating point operations. A well-formed formula sequence computes the desired result if it satisfies the following conditions:

- Each array A_j appears exactly once among the sequence of formulae.
- Except for those indices of the solution array S, each index is summed over in a single formula.
- No index appears in any formulae subsequent to summation over that index.
- Each defined function $f_r[...]$, except the last one, appears exactly once among the formulae subsequent to its definition.

Hence, a valid sequence must contain exactly $n-1$ multiplication formulae and m summation formulae, where n is the number of arrays A_j*'s* and m is the number of summation indices in the function computed by the given program fragment.

The following algorithm can be used to exhaustively enumerate all valid formula sequences:

1. Form a set of the arrays A_j's. Call each array A_i a term. Set r to zero.
2. Increment r. Then, perform either action:
   a. Generate a formula $f_r[...] = X[...] \times Y[...]$ where $X[...]$ and $Y[...]$ are any two terms in the pool and the indices for f_r are $If_r = IX \cup IY$. Replace $X[...]$ and $Y[...]$ in the pool with $f_r[...]$.
   b. If there exists a summation index (say i) that appears in exactly one term (say $X[...]$) in the pool, create a formula $f_r[...] = \sum_i X[...]$, where $If_r = IX - \{i\}$. Replace $X[...]$ in the pool by $f_r[...]$.
3. Repeat step 2 until none of the two actions can be applied, at which time a valid formula sequence is obtained. To obtain all valid sequences, exhaust all alternatives in step 2 using depth-first search.

Two formula sequences are equivalent if they have isomorphic binary trees. The enumeration algorithm discussed above is inefficient in that many equivalent formula sequences are generated by the search process. This can be avoided by creating an ordering among the arrays A_j's and the intermediate generated functions (which can be treated as new terms, numbered in increasing order as they are generated). The modified search algorithm guarantees that the same formula sequence is not evaluated more than once.

1. Form a list of the arrays A_j's. Call each A_j as term T_j. Set r and c to zero. Set d to n, the number of arrays A_j.
2. Increment r and d. Then, perform either action:
   a. Generate a formula $f_r[...] = T_a[...] \times T_b[...]$ where $T_a[...]$ and $T_b[...]$ are two terms in the list such that $a<b$ and $b>c$. The set of indices for f_r are $If_r = IX \cup IY$. Remove $T_a[...]$ and $T_b[...]$ from the list. Append to the list $T_d[...] = f_r[...]$. Set c to b.
   b. If there exists an summation index (say i) that appears in exactly one term (say $T_a[...]$) in the list and $a>c$, create a formula $f_r[...] = \sum_i T_a[...]$ where $If_r = IT_a - \{i\}$. Remove $T_a[...]$ from the list. Append to the list $T_d[...] = f_r[...]$. Set c to a.
3. Repeat step 2 until none of the two actions can be applied, at which time a valid formula sequence is obtained. To obtain all valid sequences, exhaust all alternatives in step 2 using depth-first search.

A further reduction in the cost of the search procedure can be achieved by pruning the search space by use of the following two rules:

P1: If a summation index appears in only one term, perform the summation over that index immediately, without considering any other possibilities at that step.

P2: If two or more terms have exactly the same set of indices, first multiply them together before considering any other possibilities.

It is easy to prove that the use of the pruning rules will not change the cost of the optimal formula sequence found. The pruning rules (P1 and P2) are first applied until neither of them is applicable. This effectively reduces the number of indices (rule P1) and the number of terms (rule P2) of the optimization problem. The above search algorithm is then applied to the "reduced" problem.

We have not considered storage costs in our search for an optimal sequence of formulae. A naive implementation of a sequence of formulae would involve creating a multidimensional array for each formula $f_r[...]$ in the sequence. However, some formulae can be computed as needed without requiring temporary storage for their results. Implementing a given sequence of formulae using minimum space is itself an interesting problem but will not be discussed in this paper.

5 Minimization of Communication Cost on Parallel Computers

Given a sequence of formulae that has an optimal or near-optimal cost, we now address the problem of minimizing inter-processor communication cost in implementing the computation on a message-passing parallel computer. We consider the processors to form a logical one-dimensional chain. Given a sequence of formulae to be computed, we assume that parallelism is exploited only within the computation of each formula, i.e. all processors are computing the same formula at any given time. We also assume that each input array and intermediate array (representing the intermediate functions) is either block-distributed among the processors along one of its dimensions or replicated on all processors. To simplify the presentation of the communication cost analysis, we assume that the range N_h of every index h is divisible by n_p, the number of processors. Each array X is partitioned among the processors along its distribution index $i(X)$. It is preferable to have the distribution index of X be one of the dimensions or indices of X, that is, $i(X) \in IX$, where IX is the set of indices for X. Otherwise, we have $i(X) \notin IX$, implying that a copy of X has to be replicated on every processor. If all arrays have the same distribution index and $i(X) \in IX$ for all X, no data movement among the processors will be required during execution. This is achievable if and only if there exists an index that appears in the index set of every array. When this condition cannot be satisfied, we need to determine the combination of the distribution indices for the arrays that minimizes the communication overhead.

Two types of data movements, namely redistribution and replication, may be required and the amounts of data movement can be quantified as follows. Given an array distributed along one of its dimensions, redistribution is used when it is to be rearranged among the processors so that it is distributed along another of its dimensions. Let $s(X) = \prod_{h \in IX} N_h$ be the total size of array X, and $T_{redist}(s)$ be the communication time needed to redistribute an array of size s by all-to-all personalized communication (also called total exchange), in which the size of each message is s/n_p^2. For most processor topologies, $T_{redist}(s)$ can be expressed as $C_s(n_p)t_s + C_w(n_p)st_w$ [5], where C_s and C_w are topology-dependent functions of n_p, t_s is the start-up time for a message, and t_w is the per-word transfer time. The second type of data movement is replication and is used when every processor needs a copy of the whole array. Let $T_{replicate}(s)$ be the communication time needed to replicate an array of size s by all-to-all broadcast, in which the size of each message is s/n_p. For most processor topologies, $T_{replicate}(s)$ can be expressed as $C_s'(n_p)t_s + C_w'(n_p)st_w$ [5], where C_s' and C_w' are again topology-dependent functions of n_p. For a given parallel computer with a fixed number of processors, C_s, C_w, C_s', C_w', t_s and t_w become constants. Also note that $T_{redist}(s(X))$ and $T_{replicate}(s(X))$ are independent of its distribution indices before and after the redistribution or replication.

We analyze the data movement associated with a multiplication formula and a summation formula. For a multiplication formula of the form $f_r[...] = X[...] \times Y[...]$, the amount of data movement depends on whether the distribution indices of f_r, X and Y are the same and whether we want to replicate f_r on all processors. To perform the multiplication, arrays X and Y must be first distributed along the same index, i.e. $i(X) = i(Y)$. If the desired distribution index of f_r is the same as that of the source arrays (i.e. $i(X) = i(f_r)$), no data movement is required. Otherwise, f_r can be redistributed along $i(f_r)$ after the multiplication by all-to-all personalized communication. This costs $T_{redist}(s(f_r))$, provided that $i(f_r) \in If_r$. When f_r needs to be replicated (i.e. $i(f_r) \notin If_r$), the communication cost will be $T_{replicate}(s(f_r))$.

For a summation formula of the form $f_r[...] = \sum_i X[...]$, the amount of data movement depends on whether the summation index i and the distribution indices $i(f_r)$ and $i(X)$ are the same. We would not want to distribute f_r along i since i will never appear as an index in f_r or its ancestor nodes in the binary tree representation. If f_r and X share the same distribution index, then the summation can be done without moving any data between processors. Otherwise, we have two cases. In the case where $i \neq i(X)$, we can perform summation and then redistribute the result along $i(f_r)$, which costs $T_{redist}(s(f_r))$. In the other case where $i = i(X)$, partial sums can be formed on individual processors, and then redistributed and added up to obtain the final sums. The communication cost in this case would be $T_{redist}(n_p s(f_r))$. In any case, if f_r needs to be replicated (i.e. $i(f_r) \notin If_r$), the T_{redist} term would become $T_{replicate}$.

Based on the above analysis, we can use dynamic programming to find the optimal distribution of the arrays in a bottom-up fashion:

1. Transform the given sequence of formulae into a binary tree (see Section 2).
2. Let $T(X, j)$ be the minimal total communication cost for the subtree rooted at X where X is distributed along index j. Initialize $T(X, j)$ for each leaf node X of the binary tree and each index j in the index set of X and its parent as follows:

$$T(X,j) = \begin{cases} 0 & ,j \in IX \\ T_{replicate}(s(X)) & ,j \notin IX \end{cases}$$

3. Perform a post-order traversal of the binary tree. For each internal node f_r and each index j in the index sets of f_r and its parent (or for each $j \in If_r$ if f_r is the root of the tree), calculate $T(f_r, j)$ as follows:

   Case (a): f_r is a multiplication node with two children X and Y. If $j \in If_r$, we can either have both X and Y distributed along j in which case f_r can be formed with no extra data movement, or have them distributed along another index, perform the multiplication, and redistribute the product along j. Otherwise, if $j \notin If_r$, we could distribute X and Y along any index and replicate the product on all processors. Thus,

$$T(f_r,j) = \begin{cases} min\{T(X,j) + T(Y,j), T_m + T_{redist}(s(f_r))\} & ,j \in If_r \\ T_m + T_{replicate}(s(f_r)) & ,j \notin If_r \end{cases}$$

where
$$T_m = \min_{k \in If_r} \{T(X,k) + T(Y,k)\}$$

   Case (b): f_r is a summation node over index i and with a child X. If $j \in If_r$, we have three choices. We can distribute X along j and form f_r with no extra data movement, or distribute X along i and redistribute the partial sums of f_r, or distribute X along another index and redistribute f_r along j. If $j \notin If_r$, we either distribute X along i and replicate the partial sums of f_r, or distribute X along another index and replicate f_r on all processors. Thus:

$$T(f_r,j) = \begin{cases} min\{T(X,j), T_s + T_{redist}(s(f_r)), T(X,i) + T_{redist}(n_p s(f_r))\} & ,j \in If_r \\ min\{T_s + T_{replicate}(s(f_r)), T(X,i) + T_{replicate}(n_p s(f_r))\} & ,j \notin If_r \end{cases}$$

where
$$T_s = \min_{k \in If_r} \{T(X,k)\}$$

   Note that T_m and T_s are independent of j and can be computed before $T(f_r, j)$ is evaluated for each j. Save the index k, i or j that minimize $T(f_r, j)$ into $Link(f_r, j)$.

4. When step 3 finishes for all nodes and all indices, the minimal total cost for the whole tree is $\min_{j \in IR} \{T(R, j)\}$, where R is the root of the binary tree. The index j that minimizes the total cost is the optimal distribution index for R. The optimal distribution indices for other nodes can be obtained by tracing back $Link(f_r, j)$ in a top-down manner, starting from $Link(R, j)$.

The running time complexity of this algorithm is $O(n_n n_i)$, where n_n is the number of internal nodes in the binary tree, and $n_i = \left|\bigcup_X IX\right|$ is the number of different indices in all the formulae. The storage requirement for $T(f_r, j)$ and $Link(f_r, j)$ is also $O(n_n\, n_i)$.

6 Discussion and Conclusions

In this paper, we have addressed a compile-time optimization problem that arises in the context of some computational physics applications. The computation essentially involves a multi-dimensional summation of a product of a number of array terms. Besides the typical parallel computing considerations of mapping of the data and computations, the judicious restructuring of the computations through use of algebraic properties is required in order to reduce the total number of operations. A pruning search strategy to determine the optimal restructuring of the computations has been provided. The optimal mapping of the data arrays to minimize inter-processor communication has also been addressed.

Further work on this problem is planned along several directions:

1. Generalization of the class of nested-loop computations handled, e.g. allowing inner loop bounds to be affine functions of outer loop bounds, and relaxing the current restrictions on the form of the array access functions.
2. Minimization of the amount of temporary storage required: A straightforward implementation of a sequence of formulae will require temporary intermediate arrays corresponding to each intermediate function used. The amount of storage needed can be reduced by application of further optimizations involving loop fusion.
3. Development of a system that implements the developed algorithms, and generates High Performance Fortran (HPF) code with data distribution directives from an unoptimized input nested loop of the form considered.

Acknowledgement

We thank the anonymous referee for pointing out an error in Section 5 of the submitted paper. A re-examination of the analysis has now resulted in a more efficient algorithm.

References

[1] C. N. Fischer and R. J. Leblanc Jr. *Crafting a Compiler.* Menlo Park, CA: Benjamin/Cummings, 1991.

[2] Michael R. Garey and David S. Johnson. *Computers and Intractability: A Guide to the Theory of NP-Completeness.* New York: W. H. Freeman, 1979.

[3] Ken Kennedy and Kathryn S. McKinley. Maximizing Loop Parallelism and Improving Data Locality via Loop Fusion and Distribution. *In Languages and Compilers for Parallel Computing,* August 1993, 301-320.

[4] Ken Kennedy and Kathryn S. McKinley. Optimizing for Parallelism and Data Locality. In *Proceedings of the 1992 ACM International Conference on Supercomputing,* July 1992, 323-334.

[5] V. Kumar, A. Grama, A. Gupta, and G. Karypis. *Introduction to Parallel Computing: Design and Analysis of Algorithms.* RedWood City, CA: Benjamin/Cummings, 1994.

[6] C. C. Lu and W. C. Chew. Fast Algorithm for Solving Hybrid Integral Equations. In *IEE Proceedings-H,* 140(6): 455-460, December 1993.

[7] Edmund K. Miller. Solving Bigger Problems- By Decreasing the Operation Count and Increasing the Computation Bandwidth. In *Proceedings of the IEEE,* 79(10):1493-1504, October 1991.

[8] M. Potkonjak, M. B. Srivastava, and A. P. Chandrakasan. Multiple Constant Multiplications: Efficient and Versatile Framework and Algorithms for Exploring Common Subexpression Elimination. *IEEE Transactions on Computer-aided Design of Integrated Circuits and Systems,* 15(2): 151-164, February 1996.

[9] S. Winograd. *Arithmetic complexity of computations.* Philadelphia: Society for Industrial and Applied Mathematics, 1980.

[10] M. Wolfe. *High Performance Compilers for Parallel Computing.* Addison Wesley, 1996.

[11] Michael E. Wolf and Monica S. Lam. A Data Locality Algorithm. In *Proceedings of the SIGPLAN '91 Conference on Programming Language Design and Implementation,* June 1991, 30-44.

Communication-Minimal Tiling of Uniform Dependence Loops

Jingling Xue*

Department of Mathematics, Statistics and Computing Science
University of New England, Armidale 2351, Australia

Abstract. Tiling is a loop transformation that the compiler uses to create automatically blocked algorithms in order to improve the benefits of the memory hierarchy and reduce the communication overhead between processors. Motivated by existing results, this paper presents a conceptually simple approach to finding tilings with a minimal amount of communication between tiles. The development of all results is based primarily on the inequality of arithmetic and geometric means, except for Lemma 8 whose proof relies on the concept of extremal rays of convex cones. The key insight is that a tiling that is communication-minimal must induce the same amount of communication through all faces of a tile, which restricts the search space for optimal tilings to those tiling matrices whose rows are all extremal rays in a cone. For nested loops with several special forms of dependences, closed-form optimal tilings are derived. In the general case, a procedure is given that always returns optimal tilings. A detailed comparison of this work with some existing results is provided.

1 Introduction

Prior studies have shown that blocked algorithms can improve the performance of parallel computers with a memory hierarchy [5, 6]. A block is a subarray of data and usually exhibits a high degree of data reuse, allowing better register, cache and memory hierarchy performance.

Tiling is a loop transformation that the compiler uses to automatically create blocked algorithms [7, 17]. Tiling divides the iteration space into blocks or *tiles* of the same size and shape and traverses the tiles to cover the entire iteration space. To improve cache locality of a loop nest, the compiler can find tiles so that a tile is small enough for cache to capture the available temporal reuse, improving the benefits of the memory hierarchy [3, 9, 13, 18],

Tiling is also a good paradigm for parallel computers with distributed memory. In these multicomputers, the relatively high communication startup cost makes frequent communication very expensive. Tiling can be used to reduce the communication overhead between processors [2, 10, 11, 12]; loop iterations are grouped into tiles, and communication takes place per each tile instead of per each iteration, so that communication overhead is reduced.

This paper is restricted to perfectly nested loops with constant dependences, known as *uniform dependence algorithms*. They have the characteristic that data dependences between their computations can be represented by a finite set of integer vectors, known as *dependence* or *distance vectors*. The *iteration space* of a loop nest is a discrete bounded Cartesian space defined by the loop limits of the program. For the purposes of this paper, knowing the dependence information in a program suffices. So an n-deep

* Supported by an Australian Research Council Grant A49600987.

loop nest is identified by a *dependence matrix* $D = [d_1, \cdots, d_m] \in \mathbb{Z}^{n\times m}$ whose columns are all m dependences vectors in the program. For a sequential program, all dependence vectors are lexicographically positive.

We assume that $D \in \mathbb{Z}^{n\times m}$ has full row rank, implying that $m \geqslant n$. Otherwise, we can always transform an n-deep loop nest into an $(n+\rho)$-deep loop nest consisting of n outer doall loops and ρ inner sequential loops, where ρ is the row rank of D [1]. The inner ρ loops, having a dependence matrix with full row rank, can be tiled in the normal manner.

Example 1. In the following uniform dependence algorithm:

```
do i = 0, N
   do j = 0, N
      A(i, j) = A(i − 1, j) + A(i − 1, j − 1)
```

The iteration space is a parallelogram: $\{(i,j) \mid 0 \leqslant i, j \leqslant N\}$. The dependence matrix is:

$$D = \begin{bmatrix} 1 & 1 \\ 0 & 1 \end{bmatrix}$$

A recent paper described an inspiring approach to finding tilings that minimise the communication volume of a tile when the computation volume or size of a tile is fixed [2]. That approach finds optimal tilings by first determining a tile's shape and then scaling all its sides by the same constant factor to obtain a tile of an appropriate size. The major results of that work were summarised in [2, Lemma 9 and Theorem 10], which are technically involved and do not seem to lead to an intuitive geometric interpretation.

This paper recasts and extends that work and provides new insights into the problem of finding communication-minimal tilings. Using a different formulation for finding optimal tilings, we are able to develop all results in the paper in a conceptually simpler framework, based on the inequality of arithmetic and geometric means and the concept of extremal rays of convex cones. That inequality is the basis for establishing Theorem 2 and Lemma 6 in the paper, the keystones on which all other results rest. One important new result is that a tiling that is communication-minimal must induce the same amount of communication (not the same surface area as in [13]) on all faces of a tile. This is the deep reason why the search space for optimal tilings can be restricted to a finite set of matrices whose rows are all extremal rays in a cone. By dividing programs into individual cases in terms of their dependence structures, we find optimal tilings progressively so that each case is solved based on the preceding one. For programs with several special forms of data dependences, closed-form optimal tilings are given. For programs in the general case, a procedure is given that always returns optimal tilings. Frequently, the simplest interpretation of an algebraic result is in terms of a geometric setting. Where appropriate, some geometric insights behind optimal tilings are explained.

The plan of the paper is as follows. Section 2 introduces the terminology and notations used in the paper. Section 3 discusses quickly tiling as a loop transformation. Section 4 characterises the computation and communication volumes of a tile. In Section 5, the problem of finding communication-minimal tilings is formulated as a combinatorial problem. Several concepts from higher mathematics and convex cones are introduced. We derive optimal tilings by distinguishing programs according to their data dependence structures. We first present closed-form optimal tilings for programs with several special forms of data dependences. We then discuss the general case when D is an arbitrary full row matrix. Section 6 contains a procedure for finding optimal tilings. Based on the framework developed in this paper, Section 7 compares and contrasts this work with the related work. Section 8 concludes the paper by describing some future work.

2 Notation and Terminology

$\mathbb{Z}$ and $\mathbb{Q}$ denote the set of integers and rationals, respectively. All relational operators on two vectors are component-wise. The symbol $\mathcal{I}$ denotes the identity matrix. The notation diag$(a_1, \cdots, a_n)$ denotes the square diagonal matrix with numbers $a_1, \ldots, a_n$ on its main diagonal. The transpose of a matrix A is denoted by A^T. If x and y are two vectors, $x \cdot y$ (or xy) and $x \times y$ denote the dot product and vector product of the two vectors, respectively. We use $\| \cdot \|$ for the *Euclidean norm*, i.e., $\| x \| = \sqrt{x^T x}$. If $b_1, \cdots, b_n$ are column vectors, and B is the square matrix with columns $b_1, \cdots, b_n$, then we have the *Hadamard inequality*: $|\det(B)| \leqslant \| b_1 \| \times \cdots \times \| b_n \|$ where the sign of equality holds if and only if $b_1, \cdots, b_n$ are mutually orthogonal. We write $\lceil x \rceil$ for the *ceiling* of x and $\lfloor x \rfloor$ for the *floor* of x. If x is an element of a set S, the notation $x \in S$ is used, and this notation is abused to indicate that a column vector x is a column of a matrix M, i.e., $x \in M$.

3 Iteration Space Tiling

This section discusses tiling as a loop transformation introduced in [7, 18, 19]. Tiling decomposes an n-dimensional loop nest into a $2n$-dimensional loop nest where the outer n *tile loops* step between tiles and the inner n *element loops* step the points within a tile. Figure 1(a) shows a 2×2 parallelogram tiling of the double loop in Example 1, where the tiled program is as follows:

```
do ii = 0, N, 2
   do jj = 0, N, 2
      do i = ii, min(ii + 1, N)
         do j = jj, min(jj + 1, N)
            A(i, j) = A(i - 1, j) + A(i - 1, j - 1)
```

Geometrically, tiling divides an n-dimensional iteration space into n-dimensional parallelepiped tiles of the same size and shape. Since all tiles are identical by translation, a tiling transformation can be defined either by the normal vectors to its n faces or by the edge vectors of its n edges emitting from the tile origin. Let H be the *tiling matrix* whose rows are the normal vectors of the n faces of a tile, and P be the *clustering matrix* whose columns are the n edge vectors of a tile. Figure 1(b) shows the H and P for the parallelogram tiling shown in Figure 1(a).

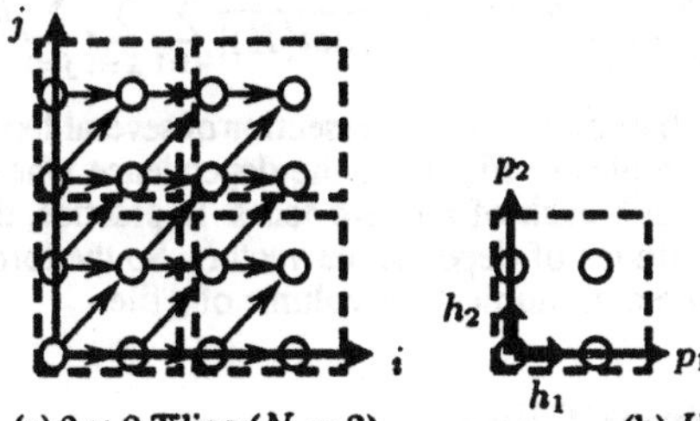

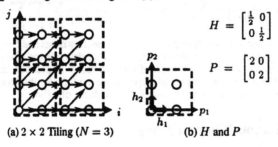

$$H = \begin{bmatrix} \frac{1}{2} & 0 \\ 0 & \frac{1}{2} \end{bmatrix} \qquad P = \begin{bmatrix} 2 & 0 \\ 0 & 2 \end{bmatrix}$$

(a) 2×2 Tiling ($N = 3$) (b) H and P

Figure 1. A parallelogram tiling of the double loop in Example 1.

A tiling transformation is defined as a one-to-one mapping from $\mathbb{Z}^n$ to $\mathbb{Z}^{2n}$ [20]:

$$I \longmapsto \begin{bmatrix} \lfloor HI \rfloor \\ I - H^{-1} \lfloor HI \rfloor \end{bmatrix}, \quad \text{where } 0 \leqslant HI - \lfloor HI \rfloor < 1$$

H is non-singular so that a tile has a bounded number of points. $P = H^{-1}$ must be integral so that all tiles contain the same number of integer points (identical by translation in $\mathbb{Z}^n$). H must also satisfy a so-called *atomic tile constraint*. Each tile is an atomic unit of work to be scheduled on a processor. Once a tile is scheduled, it runs to completion without preemption. A tile is executed only if all dependence constraints for that tile have been satisfied, implying that there must not exist any cyclic dependences on the outer n tile loops. In [7], $HD \geqslant 0$ was given as a sufficient condition for enforcing the atomic tile constraint; it also preserves the dependences of the original program [20].

4 Computation and Communication Volumes

This section discusses how to calculate the computation volume and communication volume induced by a tile, providing the basis for formulating the problem of finding communication-minimal tilings in the following section.

The number of integer points or iterations contained in a tile is called its *computation volume*. If $P = H^{-1}$ is integral, the computation volume of a tile is given by:

$$\mathcal{V}_{\text{comp}}(H) = \frac{1}{|\det(H)|} = |\det(P)|$$

The communication volume of a tile is defined as the number of dependences going into (or equivalently, leaving from) the tile; it represents the amount of data that must be communicated before a tile can be initiated in a processor. In [2, 13], the communication volume is approximated as follows (Figure 2). If d is a dependence vector, the amount of incoming messages induced by d through the face h_1 or $p_2\times\cdots\times p_n$ is equal to exactly the number of dependence sinks in the tile such that the corresponding dependence sources along d are outside the tile. (Note that some sinks are not on the surface of h_1, as Figure 2 illustrates.) This can be approximated as the number of incoming dependences d crossing the face h_1, which is equal to the volume of the parallelepiped subtended by $d, p_2, \cdots, p_n$, i.e.,

$$|\det([d, p_2, \cdots, p_n])| = |d \cdot (p_2 \times \cdots \times p_n)| = |\det(P)(h_1 \cdot d)| = \tfrac{1}{|\det(H)|} h_1 \cdot d$$

Here, we assume that $h_1 \cdot d \geqslant 0$ because we will impose $HD \geqslant 0$ later on. Hence, the communication volume induced by all dependence vectors through the face h_1 is $\frac{1}{|\det(H)|}\sum_{j=1}^{m} h_1 \cdot d_j$. Finally, the communication volume for a tile is:

$$\mathcal{V}_{\text{comm}}(H) = \frac{1}{|\det(H)|}\sum_{i=1}^{n}\sum_{j=1}^{m} h_i \cdot d_j = \frac{1}{|\det(H)|}\sum_{i=1}^{n}\sum_{k=1}^{n}\sum_{j=1}^{m} h_{i,k} d_{k,j} \quad (1)$$

As a final remark, a dependence that touches the intersection of several faces contributes multiple times in (1). As an example, in Figure 2, the dependence whose sink is the origin is counted twice, once trough each of the two faces. In practice, the tile size is sufficiently larger than the magnitudes of dependence vectors. So the formula given in (1) is a good approximation of the communication volume of a tile.

5 Communication-Minimal Tilings

Given the computation volume of a tile as a design parameter ν, this section finds tilings that yield the smallest communication volume for a tile. Formally, we provide optimal solutions to the following optimisation problem:

$$\begin{aligned} \textbf{Minimise } \mathcal{V}_{\text{comm}}(H) &= \tfrac{1}{|\det(H)|}\textstyle\sum_{i=1}^{n}\sum_{j=1}^{m}(HD)_{i,j} \\ \textbf{Subject to } \mathcal{V}_{\text{comp}}(H) &= \tfrac{1}{|\det(H)|} = \nu \\ HD &\geqslant 0 \end{aligned}$$

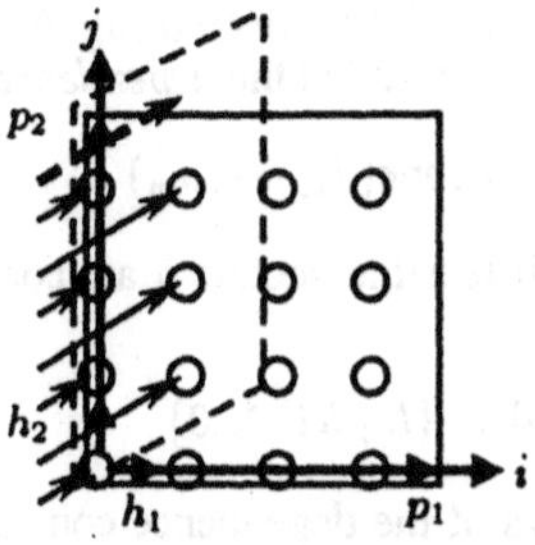

$$d = (2, 1)$$

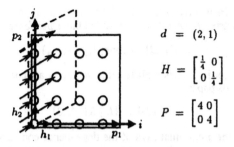

$$H = \begin{bmatrix} \frac{1}{4} & 0 \\ 0 & \frac{1}{4} \end{bmatrix}$$

$$P = \begin{bmatrix} 4 & 0 \\ 0 & 4 \end{bmatrix}$$

Figure2. Approximation of the amount of communication induced by d through the face h_1. The solid box depicts the tile at the origin. The dashed box depicts the parallelogram subtended by d and p_2, whose volume is det$([d, p_2])$=8, which measures the 8 dependences d crossing the face h_1, of which the one in the dashed arrow has its sink outside the tile.

Here, $HD \geqslant 0$ enforces the atomic tile constraint, and the problem formulation itself implies that H is non-singular. Section 6 discusses how to ensure that H^{-1} is integral.

It is clear that we can simplify (2) by making the objective function linear:

$$\begin{array}{ll} \textbf{Minimise } \mathcal{F}(H) = \sum_{i=1}^{n} \sum_{j=1}^{m} (HD)_{i,j} \\ \textbf{Subject to } \frac{1}{|\det(H)|} = \nu \\ \qquad\quad HD \geqslant 0 \end{array} \tag{2}$$

The optimal solutions to both formulations satisfy $\mathcal{V}_{\text{comm}}(H) = \frac{\mathcal{F}(H)}{|\det(H)|}$.

Note that an optimal tiling will be parameterised by the computation volume ν, and therefore represents a family of optimal solutions for different computation volumes.

At the first glance, the problem of finding optimal tilings is a difficult combinatorial problem. In this section, we show to solve this problem based primarily on the inequality of arithmetic and geometric means. In fact, this inequality is the basis for establishing Theorem 2 and Lemma 6, the key results on which all the others rest.

Lemma 1. (The Inequality of the Arithmetic and Geometric Means) *For any non-negative numbers $x_1, \cdots, x_n$, we have*

$$(x_1 \times \cdots \times x_n)^{\frac{1}{n}} \leqslant \frac{x_1 + \cdots + x_n}{n}$$

The sign of equality holds if and only if $x_1 = \cdots = x_n$.

We shall also make use of several basic concepts from convex cones [14, p. 87]. A nonempty set C in Euclidean space is called a *convex cone* if $\lambda x + \mu y \in C$ whenever $x, y \in C$ and $\lambda, \mu \geqslant 0$. A cone that is *finitely generated* by the vectors $x_1, \cdots, x_m$ is the set:

$$\text{cone}(x_1, \cdots, x_m) = \{\lambda_1 x_1 + \cdots + \lambda_m x_m \mid \lambda_1, \cdots, \lambda_m \geqslant 0\}$$

A cone that is *polyhedral* is the intersection of finitely many linear half spaces:

$$\{x \mid Ax \geqslant 0\}$$

for some matrix A. A convex cone is polyhedral if and only if it is finitely generated. Therefore, a convex cone can be represented in two different forms.

Since all dependence vectors are lexicographically positive, the dependence cone is a pointed cone with the origin as its apex. Informally, the *extremal rays* in a pointed cone are just the edges of the cone.

Two cones are frequently used in the literature on tiling. All dependence vectors in the dependence matrix D generate a cone called the *dependence cone* [21]:

$$\mathcal{C}_d(D) = \text{cone}(d_1, \cdots, d_m)$$

Let h be a row vector in H. Then all feasible vectors h are contained in a cone called the *tiling cone* in this paper:

$$\mathcal{C}_t(D) = \{h \mid hD \geqslant 0\}$$

Let $d'_1, \cdots, d'_q$ be the q extremal rays of the dependence cone and $D' = [d'_1, \cdots, d'_q]$. Let $r_1, \cdots, r_p$ be the p extremal rays of the tiling cone and $T = [r_1, \cdots, r_p]$. These two cones are related to each other in the following way:

$$\begin{array}{lclcl} \mathcal{C}_d(D) = \text{cone}(d_1, \cdots, d_m) & = & \text{cone}(d'_1, \cdots, d'_q) & = & \{h \mid \vartheta T \geqslant 0\} \\ \mathcal{C}_t(D) = \{h \mid hD \geqslant 0\} & = & \{h \mid hD' \geqslant 0\} & = & \text{cone}(r_1, \cdots, r_p) \end{array} \tag{3}$$

Techniques for constructing the extremal rays of the tiling cone from the faces of the dependence cone were described in [2, 13]. For every set of $n-1$ linearly independent dependence vectors $x_1, \cdots, x_{n-1}$ in D, compute the normal to the hyperplane spanned by these $n-1$ vectors. One solution is $r = x_1 \times \cdots \times x_{n-1}$. If $rd \geqslant 0$ for all $d \in D$, then r is an extremal ray; or if $rd \leqslant 0$ for all $d \in D$, then $-r$ is an extremal ray; otherwise $x_1 \times \cdots \times x_{n-1}$ does not define a face for the dependence cone.

Example 2. Consider the dependence matrix:

$$D = [d_1, d_2] = \begin{bmatrix} 2 & 0 \\ 1 & 1 \end{bmatrix}$$

The tiling cone has two extremal rays $r_1 = (1, 0)$ and $r_2 = (-1, 2)$. Figure 3 depicts both the dependence cone and the tiling cone defined as follows:

$$\mathcal{C}_d(D) = \text{cone}\left(\begin{bmatrix} 2 \\ 1 \end{bmatrix}, \begin{bmatrix} 0 \\ 1 \end{bmatrix}\right) = \left\{\begin{bmatrix} \vartheta_1 \\ \vartheta_2 \end{bmatrix} \middle| \vartheta_1 \geqslant 0, -\vartheta_1 + 2\vartheta_2 \geqslant 0\right\}$$

$$\mathcal{C}_t(D) = \left\{\begin{bmatrix} h_1 \\ h_2 \end{bmatrix} \middle| 2h_1 + h_2 \geqslant 0, h_2 \geqslant 0\right\} = \text{cone}\left(\begin{bmatrix} 1 \\ 0 \end{bmatrix}, \begin{bmatrix} -1 \\ 2 \end{bmatrix}\right)$$

Note that r_1 and r_2 are the normals to the two faces of the dependence cone.

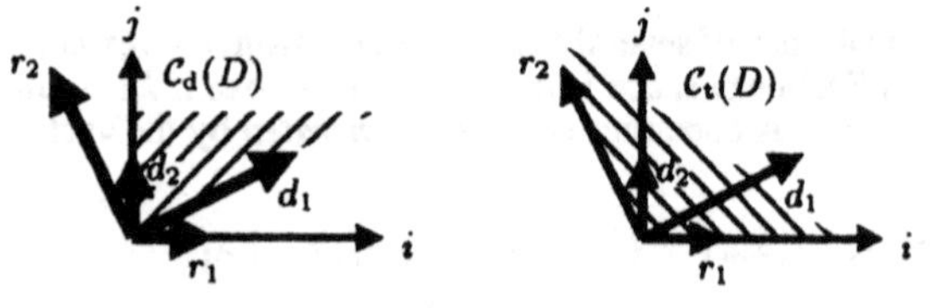

Figure3. Dependence and tiling cones for Example 2.

In the rest of this section, we focus on finding optimal solutions to (2). We distinguish programs in terms of their dependence structures. We first describe closed-form optimal tilings for programs with several special forms of dependence matrices. We then address the problem of finding optimal tilings in the general case.

5.1 D Is the Identity Matrix ($D = \mathcal{I}$)

If D is the identity matrix, the optimisation problem (2) becomes:

$$\begin{array}{l} \textbf{Minimise } \mathcal{F}(H) = \sum_{i=1}^{n} \sum_{j=1}^{m} h_{i,j} \\ \textbf{Subject to } \frac{1}{|\det(H)|} = \nu \\ H \geqslant 0 \end{array}$$

The optimal solution is found analytically based on the inequality of arithmetic and geometric means. The solution to this simpliest case provides the foundation for finding optimal solutions in three other special cases discussed shortly.

Theorem 2. *If D is the identity matrix, the optimal tiling is:*

$$H = \text{diag}\left(\sqrt[n]{\frac{1}{\nu}}, \cdots, \sqrt[n]{\frac{1}{\nu}}\right) \tag{4}$$

which has the smallest communication volume $\mathcal{V}_{\text{comm}}(H) = n\nu\sqrt[n]{\frac{1}{\nu}}$.

Proof. This is a good example to use Dijkstra's proof style [4].

$$\begin{array}{l} (\frac{1}{\nu})^{\frac{1}{n}} \\ = \{ \text{ Constraint } \frac{1}{|\det(H)|} = \nu \ \} \\ |\det(H)|^{\frac{1}{n}} \\ \leqslant \{ \text{ The Hadamard inequality } \} \\ (\| h_1 \| \times \cdots \times \| h_n \|)^{\frac{1}{n}} \\ = \{ \text{ Definition of the Euclidean norm; } H \geqslant 0 \} \\ \left(\sqrt{h_{1,1}^2 + \cdots + h_{1,n}^2} \times \cdots \times \sqrt{h_{n,1}^2 + \cdots + h_{n,n}^2}\right)^{\frac{1}{n}} \\ \leqslant \{ \text{For nonnegative integers } x_1, \cdots, x_n, \sqrt{x_1^2 + \cdots + x_n^2} \leqslant (x_1 + \cdots + x_n) \ \} \\ ((h_{1,1} + \cdots + h_{1,n}) \times \cdots \times (h_{n,1} + \cdots + h_{n,n}))^{\frac{1}{n}} \\ \leqslant \{ \text{ Lemma 1 } \} \\ \frac{(h_{1,1}+\cdots+h_{1,n})+\cdots+(h_{n,1}+\cdots+h_{n,n})}{n} \\ = \{ \sum \} \\ \frac{\sum_{i=1}^{n} \sum_{j=1}^{m} h_{i,j}}{n} \\ = \{ \mathcal{F} \} \\ \frac{\mathcal{F}(H)}{n} \end{array}$$

In the Hadamard inequality, the sign of equality holds if and only if $h_1, \cdots, h_n$ are an orthogonal basis. Since $H \geqslant 0$, the rows of H are mutually orthogonal if and only if H is a diagonal matrix (up to row permutations):

$$H = \text{diag}(h_{1,1}, \cdots, h_{n,n})$$

If H is diagonal, the second "$\leqslant$" in the above proof steps can be replaced with "=". So,

$$(\frac{1}{\nu})^{\frac{1}{n}} = |\det(H)|^{\frac{1}{n}} = (h_{1,1} \times \cdots \times h_{n,n})^{\frac{1}{n}} \leqslant \frac{h_{1,1} + \cdots + h_{n,n}}{n} = \frac{\mathcal{F}(H)}{n}$$

By Lemma 1, the sign of equality holds if and only if $h_{1,1} = \cdots = h_{n,n} = \sqrt[n]{\frac{1}{\nu}}$. This means that (4) is the optimal solution. Thus, the tiling given in (4) is optimal and it has the minimal communication volume $\mathcal{V}_{\text{comm}}(H) = n\nu \sqrt[n]{\frac{1}{\nu}}$. ■

In this special case, both the dependence cone $\mathcal{C}_{\text{d}}(D)$ and the tiling cone $\mathcal{C}_{\text{t}}(D)$ are the first orthant in the Euclidean space, a special form of a pointed cone. Note that $P = H^{-1} = \text{diag}(\sqrt[n]{\nu}, \cdots, \sqrt[n]{\nu})$. In the optimal tiling, the iteration space is tiled with rectangles of size $\sqrt[n]{\nu} \times \cdots \times \sqrt[n]{\nu}$ with the edges of a tile parallel to the natural axes, i.e., the edges of the first orthant cone. This is illustrated in Figure 4 for a two-dimensional iteration space.

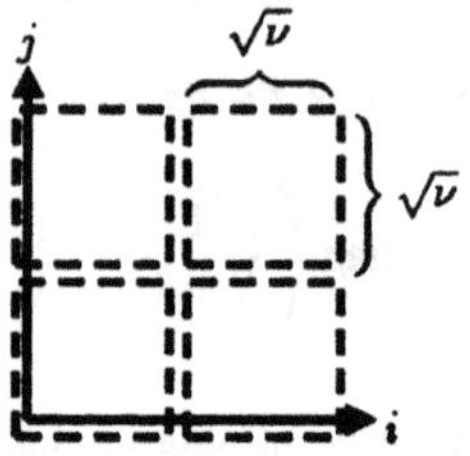

Figure4. Optimal tiling when $D \in \mathbb{Z}^{n\times n}$ is the identity matrix ($n = 2$).

5.2 D Is a Full Rank Square Matrix ($D \in \mathbb{Z}^{n\times n}$)

Theorem 3. *If D is a full rank square matrix, the optimal tiling is:*

$$H = \sqrt[n]{\frac{|\det(D)|}{\nu}}\, D^{-1} \tag{5}$$

which has the smallest communication volume $\mathcal{V}_{\text{comm}}(H) = n\nu \sqrt[n]{\frac{|\det(D)|}{\nu}}$.

Proof. If D is a full rank square matrix, so is HD. If we let $HD = H'$, which implies $\det(H)\det(D) = \det(H')$, the optimisation problem (2) is reduced to:

$$\begin{array}{ll} \textbf{Minimise} & \mathcal{F}(H') = \sum_{i=1}^{n}\sum_{j=1}^{m} h'_{i,j} \\ \textbf{Subject to} & \frac{1}{|\det(H')|} = \frac{\nu}{|\det(D)|} \\ & H' \geqslant 0 \end{array}$$

We are back to the case we solved before when the dependence matrix D is the identity matrix. By Theorem 2, the optimal solution to this problem is:

$$H' = \text{diag}\left(\sqrt[n]{\frac{|\det(D)|}{\nu}}, \cdots, \sqrt[n]{\frac{|\det(D)|}{\nu}}\right)$$

Since $HD = H'$, we conclude that the tiling given in (5) is the optimal solution to (2) and attains the smallest communication volume $\mathcal{V}_{\text{comm}}(H) = n\nu \sqrt[n]{\frac{|\det(D)|}{\nu}}$. ■

In this special case, we have

$$P = H^{-1} = \sqrt[n]{\frac{\nu}{|\det(D)|}}\, D$$

Refer to Figure 3. The dependence cone has n faces with the columns of D as its n edges. Also, the tiling cone has n faces with the rows of D^{-1} as its n edges. In the optimal tiling, the iteration space is tiled with parallelepipeds of size $\sqrt[n]{\frac{\nu}{|\det(D)|}}\, d_1 \times \cdots \times \sqrt[n]{\frac{\nu}{|\det(D)|}}\, d_n$ with its edges parallel to the columns of D. Figure 5(a) illustrates the optimal tiling for a two-dimensional iteration space by depicting the shape and size of the tile at the origin.

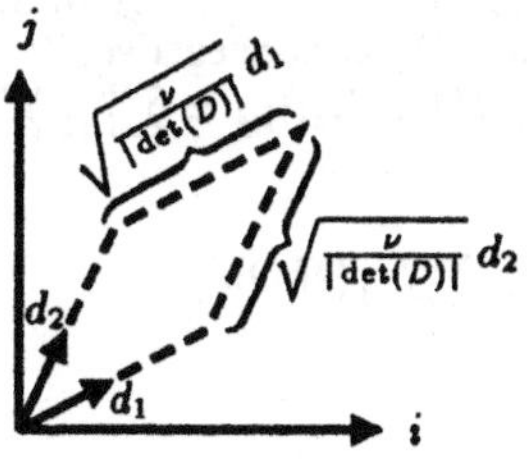

(a) For $D = [d_1, d_2]$

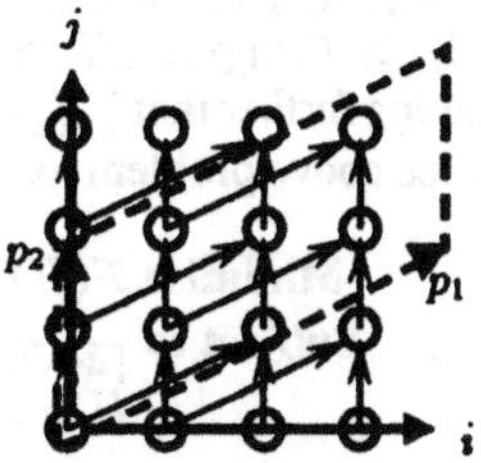

(b) For Example 3

Figure5. Optimal tiling when $D \in \mathbb{Z}^{n\times n}$ is a full rank square matrix ($n = 2$).

Example 3. By Theorem 3, the optimal tiling for Example 2 is:

$$H = \sqrt{\frac{2}{\nu}} \begin{bmatrix} \frac{1}{2} & 0 \\ -\frac{1}{2} & 1 \end{bmatrix} \qquad P = \sqrt{\frac{\nu}{2}} \begin{bmatrix} 2 & 0 \\ 1 & 1 \end{bmatrix}$$

This is illustrated in Figure 5(b) when $\nu = 8$.

5.3 D Contains an $n \times n$ Diagonal Submatrix

This section considers the case when D is nonnegative and contains an $n \times n$ diagonal submatrix. Without loss of generality, we assume that D has the form $D = [D_r, D_o]$ such that $D_r \in \mathbb{Z}^{n\times n}$ is diagonal. Let

$$\bar{D} = \text{diag}(\sum_{j=1}^{m} d_{1,j}, \cdots, \sum_{j=1}^{m} d_{n,j})$$

That is, $\bar{D}$ is the diagonal matrix whose i-th diagonal element is the sum of the i-th row of D. Note that $\bar{D} > 0$ since $D_r > 0$.

Theorem 4. *If $D = [D_r, D_o]$ as defined above, the optimal tiling is:*

$$H = \sqrt[n]{\frac{\det(\bar{D})}{\nu}}\,\bar{D}^{-1} \tag{6}$$

which has the smallest communication volume $V_{\mathrm{comm}}(H) = n\nu\sqrt[n]{\frac{\det(\bar{D})}{\nu}}$.

Proof. When $D = [D_r, D_o]$, the optimisation problem (2) can be rewritten as follows:

$$\begin{array}{ll} \textbf{Minimise} & \mathcal{F}(H) = \sum_{i=1}^{n}\sum_{j=1}^{m}(H[D_r, D_o])_{i,j} \\ \textbf{Subject to} & \frac{1}{|\det(H)|} = \nu \\ & H[D_r, D_o] \geqslant 0 \end{array}$$

$H[D_r, D_o] \geqslant 0$ can be decomposed into $HD_r \geqslant 0$ and $HD_o \geqslant 0$. Since $D_r > 0$ is diagonal, $HD_r \geqslant 0$ implies $H \geqslant 0$. Since D_o is nonnegative, $H \geqslant 0$ implies $HD_o \geqslant 0$. By noting further that $\sum_{i=1}^{n}\sum_{j=1}^{m}(H[D_r, D_o])_{i,j} = \sum_{i=1}^{n}\sum_{j=1}^{n}(H\bar{D})_{i,j}$, we can simplify the above problem to:

$$\begin{array}{ll} \textbf{Minimise} & \mathcal{F}(H) = \sum_{i=1}^{n}\sum_{j=1}^{n}(H\bar{D})_{i,j} \\ \textbf{Subject to} & \frac{1}{|\det(H)|} = \nu \\ & H \geqslant 0 \end{array}$$

which is equivalent to:

$$\begin{array}{ll} \textbf{Minimise} & \mathcal{F}(H) = \sum_{i=1}^{n}\sum_{j=1}^{n}(H\bar{D})_{i,j} \\ \textbf{Subject to} & \frac{1}{|\det(H)|} = \nu \\ & H\bar{D} \geqslant 0 \end{array}$$

This is because both $H \geqslant 0$ and $H\bar{D} \geqslant 0$ are equivalent when $\bar{D} > 0$ is diagonal, We are back to the case we solved before when the dependence matrix D is a square matrix. By Theorem 3, the tiling given in (6) is optimal and has the smallest communication volume as indicated. ∎

In this special case, we have

$$P = H^{-1} = \sqrt[n]{\frac{\nu}{\det(\bar{D})}}\,\bar{D}$$

When $D = [D_r, D_o]$, the dependence cone and tiling cone are the first orthant (Section 5.1). The optimal tiling consists of dividing the iteration space using rectangles of size $\sqrt[n]{\frac{\nu}{\det(\bar{D})}}\,\bar{d}_1 \times \cdots \sqrt[n]{\frac{\nu}{\det(\bar{D})}}\,\bar{d}_n$, with the edges of a tile parallel to the natural axes. The dependence vectors in D_r completely determine the shape of a tile – the tiling is rectangular, while those in D_o contribute only to determining the aspect ratios of a tile – the larger the sum of the i-th entries of all dependence vectors, the longer of the side of the tile along the i-th dimension.

Example 4. Consider a double loop with the dependence matrix:

$$D = [D_r, D_o] = \left[\begin{bmatrix}1 & 0\\0 & 1\end{bmatrix}, \begin{bmatrix}2 & 1\\1 & 1\end{bmatrix}\right]$$

We find that

$$\bar{D} = \begin{bmatrix} 4 & 0 \\ 0 & 3 \end{bmatrix}$$

An application of Theorem 4 yields the optimal tiling:

$$H = \begin{bmatrix} \sqrt{\frac{3}{4\nu}} & 0 \\ 0 & \sqrt{\frac{4}{3\nu}} \end{bmatrix} \qquad P = \begin{bmatrix} \sqrt{\frac{4\nu}{3}} & 0 \\ 0 & \sqrt{\frac{3\nu}{4}} \end{bmatrix}$$

5.4 *D* Contains All *n* Extremal Rays of the Dependence Cone

In this special case, the dependence cone $\mathcal{C}_d(D)$ has exactly n extremal rays and the columns of D can always be permuted so that $D = [D_r, D_o]$, where $D_r \in \mathbb{Z}^{n \times n}$ is non-singular and its columns are the n extremal rays of the dependence cone. Using the notations in (3), we have $D' = D_r$ and $T = (D_r^{-1})^T$. By the definition of D_r, $D_r^{-1}[D_r, D_o] = [\mathcal{I}, D_r^{-1}D_o]$ is nonnegative and contains the identity as a diagonal submatrix. This will enable us to reduce this case to the one solved in Section 5.3.

Example 5. Consider a triple loop with the dependence matrix:

$$D = [D_r, D_o] = \left[\begin{bmatrix} 1 & 0 & 1 \\ 1 & 1 & 0 \\ 0 & 1 & 1 \end{bmatrix}, \begin{bmatrix} 1 \\ 1 \\ 1 \end{bmatrix} \right]$$

The last column is a positive linear combination of the first three: $d_4 = \frac{1}{2}(d_1 + d_2 + d_3)$. Thus, the dependence cone, as shown in Figure 6, has three edges d_1, d_2 and d_3, and three faces are identified by their normals $d_2 \times d_3$, $d_1 \times d_2$ and $d_1 \times d_3$.

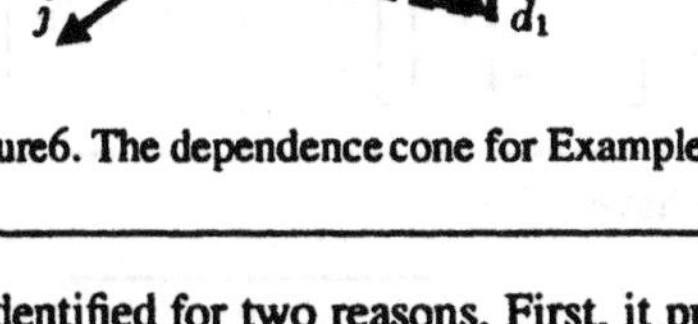

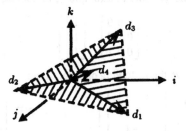

Figure6. The dependence cone for Example 5.

This special case is identified for two reasons. First, it provides insights into finding optimal tilings in the general case (to be discussed next). Second, the closed-form optimal tiling for a two-dimensional iteration space can be found more efficiently than if the approach for the general case is used. This is because if $D \in \mathbb{Z}^{2 \times m}$, we can find D_r in $O(m)$ time. In fact, the two columns in D_r can be chosen as the vectors with the largest and smallest ratios $\frac{a}{b}$ among all columns $\begin{bmatrix} a \\ b \end{bmatrix}$ in D [11].

Theorem 5. *Let $D = [D_r, D_o]$ be as defined above. Let $\bar{D}$ be the diagonal matrix whose i-th diagonal element is the sum of the i-th row of $[\mathcal{I}, D_r^{-1}D_o]$. Then the optimal tiling is:*

$$H = \sqrt[n]{\frac{|\det(\bar{D})|\det(D_r)|}{\nu}}\,\bar{D}^{-1}D_r^{-1} \tag{7}$$

which has the smallest communication volume $\mathcal{V}_{\text{comm}}(H) = n\nu\sqrt[n]{\frac{\det(\bar{D})|\det(D_r)|}{\nu}}$.

Proof. When $D = [D_r, D_o]$, the optimisation problem (2) to be solved is as follows:

$$\begin{aligned}&\textbf{Minimise } \mathcal{F}(H) = \textstyle\sum_{i=1}^{n}\sum_{j=1}^{m}(H[D_r, D_o])_{i,j}\\ &\textbf{Subject to } \tfrac{1}{|\det(H)|} = \nu\\ &\qquad H[D_r, D_o] \geqslant 0\end{aligned}$$

Letting $HD_r = H'$, we have $H[D_r, D_o] = HD_rD_r^{-1}[D_r, D_o] = HD_r[\mathcal{I}, D_r^{-1}D_o] = H'[\mathcal{I}, D_r^{-1}D_o]$. So we can reduce the above problem to:

$$\begin{aligned}&\textbf{Minimise } \mathcal{F}(H') = \textstyle\sum_{i=1}^{n}\sum_{j=1}^{m}(H'[\mathcal{I}, D_r^{-1}D_o])_{i,j}\\ &\textbf{Subject to } \tfrac{1}{|\det(H')|} = \tfrac{\nu}{|\det(D_r)|}\\ &\qquad H'[\mathcal{I}, D_r^{-1}D_o] \geqslant 0\end{aligned}$$

Because D_r are the extremal rays of the dependence cone, $D_r^{-1}D_o$ must be a nonnegative matrix. Thus, we are back to the case we solved before when the dependence matrix D contains a diagonal matrix. By Theorem 4, the optimal solution for H' is:

$$H' = \sqrt[n]{\frac{\det(\bar{D})|\det(D_r)|}{\nu}}\,\bar{D}^{-1}$$

A further use of the fact $HD_r = H'$ concludes the proof of this theorem. ∎

Example 6. Continuing the example in Example 5, we find that

$$[\mathcal{I}, D_r^{-1}D_o] = \left[\begin{bmatrix}1&0&0\\0&1&0\\0&0&1\end{bmatrix}, \begin{bmatrix}1\\1\\1\end{bmatrix}\right] \qquad \bar{D} = \begin{bmatrix}2&0&0\\0&2&0\\0&0&2\end{bmatrix}$$

We use Theorem 5 to derive the following optimal tiling:

$$H = \frac{1}{\sqrt[3]{4\nu}}\begin{bmatrix}1&1&-1\\-1&1&1\\1&-1&1\end{bmatrix} \qquad P = \sqrt[3]{4\nu}\begin{bmatrix}1&0&1\\1&1&0\\0&1&1\end{bmatrix}$$

In this special case, we have

$$P = H^{-1} = \sqrt[n]{\frac{\nu}{\det(\bar{D})|\det(D_r)|}}\,D_r\bar{D}$$

In the optimal tiling, the iteration space is tiled with parallelepipeds whose n edges are parallel to the n extremal rays of the dependence cone. In more detail, the dependence vectors in D_r completely determine the shape of a tile, and the remaining dependence vectors (i.e., those in D_o) have effects only on the aspect ratios of a tile.

5.5 D Has Full Row Rank

In all four special cases discussed above, the dependence cone always has n rays, and the n rays can always be defined by n columns of the dependence matrix D. In addition, the optimal tiling in each case is unique and enjoys a closed-form expression. In each case, the optimal tiling consists of tiling the iteration space with the n edges of a tile parallel to the n edges of the dependence cone.

In the general case, however, the dependence cone can have more than n rays (or edges), in which case, the dependence cone cannot be generated by any n columns of D. As a result, several optimal tilings may exist.

Example 7. Consider the dependence matrix:

$$D = \begin{bmatrix} 2 & 0 & 0 & 1 & 1 \\ 0 & 1 & 0 & 1 & 1 \\ 0 & 0 & 1 & -2 & 1 \end{bmatrix}$$

The dependence cone, shown in Figure 7, has four edges, which are defined by the first four dependence vectors. Thus, the dependence cone cannot be generated by any three dependence vectors. In other words, D does not contain three extremal rays generating the dependence cone. So Theorem 4 cannot be used here.

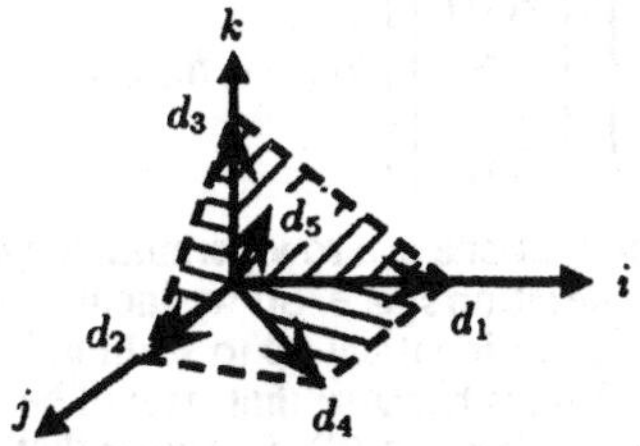

Figure7. The dependence cone for Example 7.

This section discusses how to find optimal tilings in the general case. The problem was solved in [2]. But, our solution is developed in a different and simpler framework based on Lemma 1, providing new insights into the problem of tiling nested loops in general. As an important new result, Lemma 6 shows that a tiling that is optimal must induce the same amount of communication on all faces of a tile. Lemma 7 reduces the problem of finding an optimal tiling to one of finding a matrix with the largest determinant (in absolute value). Lemma 8 further restricts the search space for optimal tilings to a finite set of matrices whose rows are all extremal rays in the tiling cone. Finally, these results are summarised in Theorem 9. This section also provides the geometric interpretation behind an optimal tiling.

Let h be a tiling vector in the tiling cone $C_t(D)$. We define:

$$c(h) = \sum_{j=1}^{m} (hD)_j$$

If h_i is the i-th row of a tiling matrix H, $\frac{c(h_i)}{|\det(H)|}$ represents the communication volume going through the face h_i.

The following lemma is proved using the inequality of arithmetic and geometric means.

Lemma 6. *Assume that D has full row rank. If H is an optimal tiling, then all faces of a tile sustain the same amount of communication, i.e.,* $c(h_1) = \cdots = c(h_n)$.

Proof. We construct a tiling H' from H as follows:

$$H' = \text{diag}\left(\frac{\sqrt[n]{c(h_1) \times \cdots \times c(h_n)}}{c(h_1)}, \ldots, \frac{\sqrt[n]{c(h_1) \times \cdots \times c(h_n)}}{c(h_n)}\right) H$$

It is clear that $|\det(H')| = |\det(H)| = \frac{1}{\nu}$, and $H'D \geqslant 0$ if and only if $HD \geqslant 0$. H and H' yield the following communication volumes for a tile, respectively:

$$\mathcal{V}_{\text{comm}}(H) = \nu(c(h_1) + \cdots + c(h_n))$$
$$\mathcal{V}_{\text{comm}}(H') = n\nu \sqrt[n]{c(h_1) \times \cdots \times c(h_n)}$$

By Lemma 1, $\mathcal{V}_{\text{comm}}(H') \leqslant \mathcal{V}_{\text{comm}}(H)$ and the sign of equality holds if and only if $c(h_1) = \cdots = c(h_n)$. This means that if $c(h_1) = \cdots = c(h_n)$ does not hold, then H is not optimal. ∎

Let G be the set of all tiling matrices, which are up to row permutations and multiplications by positive scalars, such that each tiling matrix induces the same amount of communication on all faces of a tile. G can be constructed as follows:

$$G = \left\{ \begin{bmatrix} \frac{h_1}{c(h_1)} \\ \vdots \\ \frac{h_n}{c(h_n)} \end{bmatrix} \middle| \; h_1, \cdots, h_n \in \mathcal{C}_t(D) \right\} \tag{8}$$

If two tiling matrices are such that one is a row permutation of the other, both represent exactly the same tiling to the iteration space. So we include only one of the two in G. If two tiling matrices B_1 and B_2 are identical up to scaling, it is again only necessary to include one of the two in G. This is because that, as will be shown in Lemma 7 below, an optimal tiling must have the form of (9), implying that the same H in (9) results regardless of whether B_1 or B_2 is used as B in (9).

Next, the problem of finding an optimal tiling is reduced to one of finding a matrix in G with the largest determinant in absolute value.

Lemma 7. *Assume that D has full row rank. An optimal tiling*

$$H = \sqrt[n]{\frac{1}{\nu|\det(B)|}}\, B, \quad \text{where } B \in G \tag{9}$$

has the largest $|\det(B)|$, *yielding the smallest communication volume* $\mathcal{V}_{\text{comm}}(H) = n\nu \sqrt[n]{\frac{1}{\nu|\det(B)|}}$.

Proof. By Lemma 6 and by definition of G, all optimal tilings are contained in the set:

$$\{ \sqrt[n]{\frac{1}{\nu|\det(B)|}}\, B \mid B \in G\}$$

Note that H induces the communication volume $\mathcal{V}_{\text{comm}}(H) = n\nu \sqrt[n]{\frac{1}{\nu|\det(B)|}}$ for a tile. Hence, H is optimal if and only if it has the largest $|\det(B)|$. ∎

There are infinite many matrices in G. The following lemma shows that the search space for optimal tilings can be restricted to a finite set of matrices whose rows are all extremal rays in the tiling cone.

Lemma 8. *Assume that D has full row rank. Let $B \in G$ such that some rows of B are not extremal rays in the tiling cone. Let $B' \in G$ such that the rows of B' are all extremal rays in the tiling cone. Then $|\det(B)| < |\det(B')|$.*

Proof. Since the rows of B' are all extremal rays in the tiling cone $C_t(D)$, there must exist an $n \times n$ non-singular nonnegative matrix P such that $B = PB'$. Let b_i (b'_i) be the i-th row of B (B'). From the constructions of B and B', we have $c(b_1) = \cdots = c(b_n) = 1$ and $c(b'_1) = \cdots = c(b'_n) = 1$. Since $B = PB'$, an algebraic manipulation shows that $c(b_i) = (p_{i,1} + \cdots + p_{i,n})c(b'_i)$. Hence, all entries $p_{i,j}$ of P must satisfy $0 \leqslant p_{i,j} \leqslant 1$. It suffices to prove that $|\det(P)| < 1$. According to the Hadamard inequality, $|\det(P)| \leqslant \| p_1 \| \times \cdots \times \| p_n \|$ and the sign of equality holds if and only if $p_1, \cdots, p_n$ are mutually orthogonal. Since $0 \leqslant p_{i,j} \leqslant 1, p_1, \cdots, p_n$ are mutually orthogonal if and only if P is a permutation of the identity matrix, in which case, $|\det(P)| = 1$. But this implies that the rows of $B = PB'$ are all extremal rays of the tiling cone, contradicting the assumption that some rows of H are not extremal rays. Hence, $|\det(P)| < 1$, implying that $|\det(B)| < |\det(B')|$. ■

Let R be the set of all extremal rays in the tiling cone $C_t(D)$. Let G' be the subset of G in (8) and be defined as follows:

$$G' = \left\{ \begin{bmatrix} \frac{r_1}{c(r_1)} \\ \vdots \\ \frac{r_n}{c(r_n)} \end{bmatrix} \middle| r_1, \cdots, r_n \in R \right\} \tag{10}$$

R contains a finite number of rays. So G' contains a finite number of matrices, given by $\binom{|R|}{n}$. According to (3), every tiling matrix H in G' satisfies the atomic tile constraint $HD \geqslant 0$.

Theorem 9. *Assume that D has full row rank. An optimal tiling*

$$H = \sqrt[n]{\frac{1}{\nu|\det(B)|}}\, B, \quad \text{where } B \in G'$$

has the largest $|\det(B)|$, *yielding the smallest communication volume* $V_{\text{comm}}(H) = n\nu \sqrt[n]{\frac{1}{\nu|\det(B)|}}$.

Proof. Lemmata 6, 7 and 8. ■

Example 8. Continuing Example 7, we find the four rays in the tiling cone $C_t(D)$:

$$r_1 = (0,1,0), \quad r_2 = (0,2,1), \quad r_3 = (1,0,0), \quad r_4 = (2,0,1)$$

from which we construct the four matrices contained in G' (up to row permutations):

$$B_1 = \begin{bmatrix} 0 & \frac{1}{3} & 0 \\ 0 & \frac{2}{6} & \frac{1}{6} \\ \frac{1}{4} & 0 & 0 \end{bmatrix} \qquad B_2 = \begin{bmatrix} 0 & \frac{1}{3} & 0 \\ 0 & \frac{2}{6} & \frac{1}{6} \\ \frac{2}{8} & 0 & \frac{1}{8} \end{bmatrix}$$

$$B_3 = \begin{bmatrix} 0 & \frac{1}{3} & 0 \\ \frac{1}{4} & 0 & 0 \\ \frac{2}{8} & 0 & \frac{1}{8} \end{bmatrix} \qquad B_4 = \begin{bmatrix} 0 & \frac{2}{6} & \frac{1}{6} \\ \frac{1}{4} & 0 & 0 \\ \frac{2}{8} & 0 & \frac{1}{8} \end{bmatrix}$$

We find that $|\det(B_1)| = |\det(B_2)| = 1/72$ and $|\det(B_3)| = |\det(B_4)| = 1/96$. By Theorem 9, there are two optimal tilings:

$$H_1 = \sqrt[3]{\frac{72}{\nu}} B_1 \quad H_2 = \sqrt[3]{\frac{72}{\nu}} B_2$$

Let us now explain the geometric intuition behind an optimal tiling when the dependence cone has more than n edges. In an optimal tiling

$$H = \sqrt[n]{\frac{1}{\nu|\det(B)|}}\, B \quad P = \sqrt[n]{\nu|\det(B)|}\, B^{-1}$$

the columns of H^{-1} generates a cone such that B has the largest $|\det(B)|$. This cone contains the dependence cone with its n faces coincident with some n faces of the dependence cone. The iteration space is tiled with parallelepipeds whose n edges are parallel to the n edges of this cone. The shape of a tile is completely determined by the dependence vectors of D that define B and the other dependence vectors have effects only on the aspect ratios of a tile. Take the optimal tiling H_1 for example:

$$H_1^{-1} = \sqrt[3]{\frac{\nu}{72}} \begin{bmatrix} 0 & 0 & 4 \\ 3 & 0 & 0 \\ -6 & 6 & 0 \end{bmatrix}$$

Figure 8 depicts the cone generated by the columns of H_1^{-1}; each of its three faces coincides with the identically-shaded face of the dependence cone in Figure 7:

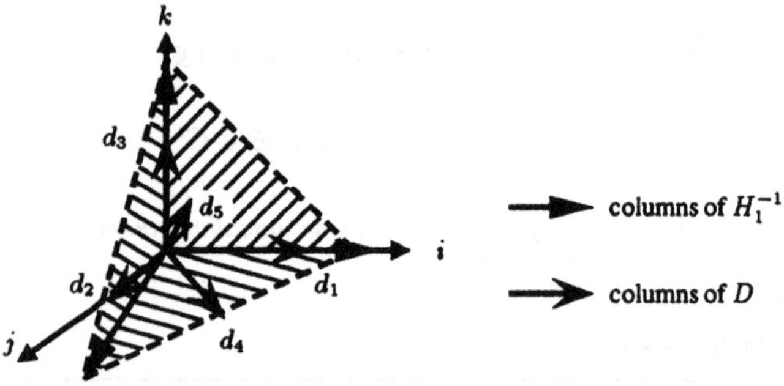

Figure8. The cone generated by the columns of H_1^{-1} for Example 8.

6 A Procedure for Finding Optimal Tilings

This section put all results in the paper together as a procedure for finding optimal tilings. Due to Section 1, we assume that the dependence matrix has full row rank.

Procedure 1 (Construction of Optimal Tilings)
Input: The dependence matrix $D \in \mathbb{Z}^{n\times m}$ with full row rank ($m \geqslant n$)
Output: All optimal solutions H to (2)

1. If D is the identity matrix, H is (4).
2. If D is a square matrix, H is (5).
3. If D is nonnegative and contains an $n \times n$ diagonal submatrix, H is (6).
4. If $D \in \mathbb{Z}^{2\times m}$, find in $O(m)$ time two linearly independent rays for the dependence cone as discussed in Section 5.4. Then, H is (7).
5. Otherwise, the following steps are performed:
   (a) Construct the set R of all extremal rays for the tiling cone $C_t(D)$ as discussed in Section 5.
   (b) Construct the set G' as defined in (10).
   (c) Generate all optimal tilings $H = \sqrt[n]{\frac{1}{\nu|\det(B)|}}\, B$, where $B \in G'$, such that B has the largest determinant $|\det(B)|$.

If H is an optimal tiling, this procedure does not guarantee that H^{-1} is integral. Note that H^{-1} is integral if B^{-1} is integral and $\sqrt[n]{\nu|\det(B)|}$ is an integer. In general, let c be the smallest positive integer such that cB^{-1} is integral. In order for H^{-1} to be integral, we must choose a computation volume from the following set:

$$\{\frac{x^n c^n}{|\det(B)|} \mid x \text{ is an positive integer}\}$$

Consider the optimal tilings in Example 7. Both B_1^{-1} and B_2^{-1} are integral. To make H_1^{-1} and H_2^{-1} integral, ν must take values from the set:

$$\{72x^3 \mid x \text{ is an positive integer}\}$$

Given an arbitrary computation volume ν, how to *best* approximate an optimal tiling H with a tiling F so that F^{-1} is integral is beyond the scope of this paper.

7 Related Work

This section reviews some existing results on tiling with particular emphasis on those aiming at finding communication-minimal tilings (in the sense of this paper).

Pioneering studies on tiling are perhaps those of Irigion and Triolet [7] and Wolfe [16, 17]. Irigion and Triolet formally defined tiling as a loop transformation that divides the iteration space using hyperplanes into parallelepiped tiles and traverses the tiles to cover the iteration space. They also introduced the three important constraints on a tiling: H must be non-singular, H^{-1} must be integral and $HD \geqslant 0$ must be true. Wolfe demonstrated the feasibility of generating blocked algorithms through strip mining and loop interchanging [17]. This consists of tiling the iteration space with rectangles using a diagonal tiling matrix:

$$H = \text{diag}(h_{1,1}, \cdots, h_{n,n})$$

and is not optimal in general. Since a tiling matrix H must satisfy $HD \geqslant 0$, this simple approach usually breaks down when the dependence matrix D contains negative entries. To alleviate this problem, Wolfe [17] proposed to first restructure (e.g. using the wavefront transformation) a loop nest and then tile the restructured program. In the extreme case along this line, Wolf and Lam [15] proceeded to first transform a loop nest into a *fully permutable loop nest* – a loop nest whose dependence matrix $D \geqslant 0$, and then settled with a rectangular tiling of the restructured program. A rectangular tiling is always feasible for a set of fully permutable loops. Wolf and Lam's approach applies to loops with iteration vectors, but was not developed to find communication-minimal tilings.

Next, we consider three recent papers on finding tilings with a minimal amount of communication. Schreiber and Dongarra were perhaps the first investigating compiler techniques for finding communication-minimal tilings [13]. In their two-step approach, they first determined the shape of a tile by minimising the ratio of the computation volume of a tile to the surface area of a tile and then attempted to adjust the aspect ratios of a tile in order to minimise the amount of local memory and communication induced by a tile. Schreiber and Dongarra formulated the problem of finding the optimal shape of a tile as follows:

Maximise $|\det(H)|$
Subject to The rows of H all have unity Euclidean norm
$HD \geqslant 0$

Essentially, the problem is to find a matrix H that has the largest determinant, subject to $HD \geqslant 0$. Unfortunately, the search space $\mathcal{C}_t(D)$ contains an infinite number of tiling matrices to be considered. In a heuristics-based procedure, they first calculated the tiling matrices whose rows are extremal rays of the tiling cone $\mathcal{C}_t(D)$ and then applied an orthogonalisation process in an attempt to maximise their determinants. This method does not yield communication-minimal tilings. For the dependence matrix in Example 2, $\mathcal{C}_t(D)$ contains two (normalised) extremal rays $(1,0)$ and $(-\frac{1}{\sqrt{5}}, \frac{2}{\sqrt{5}})$. So there is only one tiling matrix:

$$\begin{bmatrix} 1 & 0 \\ -\frac{1}{\sqrt{5}} & \frac{2}{\sqrt{5}} \end{bmatrix}$$

whose determinant is $\frac{2}{\sqrt{5}}$. Using the orthogonalisation process in [13, Section 3], the two tiling matrices with orthogonal rows are found:

$$\begin{bmatrix} 1 & 0 \\ 0 & 1 \end{bmatrix} \quad \begin{bmatrix} \frac{2}{\sqrt{5}} & \frac{1}{\sqrt{5}} \\ -\frac{1}{\sqrt{5}} & \frac{2}{\sqrt{5}} \end{bmatrix}$$

both of which have unity determinant. Scaling these two matrices to obtain the tilings with the computation volume ν yields:

$$H_1 = \sqrt{\frac{1}{\nu}} \begin{bmatrix} 1 & 0 \\ 0 & 1 \end{bmatrix} \qquad H_2 = \sqrt{\frac{1}{\nu}} \begin{bmatrix} -\frac{1}{\sqrt{5}} & \frac{2}{\sqrt{5}} \\ \frac{2}{\sqrt{5}} & \frac{1}{\sqrt{5}} \end{bmatrix}$$

Both tilings are not optimal. It can be checked that $\mathcal{V}_{\text{comm}}(H_1) = 4\sqrt{\nu}$ and $\mathcal{V}_{\text{comm}}(H_2) = \frac{8}{\sqrt{5}}\sqrt{\nu}$, while the optimal tiling given in Example 3 has the communication volume $2\sqrt{2}\sqrt{\nu}$.

There is a simple reason why Schreiber and Dongarra failed to find optimal tilings. By normalising the rows of every tiling matrix, they explicitly restricted their search for optimal tilings to those each of which induces the same surface area on all all faces of a tile. As shown in Lemma 6, *a tiling that is optimal must induce the same amount of communication not the same surface area on all faces of the tile.* By further using Lemma 8, the problem of finding optimal tilings $H = \sqrt[n]{\frac{1}{\nu|\det(B)|}}\, B$ should be formulated as follows:

Maximise $|\det(B)|$
Subject to $B \in G'$ (as in (10))
$BD \geqslant 0$

which can be solved analytically since G' contains only a finite number of elements.

Ramanujam and Sadayappan [11] required a tiling H to be a lower triangular unimodular matrix. Thus, they solved a simplified version of (2):

$$\begin{array}{ll}\textbf{Minimise} & \mathcal{V}_{\text{comm}}(H) = \frac{1}{|\det(H)|} \sum_{i=1}^{n} \sum_{j=1}^{m} (HD)_{i,j} \\ \textbf{Subject to} & HD \geqslant 0\end{array}$$

Since H is unimodular, $\frac{1}{|\det(H)|}$ can be removed from the objective function, rendering the problem a form of integer programming. The optimal solution found is scaled to obtain a tile of an appropriate size. In general, the optimality of this method is not guaranteed. For the dependence matrix in Example 4, the optimal solution to the above problem is the identity matrix. So the optimal tiling with the computation volume ν is:

$$\sqrt{\frac{1}{\nu}} \begin{bmatrix} 1 & 0 \\ 0 & 1 \end{bmatrix}$$

which yields the communication volume $7\sqrt{\nu}$, larger than the communication volume $4\sqrt{3}\sqrt{\nu}$ induced by the optimal tiling in Example 4.

The work in this paper drew its inspiration mainly from a recent work by Boulet, et al [2]. They found optimal tilings in two steps. In the first step, the optimal solutions are found to:

$$\begin{array}{ll}\textbf{Minimise} & \frac{1}{|\det(H)|^{\frac{1}{n}}} \sum_{i=1}^{n} \sum_{j=1}^{m} (HD)_{i,j} \\ \textbf{Subject to} & |\det(H)| \neq 0 \\ & HD \geqslant 0\end{array}$$

In the second step, the solutions are scaled to obtain the tiles with an appropriate size. Our problem formulation (2) is similar but with a linear objective function. The advantage is that the optimal solutions can be found analytically based primarily on the inequality of arithmetic and geometric means. It is expected that this conceptually simpler framework can provide new insights into tackling other problems in tiling nested loops. The other aspects of this work in relation to that work was already discussed at the beginning of the paper.

Finally, several researchers have studied tiling in the context of compiling programs for distributed memory machines, possibly with user-specified data decomposition directives [8, 10, 12].

8 Conclusion

Inspired by the work [2] and building on the work [13], this paper described a different but simpler approach to finding optimal tilings of iteration spaces with a minimal amount of communication through the faces of a tile. The key observation is that a tiling that is optimal must induce the same amount of communication on all faces of a tile, which reduces the search space for optimal tilings to a set of a finite number of matrices whose rows are extremal rays in the tiling cone. For nested loops with several special forms of dependences, closed-form optimal tilings were provided. In the general case, a procedure was given that is guaranteed to always find optimal tilings. Where appropriate, the geometric insights behind optimal tilings were explained. Several existing results were compared and contrasted in detail.

The problem of finding optimal tilings is a difficult non-linear combinatorial problem. But the developments of almost all results in the paper were conducted in a conceptually simple framework, based primarily on the inequality of arithmetic and geometric means and several basic concepts from convex cones. Motivated by the insights provided by this framework, we intend to pursue several related problems, including, for example, tiling of general nested loops for parallelism and locality.

References

1. U. Banerjee. *Loop Parallelization*. Kluwer Academic Publishers, 1994.
2. P. Boulet, A. Darte, T. Risset, and Y. Robert. (Pen)-ultimate tiling. *Integration, the VLSI Journal*, 17:33–51, 1994.
3. S. Carr and K. Kennedy. Compiler blockability of numerical algorithms. In *Supercomputing '92*, pages 114–124, Minneapolis, Minn., Nov. 1992.
4. E. W. Dijkstra. *Predicate Calculus and Programming Semantics*. Series in Automatic Computation. Prentice-Hall, 1990.
5. J. J. Dongarra, S. J. Hammarline, and D. C. Sorensen. Block reduction of matrices to condensed forms for eigenvalue computations. *J. of Computer Application and Mathematics*, 27:216–227, 1989.
6. K. Gallivan, W. Jalby, U. Meier, and A. H. Sameh. Impact of hierarchical memory systems on linear algebra algorithm design. *Int. J. of Supercomputer Applications*, 2:12–48, 1988.
7. F. Irigoin and R. Triolet. Supernode partitioning. In *Proc. of the 15th Annual ACM Symposium on Principles of Programming Languages*, pages 319–329, San Diego, California., Jan. 1988.
8. C. King and L. Ni. Grouping in nested loops for parallel execution on multicomputers. In *Proc. of Int. Conf. on Parallel Processing*, volume 2, pages II–31—II–38, Aug. 1989.
9. M. S. Lam, E. E. Rothberg, and M. E. Wolf. The cache performance and optimizations of blocked algorithms. In *Proc. of the 2nd International Conference on Architectural Support for Programming Languages and Operating Systems*, pages 63–74, Santa Clara, California, Apr. 1991.
10. H. Ohta, Y .Saito, M. Kainaga, and H. Ono. Optimal tile size adjustment in compiling for general DOACROSS loop nests. In *Supercomputing '95*, pages 270–27 9. ACM Press, 1995.
11. J. Ramanujam and P. Sadayappan. Tiling multidimensional iteration spaces for multicomputers. *J. of Parallel and Distributed Computing*, 16(2):108–230, Oct. 1992.
12. A. Rogers and K. Pingali. Compiling for distributed memory architectures. *IEEE Transactions on Parallel and Distributed Systems*, 5(3):281–298, Mar. 1994.
13. R. Schreiber and J. J. Dongarra. Automatic blocking of nested loops. Technical Report 90.38, RIACS, May 1990.
14. A. Schrijver. *Theory of Linear and Integer Programming*. Series in Discrete Mathematics. John Wiley & Sons, 1986.
15. M. Wolf and M. Lam. A loop transformation theory and an algorithm to maximize parallelism. *IEEE Trans. on Parallel and Distributed Systems*, 2(4):452–471, Oct. 1991.
16. M. J. Wolfe. Iteration space tiling for memory hierarchies. In G. Rodrigue, editor, *Parallel Processing for Scientific Computing*, pages 357–361, Philadelphia PA, 1987.
17. M. J. Wolfe. More iteration space tiling. In *Supercomputing '88*, pages 655–664, Nov. 1989.
18. M. J. Wolfe. *Optimizing Supercompilers for Supercomputers*. Research Monographs in Parallel and Distributed Computing. MIT Press, 1989.
19. M. J. Wolfe. *High Performance Compilers for Parallel Computing*. Addision-Wesley, 1996.
20. J. Xue. On tiling as a loop transformation. In *Proc. of the SPDP Workshop on Challenges in Compiling for Scalable Parallel Systems*, New Orleans, 1996. IEEE Computer Society Press.
21. Y.Q. Yang, C. Ancourt, and F. Irigoin. Minimal data dependence abstractions for loop transformations. In *Proc. of the 7th Workshop on Languages and Compilers for Parallel Computing*, Ithaca, Aug 1994.

Communication-Minimal Partitioning of Parallel Loops and Data Arrays for Cache-Coherent Distributed-Memory Multiprocessors *

Rajeev Barua, David Kranz and Anant Agarwal

Laboratory for Computer Science
Massachusetts Institute of Technology
Cambridge, MA 02139
Email: {barua,kranz,agarwal}@lcs.mit.edu

Abstract. Harnessing the full performance potential of cache-coherent distributed shared memory multiprocessors without inordinate user effort requires a compilation technology that can automatically manage multiple levels of memory hierarchy. This paper describes a working compiler for such machines that automatically partitions loops and data arrays to optimize locality of access.

The compiler implements a solution to the problem of finding partitions of loops and data with minimal communication. Our algorithm handles programs with multiple nested parallel loops accessing many arrays with array access indices being general affine functions of loop variables. It discovers communication-minimal partitions when communication-free partitions do not exist. The compiler also uses sub-blocking to handle finite cache sizes.

A cost model that estimates the cost of a loop and data partition given machine parameters such as cache, local and remote access timings, is presented. Minimizing the cost as estimated by our model is an NP-complete problem, as is the fully general problem of partitioning. A heuristic method which provides good approximate solutions in polynomial time is presented.

The loop and data partitioning algorithm has been implemented in the compiler for the MIT Alewife machine. Results are presented which show that combined optimization of loops and data can result in improvements in runtime by nearly a factor of two over optimization of loops alone.

1 Introduction

Cache-coherent distributed shared memory multiprocessors have multiple levels in their memory hierarchy which must be managed to obtain good performance. These levels include local cache, local memory, and remote memory that is accessed by traversing an interconnection network. Although local memory has

* This research was funded in part by ARPA contract #N00014-94-1-0985 and in part by NSF grant #MIP-9504399.

a longer access time than the cache, and the remote memory has a longer access time than local memory, the programming abstraction of shared memory hides these distinctions. Consequently, shared-memory programs written without regard to the increasing cost of access to the various levels often suffer poor performance. Fortunately, a compiler can relieve the user from the burden of managing the memory hierarchy for many classes of programs through loop partitioning and data partitioning so that the probability of access from the closest level in the memory hierarchy is maximized.

The goal of *loop partitioning* for applications with nested loops that access data arrays is to divide the iteration space among the processors to get maximum reuse of data in the cache, subject to the constraint of having a good load balance. For architectures where remote memory references are more expensive than local memory references (NUMA machines), the goal of *data partitioning* is to distribute data to nodes such that most cache misses are satisfied out of the local memory.

This paper presents an algorithm to find loop and data partitions automatically for programs with multiple loop nests and data arrays. The algorithm does not resort to square blocking when communication-free partitions do not exist. Rather, it discovers a partitioning of loops and data that minimizes communication cost over the multiple levels of memory hierarchy for the entire program.

Simultaneous partitioning of loops and data is difficult when multiple loops access the same data array with different access patterns. If a loop is partitioned in order to get good data reuse in the cache, that partition determines which processor will access each datum. In order to get good data locality, the data should be distributed to processors based on that loop partition. Likewise, given a partitioning of data, a loop should be partitioned based on the placement of data used in the loop. This introduces a conflict when there are multiple loops because a loop partition may have two competing constraints: good cache reuse may rely on one loop partition being chosen, while good data locality may rely on another.

Making cost tradeoffs in discovering *communication-minimal* partitions in the presence of multiple memory hierarchy levels requires a communication cost model. For a given loop and data partitioning, the communication cost model presented estimates the cost of executing the loop partition given the data partitions of arrays accessed in the loop and the architectural parameters of the machine, such as the cost of local and remote cache misses. Although finding communication-free partitions does not require a communication cost model, real programs often do not admit communication-free partitions.

The cost model is used to drive an iterative search procedure for finding a communication-minimal partitioning for the entire program. Although other search techniques can be used as well, the following solution is implemented in our compiler and described in this paper. We have found that this search procedure does not add much to the compilation time and it yields good results. The iterative solution has two steps: (1) an initial seed partitioning, and (2) an iterative search through the space of loop and data partitions commencing from the initial partitioning.

The iterative solution is seeded with an initial partitioning of each individual loop nest that disregards data locality. This initial loop partitioning is found using the method described in [2]. The iterative solution is also seeded with an initial data partition. This initial partitioning of each array is chosen to match the partitioning of the largest loop that accesses that array. Thus, by first partitioning each loop for cache locality, the initial seeding favors cache locality over data locality.

After the initial seeding, the iterative solution proceeds to use the cost model to repartition the loops according to the data partitions to increase the locality of access to local memory at the expense of cache locality if it results in better performance. It then repartitions the data arrays according to the resulting loop partitions to increase the cache locality. In this manner the loops and data are alternately re-partitioned, thus iteratively improving the solution. The cost model controls the heuristic search.

The algorithm has been implemented in a compiler for cache-coherent multiprocessors with physically distributed memory. The algorithm, however, is general and does not require that the target architecture have coherent caches. Parallelism in the source program is assumed to be specified using parallel do loops, either by a programmer or by a previous parallelization phase. The algorithm reported in this paper has been implemented as part of the compiler for the Alewife machine. Results from a working 16-processor machine for several real applications indicate that combined iterative optimization of loops and data can result in a decrease in runtime by nearly a factor of two over optimization of loops alone, and that a partitioning of loops for cache locality followed by partitioning data arrays according to the largest loop that accesses them, can result in improvements in runtime by a factor of about 1.4 over optimization of loops alone.

The rest of the paper describes the algorithms and the implementation, and presents several performance results. Section 2 describes related work. Section 3 overviews the notation and framework for partitioning loops and data. In particular, it shows how to derive loop partitions that minimize cache misses, and data partitions that match a given loop partition, which has the effect of minimizing remote memory accesses for a given loop partition. Note that while the above process minimizes the number of cache misses, it does not minimize overall runtime because the number of remote memory accesses is not necessarily minimized. Section 4 describes a cost model that estimates the communication cost for a given loop partition and a given data partition. This cost model is used to drive a search for a communication-minimal partitioning of loops and data arrays. Section 5 describes the iterative search method, and Section 6 presents performance results on Alewife.

2 Related Work

The problem of loop and data partitioning for distributed memory multiprocessors with global address spaces has been studied by many researchers. One approach to the problem is to have programmers specify data partitions explicitly in the program, as in Fortran-D [10, 15]. Loop partitions are usually determined by the owner computes rule. Though simple to implement, this requires the user to thoroughly understand the access patterns of the program, a task which is not trivial even for small programs. For real medium-sized or large programs, the task is a very difficult one. Presence of fully general affine function accesses further complicates the process. Worse, the program would not be portable across machines with different architectural parameters.

Ramanujam and Sadayappan [13] consider data partitioning in multicomputers and use a matrix formulation; their results do not apply to multiprocessors with caches. Their theory produces communication-free hyperplane partitions for loops with affine index expressions when such partitions exist. However, when communication-free partitions do not exist, they deal only with index expressions of the form variable plus a constant.

Ju and Dietz [11] consider the problem of reducing cache-coherence traffic in bus-based multiprocessors. Their work involves finding a data *layout* (row or column major) for arrays in a uniform memory access (UMA) environment. We consider finding data partitions for a distributed shared memory NUMA machine.

Abraham and Hudak [1] look at the problem of automatic loop partitioning for cache locality only for the case when array accesses have simple index expressions. Their method uses only a local per-loop analysis.

A more general framework for loop partitioning was presented by Agarwal et. al. [2] for optimizing for cache locality. That framework handled fully general affine access functions, i.e. accesses of the form A[2i+j,j] and A[100-i,j] were handled. However, that work found local minima for each loop independently, giving possibly conflicting data partitioning requests across loops in NUMA machines.

Another view of loop partitioning involving program transformations is presented by Carr et. al. [7]. This paper was focused on uniprocessors but their method could be integrated with data partitioning for multiprocessors as well.

The work of Anderson and Lam [4] does a global analysis across loops. It finds partitions among a space of those which satisfy a specified system of constraints, in a framework of both sequential and parallel loops. It has the following differences with our work. (1) It first tries to find a communication free solution using a iterative method, which however, is very different from ours in that it trades off parallelism until a communication free partition is found, which could sometimes result in all computation being allocated on one processor, in this first attempt. In our method, we use the iterative method to improve on the total communication cost, while maintaining load balance throughout. If no communication free partition exists, one which minimum cost, as determined by a detailed cost model, is found. [4] next attempts to use **doacross** loops to improve performance, but note that is not relevant for our programming model of only parallel loops. (2) Finally, the algorithm in [4] uses a heuristic with a greedy approach to find where data reorganization could be done to reduce communication. We concentrate on the problem of finding the best static partition. Data reorganization can be built into our method. (3) We present a cost model of wide applicability, which possibly could be used for other partitioning algorithms as well. No quantitative cost model is used in [4]'s static partitioning phase. The reorganization heuristic uses a reorganization cost, while we directly minimize loop memory access time, while is more precise. (4) It does not take into account the combined effect on performance of caches and local memories. We optimize quantitatively for both cache and data locality. (5) Unlike in [4], we allow for hyperparallelepiped data tiles, important for achieving good locality in general affine function array accesses. Results on only one program were presented.

Bixby, Kennedy and Kremer [6] present a formulation of the problem of finding data layout as a 0-1 integer programming problem. Though the problem is exponential time in the worst case, a case is made why for smaller problem sizes, the solution can be found in a reasonable amount of time. Formulating compiler problems as 0-1 integer programming problems is an exciting new approach, also used by the Stanford SUIF compiler [16]. However, a 0-1 integer programming approach is only as good as its formulation. In the case of finding loop and data partitions 0-1 programming may not be the best answer for the following reasons: (1) The formulation in [6] solves for data partitions only, which is a simpler problem. It been widely recognized [8] that for good performance, data and loop partitions need to be found simultaneously, not one following another. (2) For 0-1 formulations in general, to get one with few enough variables so as to avoid an exponential increase in solution time, we may need to simplify the problem. An exact solution to a simplified formulation could be inferior to a good heuristic's solution to a more detailed problem. For example, in [6], only two alternative partitions are examined per phase. (A phase in [6] roughly corresponds to a single set of loops nested one inside the other). (3) Hyperparallelepiped partitions are not allowed in [6], necessary for good performance on general affine functions.

Gupta and Banerjee [9] have developed an algorithm for partitioning doing a global analysis across loops. They allow simple index expression accesses of the form $c_1 * i + c_2$, but not general affine functions. They do not allow for the possibility of hyperparallelepiped data tiles, and do not account for caches.

Knobe, Lucas and Steele [12] give a method of allocating arrays on SIMD machines. They align arrays to minimize communication for vector instructions, which access array regions specified by subranges on each dimension.

Wolf and Lam [17] deal with the problem of taking sequential nested loops and applying transformations to attempt to convert them to a nest of parallel loops with at most one outer sequential loop. This technique can be used before partitioning when the programming model is sequential to convert to parallel loops, and hence complements our work.

3 Overview of the Partitioning Framework

This section overviews the notation and framework used for partitioning. The full reference presents the details[2]. The reason we describe this framework are two-fold. First, the work in [2] describes how to select loop and data partitions which optimize for cache locality. This is used by our method in computing the initial loop and data partition, used as a starting point for our heuristic search. Second, the framework in [2] on how loop and data partitions are specified, is used in our cost model in section 4 to find memory access costs considering caches, and local and remote memory.

The framework handles programs with loop nests where the array index expressions are affine functions of the loop variables. In other words, the index function **g** can be expressed as,

$$\mathbf{g}(\mathbf{i}) = \mathbf{i}\mathbf{G} + \mathbf{a} \tag{1}$$

where **G** is a $l \times d$ matrix with integer entries, **i** is the vector of loop variables and **a** is an integer constant vector of length d, termed the *offset vector*. Thus accesses of the form A[2i+j,100-i] and A[j] are handled, but not A[i^2], where i,j are nested loop induction variables. Consider the following example of a loop:

```
Doall (i=0:99, j=0:99)
  A[i,j] = B[i+j,j]+B[i+j+1,j+2]
EndDoall
```

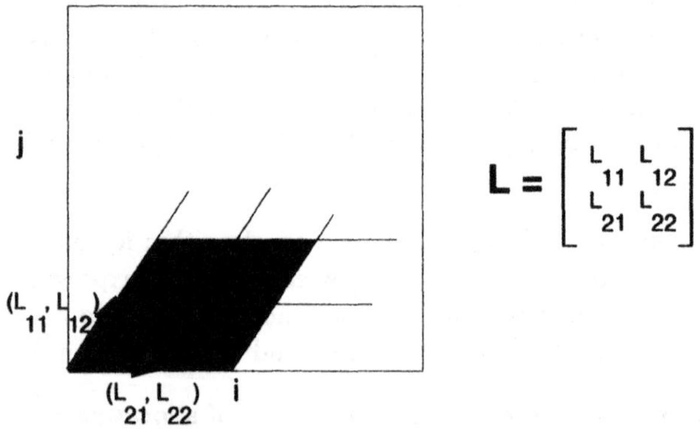

Fig. 1. Iteration space partitioning is completely specified by the tile at the origin.

A loop partition **L** is defined by a hyperparallelepiped at the origin as pictured in Figure 1. Each hyperparallelepiped represents the region executed by a different processor, and the whole loop space is tiled in this manner. The number of iterations contained in matrix **L** is $|\det \mathbf{L}|$.

The *footprint* of an iteration tile **L** with respect to an array reference is the set of points in the data space accessed by the tile through that reference. This footprint is given by **LG**, translated by **a**. A set of references to one array in one loop with the same **G** but different offsets **a** are called ***uniformly intersecting*** references. The footprints associated with such sets of references are the same shape, but are translated in the data space. They are said to be in the same *UI-set* (Uniformly Intersecting set).

This is illustrated by the above code fragment. The code has only one UI-set for array B, as the two accesses to B differ only by a constant vector. The **G** matrix for the UI-set is given by

$$\begin{bmatrix} 1 & 0 \\ 1 & 1 \end{bmatrix}.$$

For some loop tile **L** at the origin, the footprint in the data space is the union of **LG** translated by each offset in the UI-set. Since this loop has two references to **B** in the same UI-set with offsets **a** of (0,0) and (1,2), the footprint looks like that shown in Figure 2.

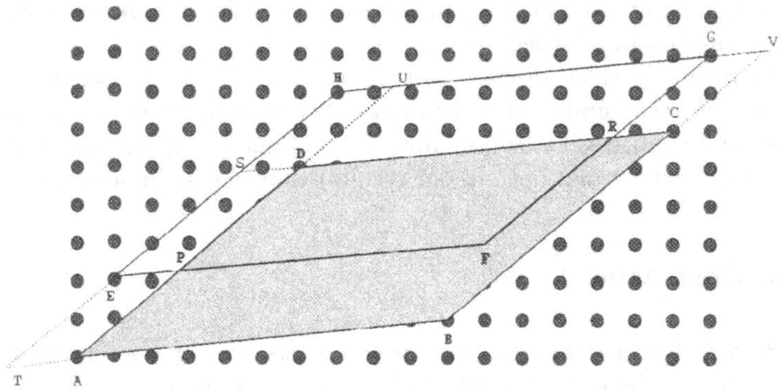

Fig. 2. Data footprint wrt $B[i+j, j]$ and $B[i+j+1, j+2]$

The total number of cache misses for a given loop nest is the number of its first time data accesses. This number is simply the size of the combined footprint with respect to all the accesses in the loop, assuming an infinitely large cache. A method to get essentially the same result with finite caches is presented in section 4. [2] shows how the combined footprint in a UI-set can be computed assuming infinite caches. It also shows how the loop partitioning **L** can be chosen to minimize the number of cache misses. Cache misses are minimized when the combined footprint with respect to all the accesses in the loop has minimum area, as the area is the number of first time data accesses. This minimizes first time (compulsory) cache misses, and hence is important for caches irrespective of size.

For cache-coherent machines with uniform-access memory (UMA), because all cache misses suffer the same cost, loop partitioning alone is sufficient. Loop partitioning performed with complete disregard to data partitioning is termed "cache-only" in our performance results in Section 6. Data partitions are done in a random manner.

The cost model also refers to the data partition **D**, relevant for NUMA machines. A matrix **D** represents a tile at the origin of the data space in the same way as **L** represents a tile at the origin of the iteration space. An array reference in a loop will have good data locality when partitions are chosen such that **LG** = **D**, and the translation offsets of the two differ by at most small constants.

In the above code, both references to B will have simultaneously good probability of being satisfied in local memory when **D** is picked to be **LG**. The only communication for B then, (that is, memory accesses to remote memory), is at the periphery of **LG**, due to small offsets. This periphery is what was minimized in [2], and is called the *peripheral footprint*. Indeed, **D** is chosen as shown above to seed the search process.

Data partitioning performed according to the loop partitioning is termed "cache + net-1" in our performance results. With data partitioning, the probability that a cache miss will be satisfied in the local memory is increased. However, although the number of cache misses satisfied in local memory is increased it is not necessarily maximized.

The following sections discuss how a cost model can be used to make a tradeoff between the number of cache misses and the number of remote memory references, and to discover a communication-minimal partitioning of loops and data (termed "cache + net-opt" in our results) that yields the lowest runtime.

4 The Cost Model

The key to a finding a communication-minimal partitioning is a cost model that allows a tradeoff to be made between cache miss cost and remote memory access cost. This cost model drives an iterative solution and is a function that takes, as arguments, a loop partition, data partitions for each array accessed in the loop, and architectural parameters that determine the relative cost of cache misses and remote memory accesses. It returns an estimation of the cost of array references for the loop.

The cost due to memory references in terms of architectural parameters is computed by the following equation:

$$T_{total\_access} = T_R(n_{remote}) + T_L(n_{local}) + T_C(n_{cache})$$

where T_R, T_L, T_C are the remote, local and cache memory access times respectively, and $n_{remote}, n_{local}, n_{cache}$ are the number of references that result in hits to remote memory, local memory and cache memory. T_C and T_L are fixed by the architecture, while T_R is determined both by the base remote latency of the architecture and possible contention if there are many remote references. T_R may also vary with the number of processors based on the interconnect topology.

n_{cache}, n_{local} and n_{remote} depend on the loop and data partitions. Given a loop partition, for each UI-set consider the intersection between the footprint (**LG**) of that set and a given data partition **D**. First time accesses to data in that intersection will be in local memory while first time references to data outside will be remote. Repeat accesses will likely hit in the cache. A UI-set may contain several references, each with slightly different footprints due to different offsets in the array index expressions. One is selected and called the base offset, or **b**. In the following definitions the symbol $\approx$ will be used to compare footprints and data partitions. $\mathbf{LG} \approx \mathbf{D}$ means that the matrix equality holds. This equality does not mean that all references in the UI-set represented by **G** will be local in the data partition **D** because there may be small offset vectors for each reference in the UI-set.

We define the functions R_b, F_f and F_b, which are all functions of the loop partition **L**, data partition **D** and reference matrix **G** with the meanings given in Section 3. For simplicity, we also use R_b, F_f and F_b, to denote the value returned by the respective functions of the same name.

Definition 1. R_b is a function which maps **L**, **D** and **G** to the number of remote references that result from a single access defined by **G** and the base offset **b**.

In other words, R_b returns the number of remote accesses that result from a single program reference in a parallel loop, not including the small peripheral footprint due to multiple accesses in its UI-set. The periphery is added using F_f to be described below.

Note that in most cases **G**'s define UI-sets: accesses to an array with the same **G** but different offsets are usually in the same UI-set, and different **G**'s always have different UI-sets. The only exception are accesses with the same **G** but large differences in their offsets relative to tile size, in which case they are considered to be in different UI-sets.

The computation of R_b is simplified by an approximation. One of the two following cases apply to loop and data partitions.

1. Loop partition **L** matches the data partition **D**, *i.e.* $\mathbf{LG} \approx \mathbf{D}$. The references in the periphery due to small offsets between references in the UI-set are considered in F_f. In this case $R_b = 0$.
2. **L** does not match **D**. This is case where the **G** matrix used to compute **D** (perhaps from another UI-set), is different from the **G** for the current access, and thus **LG** and **D** have different *shapes*, not just different offsets. In this case all references for **L** are considered remote and $R_b = |\text{Det } \mathbf{L}|$.

This is a good approximation because **LG** and **D** each represent a regular tiling of the data space. If they differ, it means the footprint and data tile differ in shape, *and do not stride the same way.* Thus, even if **L**'s footprints and **D** partially overlap at the origin, there will be less overlap on other processors.

For a reasonably large number of processors, some will end up with no overlap as shown in the example in Figure 3. Since the execution time for a parallel loop nest is limited by the processor with the most remote cache misses, the non-overlap approximation is a good one.

```
Doall (i=0:100, j=0:75)
   B[i,j] = A[i,j] + A[i+j,j]
EndDoall
```

(a) Code fragment

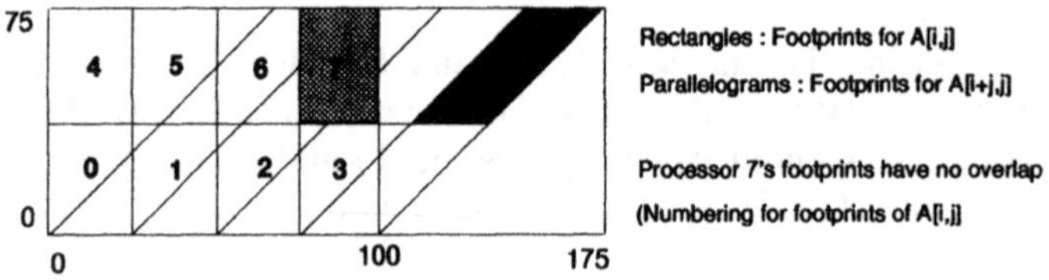

(b) Data space for Array A(8 processors)

Fig. 3. Different UI-sets have no overlap

Definition 2. F_b is the number of first time accesses in the footprint of **L** with base offset **b**. Hence:

$F_b = |\text{Det } \mathbf{L}|$

Definition 3. F_f is the difference between (1) the cumulative footprints of all the references in a given UI-set for a loop tile, and (2) the base footprint due to a single reference represented by **G** and the base offset **b**. F_f is referred to as the *peripheral footprint*.

See [2] for details on how the peripheral footprint is computed.

Theorem 4. *The cumulative access time for all accesses in a loop with partition* **L**, *accessing an array having data partition* **D** *with reference matrix* **G** *in a UI-set is*

$$T_{UI-set} = T_R(R_b + F_f) + T_L(F_b - R_b) + T_C(nref - (F_f + F_b))$$

where $nref$ is the total number of references made by **L** *for the UI-set.*

This result can be derived as follows. The number of remote accesses n_{remote} is the number of remote accesses with the base offset, which is R_b, plus the size of the peripheral footprint F_f, giving $n_{remote} = R_b + F_f$. The number of local references n_{local} is the base footprint, less the remote portion, i.e. $F_b - R_b$. Finally, number of cache hits n_{cache} is clearly $nref - n_{remote} - n_{local}$ which is equal to $nref - (F_f + F_b)$.

Sub-blocking The above cost model assumes infinite caches. In practice, even programs with moderate-sized data sets have footprints much larger than the cache size. To overcome this problem the loop tiles are ***sub-blocked***, such that each sub-block fits in the cache and has a shape that optimizes for cache locality. This optimization lets the cost model remain valid even for finite caches. It turned out that sub-blocking was critically important even for small to moderate problem sizes.

Finite caches and sub-blocking also allows us to ignore the effect of data that is shared between loop nests when that data is left behind in the cache by one loop nest and reused by another. Data sharing can happen in infinite caches due to accesses to the same array when the two loops use the same **G**. However, when caches are much smaller than data footprints, and the compiler resorts to sub-blocking, the possibility of reuse across loops is virtually eliminated.

This model also assumes a linear flow of control through the loop nests of the program. While this is the common case, conditional control flow can be handled by our algorithm. Although we do not handle this case now, an approach would be to assign probabilities to each loop nest, perhaps based on profile data, and to multiply the probabilities by the loop size to obtain an effective loop size for use by the algorithm.

5 The Multiple Loops Heuristic Method

This section describes the iterative method, whose goal is to discover a partitioning of loops and data arrays to minimize communication cost. We assume loop partitions are non-cyclic. Cyclic partitions could be handled using this method but for simplicity we leave them out.

5.1 Graph formulation

Our search procedure uses bipartite graphs to represent loops and data arrays. Bipartite graphs are a popular data structure used to represent partitioning problems for loops and data[11, 4]. For a graph G = (V_l, V_d, E), the loops are pictured as a set of nodes V_l on the left hand side, and the data arrays as a set of nodes V_d on the right. An edge e∈E between a loop and array node is present if and only if the loop accesses the array. The edges are labeled by the uniformly intersecting set(s) they represent. When we say that a data partition is ***induced*** by a loop partition, we mean the data partition **D** is the same as the loop partition **L**'s footprint. Similarly, for loop partitions induced by data partitions.

5.2 Iterative Method Outline

We use an iterative local search technique that exploits certain special properties of loops and data array partitions to move to a good solution. Extensive work evaluating search techniques has been done by researchers in many disciplines. Simulated annealing, gradient descent and genetic algorithms are some of these. See [14] for a comparison of some methods. All techniques rely on a cost function estimating some objective value to be optimized, and a search strategy. For specific problems more may be known than in the general case, and specific strategies may do better. In our case, we know the search direction that leads to improvement, and hence a specific strategy is defined. The algorithm greedily moves to a local minimum, does a mutation to escape from it, and repeats the process.

The following is the method in more detail. To derive the initial loop partition, the single loop optimization method described in Section 3 is used. Then an iterative improvement method is followed, which has two phases in each iteration: the first (forward) phase finds the best data partitions given loop partitions, and the second (back) phase redetermines the values of the loop partitions given the data partitions just determined.

We define a boolean value called the progress flag for each array. Specifically, in the forward phase the data partition of each array having a true progress flag is set to the induced data partition of the largest loop accessing it, among those which change the data partition. The method of controlling the progress flag is explained in section 5.2. In the back phase, each loop partition is set to be the data partition of one of the arrays accessed by the loop. The cost model is used to evaluate the alternative partitions and pick the one with minimal cost.

These forward and backward phases are repeated using the cost model to determine the estimated array reference cost for the current partitions. After some number of iterations, the best partition found so far is picked as the final partition. Termination is discussed in Section 5.2.

An example The workings of the heuristic can be seen by a simple example. Consider the following code fragment:

```
Doall (i=0:99, j=0:99)
  A[i,j] = i * j
EndDoall
Doall (i=0:99, j=0:99)
  B[i,j] = A[j,i]
EndDoall
```

The code does a transpose of A into B. The first loop is represented by X and the second by Y. The initial cache optimized solution for 4 processors is shown in Figure 4. In this example, as there is no peripheral footprint for either array, a default load balanced solution is picked. Iterations 1 and 2 with their forward and back phases are shown in Figure 5.

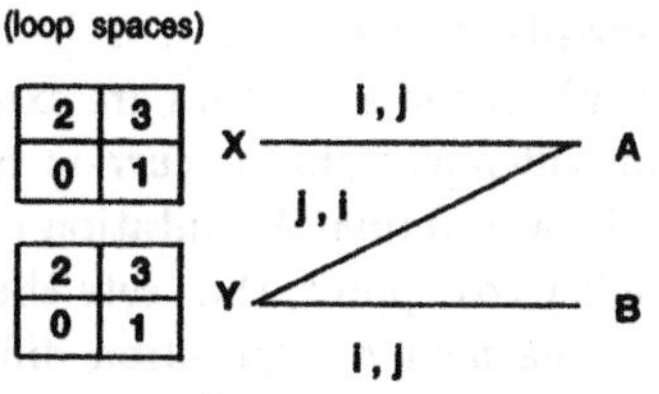

Fig. 4. Initial solution to loop partitioning (4 processors)

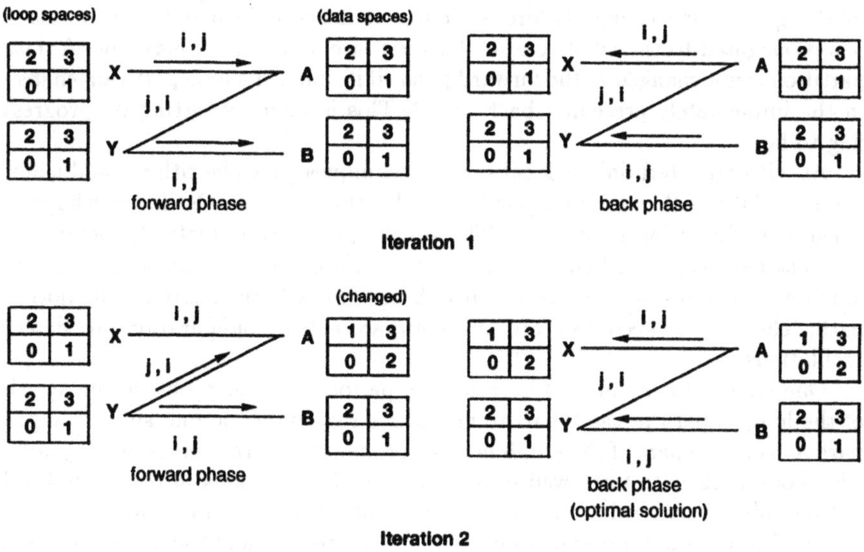

Fig. 5. Heuristic: iterations 1 and 2 (4 processors)

In iteration 1's forward phase A and B get data partitions from their largest accessing loops. Since both loops here are equal in size, the compiler picks either, and one possible choice is shown by the arrows. In 1's back phase, loop Y cannot match both A and B's data partitions, and the cost estimator indicates that matching either has the same cost. So an arbitrary choice as shown by the back arrows results in unchanged data partitions; nothing has changed from the beginning.

As explained in the next section, the choice of data partitions in the forward phase is *favored in the direction of change*. So now array A picks a different data partition from before, that of Y instead of X. In the back phase loop X now changes its loop partition to reduce cost as dictated by the cost function. This is the best solution found, and no further change occurs in subsequent iterations. In this case, this best solution is also the optimal solution as it has 100% locality. In this example a communication-free solution exists and was found. More generally, if one does not exist, the heuristic will evaluate many solutions and will pick the best one it finds.

Some Implementation Details The algorithm of the heuristic method is presented in Figure 6. Some details of the algorithm are explained here.

Choosing a data partition different from the current one is preferred because it ensures movement out of local minima. A mutation out of a local minimum is a change to a possibly higher cost point, that sets the algorithm on another path. This rule ensures that the next configuration differs from the previous, and hence makes it unnecessary to do global checks for local minima.

However, without a progress flag, always changing data partitions in the forward phase may change data partitions too fast. This is because one part of the graph may change before a change it induced in a previous iteration has propagated to the whole graph. This is prevented using a *bias rule*. A data partition is not changed in the forward phase if it induced a loop partition change in the immediately preceding back phase. This is done by setting its progress flag to false.

As with all deterministic local search techniques, this algorithm could suffer from oscillations. The progress flag helps solve this problem. Oscillations happen when a configuration is revisited. The solution is to, conservatively, determine if a cost has been seen before, and if it has, simply enforce change at all data partition selections in the next forward phase. This sets the heuristic on another path. There is no need to store and compare entire configurations to detect oscillations.

One issue is the number of iterations to perform. In this problem, the length of the longest path in the bipartite graph is a reasonable bound, since changed partitions in one part of the graph need to propagate to other parts of the graph. This bound seems to work well in practice. Further increases in this bound did not provide a better solution in any of the examples or programs tried.

In all of the small programs we tried, the heuristic found the known optimal solution. For the large applications in section 6 ,we do not know the optimal, but the heuristic found improved solutions with very high locality. Careful manual examination did not result in finding better partitions.

5.3 Algorithm Complexity

Here we show that the above algorithm runs in polynomial time in n and m, the number of loops and distributed arrays in the program. An exhaustive search guaranteed to find the optimal for this NP-complete problem is not practical.

Theorem 5. *The time complexity of the above heuristic is* $O(n^2m + m^2n)$.

To prove this, note that the number of iterations is the length of the longest acyclic path in the bipartite graph, which is upper bounded by $n + m$. The time for one iteration is the sum of the times of the forward and back phases. The forward phase does a selection among m possible loop partitions for each of n loops, giving a bound of $O(nm)$. The back phase does a selection among n

```
Procedure Do_forward_phase()
   for all d ∈ Data_set do
      if Progress_flag[d] then
         l ← largest loop accessing d which induces changed Data_partition[d]
         Data_partition[d] ← Partition induced by Loop_partition[l]
         Origin[d] ← Access function mapping of Origin[l]
         Inducing_loop[d] ← l
      endif
   endfor
end Procedure

Procedure Do_back_phase()
   for all l ∈ Loop_set do
     d ← Array inducing Loop_partition[l] with minimum cost of accessing all its data
     Loop_partition[l] ← Partition induced by Data_partition[d]
     Origin[l] ← Inverse access function mapping of Origin[d]
     if Inducing_loop[d] ≠ l then
        Progress_flag[d] ← false
     endif
   endfor
end Procedure

Procedure Partition
   Loop_set : set of all loops in the program
   Data_set : set of all data arrays in the program
   Graph_G : Bipartite graph of accesses in Loop_set to Data_set

   Min_partitions ← φ
   Min_cost ← ∞
   for all d ∈ Data_set do
      Progress_flag[d] ← true
   endfor
   for i= 1 to (length of longest path in Graph_G) do
      Do_forward_phase()
      Do_back_phase()
      Cost ← Find total cost of current partition configuration
      if Cost < Min_cost then
         Cost ← Min_cost
         Min_partitions ← Current partition configuration
      endif
      if cost repeated then              /* convergence or oscillation */
         for all d ∈ Data_set do            /* force progress */
            Progress_flag[d] ← true
         endfor
      endif
   endfor
end Procedure
```

Fig. 6. The heuristic algorithm

possible data partitions for each of m arrays, giving a bound of $O(nm)$. Thus overall the time is $O((n+m)mn) = O(n^2m + m^2n)$.

In practice, this small polynomial translated to an observed compile-time of no more than a few seconds for even large programs. In contrast, 0-1 integer programming methods inherently try to solve an NP-complete problem, and could suffer from exponential slowdown for any detailed formulation, as discussed in section 2.

6 Results

The algorithm described in this paper has been implemented as part of the compiler for the Alewife [3] machine. The Alewife machine is a cache-coherent multiprocessor with physically distributed memory. The nodes are configured in a 2-dimensional mesh network. The approximate average Alewife latencies for a 16 node machine are: 2 cycle cache hit, 11 cycle cache miss to local memory hit and 40 cycle remote cache miss. The last number will be larger for larger machine configurations or when network contention is present.

The data partitions specified by the different approaches we compare are implemented by a software page translation approach described in [5]. That is an independent piece of work, and in essence, provides an efficient addressing mechanism for any specified data partitions, by closely approximating data tile shapes by linear software pages.

We compared performance on the following applications:

Tomcatv A code from the SPEC suite. It has 12 loops and 7 arrays, all two dimensional.

Erlebacher A code written by Thomas Eidson, from ICASE. It performs 3-D tridiagonal solves using Alternating Direction Implicit (ADI) integration. It has 40 loops and 22 distributed arrays, in one, two and three dimensions.

Conduct A routine in SIMPLE, a two dimensional hydrodynamics code from Lawrence Livermore National Labs. It has 20 loops and 20 arrays, in one and two dimensions.

These programs were run using each of three compilation strategies:

cache + net-opt Uses the algorithm described in this paper, which optimizes for cache locality as well as network data locality.

cache + net-1 Uses the analysis in [2] to find loop partitions for cache locality, and then partitions each array by using the partition induced by the largest loop that accesses that array, to achieve some data locality. This analysis proceeds as in **cache + net-opt** but does only the *first* iterations' forward phase, and halts.

cache only Loop partitions as in [2] for cache locality. Allocates the data across processors randomly, thus giving poor data locality. This is implemented by using a feature of the data partition addressing mechanism used [5]. In this case, the pages are assigned to the processors in a round-robin manner,

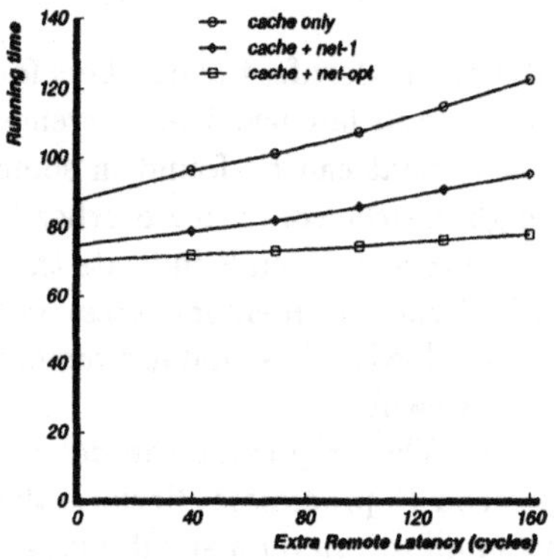

Fig. 7. Tomcatv (N = 800)

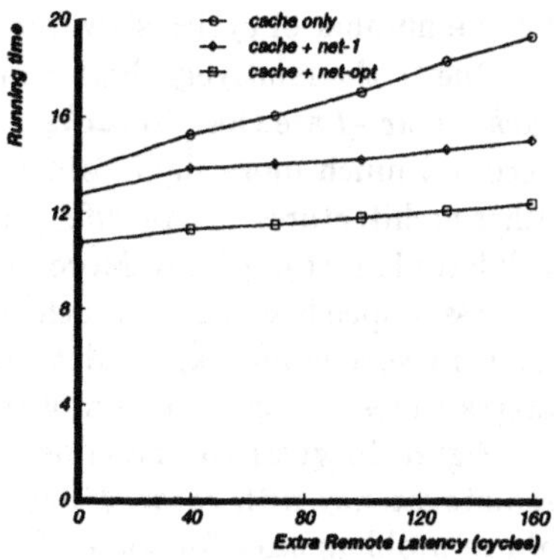

Fig. 8. Erlebacher (N = 48)

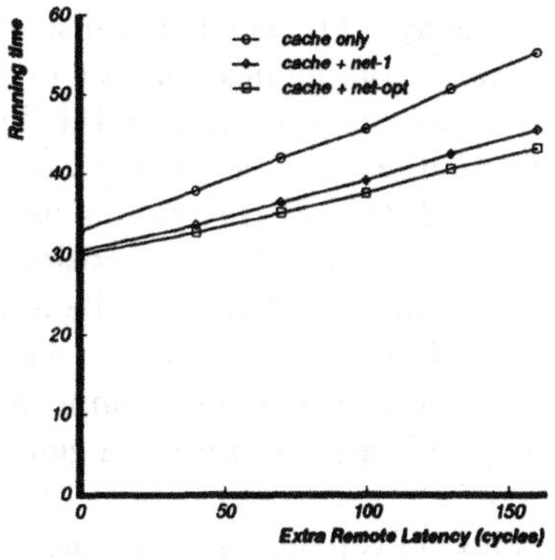

Fig. 9. Conduct (480 x 384)

Program	Problem Size	Speedup
Tomcatv	N = 192	15
Erlebacher	N = 48	10
Conduct	153 x 133	11

Fig. 10. Speedup (**cache + net-opt**) on 16 processors

effectively generating random placement from the viewpoint of any loop's accesses. This was confirmed by the statistics we collected.

Figures 7, 8 and 9 show the execution times for each application and partitioning strategy for a variety of remote latencies. The smallest latency uses the default Alewife configuration. The larger latencies were obtained by imposing a hardware-supported delay on remote cache misses. This was done by causing the processor to trap on a remote cache miss. This trap occurs at the same time that the request for data is sent to the remote node. A delay loop was then executed for the number of cycles shown in the graphs.

Due to the relatively short remote access latency in Alewife, the numbers for *cache + net-1* are close to *cache + net-opt* for the default latency. The difference becomes much more significant for longer latencies that can be found in some other architectures. In Alewife, programs with higher cache-coherency overheads will have longer latencies. More importantly, multiprocessor trends indicate that processor speeds will grow much beyond that on Alewife, but memory access and network speeds are expected to increase far more slowly, thus making remote access times a larger fraction of runtime than on Alewife.

Figure 10 gives the baseline speedup numbers. They represent the default remote latency with *cache + net-opt* optimization on 16 processors. Because the above problem sizes for some of them were too small to run on a small number of processors, these numbers are for smaller problem sizes as indicated in the table.

7 Conclusions and Summary

We have presented an algorithm to find loop and data partitions automatically for programs with multiple loop nests and data arrays. The algorithm discovers a partitioning of loops and data that minimizes communication cost over the multiple levels of memory hierarchy for the entire program. It does this by balancing the cost of cache misses and remote memory accesses using a cost function. If no communication-free partition is found, the cost function is used to guide a heuristic search through the global space of loop and data partitions. This method has been implemented as part of the compiler for the Alewife machine. We showed results from executing three applications on a real machine with 16 processors. These results indicate that significant performance improvements can be obtained by looking at data locality and cache locality in a global framework.

In the future we would like to add the possibility of copying data at runtime to avoid remote references as in [4]. This factor could be added to our cost model.

References

1. S. G. Abraham and D. E. Hudak. Compile-time partitioning of iterative parallel loops to reduce cache coherency traffic. *IEEE Transactions on Parallel and Distributed Systems*, 2(3):318–328, July 1991.
2. A. Agarwal, D.A. Kranz, and V. Natarajan. Automatic Partitioning of Parallel Loops and Data Arrays for Distributed Shared-Memory Multiprocessors. *IEEE Transactions on Parallel and Distributed Systems*, 6(9):943–962, September 1995.
3. Anant Agarwal, Ricardo Bianchini, David Chaiken, Kirk Johnson, David Kranz, John Kubiatowicz, Beng-Hong Lim, Kenneth Mackenzie, and Donald Yeung. The MIT Alewife Machine: Architecture and Performance. In *Proceedings of the 22nd Annual International Symposium on Computer Architecture (ISCA'95)*, pages 2–13, June 1995.

4. Jennifer M. Anderson and Monica S. Lam. Global Optimizations for Parallelism and Locality on Scalable Parallel Machines. In *Proceedings of SIGPLAN '93 Conference on Programming Languages Design and Implementation.* ACM, June 1993.
5. R. Barua, D. Kranz, and A. Agarwal. Communication-Minimal Partitioning of Parallel Loops and Data Arrays for Cache-Coherent Distributed-Memory Multiprocessors. Submitted for publication, June 1995.
6. R. Bixby, K. Kennedy, and U. Kremer. Automatic Data Layout Using 0-1 Integer Programming. In *Proceedings of the International Conference on Parallel Architectures and Compilation Techniques (PACT)*, pages 111–122, Montreal, Canada, August 1994.
7. Steve Carr, Kathryn S. McKinley, and Chau-Wen Tzeng. Compiler Optimization for Improving Data Locality. In *Sixth International Conference on Architectural Support for Programming Languages and Operating Systems (ASPLOS VI)*, pages 252–262, October 1994.
8. M. Cierniak and W. Li. Unifying Data and Control Transformations for Distributed Shared-Memory Machines. *Proceedings of the SIGPLAN PLDI*, 1995.
9. M. Gupta and P. Banerjee. Demonstration of Automatic Data Partitioning Techniques for Parallelizing Compilers on Multicomputers. *IEEE Transactions on Parallel and Distributed Systems*, 3(2):179–193, March 1992.
10. Seema Hiranandani, Ken Kennedy, and Chau-Wen Tseng. Compiling Fortran D for MIMD Distributed Memory Machines. *Communications of the ACM*, 35(8):66–80, August 1992.
11. Y. Ju and H. Dietz. Reduction of Cache Coherence Overhead by Compiler Data Layout and Loop Transformation. In *Languages and Compilers for Parallel Computing*, pages 344–358, Springer Verlag, 1992.
12. Kathleen Knobe, Joan Lukas, and Guy Steele Jr. Data Optimization: Allocation of Arrays to Reduce Communication on SIMD Machines. *Journal of Parallel and Distributed Computing*, 8(2):102–118, August 1990.
13. J. Ramanujam and P. Sadayappan. Compile-Time Techniques for Data Distribution in Distributed Memory Machines. *IEEE Transactions on Parallel and Distributed Systems*, 2(4):472–482, October 1991.
14. Bart Selman, Henry Kautz, and Bram Cohen. Noise Strategies for Improving Local Search. *Proceedings, AAAI*, 1, 1994.
15. C.-W. Tseng. *An Optimizing Fortran D compiler for MIMD Distributed-Memory Machines.* PhD thesis, Rice University, Jan 1993. Published as Rice COMP TR93-199.
16. R.P. Wilson, R.S. French, C.S. Wilson, S.P. Amarasinghe, J.M. Anderson, S.W.K. Tjiang, S.-W. Liao, C.-W. Tseng, M.W. Hall, M.S. Lam, and J.L. Hennessy. SUIF: An Infrastructure for Research on Parallelizing and Optimizing Compilers. *ACM SIGPLAN Notices*, 29(12):31–37, December 1994.
17. Michael E. Wolf and Monica S. Lam. A Loop Transformation Theory and an Algorithm to Maximize Parallelism. In *The Third Workshop on Programming Languages and Compilers for Parallel Computing*, August 1990. Irvine, CA.

Resource-Based Communication Placement Analysis*

Ken Kennedy and Ajay Sethi

Center for Research on Parallel Computation
Department of Computer Science, Rice University
6100 Main Street, MS 41, Houston, TX 77005

Abstract. Communication placement analysis is an important step in the compilation of data-parallel programs. However, to simplify the placement analysis, previous techniques ignored most machine-dependent resource constraints. This paper demonstrates the necessity of incorporating resource constraints in ensuring the correctness of the communication placement. It presents a new placement analysis technique that minimizes frequency of communication, eliminates redundant communication, and maximizes communication latency hiding while taking limited resources into account. The paper illustrates resource-based placement analysis in the context of placement of distributed-memory communication primitives and limited buffer size resource constraint. In addition, it shows the use of stripmining transformation in improving the efficacy of resource-based communication placement.

1 Introduction

Communication delay is the main impediment to high performance on modern parallel computers. Since most parallel machines package memory with processors, accesses to remote memory are typically an order of magnitude slower than accesses to local memory. Thus, remote accesses add communication overhead to the total execution time and, as the number of processors increase, communication overhead can dominate the execution time [14]. Reducing communication overhead is a key goal of optimizing parallel programs.

Communication overhead can be reduced in three ways: by reducing the frequency of communication, by eliminating redundant communication, and by hiding communication latency. Communication frequency can be reduced by hoisting communication to the outer-most program location. Latency hiding can

* This work was supported in part by ARPA contract DABT63-92-C-0038 and NSF Cooperative Agreement Number CCR-9120008. The content of this paper does not necessarily reflect the position or the policy of the Government, and no official endorsement should be inferred.

be achieved by initiating communication as early as possible. This exposes opportunities for overlapping communication with some intervening computation. There have been several efforts [5, 4, 7, 8] to use data-flow analysis to determine communication placement that minimizes communication overhead. However, to reduce the complexity of the problem being solved, previous frameworks ignored most machine-dependent resource constraints. This paper introduces a new framework for ***resource-based communication placement***, which takes limited resources into account.

Examples of resource constraints include cache size on distributed shared-memory systems (DSMs), in-core memory size in out-of-core computations, and the number of physical registers in register allocation. The communication placement that doesn't take resource constraints into account can prove too eager in moving communication earlier in the program. For example, prefetching data at the earliest program location can cause data to get displaced from cache even before it is used. Moreover, placing communication at the earliest location can increase demands on the system resources. An example of this is the increased buffer requirement due to unconstrained hoisting of messages out of loops. Resource constraints can affect both the performance and correctness of the placement. Prefetch placement that honors cache size resource constraint will yield better performance than the placement that doesn't.

On the other hand, and more significantly, resource-based communication placement is required to ensure the correctness of the placement. For example, buffer requirement for communication placement that does not take limited resources into account can exceed the maximum available buffer and, thus, make it impossible to execute the program; resource-based communication placement can guarantee that the memory requirement of the program does not exceed the maximum available in-core memory.

The data-flow analysis framework presented in this paper, besides eliminating partially redundant communications and maximizing latency hiding, incorporates machine-dependent resource constraints. We demonstrate our approach by imposing buffer size constraint on communication placement. The paper includes several original contributions. It presents a framework for resource-based communication placement. It shows how the problem of incorporating resource constraints into communication placement can be reduced to the problem of proper initialization of appropriate data-flow variables. It details the analysis to compute the buffer requirement for a given program. Finally, it describes how the results of resource analysis, together with the stripmining transformation, can be used to improve the efficacy of the communication placement. The communication placement analysis presented here has been implemented in the Rice Fortran D95 compiler (a High Performance Fortran [11] compiler) where it is used to determine the placement of distributed-memory communication primitives (SEND and RECV).

The rest of the paper is organized as follows. Section 2 motivates the need for resource-based communication placement with the help of benchmark programs. Sections 3 and 4 outline the underlying graph structure and our communication placement framework. Section 5 describes how resource constraints are incorporated into our placement framework. Section 6 presents the data-flow equations for resource analysis. Section 7 describes how the results of the analysis are incorporated into the placement and Section 8 gives some implementation details. Section 9 describes previous work in communication placement analysis. We conclude in Section 10 by summarizing our technique.

2 Motivating Examples

Resource constraints pose a fundamental and important issue that should be addressed by every compiler. Consider the matrix multiply program fragment shown in Figure 1(a). Let the three data arrays (a, b, and c) be of size $n \times n$ and distributed with (BLOCK, BLOCK) distribution across a 4×4 processor grid. Let the owner of c(i,j) perform the computation; thus, the references a(i,k) and b(k,j) cause off-processor accesses (we will refer to such references as "non-local" references). As shown in Figure 1(c), communication can be placed outside the loop nest. For the sake of clarity, the guards and processor loops enclosing communication primitives are not shown in the figure.

Figure 1(b) shows the non-local sections of arrays a and b required by processor (1,1) to perform its local computation; other processors need to fetch similar non-local sections of arrays a and b. In the distributed-memory systems, non-local data is communicated using messages. Now, each message has a corresponding buffer that the compiler utilizes to unpack the data received from other processor (we will refer to these buffers as non-local buffers). As can be

```
do k = 1, n
   do j = 1, n
      do i = 1, n
         c(i,j) = c(i,j) + a(i,k) * b(k,j)
      enddo
   enddo
enddo
```

(a)

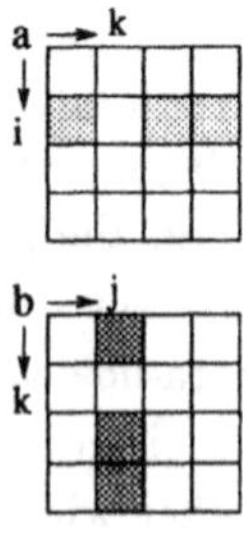

(b)

```
SEND/RECV a(i$lb:i$ub, 1:n)
SEND/RECV b(1:n, j$lb:j$ub)
do k = 1, n
   do j = j$lb, j$ub
      do i = i$lb, i$ub
         c(i,j) = c(i,j) + a(i,k) * b(k,j)
      enddo
   enddo
enddo
```

(c)

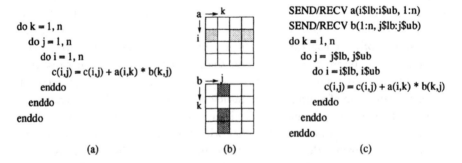

Fig. 1. (a) Original matrix multiply loop nest. (b) Non-local data accessed by processor (1,1). (c) Matrix multiply with partitioned loops.

seen from Figure 1(b), the communication placement shown in Figure 1(c) requires non-local buffers of size $3n^2/8$ per processor. On the other hand, the total size of local sections of arrays a, b, and c per processor is $3n^2/16$. Thus, the non-local buffer required by the communication placement in Figure 1(c) *triples* the memory requirement! In general, for a $p_1 \times p_2$ processor grid, the total size of local sections of arrays a, b, and c per processor is $3n^2/p_1p_2$ and the size of non-local buffers per processor is $(p_1 - 1)n^2/p_1p_2 + (p_2 - 1)n^2/p_1p_2$. Thus, for the general case, non-local buffers increase the buffer requirement by a factor of $(p_1 + p_2 + 1)/3$! In other words, the increase in buffer requirement due to non-local buffers is proportional to the dimensions of the processor grid. However, since memory is limited, it might not always be possible to have so much memory available. Therefore, the compiler needs to ensure that the non-local buffers do not cause the node codes to exceed the maximum memory available.

Note that the non-local buffer requirement would have been less if the communication were not hoisted (vectorized) to the outer-most level. For example, if both SEND a(i,k) and SEND b(k,j) (along with RECV a(i,k) and RECV b(k,j)) are placed inside the "**do** i" loop, each processor needs two buffers with only a single element each; thus, the non-local buffer requirement is 2. Also, if the communication occurs inside the "**do** j" and "**do** k" loops, the buffer requirement is $n/4 + 1$ and $n/2$, respectively. If, however, communication is placed as shown in Figure 1(c), each processor requires non-local buffers of size $3n^2/8$.

Let's assume that $n/2$ is less than the maximum memory available for non-local buffers but $3n^2/8$ exceeds the maximum. (For example, on 16 Intel iPSC/860 processors with 8 MB memory available per processor, this occurs for double precision arrays of size 1280×1280.) To find a placement that satisfies the maximum non-local buffer resource constraint, we would like the data-flow analysis to place SEND/RECV a(i,k) and SEND/RECV b(k,j) inside the "**do** k" loop. In other words, we want the compiler to incorporate resource constraints in the communication placement analysis.

However, resource constraints and latency hiding optimizations have conflicting requirements. Consider the dy3d6p subroutine, shown in Figure 2(a), from the ERLEBACHER benchmark program. Figure 2(b) shows the corresponding pseudo node code along with the communication causing references and resource-independent communication placement. The references that require off-processor data are determined based on the assumption that the owners of the *lhs* references perform the computation. For the sake of clarity, we have neither reduced/localized loop bounds nor inserted guards around the loops and communication primitives. The SENDs are placed at the beginning of the subroutine since the array uu is not modified in the subroutine and the data is received just before it is required.

```
subroutine dy3d6p
parameter (n$p = 8)
double precision uu(n,n,n)
double precision uud(n,n,n)
distribute (*,block,*) :: uu, uud
do 10 k = 1, n
  do 10 i = 1, n
    uud(i,1,k) =
         F(uu(i,2,k), uu(i,3,k),
            uu(i,n-1,k), uu(i,n,k))
    uud(i,2,k) =
         F(uu(i,1,k), uu(i,3,k),
            uu(i,4,k), uu(i,n,k))
10 continue
do 20 k = 1, n
  do 20 i = 1, n
    uud(i,n-1,k) =
         F(uu(i,1,k), uu(i,n-3,k),
            uu(i,n-2,k), uu(i,n,k))
    uud(i,n,k) =
         F(uu(i,1,k), uu(i,2,k),
            uu(i,n-2,k), uu(i,n-1,k))
20 continue
do 30 k = 1, n
  do 30 j = 3, n-2
    do 30 i = 1, n
      uud(i,j,k) =
         F(uu(i,j-2,k), uu(i,j-1,k),
            uu(i,j+1,k), uu(i,j+2,k))
30 continue
end
```

(a)

```
subroutine dy3d6p
parameter (n$p = 8,size = n/n$p)
double precision uu(n,-1:size+2,n)
double precision uud(n,size,n)
start = my$p*size
SEND uu(1:n,n-1:n,1:n) to P0 ①
SEND uu(1:n,1:2,1:n) to P_n$p-1 ②
SEND uu(1:n,size-1:size,1:n) to P_my$p+1 ③
SEND uu(1:n,start:start+1,1:n) to P_my$p-1 ④
RECV uu(1:n,n-1:n,1:n) ①
do 10 k = 1, n
  do 10 i = 1, n
    uud(i,1,k) = F(uu(i,n-1,k),
                     uu(i,n,k), ...)
    uud(i,2,k) = F(uu(i,n,k), ...)
10 continue
RECV uu(1:n,1:2,1:n) ②
do 20 k = 1, n
  do 20 i = 1, n
    uud(i,n-1,k) = F(uu(i,1,k), ...)
    uud(i,n,k) = F(uu(i,1,k),
                     uu(i,2,k), ...)
20 continue
RECV uu(1:n,size-1:size,1:n) ③
RECV uu(1:n,start:start+1,1:n) ④
do 30 k = 1, n
  do 30 j = 3, n-2
    do 30 i = 1, n
      uud(i,j,k) =
        F(uu(i,j-2,k), uu(i,j-1,k),
           uu(i,j+1,k), uu(i,j+2,k))
30 continue
end
```

(b)

Fig. 2. (a) The dy3d6p subroutine from the ERLEBACHER benchmark. (b) Resource-independent communication placement.

The communication placement shown in Figure 2(b) maximizes the latency hiding by initiating all the SENDs at the start of the subroutine. However, this placement increases the ranges over which the messages are "live". Since a message can be received any time after it has been sent, we assume that the corresponding non-local buffer is live from the time data is sent. This buffer remains live till the last use of the data. Thus, the earliest placement of SENDs increases the live ranges of non-local buffers which, in turn, results in more non-local buffers to be live simultaneously and thus increases the total memory required to allocate non-local buffers. On 8 Intel iPSC/860 processors with 8 MB memory available per processor and n = 112, the placement shown in Figure 2(b) causes the memory requirement to exceed the maximum memory available and the program can not be loaded on the cube. Therefore, although the placement in Figure 2(b) maximizes the latency hiding, it also increases the buffer requirement of the program. This example illustrates the conflicting goals of the latency hiding optimizations and resource constraints.

Our goal in this paper is to develop a placement framework that can maximize latency hiding while honoring resource constraints. For dy3d6p, this can be achieved by initiating SENDs ② – ④ after the first loop nest and by using the same memory for the non-local buffers for messages ① and ②. This decreases the memory requirement by 196 KB and the resulting program fits in the memory. In Sections 4 – 7, we describe the placement analysis that handles the above-mentioned issues.

3 Interval-Flow Graph

Our communication placement algorithm (Section 4) is based on interval analysis [1]. Interval analysis incorporates program structure into data-flow equations to enable their non-iterative and efficient solution. However, unlike classical interval analysis, we do not construct a sequence of interval graphs by recursively collapsing intervals into single nodes. Instead, we use an *interval-flow graph*, which is the control-flow graph with an interval structure imposed on it. An interval is just a collection of nodes; it is defined formally below. While solving the data-flow equations, we summarize appropriate information for an interval and propagate it to the interval header. Our interval-flow graph is similar to that used by the Give-N-Take framework [8]; it differs in the way critical edges are eliminated (see below).

The important properties of the interval-flow graph, $G = (N, E)$, are as follows. First, G is reducible; that is, each loop has a unique header node. Moreover, in this paper we assume that G corresponds to a structured program; however, the placement framework can be extended to handle jumps out of loops. Second, G is based on Tarjan intervals [13], where a Tarjan interval $T(h)$ is a set of control-flow nodes that correspond to a loop body in the program text. A Tarjan interval has a unique header node h, where $h \notin T(h)$. Third, there are no *critical edges*. A critical edge connects a node with multiple successors to a node with multiple predecessors [10]. Critical edges are eliminated by splitting edges as follows: every edge leading to a node with more than one predecessor is split by inserting a *synthetic node*. Fourth, each edge in E is classified as entry, back, or forward edge, where an entry (back) edge corresponds to the edge from

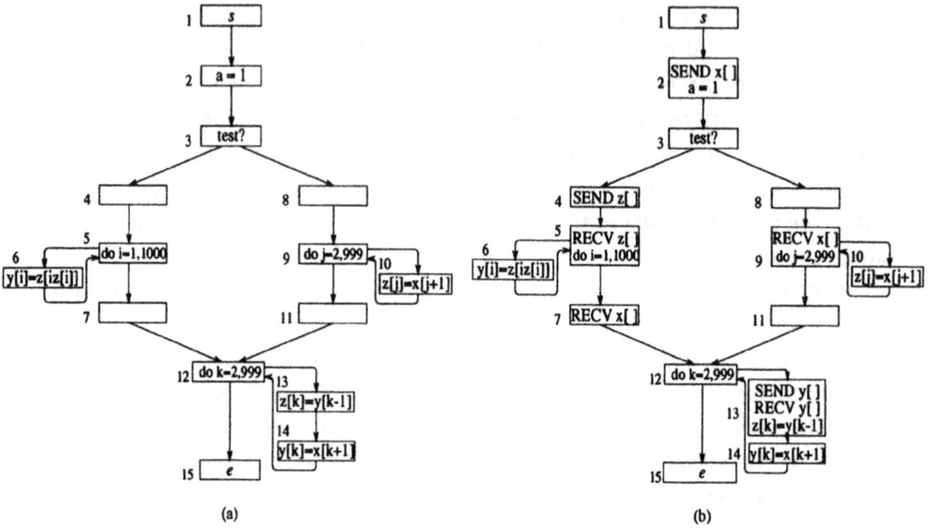

Fig. 3. (a) An example program. (b) Resource-independent communication placement.

(to) an interval header to (from) a node within the interval. All other edges are classified as forward edges. Finally, for every non-empty interval $T(h)$, there exists an unique $g \in T(h)$ such that $(g, h) \in E$; that is, there is only one back edge out of $T(h)$. This is achieved by adding a *post-body node* to $T(h)$ [8]. We assume that N has s and e as unique start and end nodes.

The graph shown in Figure 3(a) is used to illustrate resource-based communication placement. Though not shown in the figure, the graph is implicitly partitioned into intervals; each loop body in Figure 3(a) corresponds to an interval. For example, nodes 13 and 14 constitute an interval, with node 12 as the interval header. Let arrays x, y, and z (each with 1000 elements) be distributed with the same distribution (say, BLOCK distribution) across 4 processors. Also, assume that for each assignment, the *lhs* reference is made responsible for performing the computation (that is, we assume that the *owner-computes* rule is used). Thus, the *rhs* terms in nodes 6, 10, 13, and 14 correspond to non-local references. Note that the references x[j+1] and x[k+1] (nodes 10 and 14) require identical non-local data elements. Also, there is a loop-carried true dependence from node 14 to node 13 on array y; thus, the communication for the non-local reference y[k-1] needs to be placed inside the "**do** k" loop (node 12).

4 Communication Placement Framework

We now present an outline of our placement framework. To maximize latency hiding, our framework places SENDs as early as possible and RECVs as late as possible while ensuring that the buffer constraint is satisfied. To facilitate this, and unlike previous frameworks, the SEND and RECV placements are determined in two separate phases. In addition, our framework ensures that every program execution path contains matching SEND and RECV pairs; that is, SENDs and RECVs are *balanced* [8].

Before performing the placement analysis, we identify the references that cause remote accesses (that is, the non-local references). With each non-local reference, we associate a descriptor that is used to record information such as the placement of the corresponding communication primitives. For the sake of convenience, we will represent a descriptor with the corresponding non-local reference's name. Also, with each node n and descriptor d, we associate $Used(n, d)$ and $Transp(n, d)$ predicates. $Used(n, d)/Transp(n, d)$ indicate whether the data section corresponding to d is used at/not modified at n. We use array section analysis [6] to compare data sections precisely. If the data section corresponding to d is used (not modified) at n, we initialize $Used(n, d)$ ($Transp(n, d)$) to $\top$; and to $\bot$ otherwise. We use the semi-lattice $L = \{\bot, \text{UNBAL}, \top\}$.

Note that the non-local references can either correspond to *rhs* references (non-local reads) or *lhs* references (non-local writes). The benchmark programs in Section 2 had communication requirements corresponding to non-local reads. In case of non-local write, a processor computes the value(s) that need to be assigned to off-processor array element(s). The processor assigns the computed value(s) to a local copy of the data and sends back the updated copy to the owner of the data. Both non-local read and write communication instances require the placement of SEND and RECV pairs. Non-local reads require the data to be communicated *before* it is used (that is, before the off-processor data is referenced). Non-local writes, on the other hand, require the non-local data to be communicated back to the owner processor *after* it has been computed. Thus, non-local reads and writes are dual of each other.

This paper concentrates on the *before* placement problem; that is, communication placement corresponding to the non-local reads. Non-local writes require a very similar analysis. The resource-based communication placement analysis for non-local reads can be divided into following four phases.

Resource-independent send placement: First, we determine send placement without taking resource constraints into account. To determine send placement, we make two passes over the interval-flow graph. In the first pass, we traverse the interval-flow graph in reverse pre-order (backwards and inside-out) and determine the set of *safe* nodes for each SEND(d), where SEND(d) is the send primitive associated with the descriptor d. A node n is *safe* for SEND(d) if the data section corresponding to d is not modified between n and the node that uses the communicated data *and* the communicated data is used along all terminating paths starting at n. Conceptually, we place SEND(d) at the node that uses the data section corresponding to d and then hoist it up in the interval-flow graph to obtain all the nodes that are safe (that is, satisfy the safety criterion). In the second pass in this phase, we use data-flow equations to select the earliest safe node along each execution path. Since the equation for the safety criterion determines how early a SEND can be placed, we will describe the safety criterion in more detail in Section 5.

Resource analysis: We use the resource-independent send placement to compute resource usage for every node in a program (Section 6). As described in Section 2, earlier placement of SENDs increases the range over which the data, and the non-local buffers, need to be live. Longer live ranges of non-local buffers can cause more buffers to be live simultaneously and increase the total size of non-local buffers required. Thus, the placement of SEND primitives determines the total buffer usage. However, the buffer usage is independent of the receive placement because the live range of non-local buffers depend only on the last use of the communicated data and not on the placement of the RECV primitive. Thus, before performing resource analysis we determine only the resource-independent send placement.

Resource-based send placement: The buffer usage determined by the resource analysis phase is used to find the nodes that exceed the maximum buffer constraint. For each node that exceeds the resource constraint, we initialize appropriate data-flow variables (Section 7). Next, using the resource-conscious initialization of data-flow variables, we determine the resource-based send placement. This phases uses the same data-flow equations for send placement as the resource-independent send placement phase with the only difference being the initialization of appropriate data-flow variables. Note that if sufficient resources are available, our framework determines the same placement as that determined by resource-independent frameworks [8].

Latest balanced receive placement: Finally, we use the resource-based send placement to determine the corresponding receive placement. We make two passes over the interval-flow graph. In the first pass, we traverse the graph in pre-order, and for each SEND(d), we determine the nodes where RECV(d) can be placed without violating the balance criterion. The second pass determines the latest node, along each execution path, that results in balanced communication placement for each descriptor d.

Since the placement of non-local write primitives is a dual problem, resource-based communication placement for non-local writes also requires the above four phases; but, in reverse order. Thus, we first compute resource-independent receive placement (since RECVs and not SENDs determine the live ranges of non-local write buffers); second, we perform resource analysis; third, we determine resource-based receive placement; and, finally, compute the earliest balanced send placement. Details about the data-flow equations in the absence of resource constraints have been described elsewhere [9].

5 Safety Criterion

In our data-flow equations, we use SAFE(n, d) to indicate whether node n is a safe placement location for SEND(d). For descriptor d, node n can be marked *unsafe* for one of the following reasons: (1) (traditional) data-flow analysis: the communicated data corresponding to d is not used along all terminating paths starting at n or (2) dependence analysis: n is a header node and the corresponding loop carries a true dependence that affects the communication corresponding to the descriptor d. To incorporate resource constraints in our framework, we extend the safety criterion as follows. We deem a node *unsafe* if it either does not satisfy the two safety criteria mentioned above *or* (3) if it causes the non-local buffer requirement to exceed the maximum buffer available.

Criterion (1) states that node n is a safe placement location for SEND(d) if it either (a) contains an use of the communicated data ($Used(n, d) = \top$), or (b) does not modify the data being sent ($Transp(n, d) = \top$) and all its successors are safe (that is, $\bigcap_{s \in \text{SUCCS}^F(n)} \text{SAFE}(s, d) = \top$). Thus,

$$\text{SAFE}(n, d) = \text{SAFE}(n, d) \cap [Used(n, d) \cup Transp(n, d) \cap \bigcap_{s \in \text{SUCCS}^F(n)} \text{SAFE}(s, d) \cup$$
$$(Transp(\text{SUCCS}^E(n), d) \cap \text{SAFE}(\text{SUCCS}^E(n), d))]$$

where $\text{SUCCS}^F(n)$ are the forward edge successors of node n and $\text{SUCCS}^E(n)$ is the entry node successor of header node n ($\text{SUCCS}^E(n) = \emptyset$ if n is not a header node). The term $(Transp(\text{SUCCS}^E(n), d) \cap SAFE(\text{SUCCS}^E(n), d))$ indicates whether SEND(d) can be hoisted across the first node in the interval. This term allows the header nodes to hoist communication out of loops if communication can be hoisted before the first node in the loop body; that is, this term incorporates message vectorization into our placement analysis.

In the absence of resource constraints, dependence information is used to initialize SAFE variable for the header nodes. For example, the loop-carried dependence from node 14 to node 13 in Figure 3(a) causes SAFE(12, y[ ]) to be initialized to $\perp$; this indicates that it is not safe to hoist communication corresponding to array y across node 12. Further, for each node n that exceeds resource constraint(s), we initialize appropriate SAFE(n, d) variables to $\perp$ (Section 7); for every other node n and descriptor d, SAFE(n, d) is initialized to $\top$.

Figure 3(b) shows the earliest placement of SEND primitives and the latest balanced placement of RECV primitives without taking resources into account. The figure does not show the guards that enclose the communication primitives;

appropriate guards are inserted later in the code generation phase of the Fortran D95 compiler. SEND y[ ] is placed at node 13 due to the initialization described above. Since the array x is not modified in the program, SEND x[ ] can be hoisted to node 2 (by definition, we assume that every data set gets modified at the start node *s*). Also, SEND z[ ] can not be hoisted before node 4 because the communicated data is not used along the path {1,2,3,8,9,11,12,15}. Placement of RECV x[ ] depicts what we mean by the latest balanced placement; RECV x[ ] is placed at node 9 since x is used in the interval headed by the node 9. Now, since the right branch {8,9,11} of the conditional contains a matching SEND x[ ] and RECV x[ ] pair, the left branch must also contain a RECV x[ ] for balanced placement. We use data-flow equations to determine node 7 as the latest placement location. Similarly, RECV y[ ] and RECV z[ ] are placed at the latest locations (nodes 13 and 5, respectively).

6 Resource Analysis

We now describe the analysis required to compute buffer requirement for non-local read accesses. A similar analysis can be performed to determine the buffer required for non-local writes. We compute the buffer requirement for a processor by estimating the number of non-local accesses made by non-local references. However, instead of computing non-local buffer required by individual processors, we compute the *total* buffer required by all the processors. To compute the total buffer requirement, we compute the maximum non-local buffer required by a processor and multiply it by the number of processors. Though this approach forces us to over-estimate the buffer requirement in some cases (for example, in case of multi-spread communication pattern, since it does not involve all processors), we can handle the commonly occurring communication patterns such as shift, broadcast (all except one processor require same amount of non-local buffer), all-to-all communication, etc. precisely.

Let the maximum non-local buffer size allowed per processor, *maxBuffer*, be 250 array elements (for the sake of clarity, we express the size of the buffer in terms of array elements and assume that all arrays in Figure 3(a) are of the same type). Also, let the number of processors be 4. Therefore, the total buffer available among the four processors, *totalBuffer*, is 4*250 = 1000 array elements.

6.1 Resource Analysis For Individual Loop Nests

We first compute the buffer requirements for individual loop nests by ignoring the statements outside the loop nest and ensure that no single loop nest or message exceeds the specified maximum buffer. In this section, we will use "message *d*" to imply the message corresponding to the descriptor *d*. Since the loops can be nested inside other loops, we traverse the interval-flow graph in reverse pre-order.

$$\mathit{Buffer}(n) = \oplus_{s \in \text{SUCCS}^F(n)}(\mathit{Node}(n), \mathit{Buffer}_{in}(s)) \tag{1}$$

$$\mathit{Buffer}_{in}(n) = \mathit{Buffer}(n) - \sum_{d \in \text{SEND\_SET}(n)} \mathit{msg\_size}(d) \tag{2}$$

$$\mathit{Path}(n) = \max_{s \in \text{SUCCS}^F(n)} (\mathit{Path}(s), \mathit{Buffer}(n) - \sum_{d \in \text{HOISTED}(\text{HEADER}(n))} \mathit{msg\_size}(d)) \tag{3}$$

$$\mathit{Loop}(h) = \max(\mathit{Loop}(h), \mathit{Path}(n)), h = \text{HEADER}(n) \tag{4}$$

$$\mathit{Buffer}(h) = \oplus_{s \in \text{SUCCS}^F(h)}(\mathit{Loop}(h), \mathit{Buffer}_{in}(s), \otimes(\text{number-of-iterations}, \mathit{Buffer}_{in}(\text{SUCCS}^E(h)))) \tag{5}$$

$$\mathit{Total}(n) = \mathit{Path}(n) + \mathit{Total}(\text{SUCCS}^F(\text{HEADER}(n))) \tag{6}$$

$$\mathit{Avail}(n) = \mathit{total\_buffer} - \mathit{Loop}(n) - \mathit{Total}(n) \tag{7}$$

Fig. 4. Equations for computing the non-local buffer requirement.

Let $Node(n)$ be the size of the buffer required for non-local accesses at node n. For example, in Figure 3(b), $Node(13) = Node(14) = 4$ (1 array element per processor) corresponding to the references y[k-1] and x[k+1]. $Node(n) = 0$ if there are no non-local accesses at node n.

Let $Buffer_{in}(n)/Buffer(n)$ be the size of live buffers excluding/including the buffers corresponding to the messages sent at node n. Buffer required at node n, $Buffer(n)$, is the sum of the buffer requirement of node n and the size of the live messages at the exit of node n, given by $Buffer_{in}(s)$ for a forward edge successor s of n. To compute the buffer required at the start of node n, $Buffer_{in}(n)$, we subtract the total size of the messages sent at the node n. Equations 1 and 2 in Figure 4 give the corresponding equations for a non-header node n. The $\oplus$ operator takes overlapping messages into account. Section 8.1 describes its implementation in the Fortran D95 compiler. SEND_SET(n) is the set of messages sent at the nodes in $T(n) \cup \{n\}$ and $msg\_size(d)$ is the size of the message d; it is updated as communication is hoisted out of loop(s). ($T(n) = \emptyset$ if n is not a header node.) For example, since node 14 is the last node in the interval, $\text{SUCCS}^F(14)$, the forward edge successors of node 14, is $\emptyset$. Since no messages are sent at node 14, by Equations 1 and 2, $Buffer(14) = Buffer_{in}(14) = Node(14) = 4$. Now, $Buffer(13)$ is computed as follows: $Buffer(13) = \oplus(Node(13), Buffer_{in}(14)) = \oplus(4,4) = 8$ since the buffers for SEND x[ ] and SEND y[ ] do not overlap. By Equation 2, $Buffer_{in}(13) = 8 - 4 = 4$ since SEND y[ ] is placed at node 13.

Let $Path(n)$ be the maximum buffer required for the communication primitives placed on any path from n to the ***post-body node*** of the interval. As shown in Equation 3, it is computed by determining the maximum buffer at the successor nodes and comparing it with the size of messages that are live at the node and are *not* hoisted out of the enclosing loop (that is, $Buffer(n) -$

$\Sigma_{d \in \text{HOISTED}(\text{HEADER}(n))} msg\_size(d))$. For header node h, HOISTED(h) gives the messages that are hoisted out of the interval headed by the node h. Note that $Path(post\text{-}body\ node) = 0$. As an example, $Path(14) = \max(0, Buffer(14) - \Sigma_{d \in \text{HOISTED}(12)} msg\_size(d)) = \max(4 - 4) = 0$. $\Sigma_{d \in \text{HOISTED}(12)} msg\_size(d) = 4$ since SEND x[ ] has been hoisted out of loop 12. However, $Path(13) = 4$, since SEND y[ ] is placed in the loop.

Let $Loop(n)$ be the buffer size for the messages placed in the loop (interval) with header node n. $Loop(n)$ is initialized to zero for all nodes n. To compute $Loop(h)$ for header node h, we use $Path(n)$ as shown in Equation 4 in Figure 4.

As shown in Equation 5, for a header node h, $Buffer(h)$ is computed as the sum of the buffer required for messages placed inside the loop ($Loop(h)$), messages hoisted across the header node ($Buffer_{in}(s)$), and messages hoisted out of the loop ($\otimes$(number-of-iterations, $Buffer_{in}(\text{SUCCS}^E(h))$)). $Buffer_{in}(\text{SUCCS}^E(h))$ gives the size of the messages that can be hoisted across the first node in the loop body. The $\otimes$ operator determines the number of non-local accesses made in the loop by taking the overlapping messages corresponding to different references into account (see Section 8.1). As an example, node 12 in Figure 3(b) corresponds to a simple application of the $\otimes$ operator: only SEND x[ ] can be hoisted across node 13; the $\otimes$ operator recognizes that the communication pattern is shift and that only the boundary iterations need to fetch non-local data. Thus, $Buffer(12) = \oplus(Loop(12), Buffer_{in}(15), \otimes(1000, Buffer_{in}(13))) = \oplus(4, 0, 4) = 8$, where $Loop(12) = 4$ since SEND y[ ] is placed inside the loop and, as described above, $Buffer_{in}(13) = 4$.

Precise computation of *Loop*, *Buffer*, and $Buffer_{in}$ variables require the compile-time knowledge of the loop bounds and the number of processors. In case these are unknown, the compiler can either assume that all messages fit in the buffer or that no message fits in the buffer [12].

6.2 Resource Analysis Across Loop Nests

As described before, besides increasing the size of non-local buffers, earlier placement of SENDs also increases the range over which the non-local buffers need to be live and this further increase the total size of non-local buffers required. The analysis in Section 6.1 does not guarantee that the sum of buffer requirement for messages from different loop nests is less than the maximum non-local buffer. We now describe the effect of this requirement on the placement of SENDs. Let $Total(n)$ be the maximum buffer required for messages placed on any path from n to e and $Avail(n)$ be the size of the buffer available at node n.

As shown in Equation 6 in Figure 4, the size of the buffer required on a path from n to e has two components: size of the messages for a path from n to *post-body node*, $Path(n)$, and the buffer required for a path from *post-body node* to e, $Total(\text{SUCCS}^F(\text{HEADER}(n)))$.

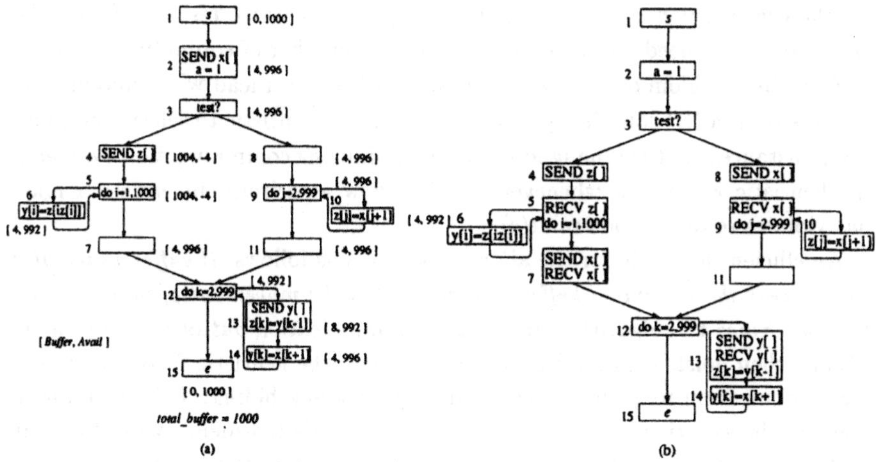

Fig. 5. (a) *Buffer* and *Avail*, respectively, are shown within brackets adjacent to the nodes. (b) Communication placement after taking resources into account.

Avail at a particular node depends on the amount of buffer reserved for messages that have a later use: the sum of buffer required to execute a path from n to e (including the buffer required at node n itself), $Total(n)$, and the buffer required for the communication primitives placed in the interval $T(n)$, $Loop(n)$; Equation 7 in Figure 4. Clearly, $Avail(e) = total\_buffer$.

Figure 5(a) shows the propagated values of *Buffer* and *Avail*. For example, $Buffer(5)$ and $Avail(5)$ are computed as follows. Since SEND z[ ] has been hoisted out of the loop, $Loop(5) = 0$; $Buffer_{in}(7) = 4$ since SEND x[ ] is live at node 7; $\text{SUCCS}^E(5) = 6$ and $Buffer_{in}(6) = 4$ because SEND z[ ] can be hoisted across node 6. Therefore, $Buffer(5) = \oplus(Loop(5), Buffer_{in}(7), \otimes(1000, Buffer_{in}(6))) = \oplus(0, 4, 1000) = 1004$ and $Avail(5) = 1000\text{-}1004 = \text{-}4$. Note that $\otimes(1000, 4) = 1000$ since, though each iteration of the "**do** i" loop potentially accesses non-local data, there are only 250 iterations per processor (due to the owner-computes rule; Section 3).

7 Taking Resources into Account

The problem of determining a placement that makes optimal use of resources while minimizing communication overheads can be shown to be NP-complete. This problem is very similar to the ones encountered in scheduling and file allocation problems [3] and can be similarly shown to be NP-complete: the knapsack problem [3] can be reduced to the problem of optimally selecting the messages that should use the available buffer at any given node. The knapsack problem is a classical problem in operations research where a scarce resource (here, the non-local buffer) needs to be allocated among a number of competing users.

Since the problem of minimizing communication overhead while maximizing buffer usage is a NP-complete problem, it requires a heuristic to select communication instances that can be ignored while minimizing communication overhead. The heuristic is invoked whenever the data-flow algorithm encounters a node that violates resource constraint(s).

An efficient heuristic for the above problem is as follows. *If buffer usage at a node exceeds the maximum buffer available, block the movement of* SENDs *across the node.* Since the algorithm first hoists communication *out* of the loop intervals and then hoists communication *across* nodes, the heuristic favors reduction of communication frequency over maximizing latency hiding. This heuristic is based on the experiences with compilation for distributed-memory machines: it has been observed that reducing frequency of communication often yields more significant benefits than the latency hiding optimization [14]. Message buffers for communication blocked at a node are deallocated. This frees up buffers and allows communication to be hoisted to the outermost placement locations.

The results of the resource analysis are used to implement the heuristic as follows. First, if $Loop(h) > total\_buffer$ (Section 6.1) for header node h then SAFE(h, d) is initialized to $\perp$ for all descriptors d. This prevents hoisting messages across node h and, thus, inhibits both further vectorization as well as movement across the node. Consider the matrix multiply example from Section 2. Recall that we had assumed that the non-local buffer requirement for communication placed outside the "**do** k" loop exceeds the maximum buffer available. In other words, *Loop*("**do** k") exceeds the resource constraint and to enforce the constraint, SAFE variables corresponding to the descriptors of arrays a and b are initialized to $\perp$. This inhibits message vectorization, as desired.

Second, the value of $Avail(n)$, as computed in Section 6.2, can be less than 0. Therefore, the actual assignment is: $Avail(n) = \max(0, Avail(n))$. If $Avail(n)$ is less than zero before the correction then n does not have sufficient buffer available to allow messages to be hoisted across it. Node 5 in Figure 5(a) is an example of such a node. To prevent messages from being hoisted across node 5, the heuristic initializes SAFE(5, x[ ]) $= \perp$. Note that since *Loop*(5) does not exceed *total_buffer*, the heuristic does *not* initialize the SAFE variables corresponding to the messages hoisted *out* of the loop to $\perp$; in other words, we allow message vectorization and only prevent messages from being hoisted across node 5.

The placement of SENDs with SAFE initialized as described above gives the resource-based placement of SEND primitives. The resource-based placement for our example program in Figure 3(a) is shown in Figure 5(b). SEND z[ ] is hoisted out of the loop and placed at node 4. However, since SAFE(5, x[ ]) $= \perp$, SEND x[ ] gets blocked at node 7. Given this SEND placement, the corresponding RECV

```
do k = 1, n
   SEND/RECV a(i$lb:i$ub, k)
   SEND/RECV b(k, j$lb:j$ub)
   do j = j$lb, j$ub
      do i = i$lb, i$ub
         c(i,j) = c(i,j) + a(i,k) * b(k,j)
      enddo
   enddo
enddo
```

(a)

```
do kk = 1, n, k$blk
   SEND/RECV a(i$lb:i$ub, kk:kk+k$blk-1)
   SEND/RECV b(kk:kk+k$blk-1, j$lb:j$ub)
   do k = kk, kk + k$blk - 1
      do j = j$lb, j$ub
         do i = i$lb, i$ub
            c(i,j) = c(i,j) + a(i,k) * b(k,j)
         enddo
      enddo
   enddo
enddo
```

(b)

Fig. 6. (a) Resource-based communication placement. (b) Resource-based stripmining transformation.

placement is determined as described in Sections 4 and 5. RECV z[ ] is placed outside and before the loop (node 5). And, as described in Section 5, RECV x[ ] is placed at node 7 to ensure balanced communication placement.

7.1 Stripmining Transformation

As described above, if *Loop*(h) exceeds the maximum buffer constraint, the placement framework inhibits message vectorization. However, to reduce communication frequency, we would like to combine as many messages as possible into a single message. To achieve this, we annotate each loop that inhibits message vectorization as a potential candidate for stripmining transformation. Stripmining reduces the frequency of communication since it allows communication primitives to be placed outside the inner stripmined loop and, thus, communicate only once for each outer stripmined loop iteration. Clearly, the stripmining (blocking) factor depends on the maximum available buffer.

An application of this transformation is the "**do** k" loop in our matrix multiply example from Section 2. As described above, *Loop*("**do** k") exceeds the resource constraint; thus the "**do** k" loop is annotated as a candidate for stripmining transformation. We then stripmine the annotated loop and hoist communication out of the inner stripmined loop which reduces the communication frequency from n to n/k$blk. The communication placement before and after stripmining transformation is shown in Figure 6.

8 Implementation details

The resource-based communication placement analysis described in the paper has been implemented in the Rice Fortran D95 compiler where it is currently used to find the placement of distributed-memory communication primitives.

To implement the resource-based placement analysis, we associate two sets of data-flow variables with each node. First, ***placement-related*** data-flow variables such as ***Used***, ***Transp***, SAFE, etc. (Sections 4 and 5). Second, ***resource analysis*** data-flow variables, such as *Node*, ***Buffer***, etc., that are used to compute resource usage for each node (Sections 6 and 7).

The data-flow variables mentioned in Sections 4 – 7 are required to determine resource-based placement of non-local read communication primitives. We associate a similar set of data-flow variables with non-local write communication placement problem. We now describe the implementation details of the buffer analysis for non-local reads.

The current implementation of the placement analysis in the Fortran D95 compiler allows the maximum non-local buffer constraint to be specified as a command-line argument at compile time. Currently, the specified total non-local buffer size is statically partitioned into non-local read and write buffer sizes. However, compiler can use sophisticated analysis to partition the total buffer size into non-local read and non-local write buffer sizes as follows: first, associate (static) communication costs with non-local reads and writes; second, compute the total non-local read and write buffer usage (without enforcing resource constraints); third, test if the total buffer usage exceeds the maximum; finally, if it does, partition the total buffer size into non-local read and write buffer sizes based on the respective buffer requirements and the associated costs.

8.1 Implementation of ⊕ and ⊗ operators

Besides the data-flow variables associated with each node, we associate two sets; one each corresponding to non-local reads and non-local writes. These sets are used to maintain the messages that are live at the current node. The set of live messages for non-local reads is used to record the communication instances for which the use of the communicated data (non-local reference) has been encountered within the current interval (that is, on any path from the node to the ***post-body node*** of the interval) but not the corresponding SEND. A message is deleted from the live message set after the corresponding SEND is encountered. It is computed by traversing the graph in reverse pre-order; thus, uses are encountered before the corresponding SENDs. Also, this allows the set to be computed in a single pass. Recall from Section 2 that the non-local buffer corresponding to a message is live between the SEND and the last use of the communicated data. In addition to the above, a message can also be deleted from the set of live messages if the buffer usage exceeds the maximum available buffer. This is because, as mentioned in Section 7, when the buffer usage exceeds the specified constraint, data-flow variables are initialized such that appropriate SENDs are *not* hoisted across the node and this forces the resource-based communication placement to insert the corresponding SENDs after the node. We incorporate this knowledge in the set of live messages by deleting the messages that get blocked at a node due to resource constraints.

To implement the ⊕ operator, we take the set of live messages at the current node and coalesce the messages in the set. Message coalescing optimization combines overlapping messages into a single message. If two non-local references require identical messages, coalescing messages, in effect, eliminates one of them. This allows the ⊕ operator to avoid counting redundant messages multiple times. To implement ⊕, then, we just calculate the total buffer required by the coalesced messages at the current node. To calculate the size of the coalesced messages, we take the loop nesting level of the node into account.

The ⊗ operator is implemented as follows. As with the ⊕ operator, we take the set of live messages at the current node and coalesce the messages. Since we take the loop nesting level into account, the ⊗ operator gets implemented automatically. For example, the size of non-local buffer corresponding to z[iz[i]] at node 6 is 4 (one non-local access times the number of processors) while at node 5 it is 1000 (since all the 250 accesses can be potentially non-local, which is then multiplied with the number of processors). Note that to compute the set of live messages at an interval header (loop) node, we merge the sets of live messages from the entry node in the interval (that is, the first node in the loop body) with the set of live messages from the successor(s) of the header node.

All the equations presented in in Section 6 inspect only a subset of incoming/outgoing edges. Also, as described above, the ⊕ and ⊗ operators can be implemented efficiently. Moreover, each of the four phases (Section 4) involved in the resource-based communication analysis make at most two uni-directional passes over G [9]. Therefore, the complexity of our algorithm is $O(E)$. Under the assumption that $O(E)$ is the same as the order of the program size [8], our algorithm has linear time complexity.

9 Related Work

The problem of data-flow based communication generation and placement has been addressed by several researchers [5, 4, 2]. However, data-flow placement frameworks to eliminate partial redundancies across loop nests were developed only recently [8, 7]. To the best of our knowledge, ours is the first effort to take resource constraints into account during communication placement. Our framework is based on Lazy Code Motion (LCM) technique [10]. Besides incorporating resources, we extended the LCM technique to determine non-atomic and balanced placement.

Give-N-Take framework [8] is the only previous framework that maximizes latency hiding while ensuring balancedness. However, it uses a complex set of inter-dependent equations to determine SEND and RECV placements at the same time. Unlike the Give-N-Take framework, we determine SEND and RECV placements using two separate uni-directional analyses. The compositional structure of our placement analysis allows us to perform resource analysis between SEND and RECV analysis phases as well as to use resource constraints to influence the SEND placement. Using resources to influence SEND placement before determining RECV placement allows us to modify SEND placements without worrying about the balancedness of the corresponding RECVs.

10 Summary

In this paper we demonstrated the importance of taking resource constraints into account during communication placement analysis. We have presented a data-flow analysis technique for resource-based communication placement. Our technique eliminates partially redundant communication and maximizes latency hiding as well as incorporates machine-dependent resource constraints. The placement framework performs SEND, RECV, and resource analysis in separate phases. A separate phase for resource analysis allows initialization of appropriate data-flow variables to take resource constraints into account. We also described the use of the stripmining transformation to improve the efficacy of communication placement.

The resource-based communication placement analysis has been implemented in the Fortran D95 compiler, where it is currently used to determine placement for distributed-memory communication primitives. Resource-based communication placement presented in this paper assumes that memory can be allocated and deallocated as required. Thus, placement of allocation and deallocation primitives depends upon the placement of communication primitives. The placement of memory management primitives is similar to the resource-based placement of communication primitives, and can be solved using the framework presented in this paper.

Though we presented the framework in the context of communication placement for distributed-memory machines, it can be used for other memory hierarchy related code placement problems that involve resource constraints. For distributed shared-memory systems, the framework can be used for prefetch placement. Satisfying both the cache size constraint and the limited number of outstanding prefetches needs to be investigated. Another potential application of the framework includes placement of I/O primitives for programs involving out-of-core I/O. Moreover, the effect of unknown (at compile time) loop bounds on the communication placement needs to be further investigated.

References

1. A. V. Aho, R. Sethi, and J. Ullman. *Compilers: Principles, Techniques, and Tools.* Addison-Wesley, Reading, MA, second edition, 1986.
2. S. Amarasinghe and M. Lam. Communication optimization and code generation for distributed memory machines. In *Proceedings of the SIGPLAN '93 Conference on Programming Language Design and Implementation*, Albuquerque, NM, June 1993.
3. M. Garey and D. Johnson. *Computers and Intractability, A Guide to the Theory of NP-Completeness.* W. H. Freeman and Co., New York, NY, 1979.
4. C. Gong, R. Gupta, and R. Melhem. Compilation techniques for optimizing communication on distributed-memory systems. In *Proceedings of the 1993 International Conference on Parallel Processing*, St. Charles, IL, August 1993.
5. E. Granston and A. Veidenbaum. Detecting redundant accesses to array data. In *Proceedings of Supercomputing '91*, Albuquerque, NM, November 1991.
6. T. Gross and P. Steenkiste. Structured dataflow analysis for arrays and its use in an optimizing compiler. *Software—Practice and Experience*, 20(2):133–155, February 1990.
7. M. Gupta, E. Schonberg, and H. Srinivasan. A unified data-flow framework for optimizing communication. In *Proceedings of the Seventh Workshop on Languages and Compilers for Parallel Computing*, Ithaca, NY, August 1994.
8. R. v. Hanxleden and K. Kennedy. Give-N-Take — A balanced code placement framework. In *Proceedings of the SIGPLAN '94 Conference on Programming Language Design and Implementation*, Orlando, FL, June 1994.
9. K. Kennedy and A. Sethi. A communication placement framework with unified dependence and data-flow analysis. In *Proceedings of the Third International Conference on High Performance Computing*, Trivandrum, December 1996.
10. J. Knoop, O. Rüthing, and B. Steffen. Optimal code motion: Theory and practice. *ACM Transactions on Programming Languages and Systems*, 16(4):1117–1155, July 1994.
11. C. Koelbel, D. Loveman, R. Schreiber, G. Steele, Jr., and M. Zosel. *The High Performance Fortran Handbook.* The MIT Press, Cambridge, MA, 1994.
12. T. Mowry, M. Lam, and A. Gupta. Design and evaluation of a compiler algorithm for prefetching. In *Proceedings of the Fifth International Conference on Architectural Support for Programming Languages and Operating Systems (ASPLOS-V)*, pages 62–73, Boston, MA, October 1992.
13. R. E. Tarjan. Testing flow graph reducibility. *Journal of Computer and System Sciences*, 9:355–365, 1974.
14. C.-W. Tseng. *An Optimizing Fortran D Compiler for MIMD Distributed-Memory Machines.* PhD thesis, Dept. of Computer Science, Rice University, January 1993.

Statement-Level Communication-Free Partitioning Techniques for Parallelizing Compilers

Kuei-Ping Shih[1], Jang-Ping Sheu[1], and Chua-Huang Huang[2]

[1] Department of Computer Science and Information Engineering
National Central University
Chung-Li 32054, Taiwan
E-mail: steven@axp1.csie.ncu.edu.tw
sheujp@csie.ncu.edu.tw

[2] Department of Computer and Information Science
The Ohio State University
Columbus, OH 43210-1277
E-mail: chh@cis.ohio-state.edu

Abstract. This paper addresses the problem of communication-free partitioning of iteration spaces and data spaces along hyperplanes. We consider statement-level partitioning for the iteration spaces. The technique explicitly formulates array references as transformations from statement-iteration spaces to data spaces. Based on these transformations, the necessary and sufficient conditions for the feasibility of communication-free hyperplane partitions are presented.

1 Introduction

It has been widely accepted that local memory access is much faster than memory access involving interprocessor communication on distributed-memory multicomputers. If data and computation are not properly distributed across processors, it may cause heavy interprocessor communication. Excessive interprocessor communication will offset the benefit of parallelization even if the program has a large amount of parallelism. Consequently, parallelizing compilers must pay more attention on the distribution of computation and data across processors to reduce the communication overhead or to completely eliminate the interprocessor communication, if possible. Communication-free partitioning, therefore, becomes an interesting and worth studying issue for distributed-memory multicomputers. In recent years, much research has been focused on the area of partitioning iteration spaces and/or data spaces to reduce interprocessor communication and achieve high-performance computing.

Ramanujam and Sadayappan [5] consider the problem of communication-free partitioning of data spaces along hyperplanes for distributed memory multicomputers. They present a matrix-based formulation of the problem for determining the existence of communication-free partitions of data arrays. Their approach proposes only the array decompositions and does not take the iteration space partitionings into consideration. In addition, they concentrate on fully parallel nested loops and focus on two-dimensional data arrays.

Huang and Sadayappan [3] generalize the approach proposed in [5]. They consider the issue of communication-free hyperplane partitioning by explicitly modeling the iteration and data spaces and provide the conditions for the feasibility of communication-free hyperplane partitioning. However, they do not deal with imperfectly nested loops. Moreover, the approach is restricted to loop-level partitioning, i.e., all statements within a loop body must be scheduled together as an indivisible unit.

Chen and Sheu [1] partition iteration space first according to the data dependence vectors obtained by analyzing all the reference patterns in a nested loop, and then group all data elements accessed by the same iteration partition. Two communication-free partitioning strategies, non-duplicate data and duplicate data strategies, are proposed in this paper. Nevertheless, they require the loop contain only uniformly generated references and the problem domain be restricted to a single perfectly nested loop. They also treat all statements within a loop body as an indivisible unit.

Lim and Lam [4] use affine processor mappings for statements to assign the statement-iterations to processors and maximize the degree of parallelism available in the program. Their approach does not treat the loop body as an indivisible unit and can assign different statement-iterations to different processors. However, they consider only the statement-iteration space partitioning and do not address the issue of data space partitioning. Furthermore, their uniform affine processor mappings can cause a large number of idle processors if the affine mappings are non-unimodular transformations.

In this paper, communication-free partitioning of statement-iteration spaces and data spaces along hyperplanes are considered. We explicitly formulate array references as transformations from statement-iteration spaces to data spaces. Based on these transformations, we then present the necessary and sufficient conditions for the feasibility of communication-free hyperplane partitions. Currently, most of the existing partitioning schemes take an iteration instance as a basic schedulable unit that can be allocated to a processor. But, when the loop body contains multiple statements, it is very difficult to make the loop be communication-freely executed by allocating iteration instances among processors. That is, the chance of communication-free execution found by using these methods is limited. For having more flexible and possible in finding communication-free hyperplane partitions, we treat statements within a loop body as separate schedulable units. Our method does not consider only one of the iteration space and data space but both of them. As in [4], our method can be extended to handle more general loop models and can be applied to programs with imperfectly nested loops and affine array references [6].

The rest of the paper is organized as follows. In Section 2, we introduce notation and terminology used throughout the paper. Section 3 describes the characteristics of statement-level communication-free hyperplane partitioning.

The necessary and sufficient conditions for the feasibility of communication-free hyperplane partitioning are presented in Section 4. Finally, the conclusions are given in Section 5.

2 Preliminaries

This section explains the statement-iteration space and the data space. It also defines the statement-iteration hyperplane and the data hyperplane.

2.1 Statement-Iteration Space and Data Space

Let $\mathbf{Q}$, $\mathbf{Z}$ and $\mathbf{Z}^+$ denote the set of rational numbers, the set of integers and the set of positive integer numbers, respectively. The symbol $\mathbf{Z}^d$ represents the set of d-tuple of integers. Traditionally, the iteration space is composed of discrete points where each point represents the execution of *all* statements in one iteration of a loop [8]. Instead of viewing each iteration indivisible, an iteration can be divided into the statements that are enclosed in the iteration, i.e., each statement is a schedulable unit and has its own iteration space. We use another term, *statement-iteration space*, to denote the iteration space of a statement in a nested loop.

The following example illustrates the notion of iteration spaces and statement-iteration spaces.

Example 1: Consider the following nested loop L_1.

$$
\begin{array}{lll}
\textbf{do } i_1 = 1, N & & \\
\quad \textbf{do } i_2 = 1, N & & \\
s_1: \quad A[i_1, -i_1 - i_2 - 1] = A[i_1 - i_2 - 1, -i_1 + i_2 + 1] + & & \\
\qquad\qquad\qquad\qquad B[i_1 + i_2, i_1 + 2i_2 - 1] & & (L_1) \\
s_2: \quad B[i_1 - i_2 + 1, i_1 - 2i_2 + 1] = A[i_2 - 1, i_1 - i_2] * & & \\
\qquad\qquad\qquad\qquad B[i_1 + i_2 - 1, i_1 + i_2 - 2] & & \\
\textbf{enddo enddo} & &
\end{array}
$$

Fig. 1 illustrates the iteration space and statement-iteration spaces of loop L_1 for $N = 5$. In Fig. 1(a), a circle means an iteration and includes two rectangles with black and gray colors. The black rectangle indicates statement s_1 and the gray one indicates statement s_2. In Fig. 1(b) and Fig. 1(c), each statement is an individual unit and the collection of statements forms two statement-iteration spaces. □

The representations of statement-iteration spaces, data spaces and the relations among them are described as follows. Let $\mathcal{S}$ denote the set of statements in the targeted problem domain and $\mathcal{D}$ be the set of array variables that are referenced by $\mathcal{S}$. Consider statement $s \in \mathcal{S}$, which is enclosed in a d-nested loop. The statement-iteration space of s, denoted by $SIS(s)$, is a subspace of $\mathbf{Z}^d$ and is defined as $SIS(s) = \{[I_1, I_2, \ldots, I_d]^t | LB_i \le I_i \le UB_i, \text{ for } 1 \le i \le d\}$, where

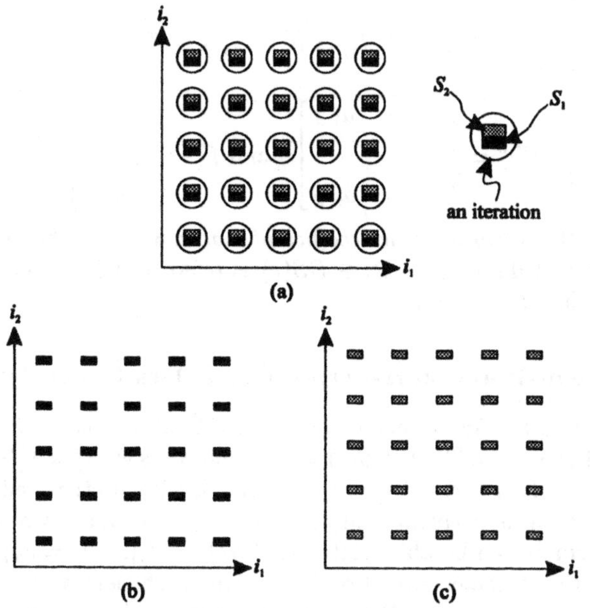

Fig. 1. Loop (L_1)'s iteration space and its corresponding statement-iteration spaces, assuming $N = 5$. (a) $IS(L_1)$, iteration space of loop (L_1). (b) $SIS(s_1)$, statement-iteration space of statement s_1. (c) $SIS(s_2)$, statement-iteration space of statement s_2.

I_i is the loop index variable, LB_i and UB_i are the lower and upper bounds of the loop index variable I_i, respectively. The superscript t is a transpose operator. The column vector $I_s = [I_1, I_2, \ldots, I_d]^t$ is called a *statement-iteration* in statement-iteration space $SIS(s)$, $LB_i \leq I_i \leq UB_i$, for $i = 1, 2, \ldots, d$. On the other hand, from the geometric point of view, an array variable also forms a space and each array element is a point in the space. For exactly describing an array variable, we use *data space* to represent an n-dimensional array v, which is denoted by $DS(v)$, where $v \in \mathcal{D}$. An array element $v[D_1, D_2, \ldots, D_n]$ has a corresponding data index in the data space $DS(v)$. We denote this data index by a column vector $D_v = [D_1, D_2, \ldots, D_n]^t$.

The relations between statement-iteration spaces and data spaces can be built via *array reference functions*. An array reference function is a transformation from statement-iteration space into data space. As most of the existing methods, we require the array references be affine functions of outer loop indices or loop invariant variables. Suppose statement s is enclosed in a d-nested loop and has an array reference pattern $v[a_{1,1}I_1 + a_{1,2}I_2 + \cdots + a_{1,d}I_d + a_{1,0},\ a_{2,1}I_1 + a_{2,2}I_2 + \cdots + a_{2,d}I_d + a_{2,0},\ \ldots,\ a_{n,1}I_1 + a_{n,2}I_2 + \cdots + a_{n,d}I_d + a_{n,0}]$, where $a_{i,j}$ are integer constants, for $1 \leq i \leq n$ and $0 \leq j \leq d$, then the array reference function can be written as:

$$Ref^{s,v}(I_s) = F^{s,v} \cdot I_s + f^{s,v},$$

where

$$F^{s,v} = \begin{bmatrix} a_{1,1} & \cdots & a_{1,d} \\ \vdots & \ddots & \vdots \\ a_{n,1} & \cdots & a_{n,d} \end{bmatrix}, \text{ and } f^{s,v} = \begin{bmatrix} a_{1,0} \\ \vdots \\ a_{n,0} \end{bmatrix}.$$

We term $F^{s,v}$ the *array reference coefficient matrix* and $f^{s,v}$ the *array reference constant vector*. If data index $D_v \in DS(v)$ is referenced in statement-iteration $I_s \in SIS(s)$, then $Ref^{s,v}(I_s) = D_v$.

2.2 Statement-Iteration Hyperplane and Data Hyperplane

A *statement-iteration hyperplane* on statement-iteration space $SIS(s)$, denoted by $\Psi(s)$, is a hyperspace [2] of $SIS(s)$ and is defined as $\Psi_h(s) = \{[I_1, I_2, \ldots, I_d]^t | \delta_1 I_1 + \delta_2 I_2 + \cdots + \delta_d I_d = c_h\}$, where $\delta_1, \ldots,$ and $\delta_d \in \mathbf{Q}$ are the coefficients of the statement-iteration hyperplane and $c_h \in \mathbf{Q}$ is the constant term of the hyperplane. The formula can be abbreviated as $\Psi_h(s) = \{I_s | \Delta \cdot I_s = c_h\}$, where $\Delta = [\delta_1, \ldots, \delta_d]$ is the statement-iteration hyperplane coefficient vector. Similarly, a *data hyperplane* on data space $DS(v)$, denoted by $\Phi(v)$, is a hyperspace of $DS(v)$ and is defined as $\Phi_g(v) = \{[D_1, D_2, \ldots, D_n]^t | \theta_1 D_1 + \theta_2 D_2 + \cdots + \theta_n D_n = c_g\}$, where $\theta_1, \ldots,$ and $\theta_n \in \mathbf{Q}$ are the coefficients of the data hyperplane and $c_g \in \mathbf{Q}$ is the constant term of the hyperplane. In the same way, the formula also can be abbreviated as $\Phi_g(v) = \{D_v | \Theta \cdot D_v = c_g\}$, where $\Theta = [\theta_1, \ldots, \theta_n]$ is the data hyperplane coefficient vector. The hyperplanes that include at least one integer point are considered in this paper.

Statement-iteration hyperplanes and data hyperplanes are used for characterizing communication-free partitioning. We discuss some of these characteristics in the next section.

3 Characteristics of Communication-Free Hyperplane Partitioning

A program execution is communication-free if all operations on each of all processors access only data elements allocated to that processor. A trivial partition strategy allocates all statement-iterations and data elements to a single processor. The program execution of this trivial partitioning is communication-free. However, we are not interested in this single processor program execution because it does not exploit the potential of parallelization and it conflicts with the goal of parallel processing. Hence, in this paper, we consider only nontrivial partitioning, in specific, hyperplane partitioning.

The formal definition of communication-free hyperplane partition is defined as below. Let *partition group*, G,

$$G = \cup_{s \in \mathcal{S}} \Psi_h(s) \bigcup \cup_{v \in \mathcal{D}} \Phi_g(v)$$

be the set of hyperplanes that should be assigned to one processor. The definition of communication-free hyperplane partition can be given as the following.

Definition 1 The hyperplane partitions of statement-iteration spaces and data spaces are said to be communication-free if and only if for any partition group $G = \cup_{s\in\mathcal{S}}\Psi_h(s) \bigcup \cup_{v\in\mathcal{D}}\Phi_g(v)$,

$$\forall I_s \in \Psi_h(s),\ Ref^{s,v}(I_s) \in \Phi_g(v),\ \forall s \in \mathcal{S}, v \in \mathcal{D}.$$

□

As mentioned above, the statement-iterations which access the same array element should be allocated to the same statement-iteration hyperplane. Therefore, it is important to decide statement-iterations that access the same array element. The following lemma states the necessary and sufficient condition that two statement-iterations will access the same array element.

Lemma 1 *For some statement $s \in \mathcal{S}$ and its referenced array $v \in \mathcal{D}$, I_s and I'_s are two statement-iterations on $SIS(s)$ and $Ref^{s,v}$ is the array reference function from $SIS(s)$ into $DS(v)$ as defined above. Then*

$$Ref^{s,v}(I_s) = Ref^{s,v}(I'_s) \Longleftrightarrow (I'_s - I_s) \in Ker(F^{s,v})$$

where $Ker(S)$ denotes the null space of S [2]. □

The proof of this lemma is referred to [6]. We explain the significance of Lemma 1 and show how this lemma can help to find communication-free hyperplane partitions. Communication-free hyperplane partitioning requires those statement-iterations that access the same array element be allocated to the same statement-iteration hyperplane. According to Lemma 1, two statement-iterations access the same array element if and only if the difference of these two statement-iterations belongs to the kernel of $F^{s,v}$. Hence, $Ker(F^{s,v})$ should be a subspace of the statement-iteration hyperplane. Since there may exist many different array references, partitioning a statement-iteration space must consider all array references appeared in the statement. Thus, the space spanned from $Ker(F^{s,v})$ for all array references appearing in the same statement should be a subspace of the statement-iteration hyperplane. The dimension of a statement-iteration hyperplane is one less than the dimension of the statement-iteration space. If there exists a statement s such that the dimension of the spanning space of $Ker(F^{s,v})$ is equal to the dimension of $SIS(s)$, then the spanning space cannot be a subspace of a statement-iteration hyperplane. Therefore, there exists no nontrivial communication-free hyperplane partitioning. From the above observation, we obtain the following theorem.

Theorem 1 *If $\exists s \in \mathcal{S}$ such that*

$$dim(span(\cup_{v\in\mathcal{D}}Ker(F^{s,v}))) = dim(SIS(s)),$$

then there exists no nontrivial communication-free hyperplane partitioning for $\mathcal{S}$ and $\mathcal{D}$. □

Example 2: Consider matrix multiplication.

```
        do i = 1, N
          do j = 1, N
            do k = 1, N
s:            C[i, j] = C[i, j] + A[i, k] * B[k, j]
        enddo enddo enddo
```

In the above program, there are three array variables, A, B, and C, with three distinct array references involved in statement s. The three array reference coefficient matrices, $F^{s,A}$, $F^{s,B}$, and $F^{s,C}$, are $\begin{bmatrix} 1 & 0 & 0 \\ 0 & 0 & 1 \end{bmatrix}$, $\begin{bmatrix} 0 & 0 & 1 \\ 0 & 1 & 0 \end{bmatrix}$, and $\begin{bmatrix} 1 & 0 & 0 \\ 0 & 1 & 0 \end{bmatrix}$, respectively. Thus, $Ker(F^{s,A}) = \{r_1[0,1,0]^t | r_1 \in \mathbf{Z}\}$, $Ker(F^{s,B}) = \{r_2[1,0,0]^t | r_2 \in \mathbf{Z}\}$, and $Ker(F^{s,C}) = \{r_3[0,0,1]^t | r_3 \in \mathbf{Z}\}$. $Ker(F^{s,A})$, $Ker(F^{s,B})$, and $Ker(F^{s,C})$ span $\mathbf{Z}^3$ which has the same dimensionality as the statement-iteration space. By Theorem 1, matrix multiplication has no nontrivial communication-free hyperplane partitioning. □

Theorem 1 can be useful for determining nested loops that have no nontrivial communication-free hyperplane partitioning. Furthermore, when a nontrivial communication-free hyperplane partitioning exists, Theorem 1 can also be useful for finding the hyperplane coefficient vectors. We state this result in the following corollary.

Corollary 1 *For any communication-free statement-iteration hyperplane* $\Psi_h(s) = \{I_s | \Delta \cdot I_s = c_h\}$, *the following two conditions must hold:*

(1) $span(\cup_{v \in \mathcal{D}} Ker(F^{s,v})) \subseteq \Psi_h(s)$,
(2) $\Delta^t \in (span(\cup_{v \in \mathcal{D}} Ker(F^{s,v})))^{\perp}$,

where $S^{\perp}$ *denotes the orthogonal complement space of* S. □

Corollary 1 gives the range of communication-free statement-iteration hyperplane coefficient vectors. It can be used for the finding of communication-free statement-iteration hyperplane coefficient vectors. On the other hand, the range of communication-free data hyperplane coefficient vectors is also given as follows.

As mentioned before, the relations between statement-iteration spaces and data spaces can be established via array references. Moreover, the statement-iteration hyperplane coefficient vectors and data hyperplane coefficient vectors are related. The following lemma expresses the relation between these two hyperplane coefficient vectors. A similar result is given in [3].

Lemma 2 *For any statement* $s \in \mathcal{S}$ *and its referenced array* $v \in \mathcal{D}$, $Ref^{s,v}$ *is the array reference function from* $SIS(s)$ *into* $DS(v)$. $\Psi_h(s) = \{I_s | \Delta \cdot I_s = c_h\}$ *and* $\Phi_g(v) = \{D_v | \Theta \cdot D_v = c_g\}$ *are communication-free hyperplane partitions if and only if* $\Delta = \alpha\Theta \cdot F^{s,v}$, *for some* α, $\alpha \neq 0$. □

By Lemma 2, the statement-iteration hyperplane coefficient vector Δ can be decided if the data hyperplane coefficient vector Θ has been determined.

If $F^{s,v}$ is invertible, the statement-iteration hyperplane coefficient vectors can be decided first, then the data hyperplane coefficient vectors can be derived by $\Theta = \alpha'\Delta(F^{s,v})^{-1}$, for some $\alpha', \alpha' \neq 0$. The range of communication-free data hyperplane coefficient vectors can be derived from this lemma. Corollary 1 shows the range of statement-iteration hyperplane coefficient vectors. The next corollary provides the ranges of data hyperplane coefficient vectors.

Corollary 2 *For any communication-free data hyperplane* $\Phi_g(v) = \{D_v | \Theta \cdot D_v = c_g\}$*, the following condition must hold:*

$$\Theta^t \in (\cup_{s \in \mathcal{S}} Ker((F^{s,v})^t))',$$

where S' denotes the complement set of S. □

The next section describes the communication-free hyperplane partitioning technique. The necessary and sufficient conditions of communication-free hyperplane partitioning for a single perfectly nested loop will be presented.

4 Communication-Free Hyperplane Partitioning for a Perfectly Nested Loop

Each data array has a corresponding data space. However, a nested loop with multiple statements may have multiple statement-iteration spaces. In this section, we will consider additional conditions of multiple statement-iteration spaces for communication-free hyperplane partitioning. These conditions are also used in determining statement-iteration hyperplanes and data hyperplanes.

Suppose $\mathcal{S} = \{s_1, s_2, \ldots, s_m\}$ and $\mathcal{D} = \{v_1, v_2, \ldots, v_n\}$, where $m, n \in \mathbf{Z}^+$. The number of occurrences of array variable v_j in statement s_i is $r_{i,j}$, where $r_{i,j} \in \mathbf{Z}^+ \cup \{0\}$, $i = 1, 2, \ldots, m$ and $j = 1, 2, \ldots, n$. If s_i does not reference v_j, $r_{i,j}$ is set to 0. The previous representation of array reference function can be modified slightly to describe the array reference of statement s_i to variable v_j in the k-th occurrence as $Ref_k^{s_i,v_j}(I_{s_i})$, where $1 \leq k \leq r_{i,j}$. The related representations will be changed accordingly, such as $Ref_k^{s_i,v_j}(I_{s_i}) = F_k^{s_i,v_j} \cdot I_{s_i} + f_k^{s_i,v_j} = D_{v_j}$.

In this section, a partition group that contains a statement-iteration hyperplane for each statement-iteration space and a data hyperplane for each data space is considered. Suppose that the data hyperplane in data space $DS(v_j)$ is $\Phi_g(v_j) = \{D_{v_j} | \Theta_j \cdot D_{v_j} = c_{g_j}\}$, for all $j, 1 \leq j \leq n$. Since $D_{v_j} = Ref_k^{s_i,v_j}(I_{s_i})$, for $i = 1, 2, \ldots, m$, $j = 1, 2, \ldots, n$ and $k = 1, 2, \ldots, r_{i,j}$ and $\Theta_j \cdot D_{v_j} = c_{g_j}$, we have

$$\begin{aligned} &\Theta_j \cdot D_{v_j} = c_{g_j} \\ \Leftrightarrow\ &\Theta_j \cdot (F_k^{s_i,v_j} \cdot I_{s_i} + f_k^{s_i,v_j}) = c_{g_j} \\ \Leftrightarrow\ &(\Theta_j \cdot F_k^{s_i,v_j}) \cdot I_{s_i} = c_{g_j} - (\Theta_j \cdot f_k^{s_i,v_j}). \end{aligned}$$

Let

$$\Delta_i = \Theta_j \cdot F_k^{s_i,v_j}, \tag{1}$$
$$c_{h_i} = c_{g_j} - (\Theta_j \cdot f_k^{s_i,v_j}). \tag{2}$$

As a result, those statement-iterations that access the data lay on the data hyperplane $\Phi_g(v_j) = \{D_{v_j} | \Theta_j \cdot D_{v_j} = c_{g_j}\}$ will be located on the statement-iteration hyperplane $\Psi_h(I_{s_i}) = \{I_{s_i} | (\Theta_j \cdot F_k^{s_i,v_j}) \cdot I_{s_i} = c_{g_j} - (\Theta_j \cdot f_k^{s_i,v_j})\}$.

To simplify the presentation, we assume all variables v_j appear in every statement s_i. To satisfy that each statement-iteration space contains a unique statement-iteration hyperplane, the following two conditions should be met.

(i) $\forall i,\ \Theta_j \cdot F_k^{s_i,v_j} = \Theta_{j'} \cdot F_{k'}^{s_i,v_{j'}},\ (j \neq j' \vee k \neq k'),$
for $j, j' = 1, 2, \ldots, n;\ k = 1, 2, \ldots, r_{i,j}$ and $k' = 1, 2, \ldots, r_{i,j'}$.

(ii) $\forall i,\ c_{g_j} - (\Theta_j \cdot f_k^{s_i,v_j}) = c_{g_{j'}} - (\Theta_{j'} \cdot f_{k'}^{s_i,v_{j'}}),\ (j \neq j' \vee k \neq k'),$
for $j, j' = 1, 2, \ldots, n;\ k = 1, 2, \ldots, r_{i,j}$ and $k' = 1, 2, \ldots, r_{i,j'}$.

Condition **(i)** can infer to the following two equivalent equations.

$$\Theta_j \cdot F_k^{s_i,v_j} = \Theta_j \cdot F_1^{s_i,v_j}, \tag{3}$$

for $i = 1, 2, \ldots, m;\ j = 1, 2, \ldots, n$ and $k = 2, 3, \ldots, r_{i,j}$.

$$\Theta_j \cdot F_1^{s_i,v_j} = \Theta_1 \cdot F_1^{s_i,v_1}, \tag{4}$$

for $i = 1, 2, \ldots, m;\ j = 2, 3, \ldots, n$. Condition **(ii)** deduces the following two equations, and vice versa.

$$\Theta_j \cdot f_k^{s_i,v_j} = \Theta_j \cdot f_1^{s_i,v_j}, \tag{5}$$

for $i = 1, 2, \ldots, m;\ j = 1, 2, \ldots, n$ and $k = 2, 3, \ldots, r_{i,j}$.

$$c_{g_j} = c_{g_1} - \Theta_1 \cdot f_1^{s_i,v_1} + \Theta_j \cdot f_1^{s_i,v_j}, \tag{6}$$

for $i = 1, 2, \ldots, m;\ j = 2, 3, \ldots, n$.

Eq. (6) can be used to evaluate the data hyperplane constant terms while some constant term is fixed, say c_{g_1}. Furthermore, we obtain the following results. For some j, c_{g_j} should be the same for all i, $1 \leq i \leq m$. Therefore,

$$c_{g_1} - \Theta_1 \cdot f_1^{s_i,v_1} + \Theta_j \cdot f_1^{s_i,v_j} = c_{g_1} - \Theta_1 \cdot f_1^{s_1,v_1} + \Theta_j \cdot f_1^{s_1,v_j}, \tag{7}$$

for $i = 2, 3, \ldots, n$ and $j = 2, 3, \ldots, n$. Eq. (7) can be further inferred to obtain the following equation:

$$\Theta_j \cdot (f_1^{s_i,v_j} - f_1^{s_1,v_j}) = \Theta_1 \cdot (f_1^{s_i,v_1} - f_1^{s_1,v_1}) \tag{8}$$

for $i = 2, 3, \ldots, m$ and $j = 2, 3, \ldots, n$.

After describing the conditions for satisfying the communication-free hyperplane partitioning constraints, we can conclude the following theorem.

Theorem 2 *Let $\mathcal{S} = \{s_1, s_2, \ldots, s_m\}$ and $\mathcal{D} = \{v_1, v_2, \ldots, v_n\}$ be the sets of statements and array variables, respectively. $Ref_k^{s_i,v_j}$ is the array reference function for statement s_i accessing array variables v_j at the k-th occurrence in s_i, where $i = 1, 2, \ldots, m$; $j = 1, 2, \ldots, n$ and $k = 1, 2, \ldots, r_{i,j}$. $\Psi_h(I_{s_i}) = \{I_{s_i} | \Delta_i \cdot I_{s_i} = c_{h_i}\}$ is the statement-iteration hyperplane in $SIS(s_i)$, for $i = 1, 2, \ldots, m$. $\Phi_g(D_{v_j}) = \{D_{v_j} | \Theta_j \cdot D_{v_j} = c_{g_j}\}$ is the data hyperplane in $DS(v_j)$, for $j = 1, 2, \ldots, n$. $\Psi_h(I_{s_i})$ and $\Phi_g(D_{v_j})$ are communication-free hyperplane partitions if and only if the following conditions hold.*

(C1) $\forall i, \Theta_j \cdot F_k^{s_i,v_j} = \Theta_j \cdot F_1^{s_i,v_j}$, for $j = 1, 2, \ldots, n$; $k = 2, 3, \ldots, r_{i,j}$.
(C2) $\forall i, \Theta_j \cdot F_1^{s_i,v_j} = \Theta_1 \cdot F_1^{s_i,v_1}$, for $j = 2, 3, \ldots, n$.
(C3) $\forall i, \Theta_j \cdot f_k^{s_i,v_j} = \Theta_j \cdot f_1^{s_i,v_j}$, for $j = 1, 2, \ldots, n$; $k = 2, 3, \ldots, r_{i,j}$.
(C4) $\Theta_j \cdot (f_1^{s_i,v_j} - f_1^{s_1,v_j}) = \Theta_1 \cdot (f_1^{s_i,v_1} - f_1^{s_1,v_1})$,
for $i = 2, 3, \ldots, m$; $j = 2, 3, \ldots, n$.
(C5) $\forall j, \Theta_j^t \in (\bigcup_{i=1}^{m} \bigcup_{k=1}^{r_{i,j}} Ker((F_k^{s_i,v_j})^t))'$.
(C6) $\forall i, \Delta_i = \Theta_j \cdot F_k^{s_i,v_j}$,
for some j, k, $j \in \{1, 2, \ldots, n\}$; $k \in \{1, 2, \ldots, r_{i,j}\}$.
(C7) $\forall i, \Delta_i^t \in (span(\bigcup_{j=1}^{n} \bigcup_{k=1}^{r_{i,j}} Ker(F_k^{s_i,v_j})))^{\perp}$.
(C8) $\forall j, j = 2, 3, \ldots, n$, $c_{g_j} = c_{g_1} - \Theta_1 \cdot f_1^{s_i,v_1} + \Theta_j \cdot f_1^{s_i,v_j}$,
for some $i, i \in \{1, 2, \ldots, m\}$.
(C9) $\forall i, c_{h_i} = c_{g_j} - (\Theta_j \cdot f_k^{s_i,v_j})$,
for some j, k, $j \in \{1, 2, \ldots, n\}$; $k \in \{1, 2, \ldots, r_{i,j}\}$.

□

Theorem 2 can be used to determine whether a nested loop is communication-free. It can also be used as a procedure of finding a communication-free hyperplane partitioning systematically. Conditions **(C1)** to **(C4)** in Theorem 2 are used for finding the data hyperplane coefficient vectors. Condition **(C5)** can check whether the data hyperplane coefficient vectors found in preceding steps are within the legal range. Following the determination of the data hyperplane coefficient vectors, the statement-iteration hyperplane coefficient vectors can be obtained by using Condition **(C6)**. Similarly, Condition **(C7)** can check whether the statement-iteration hyperplane coefficient vectors are within the legal range. The data hyperplane constant terms and statement-iteration hyperplane constant terms can be obtained by using Conditions **(C8)** and **(C9)**, respectively. If one of the conditions is violated, the whole procedure will stop and verify that the nested loop has no communication-free hyperplane partitioning.

On the other hand, combining Equations (3) and (5) together, a sufficient condition of communication-free hyperplane partitioning can be derived as follows.

$$\Theta_j(F_1^{s_i,v_j} - F_2^{s_i,v_j}, F_1^{s_i,v_j} - F_3^{s_i,v_j}, \ldots, F_1^{s_i,v_j} - F_{r_{i,j}}^{s_i,v_j},$$
$$f_1^{s_i,v_j} - f_2^{s_i,v_j}, f_1^{s_i,v_j} - f_3^{s_i,v_j}, \ldots, f_1^{s_i,v_j} - f_{r_{i,j}}^{s_i,v_j}) = 0,$$

for $i = 1, 2, \ldots, m$ and $j = 1, 2, \ldots, n$. To satisfy the constraint that Θ is a non-zero row vector, the following condition should be true.

$$Rank(F_1^{s_i,v_j} - F_2^{s_i,v_j}, \ldots, F_1^{s_i,v_j} - F_{r_{i,j}}^{s_i,v_j},$$

$$f_1^{s_i,v_j} - f_2^{s_i,v_j}, \ldots, f_1^{s_i,v_j} - f_{r_{i,j}}^{s_i,v_j}) < dim(DS(v_j)), \qquad (9)$$

for $i = 1, 2, \ldots, m$ and $j = 1, 2, \ldots, n$. Note that this condition is similar to the result in [3] for loop-level hyperplane partitioning. We conclude the following corollary.

Corollary 3 *Suppose $\mathcal{S} = \{s_1, s_2, \ldots, s_m\}$ and $\mathcal{D} = \{v_1, v_2, \ldots, v_n\}$ are the sets of statements and array variables, respectively. $F_k^{s_i,v_j}$ and $f_k^{s_i,v_j}$ are the array reference coefficient matrix and constant vector, respectively, where $i \in \{1, 2, \ldots, m\}$, $j \in \{1, 2, \ldots, n\}$ and $k \in \{1, 2, \ldots, r_{i,j}\}$. If communication-free hyperplane partitioning exists then Eq. (9) must hold.* □

Theorem 1 and Corollary 3 can be used to check the absence of communication-free hyperplane partitioning for a nested loop, because these conditions are sufficient but not necessary. Theorem 1 is the statement-iteration space dimension test and Corollary 3 is the data space dimension test. To determine the existence of a communication-free hyperplane partitioning, we need to check the conditions in Theorem 2. We show the following example to explain the finding of communication-free hyperplanes of statement-iteration spaces and data spaces.

Example 3: Reconsider loop $L1$. The set of statements $\mathcal{S}$ is $\{s_1, s_2\}$ and the set of array variables $\mathcal{D}$ is $\{v_1, v_2\}$, where $v_1 = A$ and $v_2 = B$. The occurrences of array variables are $r_{1,1} = 2$, $r_{1,2} = 1$, $r_{2,1} = 1$, and $r_{2,2} = 2$.

Since $dim(span(\cup_{j=1}^{2} \cup_{k=1}^{r_{i,j}} Ker(F_k^{s_i,v_j}))) = 1$ is less than $dim(SIS(s_i)) = 2$, for $i = 1, 2$. By Theorem 1, it may exist a communication-free hyperplane partitioning for loop L_1. Again, by Corollary 3, the loop is tested for the possible existence of a nontrivial communication-free hyperplane partitioning. For array variable v_1, the following inequality is satisfied:

$$Rank(F_1^{s_1,v_1} - F_2^{s_1,v_1}, f_1^{s_1,v_1} - f_2^{s_1,v_1}) = 1 < dim(DS(v_1)) = 2.$$

Similarly, with respect to the array variable v_2, the following inequality is obtained:

$$Rank(F_1^{s_2,v_2} - F_2^{s_2,v_2}, f_1^{s_2,v_2} - f_2^{s_2,v_2}) = 1 < dim(DS(v_2)) = 2.$$

Although Eq. (9) holds for all array variables, it still can not ensure that the loop has a nontrivial communication-free hyperplane partitioning.

Using Theorem 2, we further check the existence of a nontrivial communication-free hyperplane partitioning. In the mean time, the statement-iteration and data hyperplanes will be derived if they exist. Recall that the dimensions of data spaces $DS(v_1)$ and $DS(v_2)$ are two, Θ_1 and Θ_2 can be assumed to be $[\theta_{11}, \theta_{12}]$ and $[\theta_{21}, \theta_{22}]$, respectively. The conditions listed in Theorem 2 will be checked to determine the hyperplane coefficient vectors and constants.

By Condition **(C1)** in Theorem 2, the following equations are obtained.

$$\Theta_1 \cdot F_2^{s_1,v_1} = \Theta_1 \cdot F_1^{s_1,v_1} \; (i = 1, j = 1, \text{ and } k = 2,)$$
$$\Theta_2 \cdot F_2^{s_2,v_2} = \Theta_2 \cdot F_1^{s_2,v_2} \; (i = 2, j = 2, \text{ and } k = 2.)$$

By the Condition **(C2)** in Theorem 2,

$$\Theta_2 \cdot F_1^{s_1,v_2} = \Theta_1 \cdot F_1^{s_1,v_1} \ (i = 1 \text{ and } j = 2,)$$
$$\Theta_2 \cdot F_1^{s_2,v_2} = \Theta_1 \cdot F_1^{s_2,v_1} \ (i = 2 \text{ and } j = 2.)$$

By Condition **(C3)** in Theorem 2,

$$\Theta_1 \cdot f_2^{s_1,v_1} = \Theta_1 \cdot f_1^{s_1,v_1} \ (i = 1, j = 1, \text{ and } k = 2,)$$
$$\Theta_2 \cdot f_2^{s_2,v_2} = \Theta_2 \cdot f_1^{s_2,v_2} \ (i = 2, j = 2, \text{ and } k = 2.)$$

By Condition **(C4)** in Theorem 2,

$$\Theta_2 \cdot (f_1^{s_2,v_2} - f_1^{s_1,v_2}) = \Theta_1 \cdot (f_1^{s_2,v_1} - f_1^{s_1,v_1}) \ (i = 2 \text{ and } j = 2,)$$

Substituting $[\theta_{11}, \theta_{12}]$ and $[\theta_{21}, \theta_{22}]$ for Θ_1 and Θ_2, respectively, the above equations form a homogeneous linear system. Solving this homogeneous linear system, we obtain the general solution $(\theta_{11}, \theta_{12}, \theta_{21}, \theta_{22}) = (2r, r, 3r, -2r)$, where $r \in \mathbf{Q} - \{0\}$. Therefore, $\Theta_1 = [2r, r]$ and $\Theta_2 = [3r, -2r]$.

Next, we show Θ_1 and Θ_2 satisfy Condition **(C5)**:

$$(\cup_{i=1}^{m} \cup_{k=1}^{r_{i,1}} Ker((F_k^{s_i,v_1})^t)) = \{c_1[1,1]^t | c_1 \in \mathbf{Q} - \{0\}\},$$
$$\Longrightarrow (\cup_{i=1}^{m} \cup_{k=1}^{r_{i,1}} Ker((F_k^{s_i,v_1})^t))' = \{[r_1, r_2]^t | r_1 \neq r_2, r_1, r_2 \in \mathbf{Q} - \{0\}\},$$
$$\Longrightarrow \Theta_1^t = [2r, r]^t \in (\cup_{i=1}^{m} \cup_{k=1}^{r_{i,1}} Ker((F_k^{s_i,v_1})^t))'.$$

$$(\cup_{i=1}^{m} \cup_{k=1}^{r_{i,2}} Ker((F_k^{s_i,v_2})^t)) = \{c_2[1,-1]^t | c_2 \in \mathbf{Q} - \{0\}\},$$
$$\Longrightarrow (\cup_{i=1}^{m} \cup_{k=1}^{r_{i,2}} Ker((F_k^{s_i,v_2})^t))' = \{[r_1, r_2]^t | r_1 \neq -r_2, r_1, r_2 \in \mathbf{Q} - \{0\}\},$$
$$\Longrightarrow \Theta_2^t = [3r, -2r]^t \in (\cup_{i=1}^{m} \cup_{k=1}^{r_{i,2}} Ker((F_k^{s_i,v_2})^t))'.$$

Now the statement-iteration hyperplane coefficient vectors can be determined using Condition **(C6)** in Theorem 2.

$$\Delta_1 = \Theta_1 \cdot F_1^{s_1,v_1} = \Theta_1 \cdot F_2^{s_1,v_1} = \Theta_2 \cdot F_1^{s_1,v_2} = (r, -r)$$
$$\Delta_2 = \Theta_2 \cdot F_1^{s_2,v_2} = \Theta_1 \cdot F_1^{s_2,v_1} = \Theta_2 \cdot F_2^{s_2,v_2} = (r, r)$$

Note that the statement-iteration hyperplane coefficient vectors may be obtained using many different equations, e.g., Δ_1 can be obtained using $\Theta_1 \cdot F_1^{s_1,v_1}$, $\Theta_1 \cdot F_2^{s_1,v_1}$, or $\Theta_2 \cdot F_1^{s_1,v_2}$. Conditions **(C1)** and **(C2)** in Theorem 2 ensure that all the equations lead to the same result.

For the statement-iteration hyperplane coefficient vectors, Condition **(C7)** is satisfied:

$$span(\cup_{j=1}^{n} \cup_{k=1}^{r_{1,j}} Ker(F_k^{s_1,v_j})) = \{c_3[1,1]^t | c_3 \in \mathbf{Q} - \{0\}\},$$
$$\Longrightarrow (span(\cup_{j=1}^{n} \cup_{k=1}^{r_{1,j}} Ker(F_k^{s_1,v_j})))^{\perp} = \{[r_1, -r_1]^t | r_1 \in \mathbf{Q} - \{0\}\}$$
$$\Longrightarrow \Delta_1^t = [r, -r]^t \in (span(\cup_{j=1}^{n} \cup_{k=1}^{r_{1,j}} Ker(F_k^{s_1,v_j})))^{\perp}.$$

$$span(\cup_{j=1}^{n} \cup_{k=1}^{r_{2,j}} Ker(F_k^{s_2,v_j})) = \{c_4[1,-1]^t | c_4 \in \mathbf{Q} - \{0\}\},$$
$$\Longrightarrow (span(\cup_{j=1}^{n} \cup_{k=1}^{r_{2,j}} Ker(F_k^{s_2,v_j})))^{\perp} = \{[r_2, r_2]^t | r_2 \in \mathbf{Q} - \{0\}\},$$
$$\Longrightarrow \Delta_2^t = [r, r]^t \in (span(\cup_{j=1}^{n} \cup_{k=1}^{r_{2,j}} Ker(F_k^{s_2,v_j})))^{\perp}.$$

Next, we determine the data hyperplane constant terms. Due to the hyperplanes are related to each other, once a hyperplane constant term is determined, the other constant terms will be determined accordingly. Assuming c_{g_1} is known, c_{g_2}, c_{h_1}, and c_{h_2} can be determined using Conditions **(C8)** and **(C9)** as below:

$$\begin{aligned}
c_{g_2} &= c_{g_1} - \Theta_1 \cdot f_1^{s_1,v_1} + \Theta_2 \cdot f_1^{s_1,v_2} = c_{g_1} - \Theta_1 \cdot f_1^{s_2,v_1} + \Theta_2 \cdot f_1^{s_2,v_2} = c_{g_1} + 3r, \\
c_{h_1} &= c_{g_1} - \Theta_1 \cdot f_1^{s_1,v_1} = c_{g_1} - \Theta_1 \cdot f_2^{s_1,v_1} = c_{g_2} - \Theta_2 \cdot f_1^{s_1,v_2} = c_{g_1} + r, \\
c_{h_2} &= c_{g_2} - \Theta_2 \cdot f_1^{s_2,v_2} = c_{g_1} - \Theta_1 \cdot f_1^{s_2,v_1} = c_{g_2} - \Theta_2 \cdot f_2^{s_2,v_2} = c_{g_1} + 2r.
\end{aligned}$$

Similarly, statement-iteration and data hyperplane constant terms can be evaluated using many different equations. However, Conditions **(C3)** and **(C4)** in Theorem 2 ensure that they all lead to the same values.

It is clear that there exists at least one set of nonzero statement-iteration and data hyperplane coefficient vectors such that the conditions listed in Theorem 2 are all satisfied. By Theorem 2, this fact implies that the nested loop has a nontrivial communication-free hyperplane partitioning. The partition group is defined as the set of statement-iteration and data hyperplanes that are allocated to a processor. The partition group for this example follows. $G = \Psi_{h_1}(I_{s_1}) \cup \Psi_{h_2}(I_{s_2}) \cup \Phi_{g_1}(D_{v_1}) \cup \Phi_{g_2}(D_{v_2})$, where

$$\begin{aligned}
\Psi_{h_1}(I_{s_1}) &= \{I_{s_1} \mid [r, -r] \cdot I_{s_1} = c_{g_1} + r\} \\
\Psi_{h_2}(I_{s_2}) &= \{I_{s_2} \mid [r, r] \cdot I_{s_2} = c_{g_1} + 2r\} \\
\Phi_{g_1}(D_{v_1}) &= \{D_{v_1} \mid [2r, r] \cdot D_{v_1} = c_{g_1}\} \\
\Phi_{g_2}(D_{v_2}) &= \{D_{v_2} \mid [3r, -2r] \cdot D_{v_2} = c_{g_1} + 3r\}
\end{aligned}$$

Given loop bounds $1 \le i_1 \le 5$ and $1 \le i_2 \le 5$, for $r = 1$, the constant term c_{g_1} corresponding to statement-iteration hyperplane coefficient vector Δ_1 and Δ_2 are ranged from -5 to 3 and from 0 to 8, respectively. The intersection part of these two ranges means that the two statement-iteration hyperplanes have to be coupled together onto a processor. For the rest, just one statement-iteration hyperplane, either Δ_1 or Δ_2, is allocated to a processor. The constant terms c_{g_2}, c_{h_1}, and c_{h_2} are evaluated to the following values:

$$-2 \le c_{g_2} \le 11, \quad -4 \le c_{h_1} \le 4, \quad \text{and} \quad 2 \le c_{h_2} \le 10.$$

The corresponding parallelized program is as follows.

```
doall c = -5, 8
  do i1 = max(c - 3, 1), min(c + 1, 5)
    i2 = -i1 + c + 2
    B[i1 - i2 + 1, i1 - 2i2 + 1] = A[i2 - 1, i1 - i2] * B[i1 + i2 - 1, i1 + i2 - 2]
  enddo
  do i1 = max(c + 2, 1), min(c + 6, 5)
    i2 = i1 - c - 1
    A[i1, -i1 - i2 - 1] = A[i1 - i2 - 1, -i1 + i2 + 1] + B[i1 + i2, i1 + 2i2 - 1]
  enddo
enddoall
```

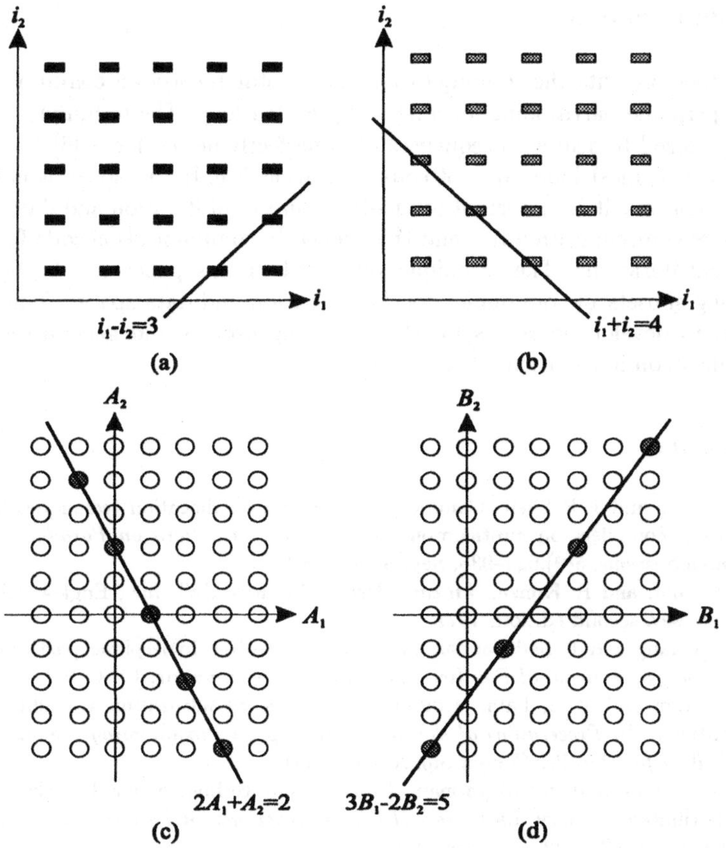

Fig. 2. Communication-free statement-iteration hyperplanes and data hyperplanes for a partition group of loop (L_1), where $r = 1$ and $c_{g_1} = 2$. (a) Statement-iteration hyperplane of $SIS(s_1)$. (b) Statement-iteration hyperplane of $SIS(s_2)$. (c) Data hyperplane of $DS(A)$. (d) Data hyperplane of $DS(B)$.

Fig. 2 illustrates the communication-free hyperplane partitionings for a particular partition group, $r = 1$ and $c_{g_1} = 2$. □

The communication-free hyperplane partitioning technique for a perfectly nested loop has been discussed in this section. Our method treats statements within a loop body as separate schedulable units and considers both iteration and data spaces at the same time. Partitioning groups are determined using affine array reference functions directly, instead of using data dependence vectors.

5 Conclusions

This paper presents the techniques for finding statement-level communication-free hyperplane partitioning for a perfectly nested loop. The technique can also be generalized to deal with sequences of imperfectly nested loops [6].

In reality, most loops are not communication-free. If a program is not communication-free, it is important to identify a subset of iteration and data spaces which are communication-free and then generate communication code for other statement-iterations. The technique presented in this paper can be used for searching subsets of communication-free iteration and data spaces. The future work is to develop heuristics for this searching process and generate efficient code when communication is inevitable.

References

1. T. S. Chen and J. P. Sheu. Communication-free data allocation techniques for parallelizing compilers on multicomputers. *IEEE Transactions on Parallel and Distributed Systems*, 5(9):924–938, September 1994.
2. K. Hoffman and R. Kunze. *Linear Algebra*. Prentice-Hall, Inc., Englewood Cliffs, New Jersey, second edition, 1971.
3. C.-H. Huang and P. Sadayappan. Communication-free hyperplane partitioning of nested loops. *Journal of Parallel and Distributed Computing*, 19:90–102, 1993.
4. A. W. Lim and M. S. Lam. Communication-free parallelization via affine transformations. In *Proceedings of the 7th Workshop on Programming Languages and Compilers for Parallel Computing*, August 1994.
5. J. Ramanujam and P. Sadayappan. Compile-time techniques for data distribution in distributed memory machines. *IEEE Transactions on Parallel and Distributed Systems*, 2(4):472–482, October 1991.
6. K.-P. Shih, J.-P. Sheu, and C.-H. Huang. Statement-level communication-free partitioning techniques for parallelizing compilers. Technical Report NCU-PPL-Tr-96-01, Dept. of Computer Science and Information Engineering, National Central University, Taiwan, 1996.
7. M. E. Wolf and M. S. Lam. A data locality optimizing algorithm. In *Proceedings of the ACM SIGPLAN'91 Conference on Programming Language Design and Implementation*, pages 30–44, June 1991.
8. M. J. Wolfe. *High Performance Compilers for Parallel Computing*. Addison-Wesley Publishing Company, 1996.

Generalized Overlap Regions for Communication Optimization in Data-Parallel Programs

A. Venkatachar, J. Ramanujam, and A. Thirumalai
Department of Electrical and Computer Engineering
Louisiana State University, Baton Rouge, LA 70803-5901, USA
http://www.ee.lsu.edu/jxr
{arun,jxr,ash}@ee.lsu.edu

Abstract. Data-parallel languages such as High Performance Fortran, Vienna Fortran and Fortran D include directives for alignment and distribution that describe how data and computation are mapped onto the processors in a distributed-memory multiprocessor. A compiler for these language that generates code for each processor has to compute the sequence of local memory addresses accessed by each processor and the sequence of sends and receives for a given processor to access non-local data. While the address generation problem has received much attention, issues in communication have not been dealt with extensively. A novel approach for the management of communication sets and strategies for local storage of remote references is presented. Algorithms for deriving communication patterns are discussed first. Then, two schemes that extend the notion of a local array by providing storage for non-local elements (called *overlap regions*) interspersed throughout the storage for the local portion are presented. The two schemes, namely *course padding* and *column padding* enhance locality of reference significantly at the cost of a small overhead due to unpacking of messages. The performance of these schemes are compared to the traditional buffer-based approach and improvements of up to 30% in total time are demonstrated. Several message optimizations such as offset communication, message aggregation and coalescing are also discussed.

1 Introduction

Programming massively parallel distributed memory machines involves partitioning data and computation across processors. Data-parallel languages like Fortran D [5], Vienna Fortran [3] and High Performance Fortran [8, 12] include directives for alignment and distribution that describe how data and computation are mapped onto the processors in a distributed-memory multiprocessor. In these languages, arrays are aligned to an abstract Cartesian grid called a *template;* the template is then distributed across the processors. The distribution of computation follows the *owner-computes* rule, *i.e.*, the processor performs only those computations (or assignments) for which it owns the left hand side variable. Access to non-local right hand side variables is achieved by inserting sends and receives. In order to generate node code we need to compute the sequence of sends and receives for a given processor to access non-local data in addition to computing the sequence of local memory addresses accessed by each processor. In addition, the compiler has to manage storage for non-local references and exploit data locality in code execution whenever possible.

Using the fact that the address generation algorithm is based on integer lattices [9, 19] and the set of array elements referenced can be generated by integer linear combinations of basis vectors for the lattice, we present algorithms for deriving the communication sets of each processor. Then, two schemes that extend the notion of a local array by providing storage for non-local elements (called *overlap regions*) interspersed throughout the storage for the local portion are presented. The two schemes, namely *course padding*

[1] Supported in part by an NSF Young Investigator Award CCR–9457768, and NSF grant CCR–9210422, and by the Louisiana Board of Regents through contract LEQSF (1991-94)-RD-A-09.

and *column padding* enhance locality of reference significantly at the cost of a small overhead due to unpacking of messages. We compare the performance of these schemes to the traditional buffer-based approach and demonstrate performance improvements of up to 30% in total time. In addition, we discuss several additional optimizations such as offset communication, message aggregation and coalescing.

Several papers have addressed the code generation problem for distributed memory machines [1, 2, 4, 7, 9, 10, 11, 14, 15, 16, 17, 18, 19, 20, 21, 22]. Many of these papers have developed good schemes for address generation but issues in communication optimization have not received much attention. Chatterjee *et al.* [4] describe the set of accesses as a finite state machine (FSM) and use the FSM to generate communication. Their model of communication is based on packing elements using an address-value pair before sending. At the receive end there is no need to unpack messages and processors use message buffers for the combined receive-execute phase. The code uses expensive conditionals and may suffer from locality when a large numbers of processors send messages. Extensions to multiple right hand side arrays and accesses have not been dealt with. Stichnoth [15] and Gupta *et al.* [7] discuss similar schemes for communication.

Kennedy, Nedeljkovic and Sethi [10] view the set of accesses as an integer lattice and make use of the repeating set of accesses. Their communication model performs packing of elements before communication. On the receive side each processor allocates overlap regions at the end of local storage (for each array) for storing non-local accesses. They then construct a table of accesses to index into the local as well as the overlap region. Their code does not require unpacking of messages but requires the added overhead of recomputing table entries; of the two tables of length k that they use, the entries in one are updated in each iteration. In effect a processor that performs N local computations computes a total of N addresses for each right hand side reference, computed using the two tables of length k. Communication generation issues are also dealt with by Thirumalai [17] and by Thirumalai, Ramanujam and Venkatachar [20]. In contrast to these papers, we present storage schemes for non-local references that help maintain data locality while reducing runtime overhead with `CYCLIC(k)` distributions. In particular, recomputing the address pattern for references is eliminated. Our approach to provide storage area for non-local references was inspired by Gerndt's work [6] on overlap regions in the context of shift communication with `BLOCK` distribution. Also, we present adaptations of these storage schemes for several communication optimizations.

This paper is organized as follows. In Section 2, we provide a short review the problem of address generation algorithm based on integer lattices. In Section 3, we present algorithms to generate the necessary communication sets; these algorithms exploit the repeating communication pattern. We show in Section 4 how to generate the sends for each processor and propose a method to directly read and execute the received elements from the buffers. In Section 5, we discuss generalized overlap regions that provide local storage for non-local references and present algorithms to unpack data. Two different schemes, namely *course padding* and *column padding* are proposed to unpack data into local storage space. In the next section, we discuss message optimizations such as coalescing, aggregation and offset communication. Experimental results are presented in Section 7 and we conclude in Section 8 with a discussion.

2 Review of lattice-based local address generation

We consider an array A identically aligned to the template T; this means that if, $A(i)$ is aligned with $T(ai + b)$, then the alignment stride $a = 1$ and the alignment offset $b = 0$. Further let this template be distributed in a block-cyclic fashion with a block size of k across p processors. This is also known as a `CYCLIC(k)` distribution [8, 12]. A typical HPF assignment statement is of the form $A(L : H : s) = \cdots$ where s is the access stride. Given an array statement with HPF-style data mappings, it is our aim to generate SPMD code along with communication for the different processors.

We treat the global address space as a two dimensional space; every element of A has an address of the form (x, y) in this space, where x is the course (or row) to which this element belongs and y is the offset of the element in that course. Given a global address i of an array element, the processor m that owns the element is $m = (i \text{ div } k) \bmod p$ and the local address of that element on processor $m = k(i \text{ div } pk) + i \bmod k$.

We [19] presented an address generation algorithm based on integer lattices. We showed that the set of array elements referenced can be generated by integer linear combinations of the basis vectors of the lattice. Let B be the basis matrix of the two dimensional space, where,

$$B = \begin{bmatrix} \alpha_1 & \beta_1 \\ \alpha_2 & \beta_2 \end{bmatrix}$$

It was shown [19] that the determinant of B is the access stride s itself. The access pattern for the array A repeats after every $\frac{s}{\text{GCD}(s,pk)}$ courses of elements. Thus, the pattern of accesses in the first $\frac{s}{\text{GCD}(s,pk)}$ courses can be used to determine the rest of the local addresses accessed. Using a transformation $T = B^{-1}$ and Fourier-Motzkin elimination [13, 22], we derive the code shown below for address pattern generation. The code for $A(L : H : s)$ is easily obtained by making minor modifications to the loop bounds of the nested loop before applying the transformation T [19].

$len = 0$
do $u = \left\lceil \frac{(-mk-k+1)\beta_1}{s_1} \right\rceil, \left\lfloor \frac{(s_1-1)\beta_2 - mk\beta_1}{s_1} \right\rfloor$
  if $\beta_1 = 0$
    $lower = \left\lceil \left(\frac{mk - u\alpha_2}{\beta_2} \right) \right\rceil$; $upper = \left\lfloor \left(\frac{mk+k-1-u\alpha_2}{\beta_2} \right) \right\rfloor$
  else
    $lower = \left\lceil \max\left(\frac{mk-u\alpha_2}{\beta_2}, \frac{-u\alpha_1}{\beta_1} \right) \right\rceil$; $upper = \left\lfloor \min\left(\frac{mk+k-1-u\alpha_2}{\beta_2}, \frac{s_1-1-u\alpha_1}{\beta_1} \right) \right\rfloor$
  endif
  do $v = lower, upper$
    $loc\_pattern_m[len] = (\alpha_1 u + \beta_1 v)k + \alpha_2 u + \beta_2 v - mk$
    $glob\_pattern_m[len] = (\alpha_1 u + \beta_1 v)pk + \alpha_2 u + \beta_2 v$
    $len = len + 1$
  enddo
enddo

3 Communication Set Generation

Communication set generation involves computing, for each processor, the set of elements to be sent, the processors to which these elements are sent, the set of elements received and the processors from which these are received. We show that there is a pattern of communication which can be exploited in communication set generation. We then present algorithms for deriving these communication patterns. The send communication pattern stores the index of the destination processor and the set of elements to be sent before the communication pattern starts repeating. The receive communication pattern on the other hand stores the index of the processor sending the data and the address of the element to be received. These communication patterns are used to derive both the send and receive communication sets for each processor. In the next sections, we use these pattern to pack and unpack messages. We discuss communication generation for the following array statement with HPF-style data mappings.

$$A(L_1 : H_1 : s_1) = \mathcal{F}\left(B(L_2 : H_2 : s_2)\right) \qquad (1)$$

where arrays A and B are distributed using a CYCLIC(k) distribution over p processors. Extensions to cases with different block sizes for the arrays as well as a different number of processors over which the arrays are distributed are straightforward and are not discussed here. Optimizations for multiple right hand side array sections are discussed in Section 5.

3.1 Receive Pattern Generation

The access pattern of the LHS array in the global address space repeats itself after pk elements are accessed, i.e. after every s_1 rows, where s_1 is the access stride of the LHS array. In order to generate the receive set, we run the code generated as described in the previous section to obtain the global address of the first pk elements accessed on the LHS. For each of these elements we calculate the processor that owns the corresponding RHS element. The pattern of elements which are needed to perform computation and are local to the processor are also computed. The length of the communication pattern, len_l, corresponds to len in the code discussed in the last section. The receive pattern generation code is shown below.

```
do j = 0, len_l − 1
    index_l = glob_LHS_pattern_m[j]
    RIndPattern_m[j] = index_r = (s_2/s_1)(index_l − L_1) + L_2
    RProcPattern_m[j] = (index_r div k) mod p
    if m = RProcPattern_m[j]
        RPattern_m[j] = (k(index_r div pk) + index_r mod k)
    endif
enddo
```

3.2 Send Pattern Generation

Our approach to the send set generation is very similar to the receive set generation shown in Section 3.1. It should be obvious that there is a one to one correspondence between the LHS array element and the RHS array elements. So the send pattern for a processor is the same as the receive pattern calculated assuming that the RHS element is actually the LHS element. Here again we notice that the send pattern should repeat after every s_2^{th} row. len_r is the length of the communication pattern which corresponds to len in the code discussed in the last section. The pattern generation code is shown below.

```
do j = 0, len_r − 1
    index_r = glob_RHS_pattern_m[j]
    SIndPattern_m[j] = index_l = (s_1/s_2)(index_r − L_2) + L_1
    SProcPattern_m[j] = (index_l div k) mod p
    if m ≠ SProcPattern_m[j]
        SPattern_m[j] = loc_RHS_pattern_m[j]
    endif
enddo
```

Example: Here we illustrate communication set generation for the array assignment statement $A(0 : H_1 : 5) = B(0 : H_2 : 3)$ where A and B are aligned identically with the template T, and $p = 4$ and $k = 8$. The elements accessed on the LHS and RHS on all processors is shown in Figure 1. Tables shown below indicate entries in the communication data structures, namely the pattern tables for processor 0.

$RIndPattern_0$	0	3	21	39	42	60	78	81
$RProcPattern_0$	0	0	2	0	1	3	1	2
$RPattern_0$	0	3		15				

$SIndPattern_0$	0	3	6	33	36	39	66	69
$SProcPattern_0$	0	0	1	2	3	0	1	2
$SPattern_0$			6	9	12		18	21

Entries in the $RIndPattern_0$ and $RPattern_0$ tables indicate the global and local indices of the elements on RHS which are needed by the LHS before the communication pattern starts repeating. Some entries in the *RPattern*$_0$ are not computed as the algorithms to be discussed in later sections do not require these elements. Similarly *SIndPattern*$_0$ and *SPattern*$_0$ tables stores the global and local indices of the elements on RHS which are accessed before the communication pattern starts repeating. Some entries in the *SPattern*$_0$ table are also not computed due to the same reasons as mentioned above. *RProcPattern*$_0$ table stores the index of processors from which processor 0 receives data and *SProcPattern*$_0$ stores the index of processors to which processor 0 sends data. These pattern tables are needed to generate the communication algorithms to be discussed in the next section.

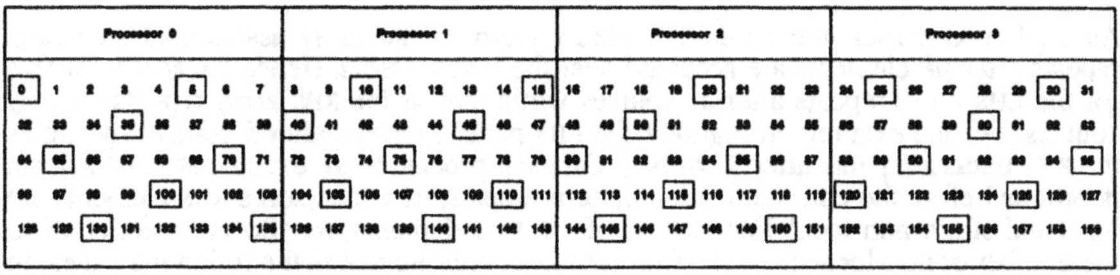

(a): Global addresses of array A accessed for $p = 4$, $k = 8$, and $s = 5$.

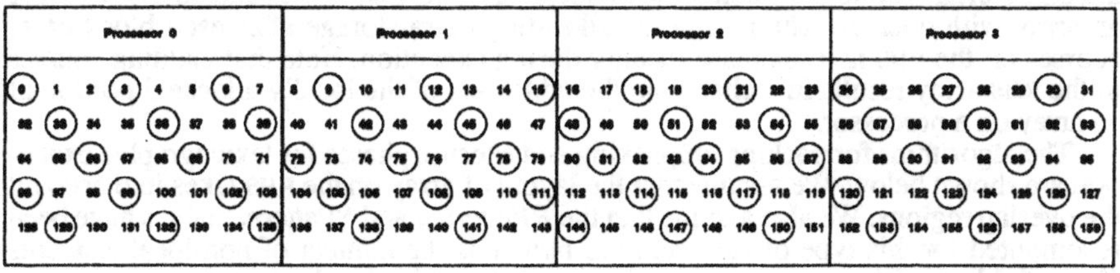

(b): Global addresses of array B accessed for $p = 4$, $k = 8$, and $s = 3$.

Fig. 1. Global addresses of arrays A and B accessed in the array statement $A(0 : H_1 : 5) = B(0 : H_2 : 3)$ with $p = 4$ and $k = 8$.

4 Generalized Overlap Regions for Block-Cyclic Distributions

In order to perform computations locally on a processor, the processor needs to receive all the non-local data using interprocessor communication. A compiler which uses owner-computes rule needs to perform all the sends and receives if lexicographic execution order has to be preserved. The communication between processors involves packing of data into buffers before being sent from one processor to another. At the receive end, the processor can either unpack the non-local elements into its local space before execution or can read directly from the receive buffers during execution.

Reading data directly out of buffers incurs no unpacking overhead but requires expensive conditionals to be executed in each iteration. In order to overcome this drawback, one can unpack the elements into overlap areas before execution. This unpacking of messages will not result in expensive conditionals and lead to improved locality of reference. In this section, we discuss two such strategies for unpacking the received elements into overlap regions.

Our algorithm unpacks the data from buffers into the local address space in order to exploit spatial locality. Since we provide storage for overlap regions, the notion of the local array has been extended; this results in a need to recompute the $RPattern_m$ and $SPattern_m$ tables. The overhead due to unpacking is significantly reduced because of the way in which the pattern table is used. Data locality is preserved because of the way we allocate storage for non-local accesses.

4.1 Course padding for overlap regions

As explained earlier, the communication pattern for an array assignment statement repeats after pk elements are accessed over the p processors. Hence the access pattern for the LHS array repeats after s_1 courses while that of the RHS array repeats after s_2 courses. For the example in Figure 1 the LHS pattern repeats after 5 courses, where as the RHS pattern repeats after 3 courses. On each processor we execute at most k local iterations before the communication pattern repeats, of which some RHS elements are local and others non-local. For each set of s_2k RHS elements, we allocate space equal to the number of non-local elements (referred to as *num_nonloc* in the following pages) in the receive index pattern. In the worst case every one of the k local iterations may require non-local RHS; thus, we might have to allocate space for at most k elements for each block of s_2 RHS courses. With course padding, after each set of s_2k local elements we allocate storage for holding non-local elements. Figure 2 shows an example of padding an array with courses. The reason for allocating extra storage after each block of s_2 courses on the RHS is to increase locality during execution. Note that padding courses in the RHS array results in a change in the addresses of the locally allocated portion of an array on a processor.

The algorithms for packing, unpacking and execute phases for lexicographic execution are shown below. We assume that the layout of array on the RHS takes into account the overlap regions. We also assume that the $RPattern_m$ and $SPattern_m$ tables have been recomputed for this type of storage. *num_nonloc* is the number of non-local elements (for each block of the communication pattern) to be padded in the new storage space before the communication pattern starts repeating. The value of *num_nonloc* is computed based on the information from the $RProcPattern_m$ table. Array elements received from processor q are in $ReceiveBuffer_q$ for each processor q where $0 \leq q \leq p-1$. *Apattern* stores the local access pattern of array A. Note that max_A is the local address of the last element of A accessed on processor m. Note that, in order to keep the presentation simple, we only present the algorithms for a full set of blocks; the code for the last incomplete block is simple and is not discussed here.

Let us consider Processor 0 from Figure 1. We have shown the computation of pattern tables for Processor 0 in Example 3.2. The array on the RHS needs to pack its elements into the $ReceiveBuffers_q$ where q is the index into the $SProcPattern_0$ table. This constitutes the packing phase (Step 3), where in, processor 0 scans its send patterns and for each non-local element i of $SPattern_0$, processor 0 packs all elements in the array section $\left(\text{SPattern}_0[i] : max_B : s_2k + \text{num\_nonloc}\right)$ into contiguous locations in the *SendBuffer* corresponding to the processor that owns $SPattern_0[i]$. This necessarily means that we make as many scans of the local space as the number of non-local elements before we pack all elements. Figure 3 shows the set of elements which are packed into *SendBuffers*. The array section involved in packing the first element to be sent to Processor 1 is (6 : 477 : 29), where 29 is the total number of elements including the space allocated for the 5 non-local elements before the pattern starts repeating.

Once all the elements to be sent have been packed, communication takes place. We do not show the communication code here. At the receiving end each processor receives all the elements from other processors in the corresponding *ReceiveBuffers*. For each access on the LHS for the first repeating set we compute and record (Step 2) the corresponding entry from the new storage space of the RHS into a table of access called the $BPattern_m$ table. This table contains the sequence of accesses to both local and received data for the first repeating set; these entries are in lexicographic order. This table is constructed only once before the unpacking stage and does not require updates such as those required by the algorithm in [10]. For the above example the entries held by the $BPattern_m$ table are shown in Figure 3. Entries (0, 3, 15) correspond to local elements where as (24, 25, 26, 27, 28) correspond to non-local elements. These entries correspond to the first repeating set of communication pattern. Step 2 illustrates the code to compute the table. The code records consecutive locations into $BPattern_m$ table if the element is non-local, since course padding schemes allocates consecutive storage for non-locals.

The unpacking stage (Step 6) looks up the entries in the $BPattern_m$ table to determine where the incoming elements are to be unpacked. For each received element i of $BPattern_m$, processor m unpacks elements from the *ReceiveBuffers* to the array section $(\text{BPattern}_m[i] : max_B : s_2k + \text{num\_nonloc})$. Figure /reffig:coupadex shows the array sections of memory into which the elements in the *ReceiveBuffers* have been unpacked. Here again we make as many scans of the local space as the number of non-local elements. Figure 3 shows the array sections into which consecutive elements from the *ReceiveBuffers* are unpacked.

Once all the elements are unpacked into the local space, the final stage (Step 7) involves lexicographic execution wherein look-ups into the $APattern_m$ and $BPattern_m$ table will determine the location of elements on both LHS and RHS. Figure 3 illustrates local addresses of both LHS and RHS which are accessed during execution using course padding scheme. All the adresses are in lexicographic order. The complete algorithm which performs packing, unpacking and execution on processor m is shown below.

Step 1: The entire local space is assumed to be reorganized in order to account for the overlap regions. We allocate extra storage equal to the number of non-local elements to be received.

Step 2: Code to compute a table to store the locations of both local and non-local accesses on RHS. This table will be used during both unpacking and execution.

```
index = s_2 k
do j = 0, sizeof(RProcPattern_m) - 1
   dest = RecvProcPattern_m[j]
   if (m = dest)
      BPattern[j] = RPattern_m[j]
   else
      BPattern[j] = index
      index = index + 1
enddo
```

Step 3: Packing: Involves packing of elements to be sent into the respective *SendBuffers*. Pattern tables discussed in Section 3.2 are used to pack these elements.

```
Scount_q = 0, where 0 <= q <= p - 1
baseadd = 0
blksize_B = s_2 k + num_nonloc
do i = 0, sizeof(SProcPattern_m) - 1
   q = SProcpattern_m[i]
   if m != q
      loc_B = SPattern_m[i]
      do j = 0, max_B / blksize_B
         address = baseadd + loc_B
         SendBuffer_q[Scount_q] = B_loc[address]
         Scount_q = Scount_q + 1
```

```
        baseadd = baseadd + blksize_B
      enddo
    endif
  enddo
```

Step 4: Send data in the *SendBuffers* to the respective processors.
Step 5: Receive data from the processors into the appropriate *ReceiveBuffers*
Step 6: Unpack: Involves unpacking non-local elements into the overlap regions allocated in the local space.

```
  count_q = 0 for 0 ≤ q ≤ p − 1
  do i = 0, sizeof(RProcPattern_m) − 1
    q = RProcPattern_m[i]
    loc_B = BPattern_m[i]
    do j = 0, max_A/(s_1 k)
      Bloc[loc_B] = ReceiveBuffer_q[count_q]
      count_q = count_q + 1
      loc_B = loc_B + s_2 k + num_nonloc
    endo
  endo
```

Step 7: Execute: Involves lexicographic order of execution.

```
  baseadd_A = baseadd_B = 0
  do j = 0, max_A/(s_1 k)
    do i = 0, sizeof(RProcPattern_m) − 1
      loc_A = APattern_m[j] + baseadd_A
      loc_B = BPattern_m[j] + baseadd_B
      Aloc[loc_A] = F(Bloc[loc_B])
    enddo
    baseadd_A = baseadd_A + s_1 k
    baseadd_B = baseadd_B + s_2 k + num_nonloc
  enddo
```

4.2 Column padding for overlap regions

In case of column padding scheme, we also allocate local storage for non-local RHS elements that are accessed. Unlike the previous unpacking strategy, the extra local storage is to the right of the local address space. The total number of extra storage space that are padded to the RHS array is equal to the number of non-local elements being accessed. There can be storage for at most k extra elements before the pattern starts repeating. The location to which the received element is to be unpacked is dependent on the address of the element being received. Figure 4(a) and (b) shows an example of padding an array with columns.

We assume that the layout of array on the RHS takes into account the overlap regions. We also assume that the *RPattern*$_m$ and *SPattern*$_m$ tables have been recomputed for this type of storage. *num_nonloc* is the number of non-local elements (for each block of the communication pattern) to be padded in the new storage space before the communication pattern starts repeating. The value of *num_nonloc* is computed based on the information from the *RProcPattern*$_m$ table. Array elements received from processor q are in *ReceiveBuffer*$_q$ for each processor q where $0 \leq q \leq p-1$. *Apattern* stores the local access pattern of array A. Note that max_A is the local address of the last element

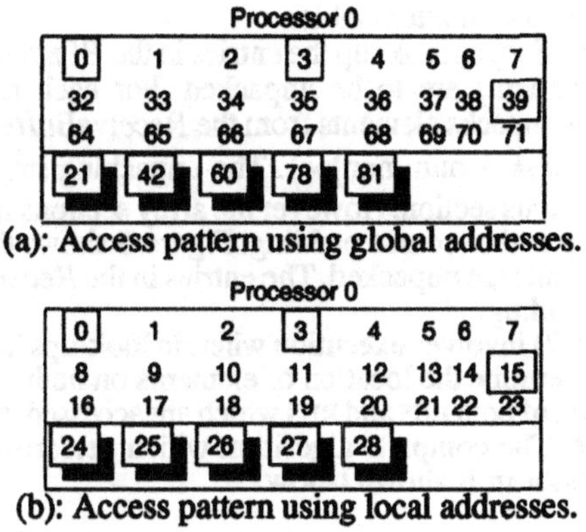

Fig. 2. RHS elements on processor 0 (using padded courses) for $A(0: \ :5) = B(0: \ :3)$, $p = 4$ and $k = 8$.

$SendBuffer_1$	6 35 64 93 122 18 47 76 105 134
$SendBuffer_2$	9 38 67 96 127 21 50 79 108 137
$SendBuffer_3$	12 41 70 99 128

BPattern	0 3 24 15 25 26 27 28

B(24:144:29) - *ReceiveBuffer*$_2(0:4)$
B(25:144:29) - *ReceiveBuffer*$_1(0:4)$
B(26:144:29) - *ReceiveBuffer*$_3(0:4)$
B(27:144:29) - *ReceiveBuffer*$_1(5:9)$
B(28:144:29) - *ReceiveBuffer*$_2(5:9)$

LHS	0 5 11 17 22 28 34 39 40 45 51 57 62 68 74 79 ······
RHS	0 3 24 15 25 26 27 28 29 32 53 44 54 55 56 57 ······

Fig. 3. Illustration of packing, unpacking and execution on processor 0 for $A(0:795:5) = B(0:477:3)$, $p = 4$ and $k = 8$.

---

of A accessed on processor m. Note that, in order to keep the presentation simple, we only present the algorithms for a full set of blocks; the code for the last incomplete block is simple and is not discussed here.

The algorithm for packing (Step 3) is exactly similar to the one discussed in Section 4.1. It is only the unpacking and execution which is different from that of course padding scheme. Figure 5 shows the elements padded into the *SendBuffers*.

At the receiving end however, we compute a table of access (Step 2) similar to the *BPattern* table as discussed in the previous section for the RHS to record the sequence of accesses to both local and received data for the first repeating set; these entries are in lexicographic order. The accesses computed, depends on the element to be received; whose information can be found from the pattern tables discussed earlier. Figure 5 shows the entries held by the *BPattern* table.

The unpacking stage (Step 6) looks up the entries in the $BPattern_m$ table to determine where the incoming elements are to be unpacked. For each received element i of $BPattern_m$, processor m unpacks elements from the *ReceiveBuffers* to the array section $(\mathrm{BPattern}_m[i] : max_B : s_2k + \mathrm{num\_nonloc})$. The unpacking strategy is similar to the one discussed in the previous section. However the array sections involved in unpacking are different when compared to course padding. Figure 5 shows the array sections into which the received elements are unpacked. The entries in the *ReceiveBuffers* are exactly the same as in course padding.

The final stage (Step 7) involves execution wherein look-ups into the $APattern_m$ and $BPattern_m$ table will determine the location of elements on both LHS and RHS. Figure 5 illustrates local addresses of both LHS and RHS which are accessed during execution using columnpadding scheme. The complete algorithm which performs packing, unpacking and execution on processor m is shown below.

Step 1: The entire local space is assumed to be reorganized in order to account for the overlap regions. We allocate extra storage equal to the number of non-local elements to be received.

Step 2: Compute *BPattern* which is the table that stores local addresses of the RHS elements needed including elements received from other processors.

Step 3: Packing: Involves packing of elements to be sent into the respective *SendBuffers*. Pattern tables discussed in Section 3.2 are used to pack these elements.

$Scount_q = 0$, where $0 \le q \le p-1$
$baseadd = 0$
$blksize_B = s_2k + num\_nonloc$
do $i = 0, sizeof(SProcPattern_m) - 1$
    $q = SProcpattern_m[i]$
    if $m \neq q$
        $loc_B = SPattern_m[i]$
        do $j = 0, \frac{max_B}{blksize_B}$
            $address = baseadd + loc_B$
            $SendBuffer_q[Scount_q] = B_{loc}[address]$
            $Scount_q = Scount_q + 1$
            $baseadd = baseadd + blksize_B$
        enddo
    endif
enddo

Step 3: Send data in the *SendBuffers* to the respective processors.

Step 4: Receive data from the processors into the appropriate *ReceiveBuffers*

Step 5: Unpack: Involves unpacking non-local elements into the overlap regions allocated in the local space.

$count_q = 0$ for $0 \le q \le p-1$
do $i = 0, sizeof(RProcPattern_m) - 1$
    $q = RProcPattern_m[i]$
    $loc_B = BPattern_m[i]$
    do $j = 0, \frac{max_A}{s_1k}$
        $Bloc[loc_B] = ReceiveBuffer_q[count_q]$
        $count_q = count_q + 1$
        $loc_B = loc_B + s_2k + num\_nonloc$
    endo
endo

Step 6: Execute: Involves lexicographic order of execution.

$baseadd_A = baseadd_B = 0$
do $j = 0, \frac{max_A}{s_1 k}$
  do $i = 0, sizeof(RProcPattern_m) - 1$
    $loc_A = APattern_m[j] + baseadd_A$
    $loc_B = BPattern_m[j] + baseadd_B$
    $Aloc[loc_A] = \mathcal{F}\left(Bloc[loc_B]\right)$
  enddo
  $baseadd_A = baseadd_A + s_1 k$
  $baseadd_B = baseadd_B + s_2 k + num\_nonloc$
enddo

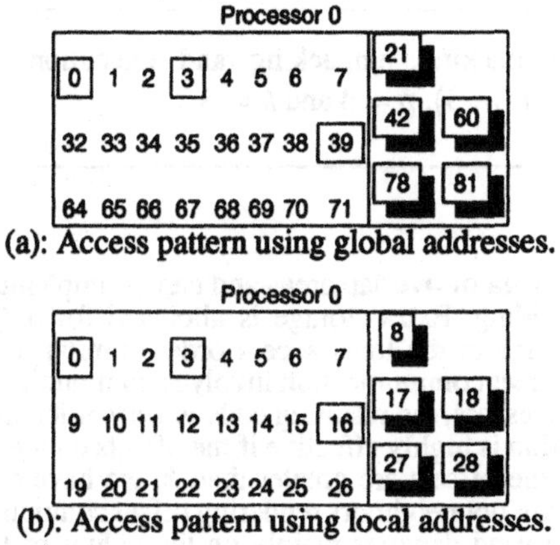

(a): Access pattern using global addresses.

(b): Access pattern using local addresses.

Fig. 4. RHS elements on processor 0 (using padded columns) for $A(0::5) = B(0::3), p = 4, k = 8$.

5 Message Optimizations

In this section, we discuss the use of message optimizations in code generation. We discuss three optimizations namely offset communication, message coalescing and aggregation. In case of multiple right hand side references to the same array, we can perform message coalescing optimization by sending only one copy of an element. We can also reduce the overhead of startup cost in communication by combining several messages—possibly due to different arrays referenced on the RHS—to be communicated between a sender and a receiver pair by performing message aggregation. We also discuss the idea of offset communication optimization which is when both LHS and RHS have the same distribution and access strides, by using the concept of overlap areas.

5.1 Offset Communication with Optimized Overlap Regions

In case of offset communication the distribution and access strides of the left and right hand side arrays are identical but have different offsets. Offset communication is

SendBuffer$_1$	6 35 64 93 122 21 50 79 108 137
SendBuffer$_2$	10 39 68 97 126 24 53 82 111 140
SendBuffer$_3$	13 42 71 100 129

BPattern	0 3 8 16 17 18 27 28

B(8:144:29) – *ReceiveBuffer*$_2$(0 : 4)
B(17:144:29) – *ReceiveBuffer*$_1$(0 : 4)
B(18:144:29) – *ReceiveBuffer*$_3$(0 : 4)
B(27:144:29) – *ReceiveBuffer*$_1$(5 : 9)
B(28:144:29) – *ReceiveBuffer*$_2$(5 : 9)

LHS	0 5 11 17 22 28 34 39 40 45 51 57 62 68 74 79 ······
RHS	0 3 8 16 17 18 27 28 29 32 37 45 46 47 56 57 ······

Fig. 5. Illustration of packing, unpacking and execution on processor 0 for $A(0:795:5) = B(0:477:3)$, $p = 4$ and $k = 8$.

---

implemented using the idea of overlap areas and can be implemented by either course padding or column padding. Extra storage is allocated for only non-local elements and this leads to a change in the local access order (similar to that with course and column padding). As offset communication involves communication between only the neighboring virtual processors, the resulting code is very efficient.

Offset communication is highly effective if the offsets on the right hand side arrays are all less than k . If the offsets are greater than k, we have communication among virtual processors that are not neighbors rendering offset communication less effective. The amount of storage used depends mainly on the values of the offsets in the RHS arrays and the stride of the LHS array. If the offsets are all less than k and s, there are no repeating elements in the non-local accesses and hence one need not perform message coalescing on the elements to be communicated. On the other hand if any of the offsets is less than k but greater than s, there might be some repeating elements in the non-local accesses due to different terms on the RHS, and message coalescing may be useful here. Hence in this case the storage space is allocated based on elements received after performing message coalescing.

Consider the array statement

$$A(L_1 : H_1 : s) = \mathcal{F}\left(B(L_2 + \theta_1 : H_2 + \theta_1 : s), \cdots, B(L_2 + \theta_r : H_2 + \theta_r : s)\right)$$

where $|\theta_i| \leq k$ and $|\theta_i| \leq s$ (for $i = 1, \cdots, r$). With course padding, the number of extra memory storage padded for every s courses of local array B is $\sum_{i=1}^{r} |\theta_i|$. In the case of column padding, local storage allocated depends on the sign of the offset. If $\theta_i < 0$ the padding column is to the left of the storage for the course; if $\theta_i > 0$ the padding column is to the right. For each s courses of local storage for the array B, we need $\sum_{i=1}^{r} |\theta_i|$ units of extra storage for non-local references. Figures 6 and Figures 7 illustrate course and column padding respectively for the following array statement which requires offset communication.

$$A(0:N:5) = \mathcal{F}\left(B(2:N+1:5), B(3:N+2:5), B(4:N+3:5)\right)$$

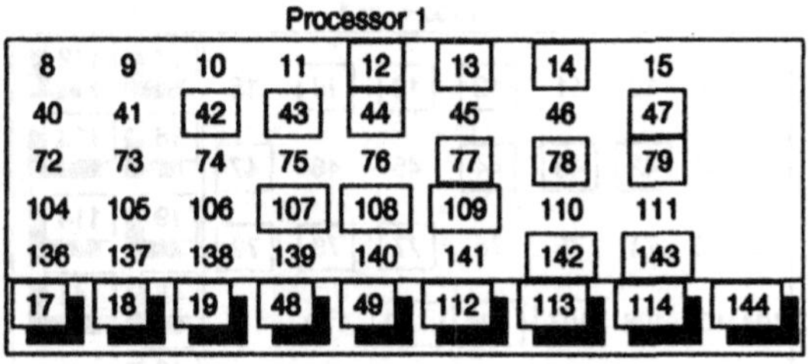

(a): Offset communication with padded courses: global address pattern.

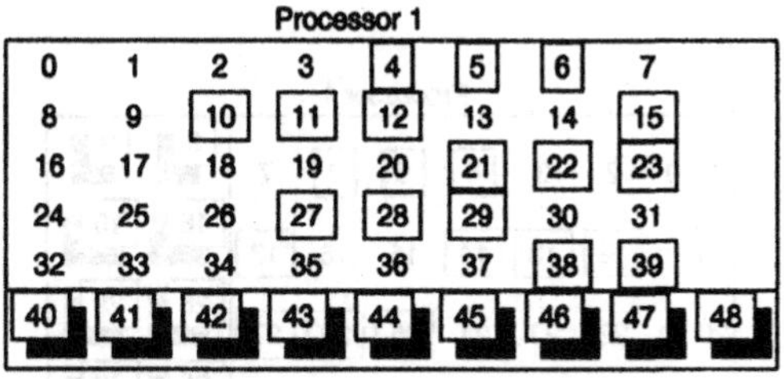

(b): Offset communication with padded courses: local address pattern.

Fig. 6. Access patterns for RHS elements on processor 1 (using offset communication using padded courses) for $A(0:N-1:5) = \mathcal{F}\left(B(2:N+1:5), B(3:N+2:5), B(4:N+3:5)\right)$, $p = 4$ and $k = 8$.

5.2 Message aggregation and coalescing

If there are references to multiple RHS arrays in a single statement, it is always better to combine all the messages going to the same processor into a single message and then send it. This optimization is called message aggregation and helps in reducing communication overhead. Message aggregation is then performed by aggregating the $SendBuffer[]_q$ (q is the receiving processor) for all the r RHS arrays on the right hand side. This results in a single message buffer being generated to be sent to a processor. In this case, the message header includes additional information that is necessary.

If there are multiple references to the same element of an array, then we can perform message coalescing and just send a single copy of the element. Here again, this optimization results in reduced communication volume. While performing message coalescing we have to keep track of the RHS array involved in sending or receiving the common element. Special message handling has to be provided at the receiving end in order to perform correct unpacking and execution.

6 Experiments

In order to verify the usefulness of overlap regions, we implemented all the above discussed algorithms and tested them for varying values of s_1, s_2 and k. Our execution model used the DAXPY operation

$$A(L_1 : H_1 : s_1) = A(L_1 : H_1 : s_1) + \mathtt{constant} * B(L_2 : H_2 : s_2)$$

In all our experiments we fixed the number of iterations per processor to be 4096. This allows us to measure the effect of the strides and block sizes for a fixed amount

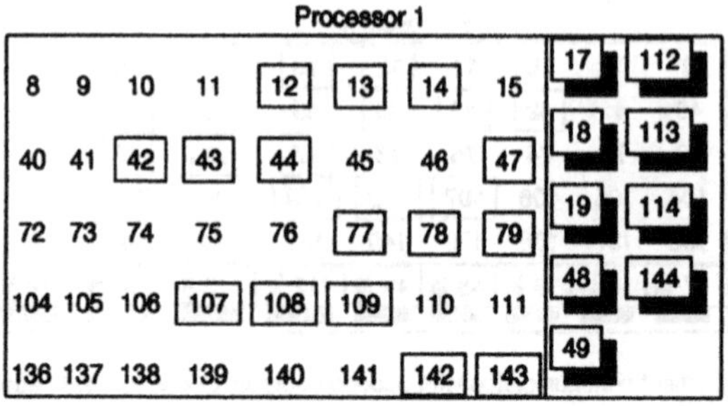

(a): Access pattern shown with global addresses for offset communication.

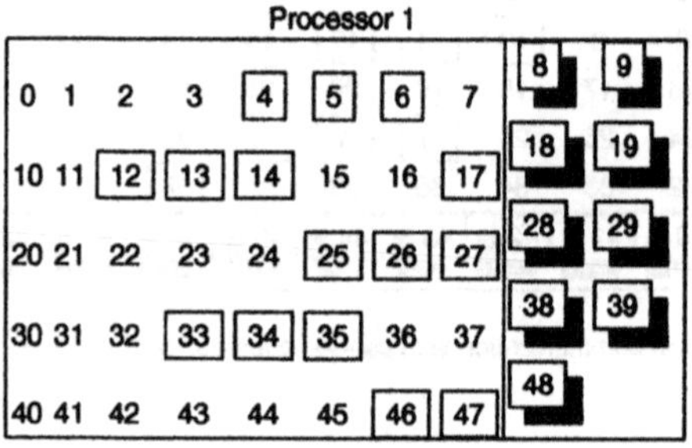

(b): Access pattern shown with local addresses for offset communication.

Fig. 7. Access patterns for RHS elements on processor 1 (using offset communication using padded columns) for $A(0:N-1:5) = \mathcal{F}\left(B(2:N+1:5), B(3:N+2:5), B(4:N+3:5)\right)$, $p = 4$ and $k = 8$.

---

of computation. We used 32 processors in the experiments. All the experiments were conducted on a single node of an IBM SP-2 using the cc compiler and -O3 optimization flag turned on. All the reported times are in microseconds. We do not discuss the communication time between processors as it varies widely across configurations and all the three methods incur the same inter-processor communication cost.

Table 1 lists the time it takes for packing, unpacking and execution (excluding unpacking overhead) for all the three methods mentioned in the paper. The model where we read directly from the buffers during execution is referred to as *buffer* in Table 1. The methods using course padding and column padding schemes are referred to as *course* and *column* respectively. Since the *buffer* scheme does not perform unpacking, the entries are dashes. The total execution time in the table corresponds to the sum of packing, unpacking and pure execution for both *course* and *column* where as it corresponds to the sum of packing and pure execution for *buffer*.

The results show that the *course* and *column* methods perform well when compared to reading data out of buffers directly. Based on the results we see a 30% improvement in the total time when compared to the *buffer* method. The low times for packing and unpacking is due to the fact that we reduced the number of look-ups in the final SPMD code and also due to the choice of building a *BPattern* table which reduces expensive runtime conditionals and recalculation of tables. Therefore, using overlap regions appears to be beneficial in executing data parallel programs on distributed-memory message passing machines. In addition, unpacking of data into overlap regions improves data locality.

Table 1. Communication packing, unpacking and execution time results (in microseconds) of our algorithms on an IBM SP-2 using the `cc` compiler and `-O3` optimization for the case $p = 32$ and number of iterations = 4096.

k	s_1	s_2	Packing			Unpacking			Execution			Total		
			buffer	column	course	buffer	column	course	buffer	column	course	buffer	column	course
4	3	5	603	126	126	-	126	126	2563	2061	2059	3166	2313	2311
	5	11	617	150	150	-	150	148	2579	2130	2157	3196	2430	2455
	9	7	612	136	136	-	135	135	2590	2145	2157	3202	2416	2428
	11	3	603	126	126	-	126	126	2596	2078	2076	3199	2330	2328
16	3	5	569	128	128	-	128	128	2502	1978	1955	3071	2234	2211
	5	11	588	155	155	-	156	138	2520	2041	1981	3108	2352	2274
	9	7	601	142	142	-	144	135	2538	2043	2023	3139	2329	2300
	11	3	569	129	129	-	128	128	2523	1980	1973	3092	2237	2230
64	3	5	562	139	139	-	138	137	2488	1935	1927	3050	2212	2203
	5	11	580	172	172	-	151	139	2496	1952	1943	3076	2275	2254
	9	7	570	154	154	-	152	142	2407	2017	1955	3077	2323	2251
	11	3	561	140	140	-	139	138	2521	1960	1953	3082	2239	2231
256	3	5	558	175	175	-	172	171	2478	1925	1923	3036	2272	2269
	5	11	579	212	212	-	179	171	2489	1923	1928	3068	2314	2311
	9	7	567	192	192	-	180	173	2404	1951	1943	3071	2323	2308
	11	3	559	181	181	-	174	173	2520	1957	1936	3079	2312	2290

7 Conclusions

In this paper, we have dealt with communication issues in code generation for data-parallel programs with block-cyclic distribution executing on distributed-memory message passing architectures. We presented a new approach for the management of communication sets and strategies for local storage of remote references. We derived algorithms for determining communication patterns. We then presented two schemes that extend the notion of a local array by providing storage for non-local elements (called *overlap regions*) interspersed throughout the storage for the local portion. The two schemes, namely *course padding* and *column padding* enhance locality of reference significantly at the cost of a small overhead due to unpacking of messages. The performance of these schemes was found to be up to 30% better than the traditional buffer-based approach. In addition, several message optimizations such as offset communication, message aggregation and coalescing were discussed. Extension of these schemes to two-level mapping is rather straightforward. Work is in progress on further message optimization issues and communication generation for more complex subscript expressions.

References

1. A. Ancourt, F. Coelho, F. Irigoin, and R. Keryell. A linear algebra framework for static HPF code distribution. To appear in *Scientific Programming*, 1996.

2. S. Benkner. Handling block-cyclic distributed arrays in Vienna Fortran 90. In *Proc. International Conference on Parallel Architectures and Compilation Techniques*, Limassol, Cyprus, June 1995.
3. B. Chapman, P. Mehrotra, and H. Zima. Programming in Vienna Fortran. *Scientific Programming*, 1(1):31–50, Fall 1992.
4. S. Chatterjee, J. Gilbert, F. Long, R. Schreiber, and S. Teng. Generating local addresses and communication sets for data parallel programs. *Journal of Parallel and Distributed Computing*, 26(1):72–84, 1995.
5. G. Fox, S. Hiranandani, K. Kennedy, C. Koelbel, U. Kremer, C. Tseng, and M. Wu. Fortran D language specification. Technical Report CRPC-TR90079, Rice University, December 1990.
6. M. Gerndt. Updating distributed variables in local computations. *Concurrency: Practice and Experience*, 2(3):171–193, September 1990.
7. S. Gupta, S. Kaushik, C. Huang, and P. Sadayappan. On compiling array expressions for efficient execution on distributed-memory machines. To appear in *Journal of Parallel and Distributed Computing*.
8. High Performance Fortran Forum. High Performance Fortran language specification. *Scientific Programming*, 2(1-2):1–170, 1993.
9. K. Kennedy, N. Nedeljkovic, and A. Sethi. A linear-time algorithm for computing the memory access sequence in data-parallel programs. In *Proc. of Fifth ACM SIGPLAN Symposium on Principles and Practice of Parallel Programming*, Santa Barbara, CA, July 1995.
10. K. Kennedy, N. Nedeljkovic, and A. Sethi. Communication generation for cyclic(k) distributions. In *Languages, Compilers, and Run-Time Systems for Scalable Computers*, B. Szymanski and B. Sinharoy (Eds.), Kluwer Academic Publishers, 1995.
11. C. Koelbel. Compile-time generation of communication for scientific programs. In *Proc. Supercomputing '91*, pages 101–110, November 1991.
12. C. Koelbel, D. Loveman, R. Schreiber, G. Steele, and M. Zosel. *High Performance Fortran Handbook*. The MIT Press, 1994.
13. J. Ramanujam. Non-unimodular transformations of nested loops. In *Proc. Supercomputing 92*, pages 214–223, November 1992.
14. C. van Reeuwijk, H.J. Sips, W. Denissen, and E. M. Paalvast. Implementing HPF distributed arrays on a message-passing parallel computer system. CP Technical Report series, TR9506, Delft University of Technology, 1995.
15. J. Stichnoth. Efficient compilation of array statements for private memory multicomputers. Technical Report CMU-CS-93-109, School of Computer Science, Carnegie-Mellon University, February 1993.
16. E. Su, A. Lain, S. Ramaswamy, D.J. Palermo, E.W. Hodges IV, and P. Banerjee. Advanced compilation techniques in the PARADIGM compiler for distributed-memory multicomputers. In *Proc. 1995 ACM International Conference on Supercomputing*, Barcelona, Spain, July 1995.
17. A. Thirumalai. Code generation and optimization for High Performance Fortran. M.S. Thesis, Department of Electrical and Computer Engineering, Louisiana State University, August 1995.
18. A. Thirumalai and J. Ramanujam. An efficient compile-time approach to compute address sequences in data parallel programs. In *Proc. 5th International Workshop on Compilers for Parallel Computers*, Malaga, Spain, pages 581-605, June 1995.
19. A. Thirumalai and J. Ramanujam. Fast address sequence generation for data-parallel programs using integer lattices. In *Languages and Compilers for Parallel Computing*, P. Sadayappan *et al.* (Eds.), Lecture Notes in Computer Science, Springer-Verlag, 1996.
20. A. Thirumalai, J. Ramanujam, and A. Venkatachar. Communication generation and optimization for HPF. In *Languages, Compilers, and Run-Time Systems for Scalable Computers*, B. Szymanski and B. Sinharoy (Eds.), Kluwer Academic Publishers, 1995.
21. A. Thirumalai and J. Ramanujam. Efficient computation of address sequences in data parallel programs using closed forms for basis vectors. *Journal of Parallel and Distributed Computing*, 38(2):188–203, November 1996.
22. M. Wolfe. *High performance compilers for parallel computing*. Addison-Wesley Publishing Co., Redwood City, CA, 1996.

Optimizing the Representation of Local Iteration Sets and Access Sequences for Block-Cyclic Distributions

Samuel P. Midkiff

IBM T.J. Watson Research, P.O. Box 704, Yorktown Height, NY 1059, *email: midkiff@watson.ibm.com*

Abstract. In this paper we investigate the optimization of state machine based representations of access sequence and local iteration set (LIS) information. Two state machine based representations are shown to have complementary strengths. We develop a third representation, the *hybrid* state machine, that utilizes the strengths of the other two methods. A new optimization is presented that allows state machine reuse across references, reducing the cost of state machine based accesses. Experimental data is presented to support the approach taken.

The block-cyclic distribution is useful for combining the load balancing characteristics of a cyclic distribution with the locality characteristics of a block distribution. Efforts to use block-cyclic distributions in HPF compilers have been hampered by the difficulty of generating efficient code.

Previous work has concentrated on efficient methods for computing either the access sequence or local iteration set (LIS) corresponding to a block-cyclic distribution. The access sequence is a sequence of offsets into a buffer that contains the block-cyclically distributed elements of an array on some processor. The LIS contains the values of the loop index variable I that access these elements. The best of these methods differ in speed by a constant factor, and there appears to be no way to make a more dramatic improvement in their speed by just tweaking the method of computing the access sequence.

In this paper we take a different tact – by improving and optimizing the representation of these solutions. Two methods to date have been used: directly using the solution to generate the desired sequence (e.g. [2, 5, 7]), or using the solution to construct a state machine, and then using that state machine to generate the access sequence (or LIS) (e.g. [1, 3]).

In this paper we give an alternate state machine representation for these sequences and provide some experimental data to characterize the relative advantages and disadvantages of the methods. Next, we present a method to mitigate a major cost of the state machine representations by allowing solutions and state machines to be reused or shared by multiple references.

Figure 1 gives an example of block-cyclic distributed data, and Figure 2 defines some symbols used in this paper.

$p = 0$	$p = 1$	$p = 2$	$p = 3$
1 2 3 4	5 6 7 8	9 10 11 12	13 14 15 16
17 18 19 20	21 22 23 24	25 26 27 28	29 30 31 32
33 34 35 36	37 38 39 40	41 42 43 44	45 46 47 48
49 50 51 52	53 54 55 56	57 58 59 60	

Fig. 1. The *cyclic(4)* distribution of the array *A(60)* onto 4 processors

Symbol	meaning
$\#p$	number of processors
bs	block size
L_b, U_b	normalised bounds on block numbers on a processor
I	loop for which the LIS is being computed
L_i, U_i	lower/upper bound/stride of I (on a processor)
L_A, U_A	lower/upper bound of array A (global space)

Fig. 2. Definition of terms used in the paper

1 Representations of access sequences and LISs

State machine representations of block-cyclic sequences were first proposed by Chatterjee, *et. al.* [1]. Some papers do not explicitly convert their solution for an access sequence or LIS into a state machine[7, 5, 2]. Nevertheless, the sequences generated by these solutions can be used to build the state machine. Using a state machine is an optimization, useful only when it simplifies code generation or allows members of the sequence to be generated more quickly. In this paper, the solution used for creating state machines is that found in [5]. The methods of [5] and [7] have the advantage of not requiring diophantine equations to be solved at run-time.

Figure 3 gives the data structures used to represent a state machine and a reference.

A *sparse* state machine includes states for every member of the sequence. The *dense* state machine uses the fact that accesses within a block always differ by c, and therefore the state machine only needs to encode the beginning element of each block. The names "sparse" and "dense" come from the observation (discussed in more detail later) that the dense machine requires fewer states, and is therefore is a denser representation of the access sequence that the sparse machine. A *hybrid* state machines combines the features of both the sparse and dense machines into a single machine. Because the dense machine is small, the resulting increment in space consumption is also small. One other change is made to allow the implementation of the machine reuse algorithm of the next section. Instead of putting the startup information for a machine in the last position of the `deltaI`, `deltaB` and `Sigma` tables, this information will be put into its own fields. This separation of the startup information from the transition tables allows the transition tables to be reused. The count field is only used with the dense state machine.

1.1 Building state machines

Figure 4 gives C code to construct a hybrid state machine, and Figure 5 gives the code for some auxiliary routines.

```
typedef struct state_machine_ {
    int block_size;
    int sub_coeff;
    int *sdeltaI, *ddeltaI; /* sparse and dense loop index increment */
    int *sdeltaB, *ddeltaB; /* sparse and dense buffer index increment */
    int *sSigma, *dSigma;   /* sparse and dense state transition table */
    int *dcount;            /* dense state transition table */
    int initialS, initialI, initialB, initialC;
} state_machine, *state_machineP;

typedef struct reference_ {
    int p, num_proc;
    int block_size;
    int gLi, gUi;
    int gLa, gUa;
    int sub_coeff, sub_const;
} reference, *referenceP;
```

Fig. 3. Representation of a reference and state machine

Construction of the sparse portion of the hybrid state machine proceeds as follows. `IncB` is a variable that gives the increment within a processor's data buffer to go from an accessed element to the next accessed element. It is initially set to zero. Next `La`, the lower bound of the array on this processor, is computed (line 7). Then, for each block b that may be on the processor, the upper and lower bound of i (the loop index variable) that accesses data in the block is computed (line 10). If `Li > Ui`, no elements in the block are accessed, and `incB` is incremented by `block_size` to skip over the entire block (lines 11, 12).

If `Ui <= Li`, then the block contains elements, and state machine tables are set. `new_state`, the offset of the first element in block `b`, is computed and `incB` is incremented by this value. Now `incB` contains the number of elements to skip over from the last access on this processor to access the first referenced element of this block. The index variable increment, buffer increment and next state in the state machine transition table are stored into `updateIs`, `updateBs` and `updateSs` respectively (lines 19, 23, 24). The state machine information for the remaining elements of the block are filled in by the "`for(i ...)`" loop (lines 36-42).

This construction is similar in spirit to that found in [3] and [1]. The major differences arise from: 1) our using a solution that is in terms of members of the LIS instead of in terms of the access sequence (i.e. `incB`); 2) accessing the

```
void
build_M(reference ref, state_machineP M) {
  int incB, slast_state, dlast_state, lastI, b, La;

  incB = 0;
  dlast_state = slast_state = M->block_size;
  lastI = 0;

  La = ref.block_size * ref.p + ref.gLa;

  for (b = 0; b < MAXINT; b++) {
     int Li, Ui;

     Li = lower_bound_i(ref, b); Ui = upper_bound_i(ref, b);

     if (Li > Ui) {
        incB = incB + ref.block_size;
     } else {
        int new_state, i, subX;
        int *updateBs, *updateCs, *updateSs, *updateIs;
        int *updateBd, *updateCd, *updateSd, *updateId;

        if (dlast_state == ref.block_size) {
           updateIs = &(M->initialI); updateBs = &(M->initialB); updateSs = &(M->initialS);
           updateId = &(M->initialI); updateBd = &(M->initialB); updateCd = &(M->initialC);
           updateSd = &(M->initialS);
        } else {
           updateIs = &(M->sdeltaI[slast_state]); updateBs = &(M->sdeltaB[slast_state]);
           updateSs = &(M->sSigma[slast_state]); updateId = &(M->ddeltaI[dlast_state]);
           updateBd = &(M->ddeltaB[dlast_state]); updateCd = &(M->dcount[dlast_state]);
           updateSd = &(M->dSigma[dlast_state]);
        }

        if (*updateBs) goto done;

        subX = ref.sub_coeff * Li + ref.sub_const;
        new_state = subX - La - ref.block_size * ref.num_proc * b;
        incB = incB + new_state;

        *updateId = Li - lastI; *updateBd = incB;
        *updateSd = new_state;  *updateCd  = Ui - Li + 1;
        dlast_state = new_state;

        for (i = Li; i <= Ui; i++) {
           *updateIs = i - lastI; *updateBs = incB;
           *updateSs = new_state; slast_state = new_state;
           lastI = i;             new_state = new_state + ref.sub_coeff;
           incB = ref.sub_coeff;
           updateIs = &(M->sdeltaI[slast_state]); updateBs = &(M->sdeltaB[slast_state]);
           updateSs = &(M->sSigma[slast_state]); }
        incB = ref.block_size - slast_state;
     }
  }
  done: if (dlast_state == M->block_size) {
           M->initialS = MAXINT; M->initialI = MAXINT; M->initialB = MAXINT;
        };
}
```

Fig. 4. Building a reusable hybrid state machine

transition tables indirectly through the *updateXx* pointers, which enables reuse of these tables in different machines (see Section 2); and 3) using `MAXINT` as the upper bound on **b**, which enhances reuse of the tables.

```
int
lower_bound_i(reference ref, int block)
{
    int num, denom, bound;

    num = -(ref.sub_coeff * ref.gLi) - ref.sub_const + ref.block_size * ref.p +
          1 + ref.block_size * ref.num_proc * block;
    denom = ref.sub_coeff;
    return ((num + denom - 1) / denom);
}

int
upper_bound_i(reference ref, int block)
{
    int num, denom;

    num = -(ref.sub_coeff * ref.gLi) - ref.sub_const + ref.block_size * ref.p +
          ref.block_size * ref.num_proc * block + ref.block_size;
    denom = ref.sub_coeff;
    return (num / denom);
}
```

Fig. 5. Some auxiliary routines used by `build_M`

Next we describe the construction of the dense portion of the hybrid state machine. The construction is similar to the sparse portion except that the "`for(i ...)`" loop no longer exists. Instead, the `updateCd` vector is given a count of the number of iterations of the I variable that can access elements of the block (line 33). From this count, the other data that would have been stored in a sparse state machine can be recreated.

With the exception of the first access into a processor's local buffer (information that is stored in the `initialB` fields), the offset of the first element in a buffer will always be less than c, the subscript coefficient. This is true because all accessed elements within a buffer are distance c apart: if an element e was more than c elements from the beginning of the block there would be another element accessed in the sequence at position $e-c$. This argument can be applied recursively until $e - c < c$. The practical consequence of this is that the dense state machine needs $c+1$ states, and not the $bs+1$ states needed by the sparse machine.

1.2 Generating access sequences from the state machines

Figure 6 shows code to generate an sequence from sparse and dense state machines, and Figure 7 gives two auxiliary routines that are used. The sparse code is straightforward, and is similar to that given in [1]. The dense code is similar, except that within a block new members of the access sequence are generated by iteration rather than referencing the state machine.

```
void
access_sparse(state_machine M, int ub, int * buffer) {
int s, base, i;

   start_machine(M, &s, &base, &i);
   while (base < ub) {
      buffer[base] = base;
      bump_sparse_index(M, &s, &base, &i);
   }
}

void
access_dense(state_machine M, reference ref, int ub, int * buffer) {
int s, base, i;

   start_machine(M, &s, &base, &i);
   while (base < ub) {
      int j, jub;
      jub = M.dcount[s];
      for (j = 0; j < jub; j++) {
         buffer[base] = base;
         base = base + ref.sub_coeff;
         i++;
      }
      bump_dense_index(M, &s, &base, &i);
   }
}
```

Fig. 6. Access sequence generation

Figure 8 gives times for generating an access sequence. The code used to gather these times differs from the code presented in the paper in three ways: 1) sparse and dense machines were generated directly and not as part of a hybrid machine; 2) the auxiliary routines have been inlined; 3) references to vector fields of the state machines were replaced with references to a pointer whose value is the base of the vector field. The code with these changes is easily generated by a compiler and the use of auxiliary routines and a `struct` representation for the state machine increases the readability of the code.

The total amount of data on each processor is 4,000 elements, and is accessed with the subscript function i. The y axis gives the time, in milliseconds, needed to perform the access, and the x axis gives the block size. Six times are plotted:

1. block: i.e. the time to do the access using a block distribution, with code using the formulation of [4]. This provides a baseline for comparison of the other methods
2. sparse: a sparse machine
3. sparse reused: a sparse machine excluding the cost of building the state machine

```
void
start_machine(state_machine M, int * s, int * bI, int * I) {
   *s = M.initialS;
   *bI = M.initialB;
   *I = M.initialI;
}

void
bump_sparse_index(state_machine M, int * s, int * bI, int * I) {
   *s = M.sSigma[*s];
   *bI = *bI + M.sdeltaB[*s];
   *I = *I + M.sdeltaI[*s];
}

void
bump_sparse_index(state_machine M, int * s, int * bI, int * I) {
   *s = M.dSigma[*s];
   *bI = *bI + M.ddeltaB[*s];
   *I = *I + M.ddeltaI[*s];
}
```

Fig. 7. Auxiliary routines

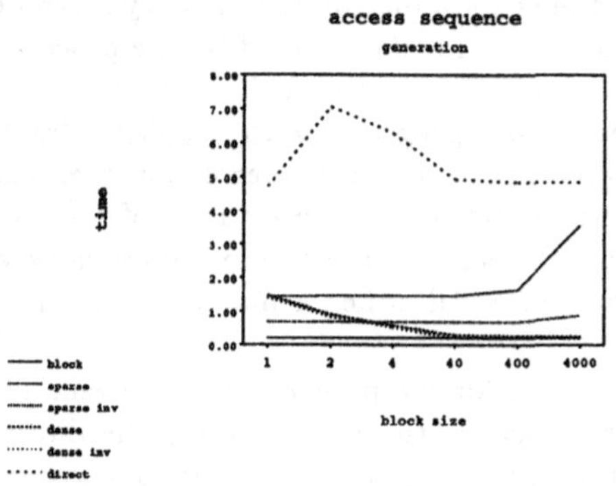

Fig. 8. Access sequence generation times

4. dense: a dense machine
5. dense reused: a dense machine excluding the cost of building the state machine
6. direct: performing the access by using the solution directly.

As can be seen, the direct time is the worst – probably because of the high cost of performing the divisions in computing the `Li` and `Ui` bounds for every block. The block time is the best, which is not surprising given that the access contains almost no overhead over simple loop iteration. Next best are the dense accesses. Because of the small number of states in the dense representation, the overhead of state machine construction is low and therefore removing the cost of state machine construction has little benefit. Finally, the sparse representation is considerably better than the direct representation, and for small block sizes is competitive with the dense representation. The reason the sparse method does well at small block sizes is that the dense method has extra overhead associated with switching between iterative code and state machine based code. As the amount of iteration decreases, the overhead of switching dominates.

Finally, removing the overhead of state machine construction eliminates approximately 50% of the cost of the sparse method, and argues for optimizations to reuse state machines across references.

From the point of view of code generation, the sparse representation is better than the dense, in that it does not require the original loop be replaced by a doubly nested loop.

1.3 Generating intersections of LIS from the state machines

Figures 9 and 10 show code to generate an intersection of two LIS's using sparse and dense state machines. This operation is necessary for at least two fundamental tasks of a compiler for a distributed memory machine. First, it is needed to find communication sets – i.e. data owned by one processor that must be sent to another processor. Second, it is needed to perform computation partitioning (i.e. scheduling of an SPMD program) with coupled subscripts. The basic idea behind both intersections is to do a list intersection over a sequence of integers. The members of the intersection are those values of I where both machines index variable values are the same. If the two machines index variables differ, then the lowest is incremented until either a match occurs or the bounds of I are exceeded.

In Figure 11, the times for the intersection are given. The direct times have been dropped for two reasons: the poor showing the direct method in the access sequence and the increasing complexity of code generation for the direct methods, which casts doubts upon its utility.

The block distribution intersection again has the best time. Intersection of a block distribution requires using the the minimum of the upper bounds as an upper bound, the maximum of the lower bounds as a lower bound, and then iterating over these computed lower and upper bounds. Thus the intersection is essentially iteration. As the block size increases, the dense method becomes increasing close to the block method, and the times converge correspondingly. Finally, the sparse method again does well for small block sizes, but as the block sizes become larger the increased cost of state machine access *vs.* incrementing an index variable, along the additional overhead of constructing the larger machines, dominates.

The effect of eliminating the overhead of state machine construction for the sparse case is less pronounced with intersection than with access sequence generation, but with large block-sizes it becomes significant.

```
void
intersect_sparse(state_machine M1, state_machine M2, reference ref1,
                 reference ref2, int buffer[]) {

   int s1, s2;    /* current state of M1 and M2 */
   int bI1, bI2;  /* buffer index for M1 and M2 */
   int I1, I2;    /* index variable value for M1 and M2 */

   start_machine(M1, &s1, &bI1, &I1);
   start_machine(M2, &s2, &bI2, &I2);

   while ((I1 <= ref1.gUi) && (I2 <= ref2.gUi)) {
      if (I1 == I2) {
         buffer[bI1] = 1;
         bump_sparse_index(M1, &s1, &bI1, &I1);
         bump_sparse_index(M2, &s2, &bI2, &I2);
      }

      if (I1 < I2) {
         bump_sparse_index(M1, &s1, &bI1, &I1);
      } else if (I1 > I2) {
         bump_sparse_index(M2, &s2, &bI2, &I2);
      }
   }
}
```

Fig. 9. Intersection of LIS using sparse state machines

1.4 Union

Figures 12 and 13 show the code to perform the union of the LIS's. The union operation is useful for performing computation partitioning over loops that contain multiple left-hand-sides.

The union operation in both the sparse and dense case is basically a two-way merge. With a union operation, it is more difficult to utilize iterative access with a block of data. The code generation appears to be so difficult as to render it impractical for incorporation within a compiler. The inability to use the iterative access, combined with the overhead of switching between increments of the index and buffer variables and state machine accesses, makes the dense machine less efficient than the sparse machine for all but large block sizes, as shown in Figure 14. And with very large block sizes, removing the overhead of machine creation makes the sparse representation useful for all block sizes examined.

1.5 Summary

The results of this section can be summarized as follows. Dense representations win in the following areas: 1) space used: space needed is proportional to the subscript expression coefficient, not the block size; 2) access time: access is faster for all but small block sizes with this representation, even when state machine construction time is not counted; 3) intersection time: intersections are much faster with this representation for all but small block sizes, again even when

```
void
intersect_dense(state_machine M1, state_machine M2, reference ref1,
                reference ref2, int * buffer) {
   int s1, s2;    /* current state of M1 and M2 */
   int bI1, bI2; /* buffer index for M1 and M2 */
   int I1, I2;    /* index variable value for M1 and M2 */

   start_machine(M1, &s1, &bI1, &I1);
   start_machine(M2, &s2, &bI2, &I2);

   while ((I1 <= ref1.gUi) && (I2 <= ref2.gUi)) {
      int lb, ub, i;
      lb = max(I1,I2);
      ub = min(I1 + M1.dcount[s1], I2 + M2.dcount[s2]);

      for (i = lb; i < ub; i++) {
         buffer[bI1] = 1;
         bI1 = bI1 + ref1.sub_coeff;
         bI2 = bI2 + ref2.sub_coeff;
      }
      if (I1 + M1.dcount[s1] == I2 + M2.dcount[s2]) {
         I1 = I1 + M1.dcount[s1];
         I2 = I2 + M2.dcount[s2];
         bump_dense_index(M1, &s1, &bI1, &I1);
         bump_dense_index(M2, &s2, &bI2, &I2);
      } else if (I1 + M1.dcount[s1] < I2 + M2.dcount[s2]) {
         I1 = I1 + M1.dcount[s1];
         bump_dense_index(M1, &s1, &bI1, &I1);
      } else if (I2 + M2.dcount[s2] < I1 + M1.dcount[s1]) {
         I2 = I2 + M2.dcount[s2];
         bump_dense_index(M2, &s2, &bI2, &I2);
      }
   }
}
```

Fig. 10. Intersection of LIS using dense state machines

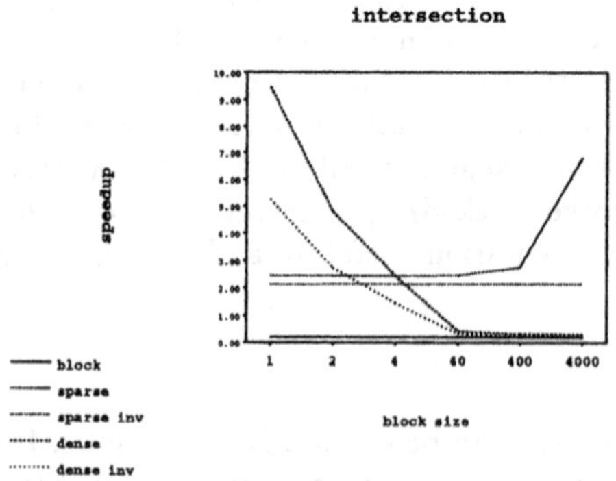

Fig. 11. Intersection generation times

```
void
union_sparse(state_machine M1, state_machine M2, int Ui, int * buffer1, int * bu
ffer2) {
   int s1, s2;      /* current state of M1 and M2 */
   int bI1, bI2;    /* buffer index for M1 and M2 */
   int i, I1, I2; /* index variable value for M1 and M2 */
   start_machine(M1, &s1, &bI1, &I1);
   start_machine(M2, &s2, &bI2, &I2);

   i = min(I1, I2);
   while (i <= Ui) {
      if (i == I1) {
         buffer1[i] = i;
         bump_sparse_index(M1, &s1, &bI1, &I1);
      }

      if (i == I2) {
         buffer2[i] = i;
         bump_sparse_index(M2, &s2, &bI2, &I2);
      }
      i = min(I1, I2);
   }
}
```

Fig. 12. Union operation with sparse machines

state machine construction time is not counted. Sparse representations win in the following areas: 1) ease of code generation. This is particularly true when unions of intersections are taken; 2) small block size access, intersection and union times; 3) union time: faster than a dense union for all but very large block sizes. To generate efficient code in all situations a hybrid state machine that combines many of the features of both the dense and sparse machines is desirable. This, in conjunction with algorithms for allowing reuse of state machines across references will allow good performance and ease of code use for all of the basic operations.

2 Reuse of state machines

This section discusses what is necessary for a single state machine to be used to generate access sequences and LIS's for multiple references. Doing this allows the cost of building a sparse machine to be amortized over multiple references, and for the resulting sparse machine operation times to more closely approximate the "no machine construction" times given in the experiment results.

The parts of the machine that will be reused are those declared to be of type "`int *`" in Figure 3. The `initial_state`, `initialI` and `intialB` fields are unique to each reference's state machine because the effort of sharing the information yields low improvements and complicates the analysis of when state machines can be shared. The `block_size` and `sub_coeff` fields are trivial to "compute" and are also duplicated.

```
void
union_dense(state_machine M1, state_machine M2, reference ref1,
                 reference ref2, int * buffer1, int * buffer2) {
   int s1, s2;    /* current state of M1 and M2 */
   int bI1, bI2;  /* buffer index for M1 and M2 */
   int i, I1, I2 ;/* index variable value for M1 and M2 */
   int cnt1, cnt2;

   start_machine(M1, &s1, &bI1, &I1);
   cnt1 = 0;

   start_machine(M2, &s2, &bI2, &I2);
   cnt2 = 0;

   i = min(I1, I2);
   while (i <= ref1.gUi) {
      if (i == I1) {
         buffer1[bI1] = bI1;
         if (cnt1 < M1.dcount[s1]) {
            I1++;
            cnt1++;
            bI1 = bI1 + ref1.sub_coeff;
         }
         if (cnt1 == M1.dcount[s1]) {
            bump_dense_index(M1, &s1, &bI1, &I1);
            cnt1 = 0;
         }
      }
      if (i == I2) {
         buffer2[bI2] = bI2;
         if (cnt2 < M2.dcount[s2]) {
            I2++;
            cnt2++;
            bI2 = bI2 + ref2.sub_coeff;
         }
         if (cnt2 == M2.dcount[s2]) {
            bump_dense_index(M2, &s2, &bI2, &I2);
            cnt2 = 0;
         }
      }
      i = min(I1, I2);
   }
}
```

Fig. 13. Union operation with dense machines

When building a shared state machine, termination will always be via the branch to done, not by exceeding the bounds of the "`for (b ...)`" loop. This allows a reference that is reusing a state machine to assume that all relevant elements have been initialized. We call such a machine *fully populated.* To see why this condition must be met, consider two references r_1 and r_2. Both references have an initial state of s, but r_1 accesses less than a full block of data. If r_2 attempts to reuse r_1's state machine, and r_2 accesses the full block of data, r_1's state machine will not be sufficient. It can be assumed that most references to block-cyclically distributed data will access many blocks, and so the penalty of requiring state machines be fully populated should normally be zero. Therefore,

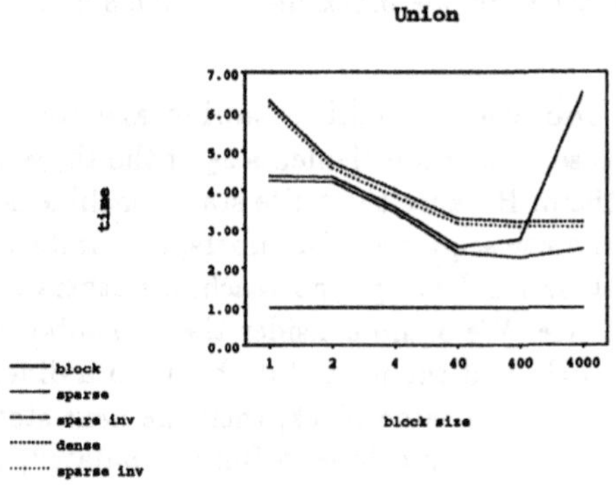

Fig. 14. Union generation times

even though it may possible to determine exactly what information should be initialized, such analysis would complicate the job of reusing state machines with little chance of an appreciable payoff.

2.1 Conditions for reuse of state machines

For a state machine to be reused, we require three conditions to be met: 1) The block size of both references must be the same; 2) the number of processors over which blocks are distributed must be the same for both references; the subscript coefficient must be the same in both references.

We now show that these conditions are sufficient for a sparse machine. The dense machine argument is similar.

The case where the state machine tables are initialized In the first case we assume that elements s_2 of the `sSigma`, `ddeltaI`, and `ddeltaB` vectors have been assigned. Are these values valid? We first examine the intra-block case, i.e. the case where the next element accessed is in the same block.

In the intra-block case, `sSigma`$[s_2]$ assigned by r_1 will be $s_2 + c$, since states correspond to buffer location, and the access stride within a block is c, and c is the same for both references. `sdeltaI`$[s_2]$ is 1, which is valid, since the I loop is normalized for both references, its stride is one, and adjacent accesses within a block correspond to adjacent iterations of the I loop. The argument for `sdeltaB`$[s_2]$ is similar to that for `sSigma`$[s_2]$.

We now consider the inter-block case, i.e. where s_2 is the last state in a block. Let s be the stride of the two references. By the intra-block case, it must also be the last state in a block for r_1. The accesses in the global space of the array will both access the elements $s_2, s_2 + s, s_2 + 2 \cdot s, \ldots$. This sequences can be continued until a block in the current processor is reached, and since the sequences are the same the element reached in the block must be the same.

The case where the state machine tables are not initialized We now consider the other case, where the elements s_2 of the three vectors have not had values assigned to them. Because the finite state machine is finite, deterministic and generates and infinite sequence of numbers, any state visited while generating a sequence must be reached by, and reach, all others that are visited while generating the sequence. We again consider the two sub-cases of the next state being in the same block, and the next state being in a different block.

If the next state is in the same block, then the next state is equal to $s_2 + c$. Since s_2 is uninitialized, the machine is fully populated, and both references have a subscript function coefficient of c, $s_2 + c$ must also be uninitialized, along with the corresponding values of $\texttt{sdeltaI}[s_2 + c]$ and $\texttt{sdeltaI}[s_2 + c]$. By the algorithm of Figure 4, these values will now be computed and set.

If the next state is in a different block, then the argument for the initialized state machine still holds. Thus the new state is reached only from the current state. Since the current state is not initialized, the new state will not be either.

2.2 Building a reusable state machine

The algorithm for building reused state machines is shown in Figure 4. If the state machine has been built by an earlier reference, only the `initial` fields, and the `block-size` and c fields will be filled in before the branch to `done` is taken. If the machine has not been built by an earlier reference, then state information will be constructed as in the algorithm of [1]. In effect, this construction interleaves the state and increment information of two or more machines within the same data structures. This further reduces the storage cost of the machines.

3 Conclusions and related work

In this paper we have described three methods of representing block-cyclic access sequence and LIS information: the sparse state machine, the dense state machine and a direct representation. The idea of a dense state machine was mentioned in [1], but its construction was not specified. We have presented experimental data to show that the two state machine representations have complementing strengths, with the weaknesses of one being covered by the strengths of the other.

To utilize the strengths of both we have developed a new representation, the *hybrid* state machine, which combines information from both state machines. This allows the best representation to be picked depending on how a particular access sequence or LIS is being used, and depending on what operations are being performed on the LIS or access sequence.

To further reduce the overhead incurred by forming the state machines, we have given conditions for showing when state machines can be reused. These conditions are easily applicable at compile-time, and should allow the number of state machines constructed at run-time for block-cyclic references to be greatly reduced. In [6], an incremental technique that allows the fast computation of the lower and upper bounds of the LIS for a block is given. Unlike the technique of this paper, this technique applies to a direct solution, not to the state machine construction. If the virtual processor method of [2] is used to build a state machine, the use of this technique will complement the reuse optimization of this paper.

As mentioned earlier, the techniques developed are applicable to a wide range of methods, including those of [7, 3, 2]. And since the same solution method is used for all representations (except, of course, the block distribution), the trends shown by the experimental results should be relatively indifferent to the particular solution used to generate the state machine.

Finally, the experimental data we presented, and that is given in [8] indicate that relative to a simple block distribution, the overheads of using a block-cyclic distribution need not be prohibitively high.

References

1. S. Chatterjee, J. R. Gilbert, F. J. E. Long, R. Schreiber, and S-H. Teng. Generating local addresses and communication sets for data-parallel programs. In *Proc. 4th annual ACM Symposium on Principles and Practice of Parallel Programming*, San Diego, CA, May 1993.
2. S.K.S. Gupta, S.D. Kaushik, C.-H. Huang, and P. Sadayappan. On compiling array expressions for efficient execution on distributed memory machines. *Journal of Parallel and Distributed Computing*, Apr 1996.
3. K. Kennedy, N. Nedeljković, and A. Sethi. A linear time algorithm for computing the memory access sequence in data-parallel programs. Technical report, Center for Research on Parallel Computation, Rice Univ., 1994. Tech Report CRPC-TR94485-S.
4. C. Koelbel and P. Mehrotra. Compiling global name-space parallel loops for distributed execution. *IEEE Trans. Parallel and Distributed Systems*, 2(4):440–451, Oct. 1991.
5. S. P. Midkiff. Local iteration set computation for block-cyclic distributions. In C. Polychronopoulos, editor, *Proceedings of the 24'th International Conference on Parallel Processing*, pages 77–84. CRC Press, Aug. 1995.
6. C.-H. Huang S.D. Kaushik and P. Sadayappan. Incremental generation of index sets for array statement execution on distributed memory machines. In K. Pingali, U. Banerjee, D. Gelernter, A. Nicolau, and D. P adua, editors, *Languages and Compilers for Parallel Computing, 7th Internationa l Workshop*, pages 251–265, Ithaca, NY, USA, August 1994.
7. A. Thirumalai and J. Ramanujam. Efficient computation of address sequences in data-parallel programs using closed forms for basis vectors. *Journal of Parallel and Distributed Computing*, 1996. To appear.
8. L. Wang, J.M. Stichnoth, and S. Chatterjee. Runtime performance of parallel array asignment: An empirical study. In *Proceedings of the 1996 ACM/IEEE Supercomputing Conference*, Nov. 1996. To Appear.

Interprocedural Array Redistribution Data-Flow Analysis

Daniel J. Palermo,[1] Eugene W. Hodges IV,[2] and Prithviraj Banerjee[3]

[1] Hewlett-Packard Company, Convex Division, Richardson, TX 75083 (palermo@rsn.hp.com)
[2] SAS Institute Inc., Cary, NC 27513 (sasehx@unx.sas.com)
[3] Northwestern University, Center for Parallel and Distributed Computing, Evanston, IL 60208 (banerjee@ece.nwu.edu)

Abstract. In High Performance Fortran (HPF), array redistribution can be described explicitly using directives (`REDISTRIBUTE` or `REALIGN`) which specify where new distributions become active or implicitly by calling functions which require different data distributions than the calling function. In order to actually compile an HPF program into an efficient form, however, both the redistribution operations as well as the possible distributions for the individual blocks of code must be known at compile-time. In this paper, we present an interprocedural data-flow framework which takes into account both explicit and implicit redistribution to automatically: (1) determine which distributions hold over specific sections of a program, (2) optimize both the inter- and intraprocedural transitions between dynamic distributions while still maintaining the original semantics of the HPF program, (3) determine when the distribution pattern specified by an HPF program causes a given array to be assigned multiple distributions due to different redistribution operations on multiple paths within a function or as a result of parameter aliasing (resulting in a non-conforming HPF program), as well as (4) convert (well behaved) dynamic HPF programs into equivalent static forms through a process we refer to as static distribution assignment (SDA) which can be used to extend the capabilities of existing subset HPF compilers that support static data distributions. As the approach presented in this paper has already been implemented as part of the PARADIGM (PARAllelizing compiler for DIstributed-memory General-purpose Multicomputers) project at the University of Illinois, examples will also be presented to demonstrate several applications of this framework.

1 Introduction

For complex programs, static data distributions may be insufficient to obtain acceptable performance on distributed-memory multicomputers. By allowing the data distribution to dynamically change over the course of a program's execution this problem can be alleviated by matching the data distribution more closely to the different computations performed throughout the program. Such dynamic partitionings can yield higher performance than a static partitioning when the redistribution is more efficient than the communication pattern required by the statically partitioned computation.

In High Performance Fortran (HPF), dynamic distributions can be described explicitly using executable redistribution directives (`REDISTRIBUTE` or `REALIGN`, which spec-

This research, performed at the University of Illinois, was supported in part by the National Aeronautics and Space Administration under Contract NASA NAG 1-613, in part by an Office of Naval Research Graduate Fellowship, and in part by the Advanced Research Projects Agency under contract DAA-H04-94-G-0273 administered by the Army Research office.

ify where new distributions become active) or implicitly by calling functions[4] (which require different data distributions than the calling function). To actually compile an HPF program into an efficient form, however, both the redistribution operations as well as the possible distributions for the individual blocks of code must be known. Since the HPF `REDISTRIBUTE` and `REALIGN` directives only specify redistribution information, both the intra- and interprocedural control flow through a program must be examined to decide exactly which redistribution operations were last performed in order to determine which distributions are active at any given point in the program.

For function calls, the distribution of the actual arguments which appear in a call to a function will not necessarily match the distribution of the dummy arguments within the function. In HPF, several different forms of distribution directives for dummy arguments are provided [11]. The distribution directive for a dummy argument may be:

prescriptive - The distribution *prescribes* the mapping of the dummy argument. Passing an actual argument with a different distribution will require redistributing the argument.

transcriptive - The distribution of the dummy argument is inherited or *transcribed* from the actual argument.

descriptive - The distribution *describes* the mapping of the dummy argument with the claim that no redistribution will take place. If an interface is present in the calling function, then this becomes a prescriptive directive.

Both prescriptive as well as descriptive arguments (with a provided interface) can have the same effect as explicit `REDISTRIBUTE` or `REALIGN` directives whereas transcriptive arguments provide a mechanism for writing functions which can accept any type of distribution. As purely descriptive directives (without an interface) do not require any additional support from an HPF compiler, they will not be discussed further in this paper.

The basic motivation for the framework presented in this paper is best summarized in the following excerpt from the HPF language specification [10]:

> *An overriding principle is that any mapping or remapping of arguments is not visible to the caller. This is true whether such remapping is implicit (in order to conform to prescriptive directives, which may themselves be explicit or implicit) or explicit (specified by `REALIGN` or `REDISTRIBUTE` directives). When the subprogram returns and the caller resumes execution, all objects accessible to the caller after the call are mapped exactly as they were before the call. It is not possible for a subprogram to change the mapping of any object in a manner visible to its caller, not even by means of `REALIGN` and `REDISTRIBUTE`.*

Interprocedural array data-flow analysis can be used to provide the correct semantics in the presence of implicit and explicit redistributions (or remappings[5]) and generate

[4] For the purposes of simplifying this discussion, the word *function* will be used throughout this paper to refer to either a Fortran program or subprogram (function or subroutine) and should be considered to be interchangeable with all of these terms.

[5] In the HPF standard [10], the word *remapping* is used to refer to *redistribution* in order to avoid associating it with only the HPF `REDISTRIBUTE` directive. For this paper, the word *redistribution* will be used equivalently to refer to remapping due to either the HPF `REDISTRIBUTE` or `REALIGN` directive.

efficient code. Such analysis avoids using either a simple copy-in/copy-out strategy or a complete redistribution of all arguments upon every entry and exit of a function. As will be shown, it is possible to optimize such interprocedural redistribution simultaneously with intraprocedural redistribution operations within the framework.

The remainder of this paper is organized as follows: related work in array redistribution and interprocedural analysis is discussed in Section 2; Section 3 presents an overview of the basic approach of the framework and the representations used in its development; the techniques for performing interprocedural array redistribution analysis are presented in Section 4; an example of the application of these techniques is given in Section 5; and conclusions are presented in Section 6.

2 Related Work

Interprocedural analysis is a useful program analysis technique that has been applied to many different applications [1]. In the area of parallel processing, it has been widely used for dependence analysis and program parallelization in the presence of function calls [3, 8, 9, 16], detecting references to stale data for improving the performance of cache coherent architectures [4], as well as for compiling static Fortran D programs [7].

The work by Hall, Hiranandani, Kennedy, and Tseng [7] defined the term *reaching decompositions* for the Fortran D decompositions (or distributions, in HPF terminology) which reach a function call site. Their work describes extensions to the Fortran D compilation strategy [17] using the reaching decompositions for a given call site to compile Fortran D programs that contain function calls as well as to optimize the resulting implicit redistribution. As presented, their techniques addressed computing and optimizing (redundant or loop invariant) implicit redistribution operations due to changes in distribution at function boundaries, but do not address many the situations which arise in HPF.

Work by Coelho and Ancourt [5] also describes an optimization for removing useless remappings specified by a programmer through explicit realign and redistribute operations. In comparison to the work in the Fortran D project, they are also concerned only with determining which distributions are generated from a set of redistributions, but instead focus only on explicit redistribution. They define a new representation called a redistribution graph in which nodes represent redistribution operations and edges represent the statements executed between redistribution operations. This representation, although correct in its formulation, does not seem to fit well with any existing analysis already performed by optimizing compilers and also requires first summarizing all variables used or defined along every possible path between successive redistribution operations in order to optimize redistribution. Even though their approach currently only performs their analysis within a single function, they do suggest the possibility of an extension to their techniques which would allow them to also handle implicit remapping operations at function calls but do not describe an approach.

The definition of reaching distributions, however, is still a useful concept. We extend this definition to also include distributions which reach any point within a function in order to encompass both implicit and explicit redistributions thereby forming the basis of the work presented in this paper. In addition to determining those distributions generated from a set of redistribution operations, this extended definition allows us to address a number of other applications in a unified framework.

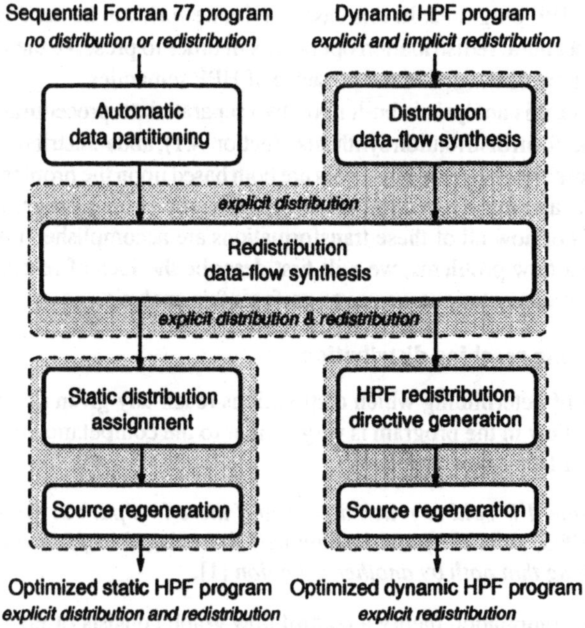

Fig. 1. Overview of the array redistribution data-flow analysis framework (shaded areas indicate components described in this paper)

3 Data Redistribution Analysis

An overall view of the array redistribution data-flow analysis framework we have developed is shown in Figure 1. In addition to analyzing HPF programs, the framework was also developed as a back-end to an automatic data partitioning system [13, 12] also developed as part of the PARADIGM compilation system [2] in order to provide a mechanism to generate fully explicit dynamic HPF programs. The shaded areas of the Figure indicate the components of the system which will be described in this paper.

The intermediate form of a program within the framework is one in which the distribution of every array at every point in the program as well as the redistribution required to move from one point to the next are explicitly known. The different paths through the framework involve passes which process the available distribution information in order to obtain the missing information required to move from one representation to another.

In HPF, dynamic distributions are described by specifying the transitions between different distributions (through explicit redistribution directives or implicit redistribution at function boundaries). Dynamic HPF programs (in which every use or definition of an array only has one reaching redistribution) can be converted to static versions (with explicit redistribution and distribution) through a process we call static distribution assignment (SDA) which will be explained later in this paper. With this framework, it is also possible to convert arbitrary HPF programs into an optimized HPF program containing only explicit redistribution directives and descriptive function arguments. The data partitioner, on the other hand, explicitly assigns different distributions to individual blocks of code serving as an automated mechanism for converting sequential Fortran programs into efficient HPF programs. In this case, the framework can be used to synthesize explicit interprocedural redistribution operations in order to preserve the meaning of what the data partitioner intended in the presence of HPF semantics.

The core of this analysis is built upon two separate interprocedural data-flow problems which perform distribution synthesis (Section 4.1), and redistribution synthesis (Section 4.2). These two data-flow problems are both based upon the problem of determining both the inter- and intraprocedural reaching distributions for a program. Before giving further details of how all of these transformations are accomplished through the use of these two data-flow problems, we will first describe the idea of reaching distributions and the basic representations we use to perform this analysis.

3.1 Computing reaching distributions

The problem of determining which distributions reach any given point taking into account control flow in the program is very similar to the computation of reaching definitions (a forward data-flow problem):

> *A definition d is said to reach a point p if there is a path in the control flow graph (CFG) from the point immediately following d to p, such that d is not* killed *along that path by another definition* [1].

In classic compilation theory a control flow graph consists of nodes (basic blocks) representing uninterrupted sequences of statements and edges representing the flow of control between basic blocks. For determining reaching distributions, an additional restriction must be added to this definition. Not only should each block B be viewed as a sequence of statements with flow only entering at the beginning and leaving at the end, but the data distribution for the arrays defined or used within the block is also not allowed to change. In comparison to the original definition of a basic block, this imposes tighter restrictions on the extents of a block. Using this definition of a block in place of a basic block results in what we refer to as the distribution flow graph (DFG). This representation differs from [5] as redistribution operations now merely augment the definition of basic block boundaries as opposed to forming the nodes of the graph.

Using this view of a block in a DFG and by viewing array distributions as definitions, the same data-flow framework used for computing reaching definitions [1] can now be used to obtain the reaching distributions by defining the following sets for each block in a function:

- DIST(B) - set of distributions present when executing block B
- REDIST(B) - set of redistributions performed upon entering block B
- GEN(B) - set of distributions generated by executing block B
- KILL(B) - set of distributions killed by executing block B
- IN(B) - set of distributions that exist upon entering block B
- OUT(B) - set of distributions that exist upon leaving block B
- DEF(B), USE(B) - set of variables defined or used in block B

It is important to note that GEN and KILL are specified as the distributions generated or killed by *executing* block B as opposed to entering (redistribution at the head of the block) or exiting (redistribution at the tail of the block) in order to allow both forms of redistribution. GEN and KILL are initialized by DIST or REDIST (depending on the current applications as described in Section 4) and may be used to keep track of redistributions that occur on entry (e.g., HPF redistribute directives or functions with prescriptive distributions) or exit (e.g., calls to functions which internally change a distribution before returning). To perform interprocedural analysis, the function itself also has IN and OUT sets, which contain the distributions present upon entry and summarize the distributions for all possible exits.

Once the sets have been defined, the following data-flow equations are iteratively computed for each block until the solution OUT(B) converges for every block B (where PRED(B) are the nodes which immediately precede B in the flow of the program):

$$\mathrm{IN}(B) = \bigcup_{P \in \mathrm{PRED}(B)} \mathrm{OUT}(P) \tag{1}$$

$$\mathrm{OUT}(B) = \mathrm{GEN}(B) \bigcup (\mathrm{IN}(B) - \mathrm{KILL}(B)) \tag{2}$$

Since the confluence operator is a union, both IN and OUT never decrease in size and the algorithm will eventually halt. By processing the blocks in the flow graph in a depth-first order, the number of iterations performed will roughly correspond to the level of the deepest nested statement, which tends to be a fairly small number on real programs [1].

As can be seen from Eqs. (1) and (2), the DEF and USE sets are actually not used to compute reaching distributions, but will have other uses for optimizing redistribution which will be explained in more detail in Section 4.2).

3.2 Constructing the distribution flow graph

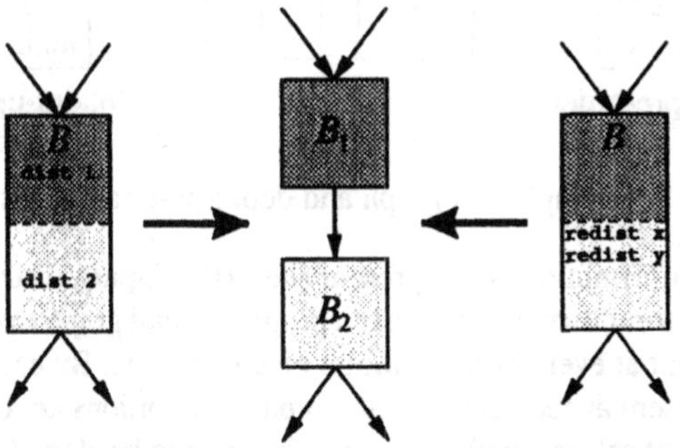

(a) Distribution split (b) Redistribution split

Fig. 2. Splitting CFG nodes to obtain DFG nodes

Since the definition of the DFG is based upon the CFG, the CFG can be easily transformed into a DFG by splitting basic blocks at points at which a distribution changes as shown in Figure 2. This can be due to an explicit change in distribution, as specified by the automatic data partitioner, or by an actual HPF redistribution directive. If the change in distribution is due to a sequence redistribution directives, the overall effect is assigned to the block in which they are contained; otherwise, a separate block is created whenever executable operations are interspersed between the directives.

4 Interprocedural Data Redistribution Analysis

Since the semantics of HPF require that all objects accessible to the caller after the call are distributed exactly as they were before the call, it is possible to first completely examine the context of a call before considering any distribution side effects due to the call. It may seem strange to say that there can be side effects when we just said that the semantics of HPF preclude it. To clarify this statement, such side effects *are* allowed to exist, but only to the extent that they are not *apparent* outside of the call. As long as the view specified by the programmer is maintained, the compiler is allowed do whatever it can to optimize both the inter- and intraprocedural redistributions so long as the resulting distributions used at any given point in the program are not changed.

Referring back to Figure 1 the core of this analysis is built upon two separate interprocedural data-flow problems which perform distribution synthesis and redistribution synthesis. These two data-flow problems are based upon the problem of determining both the inter- and intraprocedural reaching distributions for a program. An example call graph is shown in Figure 3 to help illustrate the flow of these two phases of the interprocedural analysis.

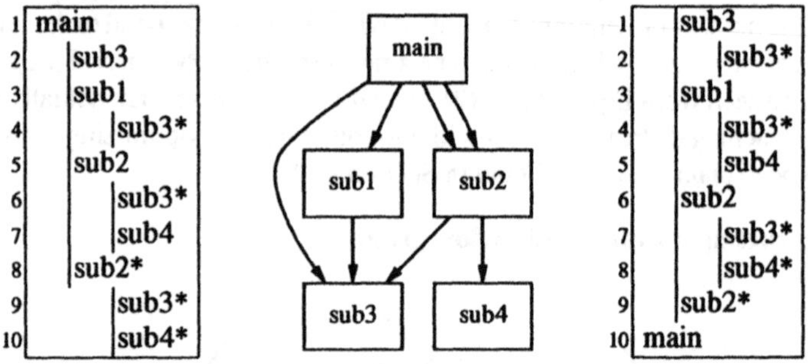

(a) Top-down (pre-order) for calling context

(b) Bottom-up (post-order) for side-effects

Fig. 3. Example call graph and depth-first traversal order

If distribution information is not present (i.e., HPF input), distribution synthesis is first performed in a top-down manner over a program's call graph to compute which distributions are present at every point within a given function. By establishing the distributions that are present at each call site, the input distributions are obtained for each of the functions which it calls as well as causes a function to be cloned if a new set of input distributions is used.[6] Redistribution synthesis is then applied in a bottom-up manner over the call graph to analyze where the distributions are actually used and synthesizing the redistribution required within a function.

Since this analysis is interested in the effects between an individual caller/callee pair, and not in summarizing the effects from all callers before examining a callee, it is not necessary to perform a topological traversal for the top-down and bottom-up passes over

[6] Because there is considerable state associated with the body of a function, it is much more efficient to record the cloned data as a separate context for the function and delay the actual cloning until later, a process which we refer to as *virtual cloning*.

the call graph. In this case, it is actually more intuitive to perform a depth-first pre-order traversal of the call graph (shown in Figure 3(a)) to fully analyze a given function before proceeding to analyze any of the functions it calls and to perform a dept-first post-order traversal (shown in Figure 3(b)) to fully analyze all called functions before analyzing the caller.

One other point to emphasize is that these interprocedural techniques can be much more efficient than analyzing a fully inlined version of the same program since it is possible to prune the traversal at the point a previous solution is found for a function in the same calling context. In Figure 3, asterisks indicate points at which a function is being examined after having already been examined previously. If the calling context is the same as the one used previously, the traversal can be pruned at this point reusing information recorded from the previous context. Depending on how much reuse occurs, this factor can greatly reduce the amount of time the compiler spends analyzing a program in comparison to a fully inlined approach.

The technique for performing distribution synthesis will be described in Section 4.1 while redistribution synthesis will be described in Section 4.2. The static HPF conversion, known as static distribution assignment (SDA), is covered in detail in Section 4.3. Since the dynamic HPF conversion only entails generating redistribution directives based on the contents of the REDIST sets, it will not be discussed further in this section. More detailed descriptions of the actual implementation of these techniques can be found in [12].

4.1 Distribution synthesis

When analyzing HPF programs, it is necessary to first perform distribution synthesis in order to determine which distributions are present at every point in a program. Since HPF semantics specify that any redistribution (implicit or explicit) due to a function call is not visible to the caller, each function can be examined independently of the functions it calls. Only the input distributions for a given function and the explicit redistribution it performs have to be considered to obtain the reaching distributions for a function.

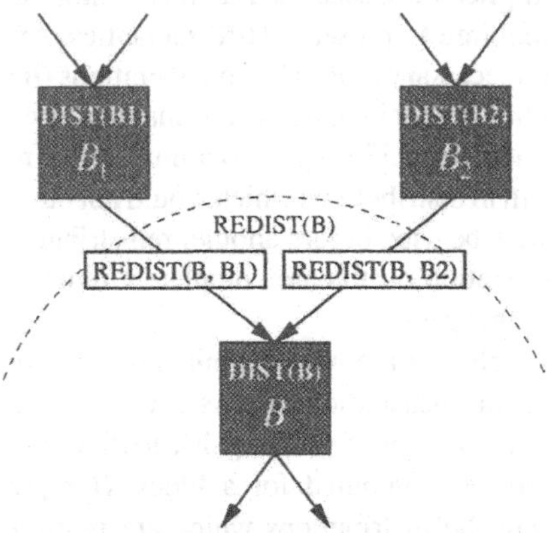

Fig. 4. Distribution synthesis (converting redistributions to distributions)

Given an HPF program, nodes (or blocks) in its DFG are delimited by the redistribution operations which appear in the form of HPF `REDISTRIBUTE` or `REALIGN` directives. As shown in Figure 4, the redistribution operations assigned to a block B represent the redistribution that will be performed when entering the block on any input path (indicated by the set REDIST(B)) as opposed to specifying the redistribution performed for each incoming path (REDIST(B, B_1) or REDIST(B, B_2) in the figure).

If the set GEN(B) is viewed as the distributions which are generated and KILL(B) as the distributions which are killed upon entering the block, this problem can now be cast directly into the reaching distribution data-flow framework by making the following assignments:

Data-flow initialization:

$$\begin{aligned} \text{REDIST}(B) &= \text{from directives} & \text{DIST}(B) &= \emptyset \\ \text{GEN}(B) &= \text{REDIST}(B) & \text{KILL}(B) &= \overline{\text{REDIST}_{var}(B)} \\ \text{OUT}(B) &= \text{REDIST}(B) & \text{IN}(B) &= \emptyset \end{aligned}$$

Data-flow solution:

$$\text{DIST(B)} = \text{OUT}(B)$$

According to the HPF standard, a REALIGN operation only affects the array being realigned while a REDISTRIBUTE operation should redistribute all arrays currently aligned to the given array being redistributed (in order to preserve any previous specified alignments). The current implementation only records redistribution information for the array immediately involved in a REDISTRIBUTE operation. This results in only redistributing the array involved in the directive and not all of the alignees of the target to which it is aligned. In the future, the implementation could be easily extended to support the full HPF interpretation of REDISTRIBUTE by simply recording the same redistribution information for all alignees for the target template of the array involved in the operation. Due to the properties of REALIGN, this will also require first determining which templates arrays are aligned to at every point in the program (using similar techniques).

4.2 Redistribution synthesis

After the distributions have been determined for each point in the program, the redistribution can be optimized. Instead of using either a simple copy-in/copy-out strategy or a complete redistribution of all arguments upon every entry and exit of a function, any implicit redistribution around function calls can be reduced to only that which is actually required to preserve HPF semantics. Any unnecessary redistribution operations (implicitly specified by HPF semantics or explicitly specified by a programmer) that result in distributions which would not otherwise be used before another redistribution operation occurs are completely removed in this pass.

Blocks are now delimited by changes in the distribution set. As shown in Figure 5, the set of reaching distributions previously computed for a block B represent the distributions which are in effect when executing that block (indicated by the set DIST$(()B)$). By first restricting the DIST(B) sets to the variables defined or used within block B, a redistribution operation will only be performed between two blocks if there is an intervening definition or use of that variable before the next change in distribution.

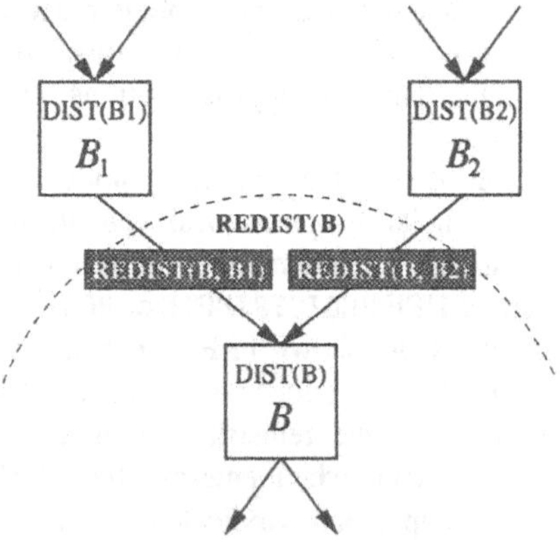

Fig. 5. Redistribution synthesis (converting distribution to redistribution)

If the set GEN(B) is viewed as the distributions which are generated and KILL(B) as the distributions which are killed upon leaving block B, this problem can now be cast directly into the reaching distribution data-flow framework by making the following initializations:

data-flow initialization:

$$\mathrm{REDIST}(B) = \emptyset \qquad \mathrm{DIST}(B) = \mathrm{DIST}(B) \bigcap (\mathrm{DEF}(B) \bigcup \mathrm{USE}(B))$$
$$\mathrm{GEN}(B) = \mathrm{DIST}(B) \qquad \mathrm{KILL}(B) = \overline{\mathrm{DIST}_{var}(B)}$$
$$\mathrm{IN}(B) = \emptyset \qquad \mathrm{OUT}(B) = \mathrm{DIST}(B)$$

data-flow solution:

$$\mathrm{REDIST}(B,P) = \mathrm{DIST}_{var}(B) \mid (\mathrm{OUT}_{var}(P) - \mathrm{DIST}_{var}(B)) \neq \emptyset \quad (\forall P \in \mathrm{PRED}(B))$$
$$\mathrm{REDIST}(B) = \bigcup_{P \in \mathrm{PRED}(B)} \mathrm{REDIST}(B,P)$$
$$= \mathrm{DIST}_{var}(B) \mid (\mathrm{IN}_{var}(B) - \mathrm{DIST}_{var}(B)) \neq \emptyset$$

We define GEN(B) and KILL(B) as the distributions which are generated or killed upon leaving block B due to the fact that we have chosen to use a caller redistributes model. As will be seen later, this exposes many interprocedural optimization opportunities and is also necessary to support function calls which may require redistribution on both their entry and exit. Since REDIST(B) is determined from both the DIST and IN sets, DIST(B) represents the distributions needed for executing block B, while the GEN, KILL sets will be used to represent the exit distribution (which may or may not match DIST).

Optimizing invariant distributions Besides performing redistribution only when necessary, it is also desirable to only perform necessary redistribution as infrequently as possible. Semantically loop invariant distribution regions can be first grown before synthesizing the redistribution operations. All distributions that do not change within a nested statement (loop or if structures) are recorded on the parent statement (or header) for that structure. This has the effect of moving redistribution operations which result in the invariant distribution out of nested structures as far as possible (as was also possible in [7]). An example of this optimization will be illustrated later in Section 5.

As a side effect, loops which are considered to contain an invariant distribution no longer propagate previous distributions for the invariant arrays. Since redistribution is moved out of the loop, this means that for the (extremely rare) special case of a loop invariant distribution (which was not originally present outside of the loop) contained within a undetectable zero trip loop, only the invariant distribution from within the loop body is propagated even though the loop nest was never executed. As this is only due to the way invariant distributions are handled, the data-flow handles non-invariant distributions as expected for zero trip loops (an extra redistribution check may be generated after the loop execution).

Multiple active distributions Even though it is not specifically stated as such in the HPF standard, we will consider an HPF program in which every use or definition of an array has only one active distribution to be well-behaved. Since PARADIGM cannot currently compile programs which contain references with multiple active distributions, this property is currently detected by examining the reaching distribution sets for every node (limited by DEF/USE) within a function. A warning is issued if any set contains multiple distributions for a given variable stating that the program is not well-behaved. An example of this situation will be illustrated later in Section 5.

In the presence of function calls, it is also possible to access an array through two or more more paths when parameter aliasing is present. If there is an attempt to redistribute one of the aliased symbols, the different aliases now have different distributions even though they actually refer to the same array. This form of multiple active distributions is actually considered to be non-conforming in HPF [11] as it can result in consistency problems if the same array were allowed to occupy two different distributions. As it may be difficult for the programmers to make this determination, this can be automatically detected by determining if the reaching distribution set contains different distributions for any aliased arrays.[7]

4.3 Static Distribution Assignment (SDA)

To utilize the available memory on a given parallel machine as efficiently as possible, only the distributions that are active at any given point in the program should actually be allocated space. It is interesting to note that as long as a given array is distributed among the same total number of processors, the actual space required to store one section of the partitioned array is the same no matter how many array dimensions are distributed.[8] By using this observation, it is possible to statically allocate the minimum amount of memory by associating all possible distributions of a given array to the same area of memory.

Static Distribution Assignment (SDA) (inspired indirectly by the Static Single Assignment (SSA) form [6]) is a process we have developed in which the names of array variables are duplicated and renamed statically based on the active distributions represented in the corresponding DIST sets. As names are generated, they are assigned a static distribution (by which we mean this new name will not change distribution during the course of the program) corresponding to the currently active dynamic distribution for the original array. Redistribution now takes the form of moving data from a statically distributed source array to another statically distributed destination array (as opposed to rearranging the data within a single array).

To statically achieve the minimum amount of memory allocation required, all of the renamed duplicates of a given array are declared to be "equivalent." The `EQUIVALENCE` statement in Fortran 77 allows this to be performed at the source level in a somewhat similar manner as assigning two array pointers to the same allocated memory as is possible in C or Fortran 90, Redistribution directives are also now replaced with actual calls to a redistribution library.

Because the different static names for an array share the same memory, this implies that the communication operations used to implement the redistribution should read all

---

[7] The `param_alias` pass in Parafrase-2 [14] is first run to compute the alias sets for every function call.

[8] Taking into account distributions in which the number of processors allocated to a given array dimension does not evenly divide the size of the dimension, or degenerate distributions in which memory is not evenly distributed over all processors, can be equivalently said that there is an amount of memory which can store all possible distributions with very little excess.

of the source data before writing to the target. In the worst case, an entire copy of a partitioned array can be buffered at the destination processor before it is actually received and moved into the destination array. However, as soon as more than two different distributions are present for a given array, the `EQUIVALENCE` begins to pay off, even in the worst case, in comparison to separately allocating each different distribution. If the performance of buffered communication is insufficient for a given machine (due to the extra buffer copy), non-buffered communication could be used instead thereby precluding the use of `EQUIVALENCE` (unless some form of explicit buffering is performed by the redistribution library itself).

```
      REAL A(N, N)
!HPF$ DISTRIBUTE (CYCLIC, *) :: A
      ...
      A(i, j) = ...
      ...
!HPF$ REDISTRIBUTE (BLOCK, BLOCK) :: A
      ...
      ... = A(i, j)
      ...
```

(a) Before SDA

```
      REAL A$0(N, N), A$1(N,N)
!HPF$ DISTRIBUTE (CYCLIC, *) :: A$0
!HPF$ DISTRIBUTE (BLOCK, BLOCK) :: A$1
      EQUIVALENCE (A$0, A$1)
      INTEGER A$cid
      A$cid = 0
      ...
      A$0(i, j) = ...
      ...
      CALL reconfig(A$1, 1, A$cid)
      ...
      ... = A$1(i, j)
      ...
```

(b) After SDA

Fig. 6. Example of static distribution assignment

In Figure 6, a small example is shown to illustrate this technique. In this example, a redistribution operation on `A` causes it to be referenced using two different distributions. A separate name is statically generated for each distribution of `A`, and the redistribution directive is replaced with a call to a run-time redistribution library [15]. The array accesses in the program can now be compiled by PARADIGM using techniques developed for programs which only contain static distributions [2] by simply ignoring the communication side effects of the redistribution call.

If more than one distribution is active for any given array reference, the program is considered to be *not well-behaved*, and the array involved can not be directly assigned a static distribution. In certain circumstances, however, it may be possible to perform code transformations to make an HPF program well-behaved. For instance, a loop that contained multiple active distributions on the entry to its body due only to a distribution from the loop back edge (caused by redistribution within the loop) that wasn't present on the loop entry would not be well-behaved. If the first iteration of that loop were peeled off, the entire loop body would now have a single active distribution for each variable and the initial redistribution into this state would be performed outside of the loop. This and other code transformations which help reduce the number of distributions reaching any given node will be the focus of further work in this area.

5 Examples

In Figure 7(a), a synthetic HPF program is presented which performs a number of different tests (described as comments in the input code) of the optimizations performed by the framework. In this program, one array, x, is redistributed both explicitly using HPF directives and implicitly through function calls using several different interfaces. Two of the functions, `func1` and `func2`, have prescriptive interfaces which may or may not require redistribution (depending on the current configuration of the input array). The first function differs from the second in that it also redistributes the array such that it returns with a different distribution than which it was called. The last function, `func3`, differs from the first two in that it has an (implicit) transcriptive interface. Calls to this function will cause it to inherit the current distribution of the actual parameters.

Several things can be noted when examining the optimized HPF shown in Figure 7(b). First of all, the necessary redistribution operations required to perform the implicit redistribution at the function call boundaries have been made explicit in the program. Here, the interprocedural analysis has completely removed any redundant redistribution by relaxing the HPF semantics allowing distributions caused by function side effects to exist so long as they do not affect the original meaning of the program. For the transcriptive function, `func3`, the framework generated two separate clones, `func3$0` and `func3$1`, corresponding to two different active distributions at a total of three different calling contexts.

Two warnings were also generated by the compiler, inserted by hand as comments in Figure 7(b), indicating that there were (semantically) multiple reaching distributions to two uses of x in the program. The first use actually does have two reaching distributions due to a conditional with redistribution performed on only one path. The second use, however, occurs after a call to a prescriptive function, `func1`, which implicitly redistributes the array to conform to its interface. Because a redistribution operation can only generate a single distribution, x can actually have only one reaching distribution, but semantically it still has two – hence the second warning.

As there are several other optimizations performed on this example, which have been described previously, we will not describe them in more detail here, but the reader is directed to the comment descriptions in the code for further information.

6 Conclusions

In this paper we have presented an interprocedural data-flow technique that can be used to transform redistribution to distributions or distributions to redistribution as well as optimize redistribution while always maintaining the semantics of the original program. Aliasing information is also used to ensure that the resulting distributions specified by the HPF program yield identical distributions for all aliased arrays. Other than for the support to physically perform redistribution in the middle of a statement (required for a return from a function call with different distributions) and support for array reshaping (which can occur through function parameters), these techniques have been fully implemented in the PARADIGM compiler [12].

Further work will also be focused on the application of code transformations (such as loop peeling) which will help reduce the number of reaching distributions to uses of variables with multiple active distributions. When it is not possible to completely eliminate such regions, code replication approaches, similar to the selective function cloning techniques used in this paper, will also be examined to allow an HPF compiler to efficiently handle such code regions (which are currently not supported in PARADIGM due to the difficulty in handling such situations).

```
      PROGRAM test
      INTEGER x(10,10)
c     *** For tests involving statement padding
      INTEGER a
!HPF$ PROCESSORS :: square(2,2)
!HPF$ DYNAMIC, DISTRIBUTE (BLOCK, BLOCK) :: x
c     *** Use of initial distribution
      x(1,1) = 1
c     *** Testing loop invariant redistribution
      DO i = 1,10
         DO j = 1,10
            a = 0
!HPF$       REDISTRIBUTE (BLOCK, CYCLIC) :: x
            x(i,j) = 1
            a = 0
         ENDDO
      ENDDO
      a = 0
c     *** Testing unnecessary redistribution
!HPF$ REDISTRIBUTE (BLOCK, CYCLIC) :: x
      if (x(i,j) .gt. 1) then
c        *** Testing redistribution in a conditional
!HPF$    REDISTRIBUTE (BLOCK, BLOCK) :: x
         x(i,j) = 2
         call func3(x,n)
      else
         x(i,j) = 3
      endif
c     *** Uses with multiple reaching distributions
      x(1,1) = 2
      call func1(x,n)
      DO i = 1,10
         DO j = 1,10
            x(j,i) = 2
         ENDDO
      ENDDO
!HPF$ REDISTRIBUTE (CYCLIC(3), CYCLIC) :: x
c     *** Testing chaining of function arguments
      call func1(x,n)
      call func2(x,n)
      call func1(x,n)
c     *** Testing loop invariant due to return
      DO i = 1,10
         DO j = 1,10
c           *** Test cloning for transcriptive functions
            call func3(x,n)
         ENDDO
      ENDDO
      a = 1
c     *** Testing unused distribution
!HPF$ REDISTRIBUTE (BLOCK, CYCLIC) :: x
      a = 0
c     *** Testing "semantically killed" distribution
!HPF$ REDISTRIBUTE (CYCLIC(3), CYCLIC) :: x
      call func3(x,n)
      END

      integer function func1(a,n)
c     *** Prescriptive function with different return
      integer n, a(n, n)
!HPF$ DYNAMIC, DISTRIBUTE (BLOCK, CYCLIC) :: a
      a(1,1) = 1
!HPF$ REDISTRIBUTE (BLOCK, CYCLIC) :: a
      a(1,2) = 1
!HPF$ REDISTRIBUTE (CYCLIC, CYCLIC) :: a
      a(1,3) = 1
      end

      integer function func2(y,n)
c     *** Prescriptive function with identical return
      integer n, y(n,n)
!HPF$ DYNAMIC, DISTRIBUTE (CYCLIC, CYCLIC) :: y
      y(1,1) = 2
      end

      integer function func3(z,n)
c     *** (implicitly) Transcriptive function
      integer n, z(n,n)
      z(1,1) = 3
      end
```

(a) Before optimization

```
      PROGRAM test
      INTEGER x(10,10)
      INTEGER a, n
!HPF$ PROCESSORS :: square(2,2)
!HPF$ DYNAMIC, DISTRIBUTE (BLOCK, BLOCK) :: x
      x(1,1) = 1
!HPF$ REDISTRIBUTE (BLOCK, CYCLIC) ONTO square :: x
      DO i = 1,10
        DO j = 1,10
          a = 0
          x(i,j) = 1
          a = 0
        END DO
      END DO
      a = 0
      IF (x(i,j) .GT. 1) THEN
!HPF$ REDISTRIBUTE (BLOCK, BLOCK) ONTO square :: x
        x(i,j) = 2
        CALL func3$0(x,n)
      ELSE
        x(i,j) = 3
      END IF
c     *** WARNING: too many dists (2) for x
      x(1,1) = 2
!HPF$ REDISTRIBUTE (BLOCK, CYCLIC) ONTO square :: x
      CALL func1(x,n)
      DO i = 1,10
        DO j = 1,10
c         *** WARNING: too many dists (2) for x
          x(j,i) = 2
        END DO
      END DO
!HPF$ REDISTRIBUTE (BLOCK, CYCLIC) ONTO square :: x
      CALL func1(x,n)
      CALL func2(x,n)
!HPF$ REDISTRIBUTE (BLOCK, CYCLIC) ONTO square :: x
      CALL func1(x,n)
!HPF$ REDISTRIBUTE (CYCLIC(3), CYCLIC) ONTO square :: x
      DO i = 1,10
        DO j = 1,10
          CALL func3$1(x,n)
        END DO
      END DO
      a = 1
      a = 0
      CALL func3$1(x,n)
      END

      INTEGER FUNCTION func1(a,n)
      INTEGER n, a(n,n)
!HPF$ DYNAMIC, DISTRIBUTE (BLOCK, CYCLIC) :: a
      a(1,1) = 1
      a(1,2) = 1
!HPF$ REDISTRIBUTE (CYCLIC, CYCLIC) ONTO square :: a
      a(1,3) = 1
      END

      INTEGER FUNCTION func2(y,n)
      INTEGER n, y(n,n)
!HPF$ DYNAMIC, DISTRIBUTE(CYCLIC,CYCLIC) ONTO square :: y
      y(1,1) = 2
      END

      INTEGER FUNCTION func3$1(n,z)
      INTEGER n, z(n,n)
!HPF$ DISTRIBUTE(CYCLIC(3),CYCLIC) ONTO square :: z
      z(1,1) = 3
      END

      INTEGER FUNCTION func3$0(n,z)
      INTEGER n, z(n,n)
!HPF$ DISTRIBUTE(BLOCK,BLOCK) ONTO square :: z
      z(1,1) = 3
      END
```

(b) After optimization

Fig. 7. Synthetic example for interprocedural redistribution optimization

(The HPF output, generated by PARADIGM, has been slightly simplified by removing unnecessary alignment directives from the figure to improve its clarity.)

References

1. A. V. Aho, R. Sethi, and J. D. Ullman. *Compilers: Principles, Techniques, and Tools.* Addison-Wesley Publ., Reading, MA, 1986.
2. P. Banerjee, J. A. Chandy, M. Gupta, E. W. Hodges IV, J. G. Holm, A. Lain, D. J. Palermo, S. Ramaswamy, and E. Su. The PARADIGM Compiler for Distributed-Memory Multicomputers. *IEEE Computer*, 28(10):37–47, Oct. 1995.
3. M. Burke and R. Cytron. Interprocedural Dependence Analysis and Parallelization. In *Proc. of the ACM SIGPLAN Symp. on Compiler Construction*, pages 162–175, Palo Alto, CA, June 1986.
4. L. Choi and P.-C. Yew. Interprocedural Array Data-Flow Analysis for Cache Coherence. In *Proc. of the 8th Work. on Langs. and Compilers for Parallel Computing*, volume 1033 of *Lecture Notes in Computer Science*, pages 81–95, Columbus, OH, Aug. 1995. Springer-Verlag. 1996.
5. F. Coelho and C. Ancourt. Optimal Compilation of HPF Remappings (Extended Abstract). Tech. Report CRI A-277, Centre de Recherche en Informatique, École des mines de Paris, Fontainebleau, France, Nov. 1995.
6. R. Cytron, J. Ferrante, B. K. Rosen, M. N. Wegman, and F. K. Zadeck. Efficiently Computing Static Single Assignment Form and the Control Dependence Graph. *ACM Trans. on Prog. Langs. and Sys.*, 13(4):451–490, Oct. 1991.
7. M. W. Hall, S. Hiranandani, K. Kennedy, and C. Tseng. Interprocedural Compilation of Fortran D for MIMD Distributed-Memory Machines. In *Proc. of Supercomputing '92*, pages 522–534, Minneapolis, MN, Nov. 1992.
8. M. W. Hall, B. R. Murphy, and S. P. Amarasinghe. Interprocedural Analysis for Parallelization. In *Proc. of the 8th Work. on Langs. and Compilers for Parallel Computing*, volume 1033 of *Lecture Notes in Computer Science*, pages 61–80, Columbus, OH, Aug. 1995. Springer-Verlag. 1996.
9. P. Havlak and K. Kennedy. Experience with Interprocedural Analysis of Array Side Effects. In *Proc. of Supercomputing '90*, pages 952–961, New York, NY, Nov. 1990.
10. High Performance Fortran Forum. High Performance Fortran Language Specification, version 1.1. Tech. report, Center for Research on Parallel Computation, Rice Univ., Houston, TX, Nov. 1994.
11. C. Koelbel, D. Loveman, R. Schreiber, G. Steele, Jr., and M. Zosel. *The High Performance Fortran Handbook.* The MIT Press, Cambridge, MA, 1994.
12. D. J. Palermo. *Compiler Techniques for Optimizing Communication and Data Distribution for Distributed-Memory Multicomputers.* PhD thesis, Dept. of Electrical and Computer Eng., Univ. of Illinois, Urbana, IL, June 1996. CRHC-96-09/UILU-ENG-96-2215.
13. D. J. Palermo and P. Banerjee. Automatic Selection of Dynamic Data Partitioning Schemes for Distributed-Memory Multicomputers. In *Proc. of the 8th Work. on Langs. and Compilers for Parallel Computing*, volume 1033 of *Lecture Notes in Computer Science*, pages 392–406, Columbus, OH, Aug. 1995. Springer-Verlag. 1996.
14. C. D. Polychronopoulos, M. Girkar, M. R. Haghighat, C. L. Lee, B. Leung, and D. Schouten. Parafrase-2: An Environment for Parallelizing, Partitioning, Synchronizing and Scheduling Programs on Multiprocessors. In *Proc. of the 18th Int'l Conf. on Parallel Processing*, pages II:39–48, St. Charles, IL, Aug. 1989.
15. S. Ramaswamy and P. Banerjee. Automatic Generation of Efficient Array Redistribution Routines for Distributed Memory Multicomputers. In *Frontiers '95: The 5th Symp. on the Frontiers of Massively Parallel Computation*, pages 342–349, McLean, VA, Feb. 1995.
16. R. Triolet, F. Irigion, and P. Feautrier. Direct Parallelization of Call Statements. *Proc. of the ACM SIGPLAN Symp. on Compiler Construction*, 21(7):176–185, July 1986.
17. C. W. Tseng. *An Optimizing Fortran D Compiler for MIMD Distributed-Memory Machines.* PhD thesis, Rice Univ., Houston, TX, Jan. 1993. COMP TR93-199.

HPF on Fine-Grain Distributed Shared Memory: Early Experience

Satish Chandra and James R. Larus

Computer Sciences Department
University of Wisconsin—Madison
1210 W. Dayton Street
Madison, WI 53706 USA
{chandra, larus}@cs.wisc.edu

Abstract. This paper examines the performance of a suite of HPF applications on a network of workstations using two different compilation approaches: generating explicit message-passing code, and generating code for a shared address space provided by a fine-grain distributed shared memory system (DSM). Preliminary experiments indicate that the DSM approach performs with usually a small slowdown compared to the message passing approach on regular programs, yet enables efficient execution of non-regular programs.

1 Introduction

High Performance Fortran (HPF) [21] is the product of many years of collective experience with compiling for distributed memory machines. Researchers and companies have built compilers that compile HPF-like languages to efficient message-passing code [8, 15, 17, 20, 30, 35]. Yet, the domain of programs for which such compilers generate efficient code is very limited: good results have been demonstrated only on *regular* programs. Programs that use complicated array subscripts, such as those in the Perfect Club benchmark suite [12], have not been successfully compiled for message-passing machines. Consequently, despite HPF's allure, compilers limit the parallel applications that can benefit from HPF.

A compiler targeting a message-passing machine converts parallel loops that manipulate data in a global address space (such as those that can be written in HPF or similar languages [20,35]) into SPMD code that, in essence, synthesizes a global name space using explicit messages [23]. Unfortunately, the compiler depends on complete and accurate program analysis [35] to generate good message-passing code. Programs that cannot be completely analyzed show poor performance [30].

An alternative approach leaves the onerous task of implementing a program's shared address space to an underlying system. With an underlying coherent shared address space, compilers can greatly expand the range of programs that they can compile efficiently, as demonstrated by the Illinois Polaris [27] and the Stanford SUIF [37] compilers, which perform reasonably well for many non-regular programs. Shared address space at the system level can also aid HPF programmers in another significant way, as many large programs could occasionally go into an explicit task parallel mode, while accessing the same data set (HPF's EXTRINSIC). For example, an FFT algorithm, often a component in

This work is supported in part by Wright Laboratory Avionics Directorate, Air Force Material Command, USAF, under grant #F33615-94-1-1525 and ARPA order no. B550, an NSF NYI Award CCR-9357779, NSF Grant MIP-9225097, DOE Grant DE-FG02-93ER25176, and donations from Digital Equipment Corporation, Sun Microsystems, and The Portland Group. The U.S. Government is authorized to reproduce and distribute reprints for Governmental purposes notwithstanding any copyright notation thereon. The views and conclusions contained herein are those of the authors and should not be interpreted as necessarily representing the official policies or endorsements, either expressed or implied, of the Wright Laboratory Avionics Directorate or the U.S. Government.

larger problems, can be written much more efficiently using task parallelism [14]. Most programmers, when writing such extrinsic routines for HPF code, would prefer to find their arrays in shared memory, than broken up and renamed by the compiler in complicated ways.

The requirement for an underlying shared address space, moreover, need not limit our choice of platforms to hardware implemented shared memory, such as the Stanford DASH [24] multiprocessor. An attractive alternative is to use a distributed shared memory (DSM) system, which implements a shared address space on top of a message-passing substrate using software, or a combination of hardware and software. Recently, researchers have demonstrated efficient implementations of fine-grain (i.e., coherence at 32-128 byte granularity) shared memory for message-passing machines. For example, the Blizzard system at Wisconsin implements, in software, coherent shared memory on a CM-5 [33], and on a cluster of workstations [32].

A key question is whether a compiler is justified in incurring the overheads of a DSM-based shared address space, in preference to low-level message passing. This paper reports an experimental study that explores this question. In this study, our platform is a cluster of SPARCstation 20 workstations connected by a Myricom Myrinet [6] network. A runtime interface, called Tempest [19], provides the primitives for communication, as well as support for shared memory implemented almost entirely in software. We modified a commercial HPF compiler—the Portland Group, Inc. (PGI) *pghpf*—to generate code for Tempest's message passing and for shared memory implemented with Tempest mechanisms. The result from our (admittedly limited) experiments is that fine-grain shared memory runs with usually a small performance degradation (0%-55% increase in execution time) compared to native message passing on regular programs, yet enables efficient execution of non-regular programs. It is important to bear in mind that our compiler and runtime system do not yet attempt DSM-specific optimizations, so the balance is likely to shift further in favor of fine-grain shared memory.

The rest of the paper is organized as follows. Section 2 discusses related work in compiling for message passing and shared memory, and briefly explains the limitations of both approaches. Section 3 describes the compiler infrastructure that we used in this study, and Section 4 describes the platform that we used to run our programs. Section 5 presents experimental results on seven benchmarks. Section 6 presents some discussion and Section 7 concludes the paper.

2 Compiling for Message Passing and Shared Memory

We first consider the problems that plague compilers for message-passing machines. In absence of a shared address space, such compilers must partition arrays into local chunks that reside in per-node memories and modify the computation to accommodate the segmented address space. Computation is usually divided using the owner-computes rule [30]. Compilers introduce explicit messages at non-local references. Since communication in this paradigm is sender-initiated, the owner of non-local data sends it to processor(s) that need it. A naive, but general technique is run-time resolution [30]. However, this scheme may cause a slow down of a factor of several hundred over uniprocessor runs. Most compilers, therefore, exploit the observation that loops with no loop-carried dependence can obtain all non-local values before executing a loop. This optimization, called message vectorization, is critical for good performance, because it replaces small, frequent messages by large, infrequent ones, permits partitioning of the loop bounds [35], and permits overlap of computation and communication. In the best case, a compiler can statically determine the non-local data requirements for each processor and place all communication outside loops. This static analysis, however, is difficult for codes that use complex array subscripts or complicated control flow. Blume and Eigenmann [5] found that many dense matrix codes in Perfect Benchmarks [12] involve such programming constructs. Even if a programmer guarantees absence of loop-carried dependence by an INDEPENDENT directive, compilers cannot always vectorize the communication (although in some cases, inspector-executor technique [20, 31] has been found useful).

Not surprisingly, the efficacy of message-passing compilation has been demonstrated only for programs that consist wholly of simple loops and simple array subscripts. Our base compiler, *pghpf*, tries to classify the communication in a parallel construct (based on array subscripts) as one of overlap-shift, section-copy, or scatter-gather, failing which, it generates scalar communication inside loops [7].

In cache-coherent shared memory, the underlying system takes responsibility of fetching the latest value of a reference, irrespective of whether it is local or remote. This simplifies the task of a compiler to spreading parallel loops among processors and inserting synchronization. However, experimental studies have shown that to obtain good performance, compilers for shared-memory machines have to be aware of the features of the underlying memory system, such as finite cache size and false sharing. Several studies have proposed and implemented data and loop transformations to increase locality of reference [3, 4, 11].

Several techniques can be used to reduce the data access costs in shared memory systems. Write-misses can be made less costly by buffering them until a sychronization point. Weaker memory consistency models [1, 16], which suffice for compiler parallelized codes, allow this optimization. Read latencies can be alleviated by judicious use of prefetching, although compiler algorithms for prefetching [26] have been few. Mirchandaney [25] and Koufaty [22] suggest augmenting their shared memory systems with a send primitive, which could reduce coherence overheads in some cases. Finally, Tseng [36] has presented a compiler algorithm to eliminate redundant barriers in compiler parallelized shared memory programs, and to replace barriers by pairwise synchronization where applicable.

In this study, we performed none of these compiler-directed optimizations. Most of these optimizations require analyses similar to those needed for message passing, and while such analyses will certainly help shared memory performance, the goal of our current experiment is to compile without deep program analyses. However, we have used an implementation of the weaker consistency model for our shared memory experiments.

3 Compiler Infrastructure

We used PGI's *pghpf* compiler (version 2.0). *pghpf* is a nearly complete implementation of HPF (it implements more that the Subset HPF). The compiler translates the input HPF to a node Fortran program containing calls to a runtime library for message passing. The node program is then compiled with PGI's *pgftn* compiler. *pghpf* performs a number of standard optimizations, most importantly message vectorization. Good performance has been reported on regular applications [7].

Our message-passing version is a straight-forward modification of *pghpf*'s runtime system to use Tempest messages. We use asynchronous transfer (with receiver side buffering) for small messages (up to 4k bytes), and synchronous unbuffered transfer for larger messages. The shared memory version involved several changes to the compiler. All distributed arrays are allocated in shared memory; replicated arrays are allocated in per-processor private memory. The compiler generates accesses to distributed arrays by their global names rather than the local equivalents. Parallel loops (arising from array statements, FORALL statements, and the INDEPENDENT directive) are separated by barriers. All statements and control structure outside parallel loops execute on all processors, except assignments to shared data, which are protected by a guard. The division of computation for parallel loops is still owner computes, in that the data distribution directives are followed to assign work to processors. Parallel loops marked INDEPENDENT are currently distributed block wise by loop index. Unlike message passing, there is no need for explicit communication.

We also modified the *pghpf* runtime code for performing reductions from a binary tree scheme into a flat reduction scheme where one processor gathers the operands from all other processors, performs the reduction, and broadcasts the result. On our eight node experiments, we found that the flat scheme significantly outperforms the binary tree on all reduction-intensive benchmarks (e.g. *gravity*, Section 5.3).

4 Experimental Platform

Our message-passing and shared-memory platforms are built on the Tempest [19] system. Tempest is an interface that provides the mechanisms needed to implement fine-grain coherent shared memory. These mechanisms include: (1) active message style message passing, (2) fine-grain access control, (3) bulk data transfer for sending large messages (4) virtual memory mechanism to map pages from the shared data segment locally. The most remarkable feature of Tempest is the fine-grain access control, which allows coherence to be maintained at the level of small blocks of memory (e.g. 128 bytes is the block size used in our experiments) in contrast to coherence at page granularity in DSMs such as Treadmarks [2]. Using these mechanisms, a coherence protocol can be written entirely in user-level software (as a library) and linked with an application; details on the implementation of a coherent protocol using Tempest mechanisms can be found elsewhere [28]. For the current set of experiments, our protocol implements a version of the weakly consistent memory model—it attempts to reduce write latency by not waiting for the write ownership grant from the home node. At synchronization points, the node waits for all pending transactions to complete. One noteworthy feature of our coherence protocol is that it uses a portion of a node's main-memory as a large level-three cache [28], for holding remote data (like COMA [34]); this alleviates the problem of throwing away expensively fetched remote data due to finite size of the level-two cache.

These experiments ran on a cluster of dual-processor SPARCstation 20 workstations running Solaris 2.4 connected by a Myrinet network (all commodity parts). This implementation (see [32] for details) uses a small custom hardware device [29] that sits on the memory bus of each workstation and accelerates access control functions. Note that the coherence protocol itself is written in unprivileged software. Purely software implementations of fine-grain access control also exist, but they generally perform slightly slower. We perform computation on only one processor of a workstation node, leaving the other for coherence protocol related tasks. Although one could use both the processors for computation, we believe that future workstations will routinely have 4 or more processors, and one of them could be spared for protocol processing without noticeable loss of compute power. Some details on various components of the system are summarized in Table 1.

Processor	66 MHz HyperSPARC (2)
Network Interface	Myricom's Myrinet
Minimum roundtrip latency for short (4 bytes) message	40 μs
Network bandwidth	20 MB/s
Read miss processing time for 128 byte block	93 μs

Table 1: Some details of the cluster configuration used.

5 Results

We present results on seven HPF applications, listed in Table 2 with their problem sizes

Application	Source of HPF version	Problem Size	Memory(Mb)
pde	Genesis. HPF by PGI	grid size 128, 40 iters	56
shallow	NCAR. HPF by PGI	grid size 513, 100 iters	14
gravity	HPF by Syracuse	grid size 128, 5 iters	17
lu	Stanford. HPF by authors	1024x1024 matrix	4
tomcatv	SPEC. HPF by PGI	grid size 257, 100 iters	4
trfd	Perfect. HPF by authors	n=50 (1275x1275)	51
lcp	HPF by authors	8k rows, 0.5%sparsity	4.5

Table 2: Application Suite

and memory usage.

For each application, we describe the structure of the application and its communication pattern. We then report the execution times on shared memory and message passing for an eight node cluster, as well as the uniprocessor times. The uniprocessor versions of programs were single processor Fortran codes obtained from the HPF program—they contain *no runtime parallelism overhead.* The uniprocessor times come from a similar workstation node containing more (96M) physical memory so none of the applications page. The times for the message passing versions are decomposed into time spent in computation and time spent in the communication libraries. Likewise, times for the shared memory versions are decomposed into time spent in computation, and time spent handling remote misses and waiting at barriers. Time spent in any reductions is counted as communication time in both versions. The speedups curves are obtained by dividing the uniprocessor execution time by the execution times for 2, 4 and 8 nodes.

5.1 PDE

PDE performs red-black successive over-relaxation on a 3 dimensional grid. Accordingly, the main data structures in this program are three 3-dimensional arrays of double precision numbers. These arrays are distributed blockwise in their third dimension, on a linear arrangement of processors. The primary source of communication in this program is the shift operation in each dimension, which causes near-neighbor communication in the third dimension (as it is distributed blockwise). The program is very communication intensive, as in each iteration, $O(n^2)$ values are communicated for $O(n^3)$ computation. With a small data set and a relatively slow communication substrate, *PDE* shows moderate speedups for both message passing and shared memory. Figure 1 summarizes the results.

Shared memory is takes about 36% more time than message passing in this case. The poor performance can be attributed to our invalidation-based coherence protocol. Previous studies [10] have shown that producer-consumer sharing behavior performs poorly with such a coherence protocol. Briefly, the standard invalidation-based protocol requires four messages to transmit a single cache line from a producer to a consumer: (1) read request from consumer, (2) reply from the producer, (3) invalidate request from the producer, and (4) acknowledgment from the consumer. Our weak consistency protocol helps overlap the delay only in steps 3 and 4. Not surprisingly, given a program dominated by producer-consumer data transfer, transparent shared memory exacts a cost in performance.

5.2 Shallow

Shallow has 14 2-dimensional arrays of single precision floating point numbers. All arrays are distributed by blocks of columns on a linear arrangement of processors. This program

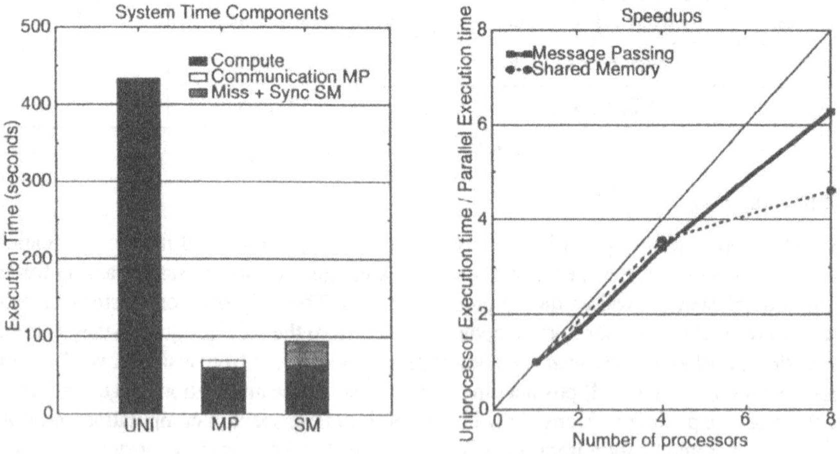

Figure 1: Performance data for *PDE*.

also performs shift communication in each dimension, causing near-neighbor communication in the second (distributed) dimension. Figure 2 presents the results.

As with *PDE* (Section 5.1), *Shallow* exhibits moderate speedups on both message-passing and shared-memory for this data-set size. A noteworthy characteristic of this application is that it exhibits message redundancy [18] across loop nests: values communicated for an earlier computation, in some cases, are still *available* (in the terminology of [18]) and need not be resent. The current version of PGI compiler does not perform message redundancy elimination of this kind. Shared memory, however, benefits from automatic caching as remote values are always available to consumers until new values are produced. In addition, *Shallow* can also benefit from message combining [9], an optimization applicable to both message passing and shared memory. Again, we have not explored this optimization yet. These observations apart, shared memory performs within 20% of message passing, even though all communication is producer-consumer.

5.3 Gravity

Gravity has two 3-d arrays and several 2-d arrays that are aligned with the last two dimensions of the 3-d arrays. In each outer time-step loop, the program iterates over the first dimension of the 3-d arrays, and performs computations on the 2-d plane formed by the second and third dimensions. These computations cause near-neighbor shift communication, and several SUM reductions in the same plane. We slightly modified the code in the mkl2 routine to work around a problem with the PGI compiler. Also, deviating from the original (*, BLOCK, BLOCK) distribution of the 3-d arrays, we used a (*, *, BLOCK) distribution; this was done to accommodate a problem with shared memory allocation in our current shared-memory compiler. Figure 3 presents the performance results.

Since this program executes reductions very frequently, both versions require an efficient mechanism. As noted earlier (Section 3), we used a flat reduction rather than a tree based reduction. In comparison with the tree reductions, the flat reductions took 44% less time

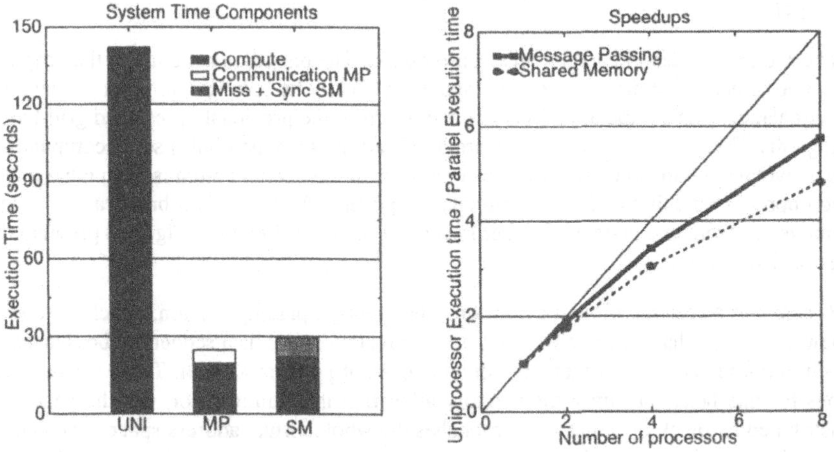

Figure 2: Performance data for *Shallow*.

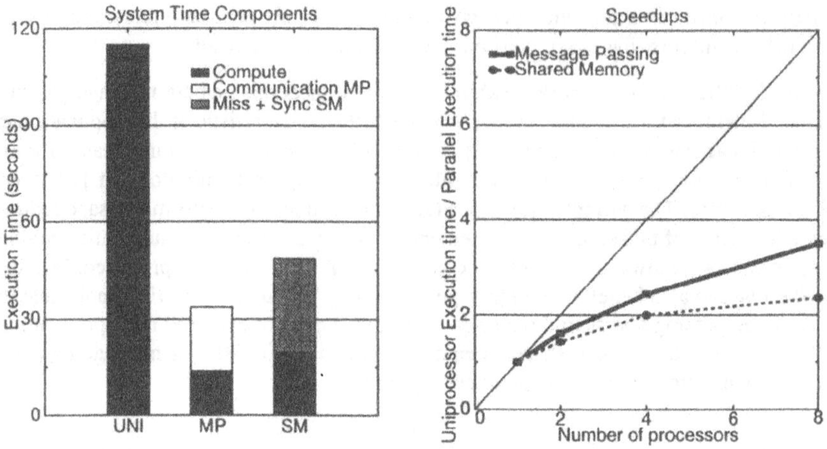

Figure 3: Performance data for *Gravity.*

for message passing and 35% less time for shared memory. Note that the shared memory reduction is not implemented solely using shared memory mechanisms. With Tempest mechanisms, this optimization is straightforward, but we expect most DSM systems to provide lower level hooks for specialized tasks such as broadcasts and reductions. The remaining communication in the program is mostly near-neighbor. As in *Shallow* (Section 5.2), both shared memory and message passing versions can benefit from message combining [9]. However, for the current data set size, both message passing and shared memory versions spend a significant amount of time in communication, and do not show good speedups. Larger data set sizes (albeit with enormous memory requirements) are likely to increase the computation to communication ratio and achieve better speedups.

5.4 LU

LU performs LU decomposition on a dense matrix. The only data structure in the program is a two dimensional matrix that is distributed cyclically by columns, in order to maintain load-balance. The computation in *LU* is distinct from the previously presented grid-based programs. Each outer iteration of the program performs (sequentially) some computation on a pivotal column, and then subtracts a multiple of the pivotal columns from the remaining unprocessed column. The communication pattern, therefore, is a broadcast of a column vector from one node to all other nodes in each outer iteration. Figure 4 presents the performance results.

LU achieves a speedup of 6 on 8 nodes for the message passing version, which is good in view of the fact that the computation on the pivotal column is a sequential bottleneck in each iteration. The shared memory version does not perform as well. There are two reasons for this behavior. Since the memory allocation is column major, and the pages are distributed by blocks, each processor touches the whole virtual address space occupied by the 2-d array. As noted in [3], this exacts a cost in memory system performance, although, in contrast with [3], we do not suffer from replacement-to-home misses.

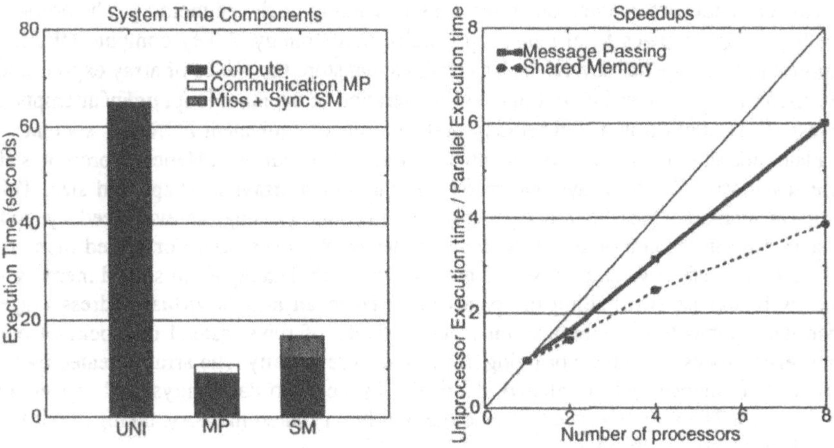

Figure 4: Performance data for *LU*

5.5 TOMCATV

Tomcatv consists of regular stencil operations on a number of 2-dimensional arrays. The distinguishing feature of *tomcatv* is that the parallelism is best exploited if the 2-dimensional arrays are distributed blockwise by rows rather than by columns. In contrast with a column-blocked distribution, the row-blocked distribution has a significant bearing on the shared memory performance. The communication in this program is primarily shift communication across the rows. Figure 5 shows the performance results.

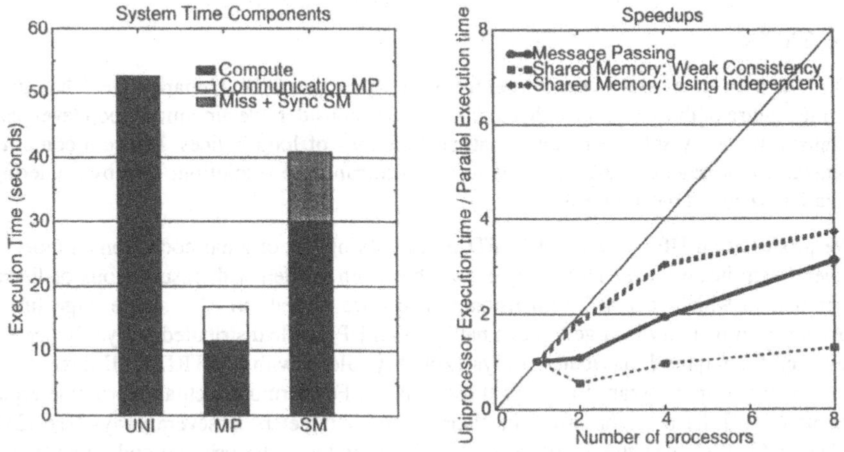

Figure 5: Tomcatv. Different versions of HPF source code are used for MP and SM (see text).

Tomcatv does not perform well on either message passing or shared memory. The problem with this program arises from *pghpf*'s parallelization strategy. A key compute-intensive loop-nest in this code has several scalar variables that store the values of array expressions to be used multiple times, but within the same iteration of the inner loop. *pghpf* attempts to express all parallelism in a Fortran loop nest in terms of equivalent FORALL statements (in a later phase, it fuses loops with identical iteration distributions). Hence, it promotes all these scalar variables to arrays that match the main data arrays in shape and size. This results in increased local data access costs for message passing, as evidenced by poor speedup even in the compute cost (only 4.7 times on 8 processors). For shared memory, this increase in effective data set size is more taxing. Our data layout in shared memory is done by blockwise distributing the pages involved in an array's virtual address range. Since the computation decomposition touches blocks of rows instead of blocks of columns, each processor ends up bringing in entire data set locally. The arrays created by the compiler are aligned and distributed identically to the main data arrays, and exacerbate this problem. The same HPF code runs quite poorly on shared memory, taking about 930 seconds (an 18 times slowdown).

Following the observation in [3], we manually rewrote *tomcatv* for shared memory so it operates in a transpose fashion. Thus, each reference a(i,j) was converted to a(j,i), making all necessary changes in the program so it computes the same result. This is the shared memory version we used for the performance data reported in Figure 5. Shared memory performs much better with this version, yet, it fails to give any speedup: the slowdown for two processors is an indication of the high data access costs caused by temporary arrays. We were, however, able to create a shared memory version which did not require this temporary storage, by using the INDEPENDENT directive. For this version, the speedup obtained by shared memory matches, and even exceeds, that of message passing. On eight nodes, the compute portion of this version runs 5.8 times faster than the uniprocessor code. Unfortunately, we were unable to convince the compiler to produce a similar message passing version for a fair comparison.

5.6 TRFD

TRFD is a quantum mechanics kernel from the Perfect Club benchmark suite. The interesting feature of this program is that although it has considerable amount of loop level parallelism, the array subscripts are not affine functions of loop indices. Hence a compiler generating message-passing code has to resort to run-time resolution, thereby rendering parallel execution meaningless.

We produced an HPF version of *TRFD* by modifying the original code from Illinois in several significant ways. The original code has been written with assumptions of linear memory, in which several 2-dimensional arrays are carved out of a single large linear array. Linear memory is largely incompatible with HPF-style distributed arrays. Hence we declared the required distributed arrays explicitly (along with DISTRIBUTE directives), and modified the program to access those instead. Furthermore, actual subroutine arguments in HPF have to conform with their formal parameters in several ways (see [21], Chapter 5). We made the appropriate changes. Finally, in the original code, two of the loops that can be executed in parallel make a procedure call (TRANSF) in their loop body. Since we wanted to use the INDEPENDENT directive for these loops, we had to inline the procedure to form the loop body. All these modifications were necessary to obtain a legal

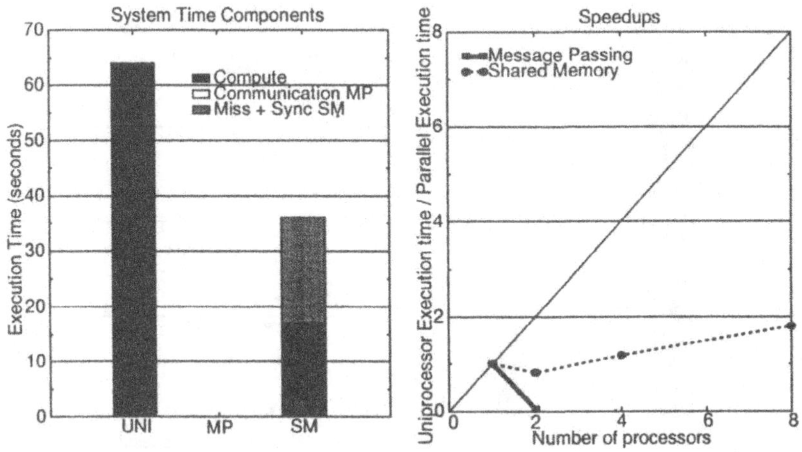

Figure 6: Performance data for *TRFD*. We could not run *TRFD* for more than 2 nodes on MP.

and efficient HPF program. The resulting HPF code manipulates a 2-dimensional array that is distributed by blocks of columns. The first loop, in subroutine INTGRL initializes the array using indirect accesses. Application-specific knowledge, or complicated dependence analysis [5] can reveal that the loop can indeed be executed in parallel. The other two loops, both of which have the TRANSF subroutine as their loop bodies, perform indirect operations only in the row dimension of the array, so all columns can be processed in parallel. Our shared memory compiler simply distributes these loops across processors (note that we use the INDEPENDENT directive). Figure 6 shows the performance numbers.

Although the program has sufficient high level parallelism, we were unable to cast the complete HPF code in terms of FORALL statements that would be accepted by the *pghpf* for efficient message passing. As a result, message passing version essentially performs the first loop sequentially, and generates calls to scalar communication in the other loops. Not surprisingly, the performance of the resulting message passing code is unacceptable: it shows a factor of 20 slowdown on a 2-node execution; we were unable to complete runs for higher number of nodes in any reasonable time. The speedup of 1.8 for shared memory, while not satisfactory, is a step towards efficiently executing non-regular programs written in HPF. This program demonstrates a case in which shared memory layer performs far better than direct message-passing code.

5.7 LCP

LCP solves the linear complementarity problem on a sparse system. The main obstacle that we encountered in writing the HPF code was the initialization. Since the input generation in done off-line, a large (4.4 Mb of binary representation) file had to be read in order to initialize all the arrays. Direct input in HPF, using an ascii version of the file, proved too slow. Instead, we declared a *shadow file* on each node, that was initialized with the contents of the input file by calling an external C function. The HPF code, then, simply reads off the values from the shadow files into distributed arrays. The data structures in the pro-

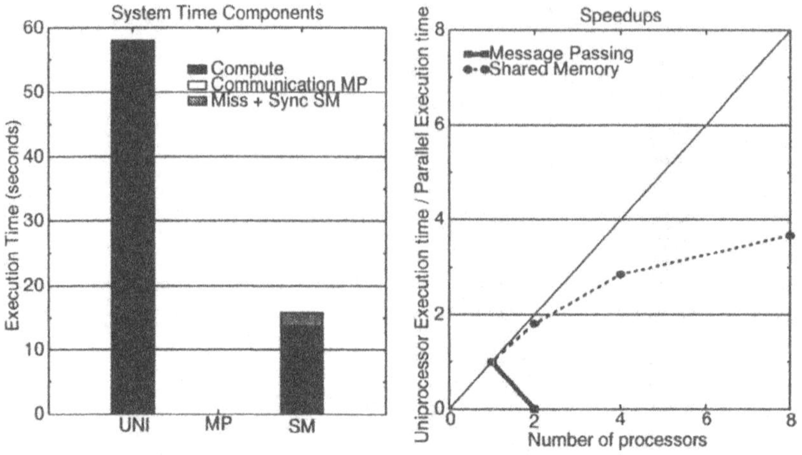

Figure 7: Performance data for *LCP*. We could not run *LCP* for more than 2 nodes.

gram consist of a sparse matrix represented by 3 arrays: an array containing the non-zero values *a*, an array containing the column index *ia* of each non zero element, and finally, and array marking the start of each new row *ja*. In addition, there is a global solution vector *xsol* that is updated once every few iterations until convergence is reached, and a local solution vector *xbar* used for intermediate values. In our implementation, we to distributed *a*, *ia* and *xbar* blockwise, and replicated *ja* and *xsol*. The computation proceeds in time steps, where in each time step, a relaxation subroutine is called five times. This routine produces new values in the local solution vector *xbar*. At the end of each time step, the local solution is committed to the global solution vector, and convergence is tested. The communication arises in updating the global solution vector, and in testing for convergence, which entails a reduction. Figure 7 presents the performance data.

Even though the arrays *a* and *ia* are read-only data, the relevant values need to reach each node once: this is an ideal case for the inspector-executor paradigm, but the current *pghpf* compiler resorts to run-time resolution for message passing. The two node execution time for message passing was about 1000 times slower than the uniprocessor case. We could not complete 8 node runs even in several hours. For the shared memory case, we are able to get some speedup (about 3.7) by the use of the INDEPENDENT directive; the accesses to *a* and *ia* are cached automatically.

6 Discussion

Tempest does not enforce a particular cache block size (unit of coherence), neither does it enforce a particular coherence policy. Although we typically use 128 byte blocks, we could use larger blocks to provide us the associated benefits of prefetching. Large blocks, however, are not a panacea, as they may hurt performance if they induce false sharing, or otherwise contribute to useless traffic. However, in most of the programs we studied, larger block size of 512 bytes helped improve shared memory performance. Figure 8 presents comparative speedup results (8 nodes) on message passing, shared memory implemented with 128 byte blocks, and shared memory implemented with 512 byte blocks. Since the block size selection is simply a matter of re-compiling user-level library code, we are justified in refining our selection of block size for an application if it improves performance. Similarly, although we have not demonstrated update-based protocols in this study, earlier experiments [13] suggest that they may improve performance over invalidation-based protocols.

7 Conclusion

The goal of this study was to compare a fine-grain distributed shared memory system with compiler implemented shared memory on message-passing hardware. Originally, we intended to address programs that have features that present message-passing compilers a continuum of challenge in static analysis. However, we found it very hard to obtain third-party HPF programs that were different from grid-based iterative computations, and were forced to produce two such programs ourselves. Perhaps this bias is due to the fact that the widely available compilers handle only "regular" programs well, and there is little motivation to use HPF for irregular codes. Thus, our current programs reflect an all-or-nothing scenario in terms of applicability of static analysis. In the set of seven programs we studied, five have a regular structure for which compiler analysis for message passing is satisfactory, even though speedups are often not. The remaining two are programs for which such analysis fails. We hope that compiler writers (and application programmers) view fine-grain DSM as a credible means for supporting a wider variety of programs.

In our limited experience, explicit message passing has a substantial advantage (up to 55%) only when an application can express all its communication as coarse-grain shifts and broadcasts. On the other hand, shared memory provides a good way of executing programs for which imperfect analysis prevents a compiler from generating good message-

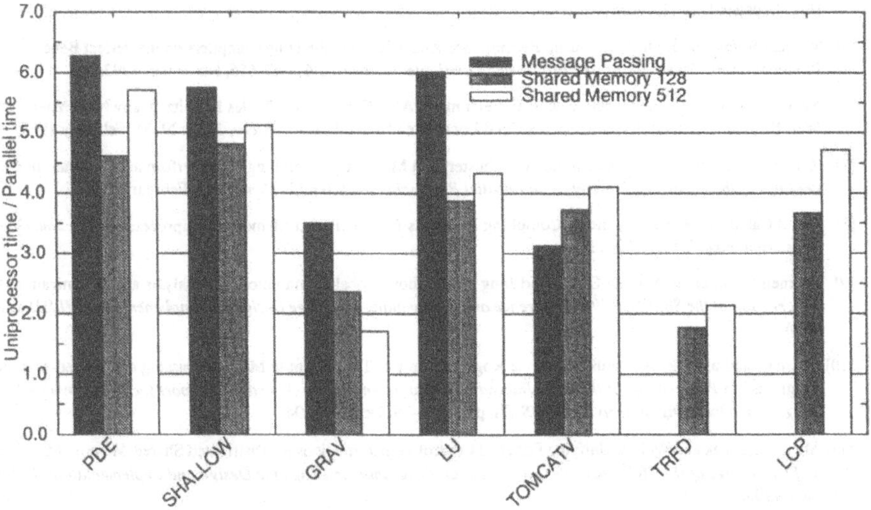

Figure 8: Comparative speedups (8 nodes) on message passing, shared memory with 128 byte cache blocks, and on shared memory with 512 byte cache blocks.

passing code. While more experimentation is undeniably required, this preliminary evidence indicates that compiler writers should consider delegating the synthesis of a shared address space to an underlying system. With the Tempest interface, a compiler can still use efficient message passing when analysis is precise and fall back on shared memory for other cases. Several methods to improve shared memory performance, such as barrier elimination and the use of update based protocols, may bridge the gap in cases in which shared memory trails message passing.

8 Acknowledgments

Yannis Schoinas, Steve Reinhardt and Marc Dionne provided invaluable assistance with using the Blizzard prototype used in this study. Krisna Kunchithapadam, Guhan Vishwanathan and Manish Gupta provided comments on earlier versions of this paper. Finally, Portland Group, Inc. provided us with their HPF compiler infrastructure, as well as prompt answers to many questions about the source code.

References

[1] Sarita V. Adve and Mark D. Hill. Weak Ordering - A New Definition. In *Proceedings of the 17th Annual International Symposium on Computer Architecture*, pages 2–14, May 1990.

[2] Cristiana Amza, Alan L. Cox, Sandhya Dwarkadas, Pete Keleher, Honghui Lu, Ramakrishnan Rajamony, Weimin Yu, and Willy Zwaenepoel. TreadMarks: Shared Memory Computing on Networks of Workstation s. *IEEE Computer*, pages 18–28, February 1996.

[3] Jennifer M. Anderson, Saman P. Amarasinghe, and Monica S. Lam. Data and Computation Transformations for Multiprocessors. In *Fifth ACM SIGPLAN Symposium on Principles & Practice of Parallel Programming (PPOPP)*, July 1995.

[4] Jennifer M. Anderson and Monica S. Lam. Global Optimizations for Parallelism and Locality on Scalable Parallel Machines. In *Proceedings of the SIGPLAN '93 Conference on Programming Language Design and Implementation (PLDI)*, pages 112–125, June 1993.

[5] William Blume and Rudolf Eigemann. Performance Analysis of Parallelizing Compilers on the Perfect Benchmarks Programs. *IEEE Transactions on Parallel and Distributed Systems*, 3(6):643–656, November 1992.

[6] Nanette J. Boden, Danny Cohen, Robert E. Felderman, Alan E. Kulawik, Charles L. Seitz, Jakov N. Seizovic, and Wen-King Su. Myrinet: A Gigabit-per-Second Local Area Network. *IEEE Micro*, 15(1):29–36, February 1995.

[7] Z. Bozkus, L. Meadows, S. Nakamoto, V. Schuster, and M. Young. Compiling High Performance Fortran. In *Proceedings of the 7th SIAM Conference on Parallel Processing for Scientific Computing*, February 1995.

[8] David Callahan and Ken Kennedy. Compiling Programs for Distributed-Memory Multiprocessors. *The Journal of Supercomputing*, 2:151–169, 1988.

[9] Soumen Chakrabarti, Manish Gupta, and Jong-Deok Choi. Global Communication Analysis and Optimization. In *Proceedings of the SIGPLAN '96 Conference on Programming Language Design and Implementation (PLDI)*, May 1996.

[10] Satish Chandra, James R. Larus, and Anne Rogers. Where is Time Spent in Message-Passing and Shared-Memory Programs? In *Proceedings of the Sixth International Conference on Architectural Support for Programming Languages and Operating Systems (ASPLOS VI)*, pages 61–75, October 1994.

[11] Michal Cierniak and Wei Li. Unifying Data and Control Transformations for Distributed Shared-Memory Machines. In *Proceedings of the SIGPLAN '95 Conference on Programming Language Design and Implementation (PLDI)*, June 1995.

[12] G. Cybenko, J. Bruner, S. Ho, and S. Sharma. Parallel Computing and the Perfect Benchmarks. Technical Report 1191, Center for Supercomputing Research & Development, University of Illinois at Urbana-Champaign, November 1991.

[13] Babak Falsafi, Alvin Lebeck, Steven Reinhardt, Ioannis Schoinas, Mark D. Hill, James Larus, Anne Rogers, and David Wood. Application-Specific Protocols for User-Level Shared Memory. In *Proceedings of Supercomputing '94*, pages 380–389, November 1994.

[14] Ian Foster. Task Parallelism and High Performance Languages. *IEEE Parallel and Distributed Technology: Systems and Applications*, 2(3):?–?, Fall 1994.

[15] Hans Michael Gerndt. *Automatic Parallelization for Distributed-Memory Multiprocessor Systems*. PhD thesis, Rheinischen Friedrich-Wilhelms-Universit"at, 1989.

[16] Kourosh Gharachorloo, Daniel Lenoski, James Laudon, Philip Gibbons, Anoop Gupta, and John Hennessy. Memory Consistency and Event Ordering in Scalable Shared-Memory. In *Proceedings of the 17th Annual International Symposium on Computer Architecture*, pages 15–26, June 1990.

[17] Manish Gupta and Prithviraj Banerjee. PARADIGM: A Compiler for Automatic Data Distribution on Multicomputers. In *Proceedings of the 1993 ACM International Conference on Supercomputing*, Tokyo, Japan, July 1993.

[18] Manish Gupta, Edith Schonberg, and Harinia Srivivasan. A Unified Framework for Optimizing Communication in Data-Parallel Programs. *IEEE Transactions on Parallel and Distributed Systems*, 7(7):689–704, July 1996.

[19] Mark D. Hill, James R. Larus, and David A. Wood. Tempest: A Substrate for Portable Parallel Programs. In *COMPCON '95*, pages 327–332, San Francisco, California, March 1995. IEEE Computer Society.

[20] Charles Koelbel and Piyush Mehrotra. Compiling Global Name-Space Parallel Loops for Distributed Execution. *IEEE Transactions on Parallel and Distributed Systems*, 2(4):440–451, October 1991.

[21] Charles H. Koelbel, David B. Loveman, Robert S. Schreiber, Guy L. Steele Jr., and Mary E. Zosel. *High Performance Fortran Handbook*. MIT Press, Cambridge, Mass., 1994.

[22] D.A. Koufaty, X. Chen, D.K. Poulsen, and J. Torrellas. Data Forwarding in Scalable Shared-Memory Multprocessors. In *Proceedings of the 1995 International Conference on Supercomputing*, page ?, 1995.

[23] James R. Larus. Compiling for Shared-Memory and Message-Passing Computers. *ACM Letters on Programming Languages and Systems*, 2(1–4):165–180, March–December 1994.

[24] Daniel Lenoski, James Laudon, Kourosh Gharachorloo, Wolf-Dietrich Weber, Anoop Gupta, John Hennessy, Mark Horowitz, and Monica Lam. The Stanford DASH Multiprocessor. *IEEE Computer*, 25(3):63–79, March 1992.

[25] Ravi Mirchandaney, Seema Hiranandani, and Ajay Sethi. Improving the Performance of DSM Systems via Compiler Involvement. In *Proceedings of Supercomputing '94*, pages 763–772, 1994.

[26] Todd C. Mowry, Monica S. Lam, and Anoop Gupta. Design and evaluation of a compiler algorithm for prefetching. In *Fifth Proceedings of Symposium on Architectural Support for Programming Languages and Operations Systems*, pages 62–73, October 1992.

[27] D. Padua, R. Eigenmann, J. Hoeflinger, P. Peterson, P. Tu, S. Weatherford, and K. Faigin. Polaris: A New-Generation Parallelizing Compiler for MPP's. Technical Report 1306, Center for Supercomputing Research & Development, University of Illinois at Urbana-Champaign, June 1993.

[28] Steven K. Reinhardt, James R. Larus, and David A. Wood. Tempest and Typhoon: User-Level Shared Memory. In *Proceedings of the 21st Annual International Symposium on Computer Architecture*, pages 325–337, April 1994.

[29] Steven K. Reinhardt, Robert W. Pfile, and David A. Wood. Decoupled Hardware Support for Distributed Shared Memory. In *Proceedings of the 23rd Annual International Symposium on Computer Architecture*, May 1996.

[30] Anne Marie Rogers. Compiling for Locality of Reference. Technical Report TR 91-1195, Department of Computer Science, Cornell University, March 1991. PhD thesis.

[31] Joel H. Saltz, Ravi Mirchandaney, and Kay Crowley. Run-Time Parallelization and Scheduling of Loops. *IEEE Transactions on Computers*, 40(5):603–612, May 1991.

[32] Ioannis Schoinas, Babak Falsafi, Mark D. Hill, James R. Larus, Christopher E. Lucas, Shubhendu S. Mukherjee, Steven K. Reinhardt, Eric Schnarr, and David A. Wood. Implementing Fine-Grain Distributed Shared Memory On Commodity SMP Workstations. Technical Report 1307, Computer Sciences Department, University of Wisconsin–Madison, March 1996.

[33] Ioannis Schoinas, Babak Falsafi, Alvin R. Lebeck, Steven K. Reinhardt, James R. Larus, and David A. Wood. Fine-grain Access Control for Distributed Shared Memory. In *Proceedings of the Sixth International Conference on Architectural Support for Programming Languages and Operating Systems (ASPLOS VI)*, pages 297–307, October 1994.

[34] Per Stenstrom, Truman Joe, and Anoop Gupta. Comparative Performance Evaluation of Cache-Coherent NUMA and COMA Architectures. In *Proceedings of the 19th Annual International Symposium on Computer Architecture*, pages 80–91, 1992.

[35] Chau-Wen Tseng. *An Optimizing FORTRAN D Compiler for Distributed Memory MIMD Machines*. PhD thesis, Rice University, January 1993. Also available as Rice CRPC-TR93291-S.

[36] Chau-Wen Tseng. Compiler Optimization for Eliminating Barrier Synchronization. In *Fifth ACM SIGPLAN Symposium on Principles & Practice of Parallel Programming (PPOPP)*, pages 144–155, August 1995.

[37] Robert P. Wilson, Robert S. French, Christopher S. Wilson, Saman P. Amarasinghe, Jennifer M. Anderson, Chau-Wen Tseng, Mary W. Hall, Monica S. Lam, and John L. Hennesy. SUIF: An Infrastructure for Reseasrch on Parallelizing and Optimizing Compilers. *ACM SIGPLAN Notices*, 29(12):31–37, December 1994.

Simple *Qualitative* Experiments with a Sparse Compiler *

Aart J.C. Bik and Harry A.G. Wijshoff

High Performance Computing Division
Department of Computer Science, Leiden University
P.O. Box 9512, 2300 RA Leiden, the Netherlands
ajcbik@cs.leidenuniv.nl

Abstract. In this paper, we present some qualitative experiments that have been conducted with a sparse compiler. This compiler can automatically transform a program operating on two-dimensional arrays into semantically equivalent code that operates on sparse storage schemes. Automatic exploitation of sparsity to reduce the storage requirements and computational time of the original program substantially reduces the complexity of developing and maintaining the program and provides more opportunities for parallelization. The experiments indicate that, in many cases, a sparse compiler is capable of transforming a dense implementation of an algorithm into efficient sparse code.

1 Introduction

Because restructuring compilers are very useful to automatically detect and exploit implicit parallelism in serial software, the question arises whether it is also possible to let a restructuring compiler convert code that operates on simple data structures into a format that exploits certain characteristics of the data operated on. In contrast to conventional restructuring compilers, mainly focusing on program transformations, this approach must allow for the application of ***data structure transformations*** as well.

For applications involving sparse matrices, this approach implies that all computations on these matrices may simply be defined on two-dimensional arrays rather than on complex data structures as has been done traditionally (see e.g. [13, 14, 17, 21, 22]). A special kind of restructuring compiler, which we will refer to as a **sparse compiler**, transforms these simple data structures into more complex sparse data structures, thereby reducing storage requirements and computational time. Analogous to the approach taken by conventional restructuring compilers, a source-to-source translation is performed. The sparse compiler automatically transforms a dense FORTRAN program operating on two-dimensional arrays into code that operates on sparse storage schemes.

* Support was provided by the Foundation for Computer Science (SION) of the Dutch Organization for Scientific Research (NWO) and the EC Esprit Agency DG XIII under Grant No. APPARC 6634 BRA III.

As depicted below, the resulting sparse code is compiled by a conventional FORTRAN compiler for a particular target architecture thereafter:

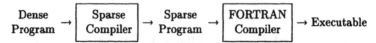

Dense Program → [Sparse Compiler] → Sparse Program → [FORTRAN Compiler] → Executable

Besides the fact that dealing with sparsity of matrices at the compilation level rather than at the programming is less error-prone, this approach has a number of other advantages. First, the complexity of writing and maintaining sparse codes is reduced substantially, which enables programmers that are not familiar with sparse matrix computations to easily produce sparse code. Second, applying data dependence analysis to the dense code usually yields more accurate information, which allows for more program transformations and may provide more opportunities for parallelization.

Because the sparse compiler can account for characteristics of both the nonzero structure and the target machine (provided that these characteristics are made available in some manner), as well as the actual operations performed while selecting a suitable sparse data structure, one dense program can be converted into a range of sparse versions, each of which is tailored for a particular instance of the same problem. Program transformations may be applied to the dense program in case this data structure selection cannot be resolved efficiently. Finally, just as traditional restructuring compilers enable the re-use of existing serial software, a sparse compiler enables the re-use of parts of existing dense code.

Elaboration of these ideas have resulted in the development and implementation of a sparse compiler. The automatic data structure selection and transformation method used by this compiler has been presented in detail in previous work [4, 5, 7]. In this paper, we present some simple *qualitative* experiments that have been conducted with this sparse compiler. The results of some simple *quantitative* experiments are presented elsewhere [6].

2 Qualitative Experiments

For each **implicitly sparse matrix** A, i.e. a matrix for which the sparsity is not explicitly dealt with, a two-dimensional array `A` is used as **enveloping data structure** in the original program. Thereupon, the sparse compiler selects a sparse storage scheme for each implicitly sparse matrix, and transforms the original code accordingly. In this section, we survey the techniques used by the sparse compiler and discuss the quality of some automatically generated sparse constructs. For a detailed discussion of the techniques, however, we refer to [2].

2.1 Associating Conditions with Statements

After the sparse compiler has identified the enveloping data structures, conditions are associated with all statements in which occurrences of these data structures appear.

For example, if we let $E(A) \subseteq \mathcal{Z}^2$ and $E(B) \subseteq \mathcal{Z}^2$ denote the index sets of the entries of two implicitly sparse matrices A and B (usually the contents of these sets are unknown until run-time), then the condition shown below is associated with the following assignment statement to indicate that only instances referring to two entries have to be executed (all other instances can be skipped):

```
X = X + 7.0 * ( A(I,K) * B(K,J) )    ← (I,K) ∈ E(A) ∧ (K,J) ∈ E(B)
```

A simple version of an attributed grammar computing conditions for assignment statements has been presented in [3]. In the current implementation, a slightly more advanced attributed grammar is used [2]. Conditions may also be associated with general IF-statements. For this purpose, for each boolean expression E, we record the conditions under which this expression may succeed or fail in two attributes E.t and E.f. Thereafter, a condition is associated with the whole IF-statement.

EXAMPLE: A somewhat contrived example to illustrate the potential of associating conditions with general IF-statements is shown below:

```
IF (A(I,J) .GT. 0.0) THEN        ← (E.t = (I,J) ∈ E(A), E.f = true)
  POS = POS + 1                  ← true
ELSEIF (A(I,J) .LT. 0.0) THEN    ← (E.t = (I,J) ∈ E(A), E.f = true)
  NEG = NEG + 1                  ← true
ELSE
  X = X + B(I,I)                 ← (I,I) ∈ E(B)
ENDIF
```

Because the condition of the first and second branch can only hold for entries of A (although the loop-body itself cannot exploit sparsity, as indicated by the condition '**true**'), whereas the ELSE-branch (although executed unconditionally) can safely be skipped for non-entries of B, the whole general IF-statement can be placed under control of the following condition:

$$(\mathtt{I},\mathtt{J}) \in E(A) \vee (\mathtt{I},\mathtt{I}) \in E(B)$$

EXAMPLE: The first branch of the following IF-statement may be skipped for non-entries of B and C, whereas the ELSE-branch (which cannot exploit sparsity) is only executed if the first boolean expression *does not hold* (hence under the condition E.f):

```
IF (A(I,J) .EQ. 0.0) THEN        ← (E.t = true, E.f = (I,J) ∈ E(A))
  X = X + B(I,I)                 ← (I,I) ∈ E(B)
  X = X + C(I,I)                 ← (I,I) ∈ E(C)
ELSE
  X = 0.0                        ← true
ENDIF
```

Hence, the following condition is associated with the whole IF-statement:

$$(\mathtt{I},\mathtt{I}) \in E(B) \vee (\mathtt{I},\mathtt{I}) \in E(C) \vee (\mathtt{I},\mathtt{J}) \in E(A)$$

In case evaluating any boolean expression may have side-effects, we conservatively associate the condition '**true**' with the whole IF-statement.

2.2 Overhead Reducing Techniques

Since skipping statement instances by means of conditionals does not reduce the execution time in general, the sparse compiler must be able to make effective use of the condition associated with each statement. Currently, the sparse compiler has the ability to apply one of the following overhead reducing techniques [2]: (i) applying so-called guard encapsulation, where a construct that iterates over the entries along an access pattern is generated, (ii) applying so-called access pattern expansion, where a sparse vector is scattered into a full-sized array before operations are applied to this vector, and gathered back into sparse storage thereafter, (iii) replacing accesses to zero regions by zero, or (iv) avoiding overhead by using static dense storage for particular regions. Techniques (i) and (ii) are important for general sparse matrices whereas the other techniques are applicable if more characteristics of the nonzero structures are known.

General Sparse Matrices In many static and simply dynamic operations [22, p10-12], the loop-body of a loop only has to be executed for the entries of an implicitly sparse matrix. This situation occurs, for instance, in the following fragment in which the elements of an implicitly sparse matrix A with enveloping data structure `A` are scaled and the position and actual value of an element with largest absolute value are determined:

```
DO I = 1, M
  DO J = 1, N
    A(I,J) = A(I,J) / 3.0                   ← (I,J) ∈ E(A)
    IF (ABS(A(I,J).GT.ABS(MX))) THEN        ← (I,J) ∈ E(A)
      II = I                                ← true
      JJ = J                                ← true
      MX = A(I,J)                           ← true
    ENDIF
  ENDDO
ENDDO
```

The first assignment statement only has to be executed for entries, since the division has no impact on zero elements. Hence, the sparse compiler associates condition '$(\texttt{I},\texttt{J}) \in E(A)$' with this assignment statement. Moreover, although none of the statements inside the one-way IF-statement can exploit sparsity (reflected by condition '**true**'), the IF-statement as a whole only has to be executed for entries, because the condition of this IF-statement always fails for zero elements. Hence, if general sparse row-wise storage is selected for A and the programmer indicates that all loop-carried data dependences may be ignored (under the assumption that *any* element with largest absolute value may be found), then encapsulation of the guard '$(\texttt{I},\texttt{J}) \in E(A)$' in the execution set of the J-loop becomes feasible. After this conversion, the J_-loop iterates over all entries within each `I`th row, of which the numerical values and column index information can be found at locations `LOW_A(I)..HGH_A(I)` in the parallel arrays `VAL_A` and `IND_A` respectively. (see [2] for more details on the sparse storage scheme selection):

```
DO I = 1, M
  DO J_ = LOW_A(I), HGH_A(I)
    J = IND_A(J_)
    VAL_A(J_) = VAL_A(J_) / 3.0
    IF (ABS(VAL_A(J_).GT.ABS(MX))) THEN
      II = I
      JJ = J
      MX = VAL_A(J_)
    ENDIF
  ENDDO
ENDDO
```

As shown below, a dense implementation of the operation $\mathbf{b} \leftarrow \mathbf{b}+A\mathbf{x}$ with A implicitly sparse can be converted similarly if general sparse *column*-wise storage is selected for the matrix:

```
DO J = 1, N                                DO J = 1, N
  DO I = 1, M                                DO I_ = LOW_A(J), HGH_A(J)
    B(I) = B(I) + A(I,J) * X(J)    →           I = IND_A(I_)
  ENDDO                                        B(I) = B(I) + VAL_A(I_) * X(J)
ENDDO                                        ENDDO
                                           ENDDO
```

After this conversion, the I_-loops implements a sparse SAXPY ($\mathbf{y} \leftarrow \mathbf{y}+\alpha\mathbf{x}$, where $\mathbf{x}$ is sparse). Likewise, if loop interchanging is applied to the original loop and general sparse row-wise storage is selected for A, then the sparse compiler generates code that implements a sequence of sparse dot products ($w = \mathbf{x} \cdot \mathbf{y}$, where $\mathbf{x}$ is sparse). Hence, in a future implementation such constructs could be replaced by calls to primitives of the sparse extensions to BLAS [10] or directly by an efficient implementation (such as the GATHER-SAXPY-SCATTER implementation of sparse SAXPY for pipelined vector processors [9, 11, 12, 16, 18]).

The conversion into sparse code becomes more complex if the condition associated with a statement in a loop consists of a conjunction of guards, such as in the following example, where arrays A and B are used as enveloping data structure of implicitly sparse matrices A and B:

```
DO I = 1, M
  DO J = 1, N
    X = X + A(I,J) * B(I,J)      ← (I,J) ∈ E(A) ∧ (I,J) ∈ E(B)
  ENDDO
ENDDO
```

If general sparse row-wise storage is selected for A and B and the data dependences caused by the accumulation may be ignored, then either the guard '$(\mathtt{I},\mathtt{J}) \in E(A)$' or '$(\mathtt{I},\mathtt{J}) \in E(B)$' can be encapsulated in the execution set of the J-loop, but not both. To prevent the situation in which a lookup would have to be performed for each entry of either A or B, the sparse compiler uses expansion. For example, if in the generated sparse code, guard '$(\mathtt{I},\mathtt{J}) \in E(A)$' is encapsulated in the execution set of the J-loop, the Ith row of B is expanded before operated upon:

```
DO I = 1, M
  CALL SSCT__(VAL_B ,IND_B, LOW_B(I), HGH_B(I), SAP_10, SWT_10)
  DO J_ = LOW_A(I), HGH_A(I)
    J = IND_A(J_)
    IF (SWT_10(J)) THEN
      X = X + VAL_A(J_) * SAP_10(J)
    ENDIF
  ENDDO
  CALL SGTH__(VAL_B ,IND_B, LOW_B(I), HGH_B(I), SAP_10, SWT_10)
ENDDO
```

The primitive SSCT scatters the I th row of B into a dense vector SAP_10, where a so-called **switch array** SWT_10 of type LOGICAL is used to locate the position of entries in the expanded vector. Note that, although matrix B remains unaffected in this loop, the gather operation is generated after the J_-loop all the same. In this manner, used elements in array SAP_10 and the switch array SWT_10 are reset to enable each subsequent expansion. Because the time required to perform each scatter and gather operation is proportional to the number of entries in the corresponding row of B, and the initial costs of resetting the full-sized arrays SAP_10 and SWT_10 can be amortized over M expansions, a construct of which the execution time is proportional to the number of entries in A and B has been obtained.

It is also difficult to make effective use of a condition that consists of a disjunction of guards, such as appearing in the following implementation of $D \leftarrow D + A + B$, where we assume that D is used to store the elements of a dense matrix D:

```
DO I = 1, M
  DO J = 1, N
    D(I,J) = D(I,J) + A(I,J) + B(I,J)      ← (I,J) ∈ E(A) ∨ (I,J) ∈ E(B)
  ENDDO
ENDDO
```

Because none of the guards dominates the condition, in this case guard encapsulation is even infeasible.[2] Clearly, performing a lookup in both A and B for each element of D would induce an unacceptable complexity. Fortunately, after this operation has been rewritten into the operations $D \leftarrow D + A$ and $D \leftarrow D + B$ using update expression splitting and loop distribution, guard encapsulation becomes feasible if general sparse row-wise storage is selected for both A and B:

```
                                       DO I = 1, M
DO I = 1, M                              DO J_ = LOW_A(I), HGH_A(I)
  DO J = 1, N                              J = IND_A(J_)
    D(I,J) = D(I,J) + A(I,J)               D(I,J) = D(I,J) + VAL_A(J_)
  ENDDO                                  ENDDO
  DO J = 1, N                     →      DO J_ = LOW_B(I), HGH_B(I)
    D(I,J) = D(I,J) + B(I,J)               J = IND_B(J_)
  ENDDO                                    D(I,J) = D(I,J) + VAL_B(J_)
ENDDO                                    ENDDO
                                       ENDDO
```

[2] Encapsulation of a conjunction or disjunction of guards could be implemented efficiently if an ordering is imposed on the entries in each sparse vector using an **in-phase scan** [13, p20-21]. Because the selection of ordered sparse storage is not supported by the sparse compiler, however, these constructs are not further considered.

In the following two fragments, the nonzero structure of each row of A is obtained by respectively performing an or- and and-operation to the nonzero structure of the original row of A and the corresponding row of B, as illustrated in figure 1:

```
      REAL A(M,N), B(M,N)
C_SPARSE(A ; B)
      ...
      DO I = 1, M
        DO J = 1, N
          A(I,J) = A(I,J) + B(I,J)
        ENDDO
      ENDDO
```

```
      REAL A(M,N), B(M,N)
C_SPARSE(A ; B)
      ...
      DO I = 1, M
        DO J = 1, N
          A(I,J) = A(I,J) * B(I,J)
        ENDDO
      ENDDO
```

Because condition '(I, J) $\in E(B)$' is associated with the assignment statement in the first loop, the sparse compiler implements $A \leftarrow A + B$ as follows if general sparse row-wise storage is selected for both implicitly sparse matrices:

```
DO I = 1, M
  CALL SSCT__(VAL_A, IND_A, LOW_A(I), HGH_A(I), SAP_10, SWT_10)
  DO J_ = LOW_B(I), HGH_B(I)
    J = IND_B(J_)
    IF (.NOT.SWT_10(J)) THEN
      SWT_10(J) = .TRUE.
      CALL SINS__(VAL_A, IND_A, LOW_A, HGH_A, I, NP_A, SZ_A, LST_A, L_, J)
    END IF
    SAP_10(J) = SAP_10(J) + VAL_B(J_)
  ENDDO
  CALL SGTH__(VAL_A, IND_A, LOW_A(I), HGH_A(I), SAP_10, SWT_10)
ENDDO
```

Consequently, the OR-operation is implemented by iterating over the entries in a row of B after the corresponding row of A has been expanded. The switch array SWT_10 is used to determine where creation occurs. After all entries in a row of B have been considered, the entries in the expanded row of A are gathered back into a sparse vector. In fact, similar implementations are obtained for adding a number of implicitly sparse matrices if first update expression splitting and loop distribution are applied (cf. previous section). In essence, these automatically generated sparse implementations are similar to the code for adding sparse matrices found in [17, p242-247], although in the latter code, symbolic and numerical operations are separated.

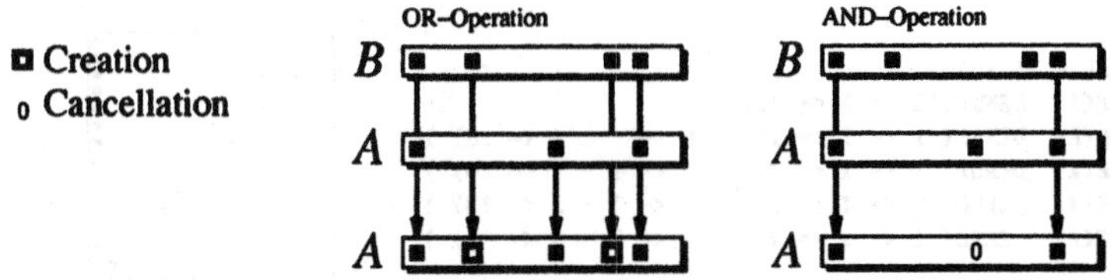

Fig. 1. OR- and AND-operation

Because condition '$(\mathtt{I},\mathtt{J}) \in E(A)$' is associated with the assignment statement in the second loop, the sparse compiler implements the scaling of matrix A with elements of B as follows if general sparse row-wise is selected for both A and B:

```
DO I = 1, M
  CALL SSCT__(VAL_B, IND_B, LOW_B(I), HGH_B(I), SAP_10, SWT_10)
  DO J_ = LOW_A(I), HGH_A(I)
    J = IND_A(J_)
    VAL_A(J_) = VAL_A(J_) * SAP_10(J)
  ENDDO
  CALL SGTH__(VAL_B, IND_B, LOW_B(I), HGH_B(I), SAP_10, SWT_10)
ENDDO
```

Hence, the situation is in fact handled as a simply dynamic operation by ignoring any cancellation caused by applying an AND-operation to the nonzero structures of a corresponding row of A and B (besides the fact that *exact* cancellation, where the subtraction of two entries is accidentally zero, is also ignored). A construct that resets some elements of the implicitly sparse matrix A is implemented similarly, i.e. the value of each entry in the regions that become zero is simply reset rather than deleting the entry explicitly, as shown below where we assume that $\mathtt{M} \leq \mathtt{N}$:

```
DO I = 1, M, 2                       DO I = 1, M, 2
  DO J = 1, I                          DO J_ = LOW_A(I), HGH_A(I)
    A(I,J) = 0.0          →              J = IND_A(J_)
  ENDDO                                  IF (J.LE.I) VAL_A(J_) = 0.0
ENDDO                                  ENDDO
                                     ENDDO
```

Structured Sparse Matrices Although in the previous section, efficient sparse code has been obtained for general sparse matrices, the sparse compiler becomes more powerful if particular characteristics of the nonzero structure of implicitly sparse matrices are accounted for during this conversion [2].

Suppose that the operation $\mathbf{b} \leftarrow \mathbf{b} + A\mathbf{x}$ is applied to a 15×15 implicitly sparse matrix A having the nonzero structure shown below. If at compile-time the matrix is available on file, the nonzero structure analyzer of the sparse compiler can identify the zero and dense regions in this matrix, and the programmer is inquired whether the zero regions will be preserved at run-time. If the matrix is not available at compile-time, this information can be supplied to the sparse compiler using the following annotations [2]:

```
      REAL A(15,15)
C_SPARSE(A: _DENSE(15 <= I <= 15))
C_SPARSE(A: _DENSE( 1 <= I <= 14,  15 <=      J <= 15) )
C_SPARSE(A: _DENSE( 1 <= I <= 14,   0 <= I - J <=  0) )
C_SPARSE(A:  _ZERO( 2 <= I <= 14,   1 <= I - J <= 13) )
C_SPARSE(A:  _ZERO( 1 <= J <= 14, -13 <= I - J <= -1) )
```

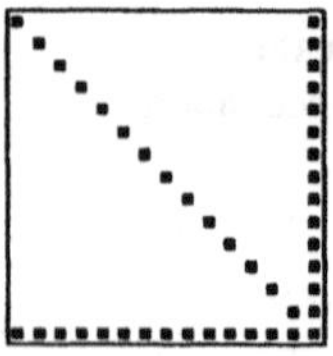

Subsequently, iteration space partitioning [2] is applied to the dense implementation to separate operations on zero regions from operations on dense regions:

```
DO I = 1, 15
  DO J = 1, 15
    B(I) = B(I) + A(I,J) * X(J)
  ENDDO
ENDDO
```

→

```
DO I = 1, 14
  DO J = 1, I-1
    B(I) = B(I) + A(I,J) * X(J)
  ENDDO
  B(I) = B(I) + A(I,I) * X(I)
  DO J = I+1, 14
    B(I) = B(I) + A(I,J) * X(J)
  ENDDO
  B(I) = B(I) + A(I,15) * X(15)
ENDDO
DO J = 1, 15
  B(15) = B(15) + A(15,J) * X(J)
ENDDO
```

Because this iteration space partitioning is successful, the sparse compiler decides to use the following static dense storage for the dense regions of A:

```
REAL       DN1_A(1:14), DN2_A(1:14), DN3_A(1:15)
COMMON /A/ DN1_A,       DN2_A,       DN3_A
```

Thereafter, all occurrences of A are either replaced by a zero constant or by an appropriate occurrence of this static dense storage. Finally, the condition of each statement in which such a replacement occurs is re-computed (thereby accounting for the constant zero and the fact that *all* elements in dense storage are entries), and redundant assignment statements and DO-loops are eliminated at compile-time:

```
DO I = 1, 14
  DO J = 1, I-1
    B(I) = B(I) + 0.0 * X(J)          ← false
  ENDDO
  B(I) = B(I) + DN2_A(I) * X(I)       ← true
  DO J = I+1, 14
    B(I) = B(I) + 0.0 * X(J)          ← false
  ENDDO
  B(I) = B(I) + DN1_A(I) * X(15)      ← true
ENDDO
DO J = 1, 15
  B(15) = B(15) + DN3_A(J) * X(J)     ← true
ENDDO
```

→

```
DO I = 1, 14
  B(I)  = B(I)  + DN2_A(I) * X(I)
  B(I)  = B(I)  + DN1_A(I) * X(15)
ENDDO
DO J = 1, 15
  B(15) = B(15) + DN3_A(J) * X(J)
ENDDO
```

Hence, the original dense implementation has been automatically converted into an implementation that is specially tailored for the particular sparse matrix. Obviously, if the characteristics of the nonzero structure that can be exploited become more complex, the transformations required to do such a conversion also become more complex [2]. This strongly motivates the use of a sparse compiler to perform this conversion.

2.3 Subroutines and Functions

Procedure cloning [8] enables the sparse compiler to apply program and data structure transformations to the code and formal arguments in all procedure clones without interfering with other uses of these subroutines and functions [2]. Because procedure cloning usually improves the results of inter-procedural constant propagation, loop bounds and subscript functions involving formal arguments may become admissible, which enables the application of more accurate program analysis and transformations.

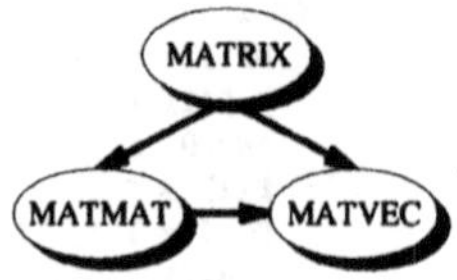

Fig. 2. Call Graph of Program **MATRIX**

Consider, for example, the following program in which annotations are used to inform the compiler about the fact that array **A** is used as enveloping data structure of an implicitly sparse matrix A in diagonal form, i.e. $a_{ij} \neq 0 \Rightarrow i = j$:

```
      PROGRAM MATRIX

      INTEGER     M, N
      PARAMETER  (M = 50, N = 100)

      REAL        A(M,M), B(M,M), C(M,M)
      REAL        D(N,N), E(N,N)
      REAL        X(N),    Y(N)

C_SPARSE(A: _ZERO ( 1-M <= I - J <=  -1))
C_SPARSE(A: _DENSE(   0 <= I - J <=   0))
C_SPARSE(A: _ZERO (   1 <= I - J <= M-1))
      ...
      CALL MATMAT(A, B, C, M)
      CALL MATMAT(D, D, E, N)
      CALL MATVEC(E, X, Y, N)
      ...

      END
```

```
      SUBROUTINE MATMAT(H, F, G, N)
      INTEGER N, I
      REAL    H(N,N), F(N,N), G(N,N)
      DO I = 1, N
       CALL MATVEC(H, F(1,I), G(1,I), N)
      ENDDO
      RETURN
      END

      SUBROUTINE MATVEC(H, R, S, N)
      INTEGER N, I, J
      REAL    H(N,N), R(N), S(N)
      DO I = 1, N
        DO J = 1, N
          S(I) = S(I) + H(I,J) * R(J)
        ENDDO
      ENDDO
      RETURN
      END
```

The call graph of this program is shown in figure 2. Here, the sparse compiler cannot bluntly apply data structure transformations to the formal arguments H in **MATMAT** and **MATVEC**, because these subroutines are also used to perform operations involving dense matrices. Therefore, the sparse compiler generates a clone **MATMAT_A000** of the subroutine **MATMAT** in which **A** is uniquely associated with the formal argument H. Moreover, since the clone calls **MATVEC** with H as first actual argument, a clone **MATVEC_A000** of **MATVEC** is also generated. The original subroutines are preserved to perform the operations $E \leftarrow E + DD$ and $\mathbf{y} \leftarrow \mathbf{y} + E\mathbf{x}$, whereas the clones are used to compute $C \leftarrow C + AB$.

If static dense storage is selected for the main diagonal of A, this data structure is placed in a named COMMON block, and the main program is converted as shown below, where the argument used to pass the whole implicitly sparse matrix has been eliminated:

```
PROGRAM MATRIX
...
REAL        DN1_A(1:50)
COMMON /A/ DN1_A
...
CALL MATMAT_A000(B, C, N)
CALL MATMAT      (D, D, E, N)
CALL MATVEC      (E, X, Y, N)
...
END
```

After iteration space partitioning has been applied to the procedure clones, and redundant assignment statements and DO-loops have been eliminated at compile-time, the sparse code shown below results. Inter-procedural constant propagation has derived the value N=50 and the formal argument H has been either eliminated or replaced by an occurrence of the selected storage scheme, made available to the subroutines using the named COMMON-block:

```
SUBROUTINE MATMAT_A000(F, G, N)
INTEGER       N, I
REAL          F(50,50), G(50,50)
REAL          DN1_A(1: 50)
COMMON  /A/ DN1_A

DO I = 1, 50
  CALL MATVEC_A000(F(1,I), G(1,I), 50)
ENDDO
RETURN
END
```

```
SUBROUTINE MATVEC_A000(R, S, N)
INTEGER       N, I, J
REAL          R(50), S(50)
REAL          DN1_A(1:50)
COMMON  /A/ DN1_A

DO I = 1, 50
  S(I) = S(I) + DN1_A(I) * R(I)
ENDDO
RETURN
END
```

A subroutine computing the product of A with another matrix and a subroutine computing the product of A with a vector tailored for the specific nonzero structure of A has been derived automatically.

2.4 An Example: Forward and Back Substitution

After a matrix A has been factorized into $A = LU$, a system $A\mathbf{x} = \mathbf{b}$ is solved by forward substitution of the system $L\mathbf{c} = \mathbf{b}$, followed by back substitution of $U\mathbf{x} = \mathbf{c}$. Dense implementations of forward and back substitution, where an in-place conversion of the vector **b** into **x** is performed, are shown below:

Forward Substitution:

```
DO I = 2, N
  DO J = 1, I-1
    B(I) = B(I) - A(I,J) * B(J)
  ENDDO
ENDDO
```

Back Substitution:

```
DO I = N, 1, -1
  DO J = I+1, N
    B(I) = B(I) - A(I,J) * B(J)
  ENDDO
  B(I) = B(I) / A(I,I)
ENDDO
```

If an annotation enforcing general sparse row-wise storage of A is used, the sparse compiler converts these fragments into the following sparse codes:

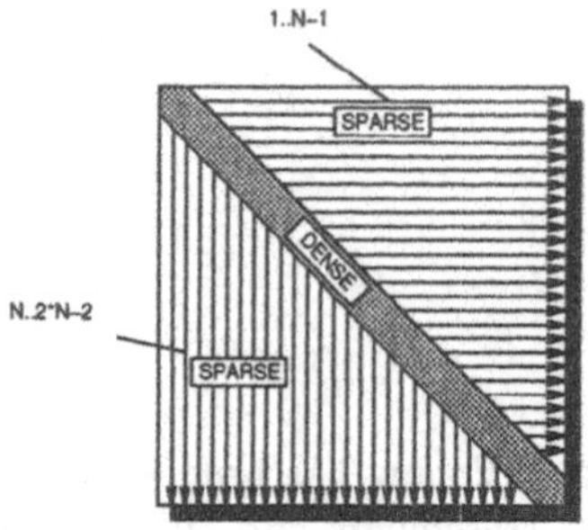

Fig. 3. LDU-Scheme

Sparse Forward:

```
DO I = 2, N
  DO J_ = LOW_A(I), HGH_A(I)
    J = IND_A(J_)
    IF (J.LE.I-1) THEN
      B(I) = B(I) - VAL_A(J_) * B(J)
    END IF
  ENDDO
ENDDO
```

Sparse Back:

```
 DO I = N, 1, -1
   IF (I+1.LE.N) THEN
     DO J_ = LOW_A(I), HGH_A(I)
       J = IND_A(J_)
       IF (I+1.LE.J) THEN
         B(I) = B(I) - VAL_A(J_) * B(J)
       END IF
     ENDDO
   ENDIF
   B(I) = B(I) / VAL_A( LKP__(IND_A,
+              LOW_A(I), HGH_A(I), I) )
 ENDDO
```

Note that although the resulting fragments strongly resemble the code generated for the product of a sparse matrix with a vector, there are some differences. First, a lookup is required in the back substitution, because the true diagonal-wise access patterns of `A(I,I)` are inconsistent with the way in which the entries of A are stored. Moreover, because the execution set of the J-loop is empty for `I=N`, the generated `J_`-loop is protected by the test '`(I+1.LE.N)`' to prevent erroneous accesses to entries in the `N`th row of the sparse matrix (although the test could be safely omitted for this particular example).[3] Finally, because *all* entries in a row are stored in a single sparse vector, the test '`(I+1.LE.J)`' remains required in the innermost DO-loop of both versions to distinguish between entries in the strict lower and upper triangular part of the matrix respectively. The fragments still exploit the sparsity of A, however, because in contrast with using the test '`(A(I,J).NE.0.0)`' in the dense case, the test in the sparse versions is only executed for entries.

If annotations enforcing the selection of a so-called LDU-scheme in which the strict lower and strict upper triangular part of the matrix are stored dynamically as a set of column- and row-wise sparse vectors, whereas static dense storage is used for the main diagonal, as illustrated in figure 3, then the sparse compiler uses loop interchanging to derive the following sparse code:

[3] The generation of this test can be avoided by peeling one iteration of the `I`-loop.

LDU Forward:

```
DO J = 1, N-1
  DO I_ = LOW_A(J+N-1), HGH_A(J+N-1)
    I = IND_A(I_)
    B(I) = B(I) - VAL_A(I_) * B(J)
  ENDDO
ENDDO
```

LDU Back:

```
DO I = N, 1, -1
  IF (I+1.LT.N) THEN
    DO J_ = LOW_A(I), HGH_A(I)
      J = IND_A(J_)
      B(I) = B(I) - VAL_A(J_) * B(J)
    ENDDO
  ENDIF
  B(I) = B(I) / DN1_A(I)
ENDDO
```

Loop interchanging has, in fact, converted the inner product formulation of forward substitution into an outer product formulation [14, p25-28]. Now, no test is required in the body of the J_-loops because entries in the strict lower and strict upper triangular part of A are stored in separate sparse vectors. Moreover, because static dense storage is used for the main diagonal of A, the lookup in back substitution vanishes. However, in this case it is essential to protect the whole J_-loop of back substitution with the test '(I+1.LE.N)', because otherwise the Nth sparse vector would be erroneously accessed, thereby inducing accesses to the first column of A.

Finally, if, for example, we know that the implicitly sparse matrix is a band matrix with semi-bandwidths 5, then we can supply this information to the sparse compiler using the following annotations:

```
      REAL      A(N,N)
C_SPARSE(A : _ZERO (1-N <= I-J <=  -6))
C_SPARSE(A : _DENSE( -5 <= I-J <=   5))
C_SPARSE(A : _ZERO (  6 <= I-J <= N-1))
```

In this case, the sparse compiler converts the original dense algorithms into the following sparse fragments:

Band Forward:

```
DO I = 2, N
  DO J = MAX(1, I-5), I-1
    B(I) = B(I) - DN1_A(J,I-J) * B(J)
  ENDDO
ENDDO
```

Band Back:

```
DO I = N, 1, -1
  DO J = I+1, MIN(N, I+5)
    B(I) = B(I) - DN1_A(J,I-J) * B(J)
  ENDDO
  B(I) = B(I) / DN1_A(I,0)
ENDDO
```

Due to data dependences, the access patterns cannot be reshaped along the diagonals. However, iteration space partitioning and the compile-time elimination of redundant assignment statements and DO-loops is still applicable to the innermost DO-loop, which also reduces the amount of operations that must be executed. Similar implementations of forward and back substitution can found in SPARSKIT and SPARK [19, 20] and in [1][17, p268-270][18].

3 Conclusions

Although developing and maintaining sparse codes is a complex and cumbersome task, only limited compiler support for sparse matrix computations has been developed in the past. We have tried to solve this omission by proposing an alternative method to develop sparse codes.

Rather than dealing with the sparsity at the programming level, as is done traditionally, the sparsity of implicitly sparse matrices is dealt with at the compilation level by a sparse compiler. Elaboration of these ideas has resulted in the development and implementation of a sparse compiler. Some initial experiments have been conducted that indicate that in many cases the sparse compiler is capable of transforming a dense fragment into code that fully exploits the sparsity of some matrices to reduce both the storage requirements as well as computational time of the original implementation. Although more experiments and probably the development of more advanced transformations and strategies to control these transformations are required to determine whether a successful conversion is also feasible for large programs, these results already indicate that a sparse compiler can be very useful during development of a sparse algorithm.

On the other hand, initial experimentation revealed shortcomings that should be fixed before sparse compilers provide a serious full alternative to explicitly dealing with sparsity at the programming level. First, although for many operations that occur frequently in numerical programs, at least one obvious dense implementation exists that is handled appropriately by the sparse compiler, there are also some operations for which any obvious dense implementation becomes translated into extremely inefficient sparse code. Any dense formulation of matrix transposition, for example, is transformed into extremely inefficient sparse code (cf. [2, ch11]). This is in strong contrast with the extremely efficient implementations of transposition that are possible for many sparse storage schemes. (see e.g. [15][17, p236-239], where applying these algorithms twice to a sparse representation can even be used to obtain *ordered* storage). Apparently there are some constructs that must be recognized explicitly by the sparse compiler to enable the generation of efficient sparse code. Another problem is that for larger problems, conflicts may arise that cannot be resolved. In these cases, it may be necessary to generate constructs that alter data structures at run-time. Finally, the current sparse compiler only has limited support to incorporate sparsity reordering methods that reduce the amount of fill-in.

Despite these shortcomings, however, we would like to stress that for many small fragments, the sparse compiler enabled us to rapidly obtain reasonably efficient sparse code which, if desired, could be further improved by hand. Consequently, even if not all shortcomings are solved in a future implementation, using a sparse compiler as a programming tool to develop new sparse algorithms seems to have some potential.

References

1. Edward Anderson and Youcef Saad. Solving sparse triangular linear systems on parallel computers. *International Journal of High Speed Computing*, 1(6):73–95, 1989.
2. Aart J.C. Bik. *Compiler Support for Sparse Matrix Computations*. PhD thesis, Department of Computer Science, Leiden University, 1996. ISBN 90-9009442-3.
3. Aart J.C. Bik and Harry A.G. Wijshoff. On automatic data structure selection and code generation for sparse computations. In Utpal Banerjee, David Gelernter, Alex

Nicolau, and David Padua, editors, *Lecture Notes in Computer Science, No. 768*, pages 57–75. Springer-Verlag, 1994.

4. Aart J.C. Bik and Harry A.G. Wijshoff. Advanced compiler optimizations for sparse computations. *Journal of Parallel and Distributed Computing*, 31:14–24, 1995.
5. Aart J.C. Bik and Harry A.G. Wijshoff. Automatic data structure selection and transformation for sparse matrix computations. *IEEE Transactions on Parallel and Distributed Systems*, 7(2):109–126, 1996.
6. Aart J.C. Bik and Harry A.G. Wijshoff. Simple *Quantitative* experiments with a sparse compiler. In A. Ferreira, J. Rolim, Y.Saad, and T. Yang, editors, *Lecture Notes in Computer Science, No. 1117*, pages 249–262. Springer-Verlag, 1996.
7. Aart J.C. Bik and Harry A.G. Wijshoff. The use of iteration space partitioning to construct representative simple sections. *Journal of Parallel and Distributed Computing*, 34:95–110, 1996.
8. Keith D. Cooper, Mary W. Hall, and Ken Kennedy. Procedure cloning. In *Proceedings of the IEEE International Conference on Computer Languages*, pages 96–105, 1992.
9. B. Dembart and K.W. Neves. Sparse triangular factorization on vector computers. In *Exploring Applications of Parallel Processing*, pages 22–25, 1977.
10. David S. Dodson, Roger G. Grimes, and John G. Lewis. Algorithm 692: Model implementation and test package for the sparse linear algebra subprograms. *ACM Transactions on Mathematical Software*, 17:264–272, 1991.
11. David S. Dodson, Roger G. Grimes, and John G. Lewis. Sparse extensions to the Fortran basic linear algebra subprograms. *ACM Transactions on Mathematical Software*, 17:253–263, 1991.
12. Iain S. Duff. The solution of sparse linear equations on the CRAY-1. In J.S. Kowalik, editor, *High-Speed Computing*, pages 293–309. Springer-Verlag, 1984. NATO ASI Series, Volume F7.
13. Iain S. Duff, A.M. Erisman, and J.K. Reid. *Direct Methods for Sparse Matrices*. Oxford Science Publications, Oxford, 1990.
14. Alan George and Joseph W.H. Liu. *Computer Solution of Large Sparse Positive Definite Systems*. Prentice-Hall, Englewood Cliffs, New York, 1981.
15. Fred G. Gustavson. Two fast algorithms for sparse matrices: Multiplication and permuted transposition. *ACM Transactions on Mathematical Software*, 4:250–269, 1978.
16. John G. Lewis and Horst D. Simon. The impact of hardware gather/scatter on sparse Gaussian elimination. *SIAM J. Sci. Stat. Comput.*, Volume 9:304–311, 1988.
17. Sergio Pissanetsky. *Sparse Matrix Technology*. Academic Press, London, 1984.
18. Youcef Saad. Krylov subspace methods on supercomputers. *SIAM J. Sci. Stat. Comput.*, 10:1200–1232, 1989.
19. Youcef Saad. SPARSKIT: a basic tool kit for sparse matrix computations. CSRD/RIACS, 1990.
20. Youcef Saad and Harry A.G. Wijshoff. Spark: A benchmark package for sparse computations. In *Proceedings of the International Conference on Supercomputing*, pages 239–253, 1990.
21. Reginal P. Tewarson. *Sparse Matrices*. Academic Press, New York, 1973.
22. Zahari Zlatev. *Computational Methods for General Sparse Matrices*. Kluwer, Dordrecht, 1991.

Factor-Join: A Unique Approach to Compiling Array Languages for Parallel Machines*

Bradford L. Chamberlain   Sung-Eun Choi   E Christopher Lewis
Calvin Lin[†]   Lawrence Snyder   W. Derrick Weathersby

University of Washington, Seattle, WA 98195-2350 USA
[†] University of Texas, Austin, TX 78712 USA

Abstract. This paper describes a new approach to compiling and optimizing array languages for parallel machines. This approach first decomposes array language operations into *factors*, where each factor corresponds to a different communication or computation structure. Optimizations are then achieved by combining, or *joining*, these factors. Because factors preserve high level information about array operations, the analysis necessary to perform these join operations is simpler than that required for scalar programs. In particular, we show how data parallel programs written in the ZPL programming language are compiled and optimized using the *factor-join* approach, and we show that a small number of factors are sufficient to represent ZPL programs.

1 Introduction

Array languages such as Fortran 90 and ZPL introduce compilation issues not encountered in the context of scalar languages such as Fortran 77 or C. Certain problems vanish, others become more complicated, and still others call for techniques not previously available. This paper shows how compilers can exploit this new context. Using the ZPL compiler as an example, we describe a new approach to compiling array languages that is particularly useful when compiling for parallel machines.

To see how an array language can simplify the compilation process, consider the problem of generating explicit interprocessor communication from a scalar language. One challenging problem in compiling scalar Fortran 77 code is performing *message vectorization* [9]—the transmission of multiple values in a single message rather than in separate messages. In scalar languages, the base unit of computation is a single value, and communication is generated per-value, making vectorization an optimization task. But in array languages the unit of computation is a contiguous sub-array, resulting in natural and automatic vectorization, as illustrated in Fig. 1.

To illustrate how an array language's high-level concepts motivate new optimizations, consider ZPL's reduce operators which combine data elements of

* This research was supported in part by ARPA Grant N00014-92-J-1824.

an array using an associative operator such as plus, logical-and, or minimum. The implementation of reduce requires local computation, a global reduction, and a broadcast. The communication components of consecutive reduces can be merged to yield significant performance improvements in much the same way that message vectorization optimizes access to consecutive scalar values. This optimization is illustrated in Fig. 2. In scalar languages, there is little chance for the compiler to optimize communication in this way. Even if the reduce concept is abstracted to a procedure, it is difficult for a compiler to recognize, much less realize, the *opportunity* to perform the optimization.

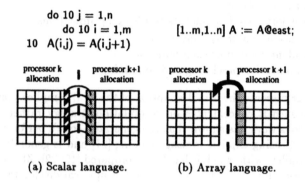

```
      do 10 j = 1,n
        do 10 i = 1,m
10    A(i,j) = A(i,j+1)
```

```
[1..m,1..n] A := A@east;
```

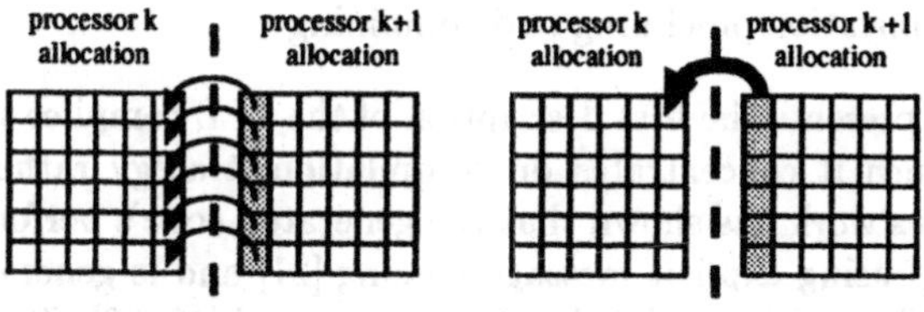

(a) Scalar language. (b) Array language.

Fig. 1. Message vectorization in parallelized Fortran 77 and ZPL.

The ZPL compiler achieves these sorts of optimizations with the *factor-join* compilation strategy in which each array operation is decomposed into basic components called *factors*. Each factor describes an elementary computation or data transfer operation, and subsequent analyses manipulate and *join* these factors as optimizations. Though more basic than ZPL array operations, the

(a) ZPL source:

```
minvel := min<<Vel;

maxvel := max<<Vel;
```

(b) Naive code generation:

```
t = DBL_MAX;
for (i=mylow; i<myhi; i++)
    t = min(t,Vel[i]);
Glob_Reduce(<t,min>);
Broadcast(<t,minvel>);
t = -DBL_MAX;
for (i=mylow; i<myhi; i++)
    t = max(t,Vel[i]);
Glob_Reduce(<t,max>);
Broadcast(<t,maxvel>);
```

(c) Optimized code generation:

```
t1 = DBL_MAX;
for (i=mylow; i<myhi; i++)
    t1 = min(t,Vel[i]);

t2 = -DBL_MAX;
for (i=mylow; i<myhi; i++)
    t2 = max(t2,Vel[i]);
Glob_Reduce(<t1,min>,<t2,max>);
Broadcast(<t1, minvel>,<t2, maxvel>);
```

(a) ZPL source. (b) Naive code generation. (c) Optimized code generation.

Fig. 2. Combining the communication portions of reductions. Notice the reduce operators in the ZPL source (a): min<< and max<<.

factors preserve the source code's high-level semantics. In contrast to this high level approach the IBM HPF compiler may lose semantic information because it *scalarizes* Fortran 90 array structures early in the compilation process [12].

The ZPL compiler thus employs standard compilation concepts and techniques, but extends them to exploit the language's abstractions and to treat arrays atomically. Our presentation of the ZPL compiler will assume an understanding of scalar compilation and concentrate only on areas of difference. These include the following.

- Internal representations, particularly the AST
- Run-time assumptions about the virtual machine
- Phases of compilation
- The factor-join technique and its resulting optimizations
  - loop fusion and array contraction
  - redundant communication removal
  - communication pipelining and combining

This paper presents the first description of the ZPL compiler's internal workings, and as such it concentrates on compilation strategy rather than performance. Previous work has shown that the generated code's performance is comparable with C using explicit message-passing [21] and is generally superior to the HPF compilers with which it has been compared [19, 22]. ZPL has also been successfully used for scientific and engineering applications [8, 18, 24], and its compiler is available on the Web.[2]

The remainder of this paper is structured as follows. Section 2 briefly introduces basic ZPL language concepts—more complete descriptions are available elsewhere [27, 20]. Section 3 describes runtime assumptions that are used in the compilation process. The compilation process itself is described in Sect. 4, with an emphasis on its structure and use of the factor-join strategy. Section 5 discusses the details of joining, and the final two sections present related work and conclusions.

2 ZPL Language Summary

ZPL is an implicitly parallel array language designed for scientific computations [27]. It is an imperative language, supporting standard data types (integer, float, char, etc.), standard operators (+, -, $*$, etc.), C-like assignment operators (+=, $*$=, etc.), procedures with by-value and by-reference parameters, recursion, a standard set of control constructs (if, for, while, etc.), and C-like I/O.

In addition, ZPL provides a number of abstractions and operations designed to simplify programming while promoting efficiency. *Regions* are a fundamental concept, implicitly specifying the parallelism in a ZPL program. A region is a set of indices and can be declared as follows. (Any text to the right of – – is a comment.)

[2] URL: http://www.cs.washington.edu/research/projects/zpl/

region R = [1..m, 1..n]; -- Declare R={(1,1), (1,2),..., (m,n)}

Regions are used to declare arrays as follows.

var A: [R] float; -- A is an m × n array of floats

Region specifiers prefix statements to define the extent of array operations. A statement whose arrays are of rank *r* requires a region specifier of rank *r*, and the array indices for which the statement is executed are the indices in the region specifier. For example, the following statement assigns the value 1 to the elements of A for the indices R = {(1,1), (1,2),..., (m,n)}.

[R] A := 1;

Dynamically scoped region specifiers allow a procedure either to supply region specifiers explicitly in its body or to inherit them from the call site. Thus, procedures can be written in a region-independent fashion and execute over different regions with each call.

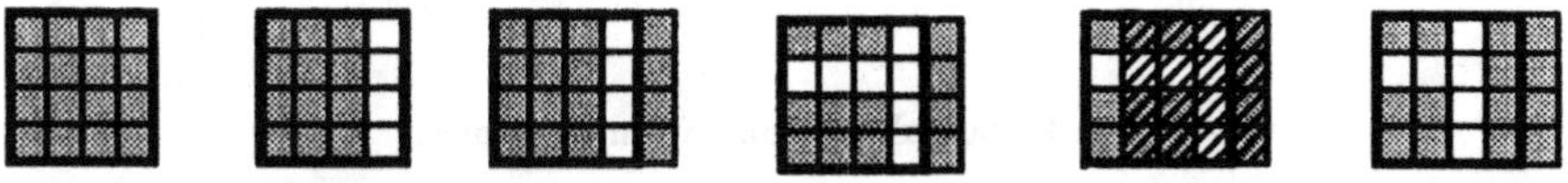

[R] A:=1 (a) [east in R] A:=0 (b) [east of R] A:=1 (c) [2,1..n] A:=0 (d) [R] ... A@east ... (e) [R] A := A@east (f)

Fig. 3. Sequence of region usage examples. Grey boxes represent the value 1 and white represents 0. The hashed area in (e) represents the elements referred to by A@east.

Regions can be expressed and manipulated in a variety of ways. Figure 3 shows a sequence of operations which use A, R and n as defined above, and east = [0,1]. Array and region names are capitalized, while scalar variables are not. In Fig. 3(a), an array assignment, as just described, sets the R region of A, to 1. Next, an assignment over the region east in R sets the column *inside* the east border to 0. In 3(c), the region east of R causes the implicit allocation of a new column adjacent to, but outside of, the east border and sets it to 1. *Dynamic regions* bind their indices at runtime. The *dynamic region* [2,1..n] in 3(d) specifies that the first n elements of the second row be set to 0. The @-operator translates the specified region, in this case R, by adding the *direction* to all indices in the region, so Fig. 3(e) uses diagonal hashing to indicate the values referenced by A@east. In 3(f), the hashed portion of the array is assigned into A, shifting the array. Notice that the values in the east of R region are unchanged because they are outside of the applied region R.

ZPL supports a full set of reduce and scan (parallel prefix) operators. For example, the following statement *reduces* A to the value of its largest element using the max reduction operator (max<<) and assigns the value to the scalar biggest.

biggest := max<<A; -- Find largest element

Other reduction operations include min<<, +<<, *<<, and &<<. Scan is similar to reduce, but it produces an array of the same shape and size as its operand, and each element contains the result of the reduction over all lower indexed elements (in row-major order).

Biggest_so_far := max||A; -- Scan finding progressively larger items

ZPL also has partial reduces and scans that apply an operator over a subset of the array's dimensions (see Fig. 4). The dimensions in brackets indicate the subset of dimensions to scan across.

1 1 1	1 2 3	1 1 1	1 2 3
1 1 1	1 2 3	2 2 2	4 5 6
1 1 1	1 2 3	3 3 3	7 8 9
A	+||[2]A	+||[1]A	+||A

Fig. 4. Partial scan operation examples.

The concepts introduced up to this point are sufficient for understanding the sample scientific computation shown in Fig. 5. This code takes as input a vector containing the sampled coordinates of an object at various times (SampleT, SampleXPos, SampleYPos). It assumes the object was at the origin at time 0 (lines 18-22) and computes the approximate velocity of the object for each sampled interval (lines 23-28). It then applies reduction operators to determine the object's minimum and maximum velocities (lines 29-30). This program will serve as a running example throughout the paper. A complete listing is provided in Appendix A.

In addition to the above operations, ZPL contains a number of expressive abstractions for array manipulation. Due to space limitations, we only give a brief survey below, but complete information is available elsewhere [27, 20].

- *Shattered control flow* – ZPL has sequential control flow as long as control statements involve only scalars (e.g., if (scalar=1) then...). Control flow can also be specified using arrays, (e.g., [R] if (Array=1) then...), so that each index in the region is given a concurrently-executing thread of control.
- *Flooding* – Arrays can be declared to be ***floodable***, causing certain dimensions to be replicated for all indices (e.g., var F:[1..m,*] float;). The flood operator (>>[R]) can be used to assign rows or columns (indicated by region R) of an array to a floodable array. For example:

  [1..m,*] F := >>[1..m,4]A; -- Flood F with column 4 of A

```
. . .
direction prev = [-1];
. . .
region R = [1..samplecount];
var SampleT, SampleXPos, SampleYPos : [R] double;
    DeltaT, DeltaXPos, DeltaYPos    : [R] double;
    XVel,YVel                       : [R] double;
    Vel                             : [R] double;
procedure VelocityStats();
          var minvel,maxvel : double;
          . . .
[R]       begin
            . . .
[prev of R]  begin
                SampleT := 0.0;
                SampleXPos := 0.0;
                SampleYPos := 0.0;
             end;
             DeltaT := SampleT - SampleT@prev;
             DeltaXPos := SampleXPos - SampleXPos@prev;
             DeltaYPos := SampleYPos - SampleYPos@prev;
             XVel := DeltaXPos/DeltaT;
             YVel := DeltaYPos/DeltaT;
             Vel := sqrt(XVel*XVel + YVel*YVel);
             minvel := min<<Vel;
             maxvel := max<<Vel;
             . . .
          end;
```

Fig. 5. Excerpt from running example in Appendix A. This ZPL code computes approximate minimum and maximum velocities of a particle from a vector of sampled positions and times.

Since F is a flood array, it has no specific number of columns, and only a single copy of its defining values is stored at each processor. This provides a highly efficient way to refer to substructures of an array. For example, after column 4 of A has been flooded into F (above), the statement [R] A:=A*F has the effect of multiplying each column of A by column 4.

- *Reflect/Wrap* – Operations are provided to simplify the computation of boundary values. When invoked in the context of an of or in region specifier, reflect and wrap cause the array's values in that region to be filled with those mirrored across the border (reflect) or from the opposite side of the array (wrap).
- *Scalars/Arrays/Indexed Arrays* – Scalars are replicated and redundantly computed. ZPL has two kinds of arrays: parallel arrays (also referred to simply as "arrays") for which indexing is not needed, and indexed arrays for which indexing is required. Parallel arrays are distributed across all processors, while indexed arrays are replicated in the same manner as scalars. Indexed arrays are commonly used as elements of parallel arrays.

This concludes our introduction to ZPL. We note that the language's operators, though very regular and structured, can be combined in non-trivial ways to implement many scientific applications. The language is not ideally suited for certain applications, particularly highly irregular codes. These are handled by ZPL's more general parent language, *Advanced ZPL* [26].

3 The ZPL Runtime

Before describing the ZPL compiler, we state a few assumptions about ZPL's runtime environment. In ZPL, the region is the basis for a program's implied parallelism. In the current implementation, the union of all regions' index sets is block distributed across a two dimensional processor mesh. Each array is allocated based on this block distribution, so all array elements with the same indices are allocated to the same processor.

This assumption leads to the trivial identification of communication—both for the compiler and the user. For example, line 28 of the running example (Vel := sqrt(XVel*XVel + YVel*YVel);) can be executed in parallel because corresponding elements of arrays Vel, XVel, and YVel are known to reside on the same processor. The shifted array reference in Line 23 (DeltaT := SampleT - SampleT@prev;) will require point-to-point communication to transfer non-local values of SampleT to adjacent processors. As a final example, line 29 (minvel := min<<Vel;) computes the minimum-reduction using collective communication involving all processors. This identification of necessary communication is crucial to the compiler's factor-join scheme, as will be seen in Sect. 4.

Although arbitrary alignment is not supported, certain optimizations, such as aligning only interacting arrays, are straightforward extensions. However, in the common case, a single global distribution scheme has proven very effective. The use of a two-dimensional block distribution of higher-dimensional regions was a decision of convenience that results in effective compilation for the common case. Higher-dimensional and alternative (e.g., cyclic, block-cyclic) distributions are a relatively straightforward extension to the existing compiler.

4 Compiler Overview

This section describes how the ZPL compiler transforms ZPL source code into a loosely synchronous SPMD C program that can then be compiled and run on any target machine. The bulk of the work is in compiling array operations into an efficient distributed scalar implementation. Since source-level scalar operations are replicated on each processor, their compilation is straightforward and will receive little attention here.

The ZPL compiler first parses the ZPL source into an abstract syntax tree (AST). The compiler preserves the source program's high-level array operations, rather than *scalarizing* them, to allow the compiler to perform optimizations at the array level. The AST is not transformed into scalar code until the generation of the ANSI C output. Additional AST nodes are introduced during the compilation process, for example to explicitly represent data transfer that is implicitly specified by the source program.

After parsing, the compiler *normalizes* the AST to produce a more uniform AST and to eliminate complex interactions between the different types of array operations. Normalization breaks heterogeneous array statements (i.e., statements containing different varieties of array operations) into a number of simpler array statements by inserting temporary scalars or arrays.

The compiler then performs optimizations using the factor-join strategy. Each normalized statement is decomposed into factors, where each factor represents an elementary array operation involving either local computation (*C-factors*) or interprocessor data transfer (*T-factors*). Because each factor represents a particular communication or computation structure, factors of the same type can always be joined. The joining of the various types of factors is discussed in Sect. 5. Figure 6 summarizes the factorization of the different types of ZPL array statements.

1	S_{array}	$\rightarrow$	$T^*_{pp} \cdot C$
2	S_{wrap}	$\rightarrow$	T_{pp}
3	$S_{reflect}$	$\rightarrow$	T_{pp}
4	S_{reduce}	$\rightarrow$	$C \cdot T_{gr} \cdot T_{bc}$
5	S_{scan}	$\rightarrow$	$C \cdot T_{gs} \cdot (C \cdot T_{gs})^* \cdot (C \cdot T_{bc} \cdot C)^* \cdot C$
6	S_{flood}	$\rightarrow$	T_{bc}

Key
C : Computation
T : Transfer
  pp : point-to-point
  bc : broadcast
  gr : global reduce
  gs : global scan
* : zero or more

Fig. 6. Rules for factoring the different types of array statements.

As an example of factorization, the compiler classifies line 28 (Vel:=sqrt(XVel*XVel+YVel*YVel);) of the running example (Fig. 5) as an element-wise array statement (S_{array}) and factors it using rule 1 (Fig. 6). This statement requires no data transfer because no communication-inducing operators are used. Thus, the compiler expands the statement into a single C-factor and no T-factors.

The correspondence between C-factors and local computation simplifies subsequent analysis. Each C-factor is represented by a *multi-loop* (or *m-loop*) node that encapsulates all information needed to generate object code, including the region over which the statement is executed and the code that forms the loop body. The AST node that is generated for this example is shown in Fig. 7(a).

As another example, consider line 23 (Delta:=SampleT-SampleT@prev;) of the running example. This statement is also classified as an array statement but requires communication because it uses the @-operator, so a multi-part T-factor representing point-to-point communication (T_{pp}) is inserted prior to its C-factor. This T-factor is represented in the AST using Send and Receive nodes[3] that

[3] The ZPL compiler actually uses the IRONMAN communication interface which is more hardware independent than a send/receive interface [7]. By using machine-dependent libraries and an unassuming interface, IRONMAN allows the same ZPL object code to exploit each machine's customized interprocessor communication features. This document uses send/receive for simplicity.

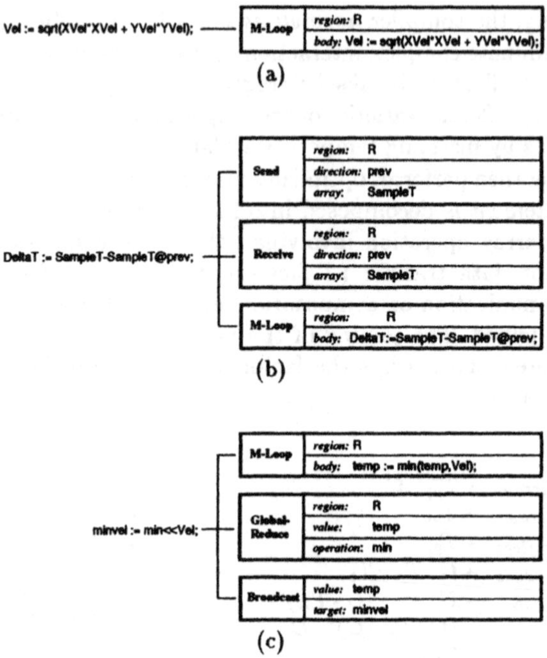
Vel := sqrt(XVel*XVel + YVel*YVel);
M-Loop
region: R
body: Vel := sqrt(XVel*XVel + YVel*YVel);
(a)
DeltaT := SampleT-SampleT@prev;
Send
region: R
direction: prev
array: SampleT
Receive
region: R
direction: prev
array: SampleT
M-Loop
region: R
body: DeltaT:=SampleT-SampleT@prev;
(b)
minvel := min<<Vel;
M-Loop
region: R
body: temp := min(temp,Vel);
Global-Reduce
region: R
value: temp
operation: min
Broadcast
value: temp
target: minvel
(c)

Fig. 7. ZPL source code and the corresponding factored AST. Note that the various node properties (e.g., *region*, *direction*, *body*) are actually pointers to symbol table entries or other parts of the AST.

describe the region, array, and direction of data transfer (Fig. 7(b)).

Some operators are translated into multiple factors. For example, the reduction in line 29 (minvel:=min<<Vel;) of the running example is factored (by rule 4, Fig. 6) into a C-factor that computes the local result for each processor and two T-factors: one to combine the local results into a global result (T_{gr}) and a second to broadcast the global result to all processors (T_{bc}). AST nodes are inserted for each of these factors, as shown in Fig. 7(c).

5 Joining Factors

This section describes how the ZPL compiler performs optimizations by manipulating C-factors and T-factors. The optimization process is simplified because only a small number of C- and T-factors are needed to represent any array operation, and because inter-statement optimizations can take place without having to consider how the many different types of array statements may interact.

5.1 Local Computation: M-Loops

As the only type of C-factor (i.e., the only way to iterate over arrays), m-loops represent the local portions of any array statement, including element-wise assignment, reductions, scans, etc. Thus, optimizing this single factor can yield substantial performance improvement. In the final compilation step, an m-loop is translated into a loop nest that executes on each processor and iterates over that processor's portion of the applicable region.

When a loop nest is generated from an m-loop, the compiler determines the nest depth, determined by the rank of the region, and iteration direction of each generated loop, as constrained by the body of the m-loop. These constraints arise from data dependences and semantic restrictions. Specifically, m-loops introduced by array statements are initially only semantically constrained, i.e., the right-hand side expression is evaulated before the left-hand side. (It is precisely this property that allows these operations to be directly parallelized.) M-loops introduced by reduce and scan operators induce a pseudo dependence due to the accumulation via an associative operator. The joining of factors introduces additional constraints, because additional dependences must be preserved.

Joining M-loops. The joining of m-loop factors has the effect of fusing loops in the object C code. Determining whether two m-loops may be legally joined is similar to the data dependence analysis required to fuse two loop nests [28]: (1) both m-loops must iterate over the same region, and (2) for the joined m-loop there must exist a loop nest that preserves the unjoined data dependences and respects semantic restrictions. This join transformation differs from traditional loop fusion in that the structure of the candidate loop nests is not fixed when the joining decision is made. There are a number of benefits to joining m-loops. Some are traditional, e.g., improved cache locality [6] and reduced loop overhead, and others are unique to the array language context, e.g., joining enables *contraction* of an array to a scalar when the array's definition only reaches uses in the same iteration.

Array Contraction. Array contraction is a well-known technique for scalar languages [28], but it is more important for array languages because the programmer has no control over the structure of the compiler-generated loops. This leads to a potential performance problem since the programmer cannot cache an array value in a *scalar* for later use in the same iteration of a loop, a common technique employed in scalar languages. Instead, the array language programmer must use whole arrays as temporaries (e.g., array Vel in the running example), which waste memory, induce contention in the data cache, and ultimately slow execution of the program. For the programmer, the only alternative to these intermediate arrays is to introduce redundant computation.

Consider the code fragment in Fig. 8(a). Figure 8(b) shows the naive code that is generated when factors are not joined. Notice that arrays XVel, YVel and Vel are used to cache computed values. If the definitions and uses of these variables can be joined into a single m-loop, then scalars can hold these values (Fig. 8(c)), as they are not live outside of the iteration. Since m-loops induced by reductions are no different from m-loops induced by element-wise assignment

```
XVel := DeltaXPos/DeltaT;
YVel := DeltaYPos/DeltaT;
Vel := sqrt(XVel*XVel + YVel*YVel);
minvel := min<<Vel;
maxvel := max<<Vel;
```

(a) ZPL source.

```
for (i=mylow; i<myhi; i++)
    XVel[i] = DeltaXPos[i] / DeltaT[i];
for (i=mylow; i<myhi; i++)
    YVel[i] = DeltaYPos[i] / DeltaT[i];
for (i=mylow; i<myhi; i++)
    Vel[i] = sqrt(XVel[i]*XVel[i]+YVel[i]*YVel[i]);
temp = DBL_MAX;
for (i=mylow; i<myhi; i++)
    temp = min(temp, Vel[i]);
< . . . data transfer code here . . .>
< . . . assignment to minvel . . .>
temp = -DBL_MAX;
for (i=mylow; i<myhi; i++)
    temp = max(temp, Vel[i]);
< . . . data transfer code here . . . >
< . . . assignment to maxvel . . . >
```

(b) Naive loop generation.

```
for (i=mylow; i<myhi; i++) {
    xvel = DeltaXPos[i] / DeltaT[i];
    yvel = DeltaYPos[i] / DeltaT[i];
    Vel[i] = sqrt(xvel*xvel+yvel*yvel);
}
temp = DBL_MAX;
for (i=mylow; i<myhi; i++)
    temp = min(temp, Vel[i]);
< . . . data transfer . . . >
< . . . assignment to minvel . . . >
temp = -DBL_MAX;
for (i=mylow; i<myhi; i++)
    temp = max(temp, Vel[i]);
< . . . data transfer code here . . . >
< . . . assignment to maxvel . . . >
```

(c) Partially optimized loop generation.

```
temp1 = DBL_MAX;
temp2 = -DBL_MAX;
for (i=mylow; i<myhi; i++) {
    xvel = DeltaXPos[i] / DeltaT[i];
    yvel = DeltaYPos[i] / DeltaT[i];
    vel = sqrt(xvel*xvel+yvel*yvel);
    temp1 = min(temp1, vel);
    temp2 = max(temp2, vel);
}
< . . . data transfer . . . >
< . . . assignment to minvel . . . >
< . . . assignment to maxvel . . . >
```

(d) Fully optimized loop generation.

Fig. 8. Effects of joining and contraction on an excerpt from the running example. A number of the array references in the bold statements become scalar references. Arrays DeltaXPos, DeltaYPos, DeltaT in the running example may be similarly contracted.

statements, array Vel may also be contracted as in Fig. 8(d). In fact, for the running example, all but the Sample arrays are eliminated by this array contraction.

We cannot independently join m-loops and perform contraction if we expect to maximize contraction. The compiler therefore joins m-loops with the goal of enabling maximal array contraction. Using a heuristic ordering of the candidate arrays, all m-loops containing a candidate array are joined if the joining enables contraction of the candidate array. This simple greedy strategy produces very high quality code [17].

Our approach not only contracts arrays that a clever scalar language programmer would, it often succeeds in non-obvious cases. There are cases when a group of m-loops may not legally be joined because they over-constrain the resulting loop nest, but simple transformations eliminate the constraints and enable the joining and contraction. The trick of eliminating the constraint is often suitably awkward that programmers are unwilling or unable to do this by hand.

Indexed Arrays. While the use of m-loops nicely encapsulates the local computation that results from array statements, the distinction between m-loops and source-level loops can produce a runtime performance penalty when these two types of loops interact. Consider the ZPL code fragment in Fig. 9(a), which uses a parallel array of indexed arrays. An m-loop will be used to iterate over the parallel array, while a source-level loop iterates over each element of the indexed array (Fig. 9(b)). The problem is that the generated code will exhibit poor cache behavior unless the source-level loop is moved inside the compiler generated loop, as in Fig. 9(c). A source-level loop is a candidate for this transformation when it iterates over an indexed array that is an element of a parallel array. The transformation is performed when all m-loops that contain the involved array may be joined.

```
region R = [1..n];
var A : [R] array [1..m] of integer;
...
[R] for i := 1 to m do
      A[i] := 1;
    end;
```

(a)

```
for (i=1; i<=m; i++)
  for (j=mylow; j<myhi; j++)
    A[j][i] = 1;
```

(b)

```
for (j=mylow; j<myhi; j++)
  for (i=1; i<=m; i++)
    A[j][i] = 1;
```

(c)

Fig. 9. The interaction of source-level loops and compiler generated loops. The ZPL source (a) will naively be compiled into the code in (b). Bringing the source-level loop inside the compiler generated loop (c) will improve cache locality.

5.2 Data Transfer

There are several types of T-factors. Point-to-point T-factors are implied by the wrap statement, the reflect statement, and the @ operator, while the remaining T-factors represent collective communication in operations such as scan, reduce and flood. A point-to-point T-factor is multi-part (send and receive), while a single T-factor can represent each variety of collective communication. This section discusses the optimization of data transfer through the manipulation of T-factors.

Data transfer can be optimized in three ways. First, redundant T-factors may be removed. A T-factor is redundant if and only if the data transfer performed by the T-factor is preceded by a T-factor that satisfies the requested data transfer. Next, T-factors involving the same source and destination processors may be combined. Finally, the components of multi-part T-factors may be pushed apart to pipeline and overlap data transfer and computation. Recall that communication in array languages is naturally vectorized, so the compiler does not perform explicit message vectorization. The removal of redundant T-factors and the combining of T-factors are exact instances of the join operation, while the pipelining of T-factors enables additional joins to occur. For convenience, we will refer to each optimization in isolation, though the actual implementation considers all three optimizations simultaneously.

Point-to-Point Communication. Point-to-point T-factors can be optimized by all three techniques. These optimizations require information about the uses and modifications of the array variables being transferred. This information is maintained in the form of def/use-sets on a *per statement* basis. Since arrays are never indexed, the compiler treats them atomically, much like scalars. Unlike languages such as Fortran 77, no index functions or loop bounds information need be examined. Rather, the region and direction indicate the slice of an array to be transferred. The compiler could perform symbolic analysis on the regions to obtain more precise def/use-sets, but this is generally not necessary as most data parallel computations use a small set of regions.

Figure 10 shows a sample code fragment that requires data transfer, along with unoptimized and optimized code generated for it. For simplicity, we again assume that the compiler generates message passing code (send and receive calls). To generate the unoptimized code in Fig. 10(b), the compiler need only generate a library call for each @ induced T-factor. The code generated in Fig. 10(c)-(e) illustrate the three data transfer optimizations performed by the compiler, which are now discussed in turn.

Removing redundant T-factors. If the T-factor due to a statement (Fig. 10, statement 4) is preceded by a T-factor that has already satisfied that data transfer (statement 3) and there are no intervening modifications to the transferred data, the T-factor for the original statement is redundant and can be eliminated (Fig. 10(c)).

Combining T-factors. If several T-factors perform data transfer on different variables in the same direction (statement 3), these T-factors my be combined (see Fig. 10(d)). T-factors from the same (as in this example) or different statements may be combined in this way.

Pipelining T-factors. The send portion of a T-factor may be pushed up to the last statement that defines the variable involved in the data transfer. This overlaps communication and computation. Statement 2 is the most recent modification of A or C before the use of A in statement 3. Therefore the pipelined T-factor can be started immediately after statement 2 (see Fig. 10(e)).

Appendix B (lines 20–23) shows the result of data transfer optimizations in the running example. Notice that the initialization of the identity elements for the reductions have been moved between the send and receive due to local joining operations. Though this is a small amount of computation, in general the separation of the send and receive may be large.

```
1  C := D;
2  A := B;

   ...

3  E := A@prev+C@prev;


4  F := A@prev;
```

(a) Original ZPL code.

```
<. . . assign C . . .>
<. . . assign A . . .>
          . . .
Send(R,<A,prev>);
Recv(R,<A,prev>);
Send(R,<C,prev>);
Recv(R,<C,prev>);
<. . . assign E . . .>
Send(R,<A,prev>);
Recv(R,<A,prev>);
<. . . assign F . . .>
```

(b) Unoptimized code.

```
<. . . assign C . . .>
<. . . assign A . . .>
          . . .
Send(R,<A,prev>);
Recv(R,<A,prev>);
Send(R,<C,prev>);
Recv(R,<C,prev>);
<. . . assign E . . .>


<. . . assign F . . .>
```

(c) Redundant T-factors removed.

```
<. . . assign C . . .>
<. . . assign A . . .>
          . . .


Send(R,<A,prev>,<C,prev>);
Recv(R,<A,prev>,<C,prev>);
<. . . assign E . . .>


<. . . assign F . . .>
```

(d) Combined T-factors.

```
<. . . assign C . . .>
<. . . assign A . . .>
Send(R,<A,prev>,<C,prev>);

          . . .

Recv(R,<A,prev>,<C,prev>);
<. . . assign E . . .>


<. . . assign F . . .>
```

(e) Pipelined T-factors.

Fig. 10. Example transformations on T-factors.

Collective Communication. Just as in the point-to-point case, collective communication T-factors of the same type are optimized by one or more of the above techniques. Any redundant T-factors may be removed, and all types of collective communication T-factors may be combined with other T-factors of the same type (see Fig. 2). The key to the optimization is that the communication patterns (each factor represents a different pattern) are exposed to the compiler. Library approaches cannot be optimized in this way, for the compiler is unaware of the libraries' contents.

Despite this fixed collective communication interface, ZPL does not lose the advantages of library support. The combined communication compiles to procedure calls in the ZPL runtime library. These procedures are optimized for the particular platform's strengths [7]. For example, on the SP2, the procedure calls are mapped to MPI library routines, while our T3D implementation uses the native SHMEM library routines [2]. In this way, a single copy of optimized code exploits the strengths of all target platform.

Though we have introduced collective communication operations as each producing a single T-factor, we often use multi-part T-factors for these operations. These multi-part factors allow for better communication hiding when implementing non-hardware supported operations (such as column broadcasts or reduces).

6 Related Work

ZPL was designed from first principles to execute efficiently across MIMD computers. There exist a number of compilation efforts that are similar in nature to that of ZPL. Several are summarized below.

The APL language supports the atomic manipulation of and computation on whole arrays [15]. APL was not designed with parallelism in mind, thus it encourages the use of locality insensitive operations. Greenlaw and Snyder demonstrate that the second most common data movement operation in APL (an array subscripted array) is very expensive on parallel machines [10]. Budd describes an APL compiler that decomposes array operations into vector operations for execution on a vector processor [5]. This fine grained approach does not extend to distributed memory or MIMD machines. Ju *et al.* describe a classification and fusion scheme for array language primitives (in APL, Fortran 90, etc.) [16]. Their fusion concept differs from our join transformation in that it only strives to eliminate intermediate storage. In addition, they assume a shared memory model and thus do not consider explicit communication. We optimize computation and communication separately.

NESL is a data-parallel programming language that emphasizes nested parallelism [4]. NESL source code is compiled to an intermediate vector-based code, called Vcode, which is either interpreted or compiled [3]. The Vcode intermediate form is well suited for vector and low-latency shared memory machines but not for distributed memory machines. The primary MIMD compilation effort is in increasing the granularity of parallelism and reducing synchronization overhead.

C* and its descendant Dataparallel C are derivatives of C with support for data parallel programming [25]. The Dataparallel C *domain* and the ZPL *region* both serve as bases for parallelism; they are used to define distributed arrays and to distribute computation. Despite this similarity, the techniques for compiling these languages greatly differ. In particular, the primary Dataparallel C compilation effort is in overcoming inefficiencies due to the sequential nature of the parent language (C) and the SIMD nature of the language itself [13]. As an example of the former, a Dataparallel C program may contain arbitrary C code, which resists static analysis due to pointer arithmetic and weak typing.

High Performance Fortran (HPF) is a language that requires the user specification of parallelism, distribution and alignment via directives in sequential Fortran 77 and Fortran 90 programs [14]. The primary compilation effort is in overcoming the sequential nature of the parent language. Arrays are manipulated at the element level, thus optimizations must be performed to vectorize communication and hoist it from inner loops. HPF and ZPL are similar in the types of parallel operations that they support, though ZPL makes clear to the programmer the execution cost of each operation [22].

Considerable research has been devoted to automatically parallelizing Fortran 77 programs [1, 23, 11]. In contrast to the ZPL approach in which the language was designed to facilitate the recognition and exploitation of parallelism, the primary effort for automatically parallelizing compilers is in recognizing, exposing and efficiently exploiting the parallelism hidden in a sequential program.

Furthermore, optimal sequential and parallel solutions to the same problem often require different algorithms, thus it seems unlikely that a compiler will be able (in general) to transform one to the other.

7 Conclusions

We have argued that when compiling for parallelism, array languages present compilers with new opportunities and challenges for optimization. The array operations of these languages make some standard optimizations (such as message vectorization) disappear, make new opportunities (such as combining reduction operations) appear, and add importance to other optimizations (such as array contraction).

We have described the factor-join approach to compiling array languages and shown how it is used to compile ZPL programs. This approach first decomposes array language constructs into a series of factors, and then joins these factors to perform various optimizations. Each factor represents a unique communication or computation structure, and only a small number of different factors are needed to describe ZPL programs. These factors cleanly separate the treatment of communication and computation. For example, C-factors represent the purely computational aspects of all operations (e.g., element-wise array assignments, reductions, scans, etc.), so optimizing C-factors simultaneously optimizes all inner loops that the compiler generates for array constructs. This factorization also simplifies the movement and joining of the data-transfer factors (T-factors). This approach provides a framework for optimizations that includes redundant communication elimination, message combining, and communication pipelining; and the use of factors abstracts common features of different optimizations. For example, the combining of collective communication operations and the combining of point-to-point communication use the same algorithm applied to different T-factors.

References

1. Saman P. Amarasinghe, Jennifer M. Anderson, Monica S. Lam, and Amy W. Lim. An overview of a compiler for scalable parallel machines. In *Sixth Workshop on Languages and Compilers for Parallel Computing*, August 1993.
2. Ray Barriuso and Allan Knies. SHMEM user's guide for C. Technical report, Cray Research Inc., June 1994.
3. G. E. Blelloch, S. Chatterjee, J. C. Hardwick, J. Sipelstein, and M. Zagha. Implementation of a portable nested data-parallel language. *Journal of Parallel and Distributed Computing*, 21(1):4–14, April 1994.
4. Guy E. Blelloch. NESL: A nested data-parallel language (version 2.6). Technical Report CMU-CS-93-129, School of Computer Science, Carnegie Mellon University, 1993.
5. Timothy A. Budd. An APL compiler for a vector processor. *ACM Transactions on Programming Languages and Systems*, 6(3):297–313, July 1984.

6. Steve Carr, Kathryn S. McKinley, and Chau-Wen Tseng. Compiler optimizations for improved data locality. In *Proceedings of the International Conference on Architectural Support for Programming Languages and Operating Systems*, October 1994. San Jose, CA.
7. Bradford L. Chamberlain, Sung-Eun Choi, and Lawrence Snyder. IRONMAN: An architecture indepedent communication interface for parallel computers. *submitted for publication*, 1996.
8. Marios D. Dikaiakos, Calvin Lin, Daphne Manoussaki, and Diana E. Woodward. The portable parallel implementation of two novel mathematical biology algorithms in ZPL. In *Ninth International Conference on Supercomputing*, 1995.
9. Michael Gerndt. Updating distributed variables in local computations. *Concurrency–Practice and Experience*, 2(3):171–193, September 1990.
10. R. Greenlaw and L. Snyder. Achieving speedups for APL on an SIMD distributed memory machine. *International Journal of Parallel Programming*, 19(2):111–127, April 1990.
11. Manish Gupta and Prithviraj Banerjee. PARADIGM: A compiler for automatic data distribution on multicomputers. In *International Conference on Supercomputing*, July 1993.
12. Manish Gupta, Sam Midkiff, Edith Schonberg, Ven Seshadri, David Shields, Ko-Yang Wang, Wai-Mee Ching, and Ton Ngo. An HPF compiler for the IBM SP2. In *Proceedings of Supercomputing '95*, December 1995.
13. Philip J. Hatcher, Anthony J. Lapadula, Robert R. Jones, Michael J. Quinn, and Ray J. Anderson. A production-quality C* compiler for hypercube multicomputers. In *Proceedings of Third ACM SIGPLAN Symposium on Principles and Practice of Parallel Programming*, April 1991.
14. High Performance Fortran Forum. *High Performance Fortran Specification Version 1.1.* November 1994.
15. Kenneth E. Iverson. *A Programming Language*. Wiley, 1962.
16. Dz-Ching R. Ju, Chaun-Lin Wu, and Paul Carini. The classification, fusion, and parallelization of array language primitives. *IEEE Transactions on Parallel and Distributed Systems*, 5(10):1113–1120, October 1994.
17. E Christopher Lewis and Calvin Lin. Array contraction in array languages. Technical report, University of Washington, Department of Computer Science and Engineering, 1996. Forthcoming.
18. E Christopher Lewis, Calvin Lin, Lawrence Snyder, and George Turkiyyah. A portable parallel n-body solver. In D. Bailey, P. Bjorstad, J. Gilbert, M. Mascagni, R. Schreiber, H. Simon, V. Torczon, and L. Watson, editors, *Proceedings of the Seventh SIAM Conference on Parallel Processing for Scientific Computing*, pages 331–336. SIAM, 1995.
19. C. Lin, L. Snyder, R. Anderson, B. Chamberlain, S. Choi, G. Forman, E. Lewis, and W. D. Weathersby. ZPL vs. HPF: A comparison of performance and programming style. Technical Report 95–11–05, Department of Computer Science and Engineering, University of Washington, 1994.
20. Calvin Lin. ZPL language reference manual. Technical Report 94–10–06, Department of Computer Science and Engineering, University of Washington, 1994.
21. Calvin Lin and Lawrence Snyder. SIMPLE performance results in ZPL. In Keshav Pingali, Uptal Banerjee, David Gelernter, Alexandru Nicolau, and David Padua, editors, *Workshop on Languages and Compilers for Parallel Computing*, pages 361–375. Springer-Verlag, 1994.

22. Ton A. Ngo. *The Effectiveness of Two Data Parallel Languages, HPF and ZPL.* PhD thesis, University of Washington, Department of Computer Science, 1996. In preparation.
23. C. D. Polychronopoulos, M. B. Girkar, M. R. Haghighat, C. L. Lee, B. P. Leung, and D. A. Schouten. The structure of Parafrase-2: an advanced parallelizing compiler for C and Fortran. In *Workshop on Languages and Compilers for Parallel Computing,* pages 423–453, 1990.
24. George Wilkey Richardson. Evaluation of a parallel Chaos router simulator. Master's thesis, University of Arizona, Department of Electrical and Computer Engineering, 1995.
25. J.R. Rose and Guy L. Steele Jr. C*: An extended C language for data parallel programming. Technical Report PL 87-5, Thinking Machines Corporation, 1987.
26. Lawrence Snyder. Foundations of practical aprallel programming languages. In Tony Hey and Jeanne Ferrante, editors, *Portability and performance for parallel processing,* pages 1–19, New York, 1994. Wiley.
27. Lawrence Snyder. *The ZPL Programmer's Guide.* May 1996.
28. Michael Wolfe. *Optimizing Supercompilers for Supercomputers.* MIT Press, Cambridge, MA, 1989.

A Sample ZPL Source Code

```
/* VelocityStats - compute approximate minimum and
   maximum velocity of particle from sample positions */

program VelocityStats;

direction prev = [-1];

config var samplecount : integer=10;
           datafile    : string="samples.dat";

region R = [1..samplecount];

var SampleT, SampleXPos, SampleYPos : [R] double;     -- samples of location (sorted by t)
    DeltaT, DeltaXPos, DeltaYPos : [R] double;        -- delta from one sample to next
    XVel,YVel : [R] double;                           -- X- and Y-components of velocity
    Vel : [R] double;                                 -- velocity


procedure VelocityStats();
          var minvel,maxvel : double; -- min/max velocities
              infile        : file;

[R]       begin
              infile := open(datafile,"r");
              read(infile,SampleT,SampleXPos,SampleYPos);
              close(infile);

[prev of R]   begin
                  SampleT := 0.0;
                  SampleXPos := 0.0;
                  SampleYPos := 0.0;
              end;

              DeltaT := SampleT - SampleT@prev;
              DeltaXPos := SampleXPos - SampleXPos@prev;
              DeltaYPos := SampleYPos - SampleYPos@prev;

              XVel := DeltaXPos/DeltaT;
              YVel := DeltaYPos/DeltaT;

              Vel := sqrt(XVel*XVel + YVel*YVel);

              minvel := min<<Vel;
              maxvel := max<<Vel;

              writeln("Minimum velocity was: ", minvel);
              writeln("Maximum velocity was: ", maxvel);
          end;
```

B Resulting Pseudo-C Code

```
integer samplecount = 10;
char * datafile = "samples.dat";
region R, prev_of_R;
double *SampleT, *SampleXPos, *SampleYPos;
double deltat, deltaxpos, deltaypos;
double xvel, yvel, vel;

void VelocityStats(void) {
    double minvel, maxvel;
    FILE * infile;
    double temp1,temp2;

    infile = fopen(datafile,"r");
    FScanParallelArray(infile,<R,SampleT>,<R,SampleXPos>,
                              <R,SampleYPos>);
    fclose(infile);

    for (i = prev_of_R.mylo; i <= prev_of_R.myhi; i++)
        SampleT[i] = 0.0;
    for (i = prev_of_R.mylo; i <= prev_of_R.myhi; i++)
        SampleXPos[i] = 0.0;
    for (i = prev_of_R.mylo; i <= prev_of_R.myhi; i++)
        SampleYPos[i] = 0.0;

    Send(R,<SampleT,prev>,<SampleXPos,prev>,
        <SampleYPos,prev>);
    temp1 = DBL_MAX;
    temp2 = -DBL_MAX;
    Receive(R,<SampleT,prev>,<SampleXPos,prev>,
            <SampleYPos,prev>);

    for (i = R.mylo; i <= R.myhi; i++) {
        deltat = SampleT[i] - SampleT[i-1];
        deltaxpos = SampleXPos[i] - SampleXPos[i-1];
        deltaypos = SampleYPos[i] - SampleYPos[i-1];
        xvel = deltaxpos/deltat;
        yvel = deltaypos/deltat;
        vel = sqrt(xvel*xvel + yvel*yvel);
        temp1 = min(temp1,vel);
        temp2 = max(temp2,vel);
    }
    Glob_Reduce(R,<temp1,min>,<temp2,max>);
    Broadcast(<temp1,minvel>,<temp2,maxvel>);
    printf("Minimum velocity was: %f\n",minvel);
    printf("Maximum velocity was: %f\n",maxvel);
}

void main(int argc,char * argv[]) {
    DistributeRegions(<R,1,m>,<prev_of_R,0,0>);
    AllocateArrays(<R,SampleT>,<R,SampleXPos>,
                   <R,SampleYPos>);
    VelocityStats();
}
```

Compilation of Constraint Systems to Procedural Parallel Programs

Ajita John and J. C. Browne

Dept. of Computer Sciences
University of Texas, Austin, TX 78712
{ajohn,browne}@cs.utexas.edu

Abstract. This paper describes the first results from research[1] on the compilation of constraint systems into task level parallel programs in a procedural language. This is the only research, of which we are aware, which attempts to generate efficient parallel programs for numerical computations from constraint systems. Computations are expressed as constraint systems. A dependence graph is derived from the constraint system and a set of input variables. The dependence graph, which exploits the parallelism in the constraints, is mapped to the target language CODE, which represents parallel computation structures as generalized dependence graphs. Finally, parallel C programs are generated. The granularity of the derived dependence graphs depends upon the complexity of the operations represented in the type system of the constraint specification language. To extract parallel programs of appropriate granularity, the following features have been included: (i) modularity, (ii) operations over structured types as primitives, (iii) definition of sequential C functions. A prototype of the compiler has been implemented. The execution environment or software architecture is specified separately from the constraint system. The domain of matrix computations has been targeted for applications. Some examples have been programmed. Initial results are very encouraging.

1 Introduction

Representing a computation as a set of constraints upon the state variables defining the solution and choosing an appropriate subset of the state variables as the input set is an attractive approach to specification of programs, but there has been little success previously in attaining efficient execution of parallel programs derived from constraint representations [1]. There are however, both motivations for continuing research in this direction and reasons for optimism concerning success. Constraint systems have attractive properties for compilation to parallel computation structures. A constraint system gives the minimum specification (See [2] for the benefits from postponing imposition of program structure) for a computation, thereby offering the compiler freedom of choice

[1] This work was supported in part through a grant from the Advanced Research Projects Office/CSTO, subcontract to Syracuse University #3531427

for derivation of control structure. Constraint systems offer some unique advantages as a representation from which parallel programs are to be derived[11]. Both "OR" and "AND" parallelism can be derived. Either effective or complete programs can be derived from constraint systems on demand. Programs for different computations can be derived from the same constraint specification by different choices of the input set of variables.

The focus of this research is to derive from constraint representations, parallel programs of execution efficiency competitive with procedural languages. This paper reports early results from this approach. The next two sections outline our approach and related work, respectively. Subsequent sections describe the constraint specification language and the compilation algorithm. We conclude the paper with performance results for some example programs and directions for future work.

2 Approach

A program is expressed as a set of constraints between the program variables and an input set consisting of a subset of the program variables. A dependence graph is derived from the program and mapped to the target language CODE [14], which expresses parallel structure over sequential units of computation declaratively as a generalized dependence graph. The software architecture or execution environment to which CODE is to compile is separately specified (SMP, DSM, NOW, etc). Finally, sequential and parallel C programs for shared memory machines like the CRAY J90, SPARCcenter 2000, and Sequent and the distributed memory PVM [10] system can be generated. An MPI [7] backend for CODE is also available.

The granularity of the derived dependence graphs depends upon the types directly represented as primitives in the constraint representation. The introduction of structured types and operations on structured types as primitives in the constraint representation give natural units of computation at a granularity appropriate for task level parallelism and avoids the problem of name ambiguity in the derivation of dependence graphs from loops over scalar representation of arrays. It also supports implementation of data parallelism, if desired[11]. The general requirements for a constraint representation which can be compiled to execute efficiently, include: (i) modularity for reusable modules, (ii) definition of sequential functions, and (iii) a rich type set. The main features of our approach are detailed in the rest of the section.

2.1 Constraint Representation

A constraint is a relationship between a set of variables. E.g. $A + B == C$ is a constraint expressing equality between C and the sum of A and B. A constraint system enumerates the relationships between the variables of the computation.

2.2 Constraint Modules

Modularity is provided by *constraint modules*, which are encapsulations of relationships between parameters and can be invoked as a constraint. Figure 1 shows a constraint specification (excluding declarations) for the non-complex roots of a quadratic equation, $ax^2 + bx + c == 0$. The specification uses a module, *DefinedRoots*. "*U*" denotes an undefined value. *sqr*, *sqrt*, and *abs* are library functions. A program specification also identifies the set of inputs. In the example, it could be $\{a, b, c\}$, or $\{a, b, r1\}$, or $\{a, b, r2\}$.

```
/* Constraint module */
DefinedRoots(a, b, c, r1, r2)
t == sqr(b) - 4 * a * c AND t >= 0 AND
2 * a * r1 == (-b + sqrt(abs(t))) AND 2 * a * r2 == -(b + sqrt(abs(t)))


/* Main */
a == 0 AND r1 == "U" AND r2 == "U"
OR
a! = 0 AND DefinedRoots(a, b, c, r1, r2)
```

Fig. 1. Quadratic Equation Solver

2.3 Translation to a Compilable Language

Encapsulated within the constraint $A + B == C$ are three assignments: $A = C - B$, $B = C - A$, and $C = A + B$; and a conditional, $A + B == C$. One of the three assignments can be extracted depending on which two of the three variables $\{ A, B, C \}$ are inputs. If all three variables are inputs, the constraint can be classified as a conditional to be checked for satisfaction. If fewer than two variables are inputs, the constraint is unresolved and no resulting program can be extracted.

A dependence graph can be derived from a set of constraints and an input set of variables. This graph ensures satisfaction of the constraints by computing values for some or all of the non-input (output) variables. In addition, parallelism in the computations is exploited. The compiler generates single-assignment variables and can extract multiple solutions on alternate paths of the dependence graph. The derivation of dependence graphs is explained in detail in Section 5.

A constraint specification represents a family of dependence graphs. Generation of all possible dependence graphs can result in combinatorial explosion. We construct only the dependence graph for a specified input set. The constraint specification can be reused for generating dependence graphs for different sets of inputs.

The dependence graph for the quadratic equation solver with the input set $\{a, b, c\}$ is shown in Figure 2. If the conditionals on an arc are satisfied, the

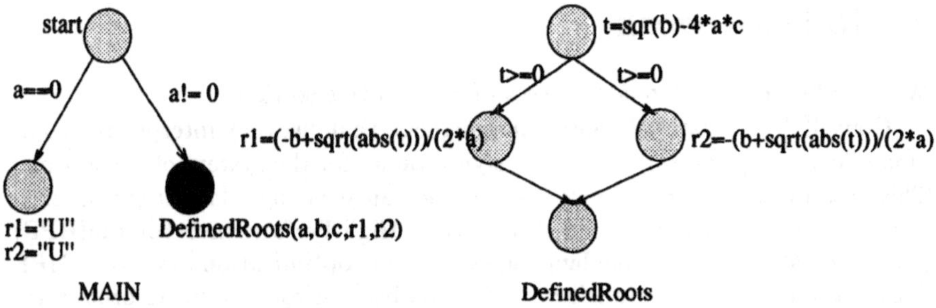

Fig. 2. Dataflow Graphs for Quadratic Equation Solver Example

corresponding destination node is executed. If a node is executed, the computations (assignments) at that node are performed. The node annotated by *DefinedRoots* in *MAIN* invokes the dependence graph corresponding to the module *DefinedRoots*. The assignments $r1 = (-b + sqrt(abs(t)))/(2 * a)$ and $r2 = -(b + sqrt(abs(t)))/(2 * a)$ are performed in parallel and the results are collected by a node.

2.4 Domain Specification: The Hierarchical Type System

The semantic domain chosen for our application programs is matrix computation. We have a built-in matrix type with its associated operations of addition, subtraction, multiplication and inverse. The matrix subtypes currently implemented in our system are lower and upper triangular and dense matrices. We plan to extend the type system to a richer class of matrices including hierarchical matrices [4]. Specialized algorithms based on the structure of the matrix can be invoked for the matrix subtypes. Other structured types such as lists, queues, trees etc. along with their associated operations could be included to broaden the class of programs which can be compactly represented.

2.5 Separate Specification of Compilation Options and the Execution Environment (Software Architecture)

To obtain architecturally optimized programs, we plan to incorporate features such as the following as part of an execution environment specification separate from the constraint specification.
(a) Specification of architecture-specific mechanisms (E.g. shared variables or messages for communication, etc).
(b) Selection of the level of granularity for operations.
(c) Option of not parallelizing a particular module.
(d) Option of selecting certain operations for executing in parallel.
(e) Choices among parallel algorithms to execute some of the operations.

3 Related work

We shall briefly sketch related pieces of work in this section.

Consul[1] is a parallel constraint language that uses an interpretive technique (local propagation) to find satisfying values for the system of constraints. This system offers performance only in the range of logic languages. Declarative extensions have been added as part of High-Performance Fortran(HPF) [15], a portable data-parallel language with some optimization directives. HPF does not support task parallelism. Also, existing control flow in its procedural programming style makes analysis for parallelism difficult. Thinglab [9] transforms constraints to a compilable language rather than to an interpretive execution environment as in many constraint systems. Kaleidoscope[8] integrates constraints with an object-oriented language and uses partial compilation for the constraints. Neither Thinglab nor Kaleidoscope is concerned with extraction of parallel structures. Vijay Saraswat described a family of concurrent constraint logic programming languages, the *cc* languages [16]. The logic and constraint portions are explicitly separated with the constraint part acting as an active data store for the logic portion of the program. Oz is a concurrent programming language based on an extension of the basic concurrent constraint model provided in [16]. The performance reported for the system is only comparable with commercial Prolog and Lisp systems [13]. Parallel logic programming [3, 6] is another area of related work. PCN [3] and Strand [6] are two parallel programming representations with a strong component of logic specification. However, both require the programmer to provide explicit operators for specification of parallelism and the dependence graph structures which could be generated were restricted to trees. Equational specifications of computations is a restriction of constraint specifications. Unity [2] is the equational programming representation around which Chandy and Misra have built a powerful paradigm for the design of parallel programs. Again, Unity requires addition of explicit specifications for parallelism.

4 Language Description

This section describes the different components of the programming system. It includes the types and their associated operations, the rules for constructing constraints, and the structure of a complete program in the system. The notations used are similar to those in the C programming language.

4.1 Types

The lowest level of the type system consists of integers, reals, characters, and arrays with the operators of addition, subtraction, multiplication, division on integers and reals. At the next level of the type hierarchy are matrices with their associated operations of addition, subtraction, multiplication and inverse. As mentioned in Section 2, the system currently supports specialized matrix types like lower and upper triangular. At the highest level of the type system are hierarchical matrices, whose individual elements are matrices.

4.2 Constraints

In our system, arithmetic expressions can be formed by using arithmetic operators and calls to library and user-defined functions (functions must have defined inverses, otherwise only a limited form of compilation can be done). In addition, expressions of the following form, using *indexed operators*, are allowed.

$$< op > \mathit{FOR}\ (< index > < b1 > < b2 >)\ X$$

An indexed operator applies a binary *op* ∈ {+, -, *, /} over an arithmetic expression, X, through a range of values, $b1$ ... $b2$, for an integer variable, *index*. E.g. + FOR (i 1 5) $A[i]$ specifies the sum of the elements in array A between positions 1-5. *b1* and *b2* have to be statically bound.
Constraints can be constructed by application of the following rules.

Rule 1: (i) $X_1\ R\ X_2$, is a constraint,
where $R \in \{ <, <=, >, >=, ==, != \}$, X_1, X_2 are arithmetic expressions.
(ii) $M_1 == M_2$ is a constraint,
where M_1, M_2 are expressions involving matrices and the matrix operators +, -, *, and Inverse.

Rule 2: (i) A AND/OR B (ii) NOT A are constraints,
where A and B are constraints.

Rule 3: Calls to user-defined constraint modules are constraints. In Figure 1, the call *DefinedRoots(a,b,c,r1,r2)* in *Main* is an application of this rule.

Rule 4: Constraints over indexed sets have the form:

AND/OR FOR (<index> <b1> <b2>) $\{ A_1, A_2, \ldots, A_n \}$

The above construct groups a set of constraints, $A_1, A_2, \ldots, A_n$, to be connected by an AND/OR connective through a range of values, $b1$ ... $b2$, for an integer variable, *index*. *b1* and *b2* have to be statically bound. This condition will be relaxed in later versions of the compiler.
An instance of Rule 4 is AND FOR (i 1 2) { A[i] == A[i-1], B[i+1] == A[i] }.
This example succinctly represents the constraints
$A[1] == A[0]$ AND $A[2] == A[1]$ AND $B[2] == A[1]$ AND $B[3] == A[2]$.

Constraints constructed from applications of Rule 1 are referred to as *simple constraints*, which form the building blocks for constraints constructed from applications of Rules 2-4.

4.3 Programs

A program in our system consists of the following constituents.
(i) Program name, global variable declarations, global input variables.

(ii) User-defined function signatures: signatures of C functions (linked during execution), which may be invoked in an arithmetic expression.

(iii) Constraint Module definitions: module name, formal parameters and their types, local variable declarations, and a body constructed from applications of Rules 1-4 in Section 4.2.

(iv) Main body of the program: constraints formed from applications of Rules 1-4 in Section 4.2.

5 Compilation

The compilation algorithm consists of the following phases.

Phase 1. The textually expressed constraint system is transformed to an undirected graph representation.

Phase 2. A depth-first search algorithm transforms the undirected graph to a directed graph.

Phase 3. With a set of input variables, the directed graph is traversed by a depth-first search to map the constraints to conditionals and computations for nodes of a generalized dependence graph.

Phase 4. Specifications of the execution environment are used to optimally select the communication and synchronization mechanisms to be used by CODE [14]. This phase is yet to be completely defined.

Phase 5. The dependence graph is mapped to the CODE parallel programming environment to produce sequential and parallel programs in C as executable for different parallel architectures.

Phases 1-5 are described in detail in Sections 5.1-5.5.

5.1 Phase 1

The textual source program is transformed to a source graph for the compiler. Starting from an empty graph, for each application of Rules 1-4 in Section 4.2, an undirected constraint graph can be constructed by adding appropriate nodes and edges to the existing graph. For each instance of a simple constraint (Rule 1), a node is created with the constraint attached to it. For each application of Rule 2, the graph is expanded as shown in Figures 3(a)-(b). For each application of Rule 3, a node is created with the constraint module call and the actual parameters attached to it. For each application of Rule 4, the graph is expanded as shown in Figure 3(c).

The different kinds of nodes in the constraint graph are (i) *simple constraint* nodes, (ii) *operator* nodes corresponding to AND/OR/NOT connectives, (iii) *call* nodes corresponding to Constraint Module Calls, and (iv) *for* nodes corresponding to indexed sets.

A set of constraint graphs is constructed from the main body and the constraint module bodies. Each graph is constructed in a hierarchical fashion. *Simple constraint* nodes and *call* nodes occur at lower levels. At higher levels, *operator* and *for* nodes connect one or more subgraphs. There will be a unique node

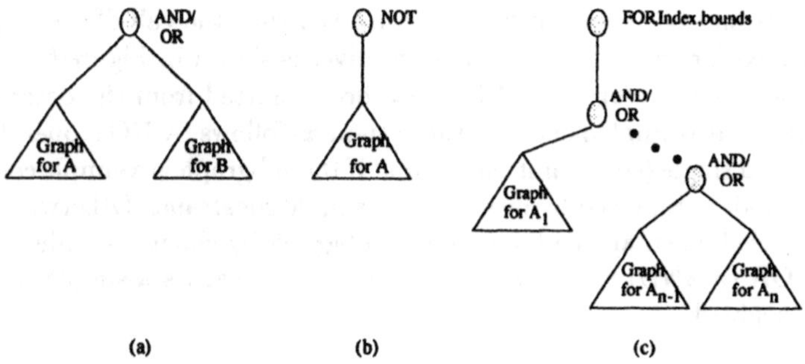

Fig. 3. Construction of Constraint Graphs for (a),(b) Rule 2 (c) Rule 4

at the highest level. The constraint graph obtained for a particular constraint specification is unique. The constraint graphs for the quadratic equation solver are shown in Figure 4.

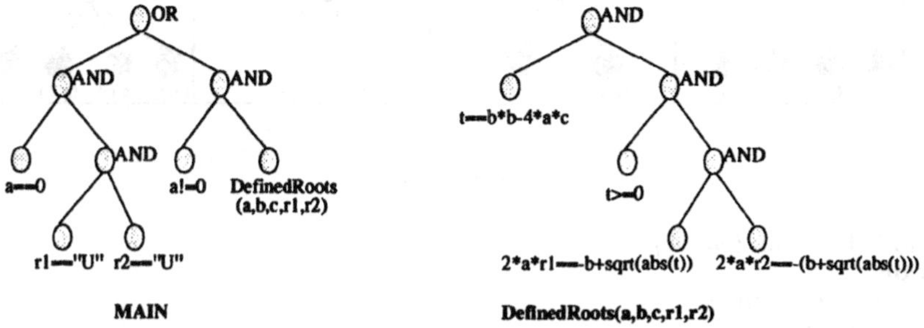

Fig. 4. Constraint Graphs for Quadratic Equation Solver

5.2 Phase 2

A depth-first traversal of each constraint graph constructs a set of directed graphs (trees). The traversal assigns constraints connected by AND operators in a constraint graph to the same node in the corresponding tree and constraints connected by OR operators in a constraint graph to nodes on diverging paths in the corresponding tree. The satisfaction of all the constraints along a path from the root to a leaf in a tree represents a satisfaction of the constraint system represented by the tree.

Figure 5 illustrates phase 2 for four base cases, where a, b, c, and d are simple constraints. The algorithm *dfs* is a generalization of Figure 5. Let v_1 be the unique node at the highest level of the input constraint graph, G. Each output tree, G^*, is initialized to a root, v_1^*. Each node in G^* can hold a list of constraints. An indexed set of constraints within a node in G^* has an associated tree obtained from the depth-first traversal of the constraint graph corresponding to constraints in the indexed set. v_c and v_c^* are the nodes currently being visited in G and G^*, respectively. dfs is invoked with the call dfs(v_1, v_1^*). The tree obtained for the quadratic equation solver is shown in Figure 6.

The case of *operator* node, NOT, has been omitted from the description of *dfs*. However, it is implemented in the system as follows. A NOT operator node operates on a single (constraint) subgraph. If the subgraph is a simple constraint, the NOT node is removed by negating the simple constraint. Otherwise, a NOT node is moved down all the levels of the subgraph by changing nodes (AND to OR and OR to AND) traversed in its path until it reaches a simple constraint, which is negated.

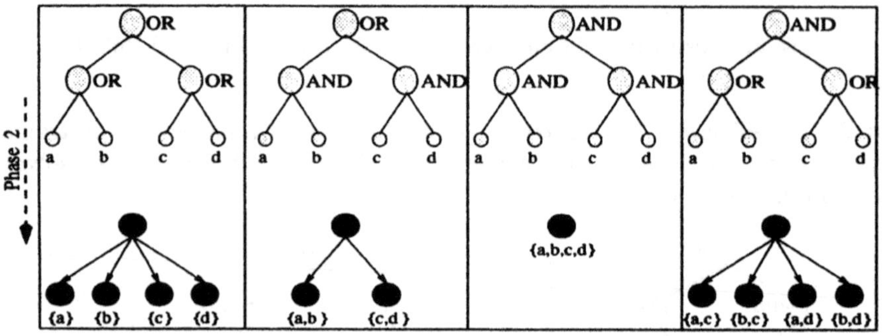

Fig. 5. Phase 2

ALGORITHM dfs (v_c, v_c^*)
begin
    visited[v_c] = true;
    Case type(v_c) of
        OR : **for each unvisited neighbor, u, of v_c do**
            if type(u) == OR dfs(u, v_c^*)
            else create node u^* in G^* as child of v_c^*;
                dfs(u, u^*);
        AND : **if there is an unvisited OR neighbor, u_1, of v_c**
            let u_2 be the other neighbor of v_c;
            let u_{11} and u_{12} be the two unvisited neighbors of u_1;
            /* transform (u_{11} OR u_{12}) AND u_2 to (u_2 AND u_{11}) OR (u_2 AND u_{12}) */
            visited[v_c] = false;
            change type of v_c to OR, remove u_1, u_2 as neighbors of v_c;
            create two unvisited AND neighbors, and_1, and_2, for v_c;
            make u_2 and u_{11} the neighbors of and_1;
            make u_2 and u_{12} the neighbors of and_2;
            dfs(v_c, v_c^*);
        else for each unvisited neighbor, u, of v_c do dfs(u, v_c^*);
        Simple_constraint : **attach constraint to v_c^*;**
        Call Node : **attach constraint module call to v_c^*;**
        For Node : **attach indexed set with index and bounds to $v_c{}^*$**
            create new root $v_i{}^*$ for tree corresponding to indexed set;
            let v_i be the node at highest level of constraint graph for indexed set;
            dfs(v_i, $v_i{}^*$);
end;

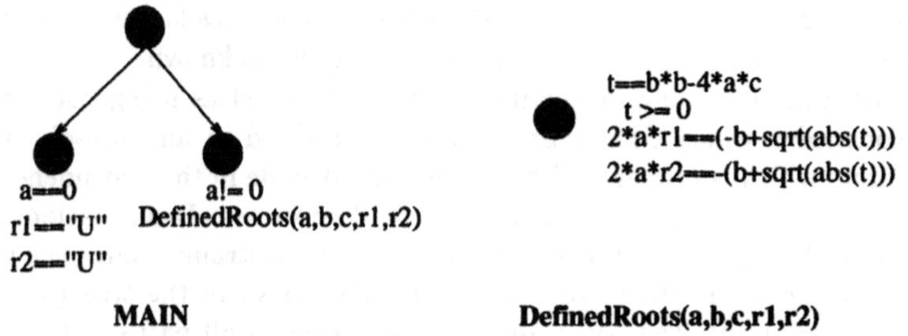

Fig. 6. Trees from Phase 2 for Quadratic Equation Solver

5.3 Phase 3

Using the input set specification, a depth-first traversal of the tree from phase 2 attempts to generate a dependence graph. The generated dependence graph is a directed graph, in which nodes are computational elements and arcs between nodes express data dependency. It has a unique *start* node. A path from the start node in the graph is a computation path. A node in the dependence graph has the form: firing rule, computation, routing rule (see Figure 7(a)). A firing rule is a condition that must hold before the node can be enabled for execution. The computation at a node is performed when the node is executed. A routing rule is a condition that must hold for the node to send data on its outgoing paths. The nodes and arcs in the tree from phase 2 correspond to the nodes and arcs, respectively, in the dependence graph.

A *known* set is associated with each node in the dependence graph. The variables in the known set at a node are *knowns* at that node. The values of these variables are known at runtime at that node. All variables not in the known set at a node are *unknowns* at that node. The input set is cast as the *known* set for the start node.

The depth-first traversal tries to generate a dependence graph with nodes that contain computations for the *unknowns*. Each node, v, in the tree from phase 2 has a set of simple constraints attached to it. When v is visited, each constraint can be *resolved* as one of the following for the corresponding node, v^*, in the dependence graph.
(i) Firing Rule: To be so classified, a constraint must have no unknowns when v is visited.
(ii) Computation: To fall into this category, a constraint must involve an equality and have a single unknown. The unknown is added to the known set for v^*.
(iii) Routing Rule: To be a routing rule, all unknown variables in the constraint must become knowns through computations at v^*.

An indexed set, AND/OR FOR (<index> <b1> <b2>) $\{A_1, A_2, \ldots, A_n\}$, is resolved if every constraint A_i resolved for all values of *index* in $b1 \ldots b2$. Resolved indexed sets are compiled to loops which iterate over values of *index* in $b1 \ldots b2$ The restrictions on the indexed set structure to be compiled successfully in our system are as follows. For all values of *index* in $b1 \ldots b2$ (a) a constraint has to have the same classification, (b) if a constraint is classified as computation, a single unique term in the constraint has to be the unknown.

Constraints involving inequalities must be resolved as firing/routing rules. Any constraint which cannot be resolved is retained in an unresolved set of constraints which is propagated down the tree. A node in the dependence graph receives the known set of its parent as its known set. Examination of each constraint at a node and in the unresolved set of constraints continues until no new variables are added to the known set. Any path in the tree that results in a leaf with unresolved constraints is abandoned. If all paths in the tree are abandoned, the user is informed of the restrictiveness of the initial input set.

When a constraint is classified as computation, it is mapped to an equation. All terms involving the single unknown in the computation are moved to the left-hand side of the equation. Currently, our system solves equations in linear unknown terms. In the future we plan to incorporate solvers for scalar types that will solve for higher powers of the unknown. If the variables in the computation are matrices, the computation is replaced by calls to specialized matrix routines in C. For example, the statement $A * x + b1 == b2$ with x as the unknown is first transformed into $A * x == b2 - b1$ and then a routine is invoked to solve for x. If A is lower (upper) triangular, then forward (backward) substitution is used to solve for x. Otherwise x is solved through an LU decomposition of A.

The dependence graphs for the quadratic equation solver with the input set $\{ a, b, c \}$ is shown in Figure 7(b).

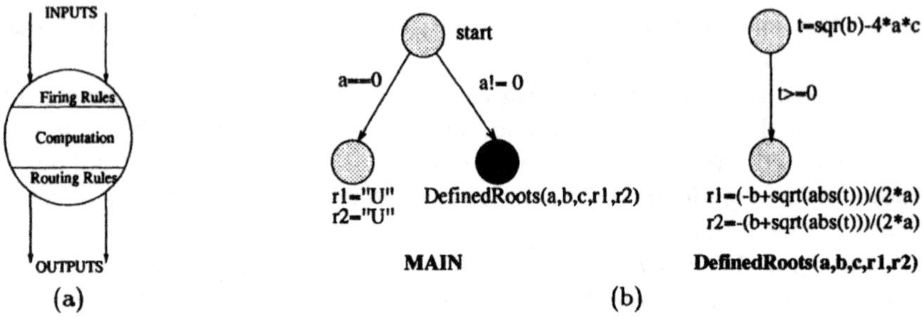

Fig. 7. (a) Dependence Graph Node (b) Dependence Graphs for Quadratic Equation Solver

5.3.1 Phase 3 for Constraint Module Calls

A constraint module call has the form $ModuleName(e_1, e_2, \ldots, e_n)$ where e_i, $1 \leq i \leq n$, is an arithmetic expression and an actual parameter. Let the formal parameters corresponding to $e_1, e_2, \ldots, e_n$ be $f_1, f_2, \ldots, f_n$, respectively. Let K be the known set at the node where the constraint module is invoked. An attempt is made to generate a dependence graph from the constraint module definition. The tree from phase 2 for the constraint module is traversed with a new known set, $K_{module} = \{ f_i \mid \{\text{all variables in } e_i\} \subseteq K \}$. The unknowns are considered to be all formal parameters not in K_{module} and the local variables in the constraint module. The depth-first traversal of the tree corresponding to the constraint module returns "True" if all the constraints in the module are resolved and every unknown parameter is computed at the end of at least one path in the resulting dependence graph (All paths not satisfying this condition are discarded). This condition is different in the dependence graph generation of the main module where all unknown variables need not be computed. The reason for imposing this condition is that the actual parameters are bound to the formal parameters at the point of call. If different sets of variables are computed in different paths of the dependence graph (as in the constraint $a == c$ OR $b == c$ with c known) it is not possible to determine statically the set of actual parameters computed in the constraint module call.

If the dependence graph generation is successful, a new set of constraints corresponding to each computed parameter is generated as follows:
$e_{k1} == Z_1$, $e_{k2} == Z_2$, ..., $e_{kp} == Z_p$, where Z_i, $1 \leq i \leq p$, are new variables generated by the compiler and $e_{k1} \ldots e_{kp}$ are the actual computed parameters. An attempt is made to resolve this set of constraints with $Z_1 \ldots Z_p$ in the known set. The set of constraints will have to be resolved as computation for all the unknowns in $e_{k1} \ldots e_{kp}$. If this is done, a call node (which invokes the dependence graph for the constraint module call) is generated. A child node of the call node receives values computed by the call node and binds them to $Z_1 \ldots Z_p$ and performs the computation generated from the new set of constraints.

If the traversal returns "False" (a dependence graph is not generated) then the current search path is discarded. Each constraint module invocation is translated as a separate program module. It might seem that many redundant translations would be performed. But a table can be maintained for each module which contains entries showing the dependence graphs generated for combinations of parameter inputs. Redundant translations can be eliminated this way.

5.3.2 Extraction of OR parallelism

Multiple paths in the dependence graph have the potential to be executed in parallel. These paths have resulted from the extraction of computation from constraints connected by OR operators.

5.3.3 Extraction of AND parallelism

The computational statements that are assigned to a node have the potential for parallel execution. Parallelism is exploited by keeping in mind that the compiler generates a single-assignment system and the lone write to a variable will appear before any reads to it. The granularity of such a scheme depends on the complexity of the functions invoked in the statements and the complexity of the operators. We have further exploited the complexity of matrix operations by splitting up the specifications, performing computations in parallel and composing them. For example, if $x = m*y+m*z$, where x, m, y, z, and b are matrices, $m*y$ and $m*z$ can be done in parallel. This leads to significant speedup since multiplication of matrices is an $O(N^3)$ operation (m, y, z being order $N \times N$).

Since $m * y$ is a primitive operation, a procedure which implements a parallel algorithm for $m * y$ can be invoked. In a later version of the compiler, provision will be made for user specification of parallelism for operations over structures. For a detailed description of the types of parallelism extracted see [11].

Parallelism in AND indexed sets: To extract parallelism, the computations within the compiled loop structures corresponding to *AND* indexed sets are examined. We discuss the case of loops with a single computation. The discussion can be generalized to the case of loops with multiple computations. Throughout this discussion, the case of array accesses will be detailed. The case of scalar accesses in loops will follow trivially since they do not involve indexed terms.

(i) If the array corresponding to the computed term is not accessed anywhere in the computation, all iterations of the loop can be executed in parallel.

(ii) If the array corresponding to the computed term is accessed in the computation and the set of accessed indices of the array are disjoint from the set of computed indices of the array, all iterations of the loop can be executed in parallel.

(iii) If cases (i) and (ii) do not hold, the loop iterations are inter-dependent and are executed sequentially.

5.4 Phase 4

We have yet to completely define Phase 4. As of now, there are provisions in the system to select certain program variables as shared variables in a shared memory environment. Also, some operations (e.g. matrix multiplication) can be chosen for parallel execution.

5.5 Phase 5

Our target for executable for constraint programs is the CODE [14] parallel programming environment. CODE takes a dependence graph as its input. The form of a node in a CODE dependence graph is given in Figure 7(a). It is seen that there is a natural match between the nodes of the dependence graph developed by the constraint compilation algorithm and the nodes in the CODE graph. The arcs in the dependence graph in CODE are used to bind names from one node to another. This is exactly the role played by arcs in the dependence graph generated by our translation algorithm. CODE produces sequential and parallel C programs for a variety of architectures.

6 Programming Examples and Results

A prototype of the compiler has been implemented in C++. A small number of examples have also been programmed and executed on the Cray J90, SPARC-center 2000, Sequent Symmetry machine and the PVM system. The next two subsections describe two examples programmed in our system.

6.1 Block Triangular Solver(BTS)

The example chosen is the solution of the $AX = B$ linear algebra problem for a known lower triangular matrix A and vector B. The parallel algorithm [5] involves dividing the matrix into blocks and a constraint program (excluding declarations) for a problem instance split into 4 blocks is shown in Figure 8. $S_0 \ldots S_3$ represent lower triangular sub-matrices along the diagonal of A that are solved sequentially, and $M_{10}, M_{20}, \ldots M_{32}$ represent dense sub-matrices within A that must be multiplied by the X sub-vector from above and the result subtracted from the X sub-vector from the left. The vector multiplications for all Ms within a column may be done in parallel. This parallelism yields an ideal asymptotic speedup of $P^2/(3P-2)$, where P is the number of processors. Ideal speedup assumes zero communication and synchronization times.

$$
\begin{array}{|l|}
\hline
(S_0 * X_0 == B_0 \ AND \\
M_{10} * X_0 + S_1 * X_1 == B_1 \ AND \\
M_{20} * X_0 + M_{21} * X_1 + S_2 * X_2 == B_2 \ AND \\
M_{30} * X_0 + M_{31} * X_1 + M_{32} * X_2 + S_3 * X_3 == B_3 \ ) \\
\hline
\end{array}
$$

Fig. 8. Specification of the BTS Algorithm as a Constraint System

The input set can be chosen as $\{ S_0, \ldots, S_3, M_{10}, M_{20}, \ldots, M_{32} \}$. The output set will be detected as $\{X_0, X_1, X_2, X_3\}$. Using an indexed set of constraints and an indexed operator, an alternate compact program is
AND FOR (i 0 3) { + FOR (j 0 i) { $A[i][j] * X[j]$ } == $B[i]$ }
where the subscripts for A, X, and B define partitions on the matrices.

Figure 9(a) gives the speedups for a 1200 × 1200 matrix on a shared memory Sequent machine. It is seen that the performance of the constraint generated code is comparable to the hand-coded program's performance. The difference in speedups is mainly due to the fact that the hand-coded program is optimized for a shared memory execution environment. (These results were obtained with an earlier version of the constraint compiler before any provision for specification of execution environments were implemented and the Sequent computer system is no longer available, now that the optimizing compiler is available.) Figure 9(b) gives the speedups for a 8800 × 8800 matrix (number of blocks=11, block size=800) on an 8-processor SPARCcenter2000. This program has been optimized for shared variables. It is to be noted that the constraint generated code performs quite well for the small number of processors available. The speedups are slightly higher than the ideal (the ideal is asymptotic) until about 7 processors, after which it drops.

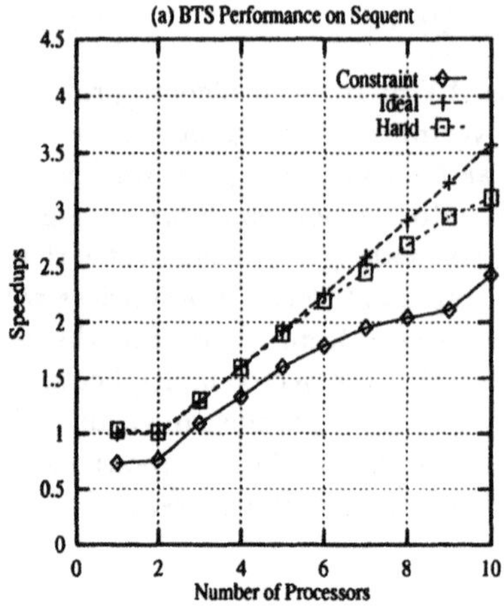

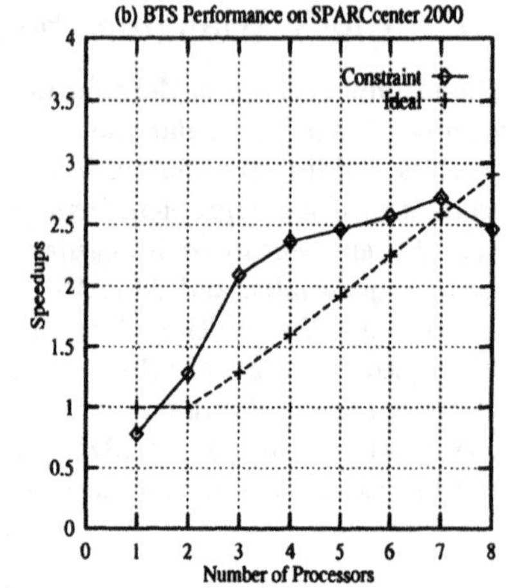

Fig. 9. Performance Results for BTS on (a) Sequent (b) SPARCcenter 2000

6.2 The Block Odd-Even Reduction Algorithm(BOER)

Consider a linear tridiagonal system $Ax = d$ where

$$A = \begin{bmatrix} B & C & 0 & 0 & \dots & 0 & 0 & 0 \\ C & B & C & 0 & \dots & 0 & 0 & 0 \\ 0 & C & B & C & \dots & 0 & 0 & 0 \\ \vdots & \vdots & \vdots & \vdots & \vdots & \vdots & \vdots & \vdots \\ 0 & 0 & 0 & 0 & \dots & C & B & C \\ 0 & 0 & 0 & 0 & \dots & 0 & C & B \end{bmatrix}$$

is a block tridiagonal matrix and B and C are square matrices of order $n \geq 2$. It is assumed that there are M such blocks along the principal diagonal of A, and $M = 2^k - 1$, for some $k \geq 2$. Thus, $N = Mn$ denotes the order of A. It is assumed that the vectors x and d are likewise partitioned, that is, $x = (x_1, x_2, \dots, x_M)^t$, $d = (d_1, d_2, \dots, d_M)^t$, $x_i = (x_{i1}, x_{i2}, \dots, x_{in})^t$, and $d_i = (d_{i1}, d_{i2}, \dots, d_{in})^t$, for $i = 1, 2, \dots, M$. It is further assumed that the blocks B and C are symmetric and commute.

A version of the parallel algorithm (taken from [12]) has a reduction phase in which the system is split into two subsystems: one for odd-indexed (reduced system) and another for even-indexed (eliminated system) terms. The reduction process is repeatedly applied to the reduced system. After $k - 1$ iterations the reduced system contains the solution for a single term. The rest of the terms can be obtained by back-substitution. The constraint specification for the problem is shown in Figure 10. The variable names, BP, CP, dP correspond to the indexed terms B,C,d in [12] and are examples of the hierarchical data type in our system (elements of BP, CP and dP are matrices). The inputs to the system are $BP[0]$, $CP[0]$ and $dP[i][0]$. *pow* is a C function implementing the arithmetic power function. The terms in bold in Figure 10 are detected by the compiler in phase 3 as the terms to be computed.

```
BP[k-1] * x[pow(2,k-1)] == dP[pow(2,k-1)][k-1] AND

AND FOR (j 1 k-1) {
   2 * CP[j-1] * CP[j-1] == BP[j] + BP[j-1] * BP[j-1] ,
   CP[j] - CP[j-1] * CP[j-1] == 0 ,
   AND FOR (i 0 pow(2,k-j)-2) {
      CP[j-1] * ( dP[i*pow(2,j) + pow(2,j-1)][j-1] + dP[i*pow(2,j) - pow(2,j-1)][j-1] ) ==
               dP[i*pow(2,j)][j] + BP[j-1] * dP[i*pow(2,j)][j-1] }} AND

AND FOR (j k-1 1) {
   AND FOR (i 0 pow(2,k-j)-1) {
      CP[j-1] * ( x[(i+1)*pow(2,j)] + x[i*pow(2,j)] ) ==
         dP[(i+1)*pow(2,j)-pow(2,j-1)][j-1] - BP[j-1] * x[(i+1)*pow(2,j)-pow(2,j-1)] }}
```

Fig. 10. Specification of the BOER Algorithm as a Constraint System

The resulting dataflow graph is shown in Figure 11(a) and corresponds to the dataflow in the algorithm in [12]. The *START* and *STOP* nodes initiate and terminate the program, respectively. A *FOR* node initiates the different iterations of a loop. The two such nodes in the figure correspond to the two outer indexed sets for index j in the constraint specification. The annotation "Replicated" on the arcs specify that the annotated arc and the destination node (shaded in Figure 11(a)) are dynamically replicated for parallel execution. The two such annotated arcs correspond to the two nested indexed sets (for index i) in the constraint specification. The nodes annotated by *BP*, *CP*, *dP*, and x compute values for parts of the corresponding variable. The nodes annotated by "Merge" collect computed results from parallel executions. It is to be noted that our compiler automatically detects the parallelism in the *for* loops in the reduction and back-substitution phases. Furthermore, it is capable of detecting the parallelism within the expression $2 * CP[j-1] * CP[j-1] - BP[j-1] * BP[j-1]$ in the computation for $BP[j]$. The authors in [12] have mentioned that the single-solution step is the major bottleneck in the algorithm. But, in our experiments we found the reduction phase resistant to scalability. This is due to the fact that the computation for $BP[j]$ and $CP[j]$ involve matrix-matrix multiplication: an $O(n^3)$ operation. This dominates the scalable part of the loop: the computation of dP, which is $O(n^2)$. In later versions of the compiler, we plan to incorporate parallel algorithms for matrix-matrix multiplication, which will overcome this bottleneck. Figure 11(b) presents the speedups over a sequential implementation of the algorithm on an 8-processor SPARCcenter 2000 for n=200 and $k = 7 (M = 127)$ and $k = 8 (M = 255)$ for the back-substitution phase of the algorithm. Note the attainment of near-linear speedup for this (relatively small) number of processors.

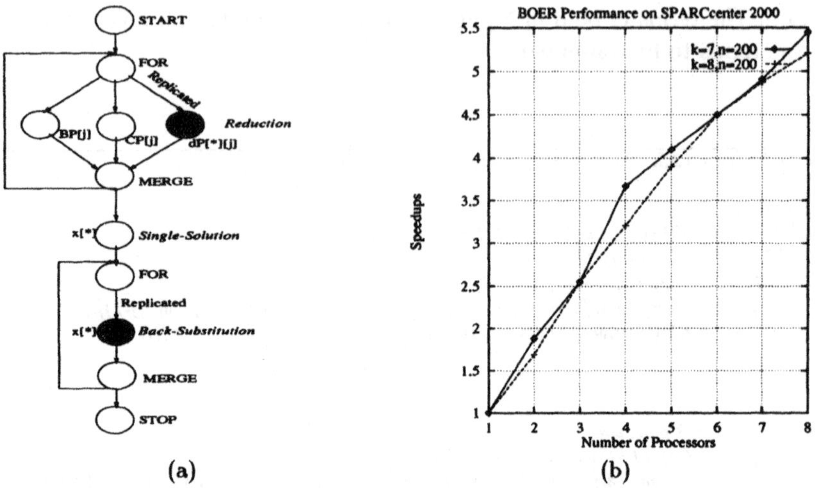

Fig. 11. BOER Program: (a)Dataflow Graph (b) Performance Results

7 Summary

Constraint programs offer a rich, relatively untapped representation of computation, from which parallelism can be readily extracted. Constraint systems with appropriate sets of input variables can be mapped to generalized dependence graphs. Coarse-grain parallelism can be extracted through modularity, operations over structured types, and specification of arithmetic functions. Data parallelism is introduced through the parallel execution of iterations of loops over computations on different partitions of matrices. By giving the programmer control over compilation choices for the execution environment, we assist in generation of architecturally optimized parallel programs. The first stage of research has established that constraint systems can be compiled to efficient coarse grained parallel programs for some plausible examples.

8 Future Research

It is clearly necessary to be able to express constraints on partitions of matrices if large scale parallelism is to be derived from constraint systems without use of the cumbersome techniques derived for array dependence analysis of scalar loop codes over arrays. There are several promising approaches: object-oriented formulations of data structures are one possibility. A simpler and more algorithmic basis for definition of constraints over partitions of matrices is to utilize a simple version of the hierarchical type theory for matrices of Collins and Browne [4].

The next steps in addition to inclusion of the hierarchical matrix type are as follows. a) Enhance the compiler with the capability of converting single-assignment variables to "destructive-update" variables so that excessive memory usage can be avoided in iterative numerical algorithms. b) Extend the AND indexed set construct to handle more general forms of constraints. c) Define and implement completely the execution environment specification.

References

1. Doug Baldwin. A status report on consul. In Nicolau Gelernter and Padua, editors, *Languages and Compilers for Parallel Computing.* MIT Press, 1990.
2. K.M. Chandy and J. Misra. *Parallel Program Design : A Foundation.* Addison-Wesley, 1989.
3. K.M. Chandy and S. Taylor. *An Introduction to Parallel Programming.* Jones and Bartlett, 1992.
4. T.S. Collins and J.C. Browne. Matrix++: An object-oriented environment for parallel high-perfomance matrix computations. In *Proc. of the Hawaii Intl. Conf. on Systems and Software,* 1995.
5. J.J. Dongarra and D.C. Sorenson. Schedule: Tools for developing and analyzing parallel fortran programs. Technical Report 86, Argonne National Laboratory, November 1986.
6. I. Foster and S. Taylor. *Strand: New Concepts in Parallel Programming.* Prentice Hall, 1990.
7. Ian Foster. *Designing and Building Parallel Programs.* Addison-Wesley, 1995.
8. B. Freeman-Benson and Alan Borning. The design and implementation of kaleidoscope '90, a constraint imperative programming language. In *Computer Languages,* pages 174–180. IEEE Computer Society, April 1992.
9. Bjorn N. Freeman-Benson. A module compiler for thinglab ii. In *Proc. 1989 ACM Conf. on Object-Oriented Programming Systems, Languages, and Applications,* October 1989.
10. Al Geist, Adam Beguelin, Jack Dongarra, Weicheng Jiang, Robert Manchek, and Vaidy Sunderam. *PVM: Parallel Virtual Machine:A Users' Guide and Tutorial for Networked Parallel Computing.* MIT Press, 1994.
11. Ajita John and J.C. Browne. Extraction of parallelism from constraint specifications. In *Proceedings of the International Conference on Parallel and Distributed Processing Techniques and Applications,* volume III, pages 1501–1512, August 1996.
12. S. Lakshmivarahan and Sudarshan K. Dhall. *Analysis and Design of Parallel Algorithms: Arithmetic and Matrix Problems.* Supercomputing and Parallel Processing. McGraw-Hill, 1990.
13. Michael Mehl, Ralf Scheidhauer, and Christian Schulte. An abstract machine for oz. In *Programming Languages, Implementations, Logics and Programs, Seventh Intl. Symposium, LNCS,* number 982. Springer-Verlag, September 1995.
14. P. Newton and J. C. Browne. The code 2.0 graphical parallel programming environment. In *Proc. of the Intl. Conf. on Supercomputing,* pages 167–177, 1992.
15. Harvey Richardson. High performance fortran: History, overview and current developments. Technical Report TMC 261, Thinking Machines Corporation.
16. Vijay A. Saraswat. *Concurrent Constraint Programming Languages.* PhD thesis, Carnegie Mellon, School of Computer Science, Pittsburgh, 1989.

A Multithreaded Substrate and Compilation Model for the Implicitly Parallel Language pH

Arvind,[1] Alejandro Caro,[1] Jan-Willem Maessen,[1] and Shail Aditya[2]

[1] MIT Laboratory for Computer Science***
[2] Hewlett-Packard Laboratories†

Abstract. We describe the compilation of the non-strict, implicitly parallel language pH to symmetric multiprocessors (SMPs). First, we introduce the λ_S calculus as a robust foundation for the semantics of pH. Next, we define a Shared-Memory Threaded (SMT) abstract machine that captures the essence of our SMP compilation target. Finally, we describe a syntax directed translation of λ_S to SMT instructions. The paper makes three important contributions: it is the first implementation of pH based on a *direct* semantics of barriers; the compilation rules generate code from λ_S without using intermediate dataflow graphs; and the multithreaded code emitted by the compiler uses *suspensive* threads.

1 Introduction

This paper describes the compilation of the pH language for symmetric multiprocessors (SMPs). pH is a parallel dialect of the functional language Haskell [9] designed to support general purpose parallel programming, including unstructured problems. Because the language is both implicitly parallel and non-strict, pH programs are highly concurrent and eminently portable across machine architectures.

The philosophy underlying the design of pH is simple: to have broad impact, parallel programming must be easy. Let the programmer concentrate on the algorithms; let the compiler worry about efficient implementation. Today, this viewpoint does not find broad acceptance in the parallel computing community. Yet, as the cost of parallel machines drops, programmability is bound to become *the* overriding concern in parallel software development. We believe the emergence of powerful, relatively affordable SMPs represents the beginning of the end for the high priesthood of parallel programming. Languages like pH, HPF, and SISAL will make parallel machines accessible to the programming masses.

The compilation scheme for pH is based on fine-grain *multithreading*. pH programs consist of a large number of threads that compute, communicate, and

*** This research was performed entirely at the MIT Laboratory for Computer Science and was supported by ARPA contract DABT63-95-C-0150. Email: {arvind,acaro,earwig}@abp.lcs.mit.edu

† Email: aditya@hplsag.hpl.hp.com

synchronize with minimal overhead. Multithreading is used because it enables the compiler to exploit the fine-grain concurrency available in a program and because it simplifies the implementation of correct language semantics.

1.1 Related Work

The history of pH, and its predecessor Id, has been closely coupled with the evolution of dataflow architectures. The dataflow execution model offers vast instruction-level parallelism but requires cheap synchronization. Custom-built dataflow machines like Monsoon [12] proved to be ideal vehicles to execute languages like Id and pH. Unfortunately, these machines were doomed by the onslaught of commercial processor technology, despite the disadvantages of the standard von Neumann architecture in a parallel setting.

Significant work has been done to implement languages like pH on standard processors. Traub's seminal work on *partitioning* [11] partially inspired the TAM work at Berkeley [7] and the pHluid work by Nikhil [8]. Both these systems convert programs into dataflow graphs with control flow information encoded as explicit "signals". The graphs are then divided into partitions, each of which is compiled into a single sequential thread. This approach to code generation suffers from several weaknesses due to its dataflow foundations. For example, the implementation of control flow makes poor use of the mechanisms offered by von Neumann processors. Also, execution efficiency on pipelined processors is hampered by short instruction sequences.

In contrast to earlier approaches, the compilation scheme described in this paper is a syntax directed translation of pH (in its kernel form) directly to multithreaded code. The compilation process avoids dataflow graphs entirely and generates code that takes advantage of the strengths of the underlying von Neumann architecture. This general approach is based on two previous research efforts: early work by Ariola and Arvind on compilation of Id to P-TAC [4]; and recent work by Aditya [1] utilizing a slightly different source language and target machine than those presented here.

The compilation of pH is also closely related to the compilation of languages like Haskell [10] and ML [3]. Non-strict languages like pH and Haskell must refer to values that have not been computed. While Haskell uses *thunks* for this purpose, pH uses memory locations extended with *presence* information instead. Being *eagerly* evaluated, pH does not need thunks. Strict languages like ML need no such mechanism because values are guaranteed to be computed before they are used. Still, compilers for all three languages address many common issues, such as optimizations for polymorphism (unboxing) and compilation for garbage collection (run-time type reconstruction).

1.2 Contributions

We make three important contributions in this paper. We present the first implementation of pH based on the precise, *direct* semantics of barriers as captured by the λ_S calculus [6]. Previous efforts, including our own Id compiler for Monsoon, used either poorly defined, ad-hoc semantics or precise semantics based on program transformations [2]. The new semantics require major changes in the implementation of free variables, bound variables, and closures.

Second, our compilation scheme generates threaded code directly from pH (λ_S), without resorting to dataflow graphs. From a theoretical point of view, we believe it is important to present pH as a language that stands on its own, apart from its dataflow roots. From an implementation point of view, we avoid many of the inefficiencies introduced into threaded code by the dataflow model of computation, and we expose many opportunities for generating better code for SMPs.

Finally, our compilation scheme makes use of ***suspensive*** threads that make optimistic assumptions about synchronization. Suspensive threads begin to execute assuming all required values have been computed and suspend only if one of these values is missing. In contrast, the non-suspensive threads used by TAM and pHluid make pessimistic assumptions about synchronization. Such a thread will begin to execute only when all the values it requires have been computed. We believe suspensive threads are superior for two reasons: overhead due to thread suspension is reduced and thread lengths increase.

1.3 Roadmap

In Sect. 2, we give a quick overview of the λ_S calculus, the kernel for the pH language. Section 3 presents a concrete view of the execution environment for compiled λ_S programs. Section 4 describes the SMT parallel abstract machine and its instruction set. In Sect. 5, we bring together λ_S and SMT by providing a syntax directed translation of the λ_S language into SMT instructions. The translation rules are designed to be simple, and as given, they produce inefficient but correct code. We mention several optimizations that can improve the quality of the code. Finally, we conclude with a discussion of the status of our implementation and directions for future work.

2 The λ_S Calculus

The λ_S calculus is a variant of the call-by-need λ calculus. The front-end of the compiler converts programs from the full pH language to the simpler λ_S representation for use in subsequent phases. The calculus captures the semantics of pH precisely, including its unique features. λ_S uses recursive let bindings to express the sharing of values in a program. It also allows reductions to occur in parallel on different parts of a term. It includes I-structure and M-structure heap operations that perform necessary synchronization within the term without the need for a separate store. Finally, it provides a direct semantics for ***barriers*** in binding groups. The syntax of the λ_S calculus is presented in Fig. 1. The detailed semantics of λ_S are beyond the scope of this paper; for a more thorough discussion, refer to [6].

E	$::= x$	:: identifier
	$\mid \lambda x.E$	:: abstraction
	$\mid x\ y$	:: application
	$\mid \{S \text{ in } x\}$	:: letrec block
	$\mid \texttt{Case}(x, E_1 \ldots E_k)$	:: integer conditional
	$\mid PF^k(x_1 \ldots x_k)$	:: k-ary primitive
	$\mid Number \mid Boolean \mid \ldots \mid Location$	:: constant
	$\mid CN^k(x_1 \ldots x_k)$	:: constructor application
	$\mid \texttt{allocate}(x)$	:: mutable allocation
	$\mid \top$	:: error value (top)
S	$::= \epsilon$	:: empty binding
	$\mid x = E$	:: identifier binding
	$\mid S\ ;\ S$	:: parallel composition
	$\mid S \text{—} S$	:: barrier, sequential composition
	$\mid \texttt{iStore}(x, y)$	:: I-structure store
	$\mid \texttt{mStore}(x, y)$	:: M-structure store
	$\mid \top_S$	:: error binding
PF^1	$::= \texttt{not} \mid \texttt{iFetch} \mid \texttt{mFetch} \mid \texttt{Prj}^1 \mid \texttt{Prj}^2 \mid \ldots$	:: unary primitives
PF^2	$::= + \mid - \mid * \mid \ldots$	:: binary primitives
CN^2	$::= Cons \mid Pair \mid \ldots$	:: data constructors

Note that all bound variables for a block are pairwise distinct. Also, the following identities apply:

$$
\begin{array}{lll}
S_1\ ;\ S_2 & \equiv S_2\ ;\ S_1 & :: \text{commutativity of ;} \\
S_1\ ;\ (S_2\ ;\ S_3) & \equiv (S_1\ ;\ S_2)\ ;\ S_3 & :: \text{associativity of ;}
\end{array}
$$

Fig. 1. Syntax of the Kernel λ_S Calculus

Though non-strict, the λ_S calculus is quite different from the formal systems underlying lazy functional languages like Haskell. The first major difference between λ_S and lazy languages is that λ_S is evaluated *eagerly*. This means that λ_S will evaluate *all* expressions, even if they are not necessary to compute a result. Lazy languages evaluate only those expressions that are absolutely necessary to produce a result.

In addition, the λ_S calculus includes *barriers* (indicated by '—'), a construct used to sequentialize the execution of statements. In the following example,

$$
\begin{array}{l}
a = \ldots; \\
b = \bot; \\
(x = \texttt{Case}(a, 7, b); \\
\text{—} \\
S\ )
\end{array}
$$

the statement x above the barrier is considered to be in the *pre-region* of the barrier. The statement S is considered to be the *post-region* of the barrier. The barrier guarantees that everything in the pre-region will be computed before the post-region is executed. This implies that, recursively, the branch selected by the Case expression must terminate before the barrier *discharges*. In this particular example, if the value of a is 1 then the barrier will discharge; if the value of a is 2, the barrier will not discharge because the evaluation of b does not terminate.

The third important difference between λ_S and lazy functional languages is that λ_S is not purely functional. It incorporates side-effects through two kinds of synchronizing memory: I-structures and M-structures. An I-structure location can be written at most once and can be read many times. If any reads occur before the single write, the reads are said to "defer" until the write occurs. The computations that performed the reads will wait until the value of the location is computed and stored in the location. An M-structure location can be read and written multiple times, but with mutual exclusion. Only one computation can read the value of an M-structure location at a time. Once the value is read successfully, subsequent readers are deferred until a value is written back. Then, only one of the deferred readers will receive the value written back while the rest remain deferred.

The source language used in the syntax directed translation presented in Sect. 5 is the λ_S calculus with two small changes. First, all barriers are named with a unique identifier, so that '—' becomes '–b–', where b is the unique identifier for the barrier. This change allows the compiler to refer to a barrier as if it were a local "variable" and allows the allocation of resources to implement the barrier. Second, all non-essential blocks—those not appearing inside Case expressions and λ-abstractions—are flattened into a single block.

3 Execution Environment

This section highlights the most interesting aspects of the execution environment for the compiled λ_S code. We assume the following about the abstract target machine: a single global memory shared by all processors; memory locations which indicate whether or not a value is present in the location (full vs. defer); and a set of registers per processor. The detailed description of the machine is left to Sect. 4. Figure 2 illustrates the run-time data structures used by a particular piece of compiled code.

3.1 Locations for Variables

The correct implementation of the semantics of λ_S requires a mechanism by which programs can refer to values without having to compute them. Consider the problem of creating a closure. A closure contains a vector of free variables that captures those pieces of the lexical environment that *may* be used by the code of the closure. What object should be stored in the closure for a free variable? We might consider storing the value of the free variable, but if the free variable

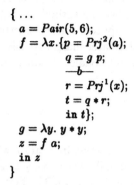

$$
\begin{array}{l}
\{\ldots \\
\quad a = Pair(5,6); \\
\quad f = \lambda x.\{p = Prj^2(a); \\
\qquad\qquad q = g\ p; \\
\qquad\qquad \text{---}b\text{---} \\
\qquad\qquad r = Prj^1(x); \\
\qquad\qquad t = q * r; \\
\qquad\qquad \mathbf{in}\ t\}; \\
\quad g = \lambda y.\ y * y; \\
\quad z = f\ a; \\
\quad \mathbf{in}\ z \\
\}
\end{array}
$$

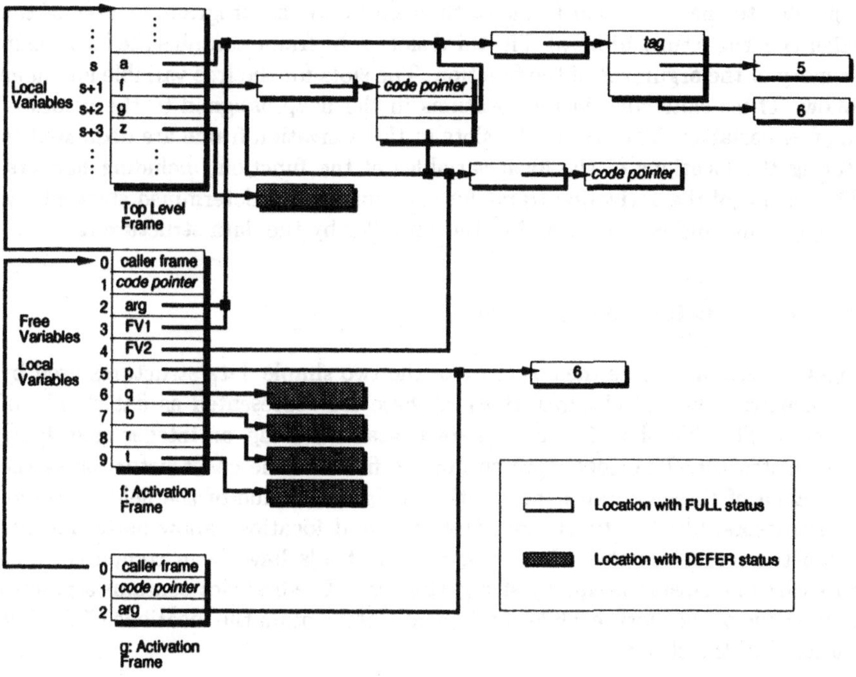

Fig. 2. Execution Environment of Compiled Code. The figure shows the state of the machine before the execution of the $*$ in function g.

is not actually used in the closure at run-time, then we will have computed its value prematurely. In other words, closures are non-strict with respect to free variables.

The correct solution to this problem requires that we store the *name* of the free variable in the closure. Suppose that every variable in a program is assigned a location in memory; a *pointer* to this location is a representation of the name of the variable. It uniquely identifies the variable, yet it is independent of whether or not the variable has been computed. This is exactly the behavior required, and the compilation rules presented later make extensive use of locations (pointers) to guarantee that barriers, conditionals, closures, and non-strict function calls behave as expected.

3.2 Activation Frames

Activation frames provide each function invocation with private space for storing local variables. In our simple compiling scheme, activation frames are allocated in the shared heap as "flat" blocks of memory. The first two slots of a frame contain a pointer to the activation frame of the caller and the program counter of the caller (*i.e.* the return address). The third slot in the frame contains the location in memory of the argument of the function. The slots for the free variable locations follow. These slots contain the locations in the heap assigned to the values of the free variables. The rest of the slots in the activation frame are dedicated to storing the locations of the local variables of the function, including barriers. The format of the activation frame for each function is determined statically at compile-time and is represented in the compiler by the data structure α.

3.3 Constructors and Closures

Figure 2 also illustrates the structure of the two simple data structures used by λ_S: constructors and closures. Both of these are represented as flat chunks of memory. The first slot of a constructor contains the *tag*, an integer identifying the constructor. The slots representing the fields of the constructor follow the tag. Each of these contains the location where the value of the field is stored. Constructors, like functions, are non-strict, and locations allow us to allocate a constructor before the values of any of its fields have been computed. The structure of a closure is equally straightforward. The first slot contains a pointer to the code of the closure while subsequent slots contain the locations of the free variables of the closure.

3.4 Barriers

The compiled code uses a counter to implement each barrier in the program. As each binding in a pre-region terminates, the associated counter is decremented. When the counter reaches zero, the barrier is effectively discharged. It is important to notice that barriers can be nested, so that different parts of the program belong to different barrier pre-regions. Any particular instance of a statement, however, is associated with only one barrier. As the program executes, the identity of the *current* barrier changes. λ_S programs are compiled so that register rB always contains the location of the current barrier.

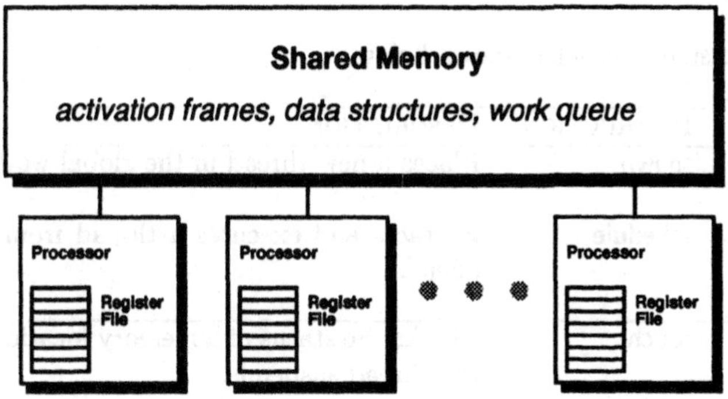

Fig. 3. SMT: A Shared-Memory Threaded Abstract Machine

4 SMT: A Shared-Memory Threaded Abstract Machine

4.1 Overview

The structure of our Shared-Memory Threaded (SMT) abstract machine is illustrated in Fig. 3. The machine consists of a number of sequential processors connected to a global shared memory. Each processor has its own register set, but all processors share a common work queue that stores tasks that are ready to run. Tasks are executed from this shared queue in a manner that guarantees fair scheduling. We chose this machine organization because we wanted to closely model a modern SMP.

Each location in the SMT shared memory can contain either a value or a list of *deferred* computations. Locations are tagged with their status, which is initially defer and changes to full when a value is stored in the location. A value is either a constant, an allocated memory location, or a barrier object.

Each SMT processor contains a register file R with a finite number of registers r0,...,rn. There are also two special registers: rB and rF. Register rB contains the location of the current barrier object. Register rF contains the location of the current activation frame.

Threads in SMT are ***suspensive***. By executing one of a small set of synchronizing instructions (touch, touchbar, take), a thread can be made to wait for a value that has not been computed. When the value is finally computed, the waiting thread is placed on the work queue. The value of register r0 in a thread is preserved across suspension points, but the values of all other registers are lost. Finally, it is the responsibility of the compiler or the programmer to ensure that all values requested will be computed eventually. Otherwise the machine will deadlock.

4.2 SMT Instruction Set

The SMT instruction set is shown below.

CLASS	INSTRUCTION	DESCRIPTION
Threads	spawn	Places a new thread in the global work queue.
	schedule	Extracts and executes a thread from the work queue.
Memory	touch	Checks the status of a memory location. If defer, the thread suspends.
	load	Reads a value from full memory into a register.
	store	Writes the contents of a register into memory.
	istore	Writes the contents of a register into memory and places deferred threads on the work queue.
	take	Reads a value in memory with mutual exclusion.
Primitives	plus, minus...	Basic arithmetic operations on registers.
	allocate	Allocates fresh memory locations from shared memory.
Control Flow	exec	Performs a "branch-and-link".
	switch	Chooses an instruction sequence to execute according to the value in a register.
Barrier	initbar	Initializes a new barrier object.
	touchbar	Checks the status of a barrier. If the barrier has not discharged, the current thread suspends.
	incbar	Increments a barrier counter.
	decbar	Decrements a barrier counter.
General	move	Transfers the contents of one register to another.
	print	Displays the contents of a register.
	halt	Stops execution on all processors.

There are four addressing modes that can be used by SMT instructions. In the following descriptions, ν represents a value, ℓ represents a memory location, σ represents shared memory (a mapping from locations to values), (rn) denotes the contents of register n, and $\underline{i}$ is a compile-time constant:

MODE	EXAMPLE	MEANING
Register	load(r0, r1)	r0 $\leftarrow \nu$, where σ[(r1) $\mapsto$ $\langle$full $\nu\rangle$]
Register Indexed	load(r0, r1[i])	r0 $\leftarrow \nu$, where σ[(r1) + $\underline{i}$ $\mapsto$ $\langle$full $\nu\rangle$]
Register Indirect	load(r0, @r1)	r0 $\leftarrow \nu$, where σ[(r1) $\mapsto$ $\langle$full $\ell\rangle$, $\ell \mapsto$ $\langle$full $\nu\rangle$]
Register Indexed Indirect	load(r0, @r1[i])	r0 $\leftarrow \nu$, where σ[(r1) + $\underline{i}$ $\mapsto$ $\langle$full $\ell\rangle$, $\ell \mapsto$ $\langle$full $\nu\rangle$]

These addressing modes apply to all instructions that are load-like, *i.e.* touch, take, etc. Addressing modes are also used in a similar way in store-like instructions such as istore, incbar, and so on.

5 Compiling λ_S for SMT

In this section, we present an overview of the compilation of λ_S to SMT instructions. The compiler generates code sequences assuming the execution environment described in Sect. 3. Due to space limitations, we present only a selected set of the full compilation rules. The entire compilation scheme is described in detail in [5].

5.1 Compiler Conventions

The compilation rules are described in terms of three translation functions: TE, TS, and TP. These functions take λ_S source code for expressions, statements, and programs respectively as input and return a sequence of abstract machine instructions as output. TE and TS are mutually recursive and are used for compiling the bulk of a λ_S program. TP (not discussed here) is used to generate the "glue" code that sets up the initial execution environment for a program. The rules are presented as if they were written in a high-level programming language and often make use of variables and block-structure.

Identifier Map. The translation functions make use of an identifier map α. The purpose of this map is to translate a source-language identifier at compile-time into an offset (slot) in the activation frame. At run-time, the slot will contain a location where the value of the identifier can be found. The contents of this map are completely static and can be generated directly from the lexical structure of the source program.

References to Code. In the compilation rules, we manipulate sequences of instructions and even store these sequences in registers and data structures. We appeal to the reader's intuition on this point. What is really stored is a *pointer* to the sequence, not the sequence itself.

Register r0. The values of all expressions are computed and placed in register r0. This allows subsequent computations to make use of the value of r0. This is particularly evident in the compilation rule for statements in Sect. 5.3.

5.2 TE: Compilation of Expressions

Identifiers. To get the value of an identifier, we must first make sure that the memory location where it is stored is full. The touch instruction performs this operation. If the location is indeed full, the load instruction proceeds. If the location is not full, the thread will suspend before the load instruction and will wait for the value of the identifier to be computed by some other thread.

$$\mathbf{TE}[x]\ \alpha = [\ \mathsf{touch}(@\mathsf{rF}[\underline{\mathsf{x}}]), \mathsf{load}(\mathsf{r0}, @\mathsf{rF}[\underline{\mathsf{x}}])\ ]$$

where $\underline{\mathsf{x}} = \alpha(x)$

Lambda Abstractions. The rule describing the compilation of lambda abstractions is perhaps the most complicated of all. Functions are responsible for allocating and initializing their own activation frames, so callers actually pass very little information to callees during the call sequence. The calling convention specifies the following contents for registers:

REGISTER	VALUE ON ENTRY	VALUE ON EXIT
r0	Argument location	Result
r1	Return instruction sequence	—
r2	Callee closure	—
rF	Caller's frame	Caller's frame
rB	Caller's barrier	Caller's barrier

The lambda compilation rule is composed of several parts described below. Most of the code is devoted to building the activation frame according to the format presented in Fig. 2:

- *body* : the body of the lambda is compiled using TE with a *modified* identifier map. This identifier map describes the locations of identifiers in the frame that will be created when the function is actually invoked.
- *savestate* : this code sequence allocates an activation frame. It saves the caller's activation frame pointer, the argument *location* (due to non-strictness), and the return instruction sequence in the new frame.
- *copyFV* : this code sequence copies the *locations*, not the values, of the free variables from the callee's closure to the activation frame.
- *locals* : this code sequence allocates space for the local variables of the function and copies these *locations* into the activation frame.

- *return* : this code sequence returns control to the caller. Notice that this code does not touch r0 since it assumes the result resides there.
- *closure* : this code sequence constructs the closure data structure which represents the lambda abstraction. It allocates a block of memory, inserts a reference to the function code, and copies the *locations* of all free variables of the function from the current frame to the closure. The location of the closure—*i.e.* the value of the lambda abstraction—is returned in r0.

$$
\begin{array}{l}
\mathbf{TE}[\![\lambda\, x.E]\!]\ \alpha = \\
\quad \{\ \textit{body} = \mathbf{TE}[\![E]\!]\ \alpha' \\
\quad\ \ \textit{savestate} = [\ \mathsf{allocate(r3,\underline{k}),store(r3,rF),move(rF,r3),store(rF[\underline{2}],r0),} \\
\qquad\qquad\qquad \mathsf{store(rF[\underline{1}],r1)}\ ] \\
\quad\ \ \textit{copyFV} = [\ \mathsf{load(r0,r2[\underline{1}]),store(rF[\underline{3}],r0),\ldots,load(r0,r2[\underline{m}]),} \\
\qquad\qquad\qquad \mathsf{store(rF[\underline{2+m}],r0)}\ ] \\
\quad\ \ \textit{locals} = [\ \mathsf{allocate(r4,\underline{n}),store(rF[\underline{3+m}],r4),plus(r4,r4,\underline{1}),store(rF[\underline{4+m}],r4),} \\
\qquad\qquad \mathsf{\ldots,plus(r4,r4,\underline{1}),store(rF[\underline{2+m+n}],r4)}\ ] \\
\quad\ \ \textit{buildframe} = \textit{savestate} + \!\!\!+\ \textit{copyFV} + \!\!\!+\ \textit{locals} \\
\quad\ \ \textit{return} = [\ \mathsf{load(r1,rF[\underline{1}]),load(rF,rF),exec(r1,\_)}\ ] \\
\quad\ \ \textit{func} = \textit{buildframe} + \!\!\!+\ \textit{body} + \!\!\!+\ \textit{return} \\
\quad\ \ \textit{closure} = [\ \mathsf{allocate(r0,\underline{m+1}),store(r0,}\textit{func}\mathsf{),} \\
\qquad\qquad\quad \mathsf{load(r1,rF[\underline{y_1}]),store(r0[\underline{1}],r1),\ldots,load(r1,rF[\underline{y_m}]),store(r0[\underline{m}],r1)}] \\
\quad\ \ \mathtt{in} \\
\qquad\quad \textit{closure} \\
\quad \}
\end{array}
$$

$$
\begin{array}{ll}
\text{where} & \underline{\mathsf{m}} = |\ FV(\lambda x.E)\ | \\
& y_1,\ldots,y_m = FV(\lambda x.E) \\
& \underline{\mathsf{y_1}} = \alpha(y_1),\ldots,\underline{\mathsf{y_m}} = \alpha(y_m) \\
& \underline{\mathsf{n}} = |\ BV(E)\ | \\
& b_1,\ldots,b_n = BV(E) \\
& \underline{\mathsf{k}} = \underline{\mathsf{m}} + \underline{\mathsf{n}} + 3 \\
& \alpha'(x) = \{\ x \mapsto 2, y_1 \mapsto 3,\ldots,y_m \mapsto 2+\underline{\mathsf{m}}, \\
& \qquad\qquad b_1 \mapsto 3+\underline{\mathsf{m}},\ldots,b_n \mapsto 2+\underline{\mathsf{m}}+\underline{\mathsf{n}}\ \}
\end{array}
$$

FV(E) denotes the free variables of expression *E*; | *FV(E)* | denotes the number of free variables; *BV(E)* denotes the set of local variables and barriers, with the exception of those that are bound inside of enclosed lambda abstractions; | *BV(E)* | denotes the number of local variables.

Application. The callee does most of the work in an application, so the caller simply loads the registers according to the calling convention. The value of f is expected to be a closure.

$$
\mathbf{TE}[\![f\ x]\!]\ \alpha = [\mathsf{touch(@rF[\underline{f}]),load(r2,@rF[\underline{f}]),load(r3,r2),load(r0,rF[\underline{x}]),exec(r3,r1)}]
$$

where $\underline{\mathsf{f}} = \alpha(f)$, $\underline{\mathsf{x}} = \alpha(x)$

Blocks. The semantics of λ_S prevent the compiler from statically determining the order in which the statements in a block will execute. Consequently, each statement is simply executed in a separate thread. This rule begins by incrementing the counter of the current barrier as a prelude to creating the thread that will execute the statements. The compilation rules maintain the invariant that for every statement in the program, there is a corresponding incbar or initbar instruction. In turn, the last instruction in the code sequence for every statement is decbar. Thus, proper barrier behavior is maintained.

$$\begin{aligned}\mathbf{TE}[\![\{S \text{ in } x\}]\!]\ \alpha = \{\ & \iota s = (\mathbf{TS}[\![S]\!]\ \alpha) +\!\!+ [\mathsf{schedule}] \\ & \iota s_x = \mathbf{TE}[\![x]\!]\ \alpha \\ & \mathtt{in} \\ & \quad [\ \mathsf{incbar}(\mathsf{rB}), \mathsf{spawn}(\iota s, \_, \mathsf{rB}, \mathsf{rF})\ ] +\!\!+ \iota s_x \\ & \}\end{aligned}$$

5.3 TS: Compilation of Statements

Parallel Statements. The code to execute each statement is placed in its own thread. It is interesting to note that we only need to include a single incbar instruction in the code sequence: we always "inherit" an incbar from a compilation rule at a higher level.

$$\begin{aligned}\mathbf{TS}[\![S_1\ ;\ S_2]\!]\ \alpha = \{\ & \iota s_1 = (\mathbf{TS}[\![S_1]\!]\ \alpha) +\!\!+ [\ \mathsf{schedule}\ ] \\ & \iota s_2 = (\mathbf{TS}[\![S_2]\!]\ \alpha) +\!\!+ [\ \mathsf{schedule}\ ] \\ & \mathtt{in} \\ & \quad [\ \mathsf{incbar}(\mathsf{rB}), \mathsf{spawn}(\iota s_1, \_, \mathsf{rB}, \mathsf{rF}), \mathsf{spawn}(\iota s_2, \_, \mathsf{rB}, \mathsf{rF})\ ] \\ & \}\end{aligned}$$

Sequential Statements. The execution of statements S_1 and S_2 is controlled by the discharge of the barrier separating them. Notice that the barrier has a unique name 'b'. Like any other local variable, it has a slot in the activation frame associated with it. The code initializes barrier b with a counter value of 1, executes the code for S_1, waits for the barrier to discharge and executes the code for S_2. The barrier guarantees that all values computed and all side-effects performed by S_1 will complete before any part of S_2 executes.

$$\begin{aligned}\mathbf{TS}[\![S_1 \text{ -}b\text{- } S_2]\!]\ \alpha = \{\ & \iota s_1 = \mathbf{TS}[\![S_1]\!]\ \alpha \\ & \iota s_2 = \mathbf{TS}[\![S_2]\!]\ \alpha \\ & \mathtt{in} \\ & \quad [\ \mathsf{initbar}(@\mathsf{rF}[\underline{\mathsf{b}}], 1, \mathsf{rB})\ ] +\!\!+ \iota s_1 +\!\!+ [\ \mathsf{touchbar}(@\mathsf{rF}[\underline{\mathsf{b}}])\ ] \\ & \quad +\!\!+ \iota s_2 \\ & \}\end{aligned}$$

where $\underline{\mathsf{b}} = \alpha(b)$

Simple Statements. The code that computes the value of expression E is compiled and combined with code that stores the value in the heap. Notice that the istore instruction assumes the value of the expression exists in register r0. Finally, the current barrier is decremented indicating the completion of the statement.

$$\mathbf{TS}[\![x = E]\!]\ \alpha = (\mathbf{TE}[\![E]\!]\ \alpha) +\!\!+ [\ \mathsf{istore}(@\mathsf{rF}[\underline{\mathsf{x}}], \mathsf{r0}), \mathsf{decbar}(\mathsf{rB})\ ]$$

where $\underline{\mathsf{x}} = \alpha(x)$

5.4 Improvements and Optimizations

The compilation scheme for λ_S described serves as a "proof of concept" of our approach. Though only a subset is presented here, the translation functions handle the entire λ_S language while maintaining correct non-strict semantics in the presence of barriers, closures, and data structures. We do not claim that the translation functions produce efficient code. We do claim, however, that the SMT model embodies the characteristics of a real machine that need to be exposed to a compiler in order to generate good code. We can improve the translation rules significantly, but we do not expect to make major changes to the SMT model in order to produce code that will run well on real SMPs. The following sections present some possible improvements to the translation rules.

Partitioning. In the context of λ_S, the goal of partitioning analysis is to replace several parallel statements with a single statement that can be compiled into one thread. Such *threaded* statements execute much more efficiently than parallel statements because they avoid the thread creation and scheduling overheads. In addition, machine-level optimizations can take advantage of the larger instruction sequences that result from threading in order to allocate resources, like registers, more efficiently.

Expanded Use of Registers. The current compilation rules use SMT registers sparingly. In particular, local variables are always read from the heap through the frames. The SMT machinery does not preclude a more aggressive use of registers, so that, for example, values computed early in a thread could be used directly from registers later in a thread. This optimization is particularly important once a partitioning transformation has been performed.

The only limitation imposed by the machine on the use of registers is that the code must be careful to save live register values across suspension points. The only general purpose register saved by suspensive instructions like touch and take is r0, so any other live registers must be stored in the activation frame of the thread explicitly.

More Efficient Activation Frame Structure. We use flat activation frames mainly to simplify the exposition of the compilation rules. To maintain this structure, however, we must perform many load and store operations when an activation frame is created. A more clever, hierarchical scheme for activation frames would significantly reduce overhead at the cost of complicating the compilation rules.

6 Conclusions

We have presented a scheme for compiling the pH language into the instruction set of an abstract parallel machine. The compilation process is based on the direct semantics of barriers, produces suspensive thread code, and avoids the pitfalls of compiling through dataflow graphs. We are currently implementing a version of the compiler described here, and we plan to generate C code for suspensive, user-level threads that are scheduled by a fast, work-stealing runtime system. We are also examining the implementation of a broad range of optimizations in this framework, including partitioning algorithms.

References

1. S. Aditya. Normalizing Strategies for Multithreaded Interpretation and Compilation of Non-Strict Languages. CSG Memo 374, MIT Laboratory for Computer Science, Cambridge, MA, May 1995.
2. S. Aditya, Arvind, and J.E. Stoy. Semantics of Barriers in a Non-Strict, Implicitly-Parallel Language. In *Proceedings of the 7th ACM Conference on Functional Programming and Computer Architecture*, La Jolla, CA, June 1995.
3. A.W. Appel. *Compiling with Continuations*. Cambridge University Press, 1992.
4. Z.M. Ariola and Arvind. Compilation of Id. In *Proceedings of the Fourth Workshop on Languages and Compilers for Parallel Computing Semantics Based Program Manipulation*, Santa Clara, CA, August 1991.
5. Arvind, A. Caro, J. Maessen, and S. Aditya. A Multithreaded Substrate and Compilation Model for the Implicitly Parallel Language pH. CSG Memo 382, MIT Laboratory for Computer Science, Cambridge, MA, July 1996.
6. Arvind, J. Maessen, R.S. Nikhil, and J.E. Stoy. λ_S: A λ-calculus with Letrec-blocks, Constants, Barriers, and Side-effects. CSG Memo 393, MIT Laboratory for Computer Science, October 1996.
7. D.E. Culler, A. Sah, K.E. Schauser, T. von Eicken, and J. Wawrzynek. Fine Grain Parallelism with Minimal Hardware Support: A Compiler-Controlled Threaded Abstract Machine. In *Proceedings of the Fourth International Conference on Architectural Support for Programming Languages and Operating Systems*, Santa Clara, CA, April 1991.
8. C. Flanagan and R.S. Nikhil. pHluid: The design of a Parallel Functional Language Implementation. In *Proceedings of the 1996 ACM SIGPLAN International Conference on Functional Programming*, Philadelphia, PA, May 1996.
9. P. Hudak, S. Peyton Jones, and P. Wadler (editors). Report on the Programming Language Haskell, A Non-strict Purely Functional Language (Version 1.2). ACM SIGPLAN Notices 27(5), May 1992.
10. S.L. Peyton Jones. *The Implementation of Functional Programming Languages*. Prentice-Hall International, London, 1987.
11. K.R. Traub. *Implementation of Non-Strict Functional Programming Languages*. MIT Press, 1991.
12. K.R. Traub, G.M. Papadopoulos, M.J. Beckerle, J.E. Hicks, and J. Young. Overview of the Monsoon Project. In *Proceedings of the 1991 IEEE International Conference on Computer Design*, Cambridge, MA, October 1991.

Threads for Interoperable Parallel Programming

L. V. Kalé, J. Yelon, and T. Knauff

Dept. of Computer Science,
University of Illinois,
Urbana Illinois 61801,
jyelon@cs.uiuc.edu, kale@cs.uiuc.edu

Abstract. Many thread packages are freely available on the Internet. Yet, most parallel language design groups seem to have rejected all existing packages and implemented their own. This is unsurprising. Existing thread packages were designed for sequential computers, not parallel machines, and do not fit well in a parallel environment. Also importantly, existing thread packages try to impose a number of design decisions, especially in regard to scheduling and preemption. Designers of parallel languages are simply not willing to have scheduling methods decided for them, nor are they willing to allow the threads package to decide how concurrency control will work. In this paper, we explore the special issues raised when threads packages are used on parallel machines, particularly as parts of new parallel languages and systems. We describe the Converse threads subsystem, whose goals are to support the special needs of parallel programs, and to support interoperability among parallel languages. We then demonstrate how the Converse threads subsystem addresses the problems created when threads are used on a parallel computer.

1 Introduction

Many parallel programming languages rely upon lightweight threads as a fundamental component. Threads are extremely useful in implementing a vast range of constructs for parallelism. Use of threads can provide a number of benefits to a parallel program, such as improved latency tolerance, higher degrees of parallelism, and the potential for adaptive scheduling. When designing a set of thread primitives, it makes sense to take into account the special needs of parallel languages. There are many such special needs: parallel language runtime systems tend to impose very strict requirements on the properties of the thread package. Since parallel languages differ so much, each language offering its own set of advantages, it becomes critical to be able to use different languages for different modules of a parallel program. As a result, future parallel applications may contain many languages, with each language's runtime system making different demands of the thread subsystem. The existing threads packages, such as those based on the POSIX threads standard, are not designed for use in parallel programs, and are thus seen to be inadequate for parallel programming. This has led the implementors of new parallel languages to develop their own thread packages tuned to the needs of their language. This obviously makes the development and maintenance of runtime systems for such languages more complex than necessary. At the same time, such specialized thread packages make it harder, if not impossible, to achieve *interoperability* across languages — i.e. allowing multiple modules written in different multi-threaded languages to coexist and interleave their execution in a single program.

In this paper, we present the design and implementation of the Converse threads subsystem, which supports such interoperability. It addresses the issues created by the diverse needs of coexisting parallel languages. The Converse threads subsystem comprises a modular and flexible thread abstraction, related facilities, and protocols, which are used in conjunction with the remainder of the Converse system to implement runtime systems of multi-threaded languages. In the remainder of this section, we examine several of the special problems created when multiple parallel languages all try to share a threads package in a single application.

1.1 Thread Scheduling

Most thread packages execute threads in a round-robin fashion. This behavior is often inappropriate for parallel languages and applications. As an example, round-robin scheduling fails to take into account the fact that parallel programs generally have critical paths, unlike sequential applications that use threads. Some applications may require a specialized scheduler with knowledge of critical paths. A second example: round-robin scheduling destroys locality of reference when large numbers of threads are being used. When hundreds of threads coexist, randomly transferring control from one to another randomizes memory access patterns, and as a consequence, cache performance is reduced to nil. Again, a customized policy with knowedge of locality may be needed for some applications. A third example: round-robin scheduling, when used with tree-search applications, tends to produce breadth-first search. This is usually undesirable, depth-first search is usually more efficient, and breadth-first sometimes overflows the available memory. Again, one needs a specialized scheduling policy. In short, round-robin scheduling may be a good general-purpose policy, but there are many cases where a customized policy is needed.

One "solution" to this problem is to add priorities to the scheduler. This provides a means by which a language can encourage the scheduler to pick the "right" thread. However, there are some cases in which priorities aren't sufficiently expressive. Two of the three cases listed above are not amenable to prioritizing. Attempting to encourage depth-first search with priorities is clumsy and is not possible unless the priorities have a large number of significant bits. Encouraging locality with priorities is not feasible. In short, priorities are quite useful for some applications, but there will be other scheduling objectives that cannot be achieved in this manner.

One could attempt to devise a more sophisticated scheduler to try to handle these complex needs. However, it is obvious that such a scheduler would be language-dependent, and therefore could not be part of the threads package. Fortunately, there is at least one threads package, QuickThreads [6], which allows one to implement one's own scheduler. Thus, each language's runtime system could contain a scheduler appropriate to its needs. Unfortunately, though, this approach causes an arbitration problem: if an applications programmer wishes to combine multiple parallel languages (with multiple runtime systems) in a single application, then that programmer must remove the schedulers from the runtime systems of the languages and write a new scheduler which is compatible with all. It is clearly undesirable to force the application programmer to undertake such a task.

One of the facilities provided by the Converse threads subsystem is a hierarchical scheduling model, which makes it possible for one module or language to implement its own scheduling behaviors without sacrificing the ability to coexist with other modules using the standard scheduler.

1.2 Portability Concerns

The second problem facing thread users today is the lack of a single threads package which runs on all platforms. Many threads packages claim to be "portable", but very few actually compile without modification on any significant number of UNIX platforms. The user who wishes to run threads on a machine with an unusual CPU, unusual compiler, or different operating system typically ends up having to do his own port of the threads package. Unfortunately, parallel machines tend to count as "unusual" in this sense: they often use custom processors, compilers, and operating systems. And, usually, it's the parallel language implementor who has to maintain the port, since thread package implementors are rarely interested in supporting some strange supercomputer to which they don't have access.

A solution to this problem is to design a threads package which can be implemented in a machine-independent manner. The machine-independent implementation may not be as efficient as the carefully tuned assembly-language implementations, however, its presence makes it possible for users of unusual parallel machines to simply plug the threads package into their application, knowing that it will work. An optimized implementation can be written later if necessary. The Converse threads subsystem can be (and has been) implemented in a fully machine-independent manner, and has been successfully tested on all the machines supported by Converse.

1.3 Preemption and Nonpreemption

There is no general consensus regarding whether or not a standardized threads package should support preemptive context-switching or not. There are strong arguments in favor of both preemptive and nonpreemptive threads.

Preemptive threads have several disadvantages in terms of convenience and efficiency. On a distributed memory machine, where concurrency control is not normally needed, preemptive threads require that one rewrite all the libraries in a reentrant fashion. This is usually achieved by adding locking to the nonreentrant routines, but the cost of of such locking can be quite significant when it surrounds an otherwise cheap routine. This performance hit is compounded by the fact that one must pay for operating system interrupts and context switching far more often than one would in a nonpreemptive system. Finally, preemptive threads can easily violate the semantics of a parallel programming language if the language was not designed for concurrent access to variables.

However, there are also strong arguments in favor of preemption. Preemption can significantly improve IO performance in systems where IO is polled. Preemption is useful for keeping priorities up to date — without preemption, high-priority tasks can end up waiting for lower-priority tasks to yield. Consider, for example, the situation in which a high-priority thread is waiting for a message. With preemption, this can be easily handled: when the message arrives, one simply preempts any low-priority thread. Preemption can significantly improve interactive response time. Finally, preemption is a required part of many parallel programming models.

Clearly, this is a tradeoff. Some runtime system designers will need preemption, others will find it unacceptable. Given this state of affairs, it doesn't make sense to design a threads package with a fixed preemption policy. In fact, in an interoperable environment, where multiple languages are linked together in a single application, it is clear that preemptive and nonpreemptive threads need to coexist. The Converse threads subsystem supports the use of preemptible and nonpreemtible threads in the same program.

1.4 Compiler-Supported Threads

Currently, most thread packages do not get any explicit support from the compiler. However, thread-packages which have the compiler's support can be significantly more efficient, as is demonstrated by such languages as Concert [11]. It therefore seems likely that popular compilers like gcc will eventually be extended to include support for high-speed threads.

However, by the time this occurs, most users will already be using a conventional thread package. If that conventional thread package has a well-designed interface, it will be possible to efficiently reimplement it as an abstraction layer on top of the high-speed compiler-supported threads. If not, then users of that thread package will need to discard their software and start over to gain the efficiency advantages of compiler-supported threads. Therefore, it is important that thread primitives be designed in such a way that they can be efficiently reimplemented with compiler support.

For a set of threads primitives to be efficient in a compiler-supported context, it must not utilize inherently expensive abstractions. If a threads package is to be reimplemented as a layer on top of an extremely fast compiler-supported threads package, it is critical that the abstractions not add excessive overhead to what could otherwise be a very fast system.

An example of a costly abstraction is the "mutex" variable. Each mutex operation is actually built from a number of simpler primitives, such as as explicit context-switching, thread queues, and monolithic monitors. By forcing a language designer to implement a basic primitive (e.g., the future) in terms of a full-featured abstraction like the mutex (when it could be implemented using much less costly abstractions) robs the language designer of needed performance.

Given the inefficiency of currently available thread packages, expensive abstractions are rarely noticed: the overhead associated with using powerful abstractions is irrelevant in comparison to the large context-switch overhead. However, when compiler-supported threads become available, software designers who used a threads package with an efficient interface will simply download a faster version of the threads package, whereas designers who used a threads package with an expensive abstraction layer will need to rewrite much code to gain the efficiency they desire.

1.5 A Model for Shared and Private Data

Designers of thread packages for workstations have clearly reached consensus regarding their model of shared and private data: global variables are to be shared among all threads, and thread-private data is to be obtained by function calls. Unfortunately, this model is unusable on parallel computers. Global sharing is simply too expensive (if available at all) to be the standard meaning for global variables. As a consequence, designers of thread packages for parallel computers have rejected the workstation-oriented model of global sharing, and without any consensus to adhere to, each thread package designer chooses a different meaning for global variables. For example, with Solaris threads, global variables turn out to be shared among all threads, while with QuickThreads on distributed memory machines, they turn out to be partially shared, and with the vendor supplied thread on the Convex Exemplar they turn out to be private.

The unfortunate consequence is this: if the programmers use a global variable in a parallel multithreaded program, their code is not portable. This is a *severe* problem, and one that can only be dealt with by the threads implementor. If the threads package does not provide a consistent interpretation of whether a given variable is to be private or shared across threads, then code using the package is *not* portable.

No solution is possible until a sharing model is adopted which is more consistent with the properties of parallel computers. Converse commits to a model which acknowledges the fact that several levels of sharing are possible, each with its own advantages. Converse therefore provides primitives to declare and access data at each level of sharing.

2 Converse Threads Subsystem

Converse [4] is a machine interface for parallel systems and languages. It seeks to achieve the following major goals:

1. portability: that programs written on top of Converse be executable without modification on a wide range of platforms,
2. generality: to be able to implement the full spectrum of parallel constructs on top of Converse.

3. interoperability: the ability for unrelated and highly dissimilar modules, often written in different parallel languages at different institutions, to *concurrently* execute, exchange data, and share the machine interface without conflicts.

Interoperability is the feature that sets Converse apart from most runtime systems — Converse provides a variety of resource arbitration techniques not found in other parallel runtime systems. Chief among these resources is CPU time itself. An important part of Converse's mechanisms for allocating and managing CPU time is the Converse threads subsystem, which is the focus of this paper. The other parts of Converse are discussed elsewhere [4].

The Converse threads subsystem is not a threads package in the traditional sense of the phrase. It includes some software, to be sure, but its goal is not just to provide some useful subroutines. Instead, it seeks to guarantee that software written with the Converse threads subsystem will be both portable and "interoperable" — in other words, it seeks to guarantee that contention over thread facilities will never be a source of incompatibility between two modules. Therefore, the Converse threads subsystem includes not just software, but also a set of "rules" which, if followed, enable threaded modules written by different research groups to coexist.

The Converse threads subsystem contains the following major components:

The Thread Objects Module: the most fundamental elements of a thread system: routines for creating threads and context switching.

A Standardized Scheduler Interface: a protocol whereby blocking routines can be written without knowing what scheduling policies are in place.

The Converse Scheduler: A scheduler provided by Converse. In addition to providing a convenient scheduler for many languages, it serves as a central clearinghouse for CPU time.

Yielding Mechanisms: A set of mechanisms that threads may use to temporarily give up control. Both nonpreemptive (manual) and preemptive (automatic) yielders are available.

A Model of Thread-Private and Thread-Shared Data: Converse defines the concepts of the address space, the processor, and the thread, and provides ways of declaring data with several levels of sharing.

The following sections describe the elements of the Converse threads subsystem in greater detail.

2.1 Thread Objects

The thread-object module, like most thread packages, provides a function for creating threads, one for destroying threads, one for explicitly transferring control to another thread, and one for retrieving the currently-executing thread. The following calls are the most important ones:

```
typedef struct CthThreadStruct *CthThread;
```

This is an opaque type defined in the Converse header files. It represents a first-class thread object. No information is publicized about the contents of a

CthThreadStruct. The fact that threads are first-class objects makes it possible to express many operations elegantly.

`CthThread CthCreate(void (*fn)(void *), void *arg, int size)`

Creates a new thread object. `CthCreate` returns the thread identifier of the newly created thread. The newly-created thread is not yet executing.

`void CthResume(CthThread t)`

Immediately context-switches (transfers control to) thread `t`. Note: normally, the user of a thread package wouldn't explicitly choose which thread to transfer to. Instead, the user would rely upon a scheduler to choose the next thread. Therefore, this routine is primarily intended for people who are implementing schedulers, not for end-users. Instead of calling `CthResume`, most threads will use a scheduler-provided function `CthSuspend` to context switch, this is described in the next section.

`CthThread CthSelf()`

Returns the currently-executing thread.

`void CthFree(CthThread t)`

Releases the memory associated with thread `t`. You may even `CthFree` the currently-executing thread, although the free will actually be postponed until the thread suspends.

2.2 Schedulers and the Standardized Scheduler Interface

We formalize the idea of a scheduler in the following manner: when a thread stops (context-switches out), another thread must take over the CPU. At that moment, a decision must be made regarding which thread will take over the CPU. Any subroutine or module making such decisions is termed a "scheduler".

Converse includes a standard scheduler. However, we recognize that the Converse scheduler uses a policy that may not be applicable to all parallel programming languages. Therefore, we allow language designers to write their own schedulers. Each thread will be managed by one scheduler, of its own choosing.

Since there will be multiple schedulers available, there is significant potential for incompatibilities. For example, suppose an implementor wished to write a subroutine that reads from the keyboard. The subroutine, upon discovering that no characters were available, would need to call some "suspend" subroutine. However, the keyboard IO routine could conceivably be called from many different languages, each using a different set of scheduling subroutines. Therefore, the keyboard IO routine would need to figure out which subroutine to call to ask for suspension. To make this feasible, we define a standardized way in which threads ask to suspend and ask to be reawakened. This interface is the "standard scheduler interface".

The standard scheduler interface consists of two functions: `CthSuspend` and `CthAwaken`. From the point of view of the thread, these methods perform as follows. When the thread wishes to block, it calls `CthSuspend()`. This causes a transfer of control to some "ready" thread. A thread `t` which has called

`CthSuspend()` is considered not-ready, and it remains not-ready until somebody calls `CthAwaken(t)`. After this time, the thread is considered ready, and it remains ready until it suspends again.

From a scheduler's point of view, the function `CthSuspend()` means "transfer control to a thread in the ready-set". `CthAwaken(t)` means "insert thread t into the ready-set". The scheduler's job is to record the contents of the ready-set, and choose elements from it as necessary.

At any given moment, each thread is connected to one scheduler. When the thread suspends, its scheduler picks the next thread. When a thread is awakened, its scheduler records the fact that it is now ready. A thread is associated with a scheduler using the function `CthSetStrategy`, described below.

The following is a brief description of the interface via which threads talk to their schedulers.

`void CthSuspend()`

Threads should call `CthSuspend` when they wish to give up control of the CPU. `CthSuspend` will then automatically transfer control to some other thread that wants the CPU. `CthSuspend` will select the thread to transfer control to by calling the scheduler-supplied, thread-specific "choosefn" described in `CthSetStrategy` below.

`void CthAwaken(CthThread t)`

Should be called only when `t` is suspended. Indicates to thread `t`'s scheduler that `t` is no longer suspended, that it needs to be selected for execution. This function actually just calls the scheduler-supplied, thread-specific "awakenfn" described in `CthSetStrategy` below.

```
void CthSetStrategy(CthThread t,
                    void (*awakenfn)(CthThread t),
                    CthThread (*choosefn)(void))
```

Specifies the scheduling functions to be used with thread `t`. Subsequent to this call, any attempt to `CthAwaken(t)` will cause then `t`'s `awakenfn` will be called. If `t` calls `CthSuspend`, then thread `t`'s `choosefn` will be called to pick the next thread. One may use the same functions for all threads (which is the common case), but the specification on a per-thread basis gives you maximum flexibility in controlling scheduling.

2.3 The Converse Scheduler

The Converse Scheduler is a fully-functional scheduler with supporting a powerful priority system, and support for a highly efficient form of stackless thread (for short, nonblocking tasks) in addition to its support for standard threads. A standard thread can be attached to the Converse scheduler using the following function:

`void CthSetStrategyDefault(CthThread t)`

After this call, the central Converse scheduler will automatically pick the next thread whenever `t` suspends or yields, and it will arrange for control to return to `t` when `t` is awakened.

The following subroutine is available for priority management:

```
void CthSetPrio(CthThread t, int strategy, int priolen, int *prio)
```

Sets the priority and queuing behavior of thread `t`. The priority is a sequence of bits representing an arbitrary-precision number. The strategy can be LIFO or FIFO (the thread is inserted on the ready queue either before or after threads of the same priority).

For many programs, the Converse scheduler will be quite sufficient in itself. It is quite common for several modules written in different multithreaded languages and running concurrently to simply share the Converse scheduler.

Although the Converse scheduler is an excellent basic scheduler, it cannot account for all the peculiarities of the languages implemented using Converse — for example, it cannot anticipate critical paths, whereas a programming language's runtime system could conceivably have good critical-path heuristics. Language designers may therefore wish to write their own schedulers to manage their own threads. In Converse's spirit of interoperability, these home-brewed schedulers must coexist with the Converse scheduler and other home-brewed schedulers. Therefore, the Converse scheduler has a second role: as a central clearinghouse for CPU time.

The principle of hierarchical scheduling is based on the idea that the scheduler is actually an allocator of CPU-time, and can be compared to memory allocators. Arranging memory allocators into hierarchies is quite common: for example, a lisp programmer might allocate memory using `cons`, which originally obtained its memory from `malloc`, which in turn obtained its memory from the UNIX primitives `brk` and `sbrk`. Hierarchical schedulers are based on exactly the same principle: initially, all CPU time is owned by the Converse scheduler. A different scheduler can request an indefinite amount of time from the central scheduler by inserting a thread into the central scheduler's queue. When the thread receives the CPU, it can then allocate time segments to other threads by calling `CthResume` to restart them. Those must eventually return control to their scheduler, which must eventually return control to the central Converse scheduler.

2.4 Yielding Mechanisms

The facilities we have shown thus far make it possible to write uninterrupted threads — threads that run continuously until they call `CthSuspend`. Such threads retain the CPU until they have no computation left to perform.

Many thread-packages use a preemptive context-switching policy. Converse, however, recognizes that preemptive context-switching can be very destructive to program correctness: it introduces a number of concurrency control issues, can destroy nonreentrant subroutines, and can violate the semantics of many parallel programming languages. On the other hand, preemptive context-switching can provide significant advantages in terms of IO performance and in terms of keeping priorities current. Therefore, Converse provides facilities for preemptive context-switching, but in a very conservative manner. Each thread must individually request preemptive behavior. If a thread does not ask to be preemptible, then that thread is not preempted. By providing preemptible threads for languages that need it, and allowing those threads to coexist with nonpreemptible threads for languages without concurrency control, Converse preserves interoperability.

Even nonpreemptible threads may wish to yield occasionally. In fact, we have found that manual yielding is sufficient for almost all purposes, and it does not create concurrency control problems. Therefore, we provide the following manual yielding mechanism.

`void CthYield()`

Temporarily suspends the current thread. This requires no additional support from the scheduling module, since it is implemented as follows: The thread simply adds itself to it's scheduler's ready-set using the scheduler's "awaken" method, and then transfers control to another thread using its schedulers "choose-next" method.

Converse provides the following facility for traditional preemptive yielding:

`void CthAutoYield(int microsec)`

Called by a thread to request "traditional" preemption. After this call, the thread that called it will be automatically preempted every `microsec` microseconds, approximately. This does not cause any other thread to be preempted.

`void CthSigYield()`

This function should be called either from inside a UNIX signal handler or a Converse event handler. (Converse generates some events, which are much like UNIX signals. Active message arrival is an example of a Converse event.) It causes the currently active thread on the current processor to yield. Accepting such yields is optional, see `CthSigYieldEnable` below. Signal-based yielding is particularly useful if the system has just received a high-priority interrupting message that needs to be processed.

`int CthSigYieldEnable(int flag)`

This functions enables preemptive yielding if `flag` is nonzero, and disables it if the flag is zero. Returns the old value of the flag. Initially, threads do not allow signal-based yielding. They must explicitly turn it on with `CthSigYieldEnable`. If a `CthSigYield` occurs and signal-based yielding is not being accepted by the current thread, the yield is delayed until the next manual yield or until signal-based yielding is enabled.

2.5 A Model of Private and Shared Data

Programming languages for uniprocessors make no presupposition about whether or not global variables, common blocks and the like are to be shared across threads. Therefore, thread-packages for parallel computers make inconsistent decisions about global variables. For example, Solaris threads [14] treats global variables as shared across threads, whereas the Convex vendor-supplied threads treat them as private. Other thread packages have other policies. The practical consequence for those attempting to write portable code is this: global variables have completely unpredictable behavior, and therefore, undefined semantics. Without a known behavior for global variables, it becomes extremely difficult to use any sort of globally-scoped data, private or shared.

Writing a useful, portable package requires a clear model of what kinds of sharing are possible. Converse identifies several levels of sharing, based on the following machine model. A parallel machine consists of a number of address spaces. Each address space contains a number of processors (or virtual processors). Each processor can support an arbitrary number of threads. The number of address spaces varies, and may be only one, likewise with the number of processors per address space. Given this machine model, there can be three kinds of variables: those where one copy per thread exists (thread-private), those with one copy per processor (processor-private), and those with one copy per address-space (shared). Converse provides macros to define variables at each level of sharing. Here are the most important macros for declaring, initializing, and accessing thread-private data:

`CtvDeclare(type, varname)`

Used in a fashion analogous to a C global variable declaration. One may place this macro at the top level of one's program to declare thread-private variables.

`CtvInitialize(varname)`

This macro must be invoked once for each thread-private variable that is declared in the program. It must be called exactly once per thread-private variable declaration, before any threads are created. It is therefore convenient to do so temporally near the start of `main`.

`CtvAccess(varname)`

Thread-private variables must be accessed with this macro. For example, to add one to the thread-private variable `X` one might say `CtvAccess(X) = CtvAccess(X) + 1`, or just `CtvAccess(X)++`.

The macros for declaring processor-private and shared variables are identical, except that they begin with `Cpv` and `Csv` respectively. With the help of these macros, it is possible for the parallel programmer to meaningfully use non-local variables.

The macros for declaring variables at each level of sharing have been carefully optimized. For example, the macro for accessing a thread-private variable takes approximately 3 Sparc instructions per fetch, which can be compared to 2 Sparc instructions for fetching a global variable.

2.6 Synchronization Mechanisms

Parallel languages use a variety of interesting and complex synchronization abstractions. It would be impossible for a threads package to provide all of them. Instead, to be usable in a parallel environment, a threads subsystem must provide efficient support for user-level implementation of synchronization abstractions. In this section, we show an implementation of such an abstraction, using the primitives described in previous chapters. The implementation illustrates the relative simplicity of building synchronization abstractions in Converse.

The synchronization mechanism we will use for demonstration purposes is the mutex. Mutexes may be in one of two states, either locked or unlocked, and they support two operations, "lock" and "unlock". A "lock" cannot proceed unless the mutex is in the unlocked state, therefore, the locking subroutine waits (blocks) until the mutex is in the unlocked state. These routines can be easily implemented using the Converse primitives. The mutex data type itself has the following structure:

```
typedef struct {
   int locked;
   queue_of_threads queue;
} *mutex;
```

If a thread (hereafter known as the "locker") wishes to lock the mutex, it must first check whether the mutex is already locked. If not, the locker can simply lock the mutex. If the mutex is already locked, however, the locker must wait for the mutex to enter the unlocked state. It pushes itself onto the queue of lockers. When the mutex is unlocked, the unlocker promises to 1, remove a locker from the queue, 2, relock the mutex on behalf of the locker, and 3, reawaken the locker. Therefore, when a locker is reawakened after being in the queue, the mutex has been locked on its behalf, and it may go on. Figure 2 shows the code executed by the locker and unlocker respectively.

```
void MutexLock(mutex m)
{
  int oldenable
    = CthSigYieldEnable(0);
  if (m->locked==0) m->locked=1;
  else {
    push(CthSelf(), m->queue);
    CthSuspend();
  }
  CthSigYieldEnable(oldenable);
}
```

```
void MutexUnlock(mutex m)
{
  int oldenable
    = CthSigYieldEnable(0);
  if (empty(m->queue))
    m->locked=0;
  else {
    CthAwaken(pop(m->queue));
  }
  CthSigYieldEnable(oldenable);
}
```

Fig. 1. Locking and Unlocking a mutex using Converse primitives.

Note that the use of CthSigYieldEnable to achieve atomicity is only correct in situations where the mutex is controlling access to processor-private data (a `Cpv` variable). If the data were shared across the node (a `Csv` variable), one would need to add a test-and-set or other interprocessor synchronization directive to the mutex implementation. (Converse provides a fairly standard set of interprocessor synchronization facilities). Note that the use of interprocessor synchronization primitives would make the lock significantly more expensive, it is therefore advantageous to be able to use this less expensive single-processor lock where appropriate. In general, the ability to design synchronization mechanisms with as little or as much generality as one needs is likely to improve the efficiency of parallel languages implemented with Converse.

3 Converse Scheduling, Messaging, and other Facilities

The thread abstractions defined above could be demonstrated in the context of a single-language uniprocessor program. However, this would not adequately demonstrate their special properties. Instead, we demonstrate them in the context of a multi-language program with message-passing and other concurrency mechanisms. Therefore, we briefly describe the Converse scheduling and messaging subsystems [4], which together with the threads make up the heart of Converse.

The Converse scheduler is much like the scheduler for a normal threads package. However, in addition to regular threads, the Converse scheduler supports stackless threads. Their lack of their own stack makes them more efficient than regular threads, though it also means they cannot suspend or yield. Their high efficiency makes it possible to use Converse's prioritized ready-queue for very small, short tasks in situations where creating a true thread for the task would be too expensive. In fact, the Converse scheduler is hand-tuned specifically for this type of thread: the very short-lived, non-blocking, rapidly-generated threads that so commonly are created by parallel programs.

The Converse scheduler provides a task pool on each processor. It repeatedly selects tasks (either threads or stackless threads) from the ready-pool and allocates time segments to them. Unlike traditional multithreaded systems, time segments can either be of a fixed length (the thread is preempted), or can be of indefinite duration (the thread runs until it decides it is ready to yield). In the case of stackless threads, however, the thread's time segment lasts until the thread completes.

The Converse messaging system is integrated with the Converse scheduling facility: it makes it possible to insert a stackless thread into another processor's ready-queue. With the ability to insert work into each other's queues, processors can easily demand arbitrary work of each other – for example, they can PUT/GET each other's memory, they can simulate the reception of MPI messages, and so forth. Most of Converse's distributed operations are built on top of this basic primitive.

To use the Converse messaging system, one first builds a "message", which is essentially a stackless thread encoded in the form of a sequence of bytes.

Messages only contain a function pointer[1] and a block of data to be passed to the function. Allocating and building the message structure is done manually by the user. One then inserts the message into another processor's ready-queue with a function similar to this one:

`void CmiSyncSend(int destPE, int size, void *msg)`

Inserts a stackless thread (as represented by the message `msg` whose size is `size` bytes) into into the ready-queue of processor `destPE`. The "sync" in the name of this functions refers only to its buffer management policy, it does *not* wait for the data to be received, it only waits for it to be extracted from the message buffer. Therefore, it returns nearly immediately. The stackless thread has extremely high priority in the target processor's ready-queue.

There are several other send-functions in Converse. Some of them perform broadcast (insertion of a stackless thread into the ready-queues of all processors). Some use varying buffer-management policies which are more efficient than this one (Converse has a variety of buffer management policies designed to minimize overhead). Further information about Converse's messaging mechansisms and buffering policies can be found in [4].

The overall structure of a Converse program can be seen in figure 3.

```
/* the following code is executed by all processors */
void user_main(int argc, char **argv)
{
  ConverseInit(argv);  /* initialize Converse runtime */
  CreateWork();        /* create some threads */
  CsdScheduler(-1);    /* run until user termination */
  ConverseExit();      /* clean up and exit */
}
```

Fig. 2. The structure of a typical program using Converse

The function `CreateWork` would be user-written. It might use `CthCreate` and `CthAwaken` to create and start some standard threads. Alternatively, it might use the messaging routines described above to create some stackless threads and insert them into the scheduler's ready-queue.

The function `CsdScheduler` is provided by Converse: it chooses threads and stackless threads from the ready-queue and allocates time segments to them. It continues until the function `CsdExitScheduler` is called by one of the threads.

In addition to its scheduler, threads, and messaging, Converse contains a number of utility modules designed to facilitate the implementation of parallel

[1] actually, a network-transmittable encoding of a function pointer.

languages. A good example of such a module would be the Converse message manager, designed to facilitate the implementation of languages with tagged message transmission. This module provides a data type, the `CmmTable`, which can store data and index it according to a set of tags. One can insert data into the table along with a sequence of integer keys, and one can then retrieve the data by specifying the keys, possibly specifying some keys as wildcards. While it would be quite feasible for the Converse user to implement this himself, it is such frequently-needed functionality that it is convenient to provide this storage structure as a part of Converse.

Collectively, the subsystems in Converse seek to provide all the facilities needed to easily implement the runtime system for a parallel programming language. The facilities are designed for ease of use, for efficiency, and to handle the resource-arbitration issues created when multiple parallel languages must coexist. In the following sections, we demonstrate how Converse can be used to implement multithreaded languages quickly and efficiently.

4 Implementing Multithreaded Languages in Converse

The purpose of this section is to explore the design of a multithreaded parallel language, and determine how this language would be implemented in an interoperable way using the facilities provided by Converse.

An interesting style of parallel programming is the model where threads on different processors communicate by sending messages to each other. Chant[2] is an example of a prominent system that supports such a capability. In this section, we describe a simple "language" that supports threads sending messages to and receiving messages from each other. This language supports a subset of the features of Chant, and so is easier to describe here. We will show how our thread interface, in conjunction with the Converse framework, facilitates implementations of such languages. The language, which we call "simple messaging plus threads" or SMT for brevity, provides the following major functions:

`CthThread CsmStartThread(void (*function)(void *), void *arg)`

This call allocates a new thread, and enters it in the main scheduler's ready-queue. When scheduled, this thread will start executing the function pointed to by `function`, with a single parameter `arg`.

`void CsmTSend(int pe, int tag, char *buffer, int size)`

A message is sent to the given processor `pe` containing `size` bytes of data from `buffer`, and tagged with the given tag. The calling thread continues after depositing the message with the runtime system.

`int CsmTRecv(int tag, char *buffer, int size, int *rtag)`

Waits until a message with a matching tag is available, and copies it into the given buffer. A wildcard value, `SMTWildCard`, may be used for the tag. In this case, any available message is considered a matching message. The tag with which the message was sent is stored in the location to which `rtag` points. The number of bytes in the message is returned.

This language has been designed to test Converse, to determine whether or not it is an adequate vehicle for implementing multithreaded parallel languages such as Chant.

The SMT runtime has been implemented with the help of mechanisms and data structures provided by Converse. Figure 3 shows a snapshot of those data structures as they might exist on some processor of a running SMT program, with each data structure labeled according to the module that supports it. In this particular snapshot, threads 1, 3, and 4 are waiting for messages: they have inserted pointers to themselves into the table of waiting threads and have suspended. Threads 2 and 6 are waiting for the CPU, they wait in the scheduler's ready-set. Thread 5 must be the currently running thread on this processor, if (as the diagram suggests) it is not stored in any synchronization structure at all. Three messages have arrived and been stored for future receipt.

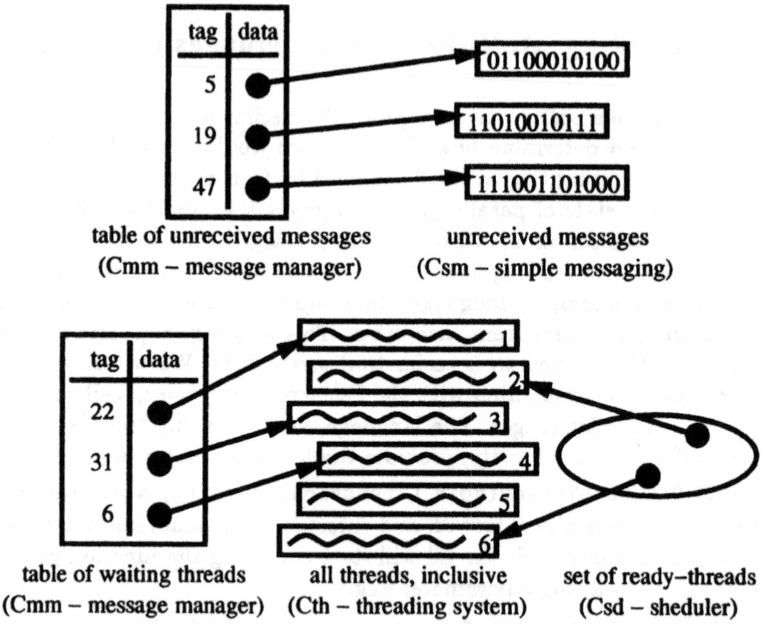

Fig. 3. Snapshot of data structures internal to Csm

The implementation of `CsmTSend` is as follows: it creates a stackless thread (also known as a Converse message), it stores the SMT message data and SMT tag in the stackless thread, and configures the thread to run an internal function `CsmTHandler`. It then inserts the stackless thread into the target processor's ready-set.

The stackless thread begins executing `CsmTHandler` on the target processor. `CsmTHandler` finds the SMT message data and SMT tag in its thread's data area, and inserts a pointer to the message data into the table of unreceived messages. It then checks to see if any `Csm` threads were waiting for the specified tag (by checking the table of waiting threads), and if so, it removes them from the table and awakens them. `CsmTHandler` returns, and the stackless thread is done.

`CsmTRecv` is implemented as follows: it first checks the table of unreceived messages, and if the message is already there, `CsmTRecv` extracts it and returns it. If not, it obtains its own thread identifier and inserts itself into the table of waiting threads. It then suspends. When it awakens, it knows that it has been awakened by `CsmTHandler`. It therefore extracts its message from the table of unreceived messages, and returns.

The `CsmStartThread` function is simply layered on top of `CthCreate` and `CthSetStrategyDefault`, it creates the thread and specifies that it should use the central Converse scheduler.

The entire code for this "runtime", which uses the message manager and the thread object, takes less than a hundred lines. The size of the runtime system would probably increase somewhat if an effort were made to optimize it, and a more sophisticated language such as Chant would require more code, but substantially less than a from-scratch implementation. The simplicity of the implementation demonstrates the success of our thread design.

Some features of Chant are not provided by SMT. For example, we have not mentioned remote thread creation. Adding such a feature can be achieved by adding a few more routines based on Converse features already described. We have also not mentioned direct thread-to-thread transmission. To provide thread-to-thread transmission, one need only make the thread identifier part of the message tag (this may require enlarging the tag). Expanding the SMT runtime to provide most of the features of the Chant runtime is straightforward.

The implementation techniques described in this section can be directly used to implement runtime systems for several thread-based languages including MultiLisp [3], Cid [10], and so forth. The ease of their implementation, using the Converse facilities, and the automatic interoperability provided by the framework, suggests that one will be able to run multilingual programs in near future, each module implemented using the language that suits its structure the best.

It is also easy to extend a language such as SMT to support prioritized threads. Of course, it is straightforward to have each thread run at a different priority level, by simply having it call `CthSetPrio`. More interestingly, we can make the priority of a thread depend on the priority of the message it is waiting for, or has just received. In such a configuration, each message will carry a priority on it, set by the sender. The message handler in the runtime, when it receives such a message, will set the priority of the waiting thread to that of the message before *awakening* it. If the message arrives before a thread starts waiting for it, the *receive* call will change the priority of the thread, and force it to yield, if necessary. Such message-induced priority will be useful, for example, to implement server threads whose priority can be dictated by its client.

5 Conclusions

We described the design and rationale of the Converse threads subsystem, a framework designed to facilitate the implementation of multithreaded parallel languages. The Converse threads subsystem is unique in that it contains support for interoperability among multiple parallel languages. The thread abstractions in Converse modularly separate the thread-scheduling functionality from the suspension and resumption mechanisms for threads. The facilities provided by the Converse threads subsystem include a highly portable thread object, a hierarchical scheduling model with a powerful top-level scheduler, routines for obtaining preemption or nonpreemption on a per-thread basis, and support for declaring thread-private variables as well as shared variables at multiple levels of sharing. The Converse threads subsystem, when integrated with the other subsystems in Converse, provides a complete framework for implementing interoperable multithreaded parallel languages. The rich set of flexible primitives ensures that a diverse set of languages, with widely varying (and possibly nonstandard) thread behaviors, can be easily implemented using Converse. The comprehensive scheduling model ensures that such languages can interoperate in a single program. We explored the implementation of the runtime system for a small multithreaded language `SMT`. In doing so, we demonstrated the feasibility and simplicity of implementing multithreaded languages using the Converse threads subsystem and the remainder of the Converse framework.

The following programming models have been implemented with the help of Converse:

- Charm++ [5], based on remote method invocation,
- IMPORT [9], a successor to Modsim, using time-warp [1] methodology,
- SMT, a message-passing threads model,
- PVM [15], a simple but popular message-passing model
- DP [7], a data-parallel Fortran-based language

Of these languages, Charm++ uses stackless threads unless the programmer explicitly creates a `Cth` thread, `DP` and `IMPORT` use stackless threads exclusively, and `SMT` and `PVM` are based upon full-fledged threads. The fact that languages of such widely varying structure can coexist under a single runtime system indicates that the goals of interoperability and generality have been fairly well attained.

Immediate goals for the Converse threads subsystem include a detailed analysis of the performance of the thread subsystem, possibly optimized implementations for specific platforms, an implementation of MPI [8] that runs within a set of threads, and a runtime layer for the multithreaded Cid [10] language.

When these are complete, the future of this research involves porting the runtime systems of a wide range of parallel languages to Converse, thereby making it possible to use what were previously isolated languages as parts of a comprehensive multi-language programming system, where one may choose the "right language for the job" on a module-by-module basis. Pre-existing libraries written in different languages can then be used in a single program. The utility of such multi-lingual programming will then be systematically examined by developing several multi-lingual applications.

Converse, including its thread subsystem, is available from the Parallel Programming Laboratory at `http://charm.cs.uiuc.edu/`.

References

1. D. Ball and S. Hoyt. The Adaptive Time-Warp Concurrency Control Algorithm. In *Proceedings of the SCS Multiconference on Distributed Simulation*, pages 174–177, 1990.
2. M. Haines, D. Cronk, and P. Mehrotra. On the design of Chant: A talking threads package. In *Proceedings of Supercomputing 1994*, Nov 1994.
3. R. Halstead. Multilisp: A Language for Concurrent Symbolic Computation. *ACM Transactions on Programming Languages and Systems*, October 1985.
4. L.V. Kalé, M. Bhandarkar, N. Jagathesan, S. Krishnan, and J. Yelon. Converse: An Interoperable Framework for Parallel Programming. In *International Parallel Processing Symposium 1996 (to appear)*, 1996.
5. L.V. Kale and Sanjeev Krishnan. Charm++ : A portable concurrent object oriented system based on C++. In *Proceedings of the Conference on Object Oriented Programmi ng Systems, Languages and Applications*, September 1993.
6. David Keppel. Tools and techniques for building fast portable threads packages. Technical Report UWCSE 93-05-06, University of Washington Department of Computer Science and Engineering, May 1993.
7. E. Kornkven and L.V. Kalé. Efficient Implementation of High Performance Fortran via Adaptive Scheduling – An Overview. In V. K. Prasanna, V. P. Bhatkar, L. M. Patnaik, and S. K. Tripathi, editors, *Proceedings of the 1st International Workshop on Parallel Processing*. Tata McGraw-Hill, New Delhi, India, December 1994.
8. Message Passing Interface Forum. *MPI: A Message-Passing Interface Standard*, May 1994.
9. Vance P. Morrison. Import/dome language reference manual. Technical report, US. Army Corps of Engineering Research Laboratory, ASSET group., 1995.
10. Rishiyur S. Nikhil. Parallel Symbolic Computing in Cid. In *Parallel Symbolic Languages and Systems*, 1995.
11. John Plevyak, Vijay Karamcheti, Xingbin Zhang, and Andrew A. Chien. A hybrid execution model for fine-grained languages on distributed memory multicomputers. In *Supercomputing '95*.
12. PORTS- POrtable Runtime System consortium. The PORTS0 Interface. Technical report, Jan 1995.
13. POSIX System Application Program Interface: Threads Extension to C Language. Technical Report POSIX 1003.4a Draft 8, Available from the IEEE Standards Department.
14. M. L. Powell, S. R. Kleiman, S. Barton, D. Shah, D. Stein, and M. Weeks. SunOS Multi-thread Architecture. In *Proceedings of the Winter 1991 USENIX Conference*.
15. V.S. Sunderam. PVM: A Framework for Parallel Distributed Computing. *Concurrency: Practice and Experience*, 2(4), December 1990.

A Programming Environment for Dynamic Resource Allocation and Data Distribution

José E. Moreira Vijay K. Naik Ravi B. Konuru
{moreira,vkn,ravik}@watson.ibm.com

IBM T. J. Watson Research Center
P. O. Box 218
Yorktown Heights, NY 10598-0218

Abstract. Dynamic resource allocation, particularly in the form of processor partitioning and scheduling, is an important factor in achieving good utilization and high performance in multiprocessor systems. We are developing a Distributed Resource Management System (DRMS) for dynamic allocation of resources during the execution of applications. DRMS provides means for applications to specify their resource requirements and for the system to manipulate resources allocated to competing jobs. DRMS also provides the programming support necessary to create *reconfigurable* applications, that can execute on time-variant processor partitions. Run-time program migration and data redistribution are performed automatically. We present performance results using application benchmarks on the first implementation of DRMS for the IBM SP2. Our performance results show that (i) the support for dynamic resource control has minimal side effects on the application performance, and (ii) the costs associated with the data redistributions and program restructuring to support changes in the processor partitions are relatively small.

1 Introduction

In the past few years, parallel and distributed computing has proved to be cost effective in many areas. In many instances, applications developed for mainframes and other supercomputers have been successfully ported onto parallel and distributed computing platforms. In spite of this impressive progress, these systems are mostly used in a mode in which a processor partition is dedicated for the life time of a job. Only after the job terminates, the resources allocated to the job are recovered and handed over to another job. As a result, resource utilization tends to be poor, especially when the demands on the system are unpredictable and dynamically changing. This situation is particularly inefficient for parallel applications that exhibit nested and variable levels of parallelism. In general, heterogeneous phases of computations in complex applications require specific resource allocation strategies. Support for this variability in the resource allocation is unavailable in existing parallel environments.

To alleviate some of these problems, and to provide a better control over parallel jobs and resource scheduling, we have developed a system called DRMS (Distributed Resource Management System) that performs dynamic resource allocation and program control. DRMS supports the efficient execution of parallel applications on *reconfigurable processor partitions*: the set of processors executing an application can change at run-time. This support consists of (i) a programming model and language extensions for the declaration of processor (resource) requirements and the data layout on those processors, (ii) a run-time system that manipulates distributed data and program reconfigurations, and (iii) a resource scheduling, control, and management system. We refer to these applications that can execute on reconfigurable processor partitions, in particular by adjusting their number of active threads, as *reconfigurable applications*. In this paper, we focus on our programming model and language extensions, and their implementation by the compiler and run-time system.

The organization of the rest of the paper is as follows. In Section 2, we describe our programming model that supports the execution of parallel jobs on time-variant resources. In Sections 3 and 4 we describe in detail the language extensions provided by DRMS to implement the programming model and the data distribution framework under which they are implemented. The DRMS architecture is outlined in Section 5 and some performance results are presented in Section 6. Section 7 discusses other related work and Section 8 concludes the paper.

2 Programming Model

The DRMS programming model is based on the SPMD programming model. In the classical SPMD model, a group of processors all execute the same code, but each processor applies this code to a different section of the data set. In our programming model, a parallel job $\mathcal{J}$ consists of the consecutive execution of $n(\mathcal{J})$ stages, that we call *schedulable and observable quanta* (SOQs). Each stage i is executed on $p(i)$ processors (and $r(i)$ resources, in general), with each of the $p(i)$ processors executing the same code for the stage. That is, each stage is executed in SPMD mode on $p(i)$ processors. The boundaries between stages are defined by *schedulable and observable points* (SOPs). At an SOP, and only at an SOP, the processor partition allocated to a job can be modified, thus enabling the following stage to execute on a different number of processors than the previous. Typically, a change in the the number of processors requires a change in the mapping of data to processors. An SOP that causes a change of processors and/or mapping of data is called a *reconfiguration point*.

For a stage i, each processor $j, j = 1, \ldots, p(i)$, has its own independent data space. We denote by $d(i,j)$ the data space of processor j in stage i. The job data space for stage i is the union of the data spaces of each processor:

$$D_{\mathcal{J}}(i) = \bigcup_{j=1}^{p(i)} d(i,j). \tag{1}$$

The data space of a processor can be divided into two parts: a private data space $d_p(i,j)$ and a shared data space $d_s(i,j)$. The private data space contains temporary data and flow control variables that are pertinent only to this processor at this stage. The shared data space contains actual problem data that is shared between adjacent stages and that may be necessary for the computations on other processors. We note that, in this context, shared data does not imply shared memory between processors. Because of replicated data, the shared data space of different processors may actually overlap. The union of the shared data spaces of individual processors form the global shared data space for a given stage:

$$D_{\mathcal{J}_s}(i) = \bigcup_{j=1}^{p(i)} d_s(i,j). \tag{2}$$

$D_{\mathcal{J}_s}(i)$ is the collection of *global* data structures of job $\mathcal{J}$ during stage i. (We use the term global in the sense that the data defined by $D_{\mathcal{J}_s}$ is global among all parallel tasks.) If the global data structures of a program are purely static, then $D_{\mathcal{J}_s}$ is an execution-time invariant. In the general case, dynamically allocated global variables can cause a change in $D_{\mathcal{J}_s}$ from stage to stage. $D_{\mathcal{J}_s}$ is the state that is preserved across reconfiguration points. Data not belonging to $D_{\mathcal{J}_s}$ is in an undefined state after a reconfiguration point.

Stage i of the computation is a well-defined unit with its own resource requirements, data distribution, and execution code. We define a stage to consist of four sections:

stage = { *resource section*; *data section*; *control section*; *computation section*; }

The *resource section* specifies the types and quantities of resources needed for the stage. Quantities can be a single value, or a range of values. The *data section* specifies the extent and partitioning among processors of the global data structures. It specifies the decomposition of the global data space $D_{\mathcal{J}_s}(i)$ into the shared data spaces $d_s(i,j)$, providing a location binding between processors and data. This decomposition is undefined after a reconfiguration point (although the data in $D_{\mathcal{J}_s}(i)$ itself is preserved), and therefore the data section must appear before global data is used. The *control section* specifies values for control variables pertinent to that stage. Control variables are used to control the flow of execution inside a stage, which may vary depending on the allocated resources and how data is partitioned. They typically define the access patterns to the global data structures, establishing an access binding between processors and data. They may also be used to define a schedule for computations and/or communications. Finally, the *computation section* specifies the computations that each processor will carry out on its section of the global data structures, and what data should be transferred from one processor to another (communications). This would correspond to a program segment in a classical SPMD program.

3 Language Extensions

DRMS language extensions implement our programming model on top of Fortran 77 and Fortran 90. The language extensions are in the form of *annotations*: source-level comments (and thus transparent to a regular compiler) that implement (i) the declaration of resource requirements, (ii) the declaration of data distributions, and (iii) interface and utility functions. Declarations of resource requirements are used to specify the number of processors (or a valid range of numbers) needed for the execution of a stage. Declarations of data distributions specify how the data is distributed among the processors executing the stage. Similar to HPF [8], we perform data distribution by first defining virtual processor grids and then distributing the data arrays onto these grids. The interface and utility functions are provided for programming convenience. We discuss some interface and utility functions, but most of them are outside the scope of this paper.

3.1 Annotations

Rather than describing each DRMS annotation exhaustively, we illustrate our language extensions with the example in Figure 1, the main loop of a Poisson solver using Jacobi relaxation. This DRMS program was obtained by modifying an explicitly parallel SPMD version that used MPL [6] for message-passing. Each iteration of the loop performs one step of the relaxation and constitutes one stage of the execution of the program. The body of the loop uses several DRMS annotations that we now describe.

```
      DO i = 1, m
c$DRMS$     RESIZE 1:16:*2
            CALL mp_environ(num_pes,my_id)
            CALL factor(num_pes, npx, npy)
c$DRMS$     PROCESSORS, DIMENSION(npx,npy) :: P
c$DRMS$     DIMENSION(n,n), DISTRIBUTE(BLOCK,BLOCK) ONTO P,
c$DRMS$     BORDERS((1,1),(1,1)) :: u0, u1
            xsize = drms_local_extent(u0,1)
            ysize = drms_local_extent(u0,2)
            IF (MOD(i,2) .eq. 0) THEN
               CALL relax(u0,u1,xsize,ysize,h)
            ELSE
               CALL relax(u1,u0,xsize,ysize,h)
            END IF
      END DO

      SUBROUTINE relax(a,b,xsize,ysize,h)
c$DRMS$ INHERIT :: a, b
      REAL a(xsize,ysize), b(xsize,ysize)
      CALL drms_update_borders(b)
      DO j = 2, ysize-1
         DO i = 2, xsize-1
            a(i,j) = h + 0.25*(b(i-1,j)+b(i+1,j)+b(i,j-1)+b(i,j+1))
         END DO
      END DO
      END
```

Fig. 1. Example of Jacobi relaxation using DRMS.

The annotations begin with `C$DRMS$` in column 1 of each line, to identify them as special purpose comments. The first annotation, `RESIZE`, is an example of a *resource specification* annotation that implements the resource section of the stage. It specifies how many processors are necessary for the execution of the stage. In this particular case, the code specifies a range of partition sizes from 1 to 16 in multiplicative steps of 2 (1,2,4,8,16). DRMS also allows the specification of ranges with additive step, ranges of powers of integers, and irregular ranges. Note that each iteration step can be executed on a processor partition of different size.

Once resource requirements are specified and a valid set of resources obtained from the system, the code declares how to distribute data onto the available processors (data section). In this example, a call to an MPL subroutine, `mp_environ()`, is used to find out how many processors were actually allocated (`num_pes`). That number is factored into two components (`npx,npy`) in an application specific way by the user-defined subroutine `factor()`, to create a two-dimensional grid `P(npx,npy)` of virtual processors. Such grids are created with a *processor declaration* annotation. The DRMS `PROCESSORS` declaration is similar to the HPF `PROCESSORS` directive [8], but, although not shown here, it also allows explicit control on the mapping of virtual to physical processors. Both one-to-one and many-to-one mappings are supported.

After the processor grid is created, the global data arrays `u0` and `u1` are declared, using a *data declaration* annotation. These arrays are specified as having a global shape `n` × `n` and `BLOCK` distribution along both axes. The shapes of the local sections for each processor are automatically computed by DRMS. If there is a change in the number of processors from iteration i to iteration $i + 1$, data are automatically moved across processors to conform to the new specification. DRMS supports all forms of data distribution of standard HPF: block, cyclic, block-cyclic, and collapsed. It also supports an additional form of regular block distribution, called `BLOCKD`, that achieves better load balancing, and two forms of irregular distributions: block-list and `ARBITRARY`. The `ARBITRARY` distribution is specially useful in manipulating sparse and unstructured computations [13]. As an additional difference from HPF, DRMS allows the declaration of *borders*. Borders are regions that extend the local section of a processor beyond the base section implied by the distribution. (Such section borders are used as programming convenience and for performance reasons in many SPMD programs.)

After data are distributed, a DRMS utility function (`drms_local_extent()`) is used to find the extents of the local sections of each processor. Those extents are used to implement the control section of the stage, by determining loop bounds for the relaxation performed in subroutine `relax`. This subroutine uses the DRMS annotation `INHERIT` to declare that the two distributed data structures, `a` and `b`, will be used inside the subroutine with their current data distribution. Before performing one step of the relaxation, the border regions have to be updated with data from the actual owners of the overlapped base section. This is accomplished with a call to `drms_update_borders()`, another DRMS utility function.

3.2 Data Distribution Forms

Let an array axis of length N (indices $1, \ldots, N$) be distributed onto a processor grid axis of length P (indices $1, \ldots, P$). The section of the array axis that is mapped to a specific processor index p ($1 \leq p \leq P$) depends on the value of p and the specific *form* of the distribution. Figure 2 gives the definition of those sections for each distribution form. The sections are given in the form of the set of indices that are mapped to processor index p. A triplet, or union of triplets, notation is used to define the set. A triplet has the form $(\alpha : \omega : \delta)$, where α is the first element, ω is the last element, and δ is the additive step between elements. We use β to denote the number of elements in a triplet ($\beta = \lfloor \frac{\omega - \alpha}{\delta} \rfloor + 1$).

4 Data Distribution Framework

To explain our support for data distribution, we start by introducing the concepts of *range* and *slice*, as applied to DRMS. A range $r = (r_1, \ldots, r_n)$ is an ordered set of

distribution form	partition for processor *p*
* (collapsed)	$(1 : N : 1)$
BLOCK	$(\alpha_p : \omega_p : 1)$ where $\left\{ \begin{array}{ll} \alpha_1 = 1 & \\ \alpha_p = \omega_{p-1} + 1, & p > 1 \\ \omega_p = \alpha_p + \beta_p - 1 & \\ \beta_p = \left\lceil \frac{N}{P} \right\rceil, & 1 \leq p \leq q \\ \beta_p = N - \left\lceil \frac{N}{P} \right\rceil q, & p = q + 1 \\ \beta_p = 0, & p > q + 1 \\ q = \left\lfloor \frac{N}{\lceil N/P \rceil} \right\rfloor & \end{array} \right\}$
BLOCKD	$(\alpha_p : \omega_p : 1)$ where $\left\{ \begin{array}{ll} \alpha_1 = 1 & \\ \alpha_p = \omega_{p-1} + 1, & p > 1 \\ \omega_p = \alpha_p + \beta_p - 1 & \\ \beta_p = \left\lfloor \frac{N}{P} \right\rfloor + 1, & 1 \leq p \leq N \bmod P \\ \beta_p = \left\lfloor \frac{N}{P} \right\rfloor, & p > N \bmod P \end{array} \right\}$
CYCLIC	$(p : \left\lfloor \frac{N}{P} \right\rfloor (P-1) + p : P),\ 1 \leq p \leq N \bmod P$ $(p : \left\lfloor \frac{N}{P} \right\rfloor (P-2) + p : P),\ N \bmod P < p \leq P$
CYCLIC(*k*)	$\bigcup_{j=1,\ \ni j \bmod P = p-1}^{\lceil \frac{N}{k} \rceil} (k(p-1) + 1 : \max(kp, N) : 1)$
BLOCK : $l(P)$ (block-list)	$(\alpha_p : \omega_p : 1)$ where $\left\{ \begin{array}{ll} \alpha_1 = 1 & \\ \alpha_p = \omega_{p-1} + 1, & p > 1 \\ \omega_p = \alpha_p + l_p - 1 & \end{array} \right\}$
ARBITRARY$(n, l(n), \mu(n))$ l = length of blocks μ = ownership mapping	$\bigcup_{j=1,\ \ni \mu_j = p}^{n} (\alpha_j : \omega_j : 1)$ where $\left\{ \begin{array}{ll} \alpha_1 = 1 & \\ \alpha_j = \omega_{j-1} + 1, & j > 1 \\ \omega_j = \alpha_j + l_j - 1 & \end{array} \right\}$

Fig. 2. Summary of distribution characteristics.

integers, in increasing order. For a range r, we denote by $|r|$ the number of elements (size) of the range. A range can be used to represent a set of indices along an axis of an array. A slice $s = (s_1, \ldots, s_d)$ is an ordered set of ranges. For a slice s, we denote by $|s|$ the number of ranges (rank) of the slice. A slice of rank d can be used to represent the indices of a d-dimensional array section, where s_1 is the range of indices along the first axis, s_2 is the range of indices along the second axis, and so on.

We define two operations on ranges: intersection and normalization. The intersection of two ranges q and r, denoted by $q * r$, is a range given by the ordered set of all elements that belong to both ranges:

$$q * r = \{x \mid (x \in q) \wedge (x \in r)\}. \tag{3}$$

The normalization of a range q with respect to a range r, denoted by q/r, is a range given by the ordered set of indices that give the location of each element of q in r. It is required that $q \subseteq r$:

$$q/r = \{i \mid r_i = q_j,\ j = 1, \ldots, q_{|q|}\}. \tag{4}$$

The intersection and normalization operations can be extended to slices s and t, of the same rank d, by performing the operations between corresponding pairs of ranges.

An array element can be referenced both by global and local indices. The global indices define the location of the element in the global problem array, which is distributed among the cooperating processors. The local indices define the location of the element in the local section of the array in that particular processor. In most cases, the shapes (extents along each dimension) of the local section and the global array are different. Let $S(p, \mathcal{D}_A)$ be the slice of global indices of the section of an array A that is mapped onto processor p in a particular distribution $\mathcal{D}_A$. This slice can be computed using the expressions in Figure 2. Also, let x be the slice of global indices of some array section of A. The slice $y = (x * S(p, \mathcal{D}_A))/S(p, \mathcal{D}_A)$ contains the local indices for all elements of x that are mapped onto p. To provide support for borders, we define $S(p, \mathcal{D}_A)$ as the slice corresponding to the base section of processor p, while $S_B(p, \mathcal{D}_a)$ corresponds to the section extended with borders.

The redistribution of an array from a current source distribution $\mathcal{D}_A$ on a processor grid P to a new target distribution $\mathcal{D}'_A$ on a processor grid Q can be accomplished by the algorithm in Figure 3(a). We use the notation $A(y)$ to represent that section of array A whose elements are given by slice y. Redistribution involves computing the old and new slices that define the sections and then performing pair-wise intersection of those slices for each pair of old (P) and new (Q) processors. This determines the data that has to be exchanged between each pair of processors in terms of the global indices. The global indices are transformed into local indices (normalization) which are then used in actual data exchange. The updating of borders for a given distribution $\mathcal{D}_A$ can be accomplished similarly. Let $B(p, \mathcal{D}_A)$ denote the set of slices that contains the global indices for all border elements of A in p (borders cannot, in general, be represented by a single slice). The algorithm in Figure 3(b) performs an update of borders on all processors. The intersection and normalization of a set of slices Σ with a single slice σ is performed by computing the intersection or normalization of each slice in Σ with σ. We have implemented the algorithms in Figure 3 in DRMS using explicit message passing to transfer data between processors. Other approaches, such as remote memory operations, can be used just as easily.

5 DRMS Architecture

Figure 4 shows the main functional components of DRMS and the primary interactions among these components. The DRMS compiler translates programs with DRMS annotations into executables that can run on reconfigurable processor partitions. The functional components that perform resource scheduling are the Resource Coordinator (*RC*), the Task Coordinators (*TC*s) and the Job Scheduler and Analyzer (*JSA*). Whereas the *RC* and *JSA* are logically centralized, there is one *TC* per node of the parallel system. The User Interface Coordinator (*UIC*) implements the system interface to users and administrators. A run-time system (RTS), linked to each application, coordinates with the external environment and propagates resource requests from the program to the resource management components of DRMS. It also implements the data distribution operations to support reconfigurable applications. The performance analysis component is handled

```
procedure Redistribute(D_A, D'_A) {
    P ← processor grid of D_A
    Q ← processor grid of D'_A
    for every processor p ∈ P {
        for every processor q ∈ Q {
            x ← S_B(q, D'_A) * S(p, D_A)
            y ← x/S_B(p, D_A)
            processor p sends A(y) to q
        }
    }
    for every processor q ∈ Q {
        for every processor p ∈ P {
            x ← S_B(q, D'_A) * S(p, D_A)
            y ← x/S_B(q, D'_A)
            processor q receives B(y) from p
        }
    }
}
```

(a)

```
procedure UpdateBorders(D_A) {
    P ← processor grid of D_A
    for every processor p ∈ P {
        for every processor q ∈ P, q ≠ p {
            x ← B(q, D_A) * S(p, D_A)
            y ← x/S_B(p, D_A)
            processor p sends A(y) to q
        }
        for every processor q ∈ P, q ≠ p {
            x ← B(p, D_A) * S(q, D_A)
            y ← x/S_B(p, D_A)
            processor p receives A(y) from q
        }
    }
}
```

(b)

Fig. 3. Algorithms for redistribution and border updating.

by the run-time performance data gatherer and the associated tools and utilities.

5.1 DRMS Compiler

The first step in compiling a DRMS annotated Fortran program consists of preprocessing the annotated program by the DRMS annotations preprocessor (DAP). DAP is built using Sage++ [7], and it generates as output a new Fortran program. This new program can then be compiled by the native Fortran compiler in our system and linked with the DRMS run-time library to produce an executable.

DAP replaces the annotations in the source Fortran code by calls to the DRMS run-time library. The calls are used to build descriptors of the distributed arrays and to provide support for resource scheduling and data distribution operations. The descriptors implement handles for the arrays that supports dynamic reshaping as dictated by changes in distribution. The local section shape $(m_1, m_2, \ldots, m_d)$, in each processor, of a global array of shape $(n_1, n_2, \ldots, n_d)$ is a function of the distribution of the array, which can change during execution of the application. To support several section shapes in the same storage area, the preprocessor declares all local section arrays as single-dimensional. It then creates a set of descriptors $(\xi_1, \xi_2, \ldots, \xi_d)$, one ξ per axis, for each distributed array. Calls are inserted to communicate to the run-time system that these descriptors are associated with this particular array. References to an array element $\mathtt{A}(i_1, i_2, \ldots, i_d)$ are translated to $\mathtt{A}(1 + \sum_{j=1}^{d}(i_j - 1)\xi_j)$ Reshaping of array A can then be performed at run-time by changing the values of the ξ_j's. When a distribute or redistribute operation is performed by the run-time system, it computes the shape vector $\mathbf{m} = (m_1, m_2, \ldots, m_d)$ of the local section. To implement column major linearization, as dictated by Fortran, it then sets

$$\xi_1 = 1$$

$$\xi_j = \prod_{k=1}^{k<j} m_k, \quad j = 2, \ldots, d.$$

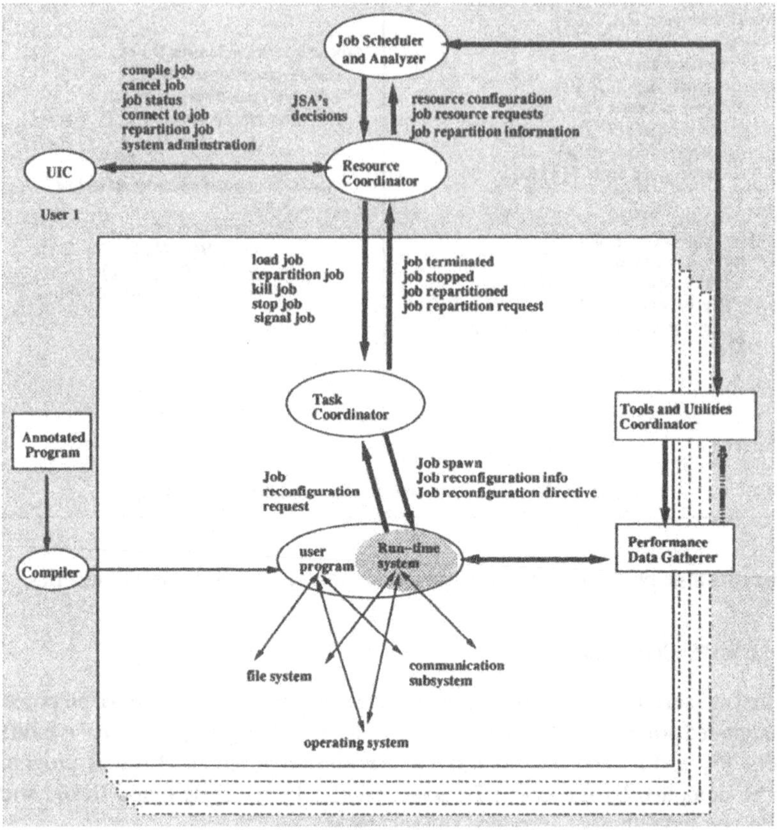

Fig. 4. DRMS Architecture

This results in a *dense storage* of the local sections: no gaps between successive columns or planes.

5.2 Run-Time System

The run-time system is responsible for supporting the distributed data structures used by the application. It builds and maintains descriptors for virtual processor grids and distributed arrays on each processor executing an application. It also performs all the necessary data movement when a data redistribution is needed, such as during a reconfiguration of allocated processors. Because it has knowledge of the distributed data, it can also perform a series of utility functions on that data.

6 Performance Evaluation

In this section, we report performance results from a set of experiments we conducted under our initial implementation of DRMS for the IBM SP2. We focused our attention on the *reconfiguration time*, the *redistribution time*, and *impact* on normal operation. We define the *reconfiguration time* for a reconfiguration operation as the elapsed time between the moment an application reaches a reconfiguration point until the moment the application is ready to continue on the new number of processors. The reconfiguration time has several components, including the *redistribution time*: the time it takes to move the data from one distribution configuration to another. Besides redistribution, we identify the following components in the reconfiguration time:

- To reconfigure a processor partition in the SP2, applications have to detach from the interconnection network. They accomplish this by exiting the code but leaving their state resident in the nodes. The "exit" component is the time elapsed from the moment *RC* instructs an application to detach from the interconnection network until the moment the *RC* detects that all nodes have detached. This requires a synchronization between the *TC*s in all nodes of the application partition.
- The "switch" component is the time it takes to update the partition tables that control message routing through the SP2 interconnection network. These tables have to be updated whenever a partition of processors is created or reconfigured.
- After the application has detached from the interconnection network and the partition tables have been updated, the application has to be restarted on the new partition. The time for this restart is the "spawn" component.
- Finally, we group all other reconfiguration costs in the "other" component. This includes the time for the application to communicate its resource requirements to the *RC*, and the time it takes for *JSA* to actually perform resource scheduling. It also includes the time for the application to reattach to its resident state (so that it can continue from where it stopped) and to perform any application specific reinitialization.

The redistribution time itself can be further subdivided into four components: (i) the "compute" time is the time to compute the slices of data that have to be exchanged among processors, as described in Section 4; (ii) the "buffer" time is the time it takes to copy data from/to their actual locations in the distributed arrays to/from intermediate buffers used for data exchange; (iii) the "message" time is the time for actual data exchange among processors using message-passing; (iv) finally, the "sync" time is the average time processors wait for the slowest processor in the redistribution, when synchronizing at the end of it.

Finally, to determine the *impact* of DRMS on normal execution, we measure the time to execute each iteration of our benchmarks between two reconfiguration points (that is, while the number of processors is constant) and compare that to the time to execute each iteration when the benchmarks are run in conventional SPMD mode on the same number of processors.

6.1 The Experimental Environment

We conducted our experiments on a 32-processor IBM SP2 with thin nodes. Each processing element on the SP2 considered in this study is IBM's RS/6000 model 390 processor (POWER2 architecture), with 64 KBytes data cache and 66.5 MHz clock speed. On the SP2, the processors are interconnected via a high performance switch (HPS). Explicit message passing is the parallel programming paradigm. In our experiments on SP2, message passing was performed by MPL. We refer the interested reader to [1] for further details on SP2. Time intervals were measured using a real time clock with resolution better than $1\mu s$. All measured intervals were greater than $100ms$.

6.2 Benchmarks

We used three application benchmarks for our measurements: (i) APPBT, (ii) APPLU, and (iii) APPSP. These benchmarks are part of the NAS parallel benchmark (NPB) suite [2]. Some intrinsic characteristics of the applications are shown in Table 1. For each application we list (i) the number of distributed arrays, (ii) the volume of problem data that has to be distributed, both in number of elements and MBytes (one element is a double-precision floating point value), and (iii) the number of iterations of the main loop (time steps) that are executed. Because of some overlap of data caused by borders, the actual volume of distributed data is, in general, dependent on the number of processors and larger than the problem data.

Table 1. Characteristics of benchmarks used to evaluate DRMS.

application	distributed arrays	distributed data (elements)	distributed data (MB)	iterations
APPBT	6	42×64^3	84	200
APPLU	5	17×64^3	34	250
APPSP	8	24×64^3	48	400

For our experiments, we started with SPMD versions of the three benchmarks that were tuned for the IBM SP2. We inserted DRMS annotations at the beginning of each time-step that allowed for a change in the number of processors allocated from that point onwards. A reconfiguration was forced every 10 iterations. For APPBT and APPSP, three-dimensional BLOCKD distributions with borders were used, while for APPLU a two-dimensional BLOCKD distribution with borders was used. The class A problem sizes [2] were utilized.

6.3 Results

In our experiments we reconfigured each application between 8 and 16, and between 16 and 32 processors. Each reconfiguration was performed at least 200 times (multiple runs of each application were necessary). We discarded the 10% smallest and largest samples and performed our analysis on the remaining (filtered) samples. The observations for this set of experiments are summarized in Table 2. Measurement results are listed in the form of mean and standard deviation ($\mu \pm \sigma$) for the filtered samples.

Table 2. Results for reconfigurations under DRMS.

application	operation $P_1 \rightarrow P_2$	reconfigure $\mu \pm \sigma(s)$	redistribute $\mu \pm \sigma(s)$	rate MB/s/PE	first $\mu \pm \sigma(ms)$	drms $\mu \pm \sigma(ms)$	spmd $\mu \pm \sigma(ms)$	%
	8 → 16	7.59 ± 2.58	2.40 ± 0.05	5.86	918 ± 77	877 ± 7	854 ± 9	3
APPBT	16 → 8	4.66 ± 0.41	2.02 ± 0.01	6.23	1657 ± 17	1627 ± 15	1596 ± 16	2
	16 → 32	9.88 ± 2.24	1.81 ± 0.04	4.34	511 ± 26	484 ± 10	471 ± 9	3
	32 → 16	11.75 ± 1.65	1.64 ± 0.02	4.29	909 ± 23	877 ± 7	854 ± 9	3
	8 → 16	6.00 ± 1.90	1.12 ± 0.01	5.36	851 ± 20	445 ± 3	452 ± 4	−2
APPLU	16 → 8	3.81 ± 0.45	1.03 ± 0.01	5.21	1291 ± 15	780 ± 3	792 ± 3	−2
	16 → 32	8.83 ± 1.98	1.04 ± 0.01	3.48	463 ± 11	251 ± 7	254 ± 7	−1
	32 → 16	11.29 ± 1.72	0.95 ± 0.01	3.16	836 ± 15	445 ± 3	452 ± 4	−2
	8 → 16	5.94 ± 1.56	1.57 ± 0.02	5.12	460 ± 20	431 ± 5	421 ± 6	2
APPSP	16 → 8	3.79 ± 0.28	1.43 ± 0.01	5.05	789 ± 6	752 ± 5	744 ± 6	1
	16 → 32	8.63 ± 1.43	1.44 ± 0.02	3.13	261 ± 7	245 ± 6	240 ± 5	2
	32 → 16	11.33 ± 1.20	1.41 ± 0.02	2.86	446 ± 6	431 ± 5	421 ± 6	2

The particular reconfigurations are identified in the "operation" column. The notation $P_1 \rightarrow P_2$ denotes a reconfiguration from P_1 (source) to P_2 (target) processors. The "reconfigure" column lists the total reconfiguration time, in seconds. The "redistribute" column lists the redistribution component of the total reconfiguration time, also in seconds. The "rate" column lists the *redistribution rate* for the operation. The redistribution rate is defined as the actual amount of distributed data in the target partition (including the overlap caused by borders) divided by the redistribution time, divided by the number of processors in the smallest (rate limiting) partition. The redistribute rate is in units of MBytes *per* second *per* processor. The "reconfigure", "redistribute", and "rate" columns characterize the intrinsic cost of a reconfiguration operation.

Columns "first", "drms", and "spmd" characterize the *impact* of DRMS on the execution of the application between reconfiguration points. Right after a reconfiguration, an application goes through a *transient* of cache misses and page faults before it reaches steady-state operation. The applications used in our studies traverse the entire data space at each iteration. Therefore, steady-state is achieved after the first iteration after a reconfiguration. Column "first" lists the execution time of the first iteration after a reconfiguration, on the destination processor partition. Columns "drms" and "spmd" list the steady-state iteration execution times for the DRMS (t_{DRMS}) and SPMD (t_{SPMD}) versions of the application, when executing on the target processor partition (P_2 processors). Iteration execution times are in milliseconds. The "%" column is a measure of how much larger the DRMS times are compared to the corresponding SPMD times. It is computed as $100 \times (t_{\text{DRMS}} - t_{\text{SPMD}})/t_{\text{SPMD}}$ and negative values indicate that the DRMS version is faster. We note that, alternatively, we could have considered the difference between the time for the first iteration after a reconfiguration and the steady state DRMS time as a part of the reconfiguration cost. This time should then be added to the "reconfigure" column.

Figure 5 shows the breakdown of reconfiguration and redistribution times into their components, for the various reconfiguration operations. The notation $P_1 : P_2$ at the top of each plot denotes a reconfiguration from P_1 to P_2 processors. The horizontal line and number at the top of each vertical bar represents the total time of each reconfiguration or redistribution. The fraction of each component is indicated by different shadings. The blank space between the top of the bar and the horizontal line, for reconfiguration, represents the "other" component. We complete our presentation of results with Tables 3 and 4, which list the mean and standard deviation for the various components of reconfiguration and redistribution. Column "%" in Table 3 is the percentage of reconfiguration time represented by the sum of the switch, exit, and spawn times.

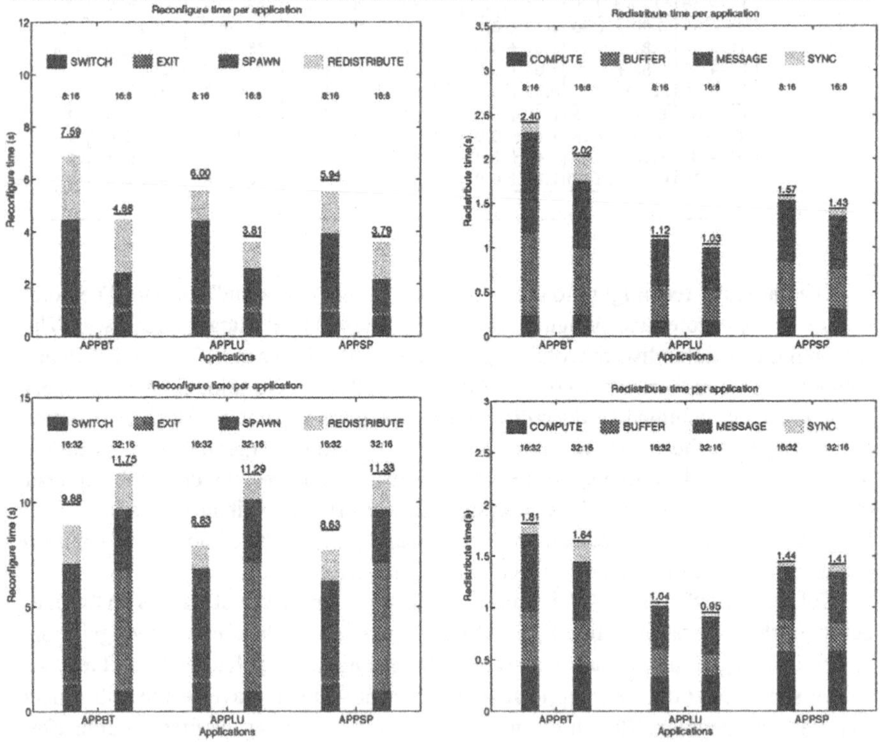

Fig. 5. Components of reconfiguration and redistribution times.

6.4 Discussion

We first note, from Table 2, that the steady-state performance of the DRMS and SPMD versions of the applications are very similar. The difference can be attributed to different

Table 3. Summary of results for reconfiguration.

application	operation	reconfigure $\mu \pm \sigma(s)$	switch $\mu \pm \sigma(s)$	exit $\mu \pm \sigma(s)$	spawn $\mu \pm \sigma(s)$	%	redistribute $\mu \pm \sigma(s)$	other $\mu \pm \sigma(s)$
APPBT	8 → 16	7.59 ± 2.58	1.11 ± 0.10	0.10 ± 0.02	3.27 ± 1.55	59	2.40 ± 0.05	0.71 ± 0.93
	16 → 8	4.66 ± 0.41	0.93 ± 0.06	0.18 ± 0.03	1.33 ± 0.20	52	2.02 ± 0.01	0.20 ± 0.14
	16 → 32	9.88 ± 2.24	1.29 ± 0.17	0.17 ± 0.01	5.62 ± 1.82	72	1.81 ± 0.04	1.00 ± 0.42
	32 → 16	11.75 ± 1.65	0.98 ± 0.08	5.75 ± 1.10	2.97 ± 1.55	83	1.64 ± 0.02	0.42 ± 1.02
APPLU	8 → 16	6.00 ± 1.90	1.05 ± 0.12	0.16 ± 0.00	3.23 ± 1.50	74	1.12 ± 0.01	0.44 ± 0.47
	16 → 8	3.81 ± 0.45	0.92 ± 0.09	0.20 ± 0.03	1.47 ± 0.27	68	1.03 ± 0.01	0.19 ± 0.08
	16 → 32	8.83 ± 1.98	1.37 ± 0.26	0.24 ± 0.01	5.22 ± 1.78	77	1.04 ± 0.01	0.96 ± 0.41
	32 → 16	11.29 ± 1.72	0.97 ± 0.08	6.14 ± 0.03	3.03 ± 1.74	90	0.95 ± 0.01	0.20 ± 0.24
APPSP	8 → 16	5.94 ± 1.56	0.95 ± 0.10	0.09 ± 0.00	2.91 ± 1.17	67	1.57 ± 0.02	0.40 ± 0.39
	16 → 8	3.79 ± 0.28	0.78 ± 0.09	0.13 ± 0.01	1.29 ± 0.18	58	1.43 ± 0.01	0.16 ± 0.03
	16 → 32	8.63 ± 1.43	1.34 ± 0.26	0.17 ± 0.00	4.76 ± 1.24	73	1.44 ± 0.02	0.92 ± 0.47
	32 → 16	11.33 ± 1.20	0.99 ± 0.08	6.10 ± 0.03	2.56 ± 0.99	85	1.41 ± 0.02	0.27 ± 0.40

Table 4. Summary of results for redistribution.

application	operation	redistribute $\mu \pm \sigma(s)$	compute $\mu \pm \sigma(s)$	buffer $\mu \pm \sigma(s)$	message $\mu \pm \sigma(s)$	sync $\mu \pm \sigma(s)$
APPBT	8 → 16	2.40 ± 0.05	0.24 ± 0.00	0.92 ± 0.00	1.15 ± 0.02	0.09 ± 0.02
	16 → 8	2.02 ± 0.01	0.24 ± 0.00	0.75 ± 0.00	0.76 ± 0.00	0.27 ± 0.01
	16 → 32	1.81 ± 0.04	0.44 ± 0.00	0.52 ± 0.00	0.76 ± 0.02	0.09 ± 0.01
	32 → 16	1.64 ± 0.02	0.45 ± 0.00	0.42 ± 0.00	0.57 ± 0.01	0.19 ± 0.01
APPLU	8 → 16	1.12 ± 0.01	0.18 ± 0.00	0.38 ± 0.00	0.54 ± 0.01	0.02 ± 0.00
	16 → 8	1.03 ± 0.01	0.18 ± 0.00	0.32 ± 0.00	0.50 ± 0.01	0.03 ± 0.00
	16 → 32	1.04 ± 0.01	0.34 ± 0.00	0.25 ± 0.00	0.43 ± 0.01	0.02 ± 0.00
	32 → 16	0.95 ± 0.01	0.35 ± 0.00	0.20 ± 0.00	0.37 ± 0.00	0.03 ± 0.00
APPSP	8 → 16	1.57 ± 0.02	0.31 ± 0.00	0.53 ± 0.00	0.70 ± 0.02	0.04 ± 0.00
	16 → 8	1.43 ± 0.01	0.31 ± 0.00	0.45 ± 0.00	0.60 ± 0.01	0.07 ± 0.00
	16 → 32	1.44 ± 0.02	0.58 ± 0.00	0.30 ± 0.00	0.52 ± 0.02	0.04 ± 0.00
	32 → 16	1.41 ± 0.02	0.59 ± 0.00	0.25 ± 0.00	0.50 ± 0.02	0.06 ± 0.00

memory access patterns caused by the dense storage used in DRMS (Section 5.1). We observe that the impact of DRMS on steady-state performance is minimal, varying from slightly slower (APPBT and APPSP) to slightly faster (APPLU). The transient penalty on the first iteration after a reconfiguration is also very small (10% or less of the iteration time) for APPBT and APPSP, but it is larger for APPLU (almost the time for one steady-state iteration).

We also observe from Table 2, for a given reconfiguration operation, that while the performance of redistribution in particular is very stable (small standard deviation), the same is not true of the reconfiguration as a whole. The variability in the reconfiguration times is caused mostly by the "spawn" and "other" components, as can be verified in Table 3. Data redistribution involves only application level communication through the HPS, which explains the low variance among the observed samples. The remaining components of reconfiguration involve communication through the Ethernet among the several modules of DRMS. This communication helps explain the larger variance observed for reconfiguration.

The switch operation involves communication of DRMS with the *partition manager*, a centralized agent in the SP2 architecture that performs the configuration of partition tables. Delays in communication with the partition manager and the load in the particular processor where it is executing are most likely the main causes for the variance in the switch time. The exit operation involves inter-*TC* synchronization over Ethernet, and we clearly observe an explosion in exit time (Figure 5) when the exit partition (source) has 32 processors. We suspect this explosion to be caused by much less efficient Ethernet communication across SP2 frames (1 frame = 16 thin nodes). The spawn time increases with the size of the processor partition being spawned (target). This occurs because the file system that contains the application executable is shared. The shared file system also explains the large variance in spawn times.

Regarding data redistribution, we note that actual message passing typically represents less than 50% of the total redistribution cost. Therefore, optimizing the computation component and eliminating some of the intermediate buffer copying can have good performance benefits. Better data agglomeration for message-passing (right now each distributed array is redistributed separately) can also help. As Table 3 shows, most of the reconfiguration time, from 52% for APPBT 16 $\rightarrow$ 8 to 88% for APPLU 32 $\rightarrow$ 16, is spent on time represented by the "exit", "switch", and "spawn" components. Therefore, these components are also high priority for optimization.

7 Related Work

The importance of dynamic and reconfigurable scheduling of processors as a way to improve application and system performance in multiprocessors has been recognized in [15, 16, 11, 5, 10, 14]. In particular, [16, 10, 11] show that dynamic partitioning of processors outperform all other space-sharing policies on uniform-access, shared-memory systems. For private-memory (message-passing) systems, it is demonstrated in [14] that dynamic reconfiguration policies outperform the other policies. Both [5] and [11] discuss research systems for shared-memory multiprocessors that support reconfiguration of the processor partition of an application during execution.

Our work differs from the previously mentioned research in that we have implemented a working environment for a production message-passing system (IBM SP2) that supports dynamic reconfiguration of processor partitions. We provide the language extensions and run-time services that allow users to easily port their existing SPMD applications to execute on reconfigurable partitions. We also provide all the resource control and scheduling mechanisms to coordinate the execution of these jobs.

The Adaptive Multiblock PARTI (AMP) library [3] supports dynamically reconfigurable applications. In AMP an application is spawned on the maximum number of processors it can run on and only a subset of the processes, corresponding to the processors actually allocated at a given time, is used for application execution. Such an approach results in performance degradation not only for the application but also interferes with the execution of other applications in multi-user environments. In general, this approach may result in scalability problems and inefficient memory utilization when the number of reconfigurable applications is large.

System-level approaches offer another way to support execution of applications on reconfigurable processor partitions, in contrast to the program-assisted approach taken by DRMS and the previously mentioned research. In these system-level approaches [12], parallel programs are decomposed into light-weight virtual processors, typically greater in number than the physical processors. Dynamic reconfiguration is then supported via application-transparent migration of these virtual processors. The disadvantages of these approaches are the need to multiplex the execution of many threads in one processor, and the negative impact on memory references caused by having each thread work on a small section of the global data space.

Extensive work has been done on language support for data distribution in multiprocessors. The data distribution in DRMS was particularly influenced by Fortran D [4] and HPF [8]. We want to emphasize that, from the language point of view, DRMS offers constructs for resource control, missing from HPF, and a much richer set of data distribution facilities. Also, DRMS annotations are targeted to explicit SPMD codes.

8 Conclusions

In this paper, we have described an implementation of DRMS (Distributed Resource Management System) for the IBM SP2, with particular emphasis on the programming interfaces for run-time resource allocations and data distributions. We have tested and validated this system using real application codes from the NAS Parallel Benchmark suite. Although our discussion in this paper has focused on processors, the framework developed under DRMS includes treatment of other types of resources in general (memory, file systems, communication channels, etc).

In addition to providing the operating system with a means for a finer control over the resources allocated to executing jobs, DRMS also makes it possible for applications to manage their resources dynamically and to manipulate their data distributions. With such dynamic control, it is possible for parallel applications to adapt to changes in the available number of processors, or to adapt to changes in the behavior of computations.

Our performance evaluation in this paper has been restricted to analyzing the effects of partition reconfiguration for codes that otherwise use a homogeneous data distribution. We have determined that DRMS has very little negative, and in some cases positive, impact on the execution of codes between reconfigurations. We have also determined the cost of reconfiguration on the IBM SP2 to be in the order of $5 - 10s$. While this cost can represent tens of iterations of our benchmarks, real production codes run for much longer time, without necessarily using much larger data spaces. Even this $5 - 10s$ cost of reconfiguration has been shown to be low enough to improve overall system performance, as measured in average job response time (the difference between job exit and arrival times), by a factor of 2 in some situations [9].

An important conclusion of this particular work is that we have demonstrated the feasibility and usefulness of our approach. We still have performance tuning and other enhancements to do, but we have laid the foundations for a dynamic resource management system that will improve utilization and performance of multiprocessor systems.

Acknowledgments: This work is partially supported by NASA under the HPCCPT-1 Cooperative Research Agreement No. NCC2-9000.

References

1. Agerwala, T., Martin, J. L., Mirza, J. H., Sadler, D. C., Dias, D. M., and Snir, M. SP2 system architecture. *IBM Systems Journal*, 34(2):152–184, 1995.
2. Bailey, D. et al. The NAS parallel benchmarks. Technical Report RNR-94-007, NASA Ames Research Center, March 1994.
3. Edjlali, E., Agrawal, G., Sussman, A., and Saltz, J. Data parallel programming in an adaptive environment. In *Proceedings of 9th International Parallel Processing Symposium*, Santa Barbara, CA, April 1995.
4. Fox, G., Hiranandani, S., Kennedy, K., Koelbel, C., Kremer, U., Tseng, C., and Wu, M. Fortran D language specification. Technical Report COMP TR90-141, Department of Computer Science, Rice University, December 1990.
5. Gupta, A., Tucker, A., and Stevens, L. Making effective use of shared-memory multiprocessors: The process control approach. Technical Report CSL-TR-91-475A, Computer Systems Laboratory, Stanford University, 1991.
6. IBM Corporation. *IBM Parallel Programming Environment for AIX, MPL Programming and Subroutine Reference*, first edition, August 1995.
7. Indiana University. *Sage++, A Class library for Building Fortran 90 and C++ Restructuring Tools*, May 1995.
8. Koelbel, C. H., Loveman, D. B., Schreiber, R. S., Steele Jr., G. L., and Zosel, M. E. *The High Performance Fortran Handbook*. The MIT Press, 1994.
9. Konuru, R. B., Moreira, J. E., and Naik, V. K. Application-assisted dynamic scheduling on large-scale multi-computer systems. In *Proceedings of Second International Euro-Par Conference (Euro-Par'96), Lyon, France*, volume 1124 of *Lecture Notes in Computer Science*, pages II:621–630, August 1996.
10. Leutenneger, S. T and Vernon, M. K. The performance of multiprogrammed multiprocessor scheduling policies. In *Proceedings of the ACM SIGMETRICS Conference on Measurement and Modeling of Computer Systems*, pages 226–236, May 1990.
11. McCann, C., Vaswami, R., and Zahorjan, J. A dynamic processor allocation policy for multiprogrammed shared-memory multiprocessors. *ACM Transactions on Computer Systems*, 11(2):146–178, May 1993.
12. McCann, C. and Zahorjan, J. Processor allocation policies for message-passing parallel computers. In *Proceedings of the ACM SIGMETRICS Conference on Measurement and Modeling of Computer Systems*, pages 19–32, May 1994.
13. Moreira, J. E., Eswar, K., Konuru, R., and Naik, V. K. Supporting dynamic data and processor repartitioning for irregular applications. In *Proceedings of Third International Workshop on Parallel Algorithms for Irregularly Structured Problems (Irregular'96), Santa Barbara, California*, volume 1117 of *Lecture Notes in Computer Science*, pages 237–238, August 1996.
14. Naik, V. K., Setia, S. K., and Squillante, M. S. Processor allocation in multiprogrammed, distributed-memory parallel computer systems. Technical Report RC 20239, IBM Research Division, October 1995. Submitted to Journal of Parallel and Distributed Computing.
15. Polychronopoulos, C. Multiprocessing versus multiprogramming. In *Proceedings of the 1989 International Conference on Parallel Processing*, volume II, pages 223–230, August 8-12 1989.
16. Tucker, A. and Gupta, A. Process control and scheduling issues for multiprogrammed shared-memory multiprocessors. In *Proceedings of the 12th ACM Symposium on Operating Systems Principles*, pages 159–166, December 1989.

Dependence Driven Execution for Data Parallelism

Suvas Vajracharya and Dirk Grunwald

University of Colorado, Campus Box 430, Boulder, Colorado 80309
{suvas,grunwald}@cs.colorado.edu

Abstract. This paper proposes an efficient run-time system to schedule general nested loops on multiprocessors. The work extends existing one-dimensional loop scheduling strategies such as static scheduling, affinity scheduling and various dynamic scheduling methods. The extensions are twofold. First, multiple independent loops as found in different branches of `parbegin/parend` constructs can be scheduled simultaneously. Secondly, multidimensional loops with dependencies and conditions can be aggressively scheduled. The ability to schedule multidimensional loops with dependencies is made possible by providing a dependence vector as an input to the scheduler. Based on this application-specific input, a continuation-passing run-time system using non-blocking threads efficiently orchestrates the parallelism on shared memory MIMD and DSM multicomputers. The run-time system uses a dependence-driven execution which is similar to data-driven and message-driven executions in that it is asynchronous. This asynchrony allows a high degree of parallelism.

1 Overview

Most loop-scheduling methods and parallel runtime systems are designed to schedule a single loop. However, loop-scheduling can also be applied to *loop nests* or general loops. Likewise, it is useful to schedule different loops in a program at the same time, even when there are data dependences between those loops.

General loop scheduling is possible if the programmer or the compiler passes application-specific dependencies to the scheduler. Parallelizing compilers can make some of this information available in the form of dependence vectors [28, 4]. By passing this information to the run-time layer, a dependence-driven run-time system can exploit application-specific parallelism in a general, portable manner. The compiler describes the parallelism *declaratively* in the form of dependence vectors. All the procedural details of synchronization and scheduling are handled by the run-time system. The compiler or programmer specifies *what* the constraints are; the run-time system effects *how* they can be satisfied. Given the dynamic nature of parallelism, we believe this is a reasonable partitioning of the scheduling process.

The proposed run-time system introduces a new method based on a dependence-driven execution. In a dependence-driven execution, an operation begins when all its dependence constraints are satisfied. The dependence constraint, in the form of a dependence vector, is an input to the system. An enabling engine matches completed loop iterations with the left hand side of the the rule which fires to enable new iterations on the right hand side. For example, the dependence rule, $(i, j) \rightarrow (i + 1, j)$, says that the system can compute iteration $(i + 1, j)$ when (i, j) completes. This allows an aggressive exploitation of application-specific parallelism. In this paper, we describe such a dependence driven runtime system. Dependence-driven execution is similar to data-driven execution used in data-flow models except that the control dependencies as well as the data dependencies are used in determining execution sequence. In the data-driven model, computations can begin when all the operands (data) of an operator are available while in a dependence-driven execution, an operation begins when all the symbolic dependency constraints are satisfied. Both of these models are characterized by asynchrony which implies a high degree of concurrency.

We expect our runtime system to be targeted by a compiler, although programs can also be constructed by hand. The proposed run-time system, DUDE (Definition-Use Description Environment) is designed to run on specific but prevalent multiprocessor architectures such as MIMD shared memory multiprocessors. This work makes no assumptions about the availability of hardware support for data-level synchronization such as full-empty bits. The contributions of this runtime system are:

- Efficient loop scheduling using a dependence-driven execution. The proposed loop scheduling schedules nested (multidimensional) loops in the presence of dependences between iterations.
- The ability to schedule different loops, as in the branches of `parbegin/parend` constructs, simultaneously.
- The run-time system is highly portable. It has been ported to the KSR-1, SGI Power Challenge, DEC Alpha multiprocessors, and Sun multiprocessors. It is currently being ported to the Hemingway DSM System.

The rest of the paper is organized as follows. Section §2 discusses related works. This is followed by section §3.1, which describes the extension of static and affinity schedulers to use data-level synchronization such that general loops can be scheduled. Section §3.2 discusses a dependence driven dynamic scheduler. In section §4, we present some experimental results. Finally, section §5 concludes the work.

2 Related Work

Our goal is to design a runtime system to efficiently schedule general loops. In this section we present related works by discussing loop scheduling methods followed by some relevant runtime systems.

2.1 Loop Scheduling Methods

Loop scheduling is the task of assigning iterations of loops to different processors to execute them in parallel. In a parallel program, three types of loops may be distinguished: *doser*, *doall* and *doacross*. *Doser* loops must be executed serially while iterations in a *doall* loop are completely independent and therefore can run in any order or in parallel. In a *doacross* loop, values assigned in one iterations are used in another iteration and therefore only partial parallelism is possible. Loops in real application can be quite baroque, as *doser* and *doall*s or *doser*'s and *doacross*s can be nested within each other arbitrarily and conditionally. Such loops are called hybrid loops. Schedulers vary in the extent that they support these various kinds of loop structures. A number of related works have focused on scheduling only a singly-nested *doall*. We discuss this next and also discuss attempts to schedule multiply-nested loops in section §2.1.

Singly-Nested Doall Loop Scheduling: Although dozens of methods have been proposed for scheduling a single `doall`, they can not be immediately applied to loop nests that have dependences carried by the inner loop. These schemes can be further divided into three types: static, dynamic and hybrid based on whether scheduling decisions are made at compile-time, runtime, or both.

Static Scheduling: At compile-time, the N iterations are divided among P processors by assigning $\frac{N}{P}$ iterations to each process. This scheme is simple and there is no runtime scheduling overhead. The disadvantage, however, is that the method cannot adapt to dynamic fluctuation of the load in the application.

Dynamic Scheduling: Dynamic assignment of iterations to processors can achieve better load balance. The simplest dynamic method is *self-scheduling* [25] where each processor grabs one iteration from the central data structure and executes that iteration. To alleviate the high cost of N synchronizations for N iterations in this approach, *fixed-size chunking* [18] was proposed, where each process grabs chunks of K iterations instead of one iteration.

If the processors do not start simultaneously or if one processor gets an expensive chunk, the potential for load imbalance still exists. In *guided-self scheduling* [22], the number of iterations assigned to a processor is a function of number iterations left to be scheduled. A variation on this method is *factoring* [17] where at each scheduling operation the scheduler computes the size of a *batch* of chunks with the motivation to reduce the number of scheduling operations. The current size of the batch is exactly half of the previous batch. Other methods in this model include *adaptive guided self-scheduling*, *trapezoidal self-scheduling* [26], *tapering* [12, 20], and *safe self-scheduling* [19].

Hybrid Methods: A compromise between purely static scheduling, which has the potential for poor load balance on irregular problems, and dynamic scheduling, is *affinity loop scheduling* [21], which takes affinity of data to processors into account. This scheme is most like chunking except that chunks have an affinity to a particular processor Another difference is that chunking is a centralized algorithm while affinity scheduling is a distributed algorithm based on work stealing.

Multiply-Nested Hybrid Loop Scheduling: The previous methods discussed loop scheduling for a simple single *doall* loop. In real applications however, the structure of loops can be quite complicated. *Doacross* loops, for example, have dependencies between iterations. Furthermore *doser*, *doacross* and *doall* loops can be nested within each other in arbitrarily complex ways.

In this section, we give an overview of static, dynamic and hybrid methods for scheduling multiply-nested loops.

Static Methods: A special case of multiply-nested loops are the one-way (or perfectly) nested *doall* loops in which there exists exactly one loop at each nest level. Given a one-way nested *doall* loop, a compile time transformation, *loop coalescing*, [23] can be used to coalesce m *doall* loops into a single *doall* with $N = \prod_{i=1}^{m}(N_i)$ iterations. This transformation then allows the application of the methods described in the previous section. A hybrid loop consisting of *doser* and *doall* can be transformed such that all *doalls* are nested within the *doser* loop by *loop interchange* [1, 28]. Other compiler transformations attempt to organize loops such that the loop with maximum parallelism is the outer loop.

Compiler transformations such as loop normalization and loop fusion can also be used to collapse a multi-dimensional iteration space to a single dimensional iteration space. In contrast, we propose the use of tree-like recursive data structures to represent multidimensional iteration space. The runtime system manipulates this structure to coalesce or divide the iteration space during scheduling. As we will describe, this allows the proposed run-time system to schedule multi-dimensional loops with dependencies across iterations and across dimensions.

Runtime Methods: Fang *et. al.* [10] described a two-level scheduling scheme for general arbitrarily nested parallel loops. Each loop *doser*, *doall* or *doacross* is termed a task. An extremely large-grain data-flow graph, where each node is an entire loop, is created. A high-level scheduler schedules these loop nodes as soon as the precedence-constraints between them are satisfied. A low-level scheduler then picks up an enabled node to schedule iterations using a singly-nested loop scheduler such as GSS. In contrast to the proposed scheduler, iterations from different loops cannot be overlapped since the low-level scheduler must schedule a loop in its entirety (by using barriers) before beginning a different loop.

Hybrid Methods: An optimized compile/run-time version of loop interchange and loop distribution called *IGSS* and *MGSS* was proposed in [27]. These schemes also allowed the scheduling of hybrid loops consisting of *doser* and *doalls*. This method is useful in cases where the number of iterations of a *doall* loop is much larger than the number of processors involved. *Doall* loops with large number of iterations are divided into pieces (usually two) and the piece are run in a interleaved fashion.

Multiple independent Loops: Graham *et al.* noticed that in many application two separate but consecutive loops may be partially independent. Normally, when consecutive loops are encountered, the system would parallelize the first loop and only when first loop is finished, the second is begun or if possible, fuse the two loops. However it may be possible to find a subset of the second loop that can run in parallel with the first loop. This can occur, for example, if the iteration space of the first loop does not subsume the iteration space of the second. These non-overlapping subsets of the computation can be recognized by the compiler and then executed in parallel with the first loop. To achieve this, it is necessary to describe regions of computations (such as the non-intersecting regions) using data descriptors. In this paper, data descriptors consist of simple rectangles although more sophisticated and exact methods available from compiler literature [2, 7, 3] could be used. In the proposed work, descriptors for iteration spaces are generated and manipulated during *run-time* by representing them using recursive structures called quad-trees. This allows (independent) portions of multiple loops to be executed in parallel.

Loops that appear in different branches *parbegin/parend* constructs are also independent and therefore can be scheduled simultaneously. We are not aware of runtime systems that efficiently supports the execution of such independent loops in parallel.

2.2 The Chores Runtime Systems

The Chores system [9] is implemented on top of Presto [5] and runs on the Sequent Symmetry. A per-processor worker (an user-level thread) grab chunks of work from a central queue using the guided self-scheduling method. As in the proposed work, the Chores system supports loop iterations with dependencies by using data-level synchronization. Data-dependent loops can be parallelized in one of two ways:

1. **Dynamic Chores**: Dynamic Chores is a very flexible and general method for implementing loop iterations with dependencies. They are particularly appropriate for recursion and functional parallelism. The generality, however, comes at the cost of forcing users to use primitive mechanisms for spawning threads, synchronizing, scheduling, and determining the appropriate granularity. Programmers need to lock the user-defined data structures to atomically decrement the counters that keep track of the number of unsatisfied precedence arcs. The *add-atom()* library call provides the means to schedule new enabled work. Dynamic Chores has the same benefits of flexibility and generality as Cilk [6], Mentat [14, 13] and Tam [8], but also suffers from the disadvantages of forcing users to use a low-level abstractions that these system provide. Users are responsible for decomposition and scheduling using the given abstractions.
2. **Indexed Chores**: Indexed chores are significantly easier to use than dynamic chores since the users need only provide the body of the loop, the range of loop iterations, and a dependence specification. The system handles synchronization, scheduling and granularity just as in DUDE.

Unfortunately, indexed chores have a limited application for multidimensional loops because ready (enabled) iterations at any given time must be contiguous such that a *single* range, consisting of a lower and an upper bound, describes the entire set of ready iterations. The single contiguous range requirement is necessary to apply guided-self scheduling. The set of enabled iterations can only grow by increasing the upper bound of the range. The enabler increases the upper bound and guided-self scheduling increases the lower bound. This method limits the amount of parallelism because the system can not enable iterations that do not fall within this range even though the dependence constraints on them are satisfied.

The more important problem with linearization (collapsing to one dimension) is that this cannot be applied to most loop structures. For example, how does one linearize complex hybrid loops? How can multi-dimensional loops with dependencies across time-steps be linearized?

We felt that the Chores scheduling model was elegant, but had some significant drawbacks that we wanted remove. First, Chores can only schedule *doacross* loops that are amenable to linearization as shown in the earlier example. For more complicated loops, programmers must resort to spawning threads and synchronizing them by hand as in dynamic chores. Chores does not discuss how multiply-nested *doall*'s or hybrid loops with *doall*'s and *doser*'s or *doser*'s and *doacross*'s or how imperfectly nested loops can be scheduled. For such cases, Chores uses a barrier synchronization which enforce false dependencies. In contrast the Jacobi method, for example, can be scheduled without using barriers in DUDE. Furthermore, DUDE presents a distributed scheduler whereas the Chores system uses a centralized.

3 The DUDE Run-time System

The DUDE runtime system is built on the top of an existing thread library, AWESIME [15], a thread library implemented in C++. Together they provide a powerful way to take advantage of both task and data parallelism in applications. In this paper, we concentrate on DUDE's data parallelism since this is the most novel aspect of the runtime system.

The proposed runtime system consists of three types of loop schedulers: static, affinity, and dynamic. The programmer or the compiler can choose one of these methods depending on the application. The next section discusses static and affinity scheduling. Section §3.2 discusses dynamic scheduling.

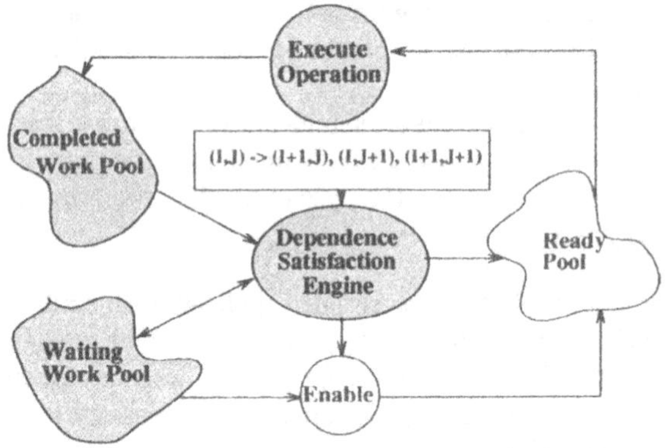

Fig. 1. Dependence-driven Execution Model

3.1 Static and Affinity Scheduling

The static and affinity schedulers in the proposed work can be broken into six parts: 1) Data decomposition, 2) Definition of loop structure, 3) Dependence specification, 4) Data distribution, 5) Data parallel operation, 6) Dependence satisfaction.

Figure 1 demonstrates the basic model. We now discuss some of the details of the different parts of the runtime system using the example of the Red/Black SOR shown in Figure 2. In the example, the methods for only the red computation are shown. The methods for black computation would be analogous to the red.

```
01 void RedSOR::main() {              // user defined loop body
02     :
03 }
00 void main(int argc, char** argv) {
01   // data decomposition
02   REDSOR=new IterCollection<REDSOR>(A,dim,BLOCK,cpus,grain);
03   BLKSOR=new IterCollection<BLKSOR>(A,dim,BLOCK,cpus,grain);
04   // dependence specification
05   SetDependence(REDSOR,BLKSOR,``(t,i,j) =>
            (t+1,i+1,j),(t+1,i-1,j),(t+1,i,j+1),(t+1,i,j-1}'');
06   // loop structure definition
07   LoopDesc *LPD=new LoopDesc(schdlr=AFFNTY,iterations=100);
08   LPD->setOp(0,REDSOR);      // specify the operations.
09   LPD->setOp(1,BLKSOR);      // do black after red.
10   LPD->add_ready_pool();     // add to system
11   Cpu.fireItUp(CPUS);        // begin parallel computation
12 }
```

Fig. 2. Parallelized Code for Red/Black SOR using Dude

Data Decomposition and Distribution: The decomposition step divides the given data into *uniform* and *fixed* sizes. In the example, this is done in lines 2-3 of Figure 2. A programmer or compiler chooses the decomposition method such as by BLOCK or CYCLIC. The decomposition methods are similar to the data decomposition and distribution utilities available in HPF [16] and pC++ [11]. One important difference, however, is that in the process of data decomposition, DUDE takes flat data and creates objects called *Iterate*s which is a tuple consisting of both data and operation. *Iterate*s defines the granularity of parallelism in DUDE. Collections of *Iterate*s, termed *Iterate-Collection*, define the operation and data for the entire data-space. An *IterateCollection* represents a parallel loop such as a *doall* or a *doacross*.

Dividing data into uniform fixed size chunks has an advantage in dependence-driven execution. The advantage is that the *Iterate*s are named simply by their indices as opposed to a range for each dimension. Consequently, the indices can be used to randomly access the *IterateCollections* which is a (multidimensional) array of *Iterate* objects. For example, if we divide a two dimensional matrix of size NxN into fixed size chunks of PxP, then the chunks can be named as (i, j) where both $i, j \in 1..\frac{N}{P}$ assuming $N \ mod \ P = 0$ (In practice, however, the granularity would be much finer than $N \ mod \ P$. This implies that the dependencies as specified in dependence rule applies to any chunks size for any granularity for applications with regular dependence structure.

Definition of Loop Structures: The loop structure is an object that brings everything together in DUDE. It contains the bounds of the loops, the scheduling method to be used, *i.e.*, static, affinity, or dynamic, and the structural information such as the way the loops are nested. After initializing this structure, the runtime system takes complete control over the scheduling and executing the loop. Loop structure initialization is shown in lines 7-9 in the example.

Dependence specification: The compiler specifies the dependence in the form of dependence vectors. Each vector in the set represents an arc from the source of the to the target of the dependency. A compiler can compute this vector by taking the difference between the iteration vectors of the source and target iterations. A good description of this dependence analysis can be found in [28] [4]. Line 5 specifies the dependences for stencil computation.

Data Parallel Operation: The runtime system handles the Data parallel operation and dependence satisfaction. When the user calls *fireItUp* as done in line 11, the data parallel operation begins. The scheduler picks up iterates from the local ready queue and invokes its *main* method which is the user-defined loop body. Next the runtime system increments a counter in the loop structure that represents the index variable of the loop. If the counter is equal to loop bound then no further action is necessary. Otherwise, we take the following step.

Dependence Satisfaction: Dependence satisfaction follows the completion of an *Iterate*. However, before dependence satisfaction procedure is begun, the scheduler must record the processor identifier on the *Iterate* so that when this *Iterate* is rescheduled, it runs on the same cpu. This improves locality when affinity scheduling is used. Next, the runtime system uses the dependence rule to find the target *Iterates* that may have been enabled as a consequence of having completed this *Iterate*. The index of the completed *Iterates* unify with the *Iterates* on the left hand side. This allows the dependence rule to fire, producing the iterates on the right hand side. In the example, when *Iterate* (t,i,j) completes , the system decrements the enable counter of *Iterates* indexed by (t+1,i,j), (t+1,i+1,j), (t+1,i,j+1), (t+1,i-1,j), and (t+1,i,j-1). We can easily retrieve these *Iterates* in static chunking by simply accessing the *IterateCollection* using these indices. If decrementing the enable counter of any of these *Iterates* makes them zero, the system adds this *Iterate* to the ready queue.

Static and affinity scheduling with or without the use of a dependence-driven execution improve data locality which reduces communications. Using a dependence-driven execution, as described above, reduces communication in two additional ways.

First, a dependence-driven execution exploits not only data locality but also temporal locality. This is because a dependence-driven execution effects a depth-first traversal of the entire iteration space; some of the subsequent computations in different time-steps can be executed before all of the data space computation have finished. The depth of execution along time-steps is only harnessed by precedence constraints. Consequently, the potential for re-use of data in the cache or registers is greater due to temporal locality. In contrast, conventional loop scheduling require all of data-space iterations to be completed before going on to the next phase. Since the entire data normally does not fit in caches, many cache faults are incurred.

Secondly, DUDE can avoid the loop coalescing, a transformation that collapses multidimensional loops into a single dimension to apply singly-nested loop schedulers.

Consequently, blocking, which is another optimization to improve data-locality, is not undone by the loop scheduler. DUDE allows the system to preserve blocking optimizations because the run-time system is designed to schedule multi-dimensional loops.

One of the contribution of this research is the ability to schedule multiple independent loops simultaneously. This is achieved in DUDE by using a polymorphic work queues. Work queues contains iterations from different loops. Each element of the work queue is an object which consists of a descriptor describing the iteration space and a virtual method called "main" which is the user defined loop body. The scheduler simply invokes the virtual method. This allows the separation of the scheduling behavior from application-specific loop behavior. This ability to schedule iterations from different loops simultaneously can be advantageous when the amount of work in a single loop is insufficient to fully utilize the available hardware resources such as CPUs.

3.2 Dynamic Scheduling

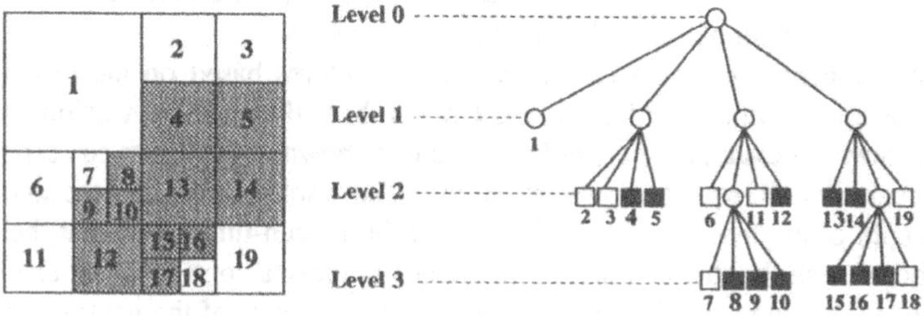

Fig. 3. A Quadtree

In the case of the dynamic scheduling, the data decomposition and data distribution is determined at run-time by the scheduler. The definition of loop structure and dependence specification remains the same as in the case of static and affinity scheduling. In dynamic scheduling, the chunk sizes are not statically determined to be uniform and fixed but varies during run-time as the scheduler sees fit for balancing the load. This introduces some difficulties. We discuss these in turn and offer a solution.

One problem is that of efficiently accessing the *Iterate*s from the pools shown in Figure 1. Indexing into and accessing the individual *Iterate*s in these pools are not as straight forward when iteration chunks sizes vary dynamically. This is because variable chunk sizes imply that random access using the array indices is no longer possible. The data descriptor, containing the range of iterations for each dimension, must be used as a key into the *Iterate* pools. The mapping function and data structure required to return an *Iterate* given a data descriptor as the key can be expensive in space and time. Since the dependence engine is in a critical section of the loop scheduler, this can be prohibitively expensive.

Put differently, an efficient way to fire the dependence rule is required. Firing the dependence rule requires unifying or matching the *lhs* and producing the *Iterate*s on *rhs*. This matching is efficient when static decomposition is used because the enabler can simply match the indices with the *lhs* of the firing rule. The firing rule applies at any granularity of chunk size – from the granularity of data points to coarse grain chunks – as long as the chunk sizes are uniform and fixed. A variable chunk size, which must be described by a range for each dimension, requires a more sophisticated and potentially inefficient firing method.

Another difficulty with dynamic scheduling is related to the tapering of the chunk sizes to balance the load. Tapering leads to a overly fine-grained computation when using a dependence-driven execution. This is not as much of a problem with singly-nested loop schedulers since the set of iterations that are ready to be scheduled become the entire contiguous set of iterations after a barrier. In contrast, in a dependence-driven execution, the order in which chunks get enabled depends on the relative order in which processors complete executing them. Consequently, the set of readied iterations at any given time will consist of dis-contiguous lists of overly fine-grained iterations. Therefore, a method for coalescing small chunks is required to avoid having to traverse long linked list of exceedingly small chunks of iterations. One solution to this, the linearization of iteration space, was presented in section §2.2. Linearization, however, leads to sequentialization or introduces false dependencies.

An alternate solution is to use spatial data-structures based on the principle of recursive decomposition called *quadtrees* (or its three dimensional version, *octree*). Figure 3 shows an example of a *quadtree*. The tree shown in the figure corresponds to the dark region in the square shown on the left. The resolution of the decomposition, *i.e.*, the depth of the tree, can be fixed or varied during run-time. Note that the nodes are numbered such that the children of any node compose a contiguous block. This is a consequence of imposing the Morton order on the elements of the iteration space at any level of the quad-tree (see the matrix in figure 3).

In the *quadtree* decomposition, each subdivision is a block divided into four equal-sized parts. Alternatively, at each subdivision, the block could be divided into two parts as in *bintree*. A comprehensive description of these data-structures can be found in [24]. These structure solve the problem of inefficient indexing into the pools of *Iterate*s because the chunk sizes are uniform at any given level. Given the level and the index, *Iterate*s from a pool can be retrieved by simply using random access. Similarly, unification with the *lhs* of the firing rules is efficient since, at any given level, the unification algorithm is same as it would be for static decomposition where grain sizes are uniform.

The hierarchical structure is also ideal for dealing with the problems of coalescing small chunks. As small chunks are enabled by dependence-driven execution, the parent, a larger chunk, can be enabled when all of its four child nodes at a finer resolution have been enabled.

We maintain a separate data structure for the purpose of keeping processor affinity information. The granularity of the chunk size for affinity maintenance need not be as fine as the granularity for scheduling and enabling the *Iterate*s. The affinity granularity is coarser than the resolution used in scheduling and enabling.

Now the quad-tree scheduling can be described as follows:

1. Construct a quad-tree for the iteration space using some minimum granularity, *i.e.*, determine the granularity of the leaf nodes.
2. During runtime, dynamically determine the scheduling granularity depending on amount of iterations left to do.
3. Assign iterations to processors at this granularity.
4. When iterations are completed, determine which new iterations can be enabled. If possible coalesce the enabled iterations.
5. Go to step two until the no new iterations can be enabled.

4 Experimental Results

We present the results of three applications using various methods on a 8 processor SGI Power Challenge. We expect the performance to scale to larger number of processors since we are using a distributed algorithm. The applications are Red/Black SOR, the Multigrid Solver and wavefront computation. We present the experimental methods before describing the applications.

4.1 Method

We present speedups of SOR, Multigrid, and wavefront on a idle machine. The speedups for Multigrid using various techniques are shown with great detail by comparing several techniques. For the other applications, the speedups for only the techniques that were competitive are shown. The variance in the all the speedup measurements were statistically insignificant. We also show the performance of various methods in the presence of noise, *i.e.*, background jobs. For this, we take the absolute times of the SOR application. The techniques are guided self-scheduling (`GSS`), static scheduling, affinity scheduling, chunking by block (`Dynamic Block`), chunking by row, linearization scheduling(`Chores`) and DUDE. To see what the benefits of coalescing are, we also show the performance of DUDE with the run-time coalescing turned off (`Dude-Nocoal`). Affinity, static, and Dude are distributed algorithms. The others are centralized.

4.2 Applications

Red/Black SOR: Red/Black SOR is an example of an algorithm that does not suffer from load-imbalance. This implies that if we use static scheduling, we would expect the processors to arrive at the barriers at approximately the same time and therefore need not idle for long periods, waiting for each other. Thus, if we can show that the DUDE's quadtree scheduling can improve upon the static scheduling in this application, then this is an indication that the performance benefits could be greater on other applications that do suffer from a load-imbalance. Results shown in Figure 4 are for a 1042x1024 matrix.

Even a static application like the Red/Black SOR can suffer from load imbalance however in presence of other applications running on the same system or when there are more processes than there are physical processors. One such environment, static scheduling does not do well as show in Table 1. This figure also shows that quadtree scheduling adapts well to such environments.

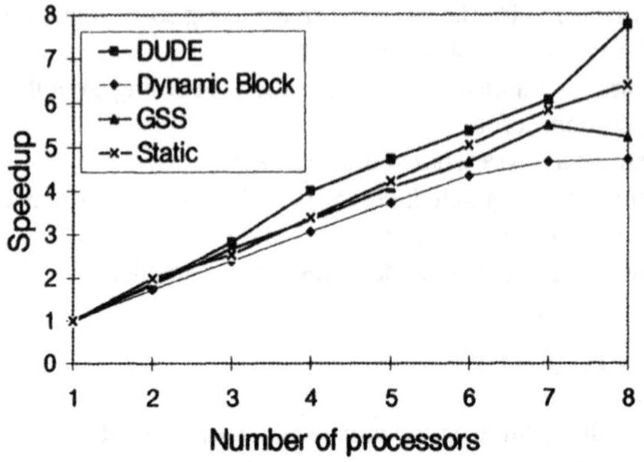

Fig. 4. Speedups of SOR on idle SGI Power Challenge

Method	Average execution time	Standard Deviation	95% Conf. Interval
Static Scheduling	8.27	2.63	0.83
DUDE Quad-tree Sched.	3.94	0.99	.31
Dynamic Block	6.75	2.49	.62
Guided Self Sched.	11.35	5.5	3.4

Table 1. Execution Times of SOR with background jobs

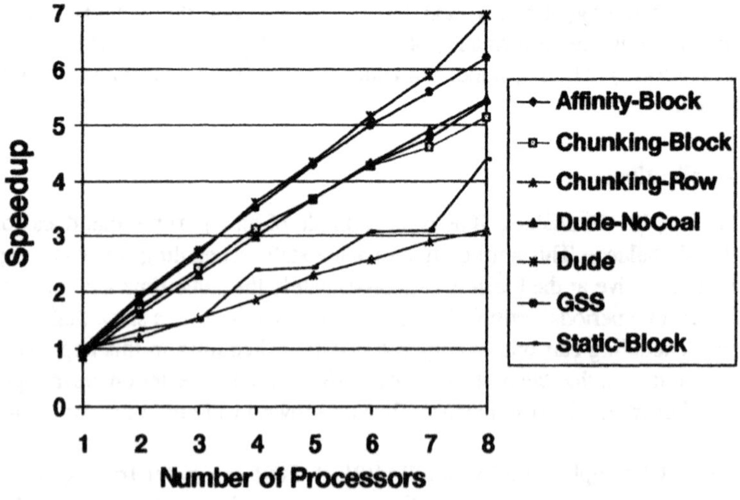

Fig. 5. Speedups of MG on idle SGI Power Challenge

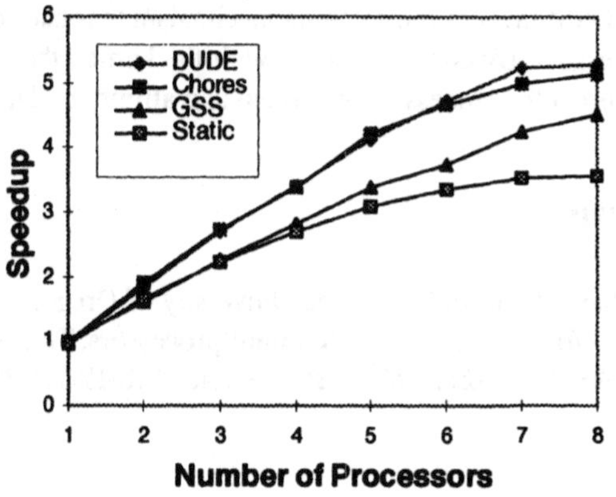

Fig. 6. Speedups of Wavefront on idle SGI Power Challenge

Wavefront The computational structure of Wavefront is representative of many algorithm such as Mean Value Analysis, pre-conditioned conjugate gradient, and least common subsequence. The amount of computation dramatically increases and decreases during run-time. The static scheduling transforms the loop to traverse the diagonals with each diagonal separated by a barrier synchronization.

Two dimensional Multigrid Solver In this application, the amount of work changes even more dramatically than in the wavefront example because the number of iterations in along consecutive time steps increases (or decreases) by a factor of four. Figure 5 shows the performance of various techniques. To see the benefits of coalescing small chunks to larger chunks, this figures also shows the performance running the same scheduler with the coalescing turned off, *i.e.*, with the chunks size fixed at an optimal granularity.

5 Conclusion

Parallelism is both application specific and dynamic. While the programmer or the compiler knows the application specific parallelism, neither can staticly assign work loads to processors because of dynamic fluctuation of interesting computations. We introduced a runtime system that uses declarative data dependence information from the compiler or programmer to capture the application specific parallelism and to dynamically assign work loads. We showed favorable performance for some sample application on architectures without special hardware for data-level synchronizations. This research also showed that general loops can be scheduled efficiently by using a declarative data dependence specification as an input to the runtime system. The communication of static information from the compiler to the runtime system was key to its generality and improved performance. A future work is to extend this idea by passing this information to lower levels such as the software DSM layer or the kernel of the operating system. By using the dependence information passed from the compiler, the runtime system can direct the software DSM layer or pre-fetching mechanism to reduce costly communications between processors. By communicating with the kernel, the runtime system can given hints to the kernel for process management and affinity of data to processors.

Acknowledgements

We would like to thank Alan Malony at the University of Oregon and Dennis Gannon at Indiana University for the use of their SGI multiprocessors. This work was funded in part by NSF grant No. ASC-9217394, ARPA contract ARMY DABT63-94-C-0029.

References

1. J.R. Allen and K. Kennedy. Automatic loop interchange. *ACM SIGPLAN Notices*, 19(6):233–246, June 1985.
2. Vasanth Balasundaram. A mechanism for keeping useful internal information in parallel programming tools: The data access descriptor. *Journal of Parallel and Distributed Computing*, 9:154–170, 1990.
3. Vasanth Balasundaram and Ken Kennedy. A technique for summarizing data access and its use in parallelism enhancing transformations. In *Proceedings of teh ACM SIGPLAN Symposium on Compiler Construction*, pages 41–53, June 1989.
4. U. Banerjee. An introduction to a formal theory of dependence analysis. *J. Supercomp.*, 2(2):133–149, August 1988.
5. B.N. Bershad, E.D. Lazowska, and H.M. Levy. PRESTO: A System for Object-Oriented Parallel Programming. *Software Practice and Experience*, 18(8):713–732, August 1988.
6. Robert D. Blumofe, Christopher F. Joerg, Bradley C. Kuszmaul, Charles E. Leiserson, Keith H. Randall, and Yuli Zhou. Cilk: An efficient multithreaded runtime system. In *Proceedings of the Fifth ACM SIGPLAN Symposium on Principles and Practice of Parallel Programming*, San Barbara, California, July 1995.
7. David Callahan. *A Global Approach to Detection of Parallelism*. PhD thesis, Rice University, April 1987.
8. D.E. Culler, A. Sah, K.E. Schauser, T. von Eicken, and J. Wawrzynek. Fine-grain parallelism with minimal hardware support: a compiler-controlled threaded abstract machine. In *Proceedings of the 4th Symposium on Architectural Support for Programming Languages and Operating Systems*, pages 164–175, Santa Clara, CA, April 1991.
9. Derek L. Eager and John Zahorjan. Chores: Enhanced run-time support fo shared memory parallel computing. *ACM. Trans on Computer Systems*, 11(1):1–32, February 1993.
10. Zhixi Fang, Peiyi Tang, Pen chung Yew, and Chuan qi Zhu. Dynamic processor self-scheduling for general parallel nested loops. *IEEE Transactions on Computers*, pages 919–929, July 1990.
11. D. Gannon and J.K. Lee. Object oriented parallelism. In *Proceedings of 1991 Japan Society for Parallel Processing*, pages 13–23, 1991.
12. Susan Graham, Steven Lucco, and Oliver Sharp. Orchestrating interactions among parallel computations. In *Proceedings of the ACM SIGPLAN '93 Conference on Programming Language Design and Implementation*, Albuquerque, NM, April 1993. ACM, ACM.
13. A. S. Grimshaw. Easy to use object-oriented parallel programming with mentat. *IEEE Computer*, pages 39–51, May 1993.

14. A. S. Grimshaw, W. T. Strayer, and P. Narayan. Dynamic object-oriented parallel processing. *IEEE Parallel and Distributed Technology: Systems and Applications*, pages 33–47, May 1993.
15. Dirk Grunwald. A users guide to awesime: An object oriented parallel programming and simulation system. Technical Report CU-CS-552-91, University of Colorado, Boulder, 1991.
16. High Performance Fortran Forum HPFF. Draft high performance fortran specificition, version 0.4. In *Proceedings of 1991 Japan Society for Parallel Processing*, page Available from anonymous ftp site titan.cs.rice.edu, 1992.
17. S. F. Hummel, Edith Schonberg, and L. E. Flynn. Factoring, a method for scheduling parallel loops. *Communications of the ACM*, 35(8):90–101, August 1992.
18. C. Kruskal and A. Weiss. Allocating independent subtasks on parallel processors. *IEEE Transactions on Software Engineering*, 11:1001–10016, October 1985.
19. Liu and et al. Scheduling parallel loops with variable length iteration execution times on parallel computers. In *Proc. 5th Intl. Conf. Parallel and Distributed Computing and System*, October 1992.
20. Steven Lucco. A dynamic scheduling method for irregular parallel programs. In *Proceedings of ACM SIGPLAN '92 Conference on Porgramming Language Design and Implementation*, pages 200–211. ACM, June 1992.
21. E.P Markatos and T. J. LeBlanc. Load Balancing vs Locality Management in Shared Memory Multiprocessors. In *Intl. Conference on Parallel Processing*, pages 258–257, St. Charles, Illinois, August 1992.
22. C. D. Polochronopoulous and D. Kuck. Guided self-scheduling: A practical scheduling scheme for parallel supercomputers. *IEEE Transactions on Computers*, 36(12):1425–1439, December 1987.
23. C. D. Polychronopoulos. Loop coalescing: A compiler transformation for parallel machines. In *Proceedings of International Conference on Parallel Processing*, August 1987.
24. Hanan Samet. *The Design and Analysis of Spatial Data Structures*. Addison-Wesley, 1990.
25. P. Tang and P.C. Yew. Processor self-scheduling for multiple nested parallel loops. In *Proc. Int. Conf. on Parallel Processing*, pages 528–535. IEEE, August 1986.
26. T.H. Tzen and L.M. Ni. Trapezoid self-scheduling: A practical scheduling scheme for parallel computers. *IEEE Transactions Parrallel Distributed Systems*, 4:87–98, January 1993.
27. Chien-Min Wang and Sheng-De Wang. A hybrid scheme for efficiently executing loops on multiprocessors. *Parallel Computing*, 18:625–637, 1992.
28. M.J. Wolfe. *Optimizing supercompilers for supercomputers*. PhD thesis, Univ. Illinois, Urbana, April 1987. Rep. 329.

σ-SSA and Its Construction Through Symbolic Interpretation*

Hideki Saito** and Constantine D. Polychronopoulos**

Center for Supercomputing Research and Development
University of Illinois at Urbana-Champaign
1308 W. Main St., Urbana, IL 61801 U.S.A.

Abstract. In this paper, we propose a new variant of SSA called σ-SSA and discuss its construction through symbolic interpretation of programs. By relaxing a condition of SSA form and without violating the fundamental property of static single assignment representation, σ-SSA form results in fewer *join* functions than the minimal SSA form.

1 σ-SSA Form

Static-Single-Assignment (SSA) form [2] is an intermediate program representation that has attracted much attention in high-performance compilers community. Due to its simplicity and straightforward derivation from the abstract syntax tree, SSA has been popular among parallelizing compiler developers. However, ambiguity in pointer dereference makes it difficult to employ SSA in C and C++ compilers, where demand for high performance is rapidly increasing.

In this paper, we propose a new variant of SSA called σ-SSA. Unlike conventional SSA form, σ-SSA is designed to integrate extensive symbolic analysis information. This information may be obtained through symbolic interpretation [4, 3] of the original program, as opposed to applying symbolic analysis after converting the program into the conventional SSA form. This approach allows us to apply sophisticated symbolic analysis techniques during the construction of the representation, making it more effective for languages with pointers. It also helps us to keep the size of the representation as small as possible from the earliest stages of compilation.

In general, all variants of SSA are characterized by Properties 1 and 2, which are essential to many of the benefits SSA offers. The SSA form proposed by Cytron *et.al.* [2] and its previously proposed variants like Gated-Single-Assignment (GSA) form use Condition 1 to subsume Property 2. However, Property 2 does not necessarily imply Condition 1. Choi *et.al.*'s *pruned*-SSA reduces the number of join functions by disregarding Condition 1 when the variable is dead at the merge point [1]. In σ-SSA, we relax Condition 1 further and place a *join* function only if the newly created version is used in the program statements (as opposed to *join* pseudo statements). In addition, we incorporate

* A more detailed report can be found in [6].

** This work is supported in part by the Office of Naval Research (ONR) under Grant No. N00014-94-1-0234, and a grant from Intel Corporation.

the intermediate results of symbolic interpretation when we compute the set of incoming definitions to the use site. For example, if the compiler can symbolically analyze the program so that only one of the possible incoming definitions (given by the conservative def-use analysis) can reach a use site of a variable, there's no need to insert a *join* function to establish Property 2 for this use site. This approach gives us a better estimate of the set of incoming definitions to the use sites especially in the presence of pointers.

Property 1 (Immortality). *A definition is never killed (except when it kills and reproduces itself due to a cross-iteration output dependence).*

Property 2 (Single Definition per Use). *There exists only one definition associated with a use of a variable, and such a definition must be delivered to the use site whenever the flow of control reaches the use site.*

Condition 1 *A join function is placed whenever two or more (different) incoming definitions of the same variable merge at a control flow confluence point.*

Figure 1(c) is an example of σ-SSA form. In this example, σ-SSA took an advantage of the fact that the two conditions are semantically (and literally) identical under any execution of the program. In general, (minimal) σ-SSA inserts a ϕ-function only when there is no "dynamically dominating" definition of the symbolic value of a variable used in an expression.

```
if (cond)
  X = 1
else
  X = 2
endif
if (cond)
  use X
else
  use X
endif
```

(a)original code

```
if (cond)
  X1 = 1
else
  X2 = 2
endif
X3 = φ(X1,X2)
if (cond)
  use X3
else
  use X3
endif
```

(b)SSA form

```
if (cond)
  X1 = 1
else
  X2 = 2
endif
if (cond)
  use X1
else
  use X2
endif
```

(c)σ-SSA form

Fig. 1. σ-SSA form

2 Construction through Symbolic Interpretation

It is straight forward to extend the symbolic interpretation scheme of Parafrase-2 [5, 3] to produce an SSA form of the original program. For each control flow confluence point, where two or more incoming interpretation environments merge, we need a ϕ-function for a variable if at least one of the incoming definitions (or versions) of a variable in the environments are identical. At the loop header, we conservatively determine whether a ϕ-function is needed for a variable by scanning the loop body . For reducible programs, such a construction scheme can always lead to the minimal SSA form.

Construction of the minimal σ-SSA form involves the following three steps at each use site of a variable. Instead of simply inserting ϕ-functions whenever multiple interpretation environments merge:

1. find definitions that yield equivalent symbolic values with the value at the use site,
2. if these definitions are found, then find a definition whose value is always available at the use site whenever the use site is executed,
3. if no definitions are left, find the best location to insert a ϕ-function.

The first step can be achieved by recording the previously computed symbolic closed form expressions for each definition (including the inserted ϕ-functions). The recorded symbolic-values can then be used for other techniques such as symbolic dependence-analysis. The second step requires a symbolic evaluation of control dependence information. The last step can be implemented by backtracking the hierarchical control flow graph from the use site towards the program entry point.

References

1. Jong-Deok Choi, Ron Cytron, and Jeanne Ferrante. Automatic construction of sparse data flow evaluation graphs. In *Proceedings of the ACM SIGPLAN Symposium on Principles of Programming Languages*, pages 55–66, June 1991.
2. Ron Cytron, Jeanne Ferrante, Barry K. Rosen, Mark N. Wegman, and F. Kenneth Zadeck. Efficiently computing static single assignment form and the control dependence graph. *ACM transactions on Programming Languages and Systems*, 13(4):451–490, October 1991.
3. Mohammad R. Haghighat. *Symbolic Analysis for Parallelizing Compilers*. PhD thesis, University of Illinois at Urbana-Champaign, 1994. Also available as a CSRD Technical Report.
4. Mohammad R. Haghighat. *Symbolic Analysis for Parallelizing Compilers*. Kluwer Academic Publishers, 1995.
5. Constantine D. Polychronopoulos, Milind Girkar, Mohammad Reza Haghighat, Chia Ling Lee, Bruce Leung, and Dale Schouten. Parafrase-2: An environment for parallelizing, partitioning, synchronizing, and scheduling programs on multiprocessors. *International Journal of High Speed Computing*, 1(1):45–72, 1989.
6. Hideki Saito and Constantine D. Polychronopoulos. σ-SSA and its construction through symbolic interpretation. Technical Report 1494, Center for Supercomputing Research and Development, University of Illinois at Urbana-Champaign, May 1996.

Compiler Support for Maintaining Cache Coherence Using Data Prefetching *
(Extended Abstract)

Hock-Beng Lim[1], Lynn Choi[2] and Pen-Chung Yew[3]

[1] Center for Supercomputing R & D, Univ. of Illinois, Urbana, IL 61801
[2] Microprocessor Group, Intel Corporation, Santa Clara, CA 95095
[3] Dept. of Computer Science, Univ. of Minnesota, Minneapolis, MN 55455

1 Introduction and Motivation

A major performance limitation in large-scale shared-memory multiprocessors is the large remote main memory latencies encountered by the processors. Private caches for processors have been used to reduce the number of main memory accesses. However, the use of private caches leads to the classic *cache coherence problem*. *Compiler-directed cache coherence* schemes [2] offer a viable solution to this problem for large-scale shared-memory multiprocessors. Although compiler-directed cache coherence schemes can improve multiprocessor cache performance, they cannot totally eliminate main memory accesses. Thus, *data prefetching* schemes have been developed to hide the memory latency.

Actually, data prefetching and compiler-directed cache coherence schemes may be combined in a complementary manner. We propose a software-only compiler-directed cache coherence scheme that incorporates data prefetching. The *Cache Coherence with Data Prefetching (CCDP)* scheme is designed for large-scale non- cache-coherent shared-memory multiprocessors that have hardware support for data prefetching. Our scheme would enable such systems to cache shared data without requiring additional hardware support.

2 Cache Coherence Enforcement by Data Prefetching

Cache coherence schemes are used to ensure that the processors will always access the most up-to-date copy of shared data. If the need to access these up-to-date shared data can be predicted in advance, then the processors can issue prefetch operations to bring these data into the caches before they are actually used. In compiler-directed cache coherence schemes, this prediction is done by using compiler analyses to identify the potentially stale data references. Data prefetching provides the additional benefit of memory latency hiding by overlapping the fetching of remote up-to-date data with computation.

* This work is supported in part by the National Science Foundation under Grant No. MIP 93-07910, MIP 94-96320, and CDA 95-02979. Additional support is provided by a gift from Cray Research, Inc and by a gift from Intel Corporation. The computing resources are provided in part by a grant from the Pittsburgh Supercomputing Center through the National Science Foundation and by Cray Research, Inc.

3 Compiler Support for the CCDP Scheme

3.1 Stale Reference Analysis

The stale reference analysis algorithm identifies the potentially stale data references in a program by detecting stale reference sequences. Three main program analysis techniques are used in stale reference analysis : ***stale reference detection***, ***array data-flow analysis***, and ***interprocedural analysis*** [1].

3.2 Prefetch Target Analysis

Since prefetch operations introduce instruction execution and network traffic overheads, it is important to minimize the number of unnecessary prefetches. The prefetch target analysis algorithm determines which potentially stale references should be prefetched. The remaining potentially stale references that are not prefetched will then be issued as either normal read operations or bypass-cache fetch operations. Our prefetch target analysis algorithm focuses on the potentially stale references in the inner loops of a program, where prefetching is most likely to contribute performance benefits. It also exploits self-spatial locality in the memory references of the program to eliminate some unnecessary prefetch operations.

3.3 Prefetch Scheduling

After identifying which potentially stale references should be prefetched, the next important task is to schedule these prefetches. There are four main design considerations for the prefetch scheduling algorithm.

First, our prefetch scheduling algorithm should ensure that the correctness of the program's memory references is not violated as a result of the prefetch operations. Second, the algorithm should improve the effectiveness of the prefetch operations so that the prefetched data will often arrive in the caches in time to be used. Third, the algorithm should take into account important hardware constraints and architectural parameters of the system, such as the size of the data cache in each processor, the size of the prefetch queue or issue buffer associated with each processor, the maximum number of outstanding prefetches allowed by the processor, and the average memory latency for a prefetch operation. Last but not least, since prefetch operations incur a significant overhead, the algorithm should try to minimize the prefetch overhead.

Our prefetch scheduling algorithm considers each inner loop and serial code section of the program, and attempts to make a good engineering decision to use one of the following prefetch scheduling techniques :

- **Vector prefetch generation**
  Gornish developed an algorithm that can be used to ***pull out*** [3] array references from loops for prefetching. We adapted his approach for the CCDP

scheme by imposing a restriction on the number of loop levels from which array references should be pulled, in order to maximize the effectiveness of the vector prefetches. We also check if the amount of data to be prefetched will exceed the available prefetch queue size or the cache size. A vector prefetch will be issued only if these hardware constraints are satisfied.

- **Software pipelining**
  Mowry [4] used software pipelining to schedule single cache-line prefetch operations. We adapted the software pipelining algorithm to suit the CCDP scheme. First, we impose a restriction that software pipelining will be used only for inner loops that do not contain branches or recursive procedure calls. Next, the number of iterations to prefetch ahead is computed and the compiler uses this information to decide whether it is profitable to use software pipelining. Finally, our algorithm considers the hardware constraints by dropping the prefetch operations when the prefetch queue is full or if the amount of data to be prefetched exceed the cache size.
- **Moving back prefetches**
  If neither vector prefetch generation nor software pipelining can be applied, then our algorithm tries to move the prefetch operations as far away as possible from the point where the data will be used. This is done in the same manner as Gornish's algorithm to ***pull back*** [3] references. To ensure correctness and to maximize the effectiveness of the prefetches, our algorithm uses a parameter to decide whether to move back a prefetch operation. The range of values for this parameter indicates the suitable range of distances to move back the prefetch operation.

4 Present and Future Work

At present, we are conducting application case studies to get quantitative measurements of the performance improvements provided by the CCDP scheme on the Cray T3D. We manually insert prefetch operations into several application benchmarks according to the CCDP scheme. In the future, we plan to do a full compiler implementation of the scheme and to study the interaction of the compiler implementation with various important architectural parameters.

References

1. L. Choi. *Hardware and Compiler Support for Cache Coherence in Large-Scale Multiprocessors.* PhD thesis, Center for Supercomputing R & D, UIUC, March 1996.
2. L. Choi, H.-B. Lim, and P.-C. Yew. Multiprocessor cache coherence : A compiler-directed approach. *To appear in IEEE Parallel & Distributed Tech.*, Winter 1996.
3. E. Gornish. Compile time analysis for data prefetching. Master's thesis, Center for Supercomputing R & D, UIUC, December 1989.
4. T. Mowry. *Tolerating Latency Through Software-Controlled Data Prefetching.* PhD thesis, Dept. of Elect. Eng., Stanford University, March 1994.

3D Visualization of Program Structure and Data Dependence for Parallelizing Compilers and Parallel Programming

Mariko Sasakura[1], Satoko Kiwada[2], Kazuki Joe[2], Tsuneo Nakanishi[2] and Keijiro Araki[3]

[1] Department of Information Technology, Okayama University, 3-1-1, Naka, Tsushima, Okayama 700, JAPAN
[2] Graduate School of Information Science, Nara Institute of Science and Technology, 8916-5, Takayama-cho, Ikoma, Nara 630-01, JAPAN
[3] Graduate School of Information Science and Electrical Engineering, Kyushu University, Kasuga Koen 6-1, Kasuga, Fukuoka 816, JAPAN

Abstract. For effective use of parallel computers, a tool which assists users to know the way of parallelization is needed. Since we believe visualization is a useful tool for parallelization, we are developing a tool named NaraView for parallelizing Fortran programs. In this paper, we propose two visualization methods in NaraView, which are 3D visualization of program structure and data dependence.

1 Introduction

Parallelizing compilers are a tool which analyzes sequential programs and restructures them to parallel forms. Although parallelizing compilers try to transform any sequential program to a parallel program automatically, they often fail to extract some kind of parallelism in the given program. One of the most significant problems is that parallelizing compilers cannot decide the best strategy for parallelization by themselves. They do not have any knowledge which part of the program should be parallelized and which transformation method should be applied to.

As a support for parallelizing compilers or parallel programming, we are developing a visualization system named NaraView, which provides an interactive compilation or programming environment for parallel computer users. By using this environment, users can instruct compilers which part should be parallelized and which transformation method should be applied to.

As kernel modules of NaraView, we propose two methods for 3D visualization in this paper: *Program structure view* and *Data dependence view*. Program structure view aims to provide users a structure map of the given program intuitively. Data dependence view aims to show data dependence among several arrays/variables with loop indexes.

2 Overview of NaraView

NaraView is a visualization system for parallelizing compilers and parallel programming, which is aimed at assisting users to detect parallelism by a glance of visualized hierarchical structures and control/data dependence graphs of given source programs.

Especially NaraView can be regarded as a visual user interface tool for a parallelizing compiler, Parafrase-2[1], which is one of the most popular parallelizing compilers in academic interests. Currently, NaraView can visualize Fortran programs by using Open-GL on SGI machines.

NaraView consists of several *views*. A *view* is a template for visualized information which is extracted from given source programs. It gives a layout for the extracted information; which parts are chosen to display and how they are placed. NaraView provides four views: (1) Source code view , (2) CFG view, (3) Program structure view and (4) Data dependence view.Users can understand the characteristics of the information through appropriate *views* and investigate the best strategy for parallelization of the given programs.

Source programs, which are going to be or have already been parallelized, are directed to NaraView to make use of the views. First, NaraView invokes Program structure view and visualizes a structure of the programs to give users an abstract and overall impression of the programs as well as clues to further investigation.

Here, we use *program structure* as following meanings: 1) the number and locations of loops and function calls and 2)the distinction between sequential and parallelized loops in the given program. We also use a *hierarchical structure* with the same meanings for nested loop structures.

Next, users specify a loop on which they want to focus. According to their indications, NaraView invokes CFG view and/or Data dependence view as well as the original source program of the loop. Using the information given by the views, they can find unnecessary data dependent parts intuitively, and improve the source program with some parallelization methods, for example.

Visualizing program structures Program structure view presents users with program flows and structures of loop hierarchies intuitively as well as visually.

Program structure view generates 3D *visible objects* which consist of a set of nodes. A node is indicated by a colored cube. Each node corresponds to a line or a chunk of source codes. Coordinates of a cube are given the following rules: a sequence of program flow (x), a measure of parallelism (y) and a level of loop hierarchy (z).

Furthermore, there are five kinds of nodes: Root node, Basic node, Parallel node, Call node and Loop node. A Root node indicates the top of the graph. A Basic and a Parallel node correspond to a statement in source codes which is executed sequentially and in parallel respectively. A Call node represents a function call. A loop is displayed as a Loop node in shallower hierarchy. A Loop node represents existence of a loop, but hides its details: its body is represented by the nodes in deeper hierarchy. The deeper nodes are connected with the loop node by arcs in order to clarify the relation between them.

Visualizing data dependence The basic idea of Data dependence view is to visualize an iteration space in three-dimension with data dependence among some arrays and/or variables. The arrays and variables are mapped on the x-y plane, called *array-variable disposition* map (AVD map), and the iteration is mapped on the z-axis lexicographically. Users can observe the relation of data dependence among each iteration and the arrays and variables. This is useful when they want to parallelize their programs with considering partitioning and allocating such data.

In Data dependence view, an access to a variable or an array element at an iteration is represented by a cube. There are three kinds of cube in this view. A blue cube represents a read access. A red cube represents a write access. And a purple cube represents read and write accesses at the same iteration.

Semi-transparent planes, which are placed perpendicularly to the z-axis, indicate the beginning of each iteration of loops. There is another plane placed perpendicularly to the z-axis, namely, AVD map. It shows a layout for arrays and variables with easy comprehension of Data dependence view.

The main purpose of this view is to visualize read and write accesses to each variable or array element. Efficient parallelization requires the knowledge about existence of anti-dependence and lifetimes of variables and array elements. In this view, NaraView draws a green pole from a red cube to a blue cube which illustrates the lifetime of a variable or array element, and a yellow pole from a blue cube to a red cube which points out existence of anti-dependence. The former is called a *lifetime pole* and the latter is called an *anti-dependence pole.*

3 Conclusion

In this paper, we proposed two methods for 3D visualization of NaraView: Program structure view and Data dependence view. The former shows users 3D *visible objects* which explain the outline of given programs for intuitive understanding, and this leads them to go down to investigate each loop which are not parallelized by compilers. The latter visualizes data dependence among arrays and variables in the loop and this allows users further investigation. Example figures generated by the views are placed at
http://www.momo.it.okayama-u.ac.jp/~sasakura/NaraView.html

References

1. Polychronopoulos, C.D. et al. "Parafrase-2: An environment for parallelizing, partitioning, synchronizing, and scheduling programs on multiprocessors", Proceedings of the 1989 International Conference on Parallel Processing, 1989.

Side Effect Analysis on User-Defined Reduction Functions with Dynamic Pointer-Linked Data Structures

Yuan-Shin Hwang and Joel Saltz

Department of Computer Science, University of Maryland, College Park, MD 20742

1 Introduction

This paper presents a simple side effect analysis algorithm to determine the side effects of programs with dynamic pointer-linked data structures. It is closely related to the compile-time conflict/interference analysis for programs with pointers [2, 4], and side effect analysis [1, 3]. The most significant difference of this algorithm from others is that a single graph, a *link graph*, is constructed for each procedure whereas others have to build a table or graph for every statement to represent alias information. The side effects of a procedure or a block of code are first gathered without concerning the aliases, and then are propagated through the links of the link graph.

Side effect analysis on user-defined reduction functions with dynamic pointer-linked data structures is used in this paper as an example application of the algorithm. User-defined reduction functions can be used to create a linked list by appending nodes, as shown in the following code fragment which is presented in Fortran 90 with the directives considered by HPF-2 project. The side effect analysis can be applied to help determine if user-defined reduction functions are safe, i.e. if they cause no side effects to any variables except the reduction variables.

```
!HPF$ INDEPENDENT
      do i = 1, no-nodes
         ...
!HPF$    REDUCE
         call append (list, node(i))
      end do
```

2 Algorithm

The algorithm to analyze side effects of a reduction function with dynamic pointer-linked data structures can be broken into three steps: (1) creating SSA (Static Single Assignment) form on pointers, (2) building a link graph, and (3) determining side effects. Two versions of the list append function *append (list, node)*, will be used as the demonstration of the algorithm.

(a)	(b)
ptr ⇒ list	ptr ⇒ list
do	do
if (.not. associated(ptr%next)) exit	if (.not. associated(ptr%next)) exit
ptr ⇒ ptr%next	ptr ⇒ ptr%next
end do	end do
ptr%next ⇒ node	allocate(ptr%next)
	ptr%next%node ⇒ node

Creating SSA Form on Pointers

A separate SSA representation will be built solely on pointers. Pointer variables are transformed in the same way as variables in regular SSA form since each pointer variable links to a memory location can be viewed as a regular variable carries a value. Furthermore, any references to linked data structures through sequences of selectors, e.g. *struct%list%next%node*, will be broken into sequences of statements such that each statement has at most one selector. The two list append functions can be transformed to the following SSA form:

(a)	(b)
ptr_1 ⇒ $list_1$	ptr_1 ⇒ $list_1$
do	do
$ptr_2 = \phi(ptr_1, ptr_3)$	$ptr_2 = \phi(ptr_1, ptr_3)$
if (.not. associated(ptr_2%next)) exit	if (.not. associated(ptr_2%next)) exit
ptr_3 ⇒ ptr_2%next	ptr_3 ⇒ ptr_2%next
end do	end do
ptr_2%next ⇒ $node_1$	allocate(ptr_2%next)
	$temp_1$ ⇒ ptr_2%next
	$temp_1$%node ⇒ $node_1$

Building Link Graphs

A link graph is built from the pointer SSA form to represent the connections among pointers. Each node in the graph corresponds to an instance of a pointer on SSA representation. Every undirected link in the graph between two nodes means that the two pointer instances might point to the same memory location caused by a pointer assignment statement that defines either instance, while the directed edges depict the connections between locations linked by selectors. The link graphs of the two link append functions are shown in the figures on the next page.

Determining Side Effects

The set of pointer variables that will be modified by assignment or pointer assignment statements is collected from the SSA form. For each pointer in the set, first mark the side effects at the corresponding node on the link graph, and then mark all the nodes that can be reached starting from the node through ε edges without passing any two ε links denoted by a ϕ sign. The marked nodes are the memory locations with side effects. From the link graphs, version (a) of the list append function causes side effects on the parameter *node* whereas version (b) does not.

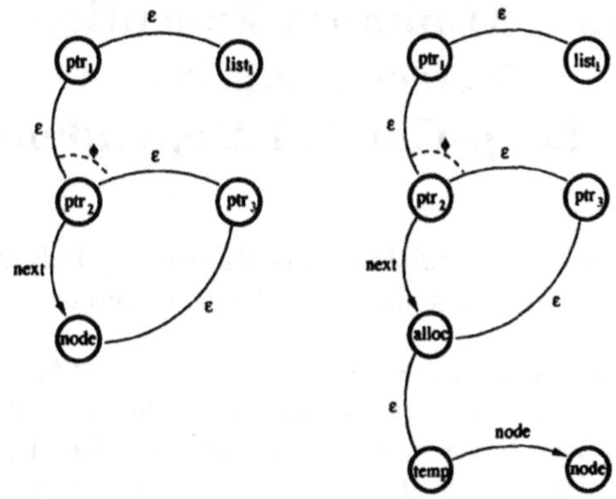

(a) Version a (b) Version b

3 Summary and Future Work

The side analysis analysis is facilitated by the construction of link graphs. The alias information can be clearly expressed by the nodes and links of the link graphs. Furthermore, the DEF-USE information of dynamic data structures can also be extracted from link graphs.

Future work of this research will be: (1) to extend the algorithm to cover interprocedural side effect analysis, (2) to development an efficient algorithm to gather interprocedural DEF-USE information of dynamic pointer-linked data structures, and (3) to implement a prototype data-parallel compiler to transform programs with user-defined reduction functions to efficient SPMD code.

References

1. Jong-Deok Choi, Michael Burke, and Paul Carini. Efficient flow-sensitive interprocedural computation of pointer-induced aliases and side effects. In *Conference Record of the Twentieth Annual Symposium on Principles of Programming Languages*, pages 232–245, January 1993.
2. Laurie J. Hendren and Alexandru Nicolau. Parallelizing programs with recursive data structures. *IEEE Transactions on Parallel and Distributed Systems*, 1(1):35–47, January 1990.
3. William Landi, Barbara G. Ryder, and Sean Zhang. Interprocedural side effect analysis with pointer aliasing. *Proceedings of the ACM SIGPLAN '93 Conference on Programming Language Design and Implementation*, pp. 56–67, June 1993.
4. James R. Larus and Paul N. Hilfinger. Detecting conflicts between structure accesses. *Proceedings of the ACM SIGPLAN '88 Conference on Programming Language Design and Implementation*, pp. 21–34, July 1988.

Estimating Minimum Execution Time of Perfect Loop Nests with Loop-Carried Dependences *

Tsuneo Nakanishi[1], Kazuki Joe[1], Constantine D. Polychronopoulos[2], Keijiro Araki[3], and Akira Fukuda[1]

[1] Graduate School of Information Science, Nara Institute of Science and Technology, 8916–5 Takayamacho, Ikoma, Nara 630–01, JAPAN
[2] Center for Supercomputing Research and Development, University of Illinois at Urbana-Champaign, 1308 West Main, Urbana, IL 61801, U.S.A.
[3] Graduate School of Information Science and Electrical Engineering, Kyushu University, 6–1 Kasuga Koen, Kasuga, Fukuoka 816, JAPAN

Abstract. We propose a scheme to estimate exact minimum parallel execution time of perfect loop nests with loop-carried dependences at iteration and instruction-level parallelism. We formulate the problem of the estimation as an integer programming problem and solve it with a branch-and-bound scheme combined with the simplex method. Execution time obtained with the proposed scheme is useful to evaluate effects of applications of various optimization or parallelizing techniques for iteration or instruction-level parallel execution of loops.

1 Introduction

Modern multiprocessors are often constructed with clusters of processors which support instruction-level parallelism (ILP). Such machines allow loops to be executed using multiple grains of parallelism (both iteration and instruction-level). So far, using complex analyses and restructuring techniques aiming at iteration-level parallelism, parallelizing compilers have laid more emphasis on exploiting and utilizing parallelism among loop iterations. Hereafter parallelizing compilers should hold it in great account to utilize ILP with iteration-level parallelism in a coupled manner; this is necessarily given the emerging parallel architectures. The quality of the parallel code generated by parallelizing compilers, which apply various restructuring and optimization techniques to loops, varies according to the order of their applications.

Considering these matters, we need a measure to evaluate the qualities of transformed codes by restructuring techniques where iteration and instruction-level parallelism is available. The critical path (CP) cost, which we mention in the next section, can be an adequate metric for this purpose.

* This work is supported by the Grant-in-Aid of Ministry of Education, Science, Sports and Culture and the Research Fellowships of the Japan Society for the Promotion of Science for Young Scientists.

2 Overview of the Proposed Scheme

Using Data Dependence Graphs: We use a more relaxed notion of data dependence graphs by assuming that the nodes of such graphs can represent computations (tasks) of any granularity — from the atomic operation to the subroutine level — in order to estimate minimum parallel execution time of perfect loop nests. A node in a data dependence graph has the execution cost (execution time) of the corresponding task as its attribute. On the other hand, an arc in the data dependence graph has the communication cost (communication time) caused by the corresponding dependence as its attribute. The CP of an acyclic data dependence graph is a path which gives the maximum total cost of the nodes and the arcs constituting the path. The CP cost of the acyclic data dependence graph is equal to the minimum parallel execution time of the code. Since the data dependence graph obtained by fully unrolling a loop nest, which we refer to *unrolled loop task graph*, is acyclic, its CP cost gives minimum parallel execution time of the loop nest. However, it is not practical in terms of computation time and storage to fully unroll loops.

The data dependence graph of a loop body, which we refer to *loop task graph*, is a compact representation and used by vectorizing and parallelizing compilers for loop restructuring in practical. However, the loop task graph is not acyclic in general. Still we cannot obtain the CP of every loop from the loop task graph for this reason, we can do that for loops which satisfy the following conditions: i)The loop nest is perfect; ii)The number of iterations of each loop in the nest is known at compile-time; iii)There is no branch in the loop body; iv)All dependences between tasks are uniform; v)All elements of any dependence distance vector are non-negative; vi)All instances of each task have the same execution time; vii)All dependences between instances of any two tasks cause the same communication overhead if their dependence distance vectors are equal. The proposed scheme is for the loop nests satisfying the above conditions.

Formulating the Problem as an Integer Programming Problem: The scheme proposed here gives the CP cost of an unrolled loop task graph without unrolling the loop at all by reducing the problem to an integer programming problem.

Fig. 1 illustrates our idea. The upper graph drawn in three-dimensional is an unrolled loop task graph whose layers correspond to iterations and are arranged in the order of the sequential execution of the loop nest. Nodes corresponding to the instances of the same task are placed at the same position in their own layers. The unrolled loop task graph is projected on the "ground" and the projection, which is the lower graph, is nothing but the loop task graph. A path of the unrolled loop task graph (thick line) is also projected. The shadow of the path can overlap on the same arc of the loop task graph multiple times. We refer the number of times of shadow overlapping on an arc to *shadow overlap degree* of the arc.

We assign a variable for the formulation to each arc of the loop task graph. When we assume values of the variables as shadow overlap degrees, the path cost is given by a linear expression with these variables. We use the linear expression as the objective function for the formulation and search for the value assignment to the variables which maximizes it. The shadow overlap degrees have two properties expressed by linear expressions.

One of them is concerning the topology of the loop task graph and the other is concerning the loop bound. We use them for the constraints of the problem. While these expressions are properties of shadow overlap degrees, they never let feasible value assignments to the variables be shadow overlap degrees given by any paths. Therefore, we may take a value assignment to the variables which satisfies the constraints but is not given by shadow overlap degrees of any path of the unrolled loop task graph as a solution of the problem.

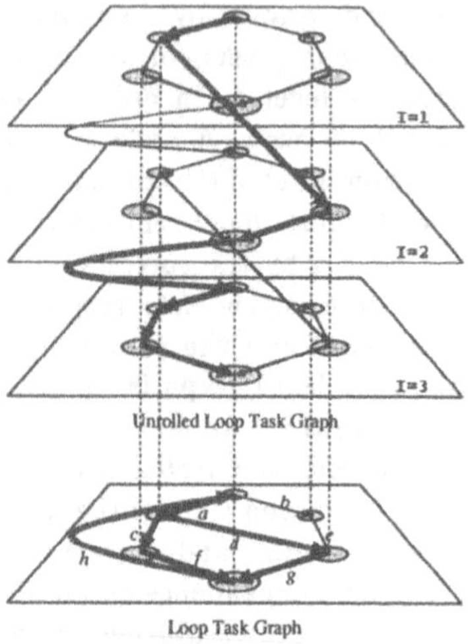

Fig.1.

We employ a branch-and-bound based algorithm combined with the simplex method to solve the integer programming problem formulated above. Still the complexity of the branch-and-bound algorithm is exponential in the worst case, our experiments with Livermore Benchmark Kernels show enough practical computation time (1.5 sec. at most on DEC3000). Moreover, their computation time does not depend on the number of iterations.

See [1] for details of our formulation and algorithm.

3 Conclusion

We proposed a scheme to evaluate the cost of a CP (minimum parallel execution time) of a perfect loop nest without actually unrolling the loops. The proposed scheme reduces the problem to an integer programming problem. Our method employs a branch-and-bound algorithm coupled with the simplex method, whose complexity has an exponential order in the worst case, to solve it. In our experiments with Livermore Benchmark Kernels, its practical computation time is reasonable enough, moreover, does not depend on the number of iterations.

References

1. T. Nakanishi, K. Joe, C. D. Polychronopoulos, K. Araki, and A. Fukuda, "Estimating Parallel Execution Time of Loops with Loop-Carried Dependences," Proc. 1996 Int'l Conf. on Parallel Processing, Vol.III, pp.61–69, Aug. 1996.

Automatic Data and Computation Partitioning on Scalable Shared Memory Multiprocessors

Sudarsan Tandri and Tarek S. Abdelrahman

Department of Electrical and Computer Engineering
The University of Toronto
Toronto, Ontario, Canada, M5S 3G4
e-mail: {tandri,tsa}@eecg.toronto.edu

1 Introduction

Scalable Shared Memory Multiprocessors (SSMMs) are becoming increasingly popular as platforms for parallel scientific computing. Recent commercial systems such as the Convex Exemplar and the Cray T3E offer not only scalability previously exclusive to distributed memory multiprocessors, but also the convenience of a single coherent view of memory. The presense of shared memory initially suggests that parallelizing compilers for SSMMs need not be concerned with the data management issues that compilers for distributed memory must contend with. However, the non-uniformity of memory accesses and limited operating system data management policies suggest that compilers should play a more active role in data management on SSMMs. A data partitioning based approach to data management can improve application performance on SSMMs [1].

In this paper, we address the problem of automatically deriving data and computation partitions for scientific applications on SSMMs. The problem of deriving optimal partitions is NP-hard [2]. Additionally, the suitability of data and/or computation partitions depends not only on data access patterns, but also on the characteristics of the target multiprocessor. A number of approaches have been proposed to tackle this problem. Bixby, et al. [3] formulate a 0–1 integer programming problem to represent all possible data partitions and their associated costs. The 0–1 problem is then solved to obtain optimal partitions. Anderson and Lam [2] propose a more efficient algebraic framework, but require run-time profiling to determine commonly executed loops. In both cases, the optimality of partitions is based on communication cost; partitions that result in less communication are considered superior.

We present a framework for deriving data and computation partitions on SSMMs. We show that communication cost alone is not adequate to assess the appropriateness of data and computation partitions; shared memory effects such as cache affinity, false sharing, synchronization and contention must also be taken into account. Furthermore, the presense of shared memory hardware makes the use of the owner-computes rule unnecessary; the performance of some applications benefit from relaxing this rule. We describe an algorithm for deriving data and computation partitions on SSMMs taking shared memory effects into account. The algorithm is computationally efficient compared to previous approaches and does not rely on run-time profiling. Experimental results from a prototype implementation of the algorithm demonstrate its effectiveness in parallelizing standard benchmarks and the necessity of taking shared memory effects into account. The results also demonstrate the computational efficiency of our framework.

2 The Algorithm

Partitions are specified by the selection of a processor geometry, the assignment of a distribution attribute to dimensions of arrays (and to parallel loops), and a mapping between array dimensions (and parallel loops) to the dimensions of the processor geometry. We introduce a new set of distribution attributes that extend well-known attributes (such as HPF's [4]) to resolve alignment conflicts between data and computations. Furthermore, explicit association between the dimensions of arrays and the dimensions of the processor geometry is used to obtain new data partitions that reduce contention and synchronization in programs on SSMMs [5].

The algorithm derives computation and data partitions for programs in which parallel loops have been identified. First, computation partitions are derived based on data access patterns in the program using the NUMA-CAG. Each node in this graph represents either an array dimension or a parallel loop. An unweighted edge connects an array dimension node to a loop node if a subscript expression in the array dimension contains the loop iterator. Array access patterns are used to assign an initial distribution attribute to each node in the graph. An iterative algorithm that utilizes our new distribution attributes is used to ensure that any two connected nodes in the NUMA-CAG have the same distribution attribute. In addition, the algorithm also maps connected nodes onto the same dimension of the processor geometry. This enhances locality and minimizes communication by allocating data and computation to the same processor.

The above use of the NUMA-CAG results in static array partitions for the entire program. Such partitions may be not be the best choice for arrays that require different partitions in different loop nests. The partitioning of *only* these arrays is re-evaluated by considering all possible partitions for each array individually using depth-first search with pruning. For example, if an array `A` requires two different partitions `D1` and `D2` in two loop nests, possible partitions evaluated are: replication, a static `D1` partition, a static `D2` partition, the static partition determined by the NUMA-CAG, and dynamic partitions obtained by re-partitioning the array between the two loop nests. The cost of a given data partition is computed using knowledge of cache, local and remote memory accesses costs as well as the costs of contention and synchronization (incurred when a loop is executed in wavefront due to data dependencies or to avoid contention). These costs are determined by a combination of analytical models and empirical evaluation of the target machine. The number of processors along each dimension of the processor geometry is selected to enhance cache affinity by examining possible processor geometry combinations for a given number of processors and the selected dimensionality of the processor geometry.

The computational complexity of the algorithm is reduced by selecting a dimensionality of the processor geometry based on the parallelism in the program, by only re-evaluating the partitions of the subset of arrays that may benefit from re-evaluation, and by using pruning to limit the number of partitions examined in each re-evaluation.

3 Results and Comparisons

The speedup of applications (only three applications are used here due to space limitations) on three SSMMs is shown in Figure 1. The speedup of the applications with data partitions is higher to the the speedup of the applications when data management is delegated to the operating system.

The impact of shared memory effects on the execution time of the well-known ADI benchmark is shown in Figure 2 for the Hector multiprocessor. A static distribution

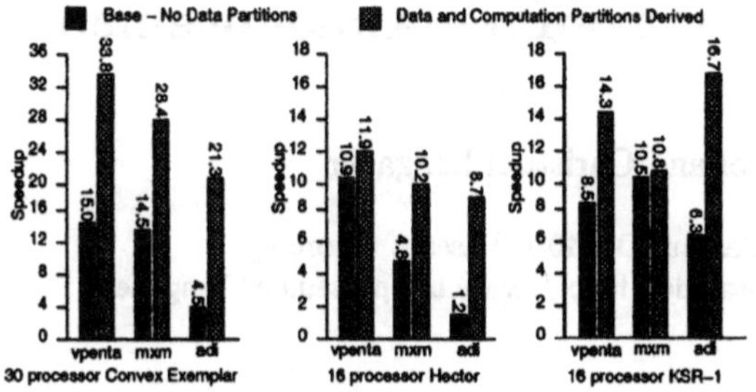

Fig. 1. Speedup of applications on three SSMMs.

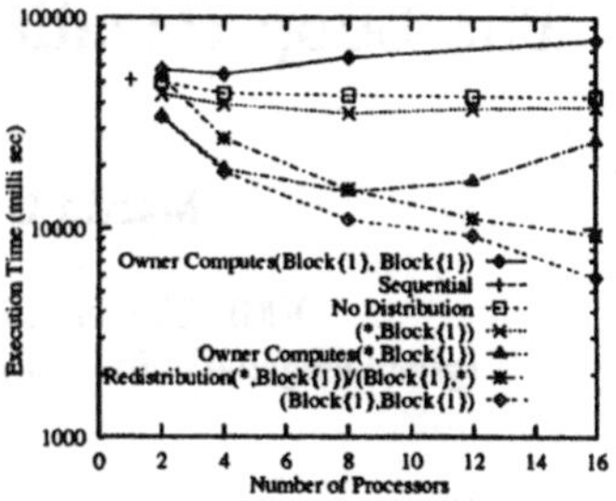

Fig. 2. Execution time of ADI.

dictated by either the first or second set of loop nests of the application results in contention and wavefront synchronization. The cost of data repartitioning between the two sets does not justify its use either. The best performance is obtained using our new data partition and a relaxed computation rule.

The computational efficiency of our framework is favorable compared to that of Bixby et al.'s approach. For example, data and computation partitions for the `vpenta` and `mxm` benchmarks are obtained directly from the NUMA-CAG (i.e., without re-evaluation), and are obtained for `ADI` after examining 116 possible partitions. This compares to solving 0–1 integer programming problems of sizes 2595×338, 170×59, 175×65, respectively. The partitions are obtained without run-time profiling.

4 Concluding Remarks

This paper presented an algorithm to automatically derive data and computation partitions taking into consideration shared memory effects. Experimental results indicate that these effects must be taken into account, and that the partitions derived by our algorithm improve the performance of the applications. A complete description of the algorithm and results can be obtained at *http://www.eecg.toronto.edu/~tsa/ca.ps*.

References

1. T. Abdelrahman and T. Wong, "Distributed array data management on NUMA multiprocessors," *Proc. of SHPCC*, pages 551–559, 1994.
2. J. Anderson and M. Lam. "Global optimization for parallelism and locality on scalable parallel machines," *Proc. of Conf. on Prog. Lang. Design and Implementation*, pp. 112–125, 1993.
3. R. Bixby, K. Kennedy, and U. Kremer. "Automatic data layout using 0–1 integer programming," *Proc. of PACT*, pp. 111–122, 1994.
4. C. Koelbel et al. *The High Performance Fortran Handbook*, The MIT Press, Cambridge, MA, 1994.
5. S. Tandri and T. Abdelrahman. "Computation and data partitioning on scalable shared memory multiprocessors," *Proc. of PDPTA*, pp. 41–50, 1995.

The Loop Parallelizer LooPo—Announcement

Martin Griebl and Christian Lengauer

FMI, Universität Passau, D–94030 Passau, Germany
{griebl,lengauer}@fmi.uni-passau.de, http://www.uni-passau.de/~lengauer

1 What is LooPo?

LooPo is a new loop parallelizing framework developed at the University of Passau to aid us in research on the space-time mapping of loop nests. LooPo is available on the Web [11] and uses only free software. It runs under SunOS 4.1.x, Solaris 2.x, and Linux.

LooPo is based on the polytope model [9]. Anybody interested in one special aspect of the parallelization can plug his/her own module into LooPo and obtains a customized source-to-source compilation environment. The central data structures (restricting the applicability of LooPo) are—according to the model—polyhedra and piecewise affine functions.

The next major version will also have the capability of parallelizing loop nests containing while loops [10].

2 The Structure of LooPo

LooPo consists of a number of modules, listed below, which transform the source program to an executable parallel target program. A front end provides the user with a graphical interface by which he/she can control LooPo. There is also a graphical displayer of index spaces and iteration dependence graphs of loop nests.

The input. LooPo accepts (possibly imperfect) loop nests in C, Fortran or a number of abstract loop notations, and declarations of functions, procedures and symbolic constants.

The inequality solvers. We considered several methods for parametric linear programming, which is the central mathematical problem of the polyhedron model [11]. The current implementation of LooPo is based on PIP and Fourier-Motzkin. *Fourier-Motzkin* is the standard doubly exponential method of polytope projection [1]. *PIP* is Feautrier's system for parametric integer programming [4].

The dependence analyzer. At present, LooPo features the dependence analysis methods described by Banerjee [1] and by Feautrier [5]. The latter allows potentially for more parallelism, due to a more precise analysis, but its application is more restricted.

The schedulers. Presently, LooPo provides three automatic schedulers. The hyperplane method of Lamport [8] handles perfectly nested for loops with uniform dependences. The Feautrier scheduler [6] determines an optimal (concave) schedule for imperfectly nested for loops with affine dependences, at the cost of a longer computation time caused by parametric integer linear programming [4]. The scheduler of Darte/Vivien [2] is fast and produces reasonably good results for arbitrary loop programs with uniform and non-uniform dependences.

The allocator. Presently, LooPo provides Feautrier's allocation method [7] which determines the placement of operations on virtual processors based on the "owner computes" rule. In addition, we have implemented the method by Darte, Dion and Robert [3] which also generates a mapping for the data.

The target code generator. The target code generation proceeds in three phases [12]: first, the statements of the source program are transformed individually. Then, these transformed statements in their respective index spaces are merged to a single target program. Finally, the target parse tree is translated to one of a variety of possible output languages, e.g., parallel C, and synchronization and communication is added if the user so desires.

Acknowledgements

We thank the LooPo team [11] and J.-F. Collard. This work received funds from DFG project RecuR and from the DAAD exchange program PROCOPE.

References

1. U. Banerjee. *Loop Transformations for Restructuring Compilers: The Foundations.* Kluwer, 1993.
2. A. Darte and F. Vivien. Automatic parallelization based on multi-dimensional scheduling. Technical Report 94-24, Laboratoire de l'Informatique du Parallélisme, Ecole Normale Supérieure de Lyon, Sept. 1994.
3. M. Dion and Y. Robert. Mapping affine loop nests: New results. In *Lecture Notes in Computer Science 919*, pages 184–189. Springer-Verlag, 1995.
4. P. Feautrier. Parametric integer programming. *Operations Research*, 22(3):243–268, 1988.
5. P. Feautrier. Dataflow analysis of array and scalar references. *Int. J. Parallel Programming*, 20(1):23–53, Feb. 1991.
6. P. Feautrier. Some efficient solutions to the affine scheduling problem. Part II. Multidimensional time. *Int. J. Parallel Programming*, 21(6):389–420, Oct. 1992.
7. P. Feautrier. Toward automatic distribution. *Parallel Processing Letters*, 4(3):233–244, 1994.
8. L. Lamport. The parallel execution of DO loops. *Comm. ACM*, 17(2):83–93, Feb. 1974.
9. C. Lengauer. Loop parallelization in the polytope model. In E. Best, editor, *CONCUR'93*, Lecture Notes in Computer Science 715, pages 398–416. Springer-Verlag, 1993.
10. C. Lengauer and M. Griebl. On the parallelization of loop nests containing while loops. In N. N. Mirenkov, Q.-P. Gu, S. Peng, and S. Sedukhin, editors, *Proc. 1st Aizu Int. Symp. on Parallel Algorithm/Architecture Synthesis (pAs'95)*, pages 10–18. IEEE Computer Society Press, 1995.
11. LooPo. http://www.uni-passau.de/~loopo/.
12. S. Wetzel. Automatic code generation in the polytope model. Diplomarbeit, Fakultät für Mathematik und Informatik, Universität Passau, 1995.

A Generalized forall Concept for Parallel Languages

P.F.G. Dechering, L.C. Breebaart, F. Kuijlman,
C. van Reeuwijk, H.J. Sips

`BoosterTeam@cp.tn.tudelft.nl`
Delft University of Technology
The Netherlands

Extended abstract

The *forall* statement is an important language construct in many (data) parallel languages [1], [2], [3], [6], [8], [9]. It gives an indication to the compiler which computations can be performed independently.

In this abstract, we will define a generalized *forall* statement and discuss its implementation. This *forall* statement has the ability to spawn more complex independent activities than can be expressed in these languages. Existing *forall* statements can be mapped to this generalized concept. The context of our *forall* statement is supplied by *V-nus*, a concise intermediate language for data parallelism [4]. The purpose of *V-nus* is providing a language platform to which other data parallel languages can be translated, and subsequently optimized.

Our *forall* statement consists of two parts: an ***index-space specification*** specifying the range of the index variable, and a ***body*** representing a block of statements. The body is parameterized with respect to, and will be executed for, every index in the index-space specification. Each separate instance of the body is called a ***body-instance***. We use denotational semantics to define the meaning of the *V-nus* language constructs. With these we can verify and optimize a *forall* statement.

It has been our goal to find a *forall* statement that complies with the following requirements: (1) The denotational semantics of a *forall* statement must represent only one possible program state change; that is, only one outcome should be possible after execution of the *forall*. (2) It must be feasible to implement the *forall* statement efficiently. This means that the administration that is needed to execute the *forall* should not use excessive amounts of computational resources. (3) The *forall* statement must be capable of representing a wide class of *forall* definitions as can be found in (data) parallel languages. (4) It must be possible to give a concise operational semantics of the *forall* statement that can easily be used in programming.

Body-instances of the *V-nus forall* statement are to be executed completely independently. By this we mean that data that can be changed by a body-instance i should not affect the outcome of another body-instance j. However, a global interference is still possible when there is a define-define dependence between the possible body-instances; i.e. two body-instances that write to the same variable. We say that a *forall* statement is deterministic if no define-define dependence is present between any two different body-instances of the *forall* statement.

We use denotational semantics, in which the meaning of a program can be expressed by the composition of the meanings of its parts, to record the concept of the *forall* statement. The semantics are described by using a difference and a merge operation on program states [5]. In order to arrive at an efficient implementation of the *forall* statement, we take the following approach. At the start of a *forall* statement the program state *ps* is preserved. For the execution of a body-instance a subset ps_i of *ps* is used for the context in which this body-instance will be executed. Only the data that is needed in the body-instance is extracted from *ps* and will be used for ps_i. Every time something needs to be read from memory, it is read from ps_i. When something needs to be written to memory, it is not only stored in ps_i, but the same store action is also performed on *ps*. In this way, each change that is made by a single body-instance is also visible in the global program state, but will not be used by the other body-instances. This is how the final program state ps' arises from the original program state *ps*, without the need for a merge or a difference operation.

The construction of ps_i is dependent on the information the compiler has about the data that is used in the body-instance. This information can be generated automatically by well-known dependence analysis techniques and by hand via pragmas. A pragma is an optional annotation for the compiler that gives additional information about a certain program construct. Pragmas that can be used for a *forall* statement specify which data should be copied in ps_i.

If a *forall* statement is not annotated by a pragma, then the local program states ps_i are created as explained above. If a pragma is present the compiler relies on this information and only copies the given data structures for the accompanying program states ps_i. In our opinion, it is more useful to specify for which data structures a dependency exists, than it is to specify those structures for which no dependency exists. The syntax of a pragma for a *forall* statement is:

<< dependsOn *Expression* >>

which expresses a dependency for the data structure(s) *Expression*. An empty list of specifications (i.e. << >>) means that no data needs to be copied. Of course, it is the responsibility of the programmer to avoid the introduction of non-determinism due to a pragma.

We end this abstract with an example of an optimization that can only be expressed by using the *V-nus forall*. Consider the following matrix operation:

```
for [j:m] {
    forall [i:n] {a[i,j] := a[i,j-1] + a[i,j+1] + a[i-1,j] + a[i+1,j] }
}
```

The optimization we have in mind is based on synchronization elimination [7]. By reversing the i and j loop the operation can be expressed as

```
forall [i:n] {
    for [j:m] {a[i,j] := a[i,j-1] + a[i,j+1] + a[i-1,j] + a[i+1,j] }
}
```

which has no computational differences in the result. Instead of executing *forall* statements in sequence, the *forall* body-instances can now be executed concurrently, yet obeying the j sequence. It is easy to see that no define-define dependence occurs, which makes it a deterministic *forall* statement. This *forall* statement is not 'valid' in the other parallel languages we refered to in this abstract.

More detailed information regarding the generalized *forall* concept can be found in our technical report [5] available at:

ftp://ftp.cp.tn.tudelft.nl/pub/cp/publications/1996/CP-96-003.ps.Z

References

1. L.C. Breebaart, P.F.G. Dechering, A.B. Poelman, J.A. Trescher, J.P.M. de Vreught, and H.J. Sips. The Booster Language, Syntax and Static Semantics. Computational Physics report series CP–95–02, Delft University of Technology, 1995.
2. P. Carlin, M. Chandy, and C. Kesselman. The Compositional C++ Language Definition. Revision 0.9 `ftp://ftp.compbio.caltech.edu /pub/CC++/Docs/cc++-def`, March 1 1993.
3. Thinking Machines Corporation. CM Fortran Programming Guide. Technical report, January 1991.
4. P.F.G. Dechering. The Denotational Semantics of Booster, A Working Paper 2.0. Computational Physics report series CP–95–05, Delft University of Technology, 1995.
5. P.F.G Dechering, L.C. Breebaart, F. Kuijlman, C. van Reeuwijk, and H.J. Sips. A Generalized forall Concept for Parallel Languages. Computational Physics report series CP–96–003, Delft University of Technology, 1996.
6. High Performance Fortran Forum. High Performance Fortran Language Specification. Technical report, November 1994.
7. A.J.C. van Gemund. *Performance Modelling of Parallel Systems.* PhD thesis, Delft University of Technology, 1996.
8. P.B. Hansen. Interference Control in SuperPascal – A Block-Structured Parallel Language. *The Computer Journal*, 37(5):399–406, 1994.
9. H. Zima, P. Brezany, B. Chapman, P. Mehrotra, and A. Schwald. Vienna Fortran – A Language Specification, version 1.1. Internal Report 21, ICASE, 1992.

Memory Optimizations In The Intel Reference Compiler

K. Sridharan
Pohua Chang
Utpal Banerjee
Ravi Narayanaswamy
Suresh Rao
Intel Architecture Lab
M/S RN6-18
2200 Mission College Blvd.
Santa Clara, CA. 95052-8119

Introduction

Instruction pipelining, superscalar implementation, and increasing clock speeds are producing dramatic increases in performance of processors. As processor performance outstrips memory performance, cache miss processing becomes a bottleneck to overall system performance. The cache miss penalty can be reduced by reducing the number of cache misses and/or reducing the cache miss repair time. The number of cache misses can be reduced by using a larger cache. However, larger cache takes up more chip space and has a slower cycle time. An alternative method to reduce the number of cache misses is to apply program transformations to reduce the number of memory references and to increase locality of references. We have implemented a number of memory optimizations in the Intel Reference C and FORTRAN Compiler. For a number of important scientific programs, the memory optimizations have been proven to be very effective.

In this paper, we will present the memory optimizations that have been implemented in the Intel Reference C and FORTRAN Compiler [1]. The optimizations include loop interchange, loop distribution, loop blocking, strip-mine-and-preload, and data alignment in COMMON blocks. The theory behind our implementation can be found in previous works. The memory dependence test is described in [16, pp. 119-124]. Loop permutation (in particular, loop interchange) is described in detail in [17, chapter 2]. Loop interchange is also described in [18, pp.98-99]. Loop distribution is described in [16, pp.187-192]. Loop blocking is described in [4]. Stripe-mine-and-preload is described in [18, pp.148]. However, the optimization decisions- when and what to apply- are our own work. We have also done extensive work to prepare loops for memory optimizations: converting pointer accesses to array accesses and non-perfectly nested loops into perfectly nested loops. The theory behind the memory dependence test in our compiler can be found in [16].

Our memory optimizations apply to perfectly nested loops only. Therefore, a phase is added to convert some non-perfectly nested loops into perfectly nested loops. There are two ways: moving some statements into inner loop, and applying loop distribution.

Compilation Time

Phase	Approximate Percentages Of Time Spent
Loop Preparation & Qualification	60
Dependence Analysis	20
Actual Loop Transformations	20

Speedups On Intel Processors

Performance results of a few benchmark programs running on a Pentium(tm) processor based system is shown in the next table. The speedups of the entire applications are not as large as that of individual loops.

However, the speedups of the entire applications are substantial enough to warrant the memory optimizations.

Program	No Memory Opti.	With Memory Opti.	Speedup
039.wave5	75 seconds	71 seconds	1.06
047.tomcatv	44 seconds	39 seconds	1.13
052.alvinn	65 seconds	54 seconds	1.20
056.ear	169 seconds	124 seconds	1.36

Performance of the memory optimizer for an i486 processor based system is shown in the next table.

Program	No Memory Opti.	With Memory Opti.	Speedup
039.wave5	321 seconds	314 seconds	1.02
047.tomcatv	139 seconds	137 seconds	1.01
052.alvinn	232 seconds	267 seconds	0.87
056.ear	857 seconds	921 seconds	0.93

Because our memory optimizer is tuned for the Pentium(tm) processor, it actually hurts i486(tm) processor performance. A major reason is that the i486(tm) processor has a write through cache. This experiment shows that memory optimizations need to be tuned for the specific cache organization to be most effective.

Compilation Time

The next table shows the compilation time, on a i486(tm) processor based machine, for each of the optimization levels. Because the memory optimizations are more effective when the procedure inlining option is turned on, we will also measure the time to perform procedure inlining optimization.

Program	Default	Inline	Inline + Memory Opti.
039.wave5	108 seconds	130 seconds	309 seconds
047.tomcatv	2 seconds	3 seconds	5 seconds
052.alvinn	2 seconds	3 seconds	8 seconds
056.ear	36 seconds	43 seconds	63 seconds

References

[1] Intel Corporation, "Intel Reference FORTRAN Compiler User's Guide for UNIX Systems," Order number 484344-002.

[2] David Callahan, Steve Carr, and Ken Kennedy, "Improving register allocation for subscripted variables," Proceedings of the ACM SIGPLAN Symposium on Programming Language Design and Implementation, 1990.

[3] Allan Porterfield, "Compiler management of program locality," Rice COMP TR-88-63, January 1988.

[4] Michael E. Wolf and Monica S. Lam, "A data locality optimizing algorithm," Proceedings of the ACM SIGPLAN Symposium on Programming Language Design and Implementation, 1991.

[5] Alvin R. Lebeck and David A. Wood, "Cache profiling and the SPEC benchmark: a case study," Technical report, University of Wisconsin, March 1992.

[6] F. E. Allen and J. Cocke, "A catalogue of optimizing transformations," in Design and Optimization of Compilers, Prentice-Hall, 1972.

[7] A. Aiken and A. Nicolau, "Loop quantization: an analysis and algorithm," Technical report 87-821, Cornell U., March 1987.

[8] D. Callahan, J. Cocke, and K. Kennedy, "Estimating interlock and improving balance for pipelined machines," Journal of Parallel and Distributed Computing, 5, 1988.

[9] M. Wolfe, "Advanced loop interchange," Proceedings of the 1986 International Conference on Parallel Processing, August 1986.

[10] J. R. Allen and K. Kennedy, "Automatic translation of Fortran programs to vector form," ACM Transactions on Programming Languages and Systems, 9(4), October 1987.

[11] M. Wolfe, "Iteration space tiling for memory hierarchies," Proceedings of the Third SIAM Conference on Parallel Processing for Scientific Computing, December 1987.

[12] A. K. Porterfield, "Software methods for improvement of cache performance on supercomputer applications," Ph.D. thesis, Rice U., May 1989.

[13] J. Ferrante, V. Sarkar, and W. Thrash, "On estimating and enhancing cache effectiveness," in Fourth Workshop on Languages and Compilers for Parallel Computing, August 1991.

[14] D. Gannon, W. Jalby, and K. Gallivan, "Strategies for cache and local memory management by global program transformations," Proceedings of the First ACM International Conference on Supercomputing, June 1987.

[15] U. Banerjee, *Dependence Analysis for Supercomputing*, Kluwer Academic Publishers, 1988.

[16] U. Banerjee, *Loop Transformations for Restructuring Compilers: The Foundations*, Kluwer Academic Publishers, 1993.

[17] U. Banerjee, *Loop Transformations for Restructuring Compilers: Loop Parallelization*, Kluwer Academic Publishers, 1994.

[18] M. Wolfe, *Optimizing Supercompilers for Supercomputers*, MIT Press, 1989.

Author Index

Lecture Notes in Computer Science

For information about Vols. 1–1179

please contact your bookseller or Springer-Verlag

Vol. 1180: V. Chandru, V. Vinay (Eds.), Foundations of Software Technology and Theoretical Computer Science. Proceedings, 1996. XI, 387 pages. 1996.

Vol. 1181: D. Bjørner, M. Broy, I.V. Pottosin (Eds.), Perspectives of System Informatics. Proceedings, 1996. XVII, 447 pages. 1996.

Vol. 1182: W. Hasan, Optimization of SQL Queries for Parallel Machines. XVIII, 133 pages. 1996.

Vol. 1183: A. Wierse, G.G. Grinstein, U. Lang (Eds.), Database Issues for Data Visualization. Proceedings, 1995. XIV, 219 pages. 1996.

Vol. 1184: J. Waśniewski, J. Dongarra, K. Madsen, D. Olesen (Eds.), Applied Parallel Computing. Proceedings, 1996. XIII, 722 pages. 1996.

Vol. 1185: G. Ventre, J. Domingo-Pascual, A. Danthine (Eds.), Multimedia Telecommunications and Applications. Proceedings, 1996. XII, 267 pages. 1996.

Vol. 1186: F. Afrati, P. Kolaitis (Eds.), Database Theory - ICDT'97. Proceedings, 1997. XIII, 477 pages. 1997.

Vol. 1187: K. Schlechta, Nonmonotonic Logics. IX, 243 pages. 1997. (Subseries LNAI).

Vol. 1188: T. Martin, A.L. Ralescu (Eds.), Fuzzy Logic in Artificial Intelligence. Proceedings, 1995. VIII, 272 pages. 1997. (Subseries LNAI).

Vol. 1189: M. Lomas (Ed.), Security Protocols. Proceedings, 1996. VIII, 203 pages. 1997.

Vol. 1190: S. North (Ed.), Graph Drawing. Proceedings, 1996. XI, 409 pages. 1997.

Vol. 1191: V. Gaede, A. Brodsky, O. Günther, D. Srivastava, V. Vianu, M. Wallace (Eds.), Constraint Databases and Applications. Proceedings, 1996. X, 345 pages. 1996.

Vol. 1192: M. Dam (Ed.), Analysis and Verification of Multiple-Agent Languages. Proceedings, 1996. VIII, 435 pages. 1997.

Vol. 1193: J.P. Müller, M.J. Wooldridge, N.R. Jennings (Eds.), Intelligent Agents III. XV, 401 pages. 1997. (Subseries LNAI).

Vol. 1194: M. Sipper, Evolution of Parallel Cellular Machines. XIII, 199 pages. 1997.

Vol. 1195: R. Trappl, P. Petta (Eds.), Creating Personalities for Synthetic Actors. VII, 251 pages. 1997. (Subseries LNAI).

Vol. 1196: L. Vulkov, J. Waśniewski, P. Yalamov (Eds.), Numerical Analysis and Its Applications. Proceedings, 1996. XIII, 608 pages. 1997.

Vol. 1197: F. d'Amore, P.G. Franciosa, A. Marchetti-Spaccamela (Eds.), Graph-Theoretic Concepts in Computer Science. Proceedings, 1996. XI, 410 pages. 1997.

Vol. 1198: H.S. Nwana, N. Azarmi (Eds.), Software Agents and Soft Computing: Towards Enhancing Machine Intelligence. XIV, 298 pages. 1997. (Subseries LNAI).

Vol. 1199: D.K. Panda, C.B. Stunkel (Eds.), Communication and Architectural Support for Network-Based Parallel Computing. Proceedings, 1997. X, 269 pages. 1997.

Vol. 1200: R. Reischuk, M. Morvan (Eds.), STACS 97. Proceedings, 1997. XIII, 614 pages. 1997.

Vol. 1201: O. Maler (Ed.), Hybrid and Real-Time Systems. Proceedings, 1997. IX, 417 pages. 1997.

Vol. 1203: G. Bongiovanni, D.P. Bovet, G. Di Battista (Eds.), Algorithms and Complexity. Proceedings, 1997. VIII, 311 pages. 1997.

Vol. 1204: H. Mössenböck (Ed.), Modular Programming Languages. Proceedings, 1997. X, 379 pages. 1997.

Vol. 1205: J. Troccaz, E. Grimson, R. Mösges (Eds.), CVRMed-MRCAS'97. Proceedings, 1997. XIX, 834 pages. 1997.

Vol. 1206: J. Bigün, G. Chollet, G. Borgefors (Eds.), Audio- and Video-based Biometric Person Authentication. Proceedings, 1997. XII, 450 pages. 1997.

Vol. 1207: J. Gallagher (Ed.), Logic Program Synthesis and Transformation. Proceedings, 1996. VII, 325 pages. 1997.

Vol. 1208: S. Ben-David (Ed.), Computational Learning Theory. Proceedings, 1997. VIII, 331 pages. 1997. (Subseries LNAI).

Vol. 1209: L. Cavedon, A. Rao, W. Wobcke (Eds.), Intelligent Agent Systems. Proceedings, 1996. IX, 188 pages. 1997. (Subseries LNAI).

Vol. 1210: P. de Groote, J.R. Hindley (Eds.), Typed Lambda Calculi and Applications. Proceedings, 1997. VIII, 405 pages. 1997.

Vol. 1211: E. Keravnou, C. Garbay, R. Baud, J. Wyatt (Eds.), Artificial Intelligence in Medicine. Proceedings, 1997. XIII, 526 pages. 1997. (Subseries LNAI).

Vol. 1212: J. P. Bowen, M.G. Hinchey, D. Till (Eds.), ZUM '97: The Z Formal Specification Notation. Proceedings, 1997. X, 435 pages. 1997.

Vol. 1213: P. J. Angeline, R. G. Reynolds, J. R. McDonnell, R. Eberhart (Eds.), Evolutionary Programming VI. Proceedings, 1997. X, 457 pages. 1997.

Vol. 1214: M. Bidoit, M. Dauchet (Eds.), TAPSOFT '97: Theory and Practice of Software Development. Proceedings, 1997. XV, 884 pages. 1997.

Vol. 1215: J. M. L. M. Palma, J. Dongarra (Eds.), Vector and Parallel Processing – VECPAR'96. Proceedings, 1996. XI, 471 pages. 1997.

Vol. 1216: J. Dix, L. Moniz Pereira, T.C. Przymusinski (Eds.), Non-Monotonic Extensions of Logic Programming. Proceedings, 1996. XI, 224 pages. 1997. (Subseries LNAI).

Vol. 1217: E. Brinksma (Ed.), Tools and Algorithms for the Construction and Analysis of Systems. Proceedings, 1997. X, 433 pages. 1997.

Vol. 1218: G. Păun, A. Salomaa (Eds.), New Trends in Formal Languages. IX, 465 pages. 1997.

Vol. 1219: K. Rothermel, R. Popescu-Zeletin (Eds.), Mobile Agents. Proceedings, 1997. VIII, 223 pages. 1997.

Vol. 1220: P. Brezany, Input/Output Intensive Massively Parallel Computing. XIV, 288 pages. 1997.

Vol. 1221: G. Weiß (Ed.), Distributed Artificial Intelligence Meets Machine Learning. Proceedings, 1996. X, 294 pages. 1997. (Subseries LNAI).

Vol. 1222: J. Vitek, C. Tschudin (Eds.), Mobile Object Systems. Proceedings, 1996. X, 319 pages. 1997.

Vol. 1223: M. Pelillo, E.R. Hancock (Eds.), Energy Minimization Methods in Computer Vision and Pattern Recognition. Proceedings, 1997. XII, 549 pages. 1997.

Vol. 1224: M. van Someren, G. Widmer (Eds.), Machine Learning: ECML-97. Proceedings, 1997. XI, 361 pages. 1997. (Subseries LNAI).

Vol. 1225: B. Hertzberger, P. Sloot (Eds.), High-Performance Computing and Networking. Proceedings, 1997. XXI, 1066 pages. 1997.

Vol. 1226: B. Reusch (Ed.), Computational Intelligence. Proceedings, 1997. XIII, 609 pages. 1997.

Vol. 1227: D. Galmiche (Ed.), Automated Reasoning with Analytic Tableaux and Related Methods. Proceedings, 1997. XI, 373 pages. 1997. (Subseries LNAI).

Vol. 1228: S.-H. Nienhuys-Cheng, R. de Wolf, Foundations of Inductive Logic Programming. XVII, 404 pages. 1997. (Subseries LNAI).

Vol. 1230: J. Duncan, G. Gindi (Eds.), Information Processing in Medical Imaging. Proceedings, 1997. XVI, 557 pages. 1997.

Vol. 1231: M. Bertran, T. Rus (Eds.), Transformation-Based Reactive Systems Development. Proceedings, 1997. XI, 431 pages. 1997.

Vol. 1232: H. Comon (Ed.), Rewriting Techniques and Applications. Proceedings, 1997. XI, 339 pages. 1997.

Vol. 1233: W. Fumy (Ed.), Advances in Cryptology — EUROCRYPT '97. Proceedings, 1997. XI, 509 pages. 1997.

Vol 1234: S. Adian, A. Nerode (Eds.), Logical Foundations of Computer Science. Proceedings, 1997. IX, 431 pages. 1997.

Vol. 1235: R. Conradi (Ed.), Software Configuration Management. Proceedings, 1997. VIII, 234 pages. 1997.

Vol. 1236: E. Maier, M. Mast, S. LuperFoy (Eds.), Dialogue Processing in Spoken Language Systems. Proceedings, 1996. VIII, 220 pages. 1997. (Subseries LNAI).

Vol. 1238: A. Mullery, M. Besson, M. Campolargo, R. Gobbi, R. Reed (Eds.), Intelligence in Services and Networks: Technology for Cooperative Competition. Proceedings, 1997. XII, 480 pages. 1997.

Vol. 1239: D. Sehr, U. Banerjee, D. Gelernter, A. Nicolau, D. Padua (Eds.), Languages and Compilers for Parallel Computing. Proceedings, 1996. XIII, 612 pages. 1997.

Vol. 1240: J. Mira, R. Moreno-Díaz, J. Cabestany (Eds.), Biological and Artificial Computation: From Neuroscience to Technology. Proceedings, 1997. XXI, 1401 pages. 1997.

Vol. 1241: M. Akşit, S. Matsuoka (Eds.), ECOOP'97 – Object-Oriented Programming. Proceedings, 1997. XI, 531 pages. 1997.

Vol. 1242: S. Fdida, M. Morganti (Eds.), Multimedia Applications, Services and Techniques – ECMAST '97. Proceedings, 1997. XIV, 772 pages. 1997.

Vol. 1243: A. Mazurkiewicz, J. Winkowski (Eds.), CONCUR'97: Concurrency Theory. Proceedings, 1997. VIII, 421 pages. 1997.

Vol. 1244: D. M. Gabbay, R. Kruse, A. Nonnengart, H.J. Ohlbach (Eds.), Qualitative and Quantitative Practical Reasoning. Proceedings, 1997. X, 621 pages. 1997. (Subseries LNAI).

Vol. 1245: M. Calzarossa, R. Marie, B. Plateau, G. Rubino (Eds.), Computer Performance Evaluation. Proceedings, 1997. VIII, 231 pages. 1997.

Vol. 1246: S. Tucker Taft, R. A. Duff (Eds.), Ada 95 Reference Manual. XXII, 526 pages. 1997.

Vol. 1247: J. Barnes (Ed.), Ada 95 Rationale. XVI, 458 pages. 1997.

Vol. 1248: P. Azéma, G. Balbo (Eds.), Application and Theory of Petri Nets 1997. Proceedings, 1997. VIII, 467 pages. 1997.

Vol. 1249: W. McCune (Ed.), Automated Deduction – CADE-14. Proceedings, 1997. XIV, 462 pages. 1997. (Subseries LNAI).

Vol. 1250: A. Olivé, J.A. Pastor (Eds.), Advanced Information Systems Engineering. Proceedings, 1997. XI, 451 pages. 1997.

Vol. 1251: K. Hardy, J. Briggs (Eds.), Reliable Software Technologies – Ada-Europe '97. Proceedings, 1997. VIII, 293 pages. 1997.

Vol. 1252: B. ter Haar Romeny, L. Florack, J. Koenderink, M. Viergever (Eds.), Scale-Space Theory for Computer Vision. Proceedings, 1997. IX, 365 pages. 1997.

Vol. 1253: G. Bilardi, A. Ferreira, R. Lüling, J. Rolim (Eds.), Solving Irregularly Structured Problems in Parallel. Proceedings, 1997. X, 287 pages. 1997.

Vol. 1254: O. Grumberg (Ed.), Computer Aided Verification. Proceedings, 1997. XI, 486 pages. 1997.

Vol. 1255: T. Mora, H. Mattson (Eds.), Applied Algebra, Algebraic Algorithms and Error-Correcting Codes. Proceedings, 1997. X, 353 pages. 1997.

Vol. 1256: P. Degano, R. Gorrieri, A. Marchetti-Spaccamela (Eds.), Automata, Languages and Programming. Proceedings, 1997. XIV, 862 pages. 1997.

Vol. 1258: D. van Dalen, M. Bezem (Eds.), Computer Science Logic. Proceedings, 1996. VIII, 473 pages. 1997.

Vol. 1259: T. Higuchi, I. Masaya, W. Liu (Eds.), Evolvable Systems: From Biology to Hardware. Proceedings, 1996. XI, 484 pages. 1997.

Vol. 1260: D. Raymond, D. Wood, S. Yu (Eds.), Automata Implementation. Proceedings, 1996. VIII, 189 pages. 1997.